INFORMATION SECURITY

DICTIONARY OF CONCEPTS, STANDARDS AND TERMS

INFORMATION SECURITY

DICTIONARY OF CONCEPTS, STANDARDS AND TERMS

Dennis Longley
Michael Shain
William Caelli

M
stockton
press

Published in the United States and Canada by
STOCKTON PRESS, 1992
257 Park Avenue South, New York, N.Y. 10010, USA

ISBN 978-0-312-08682-4

First published in the United Kingdom by
MACMILLAN PUBLISHERS LTD, 1992
Distributed by Globe Book Services Ltd
Brunel Road, Houndmills,
Basingstoke, Hants RG21 2XS, England

ISBN 978-1-349-12211-0   ISBN 978-1-349-12209-7 (eBook)
DOI 10.1007/978-1-349-12209-7

A catalogue record for this book
is available from The British Library.

Contents

Acknowledgements

The authors are indebted to Douglass L Mansur of the Lawrence Livermore National Laboratory for making available his *Glossary of Computer Security Terminology* which draws upon US Government sources not readily available outside the USA, and to Dennis Steinauer of the US National Institute of Standards and Technology for his valued comments and assistance.

The authors also wish to give their thanks to Mr Wayne Madsen for his permission to draw upon the current state of data protection legislation as described in his *Handbook of Personal Data Protection*. The list of viruses was included by kind permission of McAfee Associates. Finally our grateful thanks to Mrs Marie Sands for her invaluable assistance in producing the page proofs.

References

In this dictionary, material has been derived from a wide variety of sources. In some cases definitions are given within a particular context, and the source body of the reference is given with the definition itself (eg (FIPS), (SAA), (AR)). The references are:

AFIPS	American Federation of Information Processing Societies
AFR	US Air Force Regulation
ANSI	American National Standards Institute
AR	US Army Regulation
DCID	US Director Central Intelligence Directive
DOD	US Department of Defense
DODD	US Department of Defense Directive
DOE	US Department of Energy
FIPS	US Federal Information Processing Standards
GAO	US General Accounting Office
MTR	Mitre Corporation
NSDD-145	US National Security Decision Directive 145
OMBC	US Office of Management and Budget Circular
OPNAVINST	US Office of Naval Operations Instruction
SAA	Standards Association of Australia
TNI	Trusted Network Interpretation of the Trusted Computer System Evaluation Criteria, National Computer Security Center.

Many of the terms with references AFR, AR, DCID, DOD, DODD, DOE, FIPS, GAO, MTR, NSDD-145, OMBC and OPNAVINST are contained in the *Glossary of Computer Security Terminology* (see below) and published with the kind permission of Douglass L Mansur and Major Mary C Curtis. The original source documents for that glossary include:

Air Force Regulation 205-16 (draft).
Air Force Regulation 700-10, Information Systems Security, 3/15/85.
Army Regulation 380-380, Automation Security, 3/3/85.
Office of Management and Budget Circular A-123, Internal Control Systems, 10/28/81.
Office of Management and Budget Circular A-130, Management of Federal Information Resources, 12/12/85.
CSC-STD-001-83, DOD Trusted Computer System Evaluation Criteria 8/15/83.
CSC-STD-002-85, DOD Password Management Guideline, 4/12/85.
CSC-STD-003-85, DOD Computer Security Requirements, 6/25/85.
CSC-STD-004-85, Technical Rationale Behind CSC-STD-003-85, 6/25/85.
Director of Central Intelligence Directive 1/16-1, Security Policy on Intelligence Information in Automated Data Processing Systems and Networks, Computer Security Manual, 1/4/85.

Department of Defense Directive 5200.1-R, Information Security Program Regulation, 6/86.

Department of Defense Directive 2040.2, International Transfers of Technology, Goods, Services and Munitions, 1/17/84.

Department of Defense Directive 3200.12, DOD Scientific and Technical Information Programs, 2/15/83.

Department of Defense Directive 5200.28M, ADP Security Manual, 1/73.

Department of Defense Standard 5200.28-STD, Department of Defense Trusted Computer Systems Evaluation Criteria, 12/85.

Department of Defense Directive 5215.1, Computer Security Evaluation of Defense Directive 5230.24, Distribution Statements on Technical Documents, 11/02/84.

Department of Defense Directive 5230.25, Withholding of Unclassified Technical Data from Public Disclosure, 11/6/84.

Department of Defense Directive 7040.6, Internal Control Systems, 3/24/82.

Department of Defense Instruction 5215.2, Computer Security Technical Vulnerability Reporting Program (CSTVRP), 9/2/86.

Department of Energy Order 5635.1A, Control of Classified Documents and Information (draft).

Department of Energy Order 5636.2A, Security Requirements for Classified Automated Data Processing Systems (draft).

General Accounting Office, *Survey of Computer and Telecommunications Based Information Systems Security in the Civil Sector of the Federal Government*.

Mitre Corporation Technical Report MTR-8201, Trusted Computer Systems-Glossary, 3/81.

National Security Decision Directive 145, National Policy on Telecommunications and Automated System Security, 12/17/84.

Office of Navy Operations Instruction 5239.A, Department of the Navy Automatic Data Processing Security Program, 3/8/82.

Bibliography

Butterworths Security Dictionary. John C Fay, Butterworth Publishers, 1987.

Cipher Systems. H Beker, F Piper, Wiley.

Computers and Security. Official Journal of IFIP TC 11, North Holland.

Computers at Risk. Safe Computing in the Information Age. National Academy Press, 1991.

Computer Control Audit. W C Mair, D R Wood, K W Davis.

Computer Security for Today and Tomorrow. Proceedings of National Computer Security Conference, September 1986.

Computer Security Requirements. Guidance for Applying the Department of Defense Trusted Computer System Evaluation Criteria in Specific Environments. National Computer Security Center, 1985.

Computer Security Technology. J A Cooper, Lexington Books.

Cryptographic Checksums for Multilevel Data Security. D E Denning, Proceedings of the 1984 Symposium on Security and Privacy, IEEE Computer Society, 1984.

Cryptography and Data Security. D E R Denning, Addison Wesley Publishing Company.

Cryptography: A New Dimension in Computer Data Security. C H Meyer, S M Matyas, Wiley.

Cryptography: An Introduction to Computer Security. J Seberry and J Pieprzyk, Prentice Hall, 1989.

Data Encryption Algorithm. American National Standards Institute X3.92 - 1981.

Data Encryption Standard. FIPS PUB 46, National Bureau of Standards, 1/15/77.

Data Security in Open Systems Interconnection (OSI). W L Price, National Physical Laboratory, Teddington, UK.

DES Modes of Operation. FIPS PUB 81, National Bureau of Standards, December 1980.

Electronic Funds Transfer. Standards Association of Australia.

Financial Institution Key Management (Wholesale). American National Standards Institute X9.17.

Financial Institute Message Authentication. American National Standards Institute X9.9.

Glossary of Computer Security Terminology. Douglass L Mansur, Lawrence Livermore National Laboratory and US Department of Energy, and Major Mary C Curtis, United States Air Force.

Glossary for Computer Systems Security. FIPS PUB 39, National Bureau of Standards, 2/15/76.

Good Security Practices for Information Ownership and Classification. IBM Data Security Support Programs.

Good Security Practices for Personal Computers. IBM Data Support Security Programs. March 1982.

Guideline for Automatic Processing Risk Analysis. FIPS PUB 65, National Bureau of Standards, 1/8/79.

Guideline for Implementing and using the Data Encryption Standard. FIPS PUB 74, National Bureau of Standards, April 1981.

Inference Controls for Statistical Databases. D E Denning, J Schloerer, *Computer,* Vol 16, No 7, July 1983.

Handbook of Personal Data Protection. Wayne Madsen. Macmillan Publishers Ltd, 1992.

Information Systems Security Controls and Procedures. IBM Data Security Support Programs, February 1986.

Information Technology Security Evaluation Criteria. Provisional Harmonised Criteria. Luxembourg: Office for Official Publications of the European Community, 1991

Modes of Operation for the Data Encryption Algorithm. American National Standards Institute, X3.106 - 1983.

New Directions in Cryptography. M Hellman, W Diffie, *IEEE Transactions in Information Theory,* November 1976.

Number Theory in Science and Communications. M R Schroeder, Springer Verlag.

Overview of Computer Security. R C Summers, *IBM Systems Journal,* Vol 23, No 4, 1981.

Personal Identification Number (PIN) Management and Security. American National Standards Institute X9.8.

Secure Communications Systems. Proceedings of IEE Conference, February 1984.

Secure Speech Communications. H Beker, F Piper, Academic Press.

Security and Reliability in Electronic Systems for Payments. Published by the central banks of the Group of Ten countries and Switzerland under the aegis of the Bank for International Settlements, January 1985.

Security Considerations for Personal Computers. W H Murray, *IBM Systems Journal,* Vol 23, No 3, 1984.

Security Dictionary. R A Hofmeister and D J Prince, Howard W Sams and Co. Inc.

Some Techniques in Handling Encipherment Keys. R W Jones, *ICL Technical Journal,* November 1982.

Security for Computer Networks. D W Davies, W L Price, Wiley, 1989.

Security of Personal Computer Systems: A Management Guide. Dennis D Steinauer, NBS Special Publication 500-120, National Bureau of Standards, 1985.

Security in Computing. C P Pfleeger, Prentice Hall International Inc., 1989

Security Risk Assessment in Electronic Data Processing Systems. Data Security Support Programs, IBM.

Telecommunications: General Security Requirements for Equipment Using the Data Encryption Standard. Federal Standard 1027, Federal Telecommunications Standards Committee, April 1981.

The Considerations of Physical Security in a Computer Environment. IBM 1972.

UK Data Protection Act 1984, HMSO.

Trusted Computer System Evaluation Criteria. National Computer Security Center, 1983 (updated 1985).

Trusted Database Management System Interpretation of the Trusted Computer System Evaluation Criteria. National Computer Security Center, April 1991.

Trusted Network Interpretation of the Trusted Computer System Evaluation Criteria. National Computer Security Center, 1987.

Vocabulary and Data Elements for Wholesale Funds Transfers and Related Advices. American National Standards Institute X9.21.

A

A1. *See* DIVISION A.

A&A. *See* ADVICE AND ASSESSMENT.

aborted connection. In communications security, a disconnection which does not follow established procedures. This may occasionally result from a bad telephone connection, but more typically results when the user 'hangs up' without attempting to issue the disconnect commands.

absolute rate. In information theory, the maximum number of bits of information that could be encoded in each character assuming that all possible sequences are equally likely. If a language comprises C characters and each are equally likely to appear in any message sequence then the absolute rate of the language would be $\log_2$ C. In natural languages such as English the actual rate of the language is considerably less than the absolute rate because such languages have a high degree of redundancy. *See* RATE.

abstract data type. In data structures, a data type that is defined solely in terms of the operations, that can be performed on objects of that type, and the range of values that it can take, without regard to the method of representation of the value. *See* TYPE.

abstract syntax notation 1. In data communications, a notation devised by the ISO which may be used to describe a wide variety of data structures. When a computer system transmits a message to another system it is likely that the two systems will have idiosyncratic representations of the bits forming the various fields of the message. The abstract data notation provides for a common definition of the data structure of the message. The sending computer will convert its data structure to the form specified by the abstract syntax notation. Similarly the receiving computer will decode the incoming message, from the abstract data notation representation, to its local format. This procedure removes the requirement for systems to store an individual coding scheme for each system with which it communicates. *See* ISO.

AC. Authentication Code. *Synonymous with* MAC.

acceptability principle. In data security, security measures should not unduly interfere with the work of users while, of course, fulfilling all necessary security constraints. *See* PRINCIPLES OF SECURE SYSTEMS.

acceptable level of risk. In risk management, a judicious and carefully considered assessment by the appropriate Designated Approving Authority (DAA) that an automatic data processing (ADP) activity or network meets the minimum requirements of applicable security directives. The assessment should take into account the value of ADP assets; threats and vulnerabilities; countermeasures and their efficacy in compensating for vulnerabilities; and operational requirements. (OPNAVINST). *See* ADP, DAA, RISK, THREAT, VULNERABILITY. *Synonymous with* ACCEPTABLE RISK.

acceptable risk. *Synonymous with* ACCEPTABLE LEVEL OF RISK.

1

acceptance. In computer security, indicates a facility or system generally meets technical and performance standards but may have minor exceptions which do not keep the facility from meeting operational and security requirements. (AFR).

acceptance inspection. In computer security, the final inspection to determine if a facility or system meets the specified technical and performance standards. It is held immediately after facility and software testing and is the basis for commissioning or accepting the information system. (AFR). *See* ACCEPTANCE.

acceptance testing. A procedure to ensure that a system meets user requirements. *See* ACCEPTANCE.

access. (1) In access control, a specific type of interaction between a subject and an object that results in the flow of information from one to the other. (DOD). *See* OBJECT, SUBJECT. (2) In access control, the ability and the means necessary to approach, to store or retrieve data, to communicate with, or make use of any resource of an ADP system. (FIPS). *See* ADP, RESOURCE. (3) In computing, the manner in which files or data sets are referred to by the computer. *See* DATA SET, DIRECT ACCESS, RANDOM ACCESS, SEQUENTIAL ACCESS. (4) In access control, a specific type of interaction between a subject (i.e, person, process or input device) and an object (i.e. an AIS resource such as a record, file, program, output device) that results in the flow of information from one to the other. (DODD). *See* AIS. (5) In physical security, a mode or condition in access control equipment that allows entry into a restricted area; in this mode it is not necessary to deactivate sensors and no alarm will be activated.

access authorization. In access control, the permission granted to a subject, e.g. person, terminal, program, to perform a set of operations in the system.

Such authorizations are commonly expressed in an access privilege matrix giving details of the subjects, types of access, e.g. read, write, and time periods in which the accesses are allowed. *See* ACCESS MATRIX MODEL, SUBJECT.

access barred. In data communications, a data facility which permits a terminal installation to make outgoing, or receive incoming, calls but not both.

access card. *Synonymous with* CARD KEY.

access category. In access control, one of the classes to which a user, a program or a process in an ADP system may be assigned on the basis of the resources or groups of resources that each user, program, or process is authorized to use. (FIPS). *See* ADP, RESOURCE.

access control. (1) In computer and communications security, the prevention of unauthorized use of a resource, including the prevention of use of a resource in an unauthorized manner. (ISO). (2) In computer networks, the control of system usage, imposed by hardware, software and administrative controls. Such controls include system monitoring, user identification, ensuring data integrity, recording system access and changes and methods for granting user access. *See* HARDWARE, SOFTWARE. (3) In database security, the control of the use of the database information. Access to a particular user may be restricted both in terms of the data items that may be made available and the operations that may be performed on it, e.g. read, update etc. (4) In data security, the limiting of rights or capabilities of a subject to communicate with other subjects, or to use functions or services in a computer system or network (TNI). *See* SUBJECT. (5) In data security, restrictions controlling a subject's access to an object. *See* OBJECT, SUBJECT. (6) In information security, functions to control the flow of information between, and the use of resources by, users, processes, and objects, including the administration and verification of access rights. *See* INFORMATION TECHNOLOGY SECURITY EVALUATION CRITERIA. (7) The traditional method of protecting assets is to keep them safe from the potential wrongdoer, in other words to ensure that only duly authorized personnel are permitted access to those assets.

Traditionally access control comprised physical access control, which may be defined as 'the use of locks, guards, badges and similar administrative measures to control access to computer and related equipment'.

In computer security, where it is often possible to access stored data from a remote terminal, or over communication networks, such physical access control may provide no defence for the stored data. Logical access control, defined as 'the use of procedures related to information and knowledge' is more commonly employed.

Processes involved in access control
The processes of access control may be listed:

- allocation of privileges;
- administration of privileges;
- identification and authentication of users;
- monitoring accesses;
- limitation on the type of access;
- prevention of unauthorized access;
- revocation of access privilege.

Allocation of Privileges
The most significant decision is - who should be granted access to the assets? In the case of computer security there may be a large population of users, and a multitude of data assets. How should the decision be made that user A can access file C, and what form of access privilege should be granted, e.g read, write, execute?

There are two approaches, the first assigns some attribute to each user and each data asset, and then defines a set of system wide rules relating the type of access granted for given user attribute: data asset-attribute pair. The second approach simply permits some duly authorized person to make the decision that user A is allowed access type B to asset C.

The first approach is termed mandatory access control; it follows the line of specifying user and data asset attributes, termed security classifications. A set of system wide rules are then laid down which dictate whether or not a type of access may be granted to a (user security classification, data asset security classification) pair, an access control system must then enforce those rules. With this form of access control a central authority has the role of allocating the security classifications to users and data assets.

On the other hand discretionary access control, has no such universal rules of access; an arbitrary decision is made by some authorized person to grant or deny, a given user, a form of access to an asset. With a large population of users, and assets, the granting rights are normally delegated to owners of the data asset. In some cases the owner may also bestow the granting rights to other users, although in such cases no user should be able to bestow more rights than they themselves hold.

Mandatory access control is generally regarded as too coarse to be used by itself, and is normally used only to filter out requests. If access is granted, by the mandatory access control rules, then the discretionary access system is invoked. This combination of mandatory and discretionary access control, ensures that no owner can arbitrarily decide to make highly sensitive data available to some person who is considered to be an inappropriate user of that data. At the same time a user with a high security classification is not automatically granted access to lower classified documents; the user must demonstrate a 'need to know' to a security administrator.

Administration of Privileges

Arrangements must be made to inform users of their privileges and to hand over the means for them to exercise those privileges. It must be ensured that the privileges are handed to the right person, and that no unauthorized person has an opportunity to gain the right to access those privileges during the handover arrangements. It would also be wise to ensure that authorized recipients are aware of their security responsibilities.

Identification and Authentication of Users

When a user embarks upon accessing an asset, there is a mechanism by which the user proves the right to that access. In computer security systems there is normally a two stage process; the user first claims an identity as an individual, usually by keying in a userid, or presenting a token containing that userid, and then by proving that the individual has the right to claim the privileges corresponding to that userid. Inserting a magnetic stripe card into an ATM, followed by the keying in of a PIN, is a good example of this process.

The proof of identity is a crucial process in computer, and network, access control. If an attacker can provide the proof demanded of the legitimate user, then the security system will thereafter be completely bypassed. The proof of identity may take one of three forms, either individually, or in combination, i.e.:

- something the user knows;
- something the user possesses;
- something the user is.

When a user logs onto a computer system it is conceivable that the dialogue may actually take place with an attacker's host computer. The user could then be tricked into revealing secret information, e.g. password or PIN, and possibly even entering confidential data.

Monitoring Accesses

An effective monitoring system can form an essential feature of the access control system. The requirement for monitoring system accesses arises because:

- the system may be so inconvenient to users that it is impacting upon operating efficiency and legitimate users are tempted to adopt practices which can nullify the access control safeguards;
- it may not be possible to prevent an attacker from entering into an initial dialogue with the system;
- the identification and authentication processes may not be entirely invulnerable to attack;
- a user with a limited set of access privileges may seek to illegally extend those privileges;
- if a security incident occurs then it is essential that sufficient evidence of the incident is collected, for post hoc improvements to security, or for evidence in disciplinary proceedings;
- improvements in security procedures, or detection of attack scenarios, may be based upon some model of normal behavior of the system.

Type of Access

With computer stored data a significant degree of control on user actions can be effected. For example, in a database system, a large user population may be permitted to read the data, however, unauthorized modifications to the stored data would be totally unacceptable. In a financial environment, it will be necessary to impose strict controls on the type of transaction that may be undertaken by certain classes of users. Logical access control systems therefore commonly specify what action users may undertake in relation to a file: read, write, execute, append. The 'append' access allows a user to add additional data to a file but not to read the data or modify existing data.

Prevention of Unauthorized Access

Maintaining the security of a physical or logical access control system involves more than simply differentiating between authorized and unauthorized users. Once access has been denied it is important to ensure that the denial can be enforced.

In the case of physical access control, denial of access involves an assurance that lockable doors are not propped open, there are no means of forced entry through windows etc.

With logical access control the attacker may be able to employ extremely sophisticated means to bypass security controls. Software modification techniques such as trapdoors, Trojan Horses etc. can thwart the most carefully designed operating systems.

Revocation of Access Privileges
Deletion of a password, from a password file, requires no cooperation from the user and has no impact upon other users. However, in systems with a large population of users, and an extensive number of protected assets, it can be difficult to administer changes in access privileges. A matrix listing each user horizontally, each data asset vertically, and an entry for every user/asset privilege would be extremely sparse; users generally have access to only a minute proportion of the total assets. Such a matrix would be difficult to store, maintain and protect.

It is possible to associate a list with each asset, indicating which users have access privileges. However, if a user's privileges are to be revoked, it is necessary to examine the access list of every single asset, seeking the user's name. The alternative technique, of storing a list of permitted assets with each user, presents similar problems, if it is necessary to review the number of users with current access privileges for a particular asset.

Failure to revoke access privileges for users who have left a company is not uncommon; the consequences of such failures can be serious when the user no longer has a sense of loyalty to the organization. *See* ACCESS MATRIX MODEL, ATM, BIOMETRICS, DISCRETIONARY ACCESS CONTROL, LOGICAL ACCESS CON-TROL, MAGNETIC STRIPE CARD, MANDA-TORY ACCESS CONTROL, PASSWORD, PIN, USER ID. *Synonymous with* CONTROLLED ACCESSIBILITY.

access control list. (1) In access control, a list of entities, together with their access rights, which are authorized to have access to a resource. (ISO). (2) In access control, a list of subjects which are authorized to have access to some object. (MTR). *Compare* CAPABILITY LIST. *See* ACCESS MATRIX MODEL, OBJECT, SUB-JECT. *Synonymous with* ACCESS LIST.

access control measures. In access control, hardware and software features, physical controls, operating procedures, management procedures, and various combinations of these designed to detect or prevent unauthorized access to an ADP system and to enforce access control. (DOE).

access control mechanisms. In access control, hardware or software features, operating procedures, management procedures, and various combinations of these designed to detect and prevent unauthorized access and to permit authorized access to an ADP system. (FIPS). *See* ACCESS, ADP.

access control roster. In access control, a list of personnel, users, and so forth, that documents the degree of access and control for each person. (AFR).

access group. In access control, a class to which a user or process may be assigned; the class will possess specified access privileges to objects. *See* OBJECT.

access label. *See* LABEL.

access level. In access control, a level associated with a subject (e.g. a clearance level) or with an object (e.g. a classification level). *See* CATEGORY, CLASSIFICA-TION LEVEL, CLEARANCE LEVEL, OBJECT, SECURITY LEVEL, SENSITIVITY LABEL, SUBJECT.

access line. In data communications, a telecommunication line that continuously connects a remote station to a DSE. A telephone number is associated with such lines. *See* DSE.

access list. In access control, a catalog of users, programs, or processes and the specifications of access categories to which each is assigned. (FIPS). *See* ACCESS CATEGORY. *Synonymous with* ACCESS CONTROL LIST.

access matrix model. In access control, a model which relates subjects, objects and access types. A subject is an active entity capable of accessing objects, e.g. a program in execution, a user in a time sharing system. An object is an entity to which access is controlled, e.g. a file, memory segment, program. An access type is just a kind of access to an object, e.g. an access type to a program may be: execute, read source listing, to a file it may be: read, write, append.

The access control matrix is a two dimensional array with objects listed horizontally, subjects listed vertically and each cell contains the access type that the given subject has for the corresponding object. In practice such an array will be sparse and wasteful of memory space. In implementation, therefore, it may be represented in terms of an access control list or a capability list.

An access control list provides details of subjects and their access privileges for each object. A capability list, on the other hand, lists the objects that may be accessed by a subject and the corresponding access types. *See* ACCESS CONTROL LIST, ACCESS TYPE, CAPABILITY LIST, OBJECT, SPARSE ARRAY, SUBJECT.

access mode. (1) In access control, a distinct operation recognized by the protection mechanisms as a possible operation on an object. Read, write and append are possible modes of access to a file, while execute is an additional mode of access to a program. (MTR). *See* OBJECT. *Synonymous with* PERMISSIONS. (2) In access control, a mode of access control equipment. *See* ACCESS.

access password. In access control, a password used to authorize access to data and distributed to all those who are authorized similar access to that data. (FIPS). *See* PASSWORD.

access period. In access control, a segment of time, generally expressed on a daily or weekly basis, during which access rights prevail. (FIPS). *See* ACCESS RIGHT.

access permission. In access control, the definition of which subjects have the ability to change access modes and\or the ability to pass the ability to another subject. *See* SUBJECT.

access port. In computer security, a logical or physical identifier that a computer uses to distinguish different terminal input/output data streams. (DOD).

access right. In access control, the particular access permission (i.e. read, write, append, execute, delete, create, modify) granted to a subject in relation to an object. *See* ACCESS PERMISSION, OBJECT, SUBJECT.

access to information. In legislation, the function of providing to members of the public, upon their request, the government information to which they are entitled under law. (OMBC). *See* DATA PROTECTION, FREEDOM OF INFORMATION.

access type. In access control, the nature of an access right to a particular device, program or file; for example, read, write, execute, append, modify, delete, create. (FIPS). *See* ACCESS MODE.

accidental destruction. In data security, the unintentional overwriting or deletion of data, e.g. by faulty hardware or software. Backup is needed for recovery. *See* BACKUP/RESTORE.

accidental threat. In physical security, the threat of unintentional damage to the system arising from incorrect use of the system or natural phenomena, e.g. flood, fire etc. *Compare* ACTIVE THREAT, DELIBERATE THREAT, LOGICAL THREAT, PASSIVE THREAT, PHYSICAL THREAT. *See* THREAT.

accountability. (1) In data security, the property that ensures that the actions of an entity may be traced uniquely to that entity. (ANSI). (2) In information security, functions to record the exercising of rights to perform security relevant actions. *See* INFORMATION TECHNOLOGY SECURITY EVALUATION CRITERIA. (3) In information security, the quality or state which enables violations or attempted violations of ADP system security to be traced to individuals who may then be held responsible.(FIPS). *See* ADP.

accountability information. In computer security, a set of records, often referred to as an audit trail, that collectively provide documentary evidence of the processing or other actions related to the security of an ADP system. (DOE). *See* AUDIT TRAIL.

account balance. In banking, the aggregation of, to a total current utilization figure, for any given product. *See* CURRENT UTILIZATION, PRODUCT.

account freezing. In banking, the technique of temporarily refusing to conduct transactions of an account if an incorrect PIN is input more than a specified number of times. *See* PIN.

account identification. In banking, identification assigned by the account servicing bank to identify the account of the account owner. (ANSI). *See* ACCOUNT SERVICING BANK, PRIMARY ACCOUNT NUMBER.

account owner bank. In banking, a bank for which an account is serviced at an-

other bank. (ANSI). *See* ACCOUNT SERVICING BANK.

account servicing bank. In banking, a bank which is the depository for an account. (ANSI). *Compare* ACCOUNT OWNER BANK.

accreditation. (1) In computer security, the authorization and approval, granted to an ADP system or network to process sensitive data in an operational environment, and made on the basis of a certification by designated technical personnel of the extent to which design and implementation of the system meet prespecified technical requirements for achieving adequate data security. (FIPS). *See* APPROVAL/ACCREDITATION, CERTIFICATION, DATA SECURITY. (2) In computer security, official authorization, by the appropriate DAA, to place an automated system into operational use. This authorization is a statement that the level of residual risk in operating the system is sufficiently low to allow operation for a specified use. Accreditation is site specific and dependent on meeting local security measures and procedures. (AFR). (3) In computer security, the official authorization granted to an information system to process sensitive information in its operational environment based on comprehensive security evaluation of the system's hardware, firmware, and software security design, configuration and implementation and of the other system procedural, administrative, physical, TEMPEST, personnel and communications security controls. (AFR). *See* TEMPEST.

accreditation authority. In computer security, an official designated to accredit systems for the processing, use, storage, and production of sensitive defense material. (AR). *See* ACCREDITATION, DAA.

accreditation range. In communications security, pertaining to a range with respect to a particular network, is a set of mandatory access control levels for data storage, processing and transmission. The accreditation range will generally reflect the sensitivity levels of data that the accreditation authority believes the host can reliably keep segregated with an acceptable level of risk in the context of the particular network for which the accreditation range is given. Thus, although a host system might be accredited to employ the mandatory access control levels CONFIDENTIAL, SECRET and TOP SECRET in stand-alone operation, it might have an accreditation range consisting the single value TOP SECRET for attachment to some network. (TNI) *See* ACCREDITATION, MANDATORY ACCESS CONTROL.

accumulator circuit. In physical security, a circuit activating an alarm signal as a result of an accumulation of data from sensors.

accuracy. In information security, functions to ensure the correctness and consistency of security relevant information. *See* INFORMATION TECHNOLOGY SECURITY EVALUATION CRITERIA.

ACF2. In computer security, a data security package. *See* DATA SECURITY PACKAGE.

ACH. *See* AUTOMATED CLEARING HOUSE.

ACIA. *See* ASYNCHRONOUS COMMUNICATIONS INTERFACE ADAPTER.

ACK. *See* ACKNOWLEDGE CHARACTER.

ACK0. *See* AFFIRMATIVE ACKNOWLEDGEMENT.

ACK1. *See* AFFIRMATIVE ACKNOWLEDGEMENT.

acknowledge character. In data communications, a character transmitted by a station as an affirmative response to the station with which the connection has been set up. *Compare* NEGATIVE ACKNOWLEDGEMENT. *See* ACKNOWLEDGEMENT, STATION.

acknowledgement. In data communications, the transmission by a receiver of acknowledge characters as a response to a sender. *See* AFFIRMATIVE ACKNOWLEDGEMENT, NEGATIVE ACKNOWLEDGEMENT.

acknowledgement frame. In data communications, a packet sent from a receiver to acknowledge correct receipt of a data frame transmitted over a network. *See* DATA LINK LAYER, FRAME. *Compare* DATA FRAME.

ACM. *See* ASSOCIATION FOR COMPUTING MACHINERY.

acoustic coupler. In data communications, a device to interface an item of equipment, producing digital signals, to a telephone network. Sound transducers in the acoustic coupler produce sound tones corresponding to the digital signals; a telephone handset is placed in contact with the sound transducers so that these tones can be transferred to the telephone network. *See* MODEM, TRANSDUCER.

acoustic eavesdropping. In communications security, the interception of sound waves created by the human voice, printing, punching or transmitting equipment. *Compare* ELECTRONIC EAVESDROPPING. *See* EAVESDROPPING.

acoustic emission. In access control, a method of dynamic signature verification which monitors the sound emitted by the pen during the production of the signature. *See* DYNAMIC SIGNATURE VERIFICATION.

acquired data. In physical security, access or alarm data collected in real time and transmitted to a central alarm system for processing. *See* CENTRAL STATION.

acquirer. (1) In banking, an institution within a transaction interchange network that receives identification and authentication information from a terminal. The acquirer is responsible for obtaining payment for the card acceptor from the card issuer. (SAA). *See* CARD ACCEPTOR, CARD ISSUER, INTERCHANGE. (2) In banking, the institution, or its agent, which acquires the financial data, relating to the transaction, from the card acceptor and transfers that data into an interchange system. Any body that passes messages without regard to the financial data is not considered to be an acquirer. *See* CARD ACCEPTOR, INTERCHANGE. (3) In banking, the institution within a transaction interchange network that receives identification and authentication information from a customer. (ANSI).

activation.   In computer networks, the process by which a component of a node is made ready to perform the functions for which it was designed. *See* NODE.

active attack.   In communications security, an attack in which an opponent modifies transmitted information or injects information into the communications path. Active attacks can be subdivided into three categories:

- message stream modification;
- denial of message service;
- replay and masquerading.

Message stream modification can be aimed at changing the origination address, message contents, destination address or the order in which messages are transmitted. Denial of message service involves deleting, delaying messages or flooding the network with bogus messages.

Replay attacks are based upon the recording, and later playback, of legitimate messages. Masquerading attempts to establish communication between a genuine user and an attacker. *Compare* PASSIVE ATTACK. *See* ACTIVE WIRETAPPING, AUTHENTICATION, DELAY/DENIAL OF SERVICE,   MASQUERADING,   MESSAGE AUTHENTICATION, REPLAY.

active sensor.   In physical security, a sensor which can generate a radiation field for detection purposes. *Compare* PASSIVE SENSOR.

active threat.   (1) In risk management, the threat of deliberate unauthorized change to the state of the system. (ANSI). *Compare* PASSIVE THREAT. (2) In risk management, a potential breach of security, the nature of which, should it occur, would cause actual damage or alteration to the computer: hardware, software or data. *Compare* ACCIDENTAL THREAT, DELIBERATE THREAT, LOGICAL THREAT, PASSIVE THREAT, PHYSICAL THREAT. *See* ACTIVE ATTACK, DENIAL OF SERVICE, MASQUERADING, REPLAY, THREAT, TRAFFIC PADDING.

active wire concentrator.   In computer networks, cabinets with star connection to individual nodes. In some local area networks, they are connected in a ring thus providing a combined ring/star configuration. *See* LOCAL AREA NETWORK, NODE, RING, STAR.

active wiretapping.   (1) In computer security, the attaching of an unauthorized device, such as a computer terminal, to a communications circuit for the purpose of obtaining access to data through the generation of false messages or control signals, or by altering the communications of legitimate users. (FIPS). *See* MASQUERADING, TELEPHONE INTRUSION, WIRETAPPING. (2) In communications security, wiretapping for the purposes of obtaining access to data by the generation of false messages or control signals, alteration of communications of legitimate users or the denial of services to legitimate users. *Compare* PASSIVE WIRETAPPING. *See* DENIAL OF SERVICE, WIRETAPPING.

activity.   In computer security, a security model rule stating that once an object is made inactive, it cannot be accessed until it is made active again. (MTR). See OBJECT.

actual data transfer rate. In data communications, the average number of bits, characters or blocks, per unit time, transferred from a data source and received by a data sink. *See* SOURCE, SINK.

ACU. *See* AUTOMATIC CALLING UNIT.

ADAC. *See* ADMINISTRATIVELY DIRECTED CONTROL ACCESS.

adaptive channel allocation. In communications, a method of multiplexing where channels are allocated according to demand rather than on a fixed predetermined plan. *See* MULTIPLEXING, FREQUENCY DIVISION MULTIPLE ACCESS, TIME DIVISION MULTIPLE ACCESS.

adaptive routing. In data communications, a routing scheme for packets or messages in which the behavior adapts to network changes such as line failures or variation of the traffic pattern. *Compare* DELTA ROUTING, DIRECTORY ROUTING, FIXED ROUTING, HOT POTATO ROUTING. *See* CENTRALIZED ADAPTIVE ROUTING, MESSAGE SWITCHING, PACKET SWITCHING, ROUTING.

ADCCP. *See* ADVANCED DATA COMMUNICATIONS CONTROL PROCEDURE.

add-in. In hardware, an expansion card which slots into a computer to provide additional facilities. *See* MODEM.

additive cipher. *Synonymous with* TRANSLATION CIPHER.

add-on security. In computer security, the retrofitting of protection mechanisms, implemented by hardware or software, after the ADP system has become operational. (FIPS). *See* ADP.

address. (1) In computing, a character or group of characters that identifies a register, a particular part of storage, or some other data source or destination. (2) In computing, to refer to a device or an item of data by its address. (3) In communications, the part of the selection signals that indicates the destination of a call.

addressing. (1) In computing, the assignment of addresses to the instructions of a program. *See* ADDRESS. (2) In communications, the means whereby the originator or control station selects the unit to which it is going to send a message. *See* STATION.

address space. In architecture, the virtual memory that can be addressed by a process. The maximum size of a process address space is usually a function of the underlying hardware. (MTR). *See* VIRTUAL MEMORY.

ad hoc enquiry. In databases, a method which allows the user in a database environment to dynamically create his own view of the data and the method of retrieval for the information without intervention. (AR).

adjacent channel. In communications, the next channel, or the one in close proximity, either physically or electrically to the one in current use. *See* CHANNEL.

ADLC. *See* ADVANCED DATA LINK CONTROL.

administratively directed access control. In access control, pertaining to a system in which administrators control who can access which objects. *Compare* USER DIRECTED ACCESS CONTROL. *See* MANDATORY ACCESS CONTROL.

administrative security. In data security, the management constraints, operational procedures, accountability procedures, and supplemental controls established to provide an acceptable level of protection for sensitive data. (FIPS). *See* ACCOUNTABILITY. *Synonymous with* PROCEDURAL SECURITY.

ADP. Automatic Data Processing. *See*

AUTOMATIC DATA PROCESSING SYSTEM.

ADP availability. In computer security, the state that exists when ADP services can be obtained within an acceptable period of time. *Compare* APPLICATION CONFIDENTIALITY, APPLICATION INTEGRITY, DATA INTEGRITY. *See* ADP, DATA CONFIDENTIALITY.

ADP security. In computer security, measures required to protect against unauthorized (accidental or intentional) disclosure, modification, or destruction of ADP systems and data, and denial of service to process data. ADP security includes consideration of all hardware/software functions, characteristics, and/or features; operational procedures, accountability procedures, and access controls at the central computer facility, remote computer, and terminal facilities; management constraints; physical structures and devices; and personnel and communication controls needed to provide an acceptable level of risk for the ADP system and for the data or information contained in the system. (OPNAVINST). *See* ADP.

ADP security documentation. In computer security, documents which describe an activity's ADP security posture and include risk assessment plan and reports, security test and evaluation plans and reports, Inspector General inspection reports and findings, incident reports, contingency plans and test results, and standard operating procedures. (OPNAVINST). *See* ADP, ADP SECURITY.

ADP security staff. In computer security, individuals assigned and functioning as action officials for ADP security within their respective organization. (OPNAVINST). *See* ADP, ADP SECURITY.

ADP system security. In computer security, all of the technological safeguards and managerial procedures estab-

lished and applied to computer hardware, software, and data in order to ensure the protection of organizational assets and individual privacy. (FIPS). *See* ADP, ADP SECURITY.

advanced data communications control procedure. In data communications, pertaining to the operation of a data link using an advanced (SDLC, HDLC) protocol. *See* HDLC, PROTOCOL, SDLC.

advanced data link control. In data communications, a link protocol used in HDLC and SDLC systems. *See* HDLC, SDLC.

advice. In banking, confirmation that action has taken place. (ANSI).

advice and assessment. In computer security, a technical analysis of the computer security posture of a particular system and advice to the customer about vulnerabilities of the system. *See* VULNERABILITY.

AFCEA. Armed Forces Communications and Electronics Association.

Affirm. In computing, a formal methodology developed at the University of Southern California Information Sciences Institute (USC-ISI) for the specification and verification of abstract data types, incorporating algebraic specification techniques and hierarchical development. (MTR). *See* HDM.

affirmative acknowledgement. In data communications, the replies ACK0 and ACK1 in binary synchronous transmission indicate that the previous transmission block was accepted by the receiver and that it is ready to accept the next block. ACK0 and ACK1 sent alternately provide sequential checking for a series of replies. ACK0 is also used as an affirmative reply to a station selection signal in a multidrop circuit, or to an initialization sequence in a point to point operation. *Compare* NEG-

ATIVE ACKNOWLEDGEMENT. *See* BINARY SYNCHRONOUS COMMUNICATIONS, MULTI-DROP CIRCUIT, POINT TO POINT.

AFIPS. American Federation of Information Processing Societies Inc. A federation founded in 1961 including the American Society for Information Science, American Statistical Association, Association for Computing Machinery, Association for Education Data Systems, Data Processing Management Association, IEEE Computer Society, Instrument Society of America, Society for Computer Simulation, Society for Industrial and Applied Mathematics, Society for Information Display. It is the U.S. member of IFIP. *See* IFIP.

AFNOR. Association Francaise de NORmalisation - the French Standards Organization.

AFR. Air Force Regulation.

agency activity. In banking, activity which the bank enters on behalf of customers through which no direct risk is incurred.

aggregation. (1) In data security, individual data systems and data elements may be determined to be unclassified and to be of a specific sensitivity category. When those data are combined with other data the totality of the information may be classified or in a higher sensitivity category, with higher protection requirements. (AFR). *See* MULTILEVEL DATA-BASE SECURITY. (2) In mathematics, an abstraction, whereby a relationship between objects is regarded as a higher level object.

AGI. In computer security a virus that infects COMMAND.COM, and COM files, affects run time operation, corrupts program and OVL files and file linkage. *See* VIRUS NAMES.

aging. In data processing, identification of unprocessed or retained items in files according to their date, usually transaction date. Aging classifies items according to various ranges of dates.

AGI-Plan. In computer security, a virus that infects COMMAND.COM and COM files, affects run time operation, corrupts program and OVL files and file linkage. *See* VIRUS NAMES.

Aids. In computer security, a virus that infects COM files. *See* VIRUS NAMES.

AIM. Automatic Identification Manufacturers.

AirCop. In computer security, a virus that terminates and stays resident, infects floppy disk boot sector, corrupts boot sector and affects run time operation. *See* VIRUS NAMES.

AIS. Automated Information System.

AMAIS security. In computer security, the totality of security safeguards needed to provide an acceptable level of protection for an AIS and for data handled by an AIS. (DODD). *See* AIS.

Alabama. In computer security, a virus that terminates and stays resident, infects EXE files, affects run time operation, corrupts program, OVL files and file linkage. *See* VIRUS NAMES.

Alameda. In computer security, a virus that terminates and stays resident, infects floppy disk boot sector and corrupts boot sector. *See* VIRUS NAMES.

alarm assessment system. In physical security, a system which permits an operator to assess a previously reported alarm, e.g. a CCTV which provides images for analysis by the operator. *See* CCTV.

alarm discriminator. In physical security, a device or detector which is added to a system to reduce the probability of false alarms arising from extraneous vibrations or noise

alarm indicating device. In physical security, a visual or audible signal indicating the incidence of a fire.

alarm line. In physical security, a wired electrically supervised circuit, between a protected area and alarm receiver, used to transmit alarm signals. *See* ALARM SIGNAL.

alarm receiver. In physical security, an annunciator which also provides for the monitoring of an alarm line. It may or may not include an audible alarm device. *See* ALARM LINE, ANNUNCIATOR, AUDIBLE ALARM DEVICE.

alarm screen. In physical security, an electrified window screen which trips an alarm when cut.

alarm signal. In physical security, a visual and/or audible signal which indicates an emergency requiring immediate action (e.g. equipment failure, ingress of water, smoke, fire, line tamper or failure, unsafe equipment condition).

alarm station. In physical security, a manually operated switch or device that activates an alarm.

ALE. *See* ANNUAL LOSS EXPECTANCY.

algorithm. In computing, a finite set of well defined rules for the solution of a problem in a finite number of steps, for example, a precise description of the steps involved in determining the record with the highest value of a specified numerical attribute.

Aloha. In data communications, a communication network of ground based radio systems which employed a collision protocol to allocate the broadcast channel to users. Users transmit whenever they have data to send. If two users overlap their usage of the broadcast channel then the packets of data will be corrupted. The senders monitor the broadcast channel, if they discover that their recently transmitted packet was corrupted they wait for a random period and retransmit the packet. *See* BROADCAST, CARRIER SENSE PROTOCOL, CARRIER SENSE MULTIPLE ACCESS - COLLISION DETECTION.

alphabetic character set. A character set that contains letters but not digits. The set may contain control characters, special characters, and the space character. *Compare* ALPHANUMERIC. *See* CONTROL CHARACTER.

alphanumeric. Pertaining to a character set that contains letters, digits and usually other characters, e.g. punctuation marks. *Compare* ALPHABETIC CHARACTER SET.

alternate route. In communications, a secondary or backup route that is used if normal routing is not possible.

AM. *See* AMPLITUDE MODULATION.

ambush code. In physical security, a special code for an access control system, or digital keypad entry, which provides a remote duress alarm when input into the access control system. *See* ACCESS CONTROL, DIGITAL KEYPAD, DURESS ALARM.

amend. In banking, to amend details on the computer, for either a customer, facility or service.

American National Standards Institute. In Standards, a body that organizes committees formed of computer users, manufacturers, etc., to develop and publish industry standards, e.g. ANSI FORTRAN, ANSI Standard Code for Periodical Identification. ANSI X3 is concerned with computer and data processing standards, ANSI X9 with banking standards.

amplitude modulation. In communications, a form of modulation in which the amplitude of the carrier signal is varied in accordance with the amplitude of the modulating signal. *Compare* FREQUENCY MODULATION, PHASE MODULATION. *See* CARRIER, MODULATION.

Amstrad. In computer security, a virus that infects COM files and corrupts program and OVL files. *See* VIRUS NAMES.

analog. In computing and communications, pertaining to the form of continuously variable physical quantities. *Compare* DIGITAL. *See* ANALOG SIGNAL.

analog channel. In communications, a data channel in which the amplitude of the signal transmitted can take any value between the limits defined for the channel. Voice grade channels are analog channels. *See* ANALOG.

analog signal. A signal that varies continuously according to the information in transmission, e.g. sound waves. *Compare* DIGITAL SIGNAL. *See* ANALOG.

analog transmission. In communications, the transmission of information by analog signal. *See* ANALOG SIGNAL.

analysis. *See* COST-RISK ANALYSIS, CRYPTANALYSIS, RISK ANALYSIS.

analytical attack. In cryptanalysis, an attack in which a set of mathematical equations, obtained from the definitions of the cryptographic algorithm, are solved for the variable, or variables, representing the unknown plaintext or cryptographic key. *Compare* EXHAUSTIVE ATTACK. *See* CRYPTOGRAPHIC KEY.

ancillary equipment. In communications, equipment located on a subscriber's premises, e.g. answering devices, automatic dialers, to provide a greater utility of a communications channel for individual subscribers.

anisochronous signal. In electronics, a signal which is not related to any clock and in which transitions could occur at any instant. *See* ANISOCHRONOUS TRANSMISSION.

anisochronous transmission. In data communications, a form of data transmission, similar to asynchronous transmission, but where there can be variable time intervals between the bits within a character as well as between the characters themselves. *Compare* ASYNCHRONOUS TRANSMISSION, ISOCHRONOUS TRANSMISSION. *See* BIT.

annual loss expectancy. In risk management, a measure of the potential annual cost of a threat to system security. *See* RISK ANALYSIS, THREAT.

annunciator. In physical security, a visual or audio system which indicates a change of protection zone status in a security system. *See* PROTECTION PATTERN.

anonymous refunder. In banking, a person who moves money from one account to another outside the usual method.

ANSI. *See* AMERICAN NATIONAL STANDARDS INSTITUTE.

ANSI X.12. In standards, an ANSI standard for EDI. Unlike EDIFACT this standard deals with both the formatting and transport mechanisms of messages. Documents for the same destination or receiver are grouped within an interchange envelope, groups of the same type of documents within an interchange envelope are contained within a functional group envelope and individual documents are in turn contained in a transaction set envelope. Security of messages is discussed in X12.58, Electronic Data Interchange Security Services and the security aims to provide integrity, confidentiality and verification of the sender, but only symmetric ciphers, e.g. DES, are employed.

Filtering of the ciphertext is employed to ensure that the ciphertext comprises only characters from the permitted set for transmission. The key management is described in X.12.42. *Compare* EDIFACT. *See* DES, FILTERING, KEY MANAGEMENT, SYMMETRIC CIPHER.

ANSI X3.T1. In standards, the ANSI Technical Committee in Encryption.

ANSI X3.92 - 1981. In standards, an ANSI standard for the Data Encryption Algorithm. *See* DATA ENCRYPTION ALGORITHM.

ANSI X3.105 - 1983. In standards, an ANSI standard - Data Link Encryption. *See* OSI SECURITY.

ANSI X3.106 - 1983. In standards, an ANSI standard - Modes of operation for the Data Encryption Algorithm. *See* ANSI X3.92 - 1981, DATA ENCRYPTION ALGORITHM.

ANSI X3.118 - 1984. In standards, an ANSI standards for Personal Identification Number - PIN Pad. *See* PIN PAD.

ANSI X9.1 - 1984. In standards, an ANSI standard for Magnetic Stripe Data Content for Track 3.

ANSI X9.2 - 1980. In standards, an ANSI standard for Interchange Message Specification for debit and Credit Card Message Exchange among Financial Institutions.

ANSI X9.3 - 1981. In standards, an ANSI standard for Check Endorsements Specifications.

ANSI X9.5 - 1988. In standards, an ANSI standard for Financial Institution Numbering System (FINS).

ANSI X9.7 - 1988. In standards, an ANSI standard for Bank Check Background and Convenience Amount Field.

ANSI X9.8 - 1982. In standards, an ANSI standard for Personal Identification Number Management and Security. *See* PIN MANAGEMENT AND SECURITY.

ANSI X9.9 - 1986. In standards, an ANSI standard for Financial Institution Message Authentication. The standard deals with financial messages, including fund transfers, letters of credit, security transfers, loan agreements and foreign exchange control.

The standard defines the minimum set of message elements to be included in the authentication process. The minimum set is:

- transaction value and currency type;
- identification of credit, debit and beneficiary parties;
- value date;
- date of message origination;
- message identifier.

The standard also allows for the authentication of the entire text of the message.

The authentication ensures that the message receiver can check that its contents have not been accidentally or maliciously changed. A simple checksum provides assurance against accidental corruption, but an attacker could re-compute the checksum for an altered message. An encrypted checksum provides an assurance against malicious modification since the attacker is unable to re-compute the encrypted checksum.

The operation of the standard requires the sender to generate a Message Authentication Code (MAC) using the Data Encryption Algorithm, the MAC is included in the message forwarded to the receiving party. The receiver applies the same authentication process to the received message, using the same secret DEA key, and compares the generated MAC with that included with the message. Any discrepancy between the two MAC's indicates that one or more of the message elements included in the authentication process have been modified.

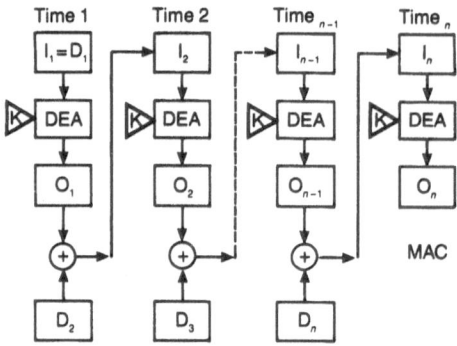

MAC

Symbols: I, input; DEA,
data encryption algorithm;
O, output; K, DEA key,
D, data block;
+, EXCLUSIVE-OR.

ANSI X9.9.

In the authentication algorithm, the message is assembled in 64-bit data blocks (T_n). The first (D_1) is passed through the DEA, which uses a secret key (K) to produce 64 bits in the output register (O_1). The second 64 bits of data (D_2) to be authenticated are bitwise 'EXCLUSIVE-OR ed' with the 64 bits in the output register, and the result is loaded into the input register (I_2). The process continues until 64 or fewer bits remain to be authenticated. The leftmost 32 bits of the final output (O_n) are taken as the MAC. The remaining 32 bits, the MAC residue, do not form part of the standard, but may be used to authenticate the sender of the message by forming a challenge to which the sender must respond.

The sender and receiver must both share a secret key and agree upon the message elements to be included in the authentication process. This key should be automatically changed on a regular basis, for example by using the procedures laid down in ANSI X9.17.

The authentication algorithm may, by bilateral agreement, be applied to the entire message or to selected message elements. If the entire message is authenticated then the body of the message must not change between the sender and receiver; header and trailer information used for transmission purposes must be omitted.

If only specific message elements are included in the authentication process then the standard defines, in detail, the minimum set of message elements and the manner in which they are edited for inclusion in the authentication algorithm. The authentication algorithm is applied using either cipher feedback or cipher block chaining modes of DES operation. The first 64 bits of data are used as the initial variable and the remaining data is then input into the encryption routine until the last data block, appended with zeros to form a 64 bit block if necessary, is processed. The leftmost 32 bits of the last output block is taken as the MAC.

See ANSI X9.17 - 1985, AUTHENTICATION, CIPHER BLOCK CHAINING, CIPHER FEEDBACK, DEA, MAC, MAC RESIDUE, VALUE DATE.

ANSI X9.12 - 1983. In standards, an ANSI standard for Specification for Fully Registered Municipal Securities.

ANSI X9.13 - 1983. In standards, an ANSI standard for Specifications for Placement and Location of MICR Printing. *See* MICR.

ANSI X9.14 - 1983. In standards, an ANSI standard for Specification for Securities Transactions Interchange Forms.

ANSI X9.16 - 1984. In standards, an ANSI standard for Formats for Message Types, Standard.

ANSI X9.17 - 1985. In standards, an ANSI standard for Financial Institution Key Management (Wholesale).

The scope of the standard is given below.

- Control during the life of the keying material to prevent unauthorized disclosure, modification or substitution.
- Distribution of keying material to permit interoperability between cryptographic key equipment or facilities using the DEA algorithm.
- Ensuring the integrity of keying material during all phases of its life, including the generation, distribution, storage, entry, use and destruction.
- Recovery in the event of failure of the key management process or when the integrity of the keying material is questioned.

The functions of the key management system are to provide keys and initialization vectors (IV) to the places required and to maintain the secrecy of keys. The measures must be aimed at the prevention of the unauthorized disclosure, modification, substitution, insertion and deletion of keys and IVs.

Keys may be distributed manually or automatically, i.e. by automated distribution. The architecture for the automated distribution is based upon the assumption that the data network shall be expandable and that a communicating pair have a key encrypting key in common, or each has a key encrypting key in common with a center.

A two or three layer key distribution architecture may be employed. With a two layer architecture the topmost layer key encrypting key is manually distributed and data keys are subject to automated distribution encrypted by the topmost layer keys. In a three layer architecture the topmost layer is again a manually distributed key encrypting key, the second layer comprises key encrypting keys

encrypted with the layer one key, and in turn, used to encrypt the third layer data keys. The architecture is designed to meet the requirements listed below.

- Communicating pairs have at least one data key which can be changed automatically.
- A data key can be used for encryption or authentication, but not both, except in the case of cryptographic service messages.
- Data keys shared by a communicating pair shall be secure from disclosure or use by a third party other than a key distribution or translation center.
- A compromise of a key shared by a communicating pair shall not compromise any third party.
- The architecture shall support communicating pairs that do not have key generation capabilities and shall support any party that wishes to initiate secure communication with any other party.
- Data keys may be sent for current or future use and key security and integrity shall be ensured.
- A key used by a communicating pair shall not be intentionally used by any other pair or by the same pair after any one of the parties has discontinued its use.
- Either party of a communicating pair may discontinue the use of a key.
- Any communicating pair may employ more than one key encrypting key.
- The architecture permits two, or three, layers of keys and in a three layer architecture the key encrypting keys may be automatically exchanged between communicating pairs.

The key and IV generation process for manual and automated distribution must ensure the protection of distribution and storage resources from unauthorized use, alteration, replacement, and destruction. Generation processes for manually distributed keys, and IVs, must be under dual control.

The automated distribution of keys may be undertaken in point to point, key distribution center or key translation center environments. In a point to point environment at least one party in a communicating pair must have the capability to generate or acquire keys and the two parties share a key encrypting key. In a key distribution center environment the parties individually share key encrypting keys with the center but not with each other. The originating party requests a data key, or data keys, from the center, providing details of the identity of the intended recipient. The center generates, or acquires, data keys. The data key is encrypted with the key encrypting key shared between the originator and center, the same data key is also encrypted with the key encrypting key shared with the intended recipient of the secure message. Both sets of encrypted keys are then forwarded to the originator. Upon receipt of the sets of encrypted data keys the originator sends the second set to the intended recipient. The key translation center environment operates in a similar manner except that the originator has the capability to generate, or acquire, a data key. In this case the originator encrypts the data key, with the key encrypting key shared with the translation center, and sends it to the center together with the identity of the intended recipient. The center decrypts the received encrypted key, re-encrypts it with the key encrypting key, shared between the center and intended recipient, and returns the result to the originator.

The keys employed in the abovementioned processes may be single keys or key pairs. A key pair comprises two independent keys; the encryption process with a key pair involves encryption with one member of the pair, decryption of the result with the second member followed by encryption with the first member again. Decryption involves the reverse processes, i.e. decryption by the first key,

encryption by the second and then decryption with the first. Encryption and decryption of key pairs with other key pairs involves the abovementioned processes on each member of the key pair and concatenation of the resulting output of the processes.

The communicating parties also employ counters to keep track of messages between specific parties. An originator updates the counter with each appropriate transmitted message and a recipient updates the 'expected count' for that originator upon receipt of a message. A recipient will take appropriate action if the count included in a message does not correspond to the 'expected count' for that originator, e.g. if the count is less than the expected count an error message will be returned to the originator. The counter value (offset) may also be combined with the key encrypting key and the result used to encrypt another key for transmission. Key notarization is a method of sealing keys with the identities of communicating pairs. A 16 byte character stream, representing the identities of each party, is produced and combined, by encryption processes, with the key encrypting key. The result of these operations produces a notarizing key used to encrypt a key encrypting key or data key.

The standard defines messages which are exchanged between communicating parties, key distribution and key translation centers. These cryptographic service messages (CSM) include: Request Service Initiation (RSI), Key Service Message (KSM), Response Service Message (RSM), Error Service Message (ESM), Disconnect Service Message (DSM), Request for Service Message (RFS), Response to Request Service Message (RTR) and Error Recovery Service Message (ERS).

A Request Service Initiation Message is an optional message requesting the initiation of a new keying relationship. A Key Service Message transfers a key from an originator to a recipient and a Response Service Message provides an authenticated response to a KSM. An error in a previous CSM is reported in an Error Service Message, and keys may be discontinued with a Disconnect Service Message.

CSMs employed in key distribution or translation center environments are:

- Request for Service Message, which sends keys, intended for the ultimate recipient, to the key translation center for translation;
- Response to Request Service Message which replies to an RFS, ERS or RSI;
- Error Recovery Service Message which reports count and key errors to the center and requests resynchronization of the count fields and re-initiation of service.

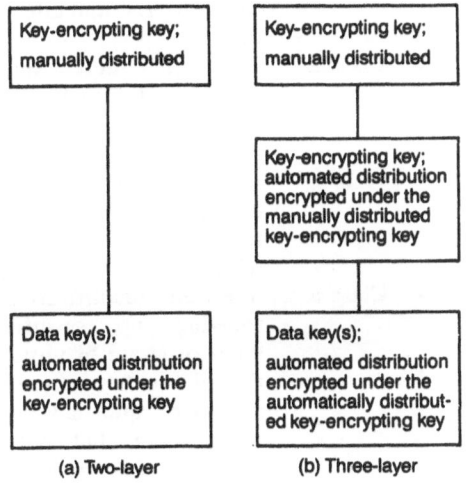

(a) Two-layer   (b) Three-layer

ANSI X9.17.
Two- and three-key distribution architecture.

See AUTHENTICATION, COMMUNICATING PAIR, CRYPTOGRAPHIC EQUIPMENT, CRYPTOGRAPHIC KEY, CRYPTOGRAPHIC SERVICE MESSAGE, DATA KEY, DEA, DUAL CONTROL, INITIALIZATION VECTOR, INTEROPERABILITY, IV, KEY ENCRYPTING KEY, KEY DISTRIBUTION CENTER, KEY GENERATOR, KEYING MATERIAL, KEY MANAGEMENT, KEY NOTARIZATION, KEY PAIR, KEY TRANSLATION CENTER, MULTIPLE DES ENCIPHERMENT, OFFSET, ORIGINATOR, POINT TO POINT, RECIPIENT, THREE LAYER ARCHITECTURE, TWO LAYER ARCHITECTURE.

ANSI X9.18 - 1986. In standards, an ANSI standard for Paper Specification for Checks.

ANSI X9.19 - 1986. In standards, an ANSI standard for Financial Institution Retail Message Authentication.

ANSI X9.20 - 1986. In standards, an ANSI standard for Securities - Institutional Delivery System.

ANSI X9.21 - 1986. In standards, an ANSI standard Vocabulary and Data Elements for Wholesale Funds Transfers and Related Advices.

ANSI X9.22 - 1986. In standards, an ANSI standard for Specifications for Standard Telex Formats for Wholesale Financial Services Messages.

ANSI X9.23 - 1988. In standards, an ANSI standard for Financial Institution Encryption of Wholesale Financial Messages.

answer back. In data communications, a signal sent by a receiving unit to the sending station for identification or to indicate it is ready for transmission. *See* VOICE ANSWER BACK.

answering. In data communications, the process of responding to a calling station to complete the establishment of a connection between data stations. *See* STATION.

Anthrax-Boot. In computer security, a virus that terminates and stays resident, infects hard disk partition table, affects run time operation, corrupts program, OVL and data files. *See* VIRUS NAMES.

Anthrax-File. In computer security, a virus that terminates and stays resident, infects COMMAND.COM, COM and EXE files, affects run time operation, corrupts program, OVL and data files. *See* VIRUS NAMES.

anti-eavesdrop device. In physical security, a device that detects the presence of covert listening units by scanning RF transmission frequencies. *See* ELECTRONIC COUNTERMEASURES SWEEPING, RF.

anti-fixed point. In cryptography, a plaintext block which is transformed into its complement by a cryptographic algorithm. In DES, if an anti-palindromic semiweak key is employed, then there are 2^{32} anti-fixed points. *Compare* FIXED POINT. *See* ANTI-PALINDROMIC KEY, COMPLEMENT, DATA ENCRYPTION STANDARD, PLAINTEXT, SEMIWEAK KEY.

anti-jam. In computer security, pertaining to special telephone dialers designed to prevent interruption of dial out by incoming calls. *See* TELEPHONE INTRUSION, TELEPHONE DIALER.

anti-palindromic key. In cryptography, a DES key in which subkey 1 is the complement of subkey 16, subkey 2 is the complement of subkey 15 etc. Four DES semiweak keys have this property. *Compare* PALINDROMIC KEY. *See* COMPLEMENT, CRYPTOGRAPHIC KEY, DATA ENCRYPTION STANDARD, SEMIWEAK KEY, SUB-KEY.

anti-passback. In physical security, pertaining to a system designed to prevent 'passing back' of an access card from an individual who has already gained entry. This measure ensures that a card used to enter an area is used to exit the area before it is reused for entry. *See* TAILGATING.

anti-surveillance. In physical security, pertaining to a system designed to prevent or detect the use of surveillance equip-

ment. *See* ANTI-EAVESDROP DEVICE.

anti-viral measures. In computer security, measures taken to prevent an attack by computer viruses and to recover from such an attack.

Although many claims for virus vaccines and virus killers were made, there is no perfect, automatic defence against the arbitrary virus. It must be recognized that there is no single attribute, which must be possessed by a virus, that is never possessed by a section of legitimate code, and there is no single action which must be performed by a virus that is never performed by a section of legitimate code.

Anti-viral products tend to fall within one of three classes:

- Class 1   infection prevention designed to stop the virus replication process and prevent initial infection;
- Class 2   infection detection, designed to pick up virus attacks soon after they happen, mark the specific component(s) infected and allow remedial action to be taken;
- Class 3   infection identification showing up specific types of strain of virus, it will identify viruses in systems and may remove them, but only works on known viruses.

Products in the first category intercept calls which appear 'suspicious' and inform the user.

An effective detection of viruses can take place after they have struck. Thus Class 2 products are less likely to have difficulty in differentiating between legitimate and malicious action. On the other hand the infection will affect at least one program; the object of the product is to warn the user at the outset of infection so that it can be prevented from spreading further, thus minimizing the damage.

One common technique of Class 2 products is to:

- compute a checksum on the 'clean' software and store the result;
- prior to the execution of the software, re-perform the checksum and compare the result with the stored result;
- allow execution to proceed if the two checksums are identical, otherwise abort execution and display a warning message.

This is an effective defence which may be deployed during normal operation. It will detect software infected by a virus which is about to spread the infection. However, like all anti-viral measures it has limitations that must be recognized:

- it will allow at least one program to be infected;
- the checksum routine must be such that it will detect very small changes in the program, this checksumming is time consuming, hence producing a irritating delay for users, some quick checksum routines are faster but can fail to detect minor program changes;
- the routine only gives an assurance of program integrity at the time of checksum comparison, if the program is infected between the time of the checksum check and program execution then a further file will be infected, i.e. a classic TOCTTOU (Time of Check to Time of Update) attack;
- some software packages, e.g. Word Perfect, modify themselves and may therefore give rise to false alarms;
- it must not be possible for the virus to recompute the checksum for infected program and then update the stored checksum.

The latter point can be met by the use of cryptographic checksums routines, and

use of a secret key which cannot be accessed by the virus.

The use of Class 3 systems which check for known virus signatures is popular because it is very user friendly. The virus signature employed in the product must identify the virus. Used wisely products in this class can be a useful adjunct to good personal computer security procedures, but they suffer from some obvious drawbacks:

- the list of virus signatures must be kept up to date;
- viruses can easily mutate to change their signatures and thus avoid detection;
- only currently known viruses will be detected.

In the case of all anti-viral products it is essential to ensure that the virus cannot take control at an early stage and effectively bypass or modify the action of the anti-viral product.

In addition to detecting viruses some products claimed to be virus killers, i.e. elimination the virus code from the disk. This action had some user appeal but it was unnecessary and contained inherent dangers to users software and data.

If a sensible backup routine is maintained, for software and data, then the surest means of killing a virus is to boot in a manner that ensures the virus cannot take control, reformat the infected disk, overwriting all files, and download software and data from an uninfected backup. Attempts to kill viruses may be incomplete; virus attacks commonly recur after apparently successful attempts to remove the sections of infected code. Virus killer products can also lead to the destruction of user data, particularly if the action of a virus, with a given signature, mutates causing a change in the nature of the virus code.

It is strongly recommended that the security procedures for personal computers, particularly those in organizations with a large population of naive computing users, be formulated to provide a defence in depth approach against virus, and other data security, events. The most important aspects of such a policy are:

- strict control on the import of software;
- central group to check and certify all new software before it is passed to users;
- information and on-line help service to users, warning of virus symptoms, advising users reporting unusual software behavior;
- strictly applied backup routines;
- recovery procedures to be undertaken by technically competent staff;
- restrictions on the use of computers by employees, e.g. forbidding use of computers for games, college assignments by part time students etc., some organizations reserve a computer for such informal use and forbid the processing of organizational data on the dedicated machine.

Encryptor boards provide a means of protecting personal computers against illicit usage, with the attendant risk of virus infection. All the software on the hard disk is encrypted and a password is required before data or programs may be inserted from a floppy disk. A legitimate user, of a machine incorporating an encryptor board, therefore has the assurance that no unauthorized user has had the opportunity to introduce infected software. *See* ENCRYPTOR BOARD, TOCTTOU PROBLEMS, VIRUS.

AOSS. In computing, Automated Office Support Systems, including stand-alone microprocessors, word processors and terminals connected to mainframes.(DOE).

API. *See* APPLICATION PROGRAM INTERFACE, AUTOMATIC PERSONAL IDENTIFICATION. *Synonymous with* BIOMETRICS.

application confidentiality. In computer security, the state that exists when application source and object code, and documentation, is held in confidence and is protected from unauthorized disclosure. *Compare* ADP AVAILABILITY, APPLICATION INTEGRITY. *See* CONFIDENTIALITY, DATA CONFIDENTIALITY, OBJECT CODE, SOURCE CODE.

application disaster recovery plan. In risk management, a plan to resume operation of an application after it has been interrupted for period of time. *See* DISASTER RECOVERY.

application integrity. (1) In computer security, those processes aimed at ensuring that an application, viewed as a system, continues to operate according to its specifications and continues to be available. *Compare* DENIAL OF SERVICE. (2) In computer security, the state that exists when the source and object code are the same as originally developed and certified/accredited or, have been modified and tested in accordance with established standards and procedures and recertified/reaccredited and have not been exposed to accidental or malicious alteration or destruction. *Compare* ADP AVAILABILITY, APPLICATION CONFIDENTIALITY. *See* DATA INTEGRITY, OBJECT CODE, SOURCE CODE.

application layer. In data communications, the topmost layer in the ISO open systems interconnections model. This layer may provide a wide variety of services to users, e.g. dealing with the problem of incompatible terminals on the network, file transfer protocols, electronic mail, etc. *Compare* DATA LINK LAYER, NETWORK LAYER, PHYSICAL LAYER, PRESENTATION LAYER, SESSION LAYER, TRANSPORT LAYER. *See* ELECTRONIC MAIL, NETWORK VIRTUAL TERMINAL, OPEN SYSTEMS INTERCONNECTION, X.400.

application process. (1) In computer

security, an untrusted process performing end user computation. *See* TRUSTED PROCESS. (2) In data communications, a part within an open system that processes information and uses Opens Systems Interconnection communication services to communicate with other application processes in other open systems. *See* OPEN SYSTEMS INTERCONNECTION.

application program. In computing, a program, usually written in house, for a specific user application, e.g. payroll.

application program interface. In computing, a set of commands that an application may make to a software module providing a defined service, e.g. a cryptographic service.

application software. In computing, routines and programs designed by, or for system users and customers. Through the use of available automated system equipment and basic software, application software completes specific, mission-oriented tasks, jobs, or functions. It can be either general purpose packages, such as demand deposit accounting, payroll, machine tool control, and so forth, or specific application programs tailored to complete a single or limited number of user functions, for example, base-level personnel, depot maintenance, missile or satellite tracking, and so forth. Except for general purpose packages that are acquired directly from software vendors or from the original equipment manufacturers (OEM), this type of software is generally developed by user either with in-house resources or through contract services. (AFR). *Synonymous with* APPLICATION PROGRAM.

approval/accreditation. In computer security, the official authorization that is granted to an ADP system to process sensitive information in its operational environment, based upon comprehensive security evaluation of the system's hardware, firmware, and software security design, configuration, and implementation and of the other system procedural, administrative, physical, Tempest, personnel and communications security controls. (DOD). *See* ACCREDITATION, TEMPEST.

approval to operate. In computer security, concurrence by the DAA that a satisfactory level of security has been provided (minimum requirements are met and there is an acceptable level of risk). It authorizes the operation of an automated system or network at a computer facility. Approval results from an analysis of the computer facility, automated system, and automatic data system certifications and the operational environment of the automated system entity by the DAA. (AFR). *See* ACCREDITATION, DAA.

approved circuit. *Synonymous with* PROTECTED WIRELINE DISTRIBUTION SYSTEM.

a priori control. In database security, a form of inference control which determines, in advance, whether or not a set of statistics can be released without causing personal disclosure. *Compare* AUDIT BASED CONTROL, MEMORYLESS CONTROL. *See* INFERENCE CONTROL, PERSONAL DISCLOSURE.

AR. Army Regulation.

Arab Virus. In computer security, a virus that terminates and stays resident, infects COM files, affects run time operation and corrupts program and OVL files. *See* VIRUS NAMES.

arbiter. In authentication, a party who keeps public data generated by users, and employed by receivers to validate signatures. *See* ARBITRATED SIGNATURE.

arbitrated signature. In authentication, a digital signature which involves a third party, the arbiter. The signed message is prepared by the sender and forwarded to the arbiter. The arbiter checks the identity of the sender, signs the message and subsequently validates it for the receiver. *Compare* UNIVERSAL SIGNATURE. *See* DIGITAL SIGNATURE.

arc-breakdown protector. In physical security, a device to protect electrical equipment against excessive voltages, such as those induced in power lines by lightning. *See* ARRESTER.

architecture. (1) *See* SECURITY ARCHITECTURE. (2) In computing, the specification of the relationships between parts of a computer system. *See* VON NEUMANN.

archive. (1) In operations, to store records or files offline. (2) In operations, the location of stored records or files.

area mat. In physical security, a thin rubber or vinyl mat, with pressure sensors, used to detect intrusions. *See* INTRUSION DETECTOR. *Synonymous with* FLOOR SENSOR.

area protection. In physical security, the use of ultrasonic, microwave, infra red or photoelectric sensors to protect a defined area. *See* INTRUSION DETECTOR. *Synonymous with* SPACE PROTECTION.

Armageddon. In computer security, a virus that terminates and stays resident, infects COMMAND.COM and COM files, affects run time operation and corrupts program and OVL files. *See* VIRUS NAMES.

arming station. In physical security, a console or keyswitch used to place an alarm system into the alarm detection mode.

ARPA. *See* DARPA.

ARPANET. In data communications, ARPA NETwork, a computer network originally established under the sponsorship of the Advanced Research Projects

Agency for the study of computer networks and computer resource sharing. Responsibility for the network was transferred to the Defense Communications Agency in 1975. Arpanet was later split into a research and development network, still named Arpanet and the Defense Data Network (DDN). *See* DDN, INTERNET, MILNET.

ARQ. *See* AUTOMATIC RETRANSMISSION REQUEST.

array. In computing, an ordered arrangement or pattern of items or numbers, e.g. a table of numbers. *See* LOOP, VECTOR.

array processor. In architecture, a computer system which is designed to perform identical operations, on elements of an array, in parallel. It may be a self contained unit or attached to a mainframe computer via an internal bus or input output port. *See* PARALLEL PROCESSING.

arrest. In computer security, the discovery of user activity not necessary to the normal processing of data which might lead to a violation of system security and force termination of the processing. (OPNAVINST).

arrester. In physical security, a nonlinear device for suppressing voltage transients that result from lightning, power surges or interference. *See* ARC BREAKDOWN PROTECTOR.

artificial intelligence. The computational reproduction of intelligent action. In practice artificial intelligence is a somewhat ill-defined discipline pertaining to many aspects of the simulation of human intellect and thought by logical systems embodied in computer programs. More precise definitions are elusive because the subject is still embryonic, with considerable disagreement amongst its own ranks as to its proper boundaries. The motivation for artificial intelligence research is twofold. On the one hand, it is pursued in the hope that the application of rigorous computational methods and their attendant logic can throw light upon the operation of the human mind. More prosaically, the predominant drive behind artificial intelligence research has been the desire to imbue machines with more flexible and informed patterns of behavior, enabling some domains of human expertise to be cheaply replicated and possibly releasing workers from hazardous or monotonous tasks. *See* EXPERT SYSTEMS.

ARU. Audio Response Unit. *See* AUDIO RESPONSE TERMINAL.

AS 2805. In standards, a set of Australian standards for Electronic Funds Transfer:

- Part 1:   Communications Interface and Data Representation;
- Part 2:   Message Structure, Format and Content;
- Part 3:   PIN Management and Security;
- Part 4:   Message Authentication;
- Part 5:   Data Encryption Algorithm;
- Part 6.1:   Key Management Principles;
- Part 6.2:   Key Management - Transaction Keys;
- Part 6.3:   Key Management - Session keys - Node to Node;
- Part 6.4:   Key Management - Session keys - Terminal to Acquirer;
- Part 7:   POS Message Content;
- Part 8:   Financial Message Content.
- Part 9:   Privacy of Communications.

See ANSI X9.17 - 1985, DATA ENCRYPTION STANDARD, KEY MANAGEMENT, MESSAGE AUTHENTICATION, TRANSACTION KEY SYSTEM.

AS 3801 - 1989. In standards, an Australian standard, Electronic data interchange for administration, commerce and transport (EDIFACT) - application level syntax rules. *Compare* AS 3802 - 1991, AS 3803 - 1991, AS 3804 - 1991, AS 3805 - 1991. *See* EDIFACT, ELECTRONIC DATA INTERCHANGE.

AS 3802 - 1989. In standards, an Australian standard, Data elements and interchange formats - information interchange-Representation of dates and times. *Compare* AS 3801 - 1991, AS 3803 - 1991, AS 3804 - 1991, AS 3805 - 1991.

AS 3803 - 1989. In standards, an Australian standard, Electronic data interchange for administration, commerce and transport (EDIFACT) - Trade Interchange Directory. *Compare* AS 3801 - 1991, AS 3802 - 1991, AS 3804 - 1991, AS 3805 - 1991. *See* EDIFACT, ELECTRONIC DATA INTERCHANGE.

AS 3804 - 1989. In standards, an Australian standard, Electronic data interchange for administration, commerce and transport (EDIFACT) - Australian port codes. *Compare* AS 3801 - 1991, AS 3802 - 1991, AS 3803 - 1991, AS 3805 - 1991. *See* EDIFACT, ELECTRONIC DATA INTERCHANGE.

AS 3805 - 1989. In standards, an Australian standard, Electronic data interchange for administration, commerce and transport (EDIFACT) - Forms design - Basic layout. *Compare* AS 3801 - 1991, AS 3802 - 1991, AS 3803 - 1991, AS 3804 - 1991. *See* EDIFACT, ELECTRONIC DATA INTERCHANGE.

ASA. In standards, American Standards Association, a body with groups responsible for the establishment of data processing standards.

ASCII. In codes, American Standard Code for Information Interchange, pronounced ASKEE. A standard data transmission code that was introduced to achieve compatibility between data devices. It consists of 7 information bits and 1 parity bit for error checking purposes, thus allowing 128 code combinations. Of these 32 are used for upper case characters and a few punctuation marks, another group of 32 characters are used for numbers, spacing and additional punctuation symbols, the third group of 32 characters are assigned to lower case characters and some rarely used punctuation symbols. The last set of 32 characters are allocated to machine and control commands, e.g. line feed, carriage return. *See* INTERNATIONAL ALPHABET NUMBER 5, PARITY CHECKING. *Synonymous with* USASCII.

ASET. In computer security, Academy of Security Educators and Trainers.

ASIS. (1) In computer security, American Society for Industrial Security. (2) American Society for Information Science.

ASN.1. *See* ABSTRACT SYNTAX NOTATION 1.

assembler. In computing, a program that translates a source program written in a low level language to machine code. *See* LOW LEVEL LANGUAGE, MACHINE CODE INSTRUCTION, SOURCE PROGRAM, TRANSLATOR.

assembly language. In computing, a language that allows a programmer to develop a machine code program using symbols and mnemonics for storage locations and operations. *Compare* HIGH LEVEL LANGUAGE. *See* LOW LEVEL LANGUAGE, MACHINE CODE INSTRUCTION, TRANSLATOR.

asset. In information security, information or resources to be protected by the technical and non-technical countermeasures of a target of evaluation. *See* INFORMATION TECHNOLOGY SECURITY EVALUATION CRITERIA, TARGET OF EVALUATION.

Association for Computing Machinery. A U.S. professional computer science organization. Its objective is to advance all aspects of information processing and to promote the interchange of such techniques between computer specialists and users.

associative law. In mathematics, a binary operation, i.e. one involving two variables, satisfies the associative law if

$$x * (y * z) = (x * y) * z$$

where x , y and z are the variables and * represents the binary operation. *Compare* COMMUTATIVE LAW, DISTRIBUTIVE LAW. *See* GALOIS FIELD.

assurance. In computer security, a measure of confidence that the security features and architecture of an AIS accurately mediate and enforce the security policy. If the security features of an AIS are relied upon to handle sensitive information and restrict user access, the features must be tested to ensure that the security policy is uncircumventably enforced during AIS operation. (DODD). *See* AIS.

asymmetric algorithm. In cryptography, a cryptographic algorithm employing a public key for encipherment and a secret key for decipherment. Together these form an asymmetric key set. (ISO). *See* ASYMMETRIC CRYPTOSYSTEM, PUBLIC KEY, SECRET KEY.

asymmetric cipher. *Compare* SYMMETRIC CIPHER. *Synonymous with* ASYMMETRIC CRYPTOSYSTEM.

asymmetric cryptosystem. In cryptography, a system in which it is computationally infeasible to deduce the enciphering key from the deciphering key and/or vice versa. *Compare* SYMMETRIC CRYPTOSYSTEM. *See* COMPUTATIONALLY INFEASIBLE, PUBLIC KEY CRYPTOGRAPHY. *Synonymous with* TWO KEY CRYPTOSYSTEM.

asymmetric key system. In cryptography, a cryptographic system that uses an encryption algorithm or key for encipherment and a second algorithm or key for decipherment. An example of the use of an asymmetrical key system is public key encryption. This allows confidential messages to be sent from the public to holder of the private key or algorithm. In some systems (especially digital signatures), the encryption algorithm or key is private and the decipher key or algorithm is public. The public and private key are sometimes referred to as the key pair. (ANSI). *Compare* SYMMETRIC KEY SYSTEM. *See* ASYMMETRIC CRYPTOSYSTEM, DIGITAL SIGNATURE, PUBLIC KEY CRYPTOGRAPHY.

async. In data communications, an abbreviation for asynchronous communication. *See* ASYNCHRONOUS TRANSMISSION.

asynchronous. Pertaining to actions and events that are not correlated with some reference time.

asynchronous attacks. (1) In computer security, a method of attempting two or more attacks at the same time in the hope that at least one will succeed whilst the others are being dealt with. *See* COMPUT-

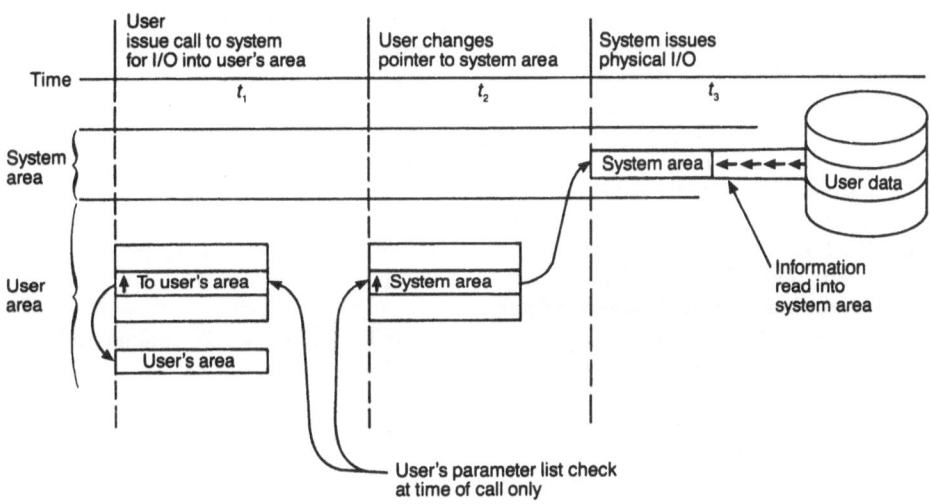

asynchronous attacks.
This attack is sometimes referred to as the time of check and time of use problem. When the parameters were originally checked by the supervisor program, they were correct. But after their check and before their use, the attacker changed them so as to circumvent some protection feature. This attack is possible because a computer is able to process I/O and relinquish control back to the user for concurrent processing. Reproduced with permission of IBM Corp.

ER FRAUD CONTROL. (2) In computer security, TOCTTOU attacks. *See* TOCTTOU PROBLEMS.

asynchronous communications interface adaptor. In hardware, a device performing a similar function to a UART. *See* UART.

asynchronous transmission. In data communications, a form of data transmission in which there can be variable time intervals between characters but the bits within a character are sent with fixed time intervals. Start and stop elements are used to indicate the beginning and end of characters. *Compare* ANISOCHRONOUS TRANSMISSION, SYNCHRONOUS TRANSMISSION.

ATM. *See* AUTOMATED TELLER MACHINE.

attack. (1) In risk management, the realization of a threat. How often a threat is realized depends on such factors as the location, type, and value of information being processed. Thus, short of moving the system or facility or radically changing its mission, there is usually no way that the level of protection can affect the frequency of attack. The exceptions to this are certain human threats where effective security measures can have a deterrent effect. The fact that an attack is made does not necessarily mean that it will succeed. The degree of success depends on the vulnerability of the system or activity and the effectiveness of existing countermeasures. (OPNAVINST). *See* ATTACKER, THREAT, VULNERABILITY.

attacker. In computer and data security, the person who attempts to overcome the computer or data security measures. *See* ATTACK, INTRUDER.

attack path. In information security, the sequence of countermeasures that an attacker must overcome to defeat the security objective of a target of evaluat-

ion. *See* INFORMATION TECHNOLOGY SECURITY EVALUATION CRITERIA, TARGET OF EVALUATION.

attack signalling. In computer security, a feature of some PPD's which provides some form of warning signal and a record of dial up attacks. *See* PORT PROTECTION DEVICE, TELEPHONE INTRUSION.

attention character. In computer security, a character that, when entered from a terminal, tells the TCB that the user wants a secure communications path from the terminal to some trusted code, in order to provide a secure service for the user, such as logging in or logging out. (MTR). *See* TCB.

attenuation. In electronics and communications, the reduction in strength of an electrical signal as it passes through a circuit or an electromagnetic wave as it propagates through a transmission medium.

attribute. In databases, a field that contains information about an entity, e.g. in a personnel database 'home address' would be an attribute of entity employee. *Compare* ENTITY, RELATIONSHIP. *See* FIELD.

AT&T. American Telephone and Telegraph.

AU. Authorized user.

audible alarm device. In physical security, a device which emits a sound to indicate an alarm condition or change in the mode of operation of a security system.

audio detection. In physical security, a technique employing a microphone, amplifier and sound actuated relay to detect noises made by an intruder in a protected area and to transmit a corresponding alarm signal. *See* ALARM SIGNAL, INTRUSION DETECTOR, AUDIO LISTEN IN.

audio listen in. In physical security, an alarm monitoring system which uses sound frequencies to detect an intrusion. The sound information is fedback to an operator at a central monitoring point. *See* audio detection, intrusion detector.

audio response terminal. In peripherals, a terminal which receives spoken information from a computer. Digitized speech in the form of words/phrases or phonemes are accessed by the program, and converted from digital to analog form for transmission. If the receiving unit is a push button telephone, with multi-frequency tones, the user can send enquiries via the push button. *See* SPEECH SYNTHESIZER, VOICE ANSWER BACK.

audio response unit. *See* VOICE ANSWER BACK.

audit. (1) In information security, functions to detect and investigate events that might represent a threat to security. *See* INFORMATION TECHNOLOGY SECURITY EVALUATION CRITERIA. (2) In computer security, to conduct the independent review and examination of system records and activities in order to test for adequacy of system controls, to ensure compliance with established policy and operational procedures, and to recommend any indicated changes in controls, policy or procedures. (FIPS). *See* AUDIT TRAIL, EXTERNAL SECURITY AUDIT, INTERNAL SECURITY AUDIT, SECURITY AUDIT.

audit based control. In database security, a form of inference control in which an audit trail is maintained so that it can be checked whether or not a query, when correlated with previously released statistics, is capable of causing a personal disclosure. *Compare* A PRIORI CONTROL, MEMORYLESS CONTROL. *See* AUDIT EXPERT, AUDIT TRAIL, INFERENCE CONTROL, OVERLAP CONTROL, PERSONAL DISCLOSURE.

audit data. In computer security, typical audit data produced in a time sharing system includes information necessary to bill users, and security logs providing lists of attempts to use privileged commands. *See* AUDIT TRAIL.

audit expert. In database security, a cell restriction technique which uses an audit trail to determine whether or not the proposed query, when correlated with data released by previous queries, can be used to disclose personal information. A binary matrix is formed with one column for each individual in the database, each row represents a basis for the set of queries deducible from the previous queries. The new query causes the matrix to be updated and if a row contains zeros in all columns except one then information, concerning the individual corresponding to that column, could be inferred from the proposed and previous queries. *Compare* CELL SUPPRESSION, GROUPING, IMPLIED QUERIES CONTROL, OVERLAP CONTROL, QUERY SET SIZE CONTROL. *See* AUDIT BASED CONTROL, CELL RESTRICTION.

auditing. In access control, the process of producing and keeping the records necessary to support accountability. *See* AUDIT, AUDIT TRAIL.

audit trail. (1) A set of records that collectively provide documentary evidence of processing used to aid in tracing from original transactions forward to related records and reports, and/or backwards from records and reports to their component source transactions. (DOD). (2) In computer security, a chronological record of system activities which is sufficient to enable the reconstruction, review, and examination of the sequence of environments and activities surrounding or leading to each event in the path of a transaction from its inception to output of final results. (FIPS). (3) In computing, the data produced as a result of a clerical or automated method for tracing the transactions affecting the contents of a record. *See* AUDIT, AUDIT TRAIL ANALYSIS, RECORD. (4) In banking, the ability to view what the system has completed in the past.

audit trail analysis. In access control, the examination of an audit trail, either manually or automatically, possibly in real time. *See* AUDIT TRAIL.

authenticate. To establish the validity of a claimed identity. (DOD). *See* AUTHENTICATION.

authentication. (1) In data security, the act of determining that a message has not been changed since leaving its point of origin. The identity of the originator is implicitly verified. (ANSI). (2) In data security, a process used, between a sender and a receiver, to ensure data integrity and to provide data origin authentication. (ISO). *See* DATA INTEGRITY, DATA ORIGIN AUTHENTICATION. (3) In data security, to establish the validity of a claimed identity (TNI). (4) In computer security, the act of identifying or verifying the eligibility of a station, originator, or individual to access specific categories of information. (FIPS) *See* ACCESS. (5) In data security, a measure designed to provide protection against fraudulent transmissions by establishing the validity of a transmission, message, station or originator. (FIPS). (6) In data security, processes that ensure everything about a teleprocessing transaction is genuine and that the message has not been altered or corrupted in transmission. The parties to the transaction must identify each other reliably, know that each message they receive comes from the other party and has not been modified, or stored earlier and replayed, by a third party. A check field can be added to the message such that the calculation of the check field depends upon the contents of the whole message, and the calculation involves a secret key. Additional information is required in the message to guard against replay of earlier messages;

time/date fields are sometimes employed for this purpose. Authentication using a secret key, shared by the sender and receiver, cannot assist in the resolution of disputes in which a receiver claims that a forged message was transmitted by the sender, or the sender disowns a messages that was actually sent, claiming that it was forged by the receiver. *See* ANSI X9.9 - 1986, CRYPTOGRAPHY, DIGITAL SIGNATURE, MAC, MESSAGE AUTHENTICATION, REPLAY, WIRETAP. (7) In computer security, the process that verifies the identity of an individual as established by an identification process. (ANSI). (8) In data security and data communications, a term that is used both to mean the prevention of undetected alteration to data and peer entity authentication. The latter meaning is commonly used in data communications where communicating parties seek mutual verification of each other's identities. The term integrity is now preferred for the process of preventing undetected alteration of data. *See* INTEGRITY, PEER ENTITY AUTHENTICATION.

authentication algorithm. In authentication, the act of determining that a message comes from a source authorized to originate messages of that type and that the message is as authorized. (ANSI). *See* MESSAGE AUTHENTICATION.

authentication element. In authentication, a contiguous group of characters which are to be protected by being processed by the authentication algorithm. *See* AUTHENTICATION ALGORITHM.

authentication equipment. In access control, equipment employed to check the authentication of a transmitted message, originator, originating system or telecommunications system, or to provide protection against fraudulent transmissions or masquerading systems.

authentication exchange. In authentication, a mechanism intended to ensure the identity of an entity by means of information exchange. *See* ACCESS CONTROL, DYNAMIC PASSWORD.

authentication information. In authentication, information used to establish the validity of a claimed identity. *See* AUTHENTICATION.

authentication key. In authentication, a cryptographic key designed to be known only to the correspondent parties. When this key and the text of the message are applied to the authentication algorithm the result will be the MAC. (ANSI). *See* ANSI X9.9 - 1986, AUTHENTICATION ALGORITHM, AUTHENTICATOR KEY, MAC.

authentication of users. In data communications, the verification that the user at the terminal corresponds to his claimed identity. *See* ACCESS CONTROL, DYNAMIC PASSWORD, PASSWORD.

authentication period. In authentication, the maximum acceptable period between any initial authentication process and subsequent re-authentication processes during a single terminal session or during the period data is being accessed. (FIPS).

authentication process. In authentication, the actions involving: (a) obtaining an identifier and a personal password from an ADP system user; (b) comparing the entered password with the stored, valid password that was issued to, or selected by, the person associated with that identifier, and (c) authenticating the identity if the entered password and the stored password are the same. (Note: If the enciphered password is stored, the entered password must be enciphered and compared with the stored ciphertext or the ciphertext must be deciphered and compared with the entered password). (FIPS). *See* PASSWORD.

authentication sequence. In authentication, the sequence used to authenticate

the identity of a subject or object. *See* OBJECT, SUBJECT.

authentication server. In authentication, a trusted facility for arbitrated digital signatures. The authentication server signs a message, from a sender, by encrypting a data block, which comprises a concatenation of the message authenticator and the sender's identity, under the arbiter's secret key. The receiver also submits the signature to the authentication server; the server deciphers the signature and supplies the sender with the authenticator and the sender's identity. Communication between users and the authentication server are encrypted under pairs of keys shared only with the individual users. *See* ARBITRATED SIGNATURE, AUTHENTICATOR, DIGITAL SIGNATURE, TRUSTED.

authenticator. (1) In authenticator, the means used to identify or verify the eligibility of a station, originator or individual to access specific categories of information. (FIPS). *See* ACCESS CONTROL. (2) In authentication, a symbol, a sequence of symbols, or a series of bits that are arranged in a predetermined manner and are usually inserted at a predetermined point within a message or transmission for the purpose of an authentication of the message or transmission. The authenticator is often a function of the complete message, or at least the security sensitive parts of it, and a secret key. Any alteration to the message, without corresponding changes to the authenticator, can thus be detected by the recipient. *See* MESSAGE AUTHENTICATION. (3) In authentication, a code in a message between the sender and receiver used to validate the source and all or part of the text of the message, based on a bilaterally agreed upon method of calculation. (ANSI). *See* MAC, TEST KEY.

authenticator key. In authentication, a cryptographic key designed to be known only to the correspondent parties. When this key and the text of the message are applied to an agreed upon algorithm the result will be the authenticator. (ANSI). *See* AUTHENTICATION KEY, BANKING NETWORKS, SWIFT.

authorization. (1) In access control, the granting to a user, a program, or a process the right of access. (FIPS). *See* ACCESS. (2) In operations, the right given to a user to communicate with or make use of a computer system or stored data. (3) The privilege granted to an individual by a designated official to access information based upon the individual's clearance and need-to-know. (DOE).

authorization code. In computing, a code used to protect against unauthorized access to data and system facilities. The code normally consists of a user id (identification) and password. *See* USER ID, PASSWORD.

authorization level. (1) In access control, a degree of security clearance. (2) In computer security, an entry point or location with a specified security rating.

authorization parameter. In banking, a value generated as a function of a card key by the card issuer and passed to the acquirer. It is used by the terminal to authenticate the card issuer and by the terminal and the acquirer as a component in key management. It is not transmitted between them. (SAA). *See* ACQUIRER, CARD ISSUER, CARD KEY, KEY MANAGEMENT.

authorization process. In access control, the actions involving: (a) obtaining an access password from an ADP system user (whose identity has already been authenticated, perhaps using a personal password), (b) comparing the access password with the password associated with the protected data, and (c) authorizing access to the data if the entered password and the stored password are the same. (FIPS). *See* AUTHORIZATION, PASSWORD.

authorized access control switch. In physical security, a device, often key operated used to switch a detection system on or off. *Synonymous with* DAY-NIGHT SWITCH, SUBSCRIBER'S UNIT.

auto-alarming switcher. In physical security, a video switcher with a facility to automatically present a CCTV camera view for a zone that has initiated an alarm via the CCTV system. *See* CCTV, VIDEO SWITCHER.

auto answer. *Synonymous with* AUTOMATIC ANSWERING.

autoclave. In cryptography, feedback in a stream cipher which renders the cryptographic bit stream dependent on the data stream. *See* CRYPTOGRAPHIC BIT STREAM, DATA STREAM, STREAM CIPHER.

auto dial. *Synonymous with* AUTOMATIC CALLING.

auto dial modem. In data communications, a modem which responds to call set up commands from a PC. It listens for the answer tone and organizes itself to accept data. In comparison, with a manual modem, the user must dial using a telephone, listen for an answer, then press the data button. *See* HAYES, MODEM, PC.

autoidentifier. In computing, a device with which a terminal automatically identifies itself to a computer.

automated audit. In auditing, an audit feature in which a review of previous steps undertaken or results previously prepared, is automatically activated at certain stages in a program or procedure.

Automated Clearing House. In banking, a set of processes which carries out the clearing of interbank payments in the form of standardized payments that can be processed by a computer.

automated error correction. In data processing, the automatic correction of errors in a transaction or record which violate some detective action.

Automated Information System. (1) An assembly of computer hardware, software, and firmware configured to collect, communicate, compute, disseminate, and/or control data. (DODD). (2) Systems which create, prepare, or manipulate information in electronic form for purposes for other than telecommunication, and includes computers, word processing systems, other electronic information handling systems, and associated equipment. (NSDD-145). *See* NSDD-145.

automated security monitoring. In computer security, the use of automated procedures to ensure that automation security controls are not circumvented. (AR).

automated system security. In computer security, all security features needed to provide an acceptable level of protection for hardware, software, and classified, sensitive unclassified or critical data, material, or processes in the system. It includes: (a) All hardware and software functions, characteristics and features. (b) Operational procedures. (c) Accountability procedures. (d) Access controls at all computer facilities. (includes those housing mainframes, terminals, minicomputers, or microcomputers). (e) Management constraints. (f) Physical protection. (g) Control of compromising emanations (Tempest). (h) Personnel and communications security (COMSEC). (i) Other security disciplines. (AFR). *See* ACCESS CONTROL, COMSEC, PHYSICAL SECURITY, TEMPEST.

automated teller machine. In peripherals, a device which provides for cash withdrawals, payment of bills, account balance enquiries, deposits and transfers of funds between accounts. *See* BANKING NETWORKS, CASH DISPENSER, PIN MAN-AGEMENT AND SECURITY, SELF BANKING. *Synonymous with* AUTOMATIC TELLER MACHINE.

automatic alarm initiating device. In physical security, a device which automatically relays an alarm signal when there is an indication of fire, smoke or water ingress. *Compare* MANUAL ALARM INITIATING DEVICE.

automatic answering. In data communications, a system in which the called station automatically responds to the calling signal, the call may be established whether or not the called station is attended. *See* CALL BACK. *Synonymous with* AUTO ANSWER.

automatic calling. In communications, a machine feature that allows a station to initiate a call automatically over a switched line. *See* AUTOMATIC CALLING UNIT, STATION. *Synonymous with* AUTO DIAL.

automatic calling unit. In data communications, a device that enables a business machine to automatically dial calls over a network. *See* AUTOMATIC CALLING, AUTOMATIC DIALER.

automatic capture. In banking, the capture of data directly from computer systems without manual intervention.

Automatic Data Processing System. An assembly of computer hardware, firmware, and software configured for the purpose of classifying, sorting, calculating, computing, summarizing, transmitting and receiving, storing, and retrieving data with a minimum of human intervention. (DOD).

automatic message switching center. In data communications, a location at which messages are automatically routed according to the information they contain. *See* MESSAGE SWITCHING.

automatic personal identification. *Synonymous with* BIOMETRICS.

automatic polling. In computing and data communications, a feature of a transmission control unit that enables it to handle negative responses to polling without interrupting the CPU. *See* CPU, POLLING.

automatic renewal clause. In risk management, a contractual clause which automatically renews a continuing agreement, e.g. for a hot or cold site. *See* COLD SITE, HOT SITE.

automatic retransmission request. In data communications, a technique to ensure accurate transmission of data. Data to be transmitted is held in a buffer until the communication link is ready to deal with it. The data is then despatched and a copy made at the same time. The copy is deposited in the buffer and erased when the sending device receives acknowledgment of correct receipt, as verified by CRC checking. If the receiving device detects an error in the data it informs the sending device which then retransmits the buffered copy. *See* CRC.

automatic teller machine. *Synonymous with* AUTOMATED TELLER MACHINE.

automation security. In data security, the measures employed to protect automation and the information handled from both hostile and benign threats and to safeguard against unauthorized exploitation through espionage, sabotage, theft, fraud, misappropriation, or misuse. Automation security applies to all ADP systems and applies to the global aspects of the security problem. Therefore, it encompasses the security management, hardware, software, procedural, communications, personnel, physical and environmental, and all other security aspects contributing to the protection of automated systems (hardware and soft-

ware), site, activity, facility, or operation as a potential target. (AR).

auto restore. In physical security, pertaining to the automatic resetting of an alarm device, within a specified period, after receipt of the alarm.

auxiliary equipment. In computing, equipment not under the direct control of the central processing unit. *See* CENTRAL PROCESSING UNIT.

auxiliary fire alarm system. In physical security, a system employing alarm initiating devices which causes the transmission of an alarm over a municipal fire alarm system to the fire station, either directly or via fire headquarters. *See* AUTOMATIC ALARM INITIATING DEVICE, MANUAL ALARM INITIATING DEVICE.

availability. (1) In computer and communications security, the property of being accessible and useable upon demand by an authorized entity. (ISO). *Compare* DENIAL OF SERVICE. (2) In computer security, the characteristic that ensures the computer resources will be available to authorized users when they need them. This characteristic protects against denial of service. (AFR). *Compare* DENIAL OF SERVICE.

availability-automated security monitoring. In information security, pertaining to the employment of automated procedures to guarantee against the circumvention of security controls within an information system.

available funds. In banking, funds available for withdrawal. (ANSI). *Synonymous with* CLEARED FUNDS.

available time. *See* UP-TIME.

AVLOS. In legislation, a U.S. database storing personal data from U.S. consular posts. *See* DATA PROTECTION - U.S.

B

B1. *See* DIVISION B.

B2. *See* DIVISION B.

B3. *See* DIVISION B.

babble. In communications, the aggregate cross talk from a number of interfering sources. *See* CROSS-TALK.

backdoor. *See* TRAPDOOR.

background job. In computing, a job of relatively low priority in a multitasking environment; computer resources are only allocated to it when they are not required for higher priority foreground tasks. *Compare* FOREGROUND PROGRAM.

backing storage. In computing, an intermediate storage medium, e.g. magnetic tape, magnetic disk etc., on to which data is entered for later processing by the central computer. *See* MAGNETIC DISK, MAGNETIC TAPE.

back office. In banking, the area where operation support is carried out, including dealing reconciliations and settlement and branch computing. *Compare* FRONT OFFICE.

backtracking. In key management, the ability to use a current key value, together with information previously transmitted or received to determine previous key values. *See* CRYPTOGRAPHIC KEY, TRANSACTION KEY SYSTEM.

backup plan. In risk management, a plan that provides the ability to conduct, by alternative means, the critical data processing workload. *See* CONTINGENCY PLANS.

backup procedures. In risk management, the provisions made for the recovery of data files and program libraries, and for restart or replacement of ADP equipment after the occurrence of a failure or of a disaster. (FIPS). *See* ADP, BACKUP/RESTORE.

backup/restore. In computing, the actions involved in transferring data from magnetic disk to tape, or disk, for off line storage, and the subsequent action of restoring the data to disk. *See* MAGNETIC DISK, MAGNETIC TAPE.

backward channel. In data communications, a channel used for supervisory or error control signals, but with a direction of transmission opposite to that in which user information is being transferred. *Compare* FORWARD CHANNEL.

backwards learning. In data communications, a method of routing in which the switching nodes are able to deduce the behavior of the network by observing the packets passing through, noting their source and the number of links through which they have travelled. *See* NODE, PACKET SWITCHING.

backward supervision. In data communications, the use of supervisory sequences sent from the slave to a master station. *See* STATION, SUPERVISORY SIGNAL.

BACS. *See* BANKERS' AUTOMATED-CLEARING SERVICES.

badge reader. In physical security, a device for reading the coded information contained on a plastic personnel identification badge. The information may be encoded with magnetic stripe, magnetic dots or proximity radio frequency circuits. *Compare* DYNAMIC PASSWORD. *See* CARD READER.

balanced circuit. In communications, a line that is terminated with a matched load.

balanced detection. In physical security, a method of detecting a false alarm by requiring that two detection events must occur within a preset time interval.

balanced transmission. In data communications, a technique for high data rates that require two wires for each signal. *Compare* UNBALANCED TRANSMISSION. *See* DATA RATE.

balancing. (1) In auditing, a method of detecting an error by testing for equality between the values of two equivalent items or a control total and one set of items. *See* BATCH BALANCING. (2) In computing, a test for equality between the values of two equivalent sets of items or one set of items and a control total.

band. In communications, a range of frequencies between two defined limits, e.g. the voice band in telephony is about 300 to 3,000 Hz. *See* Hz.

bandpass. In electronics, pertaining to an amplifier or circuit having a frequency response characteristic that is uniform, within defined limits, across a given frequency range.

bandscrambler. *Synonymous with* BANDSPLITTER.

band shift invertor. In communications security, a form of speech invertor in which a portion of the high frequency component, of the inverted signal, is frequency changed so that it is shifted to the band immediately below the lowest frequency of the inverted waveform. For example, the original speech waveform will occupy a frequency band from 300 to 3000 Hz. If a carrier frequency of 4000 Hz is employed then the inverted signal will range from 1000 (4000 - 3000) Hz to 3700 Hz. The band outside the telephone bandwidth, i.e. from 3000 to 3700 Hz, is then shifted down to 300 - 1000 Hz. The carrier frequency may be changed every 10 - 20 milliseconds, in a secret manner agreed by the transmitter and receiver, thus rendering it difficult for an interceptor to perform the same unscrambling routine as the receiver. The residual intelligibility of the transmitted signal may, however, be unacceptably high. *Compare* BANDSPLITTER. *See* CYCLICAL BAND SHIFT INVERTOR, RESIDUAL INTELLIGIBILITY, SPEECH INVERTOR, VOICE SCRAMBLING.

bandsplitter. In communications security, a form of voice scrambler in which the frequency range of the voice message is split into bands, and the bands are then interchanged. The permutations of the bands may be changed, in a sequence known only to the transmitter and receiver, every few hundred milliseconds. Individual bands may also be inverted. *Compare* BAND SHIFT INVERTOR. *See* SPEECH INVERTOR, VOICE SCRAMBLING. *Synonymous with* BANDSCRAMBLER.

bandwidth. (1) In communications, a characteristic of a communication channel that is the amount of information that can be passed through it in a given amount of time, usually expressed in bits per second. (DOD) (2) In communications, the difference between the limiting frequencies in a band. (3) In electronics, the range of frequencies within which a device can operate and

meet a specified performance characteristic.

bank. A depository financial institution. (ANSI).

bank camera. In physical security, a
surveillance camera employed in banks
that uses 16 mm. or 35 mm. film.

Bankers Automated Clearing Services.
In banking, a system set up by Bankers
Automated Clearing Services Ltd., a
company formed by the main clearing
banks with the main function to act as
an automated clearing house for standing
orders and direct debits.

banking cycle. In banking, the time
cycle in which a transaction is completed, taken to include request, processing
and identification of settlement funds for
payment products. *Synonymous with*
DOCUMENT CYCLE, PAYMENT CYCLE,
TRADE CYCLE.

banking networks. In banking, networks used by international banks to
conduct their day to day business.

Introduction
The networking requirements of the
financial sector are diverse and challen-
ging. A global bank must firstly service
its own internal communication needs
for electronic mail, management reporting and treasury operations. Secondly,
banks need to offer their customers a
variety of networked based financial
services such as cash management, EDI,
corporate treasury management and
investment services. Thirdly, and most
fundamentally, banks have to offer a
range of payment services such as ATM
(Automatic Teller Machine) systems for
retail banking, and EFT (Electronic
Funds Transfer) for wholesale banking
transactions. Moreover, banks as well as
competing amongst themselves are also
customers of each other, so they must
cooperate in transferring funds and

settling balances.
In order to achieve these objectives,
international banks interact with many
different suppliers of network services,
as well as maintaining their own individual, private networks on both a local and
global basis. The main areas of interest
in banking networks are:

• international banking networks;
• regional banking networks;
• private banking networks;
• electronic treasury management;
• EDI and future trends.

International Banking Networks
Some of the largest banks have their
own proprietary telecommunications
networks. Major US banks such as
Citibank, Chemical Bank and Chase
Manhattan use their internal networks to
link their offices and subsidiaries worldwide.
Firms that specialize in offering data
processing and communications services
also provide international connections
that can be rented by financial institutions and other bodies. Such companies
include McDonnell Douglas, GE Information Services and ADP. Essentially,
these service organizations provide an
electronic sorting office for their customers' computer messages. The service
company devises standard software and
message formats, (usually conforming to
SWIFT standards) and its central computers relay communications between the
parties. Some public telecommunications
authorities also provide commercial data
processing and transmission services.
The best known international funds
transfer system is SWIFT (Society for
Worldwide Interbank Financial Telecommunication). It is a co-operative
company incorporated in 1973 under
Belgium law by 239 banks from 15
countries (European countries, USA,
Canada). The object of the company is
to provide '...for the collective benefit
of the members of the Company, the
study, creation, utilization and operation

of the means necessary for the telecommunication, transmission and routing of private, confidential and proprietary international financial messages'.

Today SWIFT has around 2,000 shareholders (banks) and a total of 3,000 locations in some 70 countries. Users are mainly banks but also include brokers in securities, money brokers, clearing houses, travellers cheques issuers. They exchange through the SWIFT network more than 1,000,000 messages per day. The issuers can exchange between themselves nine categories of messages, the format of which is standardized and recognized by the International Standard Organization (ISO). The message types are: Customer Payments and Cheques; Customer Status; Collections and Cash Letters; Documentary Credits and Guarantees; Financial Trading; Securities; Syndications; Travellers Cheques.

A message switching system such as SWIFT needs to provide a strong level of user confidence, and it must reduce exposures to active or passive wire-tapping. Protection from this type of exposure was a fundamental business requirement, especially as the SWIFT organization assumes financial liability for transactions from the point at which they are accepted onto the SWIFT network. The transaction level security is consequently a very important feature of the system design and authentication algorithms, used to preserve both message integrity and traffic confidentiality.

Good network design, network management and network control are key features for a large network such as SWIFT and were carefully integrated to provide the necessary resilience and recovery. SWIFT in common with many of its member banks recognized the need for contingency planning, alternative network routing, and equipment redundancy. These measures are extremely important for any international message switching service, which regularly handles high volumes of financial traffic.

Users connect to SWIFT Regional Processing Centers (RPCs) in each country, by leased lines or public switched services. The RPCs provide concentration, manage the format and communications protocols. They are linked to one of SWIFT's three manned Operating Centers (OPCs). These Operating Centers are located in the US, Holland and Belgium (SWIFT Headquarters). The OPCs in turn are able to validate messages, store messages securely and finally deliver the transactions to their ultimate destination.

The entire network is managed by at least two permanently manned System Control Centers, which monitor and control the overall performance of the network. However, regular increases in business volumes have resulted in SWIFT migrating to a more modular network design, SWIFT II, which is based upon a more distributed transaction processing approach. SWIFT II allows the network to react more readily to traffic increases and to upgrades for its processing capacity. In recent years SWIFT has also reviewed security arrangements for the network to ensure that security technology advances are adequately exploited. The major aim has been to improve the operational convenience of some of the member security procedures and to enhance the automation of security management for its member's traffic.

Regional Banking Networks
Although SWIFT is extremely successful, many banks have found a need to develop shared networks among themselves, in the same country, to support fast money transfers in the local currency. The major difference is that such regional country networks can provide speedy settlement of payments or net payment values between the respective members.

Clearing houses enable debit and credit operations to be settled between banks on a net balance basis. Each member institution throws all its transfers with other members into a common pot. The clearing house does the necessary sums and comes up with the final amounts due to and from each participant at the end of the day. Typically, such arrangements are set up at national or local level. There is no comprehensive international system for clearing funds transfers.

The Clearing House Automated Payment System (CHAPS) has been operating in Britain since 1984. The system is available nationwide and transmits sterling payments electronically between banks.

CHAPS is operated by a number of settlement banks (the English and Scottish clearing banks). They communicate directly with one another via British Telecom's Packet Switch Stream Service using standardized computers and software. There is thus no central installation.

Settlement banks send messages for themselves, for other banks and for customers. Payments sent through the system are guaranteed and unconditional, and are cleared on a same-day basis. Interbank settlement is effected electronically at the end of each day, across the settlement banks' accounts held at the Bank of England.

Strong integrity features were designed to protect the large volume and value of payments which are transmitted via the CHAPS network. Every payment transaction is uniquely identified by a combination of time stamping and sequence numbering. The service employs both message authentication and encryption techniques and these are deployed to restrict any unauthorized interference with the financial transactions which are transmitted between the banks.

Frequent key exchange, of authentication keys, assist the integrity of the security design. Bilateral keys which are unique for each pair of participants are used to enhance the underlying security for the business trading relationships between the pairs of participant banks. User trust in the integrity of high level encryption keys is underpinned by placing control with the Committee of London Clearing Banks (CLCB). High level keys are distributed manually in secure, tamper resistant key transport modules, which are collected from the CLCB.

The need for traffic confidentiality between the members is met by link encryption which uses a secret encryption key between all the banks. This is achieved by an X.25 link encryption device which was developed specifically for this purpose. Additional privacy is obtained by use of the network Closed User Group (CUG) protection features, to restrict the service to bona-fide members and to limit any accidental misrouting of transactions.

CHAPS is now a major funds clearing service which handles the requirements of UK banks for interbank money transfers. However, the network itself is another link in a chain of international financial networks. Typically, member banks have their own internal and customer communication networks, from which the original payment instructions have been generated. Although this interconnection may seem transparent to either internal users or customers, many centralized, underlying system controls are used to automate sound banking control practices, prior to onward transmission. Intervention in the end-to-end process by private bank systems is a basic business requirement for automated authorization and credit limit applications for both the customer of internal users, and also for accounting purposes, see Figure 1.

The Clearing House Interbank Payments System (CHIPS) is a computerized network in the US for the transfer of international dollar payments. It links about 140 banks and other depository institutions which have offices or subsidiaries in New York City. CHIPS members are divided into settling and non--settling participants. Each of the latter

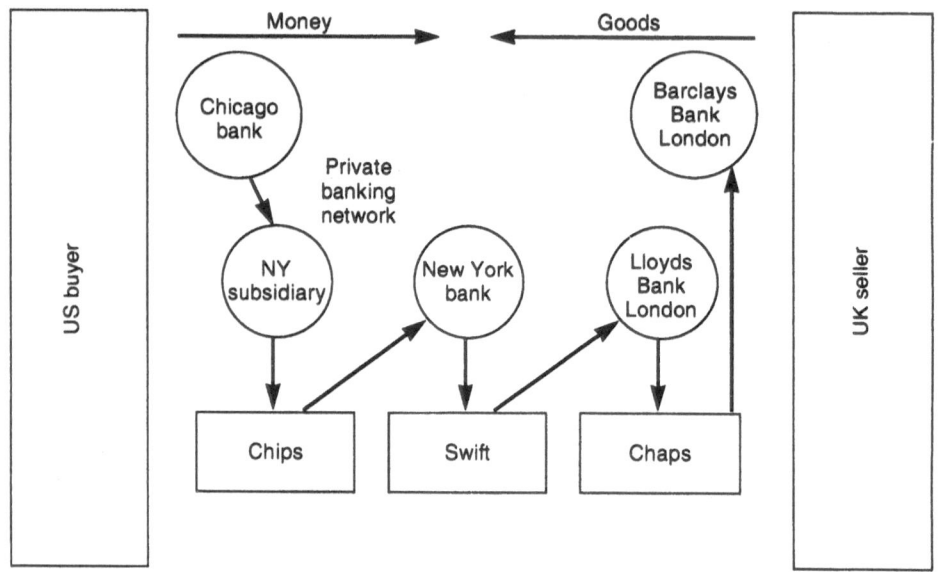

banking networks.
An illustration of how intercommunicating banking networks facilitate the payments of goods.

has an account with one of the former, which effects settlement on its behalf.

CHIPS has dual computers at its New York headquarters and a third identical system at a separate location. Messages are authenticated in accordance with ANSI X9.9. Encryption is not used. Standard message formats are employed, and many participants are able to send messages automatically from one network to another without rekeying. For example, the system accepts SWIFT identification numbers and automatically cross-references them to the CHIPS Universal Identification Numbers.

FedWire is a US funds transfer facility operated nationwide by the Federal Reserve System (the Fed) in Washington. All transactions are credit transfers, and on initiations are immediately debited to the account of the payer. A packet-switching network connects the twelve regional Federal Reserve Banks linked into the system.

Approximately 8,000 depository institutions (banks and similar deposit taking bodies) use the Fed service. The Treasury Department is also a direct participant. Many of these institutions are connected directly to Federal Reserve computers, as is the US Treasury Department.

BankWire is a private communications system serving commercial banks in US and Canadian cities. The system is used for a variety of interbank communications including funds transfers. Funds transfers can be effected on the same day by means of debits and credits to interbank demand deposit balances, and the transmitted information can include instructions to credit third parties' accounts. The service includes a specialized offering called CashWire. This provides for the net settlement of transfers on the books of the Federal Reserve.

Sagittaire is a Paris-based system which is run in co-ordination with the French SWIFT users' group, and the message standards adopted are compatible with SWIFT formats. Access is limited to banks situated in France, and the system deals exclusively with French franc settlements arising from international transfers.

The settlement procedure is managed by the Banque de France, the French central bank, and the network facilities are provided by the state-owned telecommunications authority - l'Administration des postes et telecommunications, the PTT.

Private Electronic Banking Networks

Many banks manage their own private electronic banking networks. These networks are able to deliver a large variety of automated financial products in addition to payment instructions. The users of the networks can be major corporate customers, personal customers, or bank staff. Network services are seen as an important means for a bank to maintain its competitive edge.

Large corporate customers use electronic banking services, typically for applications such as cash management, funds transfer, and balance reporting over multiple company accounts. Personal customers use the networks for services such as self service (ATMs), point of sale, and home banking applications (account enquiries, cheque books and statement ordering). Bank staff make use of internal applications for a range of internal financial products, either to react to verbal or paper requests from the customer (account opening and loan application requests).

The bank services offered are continually expanded by the industry to meet new market demands and to win new accounts. Communication networks play a key part in the delivery of these electronic products to the market place, whether this is from the home, the office, the local branch or even 'through the wall' of the local bank branch. Many banks will use private networks, which they directly manage and control.

Whilst each private network is dif-ferent, there are standardized and similar approaches to security services, the most important of which is security management. This allows the bank to control both manual and automated key management systems, large transaction processing systems, and the many users of the network. Continual expansion in the number of services and users make this requirement one of the most important considerations in the choice of a security design. Easy to use management features are recognized as the only satisfactory way to manage system security for large networks given limited human resources.

Link encryption is often used within corporate banking networks to provide transmission security, with the keys managed by the banks. This reflects the practices used on major international financial networks such as SWIFT and CHAPS.

Central security services are enforced through link encryption with host application cryptographic servers used for message authentication services. Key management techniques do vary between the banks, but RSA is now gaining favor as the preferred method for the automation and distribution of keys. A central application service usually controls customer trading limits, handles the vital transaction sequencing controls, and manages audit trail production. Frequently more than one financial product is made available to customers, and the functional authorization of user access privileges can also be vetted by the central applications.

Electronic Treasury Management

Corporate treasurers are important bank customers whose job it is to make money work for their respective corporations. They invest funds to the best possible effect, borrow on the most attractive terms, declare war on unnecessary money movements, and reduce transfer costs to the minimum. Treasury departments live on information, and in many ways they are the mirror image of the their bankers.

Electronic banking does not only cover the automated delivery and receipt of payment transactions. Increasingly, the corporate treasurer requires 'an electronic window' to the financial markets for the electronic receipt and delivery of financial data such as:

- the transmission of local currency payments (CHAPS,SAGITTAIRE, etc);
- access to account balance and transaction data, even when accounts are maintained by foreign banks;
- management control and simulation of the company's currency exposures.

EDI and Future Trends

EDI is the transmission of business data in a structured format between computers. Typically, the business data involved are purchase orders, invoices, shipping notices and remittance advices. With EDI, conventional paper documents are minimized and traditional commercial practices have to be reappraised.

In a commercial environment money can usually be analyzed as the right to a credit balance in a bank account, and therefore a debt owned by the customer. Payment of money is usually not physical delivery of tangible property but communication of data and the movement of data messages.

An instruction is given by customer to bank, and the bank effects payment by communicating to the recipient's bank. This is achieved either by means of a piece of paper such as a banker's payment, telex, EFT or some similar mechanism. Interbank settlement follows, but it is ancillary to the main commercial payment process. Payment therefore resides quite naturally within the EDI trading environment.

In essence there is no difference

between an EDI transaction and a funds transfer transaction when the latter is transmitted in a structured format between computers. In this sense, the SWIFT system, which has structured format message types for financial data, is an EDI system. However, the difference lies with the users of the system, or rather with the type of transaction transmitted through the system. While in an international funds transfer system the users are financial institutions and the transactions are related mainly to payments, in an EDI system the users can be from any type of industry and the transactions can include any type of business data.

EDI has been mainly developed in service industries, such as insurance, air transport, motor industries, and banking (SWIFT). The potential for EDI services is very large and is supported by many network providers such as GE Information Services, IBM, DEC as well as by the PTTs.

A fundamental link in the EDI trade chain is the payment function, see Figure 1. Banks have to be interested in EDI because the world of their corporate customers is changing. To be competitive banks will need to make their money transmission services available within the framework of corporate EDI networks.

SWIFT has recognized the need for a coherent set of internationally accepted technical standards to support the exchange of commercial transactions. In addition to the existing SWIFT message formats, standard interbank messages based on EDIFACT syntax have been developed. Also, standardized interchange agreements are being developed which can now form the basis of EDI agreements with whatever modifications the participants want to make.

EFT is the tool used by the banks, but within the environment of the EDI network, the EFT payment becomes an integral part of the EDI trading cycle. It is therefore a continuing and reliable function within that cycle. What EDI participating banks have to offer as their value-added service is the guaranteed element to the payment message.

EDI is both a threat and an opportunity for the banks. A threat because independent network operators, such as BT or GE Information Services, could encroach up the traditional relationship between the banks and their corporate clients, and potentially offer alternative services. EDI, however, presents an opportunity to the banks because it is a new area of business upon which additional value-added-services can be developed. The banks are well positioned to offer these services because they already have the communications infrastructure for running X.400 upon which EDI depends. Moreover, they have the experience in maintaining secure and highly dependable services. The difficulty they face is that they have to cooperate in areas where previously there has been intense competition. *See* ANSI X9.9 - 1986, ATM, BANK-WIRE, EDI, EDIFACT, EFT, CASHWIRE, CHAPS, CHIPS, CLOSED USER GROUP, FEDWIRE, KEY, LINK ENCRYPTION, MESSAGE AUTHENTICATION, RSA, SAG-ITTAIRE, SPEED, SWIFT, TAMPER RESISTANT MODULE, X.25, X.400.

bank to bank information. In banking, miscellaneous information pertaining to the transfer, that may include information specifying for which bank, or banks, the information is intended. (ANSI).

BankWire. In banking, a private telecommunication and settlement service for banks in the United States. (ANSI). *See* BANKING NETWORKS.

base. (1) In mathematics, a reference value. (2) In mathematics, a number used in the floating point representation of numbers. (3) In mathematics, the value in which a number system is established. For example, binary arithmetic uses a base of 2. *See* RADIX.

baseband. (1) In data communications, the frequency range of the information bearing signals prior to combination with carrier wave by modulation. (2) In data communications, the transmission of signals at their original frequencies, i.e. unmodulated. *See* CARRIER, MODULATION.

baseband modem. *Synonymous with* LIMITED DISTANCE MODEM.

baseline. *See* BASELINE SECURITY CONTROLS.

baseline security controls. In risk management, a set of general controls designed to provide a basic level of security in a class of systems.

basic mode link control. In data communications, control of data links by use of the control characters of the ISO-/CCITT 7 bit character set for information processing interchange. *See* CCITT, ISO-7.

basic security theorem. In computer security, a theorem which states that if a system commences in a secure state, and any transition obeys the specified security rules, then the new state will also be secure. *See* BELL LAPADULA MODEL.

basic service. In communications, a common carrier service limited to the provision of transmission capacity for the movement of information. Basic services are regulated by the FCC. *See* ENHANCED SERVICES, COMPUTER INQUIRY 1980, FCC.

batch balancing. In auditing, a comparison of items or documents processed against a predetermined control total. *See* BALANCING.

batched communication. In data communications, the transmission of a large body of data from one station to another in a network without intervening responses from the receiving unit. *Compare* INQUIRY/RESPONSE.

batch total. In computing, a total of some common component of a batch of data that enables control to be maintained over the validity of the data.

baud. In data communications, a measure of signalling speed in a digital communication circuit. The speed in bauds is equal to the number of discrete conditions or signal events per second. For example, one baud equals one bit per second in a train of binary signals. Since the baud is a measure of all the signalling elements transmitted, including those used to coordinate transmission as well as the actual message transmitted, it is not necessarily equivalent to the data signalling rate. *See* DATA SIGNALLING RATE.

baudot code. In data communications, a code for the transmission of data in which five equal length bits represent one character.

BBS. (1) Bulletin Board System. (2) Bulletin Board Software. *See* BULLETIN BOARD.

BCC. *See* BLOCK CHARACTER CHECK.

BCD. *See* BINARY CODED DECIMAL.

BCF. *See* BROMOCHLORODIFLUORO-METHANE, BYTE CIPHER FEEDBACK.

BCP. *See* BYTE CONTROL PROTOCOL.

BDN. *See* BELL DATA NETWORK.

BDSG. *See* BUNDESDATENSCHUTZGE-SETZ.

beam break. In physical security, a

technique of intruder detection that relies upon a change in a beam intensity produced by the passage of the intruder. The beam may comprise electromagnetic radiation derived from a light source, laser or radio frequency transmitter. *Compare* BREAK ALARM.

bearer. In data communications, a high bandwidth channel. *See* CHANNEL.

BeBe. In computer security, a virus that infects COMMAND.COM and COM files, affects run time operation, corrupts program, OVL and data files. *See* VIRUS NAMES.

Beeper. In computer security, a virus that terminates and stays resident, infects COM files, affects run time operation, corrupts program, OVL and data files. *See* VIRUS NAMES.

bel. In electronics and communications, the basic unit of a logarithmic scale (to base 10) used for expressing ratios of powers. Two powers, A and B are related by N bels when log (A/B) = N. *See* DECIBEL.

Bell 103. In data communications, a standard for low speed modems using frequency shift keying techniques to produce data transfer rates between 0 and 300 bits per second. *Compare* BELL 212A. *See* BITS PER SECOND, FREQUENCY SHIFT KEYING.

Bell 212A. In data communications, a standard for modems using phase shift keying to produce a data transfer rate of 1200 bits per second. *Compare* V.22. *See* BITS PER SECOND, PHASE SHIFT KEYING.

Bell Data Network. In data communications, an AT&T system intended to provide subscribers with an extensive range of communication and database access facilities.

Bell-La Padula model. (1) In computer security, a formal transition model of computer security policy that describes a set of access control rules. In this formal model, the entities in a computer system are divided into abstract sets of subjects and objects. The notion of a secure state is defined and it is proven that each state transition preserves security by moving from secure state to secure state; thus, inductively proving that the system is secure. A system state is defined to be 'secure' if the only permitted access modes of subjects to objects are in accordance with a specific security policy. In order to determine whether or not a specific access mode is allowed, the clearance of a subject is compared to the classification of the object and a determination is made as to whether the subject is authorized for the specific access mode. The clearance/ classification scheme is expressed in terms of a lattice. (DOD). *See* LATTICE, OBJECT, SIMPLE SECURITY PROPERTY, STAR PROPERTY, SUBJECT. (2) In computer security, a mathematical model dealing with mandatory and discretionary access controls; it is primarily concerned with protection against illegal disclosure of information. The report is often summarized by the two axioms:

- the simple security rule which states that a subject cannot read information for which it is not cleared ('no read up');
- the *-property which states that a subject cannot move information from an object with a higher security classification to an object with a lower classification ('no write down').

The model is of considerable significance, providing a formal model for the secure access to entities. The model does not restrict itself to computer systems, it can be applied to other forms physical security, and to procedural security.

The model also introduces the concept of a trusted system, i.e. one guaranteed not to consummate a security breaching information transfer even if it is possible.

The Bell-La Padula model is fundamental to the criteria for Class A and B systems in the Orange Book and for the many of evaluation criteria for security systems subsequently developed.

Description of the Model.
The model has the ability to represent abstractly the elements of computer systems and of security that are relevant to a treatment of classified information stored in a computer system. The essential problem is to control access to a set of passive, protected entities, termed objects, by active entities, termed subjects, based on a security policy.

The state of a system is described by a tuple (current access set, access permission matrix, level function and hierarchy) or (b, M, f, H). Each of these components of the system state are described below.

Current Access Set (b)
The purpose of an access, in the model, is to extract information from an object or to insert information into the object. Four access modes: execute, read, append and write, are defined:

- execute - neither observation nor alteration;
- read - observation with no alteration;
- append - alteration with no observation;
- write - observation and alteration.

The append mode would, for example, allow a user to add a set of statistical data into a file, without providing the facility to read data that it already contained.

A current access by a subject to an object is represented by the tuple (subject, object, access-attribute). The total set of all such tuples is the current access set of the model, i.e. the 'b' in (b, M, f, H).

Hierarchy (H)

The model imposes a structure on the objects which allows only for rooted trees or isolated points. Thus the hierarchy of objects is either that of a single isolated object, or one in which an object can have several children, but a child can have only one parent, i.e. a tree structure. Thus the particular hierarchy of objects in the system is represented by the H in the model state (b, M, f, H).

Access Permission (M)

The model includes provision for discretionary access control and the access permission is defined by a matrix M (see Fig 1):

	Program 1	Segment A	Segment B
Process 1	Read Execute	Read Write	
Process 2			Read

Bell-La Padula Model.
Fig. 1. Access Control Matrix

The columns of the matrix represent the systems objects, the rows the subjects, and the matrix entry represents the access attributes that the subject has to the corresponding object. Thus the access matrix represents the M in the model (b, M, f, H).

Level function (f)

The embodiment of security classification in the model is given by the level function f. In governmental fields people and documents are given a security designation in the form of a pair (classification, set of categories).

The classification, or clearance, is a strictly hierarchical designation e.g.
TOP SECRET > SECRET > CONFIDENTIAL > UNCLASSIFIED.

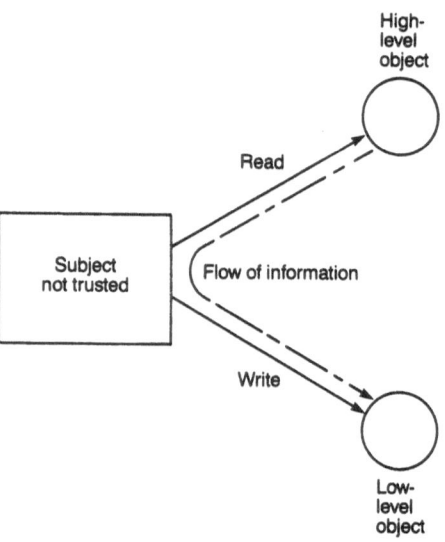

Bell-La Padula Model
Fig. 2. Information flow showing the need for the star property in order to prevent a malicious subject from extracting information from a top secret object and putting it into a confidential object. Reproduced with permission of IBM Corp.

This division is, however, too coarse and it would provide persons with a right to access based upon their security classification with no regard to their 'need to know'. The second component of the security designation is a set of categories, e.g. in military terms, Nuclear, Nato, Crypto, which represent the fields of legitimate interest of the person or the topics contained in a document (say). Thus an individual could have the security designation (SECRET, {NATO, CRYPTO}).

It is clear that there needs to be some ordering of security designations and this is achieved by the concept of domination. (class_1, category_set_1) dominates (class_2, category_set_2) if and only if:

- class_1 is greater or equal to class_2;

• category_set_1 includes category-_set_2 as a subset.

Thus (TOP SECRET, {NATO,Nuclear}) would dominate (SECRET, {NATO}).

An object will have security level designated $f_0(O_j)$. A subject (S_i) will have a (maximum) security level $f_s(S_i)$ but may elect to operate at another lower level $f_c(S_i)$, the latter is then termed the current security level of the subject. The security rules of the system may compel the user to adopt this lower designation to perform certain actions, e.g. to write to an UNCLASSIFIED file.

Thus for a given subject and object there are three security levels of significance (f_s, f_0, f_c) and these form the f term of the model (b, M, f, H).

The tuple (b, M, f, H), i.e. (security access set, access permission matrix, level function, hierarchy) represent a state of the model.

The model defines three security properties, the simple security property (ss-property), the star property (*-property) and the discretionary security property. The simple security property is satisfied if (subject, object, observe-attribute) is a current access and the security level of the subject dominates the security level of the object. In other words a subject with a low security level cannot read a highly classified file.

The star property is satisfied, in any state, if a subject has simultaneous observe access to object_1 and alter access to object_2 and the security level of object_1 is dominated by the security level of object_2. This rule is aimed at preventing a Trojan Horse operating in a process with a high security level clearance, from transferring information from a highly classified object into an object with a low security classification.

A state satisfies the discretionary security property (ds-property) if (subject_1, object_1, attribute_x) is a current access, in b, and attribute_x is recorded in the (subject_1, object_1) component

of M. In other words the entry in the discretionary access control matrix for the subject and object corresponds to the type of access being undertaken.

The system will move from one state to another as a result of a request, e.g. to add or delete an access set, and the response to that request, i.e. permitted or refused.

The basic security theorem of the model states that the security can be guaranteed systematically when each alteration to a current state does not itself cause a breach of security. The security can be guaranteed systematically if, whenever (subject, object, access attribute) is added to the current access set then the simple security property, the star security policy and the discretionary security property for that state are all satisfied. This inductive approach shows that the preservation of security from one state to another guarantees the total system security.

Compare BIBA MODEL. *See* ACCESS MATRIX MODEL, DISCRETIONARY SECURITY POLICY, DOMINATE, MANDATORY SECURITY POLICY, OBJECT, ORANGE BOOK, SIMPLE SECURITY PROPERTY, STAR SECURITY PROPERTY, SUBJECT.

beneficiary. In banking, the ultimate party to be credited or paid as a result of a transfer. (ANSI). *Synonymous with* ULTIMATE BENEFICIARY.

Berlekamp-Massey algorithm. In mathematics, an algorithm for determining the linear complexity of a finite binary sequence. *See* LINEAR COMPLEXITY.

Best Wish. In computer security, a virus that infects COMMAND.COM, COM, OVL and EXE files, affects run time operation, corrupts program, OVL and data files. *See* VIRUS NAMES.

beta testing. In reliability, testing of a product in operation by selected users before formal release.

between-the-lines entry. In computer security, access, obtained through the use of active wiretapping by an unauthorized user, to a momentarily inactive terminal of a legitimate user assigned to a communications channel. (FIPS). *See* ACCESS, ACTIVE WIRETAPPING, PIGGY-BACK ENTRY.

bias. (1) In mathematics, the condition where, during the generation of random or pseudorandom numbers, the occurrence of some numbers is more likely than others. (ISO). *See* PSEUDORANDOM NUMBER. (2) In database security, an information loss effect arising from the use of perturbation techniques in inference control. It is defined as the difference between the expectation of the perturbed statistic and its true value. *Compare* CONSISTENCY. *See* INFERENCE CONTROL, INFORMATION LOSS, PERTURBATION.

biased. In mathematics, pertaining to a process used in the generation of random numbers that is more likely to produce some numbers than others. *See* RANDOM NUMBERS.

Biba model. In access control, a model of an access control system designed to protect the integrity of data.

In this model objects and subjects have a hierarchical security classification related to their integrity or 'trustworthiness'. Thus a subject may have an integrity classification I(S), and an object an integrity classification I(O); moreover the levels are ordered so that it is possible to say, for example, that I(S) > I(O).

The Biba model has two security properties which have similar names to those employed in Bell LaPadula:

- Simple Integrity Property - if a subject S can modify an object O then I(S) > I(O);
- Integrity *-Property - if a subject S has read access to object O with integrity level I(O), S can have write access to object P only if I(O) > = I(P).

In this model a high integrity file must not be corrupted with data from a low integrity file. The simple integrity property is aimed at preventing a person, with a low integrity classification, from modifying a report with a high integrity classification. Thus, if it is important to guarantee that data in a file is only modified by highly trustworthy people, then the simple integrity model, with appropriate integrity classification of staff and files, will provide that guarantee.

The *-property is concerned with preventing the flow of relative 'suspect' information into a file with a high integrity classification. It is analogous to the Bell LaPadula *-property which aims to prevent a Trojan Horse from leaking highly confidential information into a low classified file. The Biba *-property ensures that a subject accessing a file is only permitted to write to a file of the same, or a lower integrity classification, and thus cannot corrupt a high integrity file with data derived from a less trustworthy one. *Compare* BELL LaPADULA MODEL. *See* OBJECT, SIMPLE SECURITY PROPERTY, STAR SECURITY PROPERTY, SUBJECT.

bid. In data communications, an attempt by a computer or station to gain control of a circuit so that it can transmit data.

bigram. In cryptanalysis, a pair of consecutive letters. In statistical attacks on ciphers the known frequency of various bigrams, in a given language, can be used in attempts to break the cipher. *Compare* TRIGRAM. *See* INFORMATION THEORY.

bijection. In mathematics, a function that maps a set of values {p} onto a set of values {q}, such that each set has the same number of elements and there is a one to one relationship between the elements. Thus each value in {p} is associated with just one value in {q} and vice versa.

bimetallic-type heat detector. In physical security, a heat detection device comprising a bimetallic strip, the two constituent metallic strips having different coefficients of thermal expansion. Changes in temperature cause a deflection of the strips that in turn activates an alarm.

binary. In mathematics and computing, a numbering system in which there are only two states, or conditions. The binary system is represented by the numbers 0 and 1.

binary arithmetic. In mathematics and computing, arithmetic performed with binary numbers. The arithmetic rules are extremely simple (e.g. $1 + 0 = 1$, $1 + 1 = 10$) and they can be implemented with simple logic circuits. *See* LOGIC CIRCUIT.

binary code. In codes, a coding system employing groups of the binary digits, 0 and 1, to represent a letter, digit or other character in a computer, e.g. the decimal number 6 is represented by binary 110, i.e. $(1 \times 4) + (1 \times 2) + (0 \times 1)$. *See* BINARY.

binary coded decimal. In computing, a method of representing decimal numbers where each digit of the number is represented by one nibble. The four bits of the nibble can represent numbers in the range 0 - 15 but only the representations for 0 - 9 are employed. Moreover one whole byte is sometimes used to represent the sign. This form of coding is less efficient than the various binary forms, in terms of storage space, but it allows very long decimal numbers to be precisely represented and is therefore often employed in applications in the financial

transaction areas. *See* BIT, BYTE, NIBBLE.

binary digit. In mathematics, either of the characters 0 or 1, often abbreviated to 'bit'. *See* BIT.

binary license. In computing, a form of software distribution in executable form; users are not permitted to modify the program code.

binary number. In mathematics, a number expressed in binary notation. *See* BINARY ARITHMETIC, BINARY CODE.

binary symmetric source. In cryptography, a device that, in theory, could emit a truly random sequence of binary digits. *See* BINARY DIGIT, RANDOM NUMBERS.

binary synchronous communications. In data communications, an IBM byte control protocol that sends data in frames marked by synchronization characters. After two synchronization characters, each frame has a start of header character, a header containing control and address information, a start of text character, the message text, an end of text character and a cyclic redundancy check character. The protocol supports both point to point and multipoint operation. *See* BYTE CONTROL PROTOCOL, CYCLIC REDUNDANCY CHECK, FRAME, HEADER, MULTIPOINT CONNECTION, POINT TO POINT.

binding analysis. In information security, the determination whether the totality of security enforcing functions together with the description of their interworking as described in the architectural design fulfills the totality of security objectives. *See* BINDING OF FUNCTIONALITY, INFORMATION TECHNOLOGY SECURITY EVALUATION CRITERIA.

binding of functionality. In information security, an effectiveness criterion in ITSEC. Although security functions may be suitable for their individual purposes it is possible that certain combinations of functions or mechanisms may interfere or conflict with each other. In evaluating the binding of functionality a study is undertaken of the interrelationships of security functions, and mechanisms, to ensure that they are mutually supportive and provide an effective and integrated whole. *See* INFORMATION TECHNOLOGY SECURITY EVALUATION CRITERIA, SECURITY FUNCTION, SECURITY MECHANISM.

biometrics. In access control, automated methods of verifying or recognizing a person based upon a physical or behavioral characteristics. Biometric techniques may be classified on the basis of some passive attribute of an individual, e.g. an eye retina pattern, or some unique manner in which an individual performs a task, e.g. writing a signature. The concept of using some unique physical attribute of the user has considerable attraction, from an authentication viewpoint, since there would appear to be no mechanism by which the authentication procedure could be fraudulently undertaken by an attacker. It is possible to guess a password, or steal a token, but one cannot assume the fingerprint of another.

Overview
The stages involved in the application of such a biometric access systems effectively comprise: analog capture of the users' attribute, development of a template of the user's attribute, i.e. enrolment, comparison of the input template with that of a stored value, for the authorized user, when access is requested, decision on access acceptance or rejection.

The nature of such biometric measurements is that they are likely to display variations each time that the user logs in. Variations can arise from environmental factors, such as temperature,

humidity, from the state of the user, e.g. stress, perspiration, or from the wear and tear on the measuring device.

Minor variations in the input signature should not cause a false rejection, i.e. a Type 1 error, also measured as the False Rejection Rate (FRR). On the other hand the system must not be desensitized to the point where another person's attributes are accepted as a match for the legitimate user, causing a false acceptance, or Type 2 error, also measured as the False Acceptance Rate (FAR). Reduction in Type 1 error rates can often be achieved only at the cost of increased Type 2 rates.

The analog capture mechanism must ensure a high degree of compatibility between successive measurements of the same individual's attributes, whilst guaranteeing sufficient sensitivity to minimize false acceptances. The development of a biometric template should aim to capture sufficient significant features of the analog input, to ensure that it truly identifies the user's characteristic, whilst minimizing the number of bits that must be transmitted and stored.

Comparison of input and stored template represents a pattern matching problem; the criteria for pattern matching must be such that Type 1 and Type 2 errors are simultaneously maintained at a low level.

Application
The factors to be considered in considering a biometric access control system include:

- application area;
- cost;
- Type 1 and Type 2 errors;
- throughput;
- susceptibility to external factors;
- user acceptability;
- disadvantaged users;
- responsibility to user;
- standards.

Biometric devices may be considered for a wide variety of application areas, physical access control at a point of entry, permission to conduct transactions at an ATM or EFTPOS terminal, login at a terminal, or over a network, etc. The costs associated with biometric devices includes capital cost of reader and associated template storage devices, maintenance costs, vulnerability to vandalism etc. The cost of biometric devices has, to date, restricted their usage to systems in which security is at a premium. The cost of such devices is steadily falling and it is predicted that they will be more commonly used in the future.

Enhanced security that can be achieved with biometric devices depends upon the achievement of low levels of Type 1 and Type 2 errors. It is, however, necessary to exercise caution in interpreting quoted figures for these performance factors. The measurement of Type 1 errors is comparatively straightforward. It is simply necessary to make a number of successive trials for typical users under varying conditions, temperature, humidity, physiological changes etc. However, the measurement of Type 2 errors can involve serious complications. Clearly there are two situations, one in which the characteristics of a random group of users are measured; the other in which one user deliberately attempts to masquerade as another.

The problem of assessing Type 2 error rates is that of selecting a population of users for the trials. Do the results of Type 2 trials relate to a completely random sample, or are the members of the sample selected to have characteristics close to that of the user. Conduct of Type 2 error trials with a guarantee of similarity of (say) eye retina patterns is undoubtedly a difficult task. The problem of meaningful Type 2 errors is even greater for measurement of a physical behavior. How can one ensure that the trial subjects are as skilled, at counterfeiting another's behavior, as a determined attacker. The acceptability of

Type 1 and Type 2 error rates clearly depends upon the security demanded of an application area, and the amount of user inconvenience, associated with false rejections, that can be tolerated.

Biometric systems involve the user submitting to the measurement of some physical characteristic, followed by a comparison with a stored template. Given the variables associated with the measurement, it is likely that more than one measurement will be, at least occasionally, required. This total process is likely to be more time consuming than the entry of password, or the insertion of plastic card into a reader. The acceptable time delay, associated with a biometric system, will depend upon the application area and the degree of security demanded.

The characteristics of a user, and environment of the measurement, are likely to undergo significant variation with time. A fingerprint scan will be affected by dirt, grease, perspiration, minor injury etc. The number of false rejections can be reduced by decreasing the sensitivity of the system to such variations, but this implies an increase in the probability of a Type 2 error.

Biometric systems have the advantage that they make fewer demands on the users, who do not necessarily have to remember long passwords, carry cards or undertake complicated challenge response dialogues. However, members of the public are very sensitive to the question of submitting to some form of measurement on their personal characteristics. Fingerprinting is a particularly sensitive topic, because it is commonly associated with criminals.

Access control systems that measure a user's physical characteristics can present handicapped people with difficulties or embarrassment. Voice recognition systems might well be a source of embarrassment to people with a speech impediment. The question of corporate policy, or legislation, regarding disadvantaged personnel, will clearly require careful consideration in the decision to employ biometric access systems.

If templates of users attributes are maintained at a central host, then it must be emphasized that neither the host system, nor the user, can select a different template. Unlike a password or PIN, users have no way of changing their eye retina pattern. Consider the situation that would arise if an attacker gained access to such a template. It might then be feasible for the attacker to masquerade, as the user, by simply injecting a signal, corresponding to the user's template, as if it emanated from the biometric reader. The only recourse of the host system would be to remove that template from the authorization file. The user would not only be denied access to the system, but would have no way of ever employing the eye retina scanner for access. The use of the eye retina pattern for the other eye might merely represent a temporary respite.

Biometric sensors are coming onto the market and they appear to be in advance of international standards. In a closed environment this may not be a significant factor, however, the development of such standards will become a matter of increasing urgency, however, if the systems are to be employed in major national and international networks, e.g. EDI or EFT systems. *See* EDI, EFT, EYE RETINA ANALYSIS, FAR, FRR, FINGERPRINT ANALYSIS, HAND GEOMETRY ANALYSIS, KEYSTROKE DYNAMICS ANALYSIS, SIGNATURE ANALYSIS, TEMPLATE TYPE 1 ERROR, TYPE 2 ERROR, VEINCHECK, VOICE ANALYSIS.

bipolar. In data communications, pertaining to a signal that undertakes both positive and negative values. *Compare* UNIPOLAR. *See* NONRETURN TO ZERO.

birthday problem. In mathematics, pertaining to the calculation of the probability that if n people individually select a random number in the range 1, 2 ....n^2, where $n << n^2$ then there is a significant probability that two people will select the same number. The name of the problem derives from the rather surprising fact that with a group of 23 randomly selected people there is an even chance that two of them will share a birthday.

bistatic microwave sensor. In physical security, an intruder detector device using a microwave transmitter and line of sight receiver. The total signal received comprises the vector sum of the direct signal and signals reflected from local objects. An intruder will cause a change in the received vector sum and an alarm is activated. *See* MICROWAVE SENSOR.

BISYNC. *See* BINARY SYNCHRONOUS COMMUNICATIONS.

bit. *See* BINARY DIGIT.

bit copier. In software protection, a program that reads the source disk at the bit level and writes at that level to the destination disk. If the source disk is copy protected so will be the destination disk. *See* DEMON, WEAK BITS.

bit interleaving. In data communications, a method of time division multiplexing in which the channel receives one bit in turn from each active terminal and delivers one bit in turn to each receiving terminal. *Compare* CHARACTER INTERLEAVING. *See* TIME DIVISION MULTIPLEXING.

BITNET. In data communications, Because It's Time NETwork, an international network developed for university departments.

bit oriented protocol. In data communications, a protocol that does not impose character assignments to the transmitted data bits. *Compare* CHARACTER ORIENTED PROTOCOL. *See* BIT, CHARACTER, PROTOCOL.

bit parallel, byte serial. In data communications, transmission in which the individual bits of a byte is sent on individual lines and the complete bytes are sent sequentially. *See* BIT, BYTE, PARALLEL TRANSMISSION, SERIAL TRANSMISSION.

bit rate. In data communications, the speed at which bits are transmitted over a communications link, usually expressed in bits per second (BPS). *See* BAUD, DATA TRANSFER RATE.

bit sequence independence. In data communications, pertaining to a network that enables the transfer of digital data, as a sequence of bits, without placing any restriction upon the sequence of bits. *See* BIT, TRANSPARENT DATA COMMUNICATION CODE.

bit sequence transparent. *See* BIT SEQUENCE INDEPENDENCE.

bits per inch. In computing, the number of bits recorded per inch of track on a magnetizable recording surface.

bits per second. *See* BIT RATE.

bit stream. In data communications, a binary signal without regard to grouping by character. *See* BIT.

bit string. In data communications, a string of binary digits in which each bit position is considered as an independent unit. *See* BIT, STRING.

bit stuffing. In data communications, a technique in which frames are delimited by the bit pattern e.g. 01111110. When 5 consecutive 1 bits appear in the message or control data an 0 bit is added to avoid confusion with the delimiter. *Compare* CHARACTER STUFFING. *See* SYNCHRONOUS DATA LINK CONTROL.

black. In communications security, unclassified information or equipment

and wire lines that handle encrypted classified information. (AFR). *Compare* RED.

blacklist. *Synonymous with* HOT CARD LIST.

Black Monday. In computer security, a virus that terminates and stays resident, infects COMMAND.COM, COM, EXE and OVL files, corrupts file linkage, affects run time operation, corrupts program, OVL and data files. *See* VIRUS NAMES.

blackout. In physical security, a total loss of power. *Compare* BROWNOUT.

blind dialing. In data communications, a facility of some modems which allows the modem to dial when a dial tone is supposed to be present but none is detected. This facility is important in some PBX systems that use non standard lines that certain modems will interpret as a dead line. *See* MODEM.

blob. In computer security, a destructive form of malicious code that gradually takes control over an increasing amount of memory space until the system crashes. *See* MALICIOUS CODE.

block. (1) In computing, a group of words, documents or files treated as a unit. (2) In computing, a collection of contiguous records stored as a unit. (3) In data communications, a group of bits transmitted as a unit and encoded for error control purposes. *See* ERROR DETECTION CODE.

block cancel character. In codes, a specific operational character designed to cause the portion of a block preceding it to be canceled. *See* BLOCK.

block character check. In data communications, an error control procedure used to detect errors on a block of data transmitted over a network. *See* BLOCK,

Plaintext

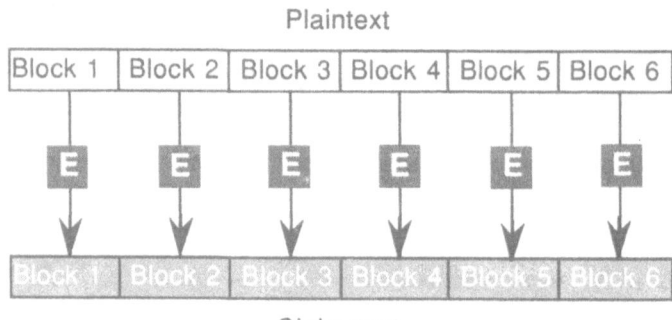

Ciphertext

block cipher.
Block ciphers encrypt each plaintext block in turn.

ERROR DETECTION CODE.

block cipher. In cryptography, a cipher in which the plaintext must be assembled into blocks with a blocksize determined by the cryptographic algorithm designer; the corresponding ciphertext block depends only upon the cryptographic key, the algorithm and the plaintext block. Thus for any given cryptographic key the cipher effectively provides a massive codebook with entries for every possible plaintext block and corresponding ciphertext block. *Compare* BLOCK CIPHER CHAINING, STREAM CIPHER. *See* CRYPTOGRAPHIC KEY, ELECTRONIC CODEBOOK.

block cipher chaining. In cryptography, a procedure using a block cipher in which the output ciphertext depends upon the key, the current and all previous plaintext blocks of the message. Chaining overcomes the cryptographic weakness of block ciphers that arises when the length of the message exceeds the blocksize and the messages are highly formatted, or contain significant redundancy.

If a ciphertext message comprises a significant number of highly formatted blocks then certain ciphertext blocks are likely to recur in successive messages, thus enabling an attacker to compile a codebook of plaintext/ciphertext pairs.

If a message has a high degree of redundancy then it will be possible for an attacker to develop a frequency analysis of plaintext segments; block ciphers will tend to produce ciphertext blocks displaying the same frequency distribution thus giving useful information to a cryptanalyst.

Chaining ensures that patterns in plaintext messages are not carried through to the ciphertext. Two identical plaintext blocks, in successive messages, will produce two dissimilar ciphertext blocks provided that the preceding plaintext blocks are not identical.

The effect of chaining is achieved by feeding back previous plaintext, or ciphertext, blocks and causing them to influence the encryption/decryption process. Previous plaintext, or ciphertext, blocks may be used to modify the key or input of the encryptor/decryptor unit. In cipher block chaining, for example, the ciphertext output is 'exclusive or-ed' with the succeeding plaintext block and the result is input into the encryption unit.

Special arrangements are required to deal with the last, short block when the length of the plaintext message is not an integral number of blocksizes. Padding with fixed, or randomly selected, characters presents one solution but this is not acceptable in cases where the ciphertext message must be of the same length as the plaintext. For example, encrypted files will need to be of the same length as the plaintext version if they are to take up occupancy of the same storage space. Two common techniques for the short block problem, that do not cause message expansion, are a stream cipher mode and ciphertext stealing.

In the stream cipher mode the last block is enciphered with a stream cipher; in ciphertext stealing the penultimate ciphertext block is caused to be of the same length as the last plaintext block.

Chaining introduces error extension; a change in a bit value of a ciphertext block will influence the deciphering process of some later blocks, but the addition or deletion of a bit will cause a complete garbling of the remainder of the received plaintext message. A chaining cipher is said to be self synchronizing if it eventually recovers from an error, in the form of a changed bit, in the transmitted ciphertext. *Compare* BLOCK CIPHER, STREAM CIPHER CHAINING. *See* BLOCKSIZE, CIPHER BLOCK CHAINING, CIPHERTEXT STEALING, ERROR EXTENSION, EXCLUSIVE OR, STREAM CIPHER.

block error rate. In data communications, the ratio of the number of blocks incorrectly received to the total number of blocks sent. *See* BLOCK.

blocking law. In legislation, a law that specifically prohibits the disclosure, copying or removal of documents to another country's authorities based on the orders to produce such documents, issued by the other country's courts or government. *See* DATA PROTECTION.

block multiplexer channel. In data communications, a multiplexer channel that interleaves blocks of data. *See* BLOCK, CHANNEL, MULTIPLEXER.

block parity. In data communications, a method of parity checking in which an error in a block of data can be detected and corrected without the block being retransmitted. *See* ERROR CORRECTION CODE, PARITY CHECKING.

blocksize. In cryptography, the number of bits in a block of a block cipher. The blocksize must be sufficiently large to thwart a message exhaustion attack. *See* BLOCK CIPHER, ELECTRONIC CODEBOOK, MESSAGE EXHAUSTION.

block sum check. *See* LONGITUDINAL REDUNDANCY CHECK.

Bloody. In computer security, a virus that encrypts itself, terminates and stays resident, infects floppy disk boot sector and hard disk partition table, corrupts boot sector, affects run time operation. *See* VIRUS NAMES.

Blood-2. In computer security, a virus that infects COM files, affects run time operation, corrupts program, OVL and data files. *See* VIRUS NAMES.

Blue Book. In database security, Trusted Database Management System Interpretation of the Trusted Computer System Evaluation Criteria. One of the Rainbow Series that is somewhat misnamed because the cover is actually pink.

The interpretation comprises two parts, two appendices, a glossary and a bibliography. The first part deals with the more general problem of security evaluation, according TCSEC, for systems that are constructed by assembling parts - hardware, firmware and software produced independently by various organizations or vendors. It introduces the concept of TCB subsets, and discusses the evaluation of a system comprising such TCB subsets, and the degree to which aspects of the TCB subset evaluation may be undertaken independently. The second part deals with the interpreted requirements for DBMS systems. *See* DBMS, ORANGE BOOK, TCB, TCB SUBSET, TCSEC, RAINBOW SERIES.

BNC connector. In communications, an industry standard coaxial cable connected to a bayonet style locking mechanism; frequently used in connecting CCTV equipment. *See* CCTV.

body print. In access control, a unique combination of physical attributes, e.g. pulse rate, respiration, that identifies a person. *See* BIOMETRICS.

book transfer. In banking, a transfer between two accounts both serviced by the bank executing the transaction. (ANSI).

boolean algebra. In mathematics, a branch of mathematics named after George Boole; it is extremely important in the study of computers. The variables in this mathematical system can only take one of two values, i.e. TRUE or FALSE, 1 or 0. There are two binary operators, AND and OR, and a single unary operator NOT. *See* BINARY ARITHMETIC, COMPLEMENT, LOGICAL EXPRESSION, LOGICAL OPERATOR, LOGIC CIRCUIT.

boolean operator. In mathematics, a logic operator, AND, OR, NOT or a combination of them, e.g. NOT AND = NAND. *See* BOOLEAN ALGEBRA, LOGICAL OPERATOR, XOR.

Boot. In computer security a virus that terminates and stays resident, infects floppy and hard disk boot sector and

hard disk partition table, affects run time operation, corrupts program, OVL and data files and file linkage. *See* VIRUS NAMES.

boot sector virus. In computer security, a virus that exploits the boot sector of a floppy or hard disk to ensure that it is activated whenever the computer is booted up from that disk. *See* VIRUS.

bounds checking. In computer security, testing of computer program results for access to storage outside of its authorized limits. (FIPS). *See* ACCESS. *Synonymous with* MEMORY BOUNDS CHECKING.

bounds register. In computer security, a hardware register that holds an address specifying a storage boundary. (FIPS). *See* BOUNDS CHECKING.

Brain. In computer security, a virus that terminates and stays resident, infects floppy disk boot sector and corrupts boot sector. *See* VIRUS NAMES.

Brain Slayer. In computer security, a virus that terminates and stays resident, infects COM and EXE and OVL files, affects run time operation, corrupts program, OVL and data files and file linkage. *See* VIRUS NAMES.

breach. In computer security, the successful and repeatable defeat of security controls with or without an arrest, that if carried to consummation, could result in a penetration of the system. Examples of breaches are: (a) Operation of user code in master mode. (b) Unauthorized acquisition of identification password or file access passwords. (c) Accessing a file without using prescribed operating system mechanisms. (d) Unauthorized access to tape library. (OPNAVINST). *See* ARREST, PENETRATION.

break. In data communications, to interrupt the transmitting end and seize control of the circuit at the receiving end.

breakable. In cryptanalysis, pertaining to a cipher in which it is possible to determine the plaintext or key from the ciphertext or to determine the key from plaintext-ciphertext pairs. *See* CRYPTO-GRAPHIC KEY, KNOWN PLAINTEXT.

break alarm. In physical security, an intruder detection alarm condition resulting from the breaking of an electric circuit, e.g. the separation of energized foils affixed to windows and window frames. *Compare* BEAM BREAK. *See* FOIL.

brevity lists. In computer security, a code system that is used to reduce the length of time required to transmit information by the use of a few characters to represent long, stereotyped sentences. (FIPS). *See* CODE SYSTEM.

Brewer-Nash. *See* CHINESE WALL MODEL.

bridge. In data communications, a device that interconnects networks. The bridge effectively comprises the data and physical link layer of the Open Systems Interconnection Reference Model and thus may interconnect networks with different data link layers. *Compare* GATEWAY, REPEATER, ROUTER. *See* DATA LINK LAYER, PHYSICAL LAYER. (2) In communications, equipment and techniques used to match circuits to each other ensuring minimum transmission impairment.

bridging sequential switcher. In physical security, a sequential video switcher with separate outputs for programmed sequence monitors and extended play monitors. Such switchers allow constant viewing of a scene selected from the standard camera sequence. *See* SEQUENTIAL SWITCHER, VIDEO SWITCHER.

British Standards Institution. In standards, the U.K. national body having a similar standards role to the American National Standards Institute.

British Telecom. The telecommunications part of the United Kingdom PTT. *See* PTT.

broadband. In communications, pertaining to transmission facilities whose bandwidth is greater than that available on voice grade circuits, and therefore capable of higher speed data transmission. *See* BANDWIDTH.

broadcast. In communications, the simultaneous transmission of data to a number of stations. *See* ALOHA, CARRIER SENSE PROTOCOL. ETHERNET, LOCAL AREA NETWORK.

bromochlorodifluoromethane. In physical security, a gas used in fire suppression. *Synonymous with* HALON 1211.

brownout. In physical security, a partial loss of power. *Compare* BLACKOUT.

browsing. (1) In data security, searching through storage to locate or acquire information, without necessarily knowing of the existence or the format of the information being sought.
(FIPS). (2) In data security, the unauthorized searching of data held on a computer, (e.g. confidential data or proprietary software). It is similar to passive wiretapping on communication channels, but is potentially more serious since data stored in a computer has a longer lifetime. Access controls are designed to prevent browsing. *See* ACCESS CONTROL, WIRETAP. *Synonymous with* SCAVENGING.

BRP. *See* BUSINESS RESUMPTION PLANNING.

BSC. *See* BINARY SYNCHRONOUS COM- MUNICATIONS.

BSI. *See* BRITISH STANDARDS INSTI- TUTION.

BT. *See* BRITISH TELECOM.

BTLE. *See* BETWEEN-THE-LINES ENT- RY.

buffer. (1) In computing, an area of storage that is temporarily reserved for use in performing an input output opera- tion, into which data is read or from which data is written. (2) In data com- munications, a storage area used to compensate for differences in the rate of flow of data, or time of occurrence of events, when transferring data from one device to another.

buffered network. In data com- munications, a system that employs buffers associated with each terminal to maximize the efficiency of the operat- ion. *See* BUFFER.

bug. (1) In communications security. *Synonymous with* ELECTRONIC LISTEN- ING DEVICE. (2) In computing, an error in a program or system. The term is reputed to have originated in the days of an electromechanical computer using re- lays. An inexplicable error was traced to the wings of an insect lodged between the contacts of a relay. *See* DEBUG, RELAY.

building security systems. In physical security, an integrated security system for an installation to provide protection against fire, smoke, intrusion, espion- age, vandalism, theft, unsafe or faulty equipment operation etc.

bulletin board. In applications, a re- mote public access system for personal computer users. A bulletin board is operated by a Sysop and provides a variety of services geared to the re- quirements of the user population. The user requires a communications software package and a modem to establish dial up connection to the system. Access to system facilities is controlled by the Sysop and users must initially be accept- ed by the Sysop and thereafter identify themselves with a password upon log in. The facilities provided by bulletin boards include:

- posting messages for other users;
- scanning and reading messages posted by other users;
- uploading and downloading files.

Users are expected to assist each other by sharing ideas, posing technical ques- tions and providing answers to posted questions based upon their knowledge and experience. The message facility can also be used for non technical matters, e.g. FOR SALE and WANTED adver- tisements, as well as an electronic mail facility.

The file transfer facility enables users to provide, and access, public domain software. Copyrighted programs can also be provided on a shareware basis, i.e. the user downloads the program and makes a voluntary donation to the sup- plier if it proves to be useful.

There has been a degree of concern in the computer security field that hackers have employed pirate bulletin boards to distribute information relevant to tele- phone intrusion, penetration software, credit card fraud, etc. and to share expertise. Moreover downloaded soft- ware may contain computer viruses. *See* ELECTRONIC MAIL, HACKER, MODEM, SYSOP, TELEPHONE INTRUSION VIRUS.

Bundesdatenschutzgesetz. In legis- lation, the German data protection law. *See* DATA PROTECTION - GERMANY.

Bundespost. The German PTT. *See* PTT.

Burger. In computer security, a virus that infects COMMAND.COM, COM and EXE files. *See* VIRUS NAMES.

burglar alarm pad. In physical security, an intruder detector comprising a support with a matrix of foil or fine wire. The footstep of an intruder breaks the foil, or wire, and an alarm is activated. *Synonymous with* GRID SENSOR. *See* FOIL.

burglary. In legislation, an illegal entry into premises with intent to commit theft.

buried-line intrusion pad. In physical security, a buried seismic-type detector comprising piezoelectric ceramic disks located within a coaxial cable. The disks are mounted between the central conductor and shield at regular intervals along the cable. Pressure from seismic motion on the disks causes them to generate alarm signals. *See* PIEZOELECTRIC DETECTOR, SEISMIC SENSOR.

burn mark. In software protection, a fingerprint technique in which a laser is used to remove a small area of magnetic material on a floppy disk. A test program will write to, and then try to read data from, this area. If the read action is successful then the disk is a copy and the protected program will be disabled. *See* EXECUTE PROTECTION.

burst. In data communications, a sequence of signals counted as a single entity in accordance with some defined criteria.

bus. (1) In data communications, a common group of hardware lines that are used to transmit information between digitally based devices or components. (2) In data communications, a network topology in which workstations are connected by T junctions to one main cable. *Compare* RING, STAR. *See* LOCAL AREA NETWORK.

business recovery planning. *Synonymous with* BUSINESS RESUMPTION PLANNING.

business resumption planning. In risk management, the arrangements for emergency operations and recovery planning. The three phases of business resumption planning are: prevention, planning and testing.

The prevention phase comprises:

threat analysis;
- physical security and protection program;
- data security and protection program.

The planning phase comprises:

- critical function/application analysis;
- design of normal and emergency procedures;
- architectures for: computer and telecommunications, manual processing and record storage;
- obtain backup resources for: off--site storage, computer processing, manual processing, data and voice communication, management control;
- arrange disaster response team staffing for: damage assessment and recovery planning, emergency operations, disaster response management.

The testing phase comprises:

- operations testing: computer processing based applications, manual processing based applications;
- simulation testing: emergency response team, disaster management team.

See CONTINGENCY PLANS, DISASTER RECOVERY PLAN. *Synonymous with* BUSINESS RECOVERY PLANNING.

bussback. In communications, the connection, by a common carrier or PTT, of the output portion of a circuit back to the input portion of a circuit. *See* LOOP-BACK TEST.

byte. (1) In computing, a binary character operated upon as a unit and usually shorter than a computer word. A byte is the smallest addressable unit of storage and is usually eight bits long. (2) The representation of a character. *See* BIT, WORD.

byte cipher feedback. In cryptography, cipher feedback in which the segments transmitted, and fed back to the shift register, are one byte in length. *See* BYTE, CIPHER FEEDBACK.

byte control protocol. In data communications, a protocol in which a message is sent with a header followed by an information field. Both the sender and receiver are required to maintain various counts and to decode control codes. *See* BINARY SYNCHRONOUS COMMUNICATIONS, HEADER, PROTOCOL.

byte mode. *Synonymous with* MULTIPLEX MODE.

byte multiplexer channel. In data communications, a multiplexer channel that interleaves bytes of data from different sources. *See* MULTIPLEXER.

byte serial transmission. In data communications, the transmission of data in which successive bytes follow one another in sequence. The individual bits of each byte may be transmitted serially or simultaneously. *See* SERIAL TRANSMISSION.

C

C1. *See* DIVISION C.

C2. *See* DIVISION C.

C2 by 92. *See* NTISSP - 200.

caboose. *Synonymous with* STOP BIT.

Caesar cipher. In cryptography, an early example of monoalphabetic, or substitution, cipher used in the Gallic wars. *See* MONOALPHABETIC CIPHER.

call. In data communications, a transmission for the purpose of identifying the transmitting station for which the transmission is intended. *See* CALL ACCEPTED SIGNAL, CALL CONTROL CHARACTER, CALL CONTROL PROCEDURE, CALL CONTROL SIGNAL, STATION.

call accepted signal. In data communications, a call control signal that is transmitted by the called DTE to indicate that it accepts the incoming call.

call back. In computer security, a procedure established for positively identifying a terminal dialing into a computer system by disconnecting the calling terminal and re-establishing the connection by the computer system's dialing the telephone number of the calling terminal. (FIPS). *See* DIAL UP CONTROL, PORT PROTECTION DEVICE, TELEPHONE INTRUSION. *Synonymous with* DIAL BACK.

call control character. In data communications, a character which is used for call control. It may be used in association with defined signal conditions on other interchange circuits. *See* CALL CONTROL SIGNAL.

call control procedure. In data communications, the implementation of a set of protocols required to establish and release a call. *See* CALL.

call control signal. In data communications, one of the set of signals necessary to establish, maintain and release a call. *See* CALL, CALL ACCEPTED SIGNAL, CALL NOT ACCEPTED SIGNAL, CALL PROGRESS SIGNAL, CALL REQUEST.

call not accepted signal. In data communications, a call control signal sent by the called DTE to indicate that the incoming call has not been accepted. *Compare* CALL ACCEPTED SIGNAL. *See* CALL CONTROL SIGNAL, DTE.

call progress signal. In data communications, a call control signal transmitted from the DCE to the calling DTE to indicate the status of the call being established, the reason why connection could not be made, or any other network condition. *See* CALL CONTROL SIGNAL, DCE, DTE.

call redirection. In data communications, a facility that allows calls to be automatically passed on to a nominated address when the recipient's user terminal is not operational. *See* CALL.

call request. In data communications, a call control signal sent by a DTE to the DCE (or network) indicating that it wishes to make a call. *See* CALL CONTROL SIGNAL, DCE, DTE.

Cambridge Ring. In data communications, a local area network standard using a coaxial cable or twisted pair ring

61

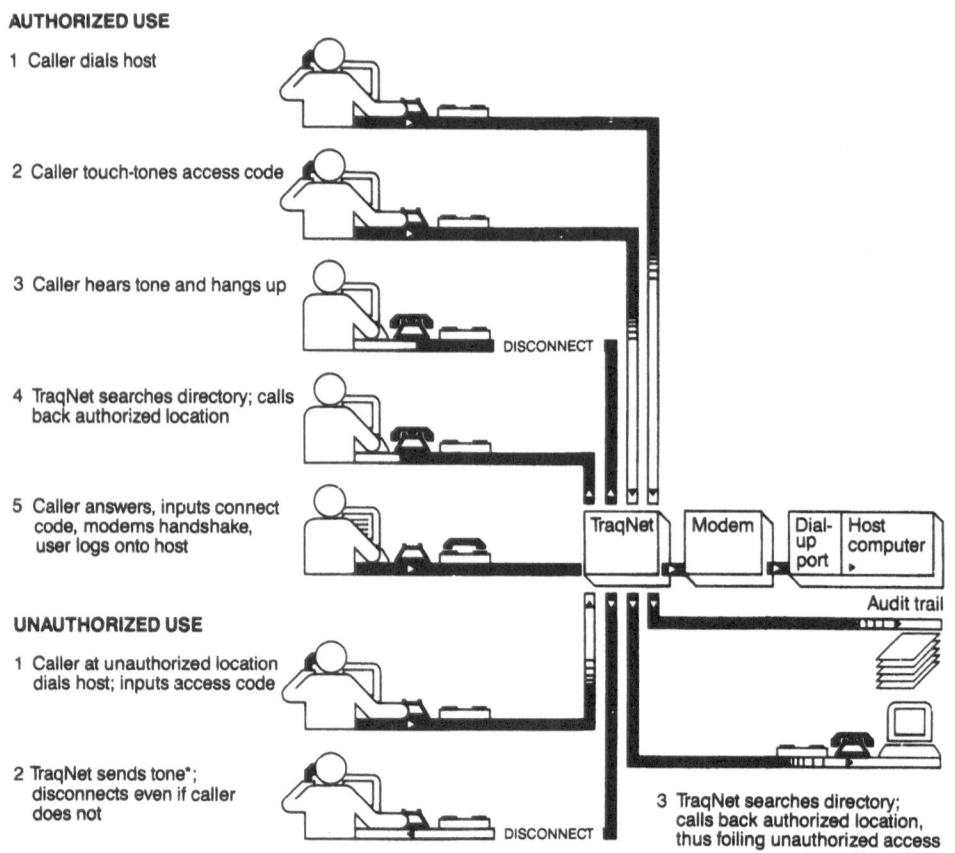

AUTHORIZED USE

1 Caller dials host

2 Caller touch-tones access code

3 Caller hears tone and hangs up
DISCONNECT

4 TraqNet searches directory; calls back authorized location

5 Caller answers, inputs connect code, modems handshake, user logs onto host

UNAUTHORIZED USE

1 Caller at unauthorized location dials host; inputs access code

2 TraqNet sends tone*; disconnects even if caller does not
DISCONNECT

TraqNet | Modem | Dial-up port | Host computer

Audit trail

3 TraqNet searches directory; calls back authorized location, thus foiling unauthorized access

call back.
The TraqNet 2000 System from LeeMah provides access control for dial-up networks.

topology and a transmission rate of 1 megabit per second. It uses a message slot protocol. *Compare* ETHERNET. *See* BIT, COAXIAL CABLE, LOCAL AREA NETWORK, MESSAGE SLOT, RING, TWISTED PAIR.

CAN. *See* CANCEL CHARACTER.

cancel call. In physical security, a facility on some telephone dialers which permits a manual override of a call initiated by an alarm. *See* TELEPHONE DIALER.

cancel character. In codes, an accuracy

control character used to indicate that the data with which it is associated is in error and is to be ignored.

cancellation. In computing, the identification of transaction documents in order to prevent their further or repeated use after they have performed their function.

Cancer. In computer security, a virus that infects COM files, affects run time operation, corrupts program, OVL and data files. *See* VIRUS NAMES.

candidate key. In databases, a key in a relational database that has the properties of a primary key. It is a combination of attributes, in a relation, that uniquely distinguishes the tuple from any other in the relation. If any attribute is dropped from the candidate key then the uniqueness property is lost. For example a personnel database may contain employee's name and date of birth as fields within a relation; two employees may have the same name and two other employees may have the same date of birth but the combination name and date of birth is likely to be a unique and hence a candidate key. *See* ATTRIBUTE, KEY, PRIMARY KEY, RELATIONAL DATABASE, TUPLE.

candidate TCB Subset. In computer security, the identification of the hardware, firmware and software that make up the proposed TCB subset, along with the identification of its subjects and objects; one of the conditions of evaluation by parts. (NCSC). *See* BLUE BOOK, OBJECT, SUBSET, TCB SUBSET.

capability. (1) In access control, a token used as an identifier for a resource such that possession of the token confers access rights for the resource. (ISO). (2) In computer security, an unforgeable ticket that is accepted by the system as incontestable proof that the presenter has authorized access to the object named by the ticket. It is often interpreted by the operating system and the hardware as an address for the object. Each capability also contains authorization information identifying the nature of the access mode (for example read mode, write mode). (MTR). *See* OBJECT.

capability list. In access control, a list of objects that may be accessed by a given subject. *Compare* ACCESS CONTROL LIST. *See* ACCESS MATRIX MODEL, CAPABILITY.

capacitance sensor. In physical security, a sensor with an action based upon the detection of changes in capacitance of a charged metallic object and ground.

capacitively coded card. In physical security, a card with information encoded in the form of capacitance sectors used in access control. *See* CARD READER.

capture. In physical security, to defeat a sensor by effecting a bypass.

card acceptor. In banking, the party accepting a credit card and presenting transaction data to an acquirer. (SAA). *Compare* CARD HOLDER, CARD ISSUER. *See* ACQUIRER.

card based mode. In banking, a mode in which transactions are initiated by the use of customer dependent data recorded onto the magnetic stripe of a plastic card. (SAA).

card encoder. In physical security, a device for placing a unique code on an access control card. *See* CARD READER.

card holder. (1) In banking, the person presenting a plastic card in payment for goods or services. *Compare* CARD ACCEPTOR, CARD ISSUER. (2) In banking, the customer associated with the Primary Account Number requesting the transaction from the card acceptor. *See* CARD ACCEPTOR, PRIMARY ACCOUNT NUMBER.

card identification code. In physical security, a numeric or alphanumeric sequence encoded onto an access card for card control and record keeping. *See* CARD READER. *Synonymous with* SYSTEM CODE.

card issuer. In banking, the institution (or its agent), that provided the card holder with the card being used in the current transaction. The institution is also responsible for paying the acquirer for goods or services on behalf of the card holder. (SAA). *Compare* CARD ACCEPTOR, CARD HOLDER. *See* ACQUIRER.

card key. (1) In banking, a key constructed from data recorded on the magnetic stripe of the plastic card. Ideally some of this data should be random. However, this is not mandatory. (SAA). *See* KEY MANAGEMENT. (2) In physical security, a plastic card containing encoded information which is used to open a locked door. *See* CARD READER. *Synonymous with* ACCESS CARD.

card mastering. In physical security, pertaining to the coding of access control cards that permits them to universally access specified groups of locks. *See* CARD READER, MASTER CODE CARD.

card reader. In physical security, a device that reads the information contained on an access control card. The information may be encoded in the card by means of a magnetic stripe, magnetic dots, punched holes, embossed printing, radio frequency circuits, capacitance sectors etc. The reader may be an intelligent reader or an on line device. The card itself may simply hold coded information or it may contain a microprocessor and RAM. *See* CAPACITIVELY CODED CARD, INTELLIGENT TOKEN, OFF LINE CARD READER, ON LINE CARD READER, MAGNETICALLY ENCODED CARD, PROXIMITY CARD READER, RAM, SINGLE VOIDING CARD READER, SMART CARD, SYSTEM CARD READER, WIPE THROUGH CARD READER.

card verification value. In banking, a check value, normally comprising three decimal digits, cryptographically derived from identifying data recorded on the magnetic stripe of a bank or credit card. The card verification value is computed in a similar manner to that of a PIN verification value. The presence of the card verification value on a card may be used as a defence against fraudulent encoding of new data on a lost or stolen card. If such a card has new data recorded on the magnetic stripe, then it is possible that in a subsequent transaction the merchant would transmit the magnetic stripe data for authorization checks but record the transaction against the account data embossed on the card. This procedure would effectively allow use of a card after its loss had been reported. With a card verification value the authorizing process computes the check value from the account identifying data, using the secret keys, and compares the result with the card verification value stored on the magnetic stripe. The card verification value provides a check against the encoding of arbitrary new account data since the attacker would have no knowledge of the cryptographic keys necessary to compute the card verification value. However, it provides no defence against data copied from another card which contains the correct card verification value. *Compare* PIN VERIFICATION VALUE. *See* CREDIT CARD, CRYPTOGRAPHIC KEY, MAGNETIC STRIPE CARD.

Carioca. In computer security, a virus that terminates and stays resident, infects COM files, affects run time operation, corrupts program and OVL files. *See* VIRUS NAMES.

carrier. In communications, a continuous frequency voltage or electromagnetic wave capable of being modulated by a second signal which carries the information to be transmitted. *See* MODULATION.

carrier detect. *Synonymous with* RECEIVED LINE SIGNAL DETECTOR.

carrier sense multiple access - collision detection. In data communications, a protocol in which a node with data to transmit listens to the network until it becomes quiet. Still listening it then transmits data, if it hears what has been transmitted then it knows that transmission is successful. Otherwise it is clear that two or more nodes have transmitted simultaneously and the collision has caused a corruption in the data. The nodes then await a random interval before attempting to retransmit. *See* ALOHA, CARRIER SENSE PROTOCOL. *Compare* CONTROL TOKEN, MESSAGE SLOT. *See* LOCAL AREA NETWORK.

carrier sense protocol. In data communications, a protocol employed in broadcast systems in which each station monitors the line to check for collisions, that corrupt their data, and then retransmit the data. *See* ALOHA, BROADCAST, CARRIER SENSE MULTIPLE ACCESS - COLLISION DETECTION.

carrier system. In communications, a method of using a single path to obtain a number of channels. Signals are modulated with a different carrier frequency for each channel and the received signals are demodulated at the receiving end. *See* CARRIER, FREQUENCY DIVISION MULTIPLEXING.

Cascade. In computer security, a virus that encrypts itself, terminates and stays resident, infects COM files, affects run time operation and corrupts program and OVL files. *See* VIRUS NAMES.

cash dispenser. In banking, a machine that provides for cash withdrawals. *See* ATM.

cash highway. In banking, a link between a cash dispenser and a depository. A bank teller could operate the cash dispenser in an insecure area with the money transferred by a high speed motor rail from a secure depository in the bank.

CashWire. In banking, the Bankwire's U.S. net settlement payment service. *See* BANKING NETWORKS, BANKWIRE.

Casino. In computer security, a virus that terminates and stays resident, infects COMMAND.COM and COM files, affects run time operation, corrupts program, OVL files and file linkage. *See* VIRUS NAMES.

Casper. In computer security, a virus that encrypts itself, infects COMMAND.COM and COM files, corrupts program, OVL, data files and file linkage, affects run time operation. *See* VIRUS NAMES.

category. (1) In data security, a grouping of objects to which a non-hierarchical restrictive label is applied (e.g. proprietary, compartmented information). Subjects must be privileged to access a category (TNI). *See* COMPARTMENT. (2) In data security, a restrictive label that has been applied to classified or unclassified data as a means of increasing the protection of and further restricting access to the data. Examples include Sensitive Compartmented Information (SCI), Proprietary Information (PROPIN), and NATO. Individuals may be given access to this information only if they have been granted formal access authorization. (AFR). *See* PROPIN, SCI. (3) In data security, a grouping of classified or unclassified but sensitive information to which an additional restrictive label is applied to signify that personnel are granted access to the information only if they have appropriate authorization. (DOD).

caution statement. In data security, a statement affixed to computer outputs which contains the highest classification being processed at the time the product was produced and a requirement that any data not requested be controlled at that level and returned immediately to the originating computer center. (AR). *See* SAFEGUARDING STATEMENT.

CB. *See* CERTIFICATION BODY.

CBC. *See* CIPHER BLOCK CHAINING.

CBMS. *See* COMPUTER BASED MESSAGE SYSTEM.

CBX. *See* COMPUTERIZED BRANCH EXCHANGE.

CCA. *See* COMMON CRYPTOGRAPHIC ARCHITECTURE.

CCEP. *See* COMMERCIAL COMSEC ENDORSEMENT PROGRAM.

CCETT. Centre Commune d'Etudes de Télévision et de Télécommunications.

CCIR. Comité Consultatif International Radio.

CCITT. . *See* COMITÉ CONSULTATIF INTERNATIONALE DE TÉLÉGRAPHIE ET TÉLÉPHONIE.

CCR. *See* CONTAINER CLEARANCE REQUIRED.

CCTA. U.K. Central Computer and Telecommunications Agency.

CCTV. *See* CLOSED CIRCUIT TELEVISION.
CCU. *See* COMMUNICATIONS CONTROL UNIT.

CDI. *See* CONSTRAINED DATA ITEM.

cell restriction. In database security, a form of memoryless control in which the decision to release a statistic is a function of the query set as compared to the table containing the statistics. *Compare* TABLE RESTRICTION. *See* INFERENCE CONTROL, LATTICE MODEL, MEMORYLESS CONTROL.

cell suppression. In database security, a form of cell restriction using a priori control, commonly used by census agencies to protect data published in tabular form. Cells, containing data from a few records, are suppressed together with associated cells which could be used to deduce the data in the suppressed cells. *Compare* AUDIT EXPERT, GROUPING, IMPLIED QUERIES CONTROL, OVERLAP CONTROL, QUERY SET SIZE CONTROL. *See* A PRIORI CONTROL, CELL RESTRICTION.

cellular radio. In communications, a method of providing a public mobile radio telephone service, e.g. for car telephones. The total area covered by the service is divided into cell clusters, typically 7, 12, 21 and 24 cells per cluster are used. The cells within a cluster share the total number of radio channels available for the service; low powered transmitters are employed so that corresponding cells in adjacent clusters, which use the same radio frequencies, do not suffer mutual interference. The cell radius may be as high as 32 kilometers in a lightly populated rural area and as low as 1.1 kilometers in densely populated city areas. To minimize co-channel interference, with small cell radii, sectored radio antenna, having a coverage angle of 120 degrees may be employed.

The cellular technique enables different conversations to use the same frequencies in areas only several miles apart. As a mobile phone user moves from one cell to another the call is handed off, i.e. the switching center compares signal strengths received at nearby cells. It searches the frequency set, of the cell receiving the strongest signal, for an open channel and commands the mobile unit to tune to that frequency. The system can now accept another call originating in the first cell on the previously occupied channel. To ensure that a minimum of calls are dropped, cells typically overlap.

When a call in progress moves into a busy cell, where there are no open channels, it can remain on its original cell until a channel opens or the user moves closer to a third cell with an open channel.

Cellular radio systems facilitate calling from a normal telephone to a mobile telephone even if the location of the called subscriber is not known and his equipment is not in use. The base station in each cell transmits regular identification signals that are constantly monitored by all mobile telephones in the area. If a mobile set

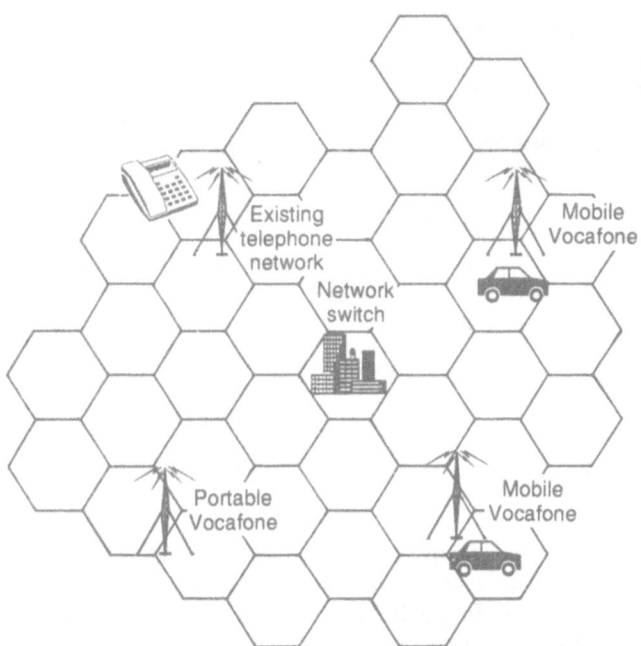

cellular radio.
Structure of a cellular radio-telephone network.

detects a change of signal, indicating that it has travelled from one cell to another, it automatically transmits a brief identification to a new base station to inform the system that it has moved and to indicate the latest location.

central computer facility. In computing, one or more computers with their peripherals and storage units, central processing units, and communications equipment in a single controlled area. This does not include remote computer facilities, peripheral devices, or terminals which are located outside the single controlled area even though they are connected to the central computer facility by approved communication links. (DCID).

centralized adaptive routing. In data communications, a method of routing in which the network routing center controls routing based on data supplied to it by each node. *Compare* DELTA ROUTING, DIRECTORY ROUTING, FIXED ROUTING,

HOT POTATO ROUTING. *See* ADAPTIVE ROUTING, NODE, ROUTING.

centralized computer network. In data communications, a computer network configuration in which a central node provides computing power, control or other services. *See* COMPUTER NETWORK, NODE.

central processing unit. In computing, the unit containing the circuits that control and perform the execution of instructions.

central station. (1) In physical security, a business or organization providing a central location for the monitoring of subscribers' alarm systems. All received alarm signals are recorded, investigated and reported to police, security or fire services. The communication links may be by telephone, radio or direct wire. The service may be provided on a regional or national basis using Wide Area Telephone Service lines. *Compare* MONITORING station. *See* GRADE AA CENTRAL STATION, GRADE A CENTRAL STATION, GRADE B CENTRAL STATION, POLICE CONNECT. (2) In physical security, a central point for an alarm system supervised by security personnel.

Central Station Electrical Protection Association. A U.S. organization to promote industry standards for central stations. *See* CENTRAL STATION.

CEPT. Conference of European PTTs. *See* PTT.

CERT. *See* COMPUTER EMERGENCY RESPONSE TEAM.

certificate. (1) In cryptography, a message which guarantees the authenticity of data contained within it. In public key cryptography it is important that a user of a public key has a guarantee of the authenticity of that key. Such a guarantee may be provided by a certificate, issued by a certification authority trusted by the users. The contents of the certificate may include the identity of the owner of the public key, the public key itself and an expiry date for that key. The data is signed with the secret key of the certification authority. A user will supply the certificate and the recipient will decrypt the certificate with the public key of the certification authority. The recipient then has the assurance that the user identity and corresponding public key has been signed by a trusted authority. *Compare* CERTIFICATION. *See* CERTIFICATE REVOCATION LIST, CERTIFICATION AUTHORITY, DIGITAL SIGNATURE, PUBLIC KEY, PUBLIC KEY CRYPTOGRAPHY, SECRET KEY. (2) In cryptography, the public key of a user, together with some other information, rendered unforgeable by a signature with the secret key of the certification authority which issued it. (ISO). *See* CERTIFICATION AUTHORITY, PUBLIC KEY, SECRET KEY.

certificate identifier. In cryptography, an identifier which is either a binary number that does not repeat during the security life of the public key/private key pair used to compute the certificate or it shall be a unique time stamp. *See* CERTIFICATE, PUBLIC KEY CRYPTOGRAPHY, SECURITY LIFE.

certificate revocation list. In cryptography, a list of revoked certificates that is transmitted by a certification authority. The list informs users that a certificate is no longer valid, e.g. due to compromise of the secret key associated with the public key signed by the certificate in question. *See* CERTIFICATE, CERTIFICATION AUTHORITY, PUBLIC KEY, SECRET KEY.

certification. (1) In cryptography, a method of testing a proposed cryptosystem by subjecting it to attacks considered most favorable to the cryptanalyst. *See* CRYPTANALYSIS, WORST CASE CONDITION. (2) In computer security, the technical evaluation, made as part of and in support of the accreditation process, that established the extent to which a particular computer system or network design and implementation meet prespecified security requirements. (FIPS). *Compare* CERTIFICATE. *See* ACCREDITATION. (3) In computer security, a statement that specifies the extent to which the security measures meet specifications. Certification is based on the results of the risk analysis performed. It does not necessarily imply a guarantee that the described system is impenetrable. It is an input to the security approval process. (AFR). *See* RISK ANALYSIS. (4) In computer security, the technical evaluation of an AIS's security features and other safeguards, made as part of and in support of the accreditation process, that establishes the extent to which a particular AIS design and implementation meet a set of specified security requirements. (DODD). *See* ACCREDITATION. (5) In computer security, an individual's formal written assurance that, based on evaluation of security tests, the classified ADP system and its environment meet the approved security specifications outlined by the ADP Security Plan. (DOE). *See* ADP SECURITY.

certification authority. In cryptography, an authority trusted by all users to create and assign certificates. (ISO). *See* CERTIFICATE, CERTIFICATE REVOCATION LIST, CERTIFICATION PATH.

certification body. In information security, a national organization responsible for administering ITSEC evaluations within that country. *Compare* INFORMATION TECHNOLOGY SECURITY EVALUATION FACILITY. *See* INFORMATION TECHNOLOGY SECURITY EVALUATION CRITERIA.

certification path. In cryptography, an ordered sequence of certificates of objects which, together with the public key of the initial object in the path, can be processed to obtain that of the final object in the path. *See* CERTIFICATE, CERTIFICATION AUTHORITY.

Certified Protection Professional. An award of the American Society of Industrial Security. *See* ASIS.

CESG. U.K. Communications Electronics Security Group.

CFB. *See* CIPHER FEEDBACK.

chaining. *See* BLOCK CIPHER CHAINING, STREAM CIPHER CHAINING.

challenge and reply authentication. *Synonymous with* CHALLENGE/RESPONSE.

challenge/response. In access control, a technique in which the host responds to a login request with a challenge to the user. The legitimate user responds to the challenge by performing a task which requires the knowledge, or access to, secret information available only to the user, and possibly the host. The user then forwards the response to the host for checking. Since the challenge is different for each challenge-response dialogue an eavesdropper cannot later masquerade as the legitimate user.

Challenge response techniques may employ either symmetric or asymmetric ciphers. Typically with a symmetric cipher the host challenge takes the form of a random number. The user encrypts the

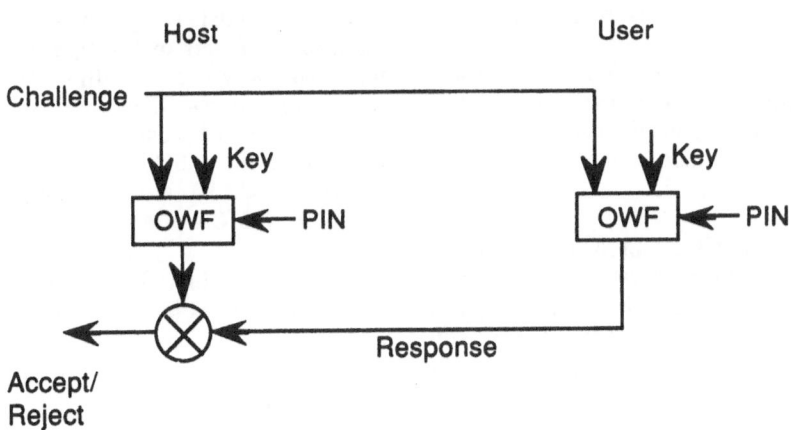

challenge/response.
Operation of challenge response system.

number with a secret key, and returns the ciphertext as the response. The host retrieves the stored secret key, corresponding to the claimed user identity, and decrypts the response. If the result is identical to the original challenge, then the host grants access.

With asymmetric ciphers the procedure is similar except that the user encrypts the challenge with a secret key and the host decrypts it with the user's public key. In this case the host does not possess the ability to masquerade as the user. *See* asymmetric cipher, DYNAMIC PASSWORD, FIAT SHAMIR ALGORITHM, PUBLIC KEY, SECRET KEY, USER ID. *Synonymous with* CHALLENGE AND REPLY AUTHENTICATION.

channel. (1) An information transfer path within a system. May also refer to the mechanism by which the path is effected. (DOD). (2) In data communications, a path along which signals can be sent, e.g. a data channel, output channel, which may either be secure or insecure against an eavesdropper. *Compare* COVERT CHANNEL. *See* EAVESDROPPING. (3) In computing, a special purpose processor and associated circuitry which has the function of controlling input output operations. *See* INPUT OUTPUT DEVICE.

channel bank. In communications, equipment performing the operation of multiplexing. Typically used for multiplexing voice grade channels. *See* MULTIPLEXER.

channel capacity. In data communications, the maximum rate at which information can be transmitted over a given channel. Channel capacity is normally measured in bauds, but may be stated in bits per second when specific terminating equipment is implied. *See* BAUD, CHANNEL.

channel isolation. In communications, a measure of the degree of cross-talk bet-

ween two channels, measured in decibels. *See* CROSS-TALK, DECIBEL.

channel overload. In data communications, a condition in which data transfer to or from a processor and I/O devices reaches a rate that approaches the capacity of the data channel. *See* I/O.

Chaos. In computer security, a virus that terminates and stays resident, infects floppy and hard disk boot sector, corrupts boot sector, affects run time operation, corrupts data files, formats or overwrites all or part of disk. *See* VIRUS NAMES.

Chaos Club. In computer security, a German club of hackers that penetrated computer systems in Europe and U.S.A. *See* HANOVER HACKER.

CHAPS. In banking, Clearing House Automated Payment System, an electronic interbank system for sending guaranteed, unconditional, sterling payments for same day settlement from one settlement bank, on behalf of itself or its customers, to another settlement bank. (ANSI). *Compare* CHIPS. *See* BANKING NETWORKS, SWIFT.

character. In data structures, a representation of the letters of the alphabet (both upper and lower case), digits 0-9 and punctuation marks. The most common representation of characters in binary notation is the ASCII code, but the EBCDIC code is also employed. *See* ASCII, EBCDIC CODE.

character assembly. In data communications, the process by which bits are put together to form characters as the bits arrive on a data link. *Compare* CHARACTER DISASSEMBLY.

character code. In codes, a method of representing characters by means of a unique set of binary digits. The two most common character codes are ASCII and

EBCDIC. *See* ASCII, EBCDIC CODE.

character disassembly. In data communications, the process by which characters are decomposed into bits for transmission over a data link. *Compare* CHARACTER ASSEMBLY. *See* BIT.

character interleaving. In data communications, a method of time division multiplexing in which the multiplexer stores a complete character before transmitting it down the line. *Compare* BIT INTERLEAVING. *See* TIME DIVISION MULTIPLEXING.

character mapping. *Synonymous with* CODE CONVERSION.

character oriented protocol. In data communications, a protocol in which the sets of bits transmitted are recognized as specific characters. *Compare* BIT ORIENTED PROTOCOL. *See* BIT, CHARACTER, PROTOCOL.

characterplexer. In data communications, a system in which data from a low speed asynchronous channel is organized on a character basis and each character is gated onto a high speed synchronous trunk. *See* ASYNCHRONOUS TRANSMISSION, SYNCHRONOUS TRANSMISSION.

character set. (1) In codes, a finite set of different characters that is considered complete for a particular application. (2) The set of characters available on a particular computer.

characters per second. In data communications, a measure of transmission rate, usually between a terminal device and a computer. *Compare* BAUD.

character stuffing. In data communications, a method of inserting additional control characters in a message so that the message does not contain the set of characters corresponding to delimiting frames with a special end of frame character. *Compare* BIT STUFFING.

character subset. In codes, a selection of characters from a character set comprising all characters which have a specified common feature. *See* CHARACTER SET.

character terminal. In data communications, a terminal which cannot form its own packets; it is connected to a PAD for connection to a packet switched network. *Compare* PACKET TERMINAL. *See* PACKET SWITCHING, PAD.

charges. In banking, fees associated with financial services. (ANSI).

check bit. In codes, a binary digit used in the process of determining the accuracy of processed or transmitted data. *Compare* CHECK DIGIT, CHECK KEY. *See* PARITY CHECKING.

check digit. In codes, one or more redundant digits used to check for the presence of errors in an associated set of digits. *Compare* CHECK BIT, CHECK KEY. *See* CHECKSUM.

check key. In codes, a group of characters, derived from and appended to a data item, that can be used to detect errors in the data item during processing. *Compare* CHECK BIT, CHECK DIGIT.

check kiting. In computer security, a form of Trojan Horse which has the effect of adding small amounts to a fraudster's account over long periods. The processing of customer cheques is deliberately delayed, and the interest earned in the intervening period credited to the fraudster's account. *Compare* SALAMI TECHNIQUE. *See* MALICIOUS CODE.

checkpoint. In computing, a control point in a program, or file, established at intervals to enable re-processing to resume from that point, instead of from the start of the program or file, should an error occur.

checkpoint restart. *See* CHECKPOINT.

checksum. (1) In authentication, a fixed length block that is produced as a function of every bit in the message. (2) In codes, the summation of a set of data items for error detection purposes. The data items are either numerals, bits or other character strings regarded as numerals for the purpose of the calculation. *See* ERROR DETECTION CODE, HASH TOTAL.

chime. In physical security, a pleasing audible signal employed in presignal systems to advise selected personnel of a fire condition prior to the sounding of the evacuation alarm. *See* PRESIGNAL SYSTEM.

Chinese Remainder Theorem. In mathematics, let $m_1, m_2,...m_k$ be k pairwise coprime integers.
Let:

$$M = m_1 \cdot m_2... \cdot m_k$$

$$x \equiv a_i \bmod m_i \quad \text{for } i = 1, 2 ... k$$
$$M_i = M/m_i \quad \text{for } i = 1, 2 ... k$$

$$M_iN_i \equiv 1 \bmod m_i \quad \text{for } i = 1, 2 ... k$$

Then
$$x \equiv p \equiv a_1M_1N_1 + a_2M_2N_2 ... a_kM_kN_k \bmod M$$

See MODULO ARITHMETIC, COPRIME.

Chinese Theorem. In number theory, an alleged test for prime numbers which states that n is prime if it divides 2^n - 2.
In fact the test fails for n = 341 which is not a prime number but does divide into 2^{341} - 2 without remainder. *See* PRIME NUMBER.

Chinese Wall model. In formal models, a formal security model defined as a confidentiality model for the commercial world.
The model uses the terms subject and object, as in Bell-La Padula, but it has a

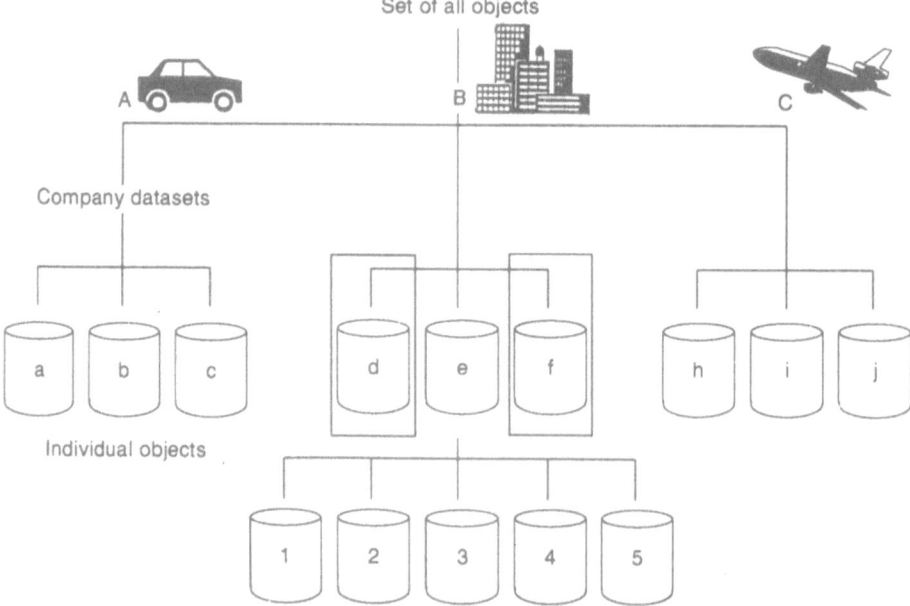

After accessing file 2, company e dataset of conflict class B analyst cannot thereafter access any objects in company d or f datasets

Chinese Wall model

significantly different concept on permitted information flows. The context of the model is that of an organization, e.g. one providing consultancy services, which stores data relating a number of client corporations. The security policy of the organization is that users should not have access relating to a corporation, if they have already accessed data from a second corporation, and the proposed access would represent a conflict of interest.

Thus a market analyst who had previously gained access to data concerning the financial affairs of car_manufacturer_A should not subsequently be permitted to access the data of car_manufacturer_B. The analyst's knowledge of the affairs of car_manufacturer_A, would be deemed to represent a conflict of interest when dealing with car_manufacturer_B.

The restriction on accesses only applies to corporations that are in some sense competitors. If two corporation were not competitors then no such conflict of interest would arise. Thus the user who had accessed car_manufacturer_A's data should not be prevented from accessing the data of hotel_group_C. The Chinese Wall model therefore partitions organizations into conflict of interest classes. The objects in the organization are organized in a hierarchy, the set of all objects is the root of the tree, the next set of nodes represent conflict classes (A,B, C), i.e. those sets of organizations which are mutual competitors, within each conflict classes there are company datasets (a,b,c....,j) which in turn contain individual objects (1,2,..5), the latter are the ultimate leaves of the tree. Initially a subject may access any object, in any dataset, in any conflict class. However, once such an access has been undertaken, the subject is subsequently restricted to accessing only objects, within the same company dataset, or objects from another hitherto unaccessed conflict class. Thus an analyst may originally access any object, e.g. file 2 from the dataset b, in conflict class A; this might correspond to the personnel file from the dataset of car_

manufacturer_B in the conflict class of car manufacturers. On the next access the analyst can only access, either any other object in car_manufacturer_B's dataset, or an object from another conflict class, e.g. object 1, from dataset a (hotel_group_A) in conflict class B (conflict class of hotel groups). The second access will subsequently also limit further accesses in conflict class B.

Thus whenever a user accesses an object, in a dataset, a Chinese Wall is built around all other datasets in the same conflict class, and the user is outside that Chinese Wall. *Compare* BELL-LA PADULA MODEL, BIBA MODELS, CLARK-WILSON MODEL, INFORMATION FLOW MODEL. *See* FORMAL MODELS.

chip card.   *Synonymous with* SMART CARD.

chip modem.   In data communications, a modem contained in a single silicon chip. *See* MODEM.

CHIPS.   In banking, Clearing House Interbank Payments System, a private telecommunications payment service operated by the New York Clearing House Association for banks in the New York area, which handles U.S. dollar payments only. (ANSI). *Compare* CHAPS. *See* BANKING NETWORKS, SWIFT.

chosen cryptogram attack.   In cryptography, an attack which claims that a message has been digitally signed by a purported signee, using the RSA algorithm. Let the public, private key and modulus used by the purported signee be E, D and n respectively. The attacker selects a number C, where $0 < C < n$, and claims that it is received ciphertext, corresponding to a message $M = C^E$ mod n. This claim is accepted since it passes the test of the digital signature.

The defence against this attack is to insist that signed messages have some degree of redundancy, since the attacker has no means of selecting the number C corresponding to a value of M with specified properties. *See* DIGITAL SIGNATURE, RSA.

chosen plaintext. In cryptanalysis, an attack in which the cryptanalyst is able to acquire ciphertext corresponding to plaintext selected by the cryptanalyst. Public key cryptosystems provide cryptanalysts with the means of acquiring an unlimited amount of chosen plaintext since the encryption key is public. *Compare* CIPHERTEXT ONLY, KNOWN PLAINTEXT. *See* PUBLIC KEY CRYPTOGRAPHY.

Christmas-J. In computer security, a virus that terminates and stays resident, infects COMMAND.COM, COM and EXE files, affects run time operation, corrupts program and OVL files. *See* VIRUS NAMES.

Christmas Violater. In computer security, a virus that infects COMMAND.COM and COM files, affects run time operation, corrupts program, OVL and data files. *See* VIRUS NAMES.

CI. *See* CARD ISSUER.

CIA. (1) U.S. Central Intelligence Agency. (2) In communications. *See* COMMUNICATIONS INTERFACE ADAPTER.

cipher. In data security, a cryptographic technique in which a sequence of bits, or characters, is changed by means of a secret transformation. A cipher encrypts a fixed sized unit of plaintext with each

operation and the length of the ciphertext is strictly related to the length of the plaintext. *Compare* CODE. *See* BLOCK CIPHER, CIPHERTEXT, CRYPTOGRAPHY, PLAINTEXT, STREAM CIPHER.

cipher block. (1) In cryptography, the result of securing a block of data by applying a cryptographic function. In general, there are the same number of bits in the block before and after processing. Typical examples of block ciphers are the ISO draft proposal, 8227: Information Processing - Data encipherment - Specification of Algorithm DEA1 (TC97/N1139) and the Data Encryption Algorithm (DEA) standard adopted by ANSI (X3.92 - 1981). (SAA). *See* BLOCK CIPHER, DEA. (2) In cryptography, a block of data produced by encrypting a prespecified length of a block of plaintext with a block cipher. The length of the cipher block may be, but is not necessarily, equal to the length of the plaintext. *See* BLOCK CIPHER, CIPHERTEXT.

cipher block chaining. In cryptography, a mode of operation which overcomes the cryptographic weakness of the electronic codebook mode. The ciphertext output is dependent upon the key and all previous plaintext blocks of the message. Thus highly formatted messages will not suffer from the repetition of ciphertext blocks experienced with the electronic codebook mode. The operation is illustrated in the diagram. A 64 bit shift register is loaded with a data block, termed the initialization vector. The first 64 bit plaintext block is

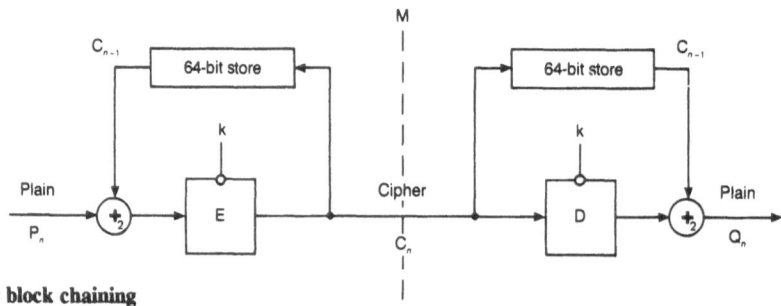

cipher block chaining

'exclusive or-ed' with the contents of the shift register and the resulting 64 bit block is encrypted using key k. The 64 bit ciphertext output is both fed into the shift register and sent to the receiver. The first cipher output C1 depends upon P1 and the initialization vector IV; the second depends upon P2 and C1 i.e. upon P2, P1 and IV.

At the receiving end the shift register is loaded with the same initialization vector IV. The first received block of ciphertext, C1, is decrypted and the output of the decryption block is 'exclusive or-ed' with the contents of the shift register IV to reproduce the first plaintext block, P1. The ciphertext block, C1, is also fed to the shift register ready for the receipt of the second cipher text block C2. The operation of cipher block chaining may be described mathematically, for encipherment:

$$C_n = ek(P_n +_2 C_{n-1})$$

where ek(M) = ciphertext produced by encryption of M with key k and $+_2$ indicates modulo 2 addition. The output of the decryption unit Q_n is given by

$$Q_n = dk(C_n) +_2 C_{n-1}$$

where $dk(C_n)$ is the data block produced by decryption of ciphertext block C_n with key k. T Hence

$$
\begin{aligned}
Q_n &= dk(ek(P_n +_2 C_{n-1})) +_2 C_{n-1} \\
&= P_n +_2 C_{n-1} +_2 C_{n-1} \\
&= P_n.
\end{aligned}
$$

Both the receiver and the sender must share the common value of the initializing variable IV, which is transmitted from the sender to receiver, normally under encipherment with a secret key. It is not strictly necessary to keep IV secret in order to protect the secrecy of the plaintext, but an attacker must be prevented from modifying the received value of IV. If an attacker can alter IV then the first output block of the received plaintext message can be changed at will by the attacker, the subsequent plaintext blocks will be unaffected. It is for this reason that IV's are normally encrypted for transmission.

CBC requires that messages comprise a multiple number of 64 bit blocks. The last block of the message may be padded with zeros but this will provide an analyst with useful information; random characters may also be employed in the place of zeros, but the receiver needs to know both that such padding is included, and the number of padding characters at the end of the message. A padding indicator may be inserted as the last character transmitted and this indicator informs the receiver of the number of padding characters. If it is important that the length of the ciphertext be equal to that of the plaintext, e.g. if an encrypted file is to occupy the storage space previously allocated to the plaintext file, then padding is not acceptable and alternative solutions, e.g. ciphertext stealing, must be employed.

A one bit error in an input plaintext message will affect every succeeding transmitted ciphertext block but will only affect the corresponding bit in the received plaintext. A loss of a bit, or the addition of a spurious bit, in the ciphertext will cause a lack of synchronism between the transmitted and received streams and will completely garble the received plaintext. If a one bit error occurs in the ciphertext then the data blocks of received plaintext will be affected. The first corrupted block will arise as a result of decryption of the changed ciphertext block and the plaintext block will be garbled, the second plaintext block will be affected by the 'exclusive or-ing' of the corrupted ciphertext block with the output of the decipherment unit. In this case only the bit of plaintext block corresponding to the corrupted bit of the ciphertext block will be affected. CBC thus exhibits error extension. *Compare* CIPHER FEEDBACK, ELECTRONIC CODEBOOK, OUTPUT FEEDBACK. *See* BLOCK CIPHER CHAINING, CIPHERTEXT, CIPHERTEXT STEALING, CRYPTOGRAPHIC KEY, DES, ERROR EXTENSION, EXCLUSIVE OR, IV, PLAIN-

TEXT, PADDING INDICATOR, SHIFT REGIST-
ER.

cipher feedback. In cryptography, a stream cipher mode of operation suitable for applications where the data cannot be formed into 64 bit blocks prior to encryption. In some applications the data is treated as individual bits, bytes or frames etc., for example a character terminal will transmit individual 8 bit characters and these characters must be transmitted as they are generated, thus they cannot be collected into 64 bit blocks for encryption.

In cipher feedback a pseudorandom stream of bits is 'exclusive or-ed' with the plaintext stream to form the ciphertext stream. At the receiving end the same pseudorandom sequence is 'exclusive or-ed' with the ciphertext stream to reproduce the plaintext. The pseudorandom sequence is generated from the ciphertext stream itself. 64 bit shift registers are initialized with an initialization vector, IV, at the transmitting and receiving ends. The content of these registers are then input to DES encryptor units, using the same secret key at the transmitter and receiver.

A segment of the DES unit 64 bit output, of the same length as the plaintext block to be enciphered, is then selected and 'exclusive or-ed' with the data stream. Thus if the data to be enciphered is in the form of 8 bit blocks then the leftmost octet of the DES 64 bit output is selected as the segment for the pseudorandom stream.

The ciphertext block, e.g. 8 bit character, is fed to the transmitter's shift register and transmitted to the receiver. At the receiving end it is fed into the receiver's shift register, and also 'exclusive or-ed' with the receiver's pseudorandom stream to produce the plaintext output.

The DES encryption effort is greater with the cipher feedback than with the CBC mode since each input block demands encryption of a 64 bit block; thus if the input is divided into bytes then encryption of 8 successive bytes requires 8 DES operations in cipher feedback and only 1 DES operation in CBC.

The initialization vector, IV, can be simply transmitted as a random 64 bit preamble to a message. If this preamble represents too large an overhead then the shift registers may be initialized with an agreed value, e.g. all zeros, and a shorter preamble transmitted; the use of a short preamble may, however, be ill-advised if the messages are highly formatted.

Cipher feedback displays error extension; a one bit error in the transmitted ciphertext will produce a corresponding one bit error in the plaintext followed by a number of garbled output blocks as the error works its way through the shift register. If the input is a byte stream then 8 garbled bytes in the output will follow the byte with the one bit error.

Compare CIPHER BLOCK CHAINING,

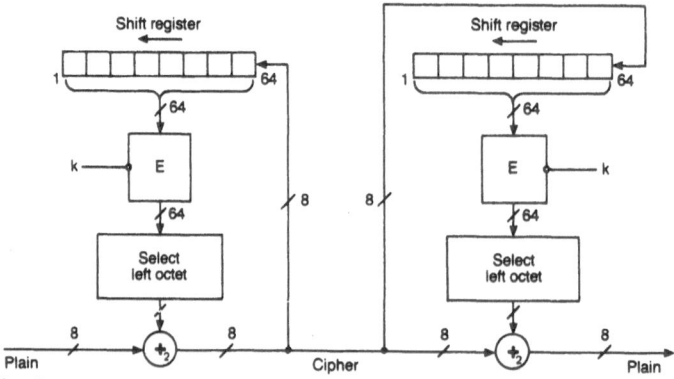

cipher feedback

ELECTRONIC CODEBOOK, OUTPUT FEED-BACK. *See* CIPHERTEXT, CRYPTOGRAPHIC KEY, DES, ERROR EXTENSION, EXCLUSIVE OR, IV, PLAINTEXT, SHIFT REGISTER, STREAM CIPHER.

cipher system. In cryptography, a cryptographic system in which cryptography is applied to plaintext elements of equal length. (FIPS). *See* CRYPTOGRAPHIC SYSTEM, CRYPTOGRAPHY, PLAINTEXT.

ciphertext. (1) In cryptography, enciphered information. (ISO). *Compare* PLAINTEXT. (2) In cryptography, unintelligible text or signals produced through the use of cipher systems. (FIPS). *Compare* PLAINTEXT. *See* cipher system.

ciphertext key auto-key cipher. In cryptography, a chaining stream cipher technique in which the ciphertext is fed back to the encryptor unit to produce the cryptographic bit stream. *See* CIPHER FEED-BACK, CRYPTOGRAPHIC BIT STREAM, STREAM CIPHER CHAINING.

ciphertext only. In cryptanalysis, an attack for which the cryptanalyst is supplied only with a quantity of ciphertext. The method of encryption, the plaintext language and some indication of the probable words or phrases may also be available. *Compare* CHOSEN PLAINTEXT, KNOWN PLAINTEXT. *See* PUBLIC KEY CRYPTOGRAPHY.

ciphertext searching. In cryptanalysis, a technique for inferring plaintext information from a mass of ciphertext. For example, browsing through a large database could reveal records with identical ciphertext blocks and hence indicate, for example, personnel with an identical set of attributes such as political affiliations, salaries, medical conditions etc. *See* BROWSING.

ciphertext stealing. In cryptography, a mode of operation in block cipher chaining which avoids message expansion. If the length of the plaintext message is not an integral number of blocksizes then bits are stolen from the penultimate ciphertext block and added to the last, short plaintext block. If the blocksize is n bits and the last block comprises j bits (j < n) then the last n-j bits are removed from the penultimate ciphertext block and added to the beginning of the last plaintext block, prior to encryption. The ciphertext message is thus of the same length as the plaintext since it also contains one short block of j bits, i.e. the penultimate block. In decipherment the last ciphertext block is deciphered before the short penultimate block. The first n-j bits of the last recovered plaintext block are then added to the j bits of the penultimate ciphertext block which is then decrypted. This technique ensures that the ciphertext message is of the same length as the original plaintext; this may be an important consideration if (say) the ciphertext is to be stored in the space originally occupied by the plaintext. *See* BLOCK CIPHER CHAINING, BLOCKSIZE.

circuit. (1) In communications, a link between two or more points. (2) In electronics, the path of an electric current in a conductor or arrangement of conductors.

circuit board. *Synonymous with* PRINTED CIRCUIT BOARD.

circuit grade. In communications, the information carrying capability of a circuit, given in terms of speed or type of signal. The grades of circuits are wide-band, voice, subvoice and telegraph. *See* WIDEBAND CHANNEL, VOICE GRADE CHANNEL, SUBVOICE GRADE CHANNEL.

circuit noise level. In communications, the ratio of the circuit noise to some reference level. The ratio is usually measured in decibels above the reference noise. *See* DECIBEL, NOISE.

circuit switched digital circuitry. In data communications, a technique for making end to end digital connections.

The user places calls normally and then employs the same connection to transmit high speed data. *See* CIRCUIT SWITCHING.

circuit switching. In data communications, a method in which a connection is established on demand, and maintained between data stations, in order to allow the exclusive use of a data circuit until the connection is released. *Compare* FAST CONNECT CIRCUIT SWITCHING, MESSAGE SWITCHING, PACKET SWITCHING. *See* DATA STATION.

circumvention. In physical security, pertaining to the use of physical avoidance techniques to prevent activating an alarm, e.g. crawling under the pattern of a motion detector. *See* MOTION DETECTOR.

Cirrus. In banking, a U.S.A. EFTPOS network. *See* EFTPOS.

CISA. Certified Information Systems Auditor.

CKDS. *See* CRYPTOGRAPHIC KEY DATA SET.

Claims Language. In information security, a semi-formal specification language, proposed by the U.K. Department of Trade and Industry. It requires the sponsor to specify security functionality using a series of templates. *See* INFORMATION TECHNOLOGY SECURITY EVALUATION CRITERIA.

Clark-Wilson model. In formal models, a formal model designed to meet the data security requirements of a commercial environment.

The bookkeeping and auditing procedures employed by companies are based upon two fundamental control procedures, certification and enforcement. Certification implies that the bookkeeping procedures have been designed and attested such that the record of financial transactions will either prove that only legitimate transactions were conducted, or indicate that some illegal action has been perpetrated; the books either balance or they do not. Thus the recording of data has an internal structure such that it accurately models the real world financial state of the organization. The means of developing this financial record must be certified by a competent authority to ensure that it meets this requirement.

The guarantee that the books balance is, however, in itself, not a sufficient guarantee that no illegal financial actions have taken place. If a person, who had committed such an illegal act, has untrammelled access, to all the financial records, then it would be possible to create an apparent state of financial integrity. For example, if it were possible to record that goods, to a given value, were received from an external source, and that due payment was made for those goods, then the financial record would give no warning of illegal activity. Such a situation would have occurred if the perpetrator were able to falsely record the receipt of the goods, and also falsely record the payment to the nonexistent supplier.

The defence against such an act lies in the separation of responsibilities; no one person should be permitted to make entries in all the books. If the person responsible for recording the receipt of goods is not authorized to make an entry regarding payment, then the false entry on receipt of goods could not be balanced by the corresponding payment entry. Thus the partial recording of an illegal act will leave the books unbalanced, providing a clue to the illicit action. Hence some form of control is required to ensure that the separation of duties is continuously enforced.

Clark and Wilson developed a formal model for computer systems which reflects the requirements of the commercial world. The Clark-Wilson model introduces two new security concepts: the Constrained Data Item (CDI) and the Transformation Procedure (TP). A CDI effectively corresponds to a defined form of entry in an account book. A TP is the only legiti-

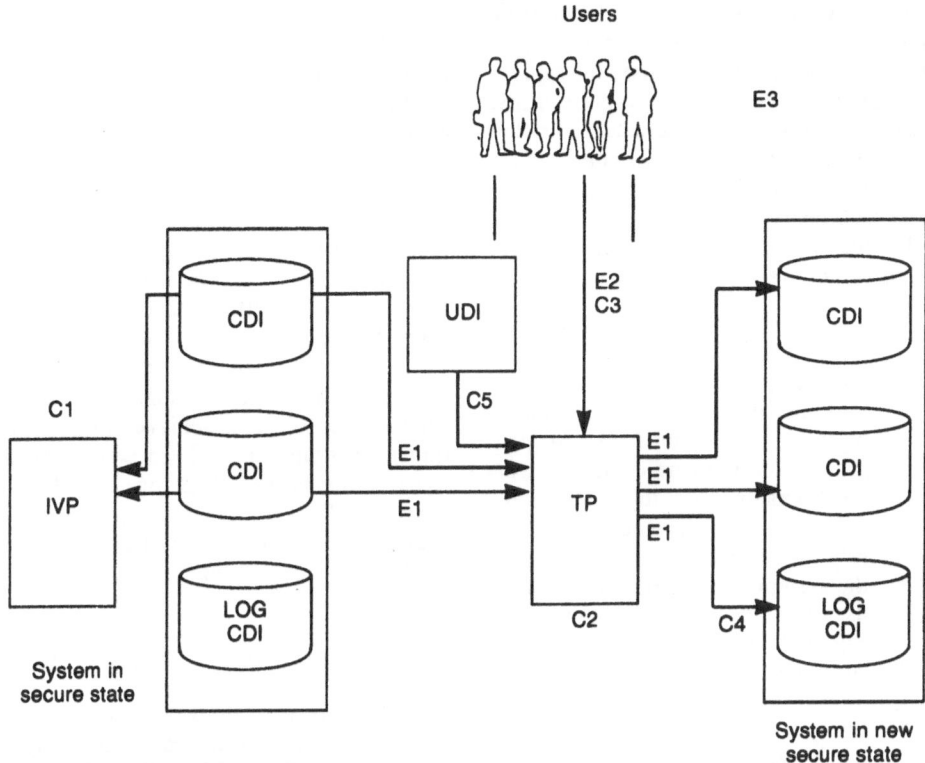

Users

E3

CDI

UDI

E2
C3

CDI

C1

CDI

C5

E1

CDI

IVP

E1

TP

E1
E1
E1

LOG
CDI

System in
secure state

C2

C4

LOG
CDI

System in new
secure state

E1 CDIs changed only by authorised TPs
E2 Users authorised for TP
E3 Users are authenticated
E4 Authorisation lists changed only by Security Officer
C1 IVP validates CDI state
C2 TPs preserve valid state
C3 Suitable separation of duty
C4 TPs write to Log
C5 TPs validate UDI

Clark-Wilson model

mate processing that may be performed on specified sets of CDIs, a TP may be likened to the performance of a double bookkeeping entry. Certification procedures are required to specify that the TPs, and related CDIs, maintain the integrity of the financial record. In addition to such certification, enforcement is required to ensure that the separation of duties rule is not violated. Thus the enforcement mechanisms restrict the TPs that may be applied to CDIs, and the users who may invoke specified TPs.

The Clark-Wilson model imposes a form of mandatory access control; in this case the access is concerned with the access of users to TPs, and TPs to CDIs. A CDI may not be accessed in an arbitrary manner for writing to other CDIs; each CDI can only be processed in a manner which meets the certification requirements. Moreover users may only invoke those TPs which satisfy the separation of duties certification requirements. These restrictions are mandatory, neither the 'owners' of CDIs nor the system administrator have the discretion to override such restrictions.

In the Clark-Wilson there are four security requirements:

- the system must separately authenticate and identify every user;
- the system must ensure that specified data items can be manipulated only by a restricted set of programs, and the data centre controls must ensure that these programs meet the well formed transaction rule (see below);
- the system must associate with each user a valid set of programs to be run, and the data centre must ensure that these sets meet the separation of duty rule;
- the system must maintain an auditing log that records every program executed, and the name of the authorizing user.

In addition to these criteria there are two further requirements for system security:

- the computer system must contain mechanisms to ensure that the system enforces its requirements;
- the mechanisms in the system must be protected against tampering or unauthorized change.

The model defines data items in the system to which the integrity rules must be applied, the so-called Constrained Data Items, CDIs. It is essential that data items regarding commercial transactions are not created, or modified, in an arbitrary manner. The state of the commercial system will be characterized by a set of CDIs, if this set meets some prespecified criteria, e.g. they represent a set of balanced books, then the system is in a secure state.

A class of procedures are required to check that the aforementioned set of CDIs do indeed correspond to such a secure state; these procedures are termed Integrity Validation Procedures, IVPs. Thus applying IVPs to a set of CDIs to ensure a secure state, is similar to checking that the books of a company balance.

Starting from a secure state is a necessary, but not sufficient, condition for some future secure state. All changes to CDIs must be such that they move the system from one secure state to another. This state of affairs is achieved by restricting all actions on CDIs to well formed transactions, termed Transformation Procedures, TPs. A TP corresponds, for example, to a double entry transaction in the bookkeeping world.

It must be recognized that not all data items entered into a system will be CDIs. Data is entered into a computer and it may by accident, or with malicious intent, fail to conform to the requirements of a CDI. The secure system must have some means of dealing with such input data, i.e. validating the input data and adding it to the current set of CDIs, or rejecting the data. Such data items are termed Unconstrained Data Items, UDIs; they are processed by a specific TP with the task of checking the data item and either accepting it as a valid CDI, i.e. transforming it to a CDI, or rejecting it.

If the system commences in a secure state, and if the only transactions permitted are guaranteed to move it into another secure state, the system security is guaranteed for any sequence of · such moves. There is an important caveat that must be associated with this argument; each TP must be performed in a strictly sequential manner, partial completion of a TP could conceivably leave the system in an insecure state, i.e. only one book entry were made. If the second TP commenced from this insecure state, then there could be no assurance on future system security.

The model deems that IVPs will validate the CDIs, i.e. ensure an initial secure state, and that TPs will move the system from one secure state to another. There are, however, two aspects of this approach to security:

- a process to certify that IVP and TPs do in fact ensure such secure actions;
- a design to enforce the security policy.

The determination that IVP and TPs ensure integrity for a given commercial system, will depend upon the particular application. Thus some authorized person, or group, must define IVP, and TPs according to the processes employed by the organization.

The certification rules of the model are:

- C1 - all IVPs must properly ensure that all CDIs are in a valid state at the time that the IVP is run;
- C2 - all TPs must be certified to be valid, i.e. they must take a CDI to a valid final state given that it is in a valid state to begin with. For each TP, and each set of CDIs that it may manipulate, the security officer must specify a relation which defines that execution. A relation is thus of the form: (TPi,(CDIa, CDIb, CDIc,...)) where the list of CDIs defines a particular set of arguments for which the TP has been certified.
- C3 - the list of relations in E2 (see below) must be certified to meet the separation of duty requirement;
- C4 - all TPs must be certified to write to an append only CDI (the log) all information,necessary to permit

the nature of the operation to be reconstructed;

- C5 - any TP that takes a UDI as an input value must be certified to perform only valid transformations, or else no transformations, for any possible value of the UDI.

The four enforcement rules of the model are:

- E1 - the system must maintain the list of relations specified in rule C2 (see above), and must ensure that the only manipulation of any CDI is by a TP, where the TP is operating on the CDI as specified in some relation;
- E2 - the system must maintain a list of relations of the form (UserID, TPi, (CDIa, CDIb, CDIc..)), which relates a user, a TP, and the data objects that the TP may reference on behalf of that user. It must ensure that only executions described in one of the relations are performed;
- E3 - the system must authenticate the identity of each user attempting to execute a TP;
- E4 - only the agent permitted to certify entities may change the list of such entities associated with other entities; specifically, the entity associated with a TP. An agent that can certify an entity may not have any execute rights with respect to that entity.

The rules C1, C2 and E1 provide the basic framework to ensure the internal consistency of the CDIs. C1 requires that a set of IVPs (Integrity Validation Procedures) be certified to the effect that they will ensure that a given set of CDIs conform to the integrity specification at the time that the IVP is run, in other words the 'books balance'. C2 similar certifies that each TPi changes the CDIs, specified in the relation (TPi,(CDIa, CDIb, CDIc,-...)), from one valid state to another. The enforcement rule E1 can be compared to (say) the enforcement of an office procedure that a sales transaction, with specified data, is processed as a double entry in the books.

E2 refers to a set of relations involving userIDs, TPs and CDIs. Rule C3 certifies that these relations correspond to the separation of duties requirements of the organization. E2 ensures that the corresponding certified set of relations are enforced, i.e. a given user is only allowed to execute a given TP using a given set of CDIs as data. E2 actually subsumes E1 but E1 has been included for ease of implementation in real systems.

E3 enforces the authentication of users, i.e. the system ensures a match between the UserID and the person claiming that identification at a terminal. C4 is a certification rule on the TPs ensuring that they log their actions thus providing an audit trail.

Data entered into the system is not guaranteed to constitute CDIs, users have the freedom to key in any characters at a terminal, such data is termed a UDI (Unconstrained Data Item). C5 is a certification rule on an edit function TP, to ensure that all entered data, i.e. UDI, is checked for conformity with a CDI and either passes the test, thus converting the UDI to a CDI, or rejects the UDI.

The last enforcement rule E4 restricts the right to modify permission lists to persons with certification rights, and such persons must not have the rights to execute TPs. *Compare* BELL-LA PADULA MODEL, BIBA MODEL, CHINESE WALL MODEL. *See* constrained data item, integrity validation procedure, transformation procedure, unconstrained data item.

Class A alarm system. In physical security, a fire protection specification that

requires alarm operation even if there is a single break, or a ground fault, in the signal line. *Compare* CLASS A FIRE, CLASS B ALARM SYSTEM.

Class A fire. In physical security, a fire of ordinary combustible material, e.g. wood, cloth, paper, plastics etc. *Compare* CLASS B FIRE, CLASS C FIRE.

Class B alarm system. In physical security, a fire protection specification that requires the detection of an alarm, a single break or a ground fault in the signal line. *Compare* CLASS A ALARM SYSTEM, CLASS B FIRE.

Class B fire. In physical security, a fire involving a vapor or flammable liquid. *Compare* CLASS A FIRE, CLASS C FIRE.

Class C fire. In physical security, a fire involving electrical energy. *Compare* CLASS A FIRE, CLASS B FIRE.

classification. (1) In data security, the assignment of information or a document to a category on the basis of its sensitivity to disclosure or to modification or destruction. Based on U.S. Executive Order 12356 dated 1982 the U.S. government classifications are: Top Secret - unauthorized disclosure could cause exceptionally grave damage to national security. Secret - unauthorized disclosure could cause serious damage to national security. Confidential - unauthorized disclosure could cause damage to national security. (2) In data security, a determination that information requires in the interest of national security, a specific degree of protection against unauthorized disclosure together with a designation signifying that such a determination has been made. Data classification is used along with categories in the calculation of risk index. (DOD).

classification level. In access control, the security level of an object. *Compare*

CLEARANCE LEVEL. *See* OBJECT.

classified computer security program. In computer security, all of the technological safeguards and managerial procedures established and applied to ADP facilities and ADP systems (including computer hardware, software, and data) in order to ensure the protection of classified information. (DOE). *See* ADP.

classified data/information. In data security, official data which has been determined to require protection in the interests of national security. (OPNAVINST).

class of service. (1) In communications, the type of communications service to which a customer subscribes. (2) In communications, the type of telephone equipment used by a customer. (3) In communications, the calling privileges and restrictions of a given line in switching.

CLC. *See* COMMUNICATIONS LINK CONTROLLER.

cleanroom approach. In computing, a software development process designed to reduce errors and increase productivity.

clearance. In access control, the authorization of a system user to access sensitive data. The U.S. Department of Defense uses several clearance levels: Uncleared (U), Unclassified Information (N), Confidential Clearance (C), Secret Clearance (S), Top Secret Clearance based on current background investigation (TS(BI)), Top Secret Clearance based on a current special background investigation (TS (SBI)), One Category (1C), Multiple Categories (MC). *See* CLEARANCE LEVEL, CONFIDENTIAL CLEARANCE, MULTIPLE CATEGORIES, ONE CATEGORY, SECRET CLEARANCE, TOP SECRET CLEARANCE, UNCLASSIFIED INFORMATION, UNCLEARED.

clearance level. In access control, the security level of a subject. *Compare* CLASSIFICATION LEVEL. *See* CLEARANCE, SUBJECT.

clear data. *Synonymous with* PLAINTEXT.

cleared funds. *Synonymous with* AVAILABLE FUNDS.

clearing. In computer security, the overwriting of classified information on magnetic media such that the media may be reused. (This does not lower the classification level of the media.) (DOE). *Compare* DEGAUSS. *See* CLEARING ADP MEDIA, OBJECT REUSE, RESIDUE.

clearing ADP media. In computer security, a procedure used to erase the classified information stored on the media, but lacking the totality of a declassification procedure. (DOD). *See* CLEARING, DECLASSIFICATION OF MAGNETIC STORAGE MEDIA.

cleartext. *Synonymous with* PLAINTEXT.

cleartext operation. In cryptography, a facility of an encryption device or scrambler to accept a cleartext message even when it is set for cipher or scrambler operation. *See* CLEARTEXT, VOICE SCRAMBLING.

clear to send. In data communications, a signal used in conjunction with another, request to send, as a handshaking protocol in half duplex operation. The signal is sent from a modem to a transmitting computer, following the receipt of a request to send, indicating that the modem is ready to receive characters for transmission. *Compare* REQUEST TO SEND. *See* HALF DUPLEX, HANDSHAKING, MODEM, RS-232C.

clear zone. In physical security, an area on either side of a perimeter barrier kept free of rubbish, trees, weeds, bushes etc. so that attempts to cross the perimeter-barrier, or to tunnel beneath, are difficult to conceal. *See* PERIMETER BARRIER.

CLEF. *See* COMMERCIAL LICENSED EVALUATION FACILITY.

clocking. In data communications, the use of clock pulses to control synchronization of data and control characters in binary synchronous communications. *See* BINARYSYNCHRONOUSCOMMUNICATIONS.

CLODO. In computer security, an early French underground organization, the committee to liquidate or neutralize computers.

closed circuit alarm. In physical security, an alarm initiated by causing a short circuit. *Synonymous with* CROSS ALARM.

closed circuit television. In physical security, a system of television cameras and monitors linked normally by cable and used for monitoring protected areas.

closed environment. In computer security, a principle that each process is given no more capabilities than it needs to perform its task. The normal state of affairs is completely disjoint, isolated processes; nothing can be shared or exchanged among processes except by explicit arrangements, all interactions being prohibited unless expressly allowed.

closed hot site. In risk management, a hot site owned by a consortium, or otherwise constructed for a specific set of companies. *Compare* OPEN HOT SITE. *See* HOT SITE.

closed security environment. In computer security, an environment that includes those systems in which both of the following conditions hold true: (a) Application developers (including maintainers) have sufficient clearances and author-

izations to provide an acceptable presumption that they have not introduced malicious logic. Sufficient clearance is defined as follows: where the maximum classification of data to be processed is Confidential or below, developers are cleared and authorized to the same level as the most sensitive data; where the maximum classification of data to be processed is Secret or above, developers have at least a Secret clearance. (b) Configuration control provides sufficient assurance that applications are protected against the introduction of malicious logic prior to and during operation of system applications. (DOD). *See* CONFIGURATION CONTROL, MALICIOUS LOGIC.

closed shop. (1) In physical security, a computer operations area with physical controls ensuring that personnel who did not require access, e.g. programmers, are restricted from entering the area. (2) In operations, a facility employing specified computing staff for design, development, testing and running of programs. *Compare* OPEN SHOP.

closed user group. In communications, a group which permits users belonging to the group to communicate with each another, but precludes communications with others who are not members of the group (TNI).

cluster. (1) In operating systems, the units of disk space allocated to a file. (2) In data communications, a group of terminal devices grouped in one specific location and interfaced to the communication facility through a cluster control unit. *See* CLUSTER CONTROL UNIT.

cluster controller. *Synonymous with* CLUSTER CONTROL UNIT.

cluster control unit. In data communications, a device that can control the input output operations of more than one terminal. *Synonymous with* CLUSTER CONTROLLER.

clutch head screw. In physical security, a screw with a nonstandard head design which requires a special screwdriver for release; it discourages tampering.

CNIL. In legislation, National Commission on Data Processing and Freedoms. *See* DATA PROTECTION - FRANCE.

CNP. *See* COMMUNICATIONS NETWORK PROCESSOR.

CNPDPI. In legislation, the Portuguese National Commission for the Protection of Automated Personal Data. *See* DATA PROTECTION - PORTUGAL.

COAM. In data communications, Customer Owned And Maintained communication equipment, e.g. terminals.

coaxial cable. In electronics, a low loss cable, used for high frequencies, which consists of a conductor within, and insulated from, a tube of braided copper.

CoCom. Coordinating Committee for Multilateral Export Controls, which began operations in 1950 to control export of strategic materials and technology to communist countries; participants include Australia, Belgium, Canada, Denmark, France, Germany, Greece, Italy, Japan, Luxembourg, the Netherlands, Norway, Portugal, Spain, Turkey, United Kingdom and the United States.

code. (1) A symbol representing data, typically to facilitate automated processing. (ISO). (2) In computing, the instructions or statements of a program, or the act of generating them. (3) In data communications, a system of symbols used to convert alphanumeric information into a form suitable for communications transmission. (4) A set of rules outlining the way in which data may be represented. *See* ASCII, BAUDOT CODE, CHARACTER CODE. (5) In data security, a method of sending secret messages. Each word or phrase is substituted by a corresponding group of symbols derived from a secret code book. *Compare* CIPHER.

code analysis. *See* STATIC ANALYSIS.

code book. In data security, a secret book used to encrypt a message and available only to the sender and receiver. For example, a word may be encrypted as its physical position and page in the codebook. *Compare* ELECTRONIC CODEBOOK.

CODEC. In communications, COder DECoder, a device to convert analog signals, e.g. speech, television, music to digital form, for transmission over a digital medium and to reconvert them back to analog form. *Compare* MODEM. *See* ANALOG SIGNAL.

code conversion. In data communications, a process for changing the bit grouping of one character in a code into the corresponding grouping for a character in a second code, e.g. from ASCII code to EBCDIC. *See* ASCII, EBCDIC CODE. *Synonymous with* CHARACTER MAPPING.

coded alarm system. In physical security, a system using pulse or frequency variations to differentiate alarms from various sensors, or protection zones, even when a single signal line is used.

coded character set. In codes, a set of rules for establishing a character set and the one to one relationships between the characters in the set and their coded representations.

coded key. In physical security, a method of access control based upon an article possessed by a user. Keys are commonly used to gain access to physical areas or equipment; a coded key can have the appearance of a conventional key but it can also store thousands or tens of thousands of bits thus providing a unique identification code. *Compare* CARD KEY.

coded system. In physical security, a system in which three or more rounds of coded alarm signals are relayed. Thereafter the fire alarm may be silenced either manually or automatically. *Compare* NONCODED SYSTEM. *See* MASTER CODED SYSTEM.

code extension character. In codes, a control character used to indicate that one or more of the succeeding code values are to be interpreted according to a special code. *See* ESCAPE CHARACTER, SHIFT CODES.

code independent system. In data communications, a mode of transmission that uses a character oriented link protocol that does not depend on the character set or code used by the source of data. *See* LINK PROTOCOL.

code level. In codes, the number of bits used to represent a character. *See* BYTE.

code review. In computer security, a technique of static evaluation in which portions of source code are evaluated to determine if they implement the design specifications and are free from errors. *Compare* PENETRATION STUDY, SOURCE CODE ANALYZER. *See* STATIC EVALUATION.

code scrambling circuit. In physical security, an electronic circuit of an access control system that allows personalized codes to be randomly reassigned upon command. *See* CARD READER.

code set. In codes, a finite and complete set of representations defined by a code. *See* CODE.

code system. (1) In computer security, any system of communication in which groups of symbols are used to represent plaintext elements of varying length (FIPS). *See* PLAINTEXT. (2) In the broadest sense, a means of converting information into a form suitable for communications or encryption, for example, coded speech, Morse Codes, teletypewriter codes. (FIPS) *See* BREVITY LISTS, ENCRYPTION. (3) In cryptography, a cryptographic system in which cryptographic equivalents (usually called code groups) typically consisting of letters, digits or both in meaningless combinations are substituted for plaintext elements which may be words, phrases, or sentences. (FIPS). *See* CODE.

code value. In codes, one element of a code set, e.g. the eight bit binary digit code value for the delete character.

coercive force. In electronics, a negative or reverse magnetic force applied for the purpose of reducing magnetic flux density. (DOD). *See* COERCIVITY, DEGAUSS.

coercivity. (1) In electronics, the measure of the amount of coercive force required to reduce magnetic flux density to zero. Often used to represent the ease with which magnetic ADP media can be degaussed. (DOD). *See* COERCIVE FORCE, DEGAUSS. (2) In electronics, the reverse magnetic field necessary to reduce the magnetic flux to zero, after the field has been increased to produce flux saturation and then reduced to zero.

cold site. In risk management, a center with the necessary shell facilities to provide a location for the operation of a computer center following a computer disaster. It will provide office and machine space, power supplies, air conditioning, raised floors, wiring etc. but usually few or no computer processors. Membership of an organization providing the cold site will be limited as will the length of use of such sites. *Compare* HOT SITE, WARM SITE. *See* CONTINGENCY PLANS. *Synonymous with* SHELL SITE.

cold standby. In reliability, the use of a backup computer in the event of a failure in the main system. Any data in the main memory of the computer at the time of failure, and not recorded in backing storage, will be lost. *Compare* WARM STAND-BY, HOT STANDBY.

cold start. In computer security, the activity that must be taken following a serious failure in a computer system when the direct access storage is inaccessible and recent transactions may have been lost. The system is reloaded and started in IPL mode. *See* IPL.

collusion. In legislation, an action of two or more persons collaborating for fraudulent purposes.

Colossus. In cryptography, an electronic special purpose computer built by the U.K. Post Office Research Station during World War II and used for cryptanalysis of German ciphers.

combination smoke detector. In physical security, a smoke detector comprising both ionization and photoelectric detectors. *See* IONIZATION SMOKE SENSOR, PHOTOELECTRIC BEAM SMOKE DETECTOR.

combinatorics. In mathematics, a branch of mathematics dealing with enumeration and counting problems.

combined alarms. In physical security, a system which only activates alarms upon combinations of alarm signals from specific sensors.

combined station. In data communications, the station used in HDLC procedures. A combined station generates and interprets both commands and responses. *See* HDLC.

COMINT. Communications Intelligence.

Comité Consultatif Internationale de Télégraphie et Téléphonie. In communications, an international advisory and

consultative body established under the aegis of the United Nations to recommend international communications standards. *See* PROTOCOL STANDARDS.

Commercial COMSEC Endorsement Program. A program established by the NSA for the protection of government information. *See* NSA COMSEC MODULE.

commercial licensed evaluation facility. In information security, a facility licensed in the U.K. to conduct security evaluations. *Compare* INFORMATION TECHNOLOGY SECURITY EVALUATION FACILITY. *See* INFORMATION TECHNOLOGY SECURITY EVALUATION CRITERIA.

commit. In databases, a command to update the database according to the set of transactions input to the system. *Compare* ROLLBACK.

common carrier. In communications, a company whose business is to supply communication facilities to the public. The term is derived from the interstate commerce concept of carrying goods. In the U.S. a communication common carrier comes under the jurisdiction of relevant state organizations and if it operates interstate facilities it will be subject to FCC regulations. Common carriers can carry telemetry, facsimile, television and data messages. *Compare* VANS. *See* FCC, TELEMETRY, PTT.

common cryptographic architecture. In cryptography, the cryptographic architecture developed for IBM systems. *See* CONTROL VECTOR.

communicating pair. In key management, the logical parties who have previously agreed to exchange data. A party and a center exchanging cryptographic service messages do not constitute a communicating pair. (ANSI). *See* CRYPTOGRAPHIC SERVICE MESSAGE, LOGICAL

PARTY.

communication. The process of transferring information in the various media from one point, person or device to another. *See* TELECOMMUNICATIONS.

communication channel. In data communications, the physical media and devices which provide the means for transmitting information from one component of a network to (one or more) other components (TNI). *Compare* COMMUNICATION LINK.

communication link. The physical means of connecting one location to another for the purpose of transmitting and receiving information. *Compare* COMMUNICATION CHANNEL.

communication processor. *See* FRONT END PROCESSOR.

communication scanner. In data communications, a device that monitors lines for service requests.

communications computer. In data communications, a computer which manages the control of lines and the routing of data in a network. *See* ROUTING.

communications control unit. In data communications, a device that controls the transmission of data over lines in the network.

communication server. *Synonymous with* GATEWAY.

communication service. In banking, a service that moves messages among subscribers, including funds transfer transactions that are subject to settlement by other means. (ANSI).

communications link controller. In data communications, an intelligent unit which provides line oriented interface functions, e.g. error detection, synchronization, acknowledgements, between a group of modems and a computer or communications network processor. *See* COMMUNICATIONS NETWORK PROCESSOR.

communications medium. In data communications, the circuits that interconnect networks, terminals, or network physical devices. These circuits may be logical or physical and provide end-to-end paths between communicating processes.

communications network processor. In data communications, an intelligent unit which performs interface functions, e.g. buffering, code conversion, queue management, between a computer and one or more communications link controllers. *See* COMMUNICATIONS LINK CONTROLLER.

communications security. (1) The protection resulting from all measures designed to deny unauthorized persons information of value which might be derived from the possession and study of telecommunications, or to mislead unauthorized persons in their interpretation of the results of such possession and study. Communications security includes cryptosecurity, transmission security, emission security, and physical security of communications security materials and information. (OPNAVINST). *See* CRYPTOGRAPHY, PHYSICAL SECURITY, TEMPEST. (2) The protection that ensures the authenticity of telecommunications and that results from the application of measures taken to deny unauthorized persons information of value which might be derived from the acquisition of telecommunications. (FIPS).

communication theory. In mathematics, the topic dealing with the transmission of messages in the presence of noise. *See* INFORMATION THEORY, NOISE.

commutative law. In mathematics, a binary operation, i.e. one involving two variables, satisfies the commutative law if $x * y = y * x$ where x and y are the variables and * represents the binary operation. *Compare* ASSOCIATIVE LAW, DISTRIBUTIVE LAW. *See* GALOIS FIELD.

compartment. In data security, a designation applied to a type of sensitive information, indicating the special handling procedures to be used for the information and the general class of people who may have access to the information. It can refer to the designation of information belonging to one or more categories (TNI). *See* CATEGORY.

compartmentalization. (1) In computer security, the isolation of the operating system, user programs, and data files from one another in main storage in order to provide protection against unauthorized or concurrent access by other users or programs.(FIPS). *See* ACCESS. (2) In data security, the breaking down of sensitive data into small, isolated blocks for the purpose of reducing risk to the data. (FIPS) (3) In physical security, a principle of design that a failure or a harmful event in one part of a system should not be allowed to spread into another part of the system, e.g. smoke or harmful gases should not be allowed to spread outside a given area. *See* HARMFUL EVENT.

compartmented security mode. (1) In computer security, the mode of operation which allows the system to process two or more types of compartmented information (information requiring a special authorization) or any one type of compartmented information with other than compartmented information. In this mode, all system users need not be cleared for all types of compartmented information processed, but must be fully cleared for at least Top Secret information for unescorted access to the computer. (DOD). *See* COMPARTMENTALIZATION.

compatibility. (1) In data communications, pertaining to pairs of devices that have met the requirements for code, speed and signal level conversion to enable direct interconnections. (2) In computing, pertaining to machines on which programs may be interchanged without appreciable modification.

compiler. In computing, a program designed to translate a high level language source program into a corresponding machine code program. *See* HIGH LEVEL LANGUAGE, MACHINE CODE INSTRUCTION, SOURCE PROGRAM.

complement. In mathematics, to change a bit from 0 to 1 or vice versa in binary arithmetic. *See* BOOLEAN ALGEBRA. (2) In mathematics, a number that is derived by subtracting the given number from another specified number. Often used in the representation of negative numbers.

complete mediation. In computer security, principle of complete mediation, one of the principles of secure systems which states that checks for access, against access control information, must be performed under all circumstances including normal operation, maintenance, recovery etc. *See* PRINCIPLES OF SECURE SYSTEMS.

completeness check. In computing, a test that data entries are made in fields which cannot be processed in a blank state. *See* FIELD.

complete set of residues. In number theory, a set of residues $(r_1, r_2..r_n)$ for a given integer n such that for each value of an integer b there is only one value, r_i, where b is congruent to r_i modulo n. *See* CONGRUENT, RESIDUE.

complexity. In mathematics, pertaining to the difficulty of computational problems as measured by the resources required to complete the computation. It is an area of active research and has applications in the field of cryptography amongst others. *Compare* COMPLEXITY

ANALYSIS. *See* CRYPTOGRAPHY.

complexity analysis. In computer security, a method of static analysis which identifies modules within the software that have a high degree of complexity according to some measure, e.g. the number of control paths in the module. *Compare* COMPLEXITY. *See* STATIC ANALYSIS.

compliance testing. In computer security, detailed checking of a relatively small volume of transactions so that the auditor can discover if the controls built into the system have operated properly. *Compare* SUBSTANTIVE TESTING.

component. In data communications, a device or set of devices, consisting of hardware, along with its firmware, and /or software that performs a specific function on a computer communications network. A component is a part of a larger system, and may itself consist of other components. Examples include modems, telecommunications controllers, message switches, technical control devices, host computers, gateways, communications subnets etc. (TNI) *See* GATEWAY, HOST COMPUTER, MESSAGE SWITCHING, MODEM.

component reference monitor. In access control, an access control concept referring to an abstract machine that mediates all accesses to objects within a component by subjects within the component. *See* COMPONENT, REFERENCE MONITOR.

composite. In number theory, an integer that is divisible, without remainder, by another integer other than 1. *Compare* PRIME NUMBER.

compromise. In data security, a violation of the security system such that an unauthorized disclosure of sensitive information may have occurred (TNI). *See* SENSITIVE INFORMATION. (2) In data security, an unauthorized disclosure or loss of sensitive information. (FIPS). *See* SENSITIVE INFORMATION. (3) In data security, pertaining to the unauthorized disclosure of sensitive information. An adversary may achieve this disclosure by wiretapping, covert channels, a Trojan Horse or message misrouting. Wiretapping provides direct access to information transmitted over a network. Covert channels allow protected information to be signalled to an attacker by monitoring changes in shared resources etc. A Trojan Horse can collect sensitive information and release it to the attacker upon receipt of coded signals from the attacker. Messages can also be misrouted and leave the network at unauthorized locations. *See* COVERT CHANNEL, TROJAN HORSE, WIRETAP. (3) In database security, *Synonymous with* PERSONAL DISCLOSURE.

compromising emanations. (1) In computer security, unintentional data related or intelligence bearing signals which, if intercepted and analyzed, disclose the classified information transmission received, handled or otherwise processed by any information processing equipment. TEMPEST is an unclassified short name referring to investigations and studies of compromising emanations. It is sometimes used synonymously for the 'compromising emanations' (OPNAVINST). *See* TEMPEST, VAN ECK PHENOMENON. (2) In computer security, electromagnetic emanations that may convey data and that, if intercepted and analyzed, may compromise sensitive information being processed by any ADP system. (FIPS). *See* COMPROMISE, ELECTROMAGNETIC EMANATIONS, SENSITIVE INFORMATION, TEMPEST PROOFING, VAN ECK PHENOMENON.

COMPUSEC. In computer security, the U.S. NSA computer security program. *Compare* COMSEC, INFOSEC.

computationally infeasible. In cryptanalysis, pertaining to a computation that is theoretically achievable but which is infeasible in terms of the time taken to perform it with the current or predicted power of computers.

computationally secure. In cryptanalysis, pertaining to a cipher that cannot be broken by systematic analysis with available resources. *Synonymous with* COMPUTATIONALLY STRONG.

computationally strong. *Synonymous with* COMPUTATIONALLY SECURE.

computer. (1) A device which performs prespecified computations on any valid set of input data and delivers results within defined levels of accuracy. (2) A term which is used for an electronic digital computer. *See* ELECTRONIC DIGITAL COMPUTER, MICROCOMPUTER.

computer abuse. (1) In legislation, wilful or negligent unauthorized activity that affects the availability, confidentiality, or integrity of computer resources.

Computer abuse includes fraud, embezzlement, theft, malicious damage, unauthorized use, denial of service, and misappropriation. Levels of computer abuse are: (a) Minor abuse - acts that represent management problems, such as, printing calendars or running games, that do not impact system availability for authorized applications; (b) Major abuse - unauthorized use (possibly criminal), denial of service, and multiple instances of minor abuse to include waste; (c) Criminal act - fraud, embezzlement, theft, malicious damage, misappropriation, conflict of interest, and unauthorized access to classified data. (AFR). *See* DENIAL OF SERVICE. (2) In computer security, pertaining to the theft, fraud, embezzlement or damage in connection to computers including:

- unauthorized manipulation of computer input or output;
- unauthorized access to the system through terminals;

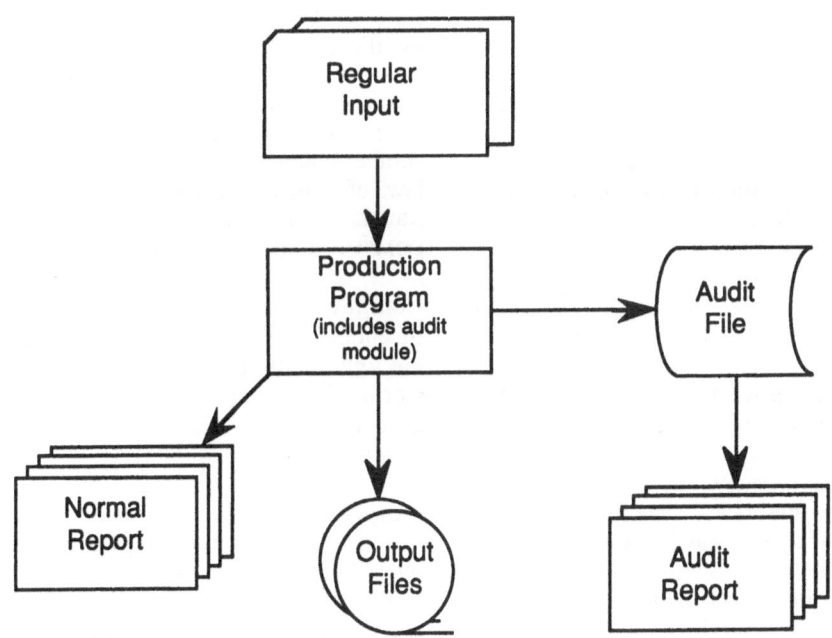

computer audit packages
Integrated audit monitor

- unauthorized modification or use of application programs;
- trespass on a data processing installation and/or theft of equipment, files or output;
- sabotage of a computer installation's equipment;
- unauthorized data interception.

See COMPUTER FRAUD CONTROL, COMPUTER SECURITY.

computer audit enquiry packages. In auditing, computer audit software packages that contain a number of standard features and can be parameterized to meet an auditors requirements. *See* COMPUTER AUDIT PACKAGES.

computer audit packages. In auditing, software for use by auditors which typically contains facilities for the:

- comparison of program or data files, and reporting of any variations;
- sampling of records on a predetermined or random basis;
- selection and reporting of records that fail to satisfy specified criteria;
- re-performance of critical calculations for verification;
- stratification and analysis of large data files.

See COMPUTER AUDIT ENQUIRY PACKAGES, EXTERNAL AUDITOR, INTERNAL AUDITOR.

computer based message system. *Synonymous with* ELECTRONIC MAIL.

computer bureau. In legislation, as defined by the U.K. Data Protection Act 1984, a person carries on a computer bureau if he provides other persons with services in respect of data, and a person provides such services if:

- as agent for other persons he causes

them to be processed; or
- he allows other persons to use equipment in his possession for the processing.

See DATA, DATA PROTECTION.

computer crime. (1) In legislation, according to the United States Department of Justice's Computer Crime: Criminal Justice Resource Manual (1979) - any illegal act for which knowledge of computer technology is essential for successful prosecution. Computer crime includes crimes and alleged crimes that may involve computers not only actively but also passively when usable evidence of the acts resides in computer stored form. (2) In legislation, fraud, embezzlement unauthorized access, and other 'white collar' crimes committed with the aid of or directly involving a computer system and/or network. (GAO). (3) In legislation, a misleading term because it is sometimes employed to cover unauthorized activities which do not meet the legal definition of a crime. The issue is further complicated by the absence of agreement on international criminal law. An individual committing fraud at a terminal on a network by manipulating a computer in another country need not be breaking the law of either country. *See* COMPUTER ABUSE, COMPUTER FRAUD CONTROL, COMPUTER SECURITY.

Computer Emergency Response Team. In computer security, a team formed in the light of the experience of the Morris worm to provide rapid response to attacks on computer networks and systems. *See* MORRIS WORM.

computer facility. Physical resources that include structures or parts of structures to house and support capabilities. For small computers, stand-alone systems, and word processing equipment, it is the physical area where the computer is used. (AFR).

computer fraud control. In computer security, the measures of effective control against computer fraud include:

- prevention or reduction;
- segregation of duties;
- control of input and output;
- control of amendments;
- structured walk through;
- good documentation;
- job rotation;
- split knowledge or dual control;
- increasing the difficulty of concealment/realization;
- good personnel procedures;
- fidelity guarantee and computer crime insurance;
- early detection;
- monitoring of access violations;
- reviewing unusual circumstances;
- audit trails;
- fraud detection models;
- employer response;
- public prosecution.

Preventive measures against the occurrence of fraud should be adopted and if completely comprehensive measures prove to be excessively expensive or counterproductive then the alternative strategy of measures designed to reduce the frequency and magnitude of fraud should be employed.

Duties of staff should be segregated so that no one individual has a sufficient span of control to perpetrate a fraud. Increasing the minimum number of collaborators necessary to operate a fraud will both reduce the possibility of its occurrence and facilitate detection of the abuse.

The processes concerned with entering data into the computer, e.g. invoice details, or accepting the outputs from the computer, e.g. payment checks, are extremely sensitive and must be closely controlled. Any amendments to programs, data or procedures should be independently checked. Structured walkthroughs of system testing should be undertaken to ensure that the computer operation is understood by more than one individual. Auditors should be involved in system design and acceptance testing to seek out potential loopholes.

Good documentation ensures that information on the system operation is widely available and is not the sole domain of one individual. Job rotation should be practiced to avoid situations in which individuals have the temptation and opportunity to seek out system weaknesses; employees should also be compelled to take their vacations. Dual control of sensitive activities involving financial, cryptographic key management operations etc., ensures that no one individual has the power to compromise the system. Situations in which an offender, caught in the act, can claim that a genuine error occurred must be avoided. Clear disciplinary guidelines must be issued to notify the fact that certain actions, e.g. entry to a sensitive area, are forbidden. Good personnel procedures to vet potential employees, maintain the loyalty of current employees, detect changes in employee behavior, minimize potential damage by dismissed employees etc. must be undertaken. Fidelity guarantees for staff controlling sensitive operations and computer crime insurance should be considered.

Early detection of fraud attempts, e.g. detection of experiments with system controls, may be achieved by effective monitoring of the system. All access violations, e.g. unsuccessful attempts to enter passwords, attempts to access privileged operations should be monitored and investigated. A review of unusual incidents and patterns of behavior, changes in personal habits or circumstances can lead to early detection of fraud in some cases. The audit trails employed should be adequate for security purposes and exception reports regularly monitored and reviewed. Fraud detection models can be developed to indicate variances in the operation of a system or significant variances between compatible parts of the system, e.g. the pattern of transactions in different company sites. Employers should respond to fraud by employees by ensuring that references to other employers provide adequate warning of employee misdeeds and prosecution of offenders will serve to deter other potential offenders. *See* AUDIT TRAIL.

computer inquiry 1980. In the U.S. an FCC decision to restrict common carrier regulation only to the carrier's provision of basic services, and to free enhanced services from regulation. This decision encouraged competition in the telecommunications market and increased the range of customer services and equipment. *See* BASIC SERVICE, COMMON CARRIER, ENHANCED SERVICES.

computerized branch exchange. *Synonymous with* PRIVATE AUTOMATIC BRANCH EXCHANGE.

computer matching. In legislation, the comparison of two or more sets of data files to search for individuals included in both or all sets. *See* DATA PROTECTION, LINKAGE.

Computer Misuse Act 1990. In legislation, U.K. legislation which deals with the problem of computer misuse. It defines offenses dealing with hackers, creators of computer viruses, worms and other threats.

computer network. *See* DATA COMMUNICATIONS.

computer security. (1) The protection of computers and their services from all natural and human-made hazards and provide an assurance that the computer performs its critical functions correctly and there are no harmful side-effects. It includes providing for information accuracy. *Compare* DATA SECURITY, INFORMATION SECURITY. (2) The protection of the information and physical assets of a computer system. The protection of information aims to prevent the unauthorized disclosure, manipulation, injection, destruction or alteration of data. The protection of physical assets implies security measures against theft, destruction or misuse of equipment, i.e. processors, peripherals, data storage media, communication lines and interfaces.

Unauthorized disclosure of information can be considered in relation to the disclosure of classified, protected or proprietary data. Military organizations, businesses, government offices etc., will have confidential data that is not to be revealed to unauthorized persons. Data protection and privacy legislation places a responsibility upon holders of personal data to maintain the confidentiality of that data; failure to do so can, under the terms of such legislation, result in legal action against the data holder. Proprietary information, e.g. software, databases accessed by commercial on line information retrieval systems etc., constitute the major assets of software houses and electronic publishers; protection against illicit disclosure is vital for the financial wellbeing of such institutions.

Data manipulation refers to changing some attribute of data, such as security classification, file access privileges or data destination, which causes the data to be made available to illicit users or to be handled in an unauthorized manner.

Electronic and magnetic storage devices are designed to handle extremely volatile information. Whilst the destruction of paper stored data can be a surprisingly difficult, time consuming task, it is possible to destroy computer based information by a short section of code instructing an overwriting action, by removal of power from volatile storage, degaussing magnetic storage media or simply stealing a box of floppy disks. The damage suffered by the erstwhile owner of the data may be out of all proportion to the benefit, if any, gained by the attacker or the effort required for the attack.

Unauthorized injection of data may result in the illicit insertion of an item in a database. Unauthorized alteration can

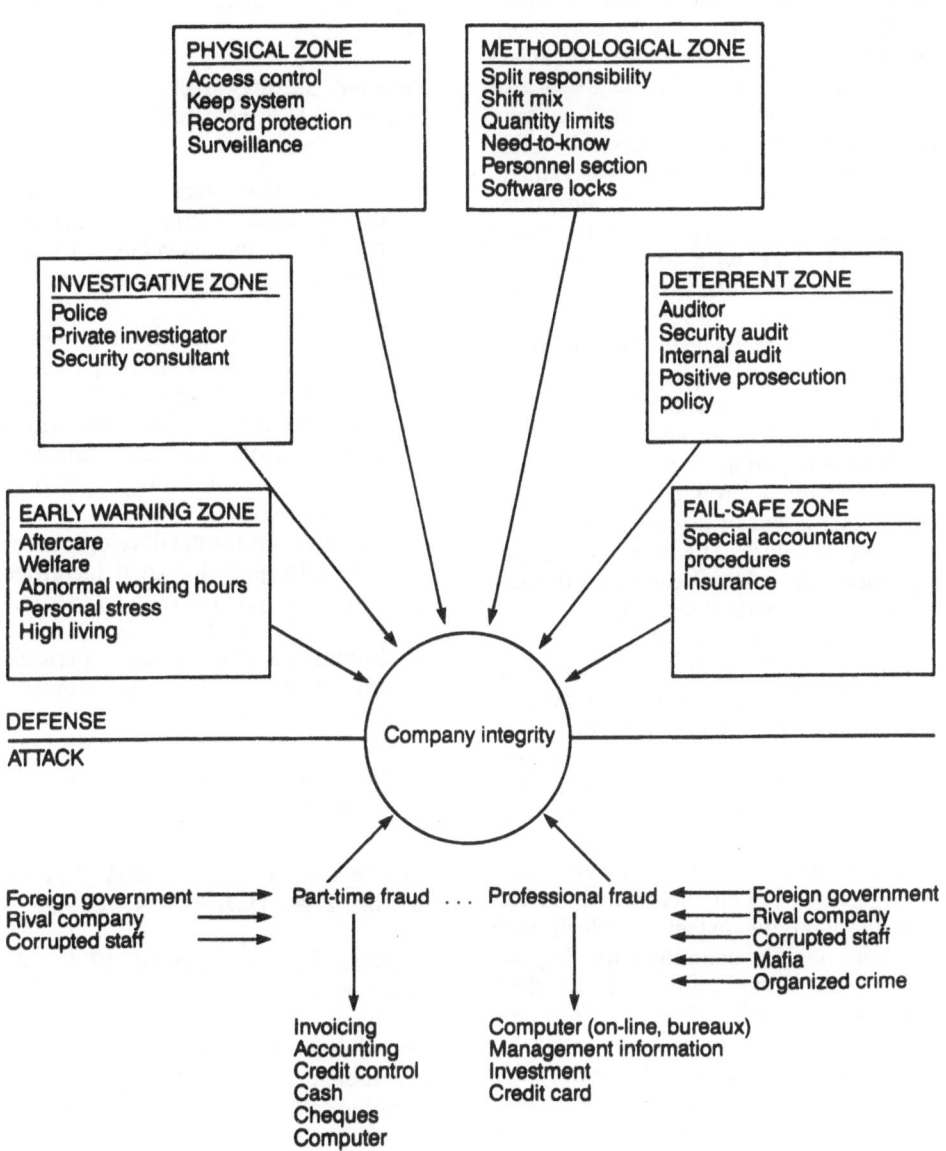

PHYSICAL ZONE
Access control
Keep system
Record protection
Surveillance

METHODOLOGICAL ZONE
Split responsibility
Shift mix
Quantity limits
Need-to-know
Personnel section
Software locks

INVESTIGATIVE ZONE
Police
Private investigator
Security consultant

DETERRENT ZONE
Auditor
Security audit
Internal audit
Positive prosecution
policy

EARLY WARNING ZONE
Aftercare
Welfare
Abnormal working hours
Personal stress
High living

FAIL-SAFE ZONE
Special accountancy
procedures
Insurance

DEFENSE

Company integrity

ATTACK

Foreign government
Rival company
Corrupted staff

Part-time fraud ... Professional fraud

Foreign government
Rival company
Corrupted staff
Mafia
Organized crime

Invoicing
Accounting
Credit control
Cash
Cheques
Computer

Computer (on-line, bureaux)
Management information
Investment
Credit card

computer security.
Copyright Kluwer Publishing Limited - source:
Handbook of Security

produce considerable personal or financial benefit to an attacker, and/or corresponding disadvantage to the holder or subject of the data; moreover, in the absence of special precautions such alterations may pass undetected. Bank account information, examination marks, credit ratings, criminal records, financial transactions and medical records represent information that people may wish to alter for their own benefit, or to the detriment of another.

Physical assets security involves traditional security techniques which may be less esoteric, than those of the information security field, but are no less important. Theft of computing or associated equipment can often produce a loss to the owner that is out of all proportion to the benefit to the thief. The malicious theft of a printed circuit board can close down a computer center for some hours.

Destruction of equipment can be accidental (natural disaster, fire, flood etc.) or intentional (vandalism, terrorist action). The loss suffered by the organization can far exceed that of the cost of the equipment destroyed. Non malicious misuse of computer or communication equipment can arise from employees conducting private businesses or simply playing computer games. Their deleterious effects depend upon the extent to which such activities impinge upon the normal operation of the organization, e.g. do these activities seriously affect the response time of the computer or occupy valuable disk storage space; or to the extent that they raise operating costs, e.g. public network communication charges. Such misuse of computing facilities may also increase the danger of the introduction of computer viruses.

Malicious misuse of facilities can be aimed at deliberate overloading of the computer/communication system or attacking the reputation of the organization, e.g. hackers misusing a computer and publicizing their exploits. *See* ACCESS CONTROL, COMPROMISE, DATA, DATA PROTECTION, DATA SUBJECT, DATA USER, DISCLOSING, HACKER, PERSONAL DATA, RISK ANALYSIS.

Computer Security Act of 1987. In legislation, a U.S. act which, includes the provisions, inter alia:

- Assignment of responsibility for the development of computer security guidelines and standards to the National Institute of Standards and Technology.
- Requirement that within six months after enactment of the Act, Federal agencies shall have identified existing and planned systems which contain (will contain) sensitive information, including personal information.
- Requirement for the development of a security plan for each identified computer system within one year of the enactment of the Act.
- Requirement for mandatory periodic training in computer security awareness and accepted computer security practice of all employees who are involved with the management, use or operation of Federal computer systems.

Compare COMPUTER SECURITY ACT OF 1988. *See* DATA PROTECTION - U.S.A.

Computer Security Act of 1988. In legislation, a U.S act which established the Computer System Security and Privacy Advisory Board under the aegis of the National Institute of Standards and Technology. *Compare* COMPUTER SECURITY ACT OF 1987.

computer security incident. In computer security, an adverse event associated with an ADP system: (a) that is a failure to comply with Departmental security regulations or directives; (b) that results in suspected or actual compromise of classified information; or (c) that results in the misuse, loss or damage of government property or information. (DOE). *See* ADP.

computer security plan. In computer security, a record of an organization's approach to security for reference by auditors, users, security staff etc. The plan should contain specifications of hardware, software, type of data, physical location, communication networks and details of security personnel. The security measures applying to personnel: i.e. access to equipment, data, processes, should be stated together with details of techniques employed for communications security, information security access control and emanation security. Details of emergency procedures, contingency plans, backup provisions, disaster recovery plans and training procedures should also form part of the security plan. *See* CONTINGENCY PLANS, COMPROMISING EMANATIONS, DISASTER RECOVERY PLAN.

computer security specialist. In computer security, a person with operational or consulting responsibilities for planning, implementation, installation, operation and evaluation of security safeguards and controls.

computer security subsystem. In computer security, additional facilities in the form of hardware, software or firmware that may be added to a system to enhance its security. *See* FIRMWARE, HARDWARE, SOFTWARE.

computer software quality. In reliability, the degree to which the attributes of the software enable it to perform its specified end item use. *Synonymous with* SOFTWARE QUALITY.

computer virus. *See* VIRUS.

COMSEC. In communications security, U.S. NSA communications security program. *Compare* COMPUSEC, INFOSEC. *See* COMMUNICATIONS SECURITY, NSA COMSEC MODULE.

concealment system. In data security, a method of achieving confidentiality in

which the existence of sensitive information is hidden by embedding it in irrelevant data. (FIPS). *See* CONFIDENTIALITY, SENSITIVE INFORMATION.

concentrator. In data communications, a device that buffers incoming data and retransmits it over appropriate output lines.

conceptual design. An application system described and presented in a form suitable for users.

conditioning. In data communications, procedures to ensure that transmission impairment on a circuit lie within limits specified in a tariff. Conditioning is used on telephone lines, leased for data transmission, to improve the transmission speed.

conductive radiation. In communications security, the transmission of information bearing signals back through the mains or supply lines not intended for the transmission of information. *See* TEMPEST PROOFING.

conductive shielding. In electronics, a special material placed around a component to prevent it from emitting EMI /RF radiation. *See* EMI/RF RADIATION, SHIELDING EFFECTIVENESS.

Confidential. *See* CLASSIFICATION.

confidential clearance. In access control, a U.S. Department of Defense clearance which requires U.S. citizenship and typically some limited records checking. In some cases, a national agency check is required. *Compare* MULTIPLE CATEGORIES, ONE CATEGORY, SECRET CLEARANCE, TOP SECRET CLEARANCE, UNCLASSIFIED INFORMATION, UNCLEARED. *See* CLEARANCE.

confidentiality. (1) In data security, the computer security characteristic that ensures individuals are given access to computer resources based on security clearance and need-to-know. This characteristic protects against compromise and inadvertent disclosure. (AFR). *See* DATA CONFIDENTIALITY, NEED-TO-KNOW. (2) In data security, a concept that applies to data that must be held in confidence and that describes the status and degree of protection that must be provided for such data about individuals as well as organizations. (FIPS). *See* DATA CONFIDENTIALITY. (3) In data security, the property that information is not made available or disclosed to unauthorized individuals, entities or processes (TNI). *See* DATA CONFIDENTIALITY.

configurably dumb terminal. In computer security, a terminal which may have extensive processing and storage facilities but these can be disabled to render the unit dumb, i.e. have no programmable memory, for computer security purposes. *See* DUMB DEVICE.

configuration control. In computer security, the management of changes made to a system's hardware, software, firmware, and documentation throughout the development and operational life of the system. (DOE). *See* CONFIGURATION MANAGEMENT.

configuration management. (1) In computer security, the process of controlling modifications to the system's hardware, firmware, software, and documentation which provides sufficient assurance the system is protected against the introduction of improper modification before, during, and after system implementation. (AFR). *See* CONFIGURATION CONTROL. (2) In computer security, the use of procedures appropriate for controlling changes to a system's hardware and software structure for the purpose of insuring that such changes will not lead to decreased data security. (OPNAVINST)

confinement. (1) In data security, keep-

ing data within its proper security level. *Compare* DATA LEAKAGE. (2) In computer security, allowing a process executing a borrowed program (in general, an arbitrary program) to have access to data, while ensuring that the data cannot be misused, altered, destroyed or released. (MTR)

confinement channel. *See* COVERT CHANNEL.

confinement property. *Synonymous with* STAR PROPERTY.

confirmed service. In data communications, a service in which the sender issues a request, an indication of the request is passed to the intended recipient who replies with a response causing a confirmation to be passed to the sender. *Compare* UNCONFIRMED SERVICE.

confusion. (1) In cryptography, a technique in which the strength of a cipher system is increased by producing a complex relationship between the ciphertext and the cryptographic key. *Compare* DIFFUSION. *See* CIPHERTEXT, CRYPTOGRAPHIC KEY, STRENGTH. (2) In cryptography, a characteristic of a cipher which makes each letter of the cryptogram dependent on all the characters of the key. *See* CRYPTOGRAM, CRYPTOGRAPHIC KEY.

congruent. In mathematics, given integers b,c, and $n \neq 0$, then b is congruent to c modulo n if and only if for some integer m, $b-c = mn$.

connection. In data communications, a liaison, in the sense of a network interrelationship, between two hosts for a period of time. The liaison is established (by an initiating host) for the purpose of information transfer (with the associated host); the period of time is the time required to carry out the intent of the liaison (e.g. transfer of file, a chatter session, delivery of mail). In many cases, a connection will coincide with a host-host connection established via TCP or equivalent protocol. However a connection (liaison) can also exist when only a protocol such as IP is in use (IP has no concept of a connection that persists for a period of time). Hence the notion of connection as used here is independent of the particular protocols in use during a liaison of two hosts (TNI). *See* PROTOCOL, TCP/IP.

connectionless service. In data communications, a communication service in which each packet of information is transmitted as a separate entity, through the network, to its destination. Packets need not travel through the same path and may not arrive at the destination in the same order as transmission. *Compare* CONNECTION ORIENTED SERVICE. *See* DATAGRAM SERVICE.

connection oriented service. In communications, a communication service in which the sending unit establishes a connection, uses the connection for the period of information transfer and then terminates the connection. A simple telephone call is an example of a connection oriented service. *Compare* CONNECTIONLESS SERVICE.

consistency. In database security, pertaining to the lack of contradictions or paradoxes which arise when perturbation techniques are used for inference control. Such techniques can, for example, cause an average value returned in response to a query to differ from the average value computed by dividing the returned sum by the returned count. *Compare* BIAS. *See* INFERENCE CONTROL, PERTURBATION.

console. In peripherals, the controlling terminal of a computer system.

constant ratio code. *Synonymous with* M OUT OF N CODE.

constrained data item. In formal models, a term used in the Clark-Wilson model, it represents the data items that must be maintained in a given relationship to each other, e.g. to correspond with balanced books in an accounting system. *Compare* UNCONSTRAINED DATA ITEM. *See* CLARK-WILSON MODEL.

construction vulnerability. In information security, a vulnerability that takes advantage of some property of the target of evaluation that was introduced during its construction. *Compare* EXPLOITABLE VULNERABILITY, OPERATIONAL VULNERABILITY, POTENTIAL VULNERABILITY. *See* INFORMATION TECHNOLOGY SECURITY EVALUATION CRITERIA, TARGET OF EVALUATION, VULNERABILITY.

contactless smart card. In access control, a form of a smart card that does not require direct electrical contact to transfer data between the smart card and the reader. The card is placed in close proximity to a card coupler and data is exchanged via an inductive radio frequency field. This card has the advantage that there is no wear and tear on mechanical contacts. *See* SMART CARD.

contained. A state of being within limits, as within system bounds, regardless of purpose or functions, and includes any state of storage, use, or processing. (OPNAVINST, DODD).

container. In data security, a multilevel information structure. A container has a classification and may contain objects (each with its own classification) and/or other containers. *See* CONTAINER CLEARANCE REQUIRED, LANDWEHR'S SECURITY MODEL FOR MILITARY MESSAGE SYSTEMS, MULTILEVEL DEVICE, OBJECT.

container clearance required. In data security, an attribute of some containers where it is important to require minimum clearance, so that if a user does not have, at least, this clearance, that user cannot view any of the entities within the container. *See* CONTAINER, LANDWEHR'S

100 contamination

SECURITY MODEL FOR MILITARY MESSAGE SYSTEMS.

contamination. (1) In computer security, a situation in which the data or program of one user impacts upon that of another, in an undesirable manner, either accidentally or intentionally. (2) In data security, the introduction of data of one sensitivity and need-to-know with data of a lower sensitivity or different need-to-know. This can result in the contaminating data not receiving the required level of protection. (AFR). *See* DATA CONTAMINATION, NEED-TO-KNOW, SENSITIVITY LABEL.

content dependent access control. In access control, access control in which access is determined by the value of data to be accessed. (NCSC). *Compare* CONTEXT DEPENDENT ACCESS CONTROL.

contention. (1) In data communications, a situation in which two or more devices simultaneously attempt to access a common piece of equipment, e.g. two terminals attempting to access a processing unit. (2) In data communications, a method of line control on which terminals request or bid to transmit. If the channel is not available the terminals must wait until it is free. *See* CONTENTION CONTROL.

contention control. In data communications, a control strategy for a local area network in which any node that wishes to transmit does so. If two nodes transmit at the same time a collision occurs and both messages are garbled. The transmitting nodes detect the collision and await a random interval before retransmitting the message. *See* CARRIER SENSE MULTIPLE ACCESS - COLLISION DETECTION, CARRIER SENSE PROTOCOL, CONTENTION, LOCAL AREA NETWORK.

contention delay. In data communications, the time spent waiting for a facility that is occupied by other using devices. *See* CONTENTION.

context dependent access control. In access control, access control in which access is determined by the specific circumstances under which the data is being accessed. (NCSC). *Compare* CONTENT DEPENDENT ACCESS CONTROL.

contingency management. In risk management, management of all the actions to be taken before during, and after a disaster (emergency condition), along with documented, tested procedures which, if followed, will ensure the availability of critical ADP systems and which will facilitate maintaining the continuity of operations in an emergency situation. (DOE). *See* ADP, CONTINGENCY PLANS.

contingency plans. (1) In risk management, a plan for emergency response, backup operations, and post-disaster recovery maintained by an ADP activity as a part of its security program. A comprehensive consistent statement of all the actions (plans) to be taken before, during, and after a disaster (emergency condition), along with documented, tested procedures which, if followed, will ensure the availability of critical ADP resources and which will facilitate maintaining the continuity of operations in an emergency situation. (OPNAVINST). *See* ADP, CONTINGENCY MANAGEMENT. (2) In risk management, the plans produced by an organization to respond to the range of incidents, accidents and disasters that could occur: mistakes by operating staff, loss of personnel due to sickness, death or strikes, hacker activity, theft, fraud, vandalism, alteration or destruction of software or data, fire, flood, power failure, excessive weather conditions, electrical disturbances, failure of environmental protection (airconditioning, fumes, dust), terrorist attack, aircraft, vehicle, meteorite or satellite impact, chemical spillage, building construction failure, nuclear reactor incidents or other radiation effects, earthquakes, volcanos, avalanches etc.

The response to such phenomena should be detailed, e.g. personnel responsibilities, backup procedures, mutual aid agreements, alternative communication facilities, alternative processing facilities, insurance, testing plans etc.

Specialist organizations provide a range of facilities for recovery management. A hot site provides a fully equipped center with comparable processing power available for a specified limited period. Alternatively a shell facility, or cold site, comprises computer and office accommodation, power supplies, raised floors etc. to house an organization's hardware, but no processing power. Other services provided by such specialist organizations include consulting, matching companies with those with excess compatible facilities, etc.

Contingency planning must also include backup procedures and alternative storage for magnetic media, documentation, system wiring plans etc. *See* BUSINESS RESUMPTION PLANNING, COLD SITE, DISASTER RECOVERY PLAN, EMERGENCY RESPONSE PLAN, HOT SITE, RISK ANALYSIS.

contingency program. In computer security, the day to day activities and procedures, e.g. backing up of critical data files, that fulfil the requirements of recoverability. *Compare* CONTINGENCY PLANS.

continuity check. In data communications, a check made to verify that an information path exists in a channel or channels. *See* CHANNEL.

continuity of operations. In risk management, the maintenance of essential services for an information system after a major failure at an information center. The failure may result from natural causes (such as fire, flood or earthquakes) or from deliberate events (such as sabotage). (GAO) *See* CONTINGENCY PLANS.

continuous synchronization. In communications security, a technique of voice scrambling in which the synchronization information, necessary for decryption of the received message, is transmitted continuously, or at intervals, throughout the message. *Compare* INITIAL SYNCHRONIZATION. *See* VOICE SCRAMBLING.

continuous wave. In data communications, pertaining to a transmission technique in which a constant carrier wave is turned on and off in patterns to represent the signal.

control cabinet. In physical security, a centrally located unit which receives and interprets alarm signals from a protected area and supervises the alarm lines. The unit will contain the requisite power supplies, relays, amplifiers etc. *See* ALARM LINE.

control character. In codes, a character whose occurrence in a particular context initiates a control action, e.g. carriage return on a printer.

control flow analysis. In computer security, a method of static analysis, which checks the control structure of high level programs. This technique provides checking of programs for improper subprogram usage and violations of control standards. *See* STATIC ANALYSIS.

controllable isolation. In computer security, controlled sharing in which the scope or domain of authorization can be reduced to an arbitrarily small set or sphere of activity. (FIPS). *See* AUTHORIZATION, CONTROLLED SHARING.

controlled access. *Synonymous with* ACCESS CONTROL.

controlled access area. In physical security, either part or all of an environment where all types and aspects of an access are checked and controlled. (AFR). *See* CONTROLLED AREA.

controlled accessibility. *Synonymous with* ACCESS CONTROL.

controlled area. In physical security, an area within which uncontrolled movement does not permit access to classified information and which is designed for the principal purpose of providing administrative control, safety, or a buffer area of security restrictions for Limited Exclusion Areas. This area may be protected by physical security measures, such as sentries and fences. (OPNAVINST)

controlled rounding. In database security, a form of result based perturbation in which the statistics are rounded in such a manner that the sum of rounded numbers is equal to the rounded sum of the numbers. *Compare* RANDOM ROUNDING, SYSTEMATIC ROUNDING. *See* INFERENCE CONTROL, RESULT BASED PERTURBATION, PERTURBATION.

controlled security mode. (1) In computer security, a mode of operation where internal security controls prevent inadvertent disclosure. Personnel, physical, and administrative controls prevent attempts to gain unauthorized access. The system may have users with access to the system who have neither the security clearance nor need-to-know for all classified information in the system. Access shall be limited to users with a minimal security clearance of one less than the highest classified information processed. (AFR). *See* ADMINISTRATIVE SECURITY, NEED-TO-KNOW, PHYSICAL SECURITY. (2) In computer security, the mode of operation that is a type of multilevel security mode in which a more limited amount of trust is placed in the hardware/software base of the system, with the resultant restrictions on the classification levels and clearance levels that may be supported. (DOD). (3) In computer security, an ADP system is operating in the controlled security mode when at least some personnel (users) with access to the system have neither a security clearance nor a need-to-know for all classified material then contained in the ADP system. However, the separation and control of users and classified mater-

ial on the basis, respectively, of security clearance and security classification is not essentially under operating system control as in the multilevel security mode. (OPNAVINST). *See* ADP, MULTILEVEL SECURITY MODE, NEED-TO-KNOW CLASSIFICATION, CLEARANCE.

controlled sharing. In computer security, the condition which exists when access control is applied to all users and components of a resource-sharing ADP system. (FIPS). *See* ACCESS CONTROL, ADP, RESOURCE SHARING.

controlled space. In physical security, the three-dimensional space surrounding equipment that processes national security information within which unauthorized personnel are: (a) denied unrestricted access and (b) enter escorted by authorized personnel or under continual physical or electronic surveillance. (AFR). *See* CONTROL ZONE.

controller. In data communications, a device, which may contain a stored program, that directs the transmission of data over a network.

control mode. In data communications, a necessary state for all terminals on a line to allow line control actions or terminal selection to occur.

control panel. *See* CONTROL CABINET.

control station. In communications, a network station responsible for control procedures, e.g. polling, selecting, recovery and for recovery from abnormal situations such as contention.

control token. In data communications, a bit pattern passed around a local area network for control purposes. Any node, upon receiving the control token, may remove it from the network, send a message and then pass on the control token. *Compare* DAISY CHAIN, MESSAGE SLOT. *See* LOCAL AREA NETWORK.

control vector. In key management, a non secret cryptographic variable, employed in the IBM common cryptographic architecture, to control key usage.

The control vector comprises a 64 bit, 128 bit or > 128 bit field which provides detailed information to be associated with a cryptographic key, or a general cryptographic variable. The tuple (C,K) comprises the control vector and associated key K is designed so that cryptographic processing, involving the key K, can only be performed if the requested processing is authorized by the control vector.

The control vector is supplied in plaintext and may therefore be interpreted outside special purpose cryptographic hardware. It must however be coupled with the key, or in the general case cryptographic variable, in such a manner that a different control vector cannot be substituted for the original value. This may be achieved by combining the control vector with the double length key encrypting key, KK, used to protect the K in storage or transmission. Alternatively an authentication code based upon the values of both C and K may be associated with the control vector.

The method of combining the control vector with key encrypting KK involves producing a 128 bit hash function of the control vector. In the case of a 64 bit data structure, the control vector is concatenated with itself and then a two bit extension field is set to indicate that the control vector was derived from a 64 bit field. For a 128 bit control vector the hash function is an identity function, and then the extension field is set to indicate that the original data structure was 128 bits. A cryptographic hashing function is used for data structures in excess of 128 bits to produce a 128 bit field, and again the extension field is set to indicate that the original data structure was in excess of 128 bits in length. The result of the hash function operations, discussed above, is then added modulo 2 to the DES key encrypting key KK; the resultant 128 bit key is employed to encrypt the key K.

Thus if an illegitimate control vector is supplied with the key K, then the key encrypting key, formed by modulo addition of KK with the hashed control vector, will not correspond with the key, used originally to encrypt K, and the resultant decryption operation will produce a spurious value of K. *Compare* TAGGED KEYS. *See* COMMON CRYPTOGRAPHIC ARCHITECTURE, CRYPTOGRAPHIC VARIABLE, DES, KEY ENCRYPTING KEY.

control zone. In physical security, the space, expressed in feet of radius, that surrounds equipment that is used to process sensitive information and that is under sufficient physical and technical control to preclude an unauthorized entry or compromise. (FIPS). *See* COMPROMISE, CONTROLLED SPACE, SENSITIVE INFORMATION. *Synonymous with* SECURITY PERIMETER.

Convention on Mutual Administrative Assistance in Tax Matters. In legislation, an agreement between countries which authorizes the automatic exchange of tax data without the consent of the data subject. *See* DATA PROTECTION, DATA SUBJECT.

conversation. In data communications, an interactive exchange of information between two systems or two systems users.

converter. *See* CODE CONVERSION.

cookie monster. In computer security, a form of malicious code which caused a graphic of a 'cookie monster' to appear on computer terminal screens, together with the text 'I want a cookie'. The graphic gradually devours the displayed text until the user inputs 'Cookie' at the terminal keyboard. *Compare* FLYING DUTCHMAN. *See* MALICIOUS CODE.

Co-ordinated Universal Time. The time scale maintained by the Bureau International de L'Heure (International Time

Bureau) that forms the basis of a co-ord-inated dissemination of standard frequen-cies and time signals. (ISO). *Synonymous with* GREENWICH MEAN TIME.

coprime. In number theory, pertaining to a pair of integers with a greatest common divisor of 1, e.g. 8 and 15. *See* GREATEST COMMON DIVISOR, PRIME NUMBER. *Synonymous with* MUTUALLY PRIME.

coprocessor. In computing, a form of multiprocessing where two or more pro-cessors share the same instruction stream. *See* PROCESSOR.

copy protected. In data security, soft-ware distributed on diskettes rendered 'uncopyable' by physical means. *See* COPY PROTECTION, SOFTWARE PROTECT-ION, UNPROTECT.

copy protection. In software protection, techniques used to prevent the unauthor-ized duplication of software. The term is a misnomer since any program can be copied, but with certain protection meas-ures, it may not be executable after it is copied. *Compare* EXECUTE PROTECTION. *See* COPY PROTECTED.

copyright. In legislation, the right to prevent copying. The copyright owner has the right to prevent copying of the form, in which an idea is expressed, but not the idea itself. Computer programs are prot-ected under the same laws which cover literary works in those countries that have copyright legislation. However the use of an idea, or an algorithm, obtained by studying source code of a copyrighted program is not, in itself, an infringement of copyright.

cord trap. In physical security, a simple intruder detector device comprising a cord stretched across a protected area and connected to switches at either end. A displacement of the cord activates an alarm.

core. In communications, the central primary light conducting region of an optical fiber. *See* FIBER OPTICS.

coroutine. In computing, a procedure that can pass control to any other co-routine, suspend itself and continue later. *Compare* SUBROUTINE. *See* PROCEDURE.

corporate security policy. In information security, the set of laws, rules and practices that regulate how assets including sensitive information are man-aged, protected and distributed within a user organization.

corrective maintenance. In computing, the activity of detecting, isolating and correcting failures after occurrence. *Com-pare* PREVENTIVE MAINTENANCE.

correctness. In computer security, in a strict sense, the property of a system that is guaranteed as a result of formal verifi-cation activities. Correctness is not an absolute property of a system, rather it implies the mutual consistency of a speci-fication and its implementation. (MTR). *See* FORMAL PROOF, FORMAL VERIFICA-TION, PROOF OF PROGRAM CORRECTNESS, VERIFICATION.

correctness proof. In computer security, a mathematical proof of consistency bet-ween a specification and its implemen-tation. It may apply at the security model-to-formal specification level, at the formal specification-to-HOL code level, at the compiler level or at the hardware level. For example, if a system has a verified design and implementation, then its over-all correctness rests with the correctness of the compiler and hardware. Once a system is proved correct, it can be expect-ed to perform as specified, but not neces-sarily as anticipated if the specifications are incomplete or inappropriate. (MTR). *See* FORMAL SECURITY POLICY MODEL, PROOF OF PROGRAM CORRECTNESS, VERI-FICATION.

correct refinement. In information security, the refinement of a function described at one abstraction level is said to be correct if the totality of effects described at the lower abstraction level at least exhibits all the effects described at the higher abstraction level. *See* INFORMATION TECHNOLOGY SECURITY EVALUATION CRITERIA.

correspondent banks. In banking, banks that have exchanged authorized signature lists or codes or both, or engage in an exchange of services, or have an account or accounts with each other, or any combination thereof. (ANSI).

corrupt data. In data security, pertaining to data that is accidentally or maliciously modified, e.g. by active wiretapping. *See* DATA INTEGRITY, ACTIVE WIRETAPPING.

corruption. In computing and data communications, pertaining to data that has been changed in an undesired manner either during transmission or in storage, e.g. a corrupt floppy disk. *See* FLOPPY DISK.

cost-risk analysis. In risk management, the assessment of the costs of potential risk or loss or compromise of data in an ADP system without data protection versus the cost of providing data protection. (FIPS). *See* ADP, COMPROMISE, RISK ANALYSIS.

COTS. In computing, Commercial Off The Shelf, pertaining to software that may be obtained from a vendor.

counter. In cryptography, an incrementing count used between two parties to control successive key distributions. (ISO). *See* KEY MANAGEMENT.

countermeasure. (1) In risk management, any method: physical, hardware, software, personnel, procedural etc., used to counteract a threat to the system. *See* THREAT. (2) In information security, a

technical or non-technical security measure contributing to the security objective of a target of evaluation. *See* INFORMATION TECHNOLOGY SECURITY EVALUATION CRITERIA, TARGET OF EVALUATION.

counterparty. In banking, the customer with whom the bank concludes a transaction. *See* COUNTERPARTY GROUP.

counterparty group. In banking, the amalgamation of counterparties into generic groups, e.g. industry, country. *See* COUNTERPARTY.

counterparty risk. *See* COUNTERPARTY. *Synonymous with* CREDIT RISK.

country of domicile. In banking, the country in which the customer is based. *Synonymous with* COUNTRY OF RESIDENCE.

country of residence. *Synonymous with* COUNTRY OF DOMICILE.

cover payment. In banking, reimbursement of a correspondent bank for a payment. (ANSI). *See* CORRESPONDENT BANKS.

covert. Disguised.

covert channel. In computer security, a communication channel that allows a process to transfer information in a manner that violates the system's security policy. A covert channel typically communicates by exploiting a mechanism not intended to be used for communication (TNI). *Compare* COVERT CHANNEL. *See* COVERT STORAGE CHANNEL, COVERT TIMING CHANNEL, SECURITY POLICY.

cover time. In cryptography, the length of time that it is believed a cipher will resist a particular attack. *See* MINIMAL COVER TIME.

covert storage channel. In computer security, a covert channel that involves the direct or indirect writing of a storage location by one process and the direct or indirect reading of the storage location by another process. Covert storage channels typically involve a finite resource (e.g. sectors on a disk) that is shared by two subjects at different security levels. (DOD). *Compare* COVERT TIMING CHANNEL. *See* CHANNEL.

covert timing channel. In computer security, a covert channel in which one process signals information to another by modulating its own use of system resources (e.g. CPU time) in such a way that this manipulation affects the real response time observed by the second process. (DOD). *Compare* COVERT STORAGE CHANNEL. *See* CHANNEL.

CPP. *See* CERTIFIED PROTECTION PROFESSIONAL.

CPU. *See* CENTRAL PROCESSING UNIT.

cracker. In legislation, a hacker who specializes in overcoming software protection systems. *Compare* CRASHER. *See* HACKER.

CRAMM. In risk management, a risk analysis methodology. *See* RISK ANALYSIS METHODOLOGIES.

crash. In computer security, a breakdown caused by software or hardware failure. *See* CRASHER.

crasher. In legislation, a hacker who deliberately attempts to cause serious interference to the operation of the computer system. *Compare* CRACKER. *See* HACKER.

CRC. *See* CYCLIC REDUNDANCY CHECK.

credentials. (1) In authentication, data that is transferred to establish the claimed identity of an entity. (ISO). (2) In access control, data, passed from one entity to another, that is used to establish the sen-

ding entity's access rights. *See* ACCESS RIGHT.

credit advice. In banking, advice by the account servicing bank of a credit to the account of the receiver (account owner). (ANSI). *See* ACCOUNT SERVICING BANK.

credit card. In banking, a card which enables the subscriber to purchase goods or services from a variety of outlets and then refund the appropriate financial institution, on a periodic basis. *Compare* DEBIT CARD.

credit party. In banking, the party to be credited or paid by the receiving bank. (ANSI). *Compare* BENEFICIARY, DEBIT PARTY.

credit risk. In banking, the risk accruing through the ability of the counterparty to honor his payment obligations. *See* COUNTERPARTY. *Synonymous with* COUNTERPARTY RISK.

criteria. In information security, pertaining to the definitions of properties and constraints to be met by system functionality and assurance. *See* ITSEC, TCSEC.

critical data processing workload. In risk management, that portion of the total workload which will generate serious loss if disrupted for a specified period of time. *See* CRITICAL FUNCTIONS, CRITICALITY, CRITICAL PROCESSING.

critical functions. In operations, elements vital to an organizations operations and possibly to its survival. *See* CRITICAL DATA PROCESSING WORKLOAD, CRITICALITY, CRITICAL PROCESSING.

criticality. In computer security, a concept related to the mission the automated system supports and the degree that the mission is dependent upon the system. This degree of dependence corresponds to the effect on the mission in the event of denial of service, modification, or destruction of data or software. (AFR). *See* CRITICAL DATA PROCESSING WORKLOAD, CRITICAL PROCESSING.

critical processing. In computer security, applications defined as being of such importance in the operation of an organization that little or no loss of availability is acceptable. *Compare* DISCRETIONARY PROCESSING. *See* CRITICAL DATA PROCESSING WORKLOAD, CRITICAL FUNCTIONS.

critical technology. Technologies that consist of (a) arrays of design and manufacturing know-how (including technical data), (b) keystone manufacturing, inspection, and test equipment; (c) keystone materials, and (d) goods accompanied by sophisticated operation, application, or maintenance know-how that would make a significant contribution to the military potential of any country or combination of countries and that may prove detrimental to the security of the United States. (DODD). *See* KEYSTONE EQUIPMENT, KNOW-HOW. *Synonymous with* MILITARY CRITICAL TECHNOLOGY.

CRL. *See* CERTIFICATE REVOCATION LIST.

cross alarm. *Synonymous with* CLOSED CIRCUIT ALARM.

crossfire. *Synonymous with* CROSS-TALK.

cross-talk. In communications, an unwanted transfer of energy from one communications channel to another channel. (FIPS). *Synonymous with* CROSSFIRE.

cross zone. (1) In physical security, a fire alarm circuit that requires signals from two different sensors for activation. (2) In physical security, circuitry for combining alarm signal inputs to produce specified outputs. *See* COMBINED ALARMS.

cryptanalysis. (1) In cryptology, the analysis of a cryptographic system, and/or

its inputs and outputs to derive confidential variables and/or sensitive data including cleartext. (ISO). *See* CLEARTEXT. (2) In cryptology, the steps and operations performed in converting encrypted messages into plaintext without initial knowledge of the key employed in the encryption algorithm. (FIPS). *See* CHOSEN PLAINTEXT, CIPHERTEXT ONLY, ENCRYPT, ENCRYPTION ALGORITHM, KEY, KNOWN PLAINTEXT, PLAINTEXT.

cryption. In cryptography, the process of encryption or decryption. *See* DECRYPT, ENCRYPT.

cryptogram. In cryptography, an encrypted message. *Synonymous with* CIPHERTEXT.

cryptogram space. In cryptography, the total set of ciphertext messages that can be produced by encrypting all messages in the message space with all the keys in the key space. *Compare* MESSAGE SPACE, KEY SPACE.

cryptographic algorithm. In data security, a set of rules specifying the procedure required to encipher and decipher data. *See* CIPHER.

cryptographic API. In cryptography, cryptographic Application Programming Interface, an interface between application programs, and cryptographic services, that enables application programs to make calls for cryptographic services in a defined format. It allows application programs to invoke cryptographic services in a manner according to predefined command formats and thus relieves the application programmer from much of the cryptographic implementation detail, key management etc. The cryptographic API also enhances the interoperability and portability of user programs. *See* COMMON CRYPTOGRAPHIC ARCHITECTURE.

cryptographic authentication. In authentication, the use of encryption related techniques to provide authentication. *See* MESSAGE AUTHENTICATION.

cryptographic bit stream. In cryptography, the stream of bits which is combined with the plaintext to form the ciphertext in stream cipher. *See* STREAM CIPHER. *Synonymous with* KEY STREAM.

cryptographic checkfunction. In cryptography, information which is derived by performing a cryptographic process on data; it is therefore a result of a mathematical function of the key and data. *See* CRYPTOGRAPHIC KEY, MAC. *Synonymous with* CRYPTOGRAPHIC CHECKSUM.

cryptographic checksum. In cryptography, a checksum computed using a secret key. *See* CHECKSUM, MAC. *Synonymous with* CRYPTOGRAPHIC CHECKFUNCTION.

cryptographic checkvalue. In cryptography, information which is derived by performing a cryptographic transformation on a data unit. (ISO). *Synonymous with* CRYPTOGRAPHIC CHECKSUM.

cryptographic control. In cryptography, the use of cryptographic techniques to protect information when transmitted over a link or when stored in a computer. *See* WIRETAPPING.

cryptographic device. In cryptography, an implementation of a cryptographic procedure.

cryptographic equipment. In key management, a device wherein cryptographic functions (e.g. encryption, authentication, key generation) are performed. (ANSI). *See* AUTHENTICATION, CRYPTOGRAPHIC FACILITY, ENCRYPTION, KEY GENERATION.

cryptographic facility. In key management, a tamper resistant module containing a unit which can perform a cryptographic algorithm, e.g. DES, and also

contains storage for a limited number of keys. In a typical operation a data key, encrypted under a master key, is presented to the unit together with data encrypted under the data key. The master key is held in non-volatile storage within the unit. A two-stage operation first decrypts the data key using the master key and then decrypts the data with the data key. Thus the data key is never revealed outside the facility. *See* KEY ENCRYPTING KEY, KEY MANAGEMENT, TAMPER RESISTANT MODULE. *Synonymous with* CRYPTOGRAPHIC EQUIPMENT.

cryptographic key. (1) In cryptography, a parameter used in conjunction with an algorithm for the purpose of validation, authentication, encipherment, decipherment, signature construction or deconstruction. (ISO) *See* AUTHENTICATION, CRYPTOGRAPHIC ALGORITHM, DECIPHERMENT, ENCIPHERMENT, SIGNATURE CONSTRUCTION, SIGNATURE DECONSTRUCTION VALIDATION. *Synonymous with* KEY. (2) In cryptography, a parameter (e.g., a secret 64-bit number for DES) used by a cryptographic process that makes the process completely defined and usable only by those having that key. (FIPS). (3) In cryptography, a parameter that determines the transformation from plaintext to ci-phertext and vice versa. A DEA key is a 64 bit parameter consisting of 56 independent bits and 8 bits which may be used as parity bits. (ANSI). *See* CIPHERTEXT, DEA, PARITY BIT.

cryptographic key data set. In key management, a set of keys encrypted under key encrypting keys and held in backing storage. *See* BACKING STORAGE, KEY ENCRYPTING KEY.

cryptographic keying material. *See* KEYING MATERIAL.

cryptographic period. In cryptography, a specified period of time, period of usage, or number of events within which a cryptographic key will be changed. *See* CRYPTOGRAPHIC KEY.

cryptographic seal. *See* DIGITAL SIGNATURE.

cryptographic service message. In key management, a message for transporting keys or related information used to control a keying relationship. (ANSI). *See* ANSI X9.17 - 1985, CRYPTOGRAPHIC KEY, KEYING RELATIONSHIP, SERVICE MESSAGE.

cryptographic system. (1) In cryptography, in formal terms a cryptographic system comprises five components:
- a message space;
- a ciphertext space;
- a key space;
- a family of enciphering transformations;
- a family of deciphering transformations.

The message space comprises the total set of messages that can be encrypted etc. The enciphering transformation employs an enciphering key, in the key space, to map a message in the message space into a ciphertext in the ciphertext space, the deciphering algorithm performs the reverse transformation, with the corresponding deciphering key.

In general, cryptographic systems should satisfy the requirements that:

- the enciphering and deciphering algorithms should be efficient for all keys;
- the system should be simple to operate;
- the security should depend upon the secrecy of the keys and not upon the secrecy of the enciphering or deciphering algorithms.

See MAPPING. (2) In cryptography, the documents, devices, equipment, and associated techniques that are used as a unit to provide a single means of encryp-

tion (enciphering or encoding). (FIPS). *See* ENCODE, ENCRYPT.

cryptographic throughput factor. In cryptography, a measure of message expansion produced by padding. It is defined as the ratio of the length, in bits, of the message to the corresponding length, in bits, of the corresponding ciphertext. *See* PADDING.

cryptographic transparency. In cryptography, a technique in which a privileged user can access enciphered material in a deciphered state without being conscious of the decryption process.

cryptographic variable. In cryptography, a parameter of a cryptographic algorithm that provides security because of its secrecy, e.g. the private key in a public key cryptosystem. *See* CRYPTOGRAPHIC KEY, PUBLIC KEY CRYPTOGRAPHY.

cryptography. (1) In cryptology, the discipline which embodies principles, means and methods for the transformation of data in order to hide its information content, prevent its undetected modification and/or prevent its unauthorized use. (ISO). (2) In cryptology, the art or science which treats of the principles, means, and methods for rendering plaintext unintelligible and for converting encrypted messages into intelligible form. (FIPS). *See* ENCRYPT, PLAINTEXT. (3) In cryptology, the science and study of secret writing. A cipher is a secret method of writing, whereby plaintext (or cleartext) is transformed into ciphertext. The process of transforming plaintext into ciphertext is called encipherment or encryption; the reverse process of transforming ciphertext into plaintext is called decipherment or decryption. Both encipherment and decipherment are controlled by one or more cryptographic keys.

Classical cryptography provided secrecy for information sent over channels where eavesdropping and message interception

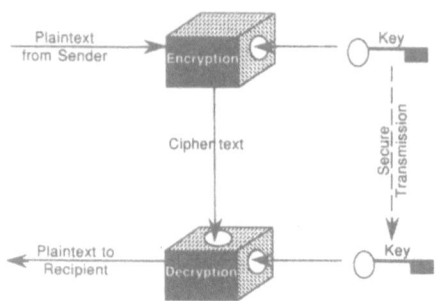

Figure 7.1 Encryption and Decryption

cryptography

were possible. The sender selected a cipher and encryption key, and either gave it directly to the receiver or else sent it indirectly over a slow but secure channel, typically a trusted courier. Messages and replies were transmitted over the insecure channel in ciphertext.

A cryptographic system is analogous to a resettable combination lock used to secure a safe. The combination is kept secret and can be changed whenever it is suspected of having fallen into the wrong hands. Even though unauthorized persons know the set of all possible keys or combinations, they may be unable to discover the exact combination with a reasonable expenditure of time and money. The effort to try all possible combinations is a measure of the security of the lock, or cipher.

Modern cryptography protects data transmitted over high-speed links or information stored in computer systems. There are two principal objectives: secrecy and authenticity. Secrecy aims to ensure that data is only disclosed to an authorized individual or process. Authenticity relates to:

- proving the identity of an individual or system;
- proving that the originator of data is the purported identity;
- proving that the contents of data have not been illicitly modified.

Modern ciphers, such as the Data Encryption Standard, FEAL or RSA, offer a high degree of security and can, under normal circumstances, only be broken by an attacker with knowledge of the key being used. In general, the algorithm used for encryption/decryption with modern cryptosystems is published, but the key is kept secret. *See* CRYPTANALYSIS, CRYPTOGRAPHIC KEY, CRYPTOLOGY, DATA ENCRYPTION STANDARD, DIGITAL SIGNATURE, KEY MANAGEMENT, PUBLIC KEY CRYPTOGRAPHY, RSA.

crypto-key. *Synonymous with* CRYPTOGRAPHIC KEY.

cryptology. The field that encompasses both cryptography and cryptanalysis. (FIPS). *See* CRYPTANALYSIS, CRYPTOGRAPHY.

cryptomanagement. In cryptography, the procedures which must be implemented and operated to ensure that cryptographic systems provide the required degree of security.

crypto-operation. In cryptography, the functional application of cryptographic methods. (a) Off-line. Encryption or decryption performed as a self-contained operation distinct from the transmission of the encrypted text, as by hand or by machines not electrically connected to a signal line. (b) On-line. The use of crypto equipment that is directly connected to a signal line, making continuous processes of encryption and transmission or reception and decryption. (AR). *See* OFF LINE CRYPTO-OPERATION, ON LINE CRYPTO-OPERATION.

cryptoperiod. In key management, the time span during which a specific key is authorized for use or in which the keys for a given system may remain in effect. (ANSI). *See* CRYPTOGRAPHIC KEY.

cryptosystem. *See* CRYPTOGRAPHIC SYSTEM.

cryptotext. *Synonymous with* CIPHER-TEXT.

CSDC. *See* CIRCUIT SWITCHED DIGITAL CIRCUITRY.

CSM. Cryptographic Service Message. *See* ANSI X9.17 - 1985, CRYPTOGRAPHIC SERVICE MESSAGE.

CSMA-CD. *See* CARRIER SENSE MULTIPLE ACCESS - COLLISION DETECTION.

CSTVRP. Computer Security Technical Vulnerability Reporting Program.

CTS. *See* CLEAR TO SEND.

CUG. *See* CLOSED USER GROUP.

current utilization. In banking, the amount actually running at present; this will be the original amount drawn (original commitment if fully drawn) less any repayments received. *Synonymous with* LOAN UTILIZATION.

Curse Boot. In computer security, a virus that terminates and stays resident, infects floppy and hard disk boot sector, corrupts boot sector and affects run time operation. *See* VIRUS NAMES.

custodian of data. In data security, the individual or group that has been entrusted with the possession of, and responsibility for, the security of specified data.

customer. (1) In computer security, a person or organization who receives products that an automated system produces, but who does not have access to the system. (AFR). *Compare* USER. *See* ACCESS. (2) In banking, the individual initiating a transaction. (ANSI)

customer code. In physical security, a code used in alarm or access control systems to identify a piece of equipment or customer. *See* ACCESS CONTROL.

customer type. In banking, the peer group in which a customer resides, e.g. private bank, state utility.

cutoff frequency. In electronics, the upper or lower frequency limits of the useful frequency band of a filter. *See* FILTER.

CVV. *See* CARD VERIFICATION VALUE.

cyclical band shift invertor. In communications security, a form of band shift invertor in which the carrier frequencies are selected by the output of a pseudorandom number generator. *See* BAND SHIFT INVERTOR, SPEECH INVERTOR, VOICE SCRAMBLING.

cyclic code. *See* GRAY CODE.

cyclic redundancy check. In codes, a method for detecting errors in the transmission or transfer of data using a polynomial code and a cyclic check character. *See* ERROR DETECTION CODE, POLYNOMIAL CODE.

D

D. *See* DIVISION D.

DAA. (1) In cryptography, data authentication algorithm. *See* AUTHENTICATION. (2) In computer security, *See* DESIGNATED APPROVING AUTHORITY. (3) In communications, *See* DATA ACCESS ARRANGEMENT.

DAC. (1) Data Authentication Code. *Synonymous with* MAC. (2) In access control. *See* DISCRETIONARY ACCESS CONTROL.

daemon. (1) In computing, a suspended process that waits for a certain kind of event to occur, it is then automatically actuated, performs its job and either terminates or suspends itself in wait for the next event. *Compare* DEMON, TROJAN HORSE. *See* MORRIS WORM. (2) In computer security. *Synonymous with* INTERNAL SUBJECT.

daisy chain. In data communications, a technique in a local area network to pass permission for a node to transmit; dedicated wires are used to pass control information from one node to the next. *Compare* CONTROL TOKEN, MESSAGE SLOT. *See* LOCAL AREA NETWORK.

Dark Avenger. In computer security, a virus that terminates and stays resident, infects COMMAND.COM, COM, EXE and OVL files, affects run time operation, corrupts program and OVL files and file linkage. *See* VIRUS NAMES.

DARPA. Defense Advanced Research Projects Agency, originally ARPA. *See* ARPA.

dasd. In computing, direct access storage device.

data. (1) Information with a specific physical representation. (DOD). (2) A representation of facts, concepts, information, or instructions in a manner suitable for communication, interpretation, or processing by humans or by an AIS. (DODD). (3) Programs, files or other information stored in, or processed by, a computer system. (FIPS). (4) Information with a specific representation (loosely used to denote any or all information that can be produced, processed, stored or produced by a computer). (DOD). (5) In legislation, as defined by the U.K. Data Protection Act 1984, information recorded in a form in which it can be processed by equipment operating automatically in response to instructions given for that purpose. *See* DATA PROTECTION. (6) A representation of facts, concepts, or instructions in a formalized manner in order that it may be communicated, interpreted, or processed by human or automatic means. *Compare* INFORMATION.

data above voice. In data communications, a system for carrying digital data on a portion of the microwave radio spectrum above the frequency used for voice transmission. *Compare* DATA IN VOICE, DATA UNDER VOICE.

data access arrangement. In communications, a unit containing an isolation transformer, for interconnecting user equipment to a telephone network. It is designed to prevent harmful voltages or signals entering the network.

data access management. See MO-DEM.

data acquisition. In computing, the process of identifying, isolating and gathering source data to be centrally processed. *See* DATA CAPTURE.

databank. *Synonymous with* DATA-BASE.

database. (1) An extensive and comprehensive set of records collected and organized in a meaningful manner to serve a particular purpose. (DODD). (2) In computing, a collection of stored operational data used by the applications system of an enterprise. The precursor of database systems was sets of individual files maintained by departments of the enterprise for prespecified purposes and processed by individual application programs. This arrangement was inefficient in terms of the programming effort required to operate the system, failed to provide the management with the whole range of information available from the stored data and was too inflexible for evolving enterprises.

Database systems integrate stored data and special software termed database management systems provide a buffer between the stored data and application programs.

The advantages gained from this approach are:

- the physical storage systems are decoupled from the application program;
- the redundancy of stored data can be reduced;
- problems of inconsistency in the stored data are reduced;
- stored data can be shared amongst users;
- data control standards can be enforced;
- security restrictions can be applied;
- data integrity can be maintained;
- ad hoc enquiries are facilitated.

The presence of the database management system implies that individual programs can communicate data to the database management system that has responsibility for accessing, or updating,

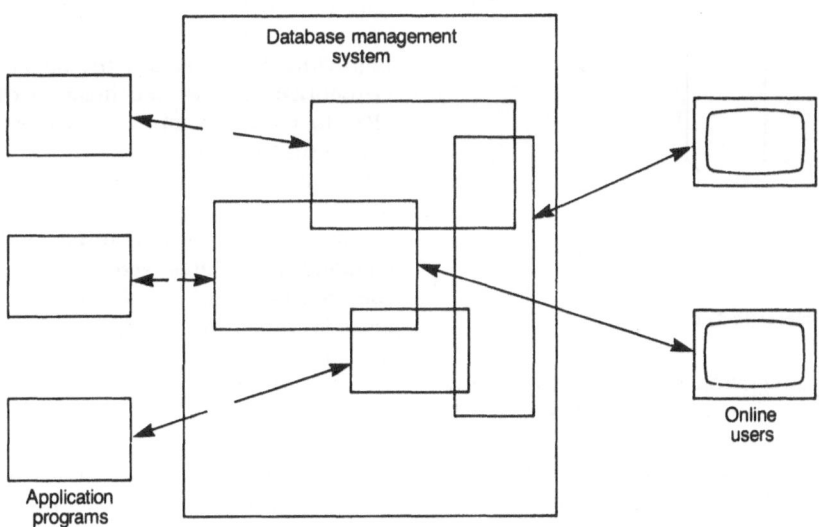

database.
Fig. 1. Unintegrated system of files

the corresponding item in physical storage. This physical data independence allows the physical storage arrangements to be changed, e.g. to accommodate larger masses of data or to optimize data access, without modification to the application programs.

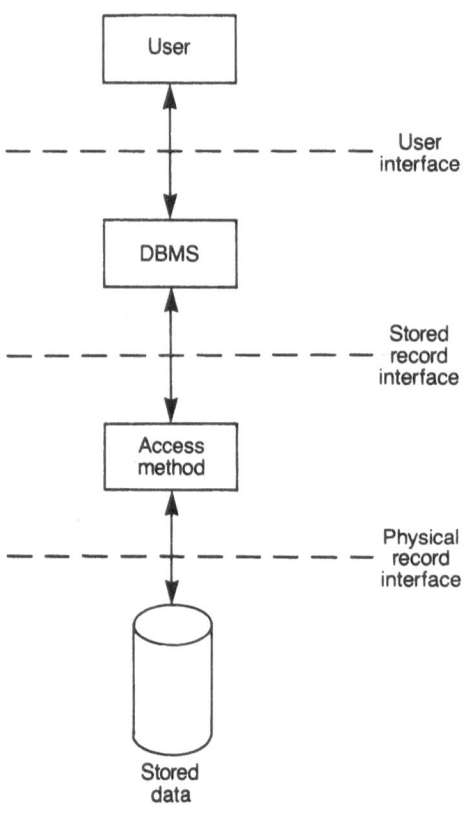

database.
Fig. 2. Integrated data.

The integration of stored data ensures that data items are not unnecessarily duplicated across files, e.g. employee information stored on personnel and payroll files. This reduction in data redundancy also minimizes the danger of data inconsistency, e.g. if the personnel department updated its file when an employee resigned then there would be an inconsistency with the corresponding item on the payroll file until the accounts department took the same action.

Sharing of data between departments is obviously facilitated by the database approach and this provides more relevant information for managers, e.g. it is possible to correlate details of employee qualifications with salary.

The major advantage of database systems became apparent as the volume of stored data increased and the systems moved from batch to interactive modes. The dangers of incorrect, invalid or insecure data becomes acute in these circumstances but with an integrated store of data it is possible to assign responsibility for overall control of the database to a database administrator (DBA). The DBA is given the authority and responsibility to ensure that the installation standards are enforced. This overcomes the problems arising from idiosyncratic data formats produced by individual programmers and facilitates both maintenance and data interchange between installations.

The value and confidential nature of corporate data has compelled organizations to adopt stricter attitudes to data access. The existence of a central electronic store has enhanced the dangers of unauthorized access; the function of the DBA to enforce central control is thus vital to organizations.

It is important to protect the data from accidental as well as malicious damage and the DBA must initiate and enforce operating procedures and validity controls that minimize the danger of incorrect insertions or modifications, e.g. input data is rejected if it is in an incorrect format or does not conform to prespecified criteria.

The initial developments of databases concentrated upon the design of the interrelationships between data items and the optimization of access strategies. The two major approaches were hierarchical and network databases. The former have a tree structure and individual items are accessed by searches along branches, from parent to child nodes, whereas network databases allow pointers between data items that contravene the tree requirements of only one parent per node.

Indexes and inverted files greatly facilitate access to individual items and reduce time consuming multiple disk accesses. Inverted files permit fast searches on attributes other than the primary key. For example, if an employee file is sorted alphabetically by employee name then a search for all the employees in a particular department involves a comprehensive search of all the employees in the organization; an inverted file containing department and employee name, sorted by department name, would provide the necessary information in a fraction of the time.

The aforementioned approaches to database design, however, imposed a rigid structure on the database and led to very complex indexing arrangements. The relational database concept introduced by E. F. Codd revolutionized database concepts and removed the demand for complex indexes.

The relational database is based upon the simplest possible data structure, i.e. tables or flat files. These tables, termed relations, can be manipulated to provide a view of the data appropriate to the particular application. This development provides yet a further degree of data independence, i.e. logical data independence. The users can be effectively provided with an individual database, that is a subset of the total database, geared to their particular requirements. This individual database does not involve any physical partitioning or rearrangement of the stored data; it does not therefore reintroduce the dangers of duplication or inconsistency inherent in the production of multiple 'private' databases.

The provision of local views also simplifies security procedures since individual users are only provided with a subschema consistent with their security grading.

The modern trend is to employ relational databases accessed interactively with simple query languages or processed by fourth generation languages. Whereas earlier databases were primarily processed by application programs in batch mode, current systems are designed to support both this mode and on line access for ad hoc queries, and updates, by a large and diffuse user population.

The on line access in a multiuser environment demands both a simple user interface and a sophisticated database management system that guarantees security and integrity under all operating conditions. The database must be protected against aborted transactions that could leave it in an inconsistent state, e.g. a partial bank transaction that credits one account but does not debit another corresponding one.

It must also be possible to reconstruct the database in the case of system failure. Concurrent users must be protected against mutual interference particularly if both are updating the same record.

The total population of database users is expanding rapidly. At one end of the spectrum there are massive databases designed for corporate bodies and public databases serving national and international users. At the other, there are a multiplicity of microcomputer database management systems designed for small businesses and professional users, e.g. dBase. *See* APPLICATION PROGRAM, DBA, FLAT FILE, FOURTH GENERATION LANGUAGE, HIERARCHICAL DATABASE, INVERTED FILE, LOGICAL DATA INDEPENDENCE, LOCKOUT, NETWORK DATABASE, DATA INDEPENDENCE, PRIMARY KEY, QUERY LANGUAGE, RELATIONAL DATABASE, ROLLBACK, SCHEMA, SUBSCHEMA, TREE STRUCTURE. *Synonymous with* DATABANK.

database administrator. In computing,

a person who is responsible for a database system, particularly for defining the rules by which data is accessed, modified and stored. *See* DATABASE.

database language. *See* DATABASE MANAGEMENT SYSTEM, DATA DESCRIPTION LANGUAGE, DATA MANIPULATION LANGUAGE, QUERY LANGUAGE.

database management system. In databases, a set of programs that facilitates the creation and maintenance of a database and the execution of programs accessing the database. *See* DATA INDEPENDENCE.

database security. The application of databases has increased rapidly in recent years; there has been a proliferation of individual databases on micro- and minicomputers, and an expansion in the capacity of large systems serving organizational, national and international user populations.

Overview
The integration of an organization's files, into a single database, increases the risk of unauthorized access and malicious modification of the organization's data. Moreover the advent of data protection legislation places a legal responsibility on holders of personal data to protect that information against malicious modification and unauthorized access. Thus the problems of database security are increasing both in terms of the magnitude of the problem and the penalties associated with inadequate security.

Ideally the security arrangements for a database should meet the requirements listed below.

- No person or groups of persons should be able to illegally access, modify, add or delete the data.
- No unauthorized person, or unauthorized group of persons, should be able to infer the value of a confidential item by manipulating queries or performing computations on released data.
- The security arrangements should be flexible and users provided with privileges appropriate to their function and needs.
- The security mechanisms should not significantly degrade the performance of the DBMS.
- The accessibility of the system should not be reduced for legitimate users.
- There should be no significant expansion of stored data.
- The cost of the security arrangements should not be incompatible with the function of the database.

The security problems for all databases fall into two broad categories: integrity preservation and security, but the nature of the problem is related to the function, size and user population of the database. Integrity preservation concerns the preservation of the database contents against non-malicious errors. Security is concerned with access control, i.e. the database is only viewed and/or modified by authorized users. Integrity preservation is the responsibility of the DBMS; the database contents must be protected against errors arising from miskeying, update inconsistency, partially aborted updates etc. Security of the database system is designed to ensure that database access is prevented for unauthorized users, malicious or otherwise.

The database contents must be protected against accidental modification by naive users, program errors etc., as well as against the attacker. The security against malicious access may be categorized as DBMS access control, file encryption, inference control and filters for multilevel systems.

DBMS Access Control
A DBMS provides an interface be-

tween a user and the data files; it is therefore possible for the DBMS to create a view of the database appropriate to a particular user. Thus the DBMS can effectively provide each user with a personal, restricted database containing only those data items that correspond to the user's level of privilege. The DBMS cannot, however, provide a guarantee of security in all circumstances. The limitations of database security are:

- it is sometimes possible for users to bypass the DBMS and access the database files directly;
- statistical databases may be manipulated to reveal information concerning individuals;
- a DBMS may be unable to prevent users deducing classified information by manipulating enquiries within their level of privilege;
- attackers can insert Trojan Horses within the DBMS;
- the DBMS may be too complex to permit formal verification of security procedures.

If a database is contained in a computer system where users have separate access to the operating system, or the media containing the data files, then an attacker may simply bypass the DBMS and access the data files directly. For example, a floppy disk containing a set of microcomputer database files may be removed from the computer and subjected to a detailed study on an attacker's microcomputer.

Encryption
The data may be encrypted to prevent a direct attack; however, such encryption immediately impacts upon the DBMS operation and there are a number of constraints on the encryption algorithm and the mode of encryption.

- The encryption system should be theoretically secure or involve a

high work factor to break. Stored data often has a value over an extended period, and is therefore susceptible to cryptanalysis that may require an extensive time period.

- Encryption, and particularly, decryption times should not materially affect the on line user operation. Encryption may, in some systems, be performed on batches of data updates, but decryption time will directly impact upon normal user accesses.
- The encrypted data should not occupy a significantly larger volume than the cleartext data.
- The encryption must be record based so that the DBMS is not compelled to retrieve a large volume of data in order to decrypt a record.
- The encryption scheme must be compatible with the DBMS facility to provide user subschemas.
- Fields within the database should be encrypted with different keys. Thus a user who gains illegal access to encrypted classified fields should be unable to deduce their plaintext values by authorized manipulations on other fields.
- The record should itself be encrypted as an entity. If the record merely comprised a collection of individually encrypted fields, then there exists the dangers of substitution of an encrypted field from one record to another, and pattern matching. In the latter case a user might be able to match the values of fields in different records; if the matched encrypted field existed in a record within the user's level of privilege then it would be possible to deduce the value of the matched ciphertext field.
- The encryption scheme should permit users to be given a variety of levels of read and write privileges.

- The DBMS must not be compelled, by the encryption scheme, to maintain duplicate copies of data items in order to allow different subschema to be presented.
- It should be possible to operate the encryption scheme with partially completed records.

Inference Control - Overview

Some database security systems do not encrypt the stored data but constrain the user to access the database via the DBMS. In these cases the DBMS may itself be manipulated to reveal secret information.

A particular case, in point, arises where users can legitimately obtain statistical data, concerning a given user population, but are not authorized to access the personal details of an individual within that population. Thus it may be legitimate to access the incidence of a disease within a town but it should not be possible to determine, whether or not, a particular inhabitant of the town has contracted the disease in question. This aspect of database security is termed inference control.

It is not sufficient to set a lower limit on the number of records that can be associated with a query, since overlapping queries can still be used to deduce information concerning an individual. For example, if a lower limit of 100 records per query is set, then 'A Smith' can legitimately access the average salary of 99 employees and 'A Smith'. A second query on the average salary of the same individuals and 'B Jones' provides sufficient information for 'A Smith' to infer 'B Jone's' salary. If the system sets a lower limit on the number of records associated with a query, and the maximum number of common elements in two queries, then an attacker will be compelled to make a large number of queries to infer an item concerning an individual, making the attacker's problem more difficult but not impossible.

Inference control techniques may be judged in terms of security, information loss and cost. Security relates to the relative number of sensitive statistics that can be deduced by manipulation of legitimate queries, and the difficulty of doing so. Information loss is a measure of the number of non-sensitive statistics that are unnecessarily restricted by the control. The cost of inference control arises from the implementation of the control system and the computational/storage overhead in assessing whether or not queries may be processed.

The techniques of inference control may be classified as:

- restriction on the set of allowable queries;
- the addition of noise to released statistics.

Inference Control - Restriction on Allowable Queries

In the study of restrictions on the allowable queries it is useful to represent the database as a lattice model.

Consider a statistical database containing details of a survey population with attributes age and salary. The age attribute is divided into ranges 0 - 20, 21 - 40, 41 - 60, 61 - 80, and the salary into ranges 0 - 20 000, 20 001 - 40 000, 40 001 - 60 000, and 60 001 - 80 000. The lattice model for this database is illustrated in Fig. 1. The database may represent the number of people within each of these attribute ranges, and this situation can be represented as a two dimensional table with each cell containing the corresponding counts. A coarser version of the data can be derived by considering either the age, or salary, alone. In this case the tables provide only details of the number of people in a given age or salary range (see Fig. 1), i.e. the figures in the cells of these table represent the sum of the columns (for age), or rows (for salary), of the two dimensional table.

At the top of the lattice model is a

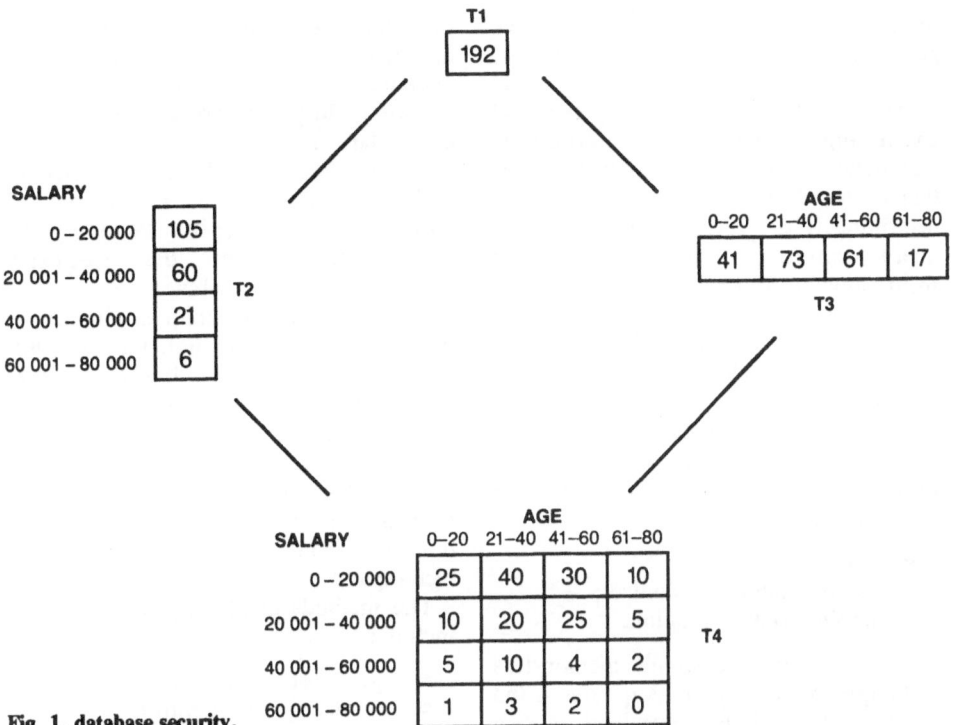

Fig. 1. database security. Lattice model.

single cell table that simply gives the count of the number of people in the survey population. The table at the bottom of the lattice is the one that is most likely to be capable of revealing information about an individual. It is clear, for example, that only one person of the survey population, in the age range 0 - 20, has a salary between 60,001 and 80,000. Suppose that there were a third attribute in the database, e.g. number of criminal convictions, it would then be possible to deduce the number of criminal convictions for an individual if it were known that the individual was aged between 0 and 20 and had a salary in the range 60 001 - 80 000.

The tables higher in the lattice do not provide such fine detail, e.g. the age table only gives information on the age distribution of the user population, with no correlation to salary. The sensitivity of a statistic may be defined by the n-respondent, k%-dominance criterion, i.e. a sensitive statistic is one in which n or fewer records constitute more than k% of the total.

The disclosure risk of a table is given by the percentage of sensitive cells of the table. Compromise, or personal disclosure, occurs when it is possible to infer a hitherto unknown statistic about an individual. Negative disclosure arises when the statistic can be used to infer that the individual does not have a particular attribute, e.g. in Fig. 1 any individual over the age of 60 cannot be earning more than 60 000.

Restriction techniques, in inference control, may be applied at the table or cell level, and are designed to prevent access to tables or cells that contain sensitive statistics. The techniques of table or cell restriction are categorized as memoryless, audit based and a priori.

Memoryless techniques use criteria based neither upon the maintenance of a record of the previous queries posed nor a list of permitted statistics, i.e. the decision to allow a query is made at the time that the query is posed and no pre-computation of the criteria is undertaken. Audit based controls maintain a record of queries and attempt to determine if the result of the proposed query, correlated with data obtained from previous queries, could lead to a compromise. A priori controls determine in advance whether or not a given set of statistics can be released without causing a compromise.

Table restriction determines whether or not a particular table can be provided to answer queries; the three common techniques are :

- order control;
- relative table size control;
- explicit risk estimation.

Order control is a simple memoryless technique that only permits queries if the number of attributes contained therein do not exceed some specified value. This technique effectively restricts the database representation to the upper tables of the lattice model. For example if only one attribute is permitted in a query then only the three upper tables of Fig. 1 (i.e. T1, T2 and T3), could be accessed. This technique does not, however, consider the number of cells in a table, in relation to the total number of records. A two dimensional table with 100 cells for a set of 200 records is more likely to lead to compromise than the same table serving 10 000 records. Similarly a reduction in the number of cells, by recording attributes over larger ranges (e.g. 0 - 40000 instead of 0 - 20000) can reduce the danger of compromise for a given multidimensional table.

Relative table size control, also known as s_m/N criterion, is based upon the ratio of the number of cells in a table to the total number of records. If the average number of records associated with a cell falls below some threshold value then the table is restricted. This control takes no account of the distribution of records over the table, e.g. in Fig. 1 very young and very old people are unlikely to earn high salaries.

Various techniques have been tried to explicitly determine the risk associated with the release of a given table, e.g. by a consideration of the frequency distribution of the attributes.

Cell restriction techniques attempt to determine whether, or not, the availability of a particular cell is likely to lead to the disclosure of personal data. With these techniques the decision is taken to suppress a particular cell, or group of cells, rather than the whole table; the information loss is therefore less than that associated with table restriction techniques.

The methods employing this approach include:

- query set size control;
- implied queries control;
- overlap control;
- audit expert;
- cell suppression;
- grouping.

Query set size control is a simple memoryless cell restriction technique that does not permit queries relating to a very low, or a very high proportion, of the appropriate records in the database. The restriction on queries that constitute a very low proportion of the records is self-evident; the restriction on queries that constitute a very high proportion of records arises because it is possible to infer the data contained in the records not included in the query. Thus a query over 99 of 100 records, followed by a second identical query over the whole 100 records, provides direct information on the record omitted from the first query. It is possible to subvert this control by the use of trackers to pad out the number of records in a query. For example in Fig. 1 a query on the number of people in the age range 0 -20, with salary between 60 000 and 80 000 may well be rejected by this control. However if the query is applied to a salary range of 0 - 20 000 as well as 60 000 to 80 000 then it could well be permitted. A second permissible query on the tracker, i.e. age 0 - 20, salary 0 - 20 000 can then be used to infer the sensitive statistic.

Implied queries control restrictions attempt to thwart tracker attacks by checking sizes of implied query sets for each query. An implied query set is one that can be computed from the actual query and other permissible queries. This technique, however, can demand excessive computation since there may be many implied query sets for each individual query.

Overlap query control uses an audit trail and restricts queries in which the query sets have more than a small specified number of records in common. This technique can, however, cause excessive information loss, e.g. a query covering a substantial part of the database can cause virtually any other associated query to be forbidden.

An audit trail is used, in the audit expert technique, to develop a binary matrix that indicates whether or not a given query could reveal information about an individual. The columns of the binary matrix correspond to individuals; the rows represent a basis for the set of queries deducible from previous queries. If a query results in a matrix update with a row containing all zeros, except for one column, then that query could disclose information on the individual corresponding to that column.

An a priori method is used to determine that cells are to be suppressed in the cell suppression technique. It is not sufficient to withhold information in an individual cell because that data can be easily deduced from higher level tables in the lattice. For example, consider table T4 (Fig. 1), if the cell, corresponding to age 0 - 20, salary 60,001 - 80,000, is left blank then the data can be deduced by simply summing the rem-

aining cells in the age column and subtracting the result from the 0 - 20 cell in higher level table T3. Adjoining cells of T4 are therefore also suppressed until the sensitive statistic is protected. The a priori computations can be performed once for the complete database and do not therefore involve excessive computation for each query. However, the total computational load may be infeasible if the statistics are released for a large number attributes, or if the database is subject to many updates.

In the grouping, or rolling up, technique attributes are grouped together to ensure that no cell can reveal personal data. Thus in Fig. 1 a grouping of the higher salary ranges into a single range of 40 001 to 80 000 would ensure that no cell corresponded to less than 2 records.

Inference Control - Addition of Noise
Perturbation techniques modify the statistics returned to the user in such a manner that the information supplied is adequate for its intended purpose but cannot be manipulated to reveal accurate data concerning an individual. For example, the danger of compromise can be reduced by adding random numbers, or noise, to individual data items as they are extracted by the selection criteria and used to compute an overall statistic, e.g. an average. The total effect of the random numbers, that will have both positive and negative values, should not materially affect the computed statistic. However, it is sufficient to render any illegitimately deduced data, that may for example be the difference of two large perturbed numbers, meaningless.

The disadvantage of perturbation techniques is that they can cause information loss due to bias and consistency factors. Bias is the difference between the expectation of the perturbed statistic and its true value. Lack of consistency refers to the contradictions that can arise when a repetition of the same query produces different results, e.g. the returned average value can differ from the average computed by dividing the result of queries producing the sum and count respectively.

Perturbation techniques can be classified as record or result based. In record based queries either a sample of the records, satisfying the query, are selected and the overall statistic is estimated from the sample, or the individual records are perturbed, as they are used to compute the statistic. Result based methods apply perturbation to the result of the query after it has been correctly computed, e.g. by rounding off the result.

The record based perturbation techniques are: random sample queries and random data perturbations. In the case of random sample queries a selection procedure is applied to each record as it is extracted by the query criteria. The selection criteria determine whether or not the record is to be used on the desired statistic. The statistic is estimated from a sample of the query set and it is therefore difficult, if not impossible, to identify the data of an individual record.

Random data perturbation adds a random number to the data, of each record that is extracted, to compute the overall statistic. This technique is subject to averaging attacks in which the same query is repeated several times so that the total effect of the added noise can be successively reduced. A second disadvantage of this technique is that it can cause difficulties for users in terms of inconsistencies, e.g. it is possible for negative counts to be returned.

Result based perturbation techniques are:

- systematic rounding;
- systematic ranges;
- random rounding;
- controlled rounding.

Systematic rounding involves rounding off data according to some predetermined value. This technique can lead to inconsistency, e.g. the rounded sum of

numbers can differ from the sum of rounded numbers.

The presentation of systematic rounded data may be provided in the form of systematic ranges, thus if the number 13 is rounded to the nearest multiple of 5 then it is represented by the range 10-14, instead of the number 15.

Random rounding selects randomly the lower or upper extreme of the rounding range, e.g. the number 7 may be represented by 5 or 10. This technique is unbiased but to avoid inconsistencies the result of rounding should be such that equivalent queries always give the same result.

Controlled rounding avoids the inconsistency of rounded sums that differ from the sum of the rounded numbers.

Filters

The security of large database systems, employed by users with differing security classifications, poses particular problems. The complexity of a large DBMS mitigates against formal verification procedures that would give an assurance that data with a security classification of d is never delivered to a user with a security classification less than d. There are four kinds of attack that can lead to the unauthorized disclosure of classified data:

- direct access;
- indirect access by inference,
- Trojan Horse direct release;
- Trojan Horse leakage.

The direct access threat simply responds to a user's request for data at a classification level greater than that authorized for the user. An indirect attack by inference enables a user to pose a query involving selection of records according to the value of data items that have a higher classification than that of the user. The actual data returned to the user is at the user's authorized level but it enables the user to infer information of a higher security level. For example, if the names of certain weapon systems are top secret, but those of the component suppliers for the manufacture of those systems are only classified as confidential, then a query on the names of suppliers for the top secret weapon system ZEUS will reveal the list of suppliers for that top secret system.

Trojan Horses in the DBMS can seek out classified data and make it available to unauthorized users. A Trojan Horse direct attack supplies classified information by changing its security label or relocating the data into a record with a lower security classification. A Trojan Horse leakage attack encodes classified information and supplies it to the unauthorized user, apparently as a response to a legitimate query. The user then decodes the response and extracts the classified information. For example, the Trojan Horse user might set up an unclassified table with 26 names of towns. If the Trojan Horse needs to release a name, that has a top secret connotation, then it would encode the name into numbers, with each letter replaced by a number representing its alphabetic position, and then return the towns corresponding to those numbers.

The threats to a multilevel database are such that it is extremely difficult to design a DBMS that will guarantee the system security. A proposed approach separates out the security function and entrusts it to a filter located between the user and the DBMS. The separation of database access and security checking system implies that the formal security verification need only be applied to the filter and thus need not extend to the complex software of the DBMS.

In one approach the filter applies a cryptographic checksum to each item of data that is to be labelled with a security classification. The checksum is effectively a MAC computed over the data item, and classification label, using a secret key known only to the filter. The data itself is stored in clear and can therefore be manipulated by the DBMS;

any unauthorized attempt to modify stored data, or to change its security classification, will however be detected by the filter when it validates the checksum. This technique, termed integrity locking, has been nicknamed spray paint because each item of data is indelibly colored with its classification.

The filter is responsible for checking the security classification of data and comparing it with that of the user before releasing it. The classification label may be stored with the data in clear or encrypted form, or the labels may be stored within the filter. The former opens up the danger of attacks by a Trojan Horse that captures and releases highly classified data. Simple encryption of the labels with a single key is insecure because all top secret labels (say) will have the same ciphertext value. In these circumstances an attacker could collaborate with a Trojan Horse to determine the ciphertext classification labels, e.g. by inserting items with low classification labels so that the Trojan Horse could develop a list of the ciphertext version of such labels and hence determine the corresponding ciphertexts of higher level classifications.

The security of the labels can be increased by using a cryptographic key that is a function of a secret key and the data itself, e.g. the record id and attribute name; this technique effectively provides a separate key for each individual classification label. The label can also be separated entirely from the data and stored in the secure filter. The main disadvantage of this approach is that it increases the functions of the filter to storage and retrieval of labels, this will necessarily add to the complexity of the filter software and conflicts with the concept that the filter should be simple enough to permit formal security verification.

The classification labels can be applied to whole relations, attributes, records or individual data items. Likewise the cryptographic checksums may be applied at the relation, attribute, record or data item level. The data delivered to the filter must be such that the checksum can be computed and validated, if the checksum is computed over a large body of data then a simple query, involving one data item, will involve retrieval and transfer of large data blocks to the filter. On the other hand checksums computed over single data items introduce the danger that such items may be illegally transferred from one record to another.

The function of the filter is to compute checksums using a stored secret key, to validate the checksums of data returned to it by the DBMS and to determine whether or not the response to queries lies within the user's level of privilege. The functions of the filter should be kept as simple as possible to facilitate the formal verification of its security. Thus the filter should not have the complex accessing and retrieval functions of the DBMS. However Trojan Horse attacks are still possible if the security labels and checksums are not stored by the filter independent of the DBMS data handling. A Trojan Horse could, for example, simply fail to update the security classification of a data item. Thus if the Trojan Horse detects that the filter has changed the checksum of some data item, when the data itself is unchanged, then it is clear that the classification has been changed. The Trojan Horse could then simply restore the previous checksum, and its encrypted classification label, to its original value and the filter would be unable to detect the actions of the Trojan Horse.

Trojan Horse attacks are difficult to suppress even if the filter has the extended task of storing labels and checksums. For example an attack could follow the stages:

- (i) a Trojan Horse collaborator initiates a query that causes the DBMS to retrieve a set of records with varying security classifications;

- (ii) the Trojan Horse notes all these records;
- (iii) the filter passes only those records within the user's security clearance;
- (iv) the user then makes a query that only returns those records released by the filter in response to the first query;
- (v) the Trojan Horse notes the sets of records accessed by the DBMS for the second query and deletes them from the set collected in (ii);
- (vi) the Trojan Horse leaks the remaining higher classification records to the user.

See A PRIORI CONTROL, ATTRIBUTE, AUDIT BASED CONTROL, AUDIT EXPERT, AUDIT TRAIL, BIAS, CELL RESTRICTION, CELL SUPPRESSION, COMPROMISE, CONSISTENCY, CONTROLLED ROUNDING, CRYPTOGRAPHIC CHECKSUM, DATA PROTECTION, DBMS, DISCLOSURE RISK, FIELD, FILTER, GROUPING, IMPLIED QUERIES CONTROL, INFERENCE CONTROL, INFORMATION LOSS, KEY MANAGEMENT, LATTICE MODEL, MEMORYLESS CONTROL, MULTILEVEL DATABASE SECURITY, NEGATIVE DISCLOSURE, N-RESPONDENT, K%-DOMINANCE, OPERATING SYSTEM, ORDER CONTROL, OVERLAP CONTROL, PERSONAL DISCLOSURE, QUERY SET SIZE CONTROL, RANDOM DATA PERTURBATION, RANDOM ROUNDING, RANDOM SAMPLE QUERIES, RECORD, RELATIVE TABLE SIZE CONTROL, SENSITIVE STATISTIC, SPRAY PAINT, STATISTICAL DATABASE, SUBSCHEMA, SYSTEMATIC RANGES, SYSTEMATIC ROUNDING, TABLE RESTRICTION, TRACKER, TROJAN HORSE, UPDATE INCONSISTENCY, VIEW, WORK FACTOR.

data bits. In data communications, the number of bits transmitted per character, not including checking and timing bits. See BIT.

data bus coupler. In communications, a component that interconnects a number of optical waveguides and provides an inherently bidirectional system by mixing and splitting all signals in it. *See* DATA BUS, FIBER OPTICS.

data capture. In computing, the act of obtaining data by means of peripheral devices, e.g. a point of sale terminal. *See* POINT OF SALE TERMINAL.

data carrier detect. In data communications, an interface signal from a modem to a DTE indicating that a carrier signal of adequate quality is being received. *See* CARRIER, DTE.

data cell. In computing, the smallest unit of data that cannot be further subdivided, e.g. a bit. *See* BIT.

data chain. In computing, blocks of data linked together by pointers.

data channel. *See* CHANNEL.

data circuit. In data communications, a circuit that enables two way communication to be carried out between any two data terminating devices such as teleprinters, computers, visual display units, etc.

data circuit terminating equipment. In data communications, a piece of equipment located at either end of a data circuit that provides all the functions needed to establish, maintain and terminate a connection. It also carries out the signal conversion and coding between the data terminal equipment and the telephone line. *Compare* DATA TERMINAL EQUIPMENT. *See* MODEM.

data collection. In computing, an activity in which data from several locations is accumulated at one place prior to processing.

data communications. The exchange of messages, encoded in the form of binary data, between two normally geo-graphically separate communicating parties (or end users) over a communications network.

Overview
The communicating parties may be people or computer based applications such as transaction processing systems. The types of messages to be exchanged include:

- voice (e.g. telephone conversation);
- data (e.g. Automatic Teller Machine transaction);
- video (e.g. television);
- graphics (e.g. facsimile);
- text (e.g. contents of a book);

or any combination of these.

Associated with each communicating party there is an end user device through which the communication occurs or which supports the communicating applications. In the case of a telephone conversation the end user devices are the telephone handsets, whilst in the case of a banking transaction, the end user devices are Automatic Teller Machines (ATM) and some form of host computer system supporting the ATM banking application (Fig. 1).

A communications network is an interconnected set of physical components which transport the messages between the end user devices according to a previously agreed set of 'quality of service' parameters. These parameters determine the extent to which:

- the service provided by the communications network is subject to interruption or loss of continuity (network service availability/ reliability);
- the privacy of the messages being exchanged may be compromised (message confidentiality);
- the messages being exchanged are subject to corruption or modification (message integrity);

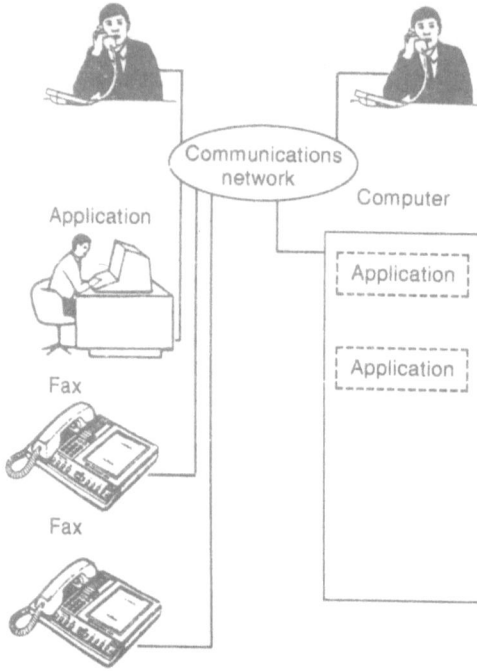

Fig. 1. Communication network

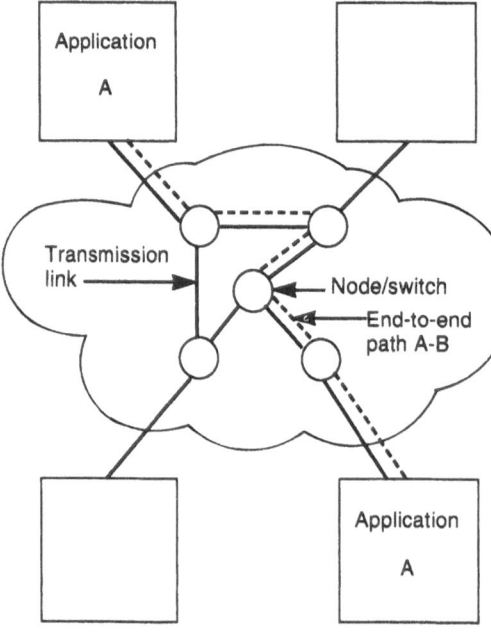

Fig. 2(a). Switched network

• the time delays in delivering the messages across the communications network.

The set of physical components which comprise a communications network include transmission links and network nodes. Transmission links are the paths over which the messages travel as they traverse the communications network. A variety of transmission media is used to provide transmission links including copper wire (twisted pair cables, coaxial cables), glass (optical fiber cables) and air/ vacuum (for the transmission of electromagnetic radiation).

Network nodes, also termed switches or Interface Message Processors (IMP), are typically computer processors that terminate individual transmission link segments, and which route messages between the end user devices. They also provide the interface between the end user devices and the communications network.

Networks

The two basic types of communications networks are switched communications networks, and broadcast communications networks.

A switched communications network (Fig. 2a) comprises a concatenated set of network nodes and transmission link segments that together provide an end-to-end path for the exchange of messages between end user devices. An example of this type of network is the Public Switched Telephone Network (PSTN) used for voice communications. Another important type of switched network, designed for data messages (e.g. financial transactions in a banking network), is a Packet Switched Data Network (PSDN).

In a broadcast communications network there is a single shared transmission link between all the end user devices. Examples of this type of network include satellite systems, the cellular mobile telephone network (Fig. 2b) and Local Area Networks (LANs) (Fig. 2c).

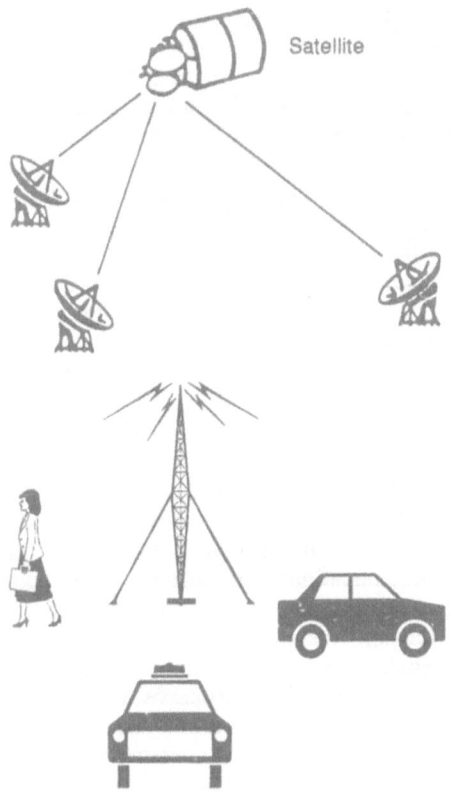

Fig. 2(b) Broadcast network

Transmission Signals

The network node connects the end user devices to the network. It converts messages from the type and format employed by end user devices into physical transmission signals so that they may be transmitted across a transmission link segment. The messages to be transmitted are either digital (e.g. a file of information stored in a computer system) or analog (e.g. a voice conversation). Examples of physical transmission signals include voltage levels on an electrical conductor, the intensity of a light beam in an optical fibre, and radio waves. The physical transmission signals are also either digital (i.e. one in which the signal level has only discrete values) or analog (i.e. one in which the signal level varies continuously).

Early communications networks designed for voice communications used analog transmission signalling techniques. Hence such networks required the conversion of data messages, generated by digital computer systems, to analog transmission signals. This process is termed modulation and is performed by a modem (modulator/demodulator). Modern communications networks, on the other hand, are designed to use digital transmission technologies and are therefore essentially a bit transport system. In using these networks, analog messages such as voice conversations and video must first be converted to digital transmission signals using a codec (coder/decoder). Pulse Code Modulation (PCM) is commonly used to convert an analog signal to digital form.

Communication Protocols

A communications network is required to provide a service to the end user devices that satisfies a specified set of the 'quality-of-service' criteria such as message integrity.

A number of processes are required to enable a communications network to control and manage the transport of messages between the end user devices. These processes are implementations of rules (or protocols) which specify, for example:

- how the overall exchange of messages is to be managed;
- the format of the messages to be exchanged;
- how messages are to be addressed and routed;
- procedures to detect transmission errors and to initiate corrective action, i.e. error control;
- procedures for preventing the sending node from overwhelming the receiving node by transmitting more data than the receiving node can process, i.e. flow control.

The total set of rules governing the interchange of information between end user devices, particularly for data applications, is potentially extremely large. Hence the rules are typically grouped into layers, where a given protocol layer contains a set of related functions (e.g. the exchange of data across a single transmission link, message routing across a network).

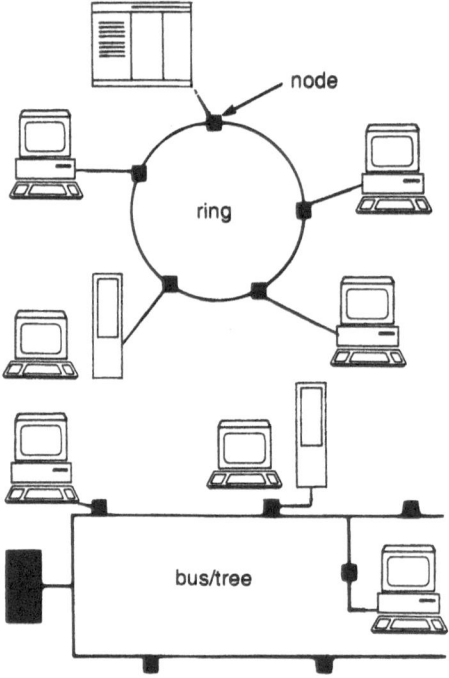

data communication
Fig. 2(c). Local area network

The layers constitute a protocol hierarchy or communications architecture. Examples of layered communications architectures include System Network Architecture (SNA) developed by IBM, Transmission Control Protocol/ Internet Protocol (TCP/IP) developed by the U.S. Department of Defence and the Reference Model for Open Systems Interconnection (OSI RM) (Fig. 3) developed under the aegis of the International Standards Organization.

The OSI RM communications architecture provides a basis for discussion of the general characteristics of such architectures. For example, the physical level protocols (the physical layer) specify how both control and data signals are to be represented (e.g. the value of the voltage levels for logical 0 and 1). In addition the physical layer defines other transmission signal characteristics such as the time duration of a signal and the sequence of signals required to effect a transfer of data. The physical layer also specifies mechanical characteristics such as the dimensions of the transmission link connectors and the number and arrangement of pins and sockets. One of the most widely used physical interface standards is the Electronic Industries Association (EIA) RS-232-C.

The role of the data link layer in the communications architecture is to control and manage the process of data exchange (as distinct from transmission signals) over a single transmission link. A fundamental requirement is to place suitable delimiters around the transmitted data segments to ensure synchronization between sender and receiver. In asynchronous transmission the transmitted data segments are single (e.g. 8 bit) character delimited by start and stop bits. The characters are transmitted independently (asynchronously) across the transmission link. In (bit-oriented) synchronous transmission the unit of data transfer is a transmission frame which is delimited by a separate reserved bit pattern known as a flag field (Fig. 4). A transmission frame containing end user message segments may be of arbitrary length but is typically in the range 500-2000 bits.

The data link layer is responsible for maintaining the integrity of the individual data segments transmitted over the link. To this end each data segment (i.e. character or frame) carries additional error-control information (generated by the transmitting node) which enables the receiving node to verify (to a required degree) that there has been no corrup-

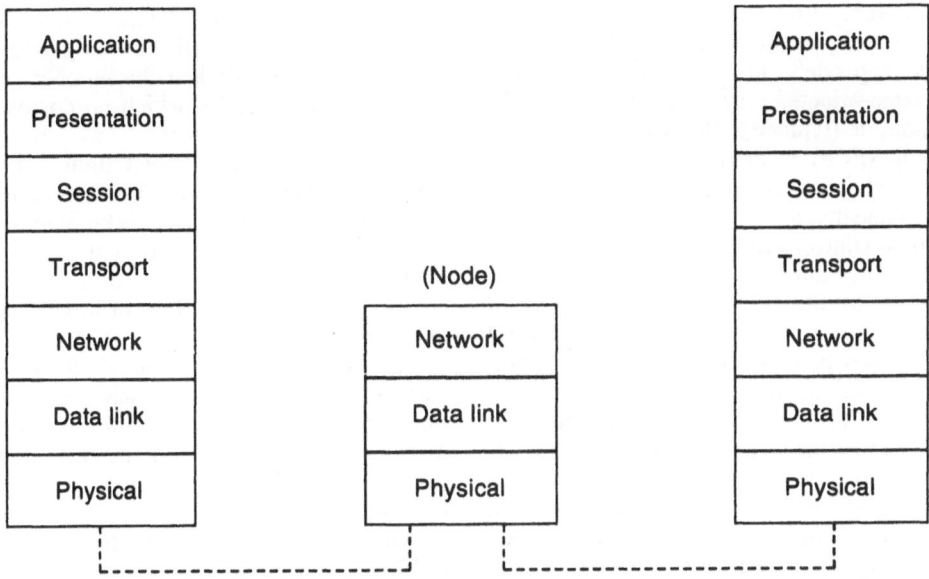

Fig. 3. Communication architecture

01111110 Flag (8 bits)	Address (8 bits)	Control (8 bits)	Information	Frame checksum (FCS) (16 bits)	01111110 Flag (8 bits)

Control:

I: information	0	N(S)		P/F	N(R)
S: supervisory	1	0	S	P/F	N(R)
U: Unnumbered	1	1	M	P/F	M

Fig. 4. Transmission frame

tion of the data segments during transmission. For asynchronous character-oriented transmission a single parity-bit is appended to each character. For frame-oriented synchronous transmission, a (typically 16 bit) frame checksum (FCS) is used to verify each individual data segment.

Transmission frames also carry additional control information, in the form of sequence numbers, used by the receiving node to detect loss or duplication of frames. In forward error control schemes there is sufficient error control information, in each data segment, to enable the receiving node to detect a transmission error in that data segment, and to attempt to correct the error. Feedback error control schemes require the receiving node to acknowledge the receipt of correct and in-sequence data segments, or to request retransmission in the event that a problem is detected (e.g. corrupt data segments, lost or duplicated data segments).

At the data link level, the sending node exercises an additional level of error control over the transmission process through a 'time out' mechanism. If an acknowledgment for a data segment is not received within a predefined time interval, the sending node initiates corrective action, such as automatically retransmitting the data segment (up to a specified limit).

Flow control is implemented at the data link level, in one of two ways. In the first, the receiving node transmits a supervisory/ control data segment, (e.g. an XOFF control character for asynchronous transmission, a Receiver Not Ready (RNR) frame for synchronous transmission), to the sending node in order to inhibit further transmission. When the receiving node is ready for further transmissions it sends a corresponding supervisory/ control data segment, (e.g. an XON control character for asynchronous transmission, a Receiver Ready (RR) frame for synchronous transmission).

In the second basic flow control mechanism, employed in frame oriented transmission schemes, the sending node ceases transmission when the number of transmitted frames, for which no corresponding acknowledgment has been received, attain a predefined limit. The limit is termed a Send Window and transmission resumes as acknowledgments arrive at the receiving node.

The data link layer also controls access to the transmission link in broadcast networks (e.g. Local Area Networks) where a number of terminal devices share the common link. Schemes for link access arbitration include polling mechanisms, token passing mechanisms (as used in token ring and token bus LANs), and contention mechanisms such as the Carrier Sense Multiple Access/ Collision Detection (CSMA/CD) used in the Ethernet LAN system.

The primary function of the network layer, in the architecture of Fig.3, is to provide end-to-end routing of data segments, between the end user devices, through the communications network. This requirement for routing capabilities arises in switched communications networks, i.e. networks in which an end-to-end path is created by a concatenated set of transmission links and nodes (e.g. a Packet Switched Data Network PSDN). In such networks a communications network node may have a choice of number of transmission links leading to the final destination.

At the network layer level the data segments are called packets and a single packet is typically less than 2000 bits in length. Depending on the type of messages being exchanged between the end user devices, a packet may contain a complete message or part of a message.

The network layer operates in one of two basic modes. In a virtual circuit (or connection-oriented) mode the end user devices first exchange supervisory/ control packets which establish an end-to-end path between the end user devices. Once the route through the communications network is established, all subsequent packets containing messages between the end user devices use this route. This is similar in operation to the Public Switched Telephone Network (PSTN) in which an end-to-end circuit is established between the end user devices at the time of call connection.

The other basic mode of operation of the network layer is a datagram (or connectionless) mode. In this mode the packets (or datagrams) containing messages are treated by the network nodes as self-contained entities. Each packet is routed independently through the network and end-to-end delivery is on a 'best-effort' basis. Hence, in a datagram mode of operation, packets may arrive in any sequence whereas in a virtual circuit mode of operation, the packet sequence is maintained. A datagram mode of operation is analogous to the postal system.

The primary goals in network routing are to deliver the packets reliably (and correctly) across the network with minimal delay and at least cost. A number of different routing strategies have been developed to achieve these goals, although most rely on some form of directory (or table) stored in each network node. At the simplest level, the directory contains a static set of information indicating which transmission link is to be selected to reach a particular node. This 'fixed-routing' (Fig. 5) scheme has the advantage of simplicity, it provides poor performance in peak load situations (i.e. during periods of heavy congestion) and also a lack of resilience to component failure. Alternative strategies use a variety of adaptive techniques which enable network nodes to monitor network conditions through the exchange of supervisory/ control information and to react dynamically.

The primary function of the Transport Layer in this illustration is to provide end-to-end management of the exchange of messages between the end user devices. The requirement for such ex-

change management functions (e.g. end-to-end message integrity) arises in the case of a communications network using a datagram (connectionless) mode of operation at the network layer level, where there can be no guarantee that the totality of packets will be delivered. Similarly in a virtual circuit (connection-oriented) mode, a network node may encounter hardware, software, or transmission problems which require it to reset either a single virtual circuit connection or multiple connections.

As part of its management role, the Transport Layer may be required to partition the messages, from the end user devices, into data segments of a size which satisfies the packet requirements of the Network Layer. It then appends to each such data segment supervisory/error-control information such as a computed checksum and data segment sequence numbers. The checksum procedure enables the corresponding Transport Layer in the receiving party to detect transmission errors which have not been detected by the error-control procedures in the Data Link Layers. The data-segment sequence numbering information enables the detection of lost or duplicate data segments.

The Session, Presentation, and Application layers in the OSI Reference Model provide functions which relate to the management of an application being used by the end user devices.

The CCITT X.25 standard is a widely used standard for accessing packet switched networks. The standard defines a three layer protocol for a virtual circuit mode of operation incorporating a physical level, a link level and a packet level.

The Transmission Control Protocol/Internet Protocol (TCP/IP) developed by the U.S. Department of Defence provides functions similar to those described for the Transport and Network layers in the example above. In the TCP/IP architecture, the Internet Proto-

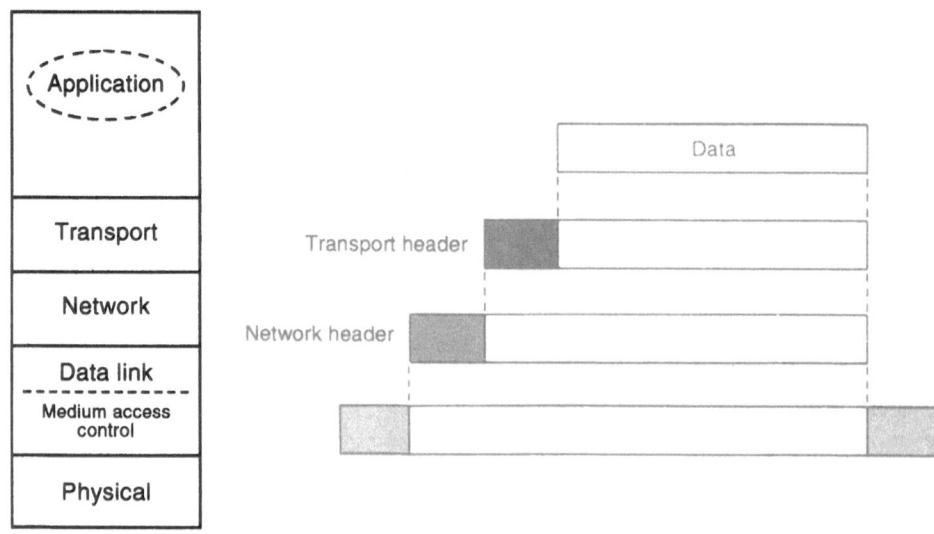

Fig. 5. Protocol hierarchy

col (IP) layer provides a datagram (connectionless) service to the Transmission Control Protocol (TCP) layer. The TCP layer provides for reliable end-to-end error control and flow control.

Integrated Services Digital Network (ISDN) is an important development in data communications; all the signalling and switching functions of the network are performed using digital techniques. This will make a substantial impact on the range of services offered by the network and the cost and reliability of those services. See APPLICATION LAYER, ASYNCHRONOUS TRANSMISSION, ATM, CCITT, CELLULAR RADIO, CODEC, CONNECTIONLESS SERVICE, CSMA-CD, DATAGRAM, DATA LINK LAYER, ETHERNET, FIBER OPTICS, FIXED ROUTING, FLOW CONTROL, FORWARD ERROR CONTROL, LOCAL AREA NETWORK, INTERFACE MESSAGE PROCESSOR, INTERNATIONAL STANDARDS ORGANIZATION, ISDN, MODEM, NETWORK LAYER, OPEN SYSTEMS INTERCONNECTION, PACKET, PACKET SWITCHING NETWORK, PHYSICAL LAYER, POLLING, PRESENTATION LAYER, PROTO-COL, PULSE CODE MODULATION, RS-232C, SESSION LAYER, SLIDING WINDOW PROTOCOL, START BIT, STOP BIT, SYNCHRONOUS TRANSMISSION, SYSTEM NETWORK ARCHITECTURE, TOKEN RING, TOKEN BUS, TRANSMISSION CONTROL PROTOCOL/INTERNET PROTOCOL, TRANSPORT LAYER, VIRTUAL CIRCUIT, XON-XOFF PROTOCOL, X.25.

data compression. (1) In codes, the reduction of the size of data by coding techniques that exploit redundancies in the data. *See* REDUNDANCY. (2) In computing, a technique that saves storage space by eliminating gaps, empty fields, redundancies, or unnecessary data to shorten the length of records or blocks. *See* NULL SUPPRESSION.

data confidentiality. In data security, the state that exists when the data is held in confidence and protected from unauthorized disclosure. *Compare* DATA INTEGRITY. *See* ADP AVAILABILITY, APPLICATION CONFIDENTIALITY, APPLICATION INTEGRITY, CONFIDENTIALITY.

data connection. In data communications, the interconnection of a number of circuits designed to carry data signals. Special switching equipment is required so that data may be transmitted between data terminal equipment. *See* DATA TERMINAL EQUIPMENT, SWITCHING.

data contamination. In computer security, a deliberate or accidental process or act that results in a change in the integrity of the original data. (FIPS). *See* DATA DIDDLING.

data corruption. In data security, a deliberate or accidental violation of data integrity. *See* DATA INTEGRITY.

data coupler. In data communications, a device that enables the connection of customer provided modems to the telephone network. It limits the power applied to the line and provides network control and signalling functions. *See* MODEM.

Datacrime. In computer security, a virus that encrypts itself, infects COM files, corrupts program and OVL files, formats and overwrites all or part of disk. *See* VIRUS NAMES.

Datacrime-B. In computer security, a virus that encrypts itself, infects COM files, corrupts program and OVL files, formats and overwrites all or part of disk. *See* VIRUS NAMES.

Datacrime II. In computer security, a virus that encrypts itself, infects COM and EXE files, corrupts program and OVL files, formats and overwrites all or part of disk. *See* VIRUS NAMES.

Datacrime II-B. In computer security, a virus that encrypts itself, infects COMMAND.COM, COM files and EXE files, corrupts program and OVL files, formats and overwrites all or part of disk. *See* VIRUS NAMES.

data-dependent protection. In data security, protection of data at a level commensurate with the sensitivity level of the individual data elements, rather than with the sensitivity of the entire file that includes the data elements. (FIPS).

data description language. In databases, the language for describing the data. Such languages will provide very detailed definitions of the structures and relationship of the data.

data dictionary. In databases, a centralized repository of information about the stored data, providing details of the meaning, relationship to other data, origin, usage and format. *See* DBA, DATABASE MANAGEMENT SYSTEM.

data diddling. In data security, the changing of stored data values for illegal purposes. *See* DATA CONTAMINATION, DATA INTEGRITY.

data element. *Synonymous with* DATA ITEM.

data-encrypting key. In key management, a cryptographic key used for encrypting (and decrypting) data.(FIPS) *Compare* KEY-ENCRYPTING KEY. *Synonymous with* PRIMARY KEY.

data encryption algorithm. In cryptography, an ANSI encryption standard, ANSI X3.92 - 1981, identical to the cryptographic function that forms part of the data encryption standard, FIPS Pub 46. *See* ANSI, DATA ENCRYPTION STANDARD.

data encryption standard. In cryptography, the Data Encryption Standard specifies an algorithm to be implemented in electronic hardware devices and used for the cryptographic protection of computer data. The algorithm is a product cipher employing 64 bit data blocks and a 64 bit key. The standard was published by the National Bureau of Standards in January 1977, as FIPS Publication 46. It became mandatory for U.S. Federal agencies in June 1977.

DES is based upon an earlier product cipher, named Lucifer and developed by IBM. It uses 64 bit data blocks and a 64 bit key, the cryptographic key, however, employs 8 parity bits and thus from a cryptographic viewpoint it is only a 56 bit key. The flow of data in the DES algorithm is illustrated in Fig.1.

The data is subjected to transpositions and substitutions in P boxes (IP, IP^1, E and P) and S boxes respectively. The key is also subjected to transpositions in permutation boxes PC1, PC2 and shift registers C and D. There are 16 rounds of operation for the data and each round involves operations with a different 48 bit key developed from the original 64 bit cryptographic key. The operations on the data are illustrated in the ladder diagram of Fig. 2.

The input data block is first subjected to a straight permutation, IP. In this case the bits are simply rearranged as shown in Table 1.

Table 1
IP

58	50	42	34	26	18	10	2
60	52	44	36	28	20	12	4
62	54	46	38	30	22	14	6
64	56	48	40	32	24	16	8
57	49	41	33	25	17	9	1
59	51	43	35	27	19	11	3
61	53	45	37	29	21	13	5
63	55	47	39	31	23	15	7

Thus the first octet of the input appears in bit positions 40, 8, 48, 16, 56, 24, 64 and 32 of the output respectively. Neither this permutation nor the input to it is affected by the key; it is said to have been included for convenience of implementation but it has no cryptographic function. The output of this stage is split into two 32 bit blocks, the left hand block is passed to 32 bit regis-

ter L32, and the right hand to R32. The 32 bits of R32 are then subjected to the expanded permutation E (Table 2).

Table 2
E

32	1	2	3	4	5
4	5	6	7	8	9
8	9	10	11	12	13
12	13	14	15	16	17
16	17	18	19	20	21
20	21	22	23	24	25
24	25	26	27	28	29
28	29	30	31	32	1

In this case some of the inputs appear in 2 output positions, e.g. bit 4 occurs in output positions 5 and 7. In this way the 32 bit input block is both transposed and expanded into a 48 bit output block. The output of the E block is added modulo 2 to the first stage output of the key generator and the result is subjected to a substitution cipher in eight S boxes. These S boxes operate in parallel, each accepting 6 bit inputs and generating 4 bit outputs (Table 3).

The 48 bit input is divided into eight 6 bit blocks, each of which enters one of the S boxes. Each S box may be considered as a ROM containing data organized in 4 rows and 16 columns, thus each position in the matrix for the S box corresponds to one of the 64 possible inputs. The matrix element is determined by the row, selected by bits 1 and 6 of the input, e.g. 1xxxx0 selects row 2. Bits 2..5 of the input determine the column of the matrix element, e.g. if the first 6 bit block of the input is 110 000 then row 2 (10) column 8 (1000) of the first S box is selected giving output 1111 (decimal 15).

The 4 bit outputs of the 8 S boxes are collected to form a 32 bit output block which is then subjected to straight permutation P (Table 4). This permutation simply transposes the 32 bit input giving a 32 bit output, e.g. bit 1 of the input is transposed to bit 9 of the output. The 32 bit output of P is exclusive or'ed to the contents of the L32 register and the result is placed in a temporary 32 bit store.

Table 3
S Boxes
Columns

0	1	2	3	4	5	6	7	8	9	10	11	12	13	14	15
14	4	13	1	2	15	11	8	3	10	6	12	5	9	0	7
0	15	7	4	14	2	13	1	10	6	12	11	9	5	3	8
4	1	14	8	13	6	2	11	15	12	9	7	3	10	5	0
15	12	8	2	4	9	1	7	5	11	3	14	10	0	6	13
15	1	8	14	6	11	3	4	9	7	2	13	12	0	5	10
3	13	4	7	15	2	8	14	12	0	1	10	6	9	11	5
0	14	7	11	10	4	13	1	5	8	12	6	9	3	2	15
13	8	10	1	3	15	4	2	11	6	7	12	0	5	14	9
10	0	9	14	6	3	15	5	1	13	12	7	11	4	2	8
13	7	0	9	3	4	6	10	2	8	5	14	12	11	15	1
13	6	4	9	8	15	3	0	11	1	2	12	5	10	14	7
1	10	13	0	6	9	8	7	4	15	14	3	11	5	2	12
7	13	14	3	0	6	9	10	1	2	8	5	11	12	4	15
13	8	11	5	6	15	0	3	4	7	2	12	1	10	14	9
10	6	9	0	12	11	7	13	15	1	3	14	5	2	8	4
3	15	0	6	10	1	13	8	9	4	5	11	12	7	2	14
2	12	4	1	7	10	11	6	8	5	3	15	13	0	14	9
14	11	2	12	4	7	13	1	5	0	15	10	3	9	8	6
4	2	1	11	10	13	7	8	15	9	12	5	6	3	0	14
11	8	12	7	1	14	2	13	6	15	0	9	10	4	5	3
12	1	10	15	9	2	6	8	0	13	3	4	14	7	5	11
10	15	4	2	7	12	9	5	6	1	13	14	0	11	3	8
9	14	15	5	2	8	12	3	7	0	4	10	1	13	11	6
4	3	2	12	9	5	15	10	11	14	1	7	6	0	8	13
4	11	2	14	15	0	8	13	3	12	9	7	5	10	6	1
13	0	11	7	4	9	1	10	14	3	5	12	2	15	8	6
1	4	11	13	12	3	7	14	10	15	6	8	0	5	9	2
6	11	13	8	1	4	10	7	9	5	0	15	14	2	23	12
13	2	8	4	6	15	11	1	10	9	3	14	5	0	12	7
1	15	13	8	10	3	7	4	12	5	6	11	0	14	9	2
7	11	4	1	9	12	14	2	0	6	10	13	15	3	5	8
2	1	14	7	4	10	8	13	15	12	9	0	3	5	6	11

The contents of the register R32 are transferred to the L32 register and R32 is then updated with the contents of the temporary 32 bit register. This completes the first of the 16 rounds; the key generator then produces a new 48 bit key and the process is repeated with the new contents of L32 and R32.

After 16 such iterations the contents of the L and R registers are cross-fed into the right and left hand 32 bit input blocks of IP⁻¹ permutation box, which produces the inverse permutation of IP and the output of the encryption routine.

Table 4
P

16	7	20	21
29	12	28	17
1	15	23	26
5	18	31	10
2	8	24	14
32	27	3	9
19	13	30	6
22	11	4	25

The DES key has 64 bits but only 56 bits may be independently selected, the remaining 8 bits are parity bits and therefore have no cryptographic function. The key generator accepts a 64 bit key input into the permutation box PC1 where every eighth bit is discarded and the remaining bits are permuted according to the data in Table 5, i.e. bit 57 appears as output bit 1, bit 8 is discarded and bit 9 is transposed to bit 7.

Table 5
PC1

	57	49	41	33	25	17	9
	1	58	50	42	34	26	18
C	10	2	59	51	43	35	27
	19	11	3	60	52	44	36
	63	55	47	39	31	23	15
	7	62	54	46	38	30	22
D	14	6	61	53	45	37	29
	21	13	5	28	20	12	4

The leftmost 28 bits of the output are transferred to shift register C and the rightmost to shift register D. The data in these registers is shifted to the left 1 or 2 bits, prior to each of the 16 rounds, (Table 6).

The contents of these registers are then fed into selected permutation box PC2 (Table 7) providing a 48 bit key output which is exclusive or'ed with the output of the E permutation.

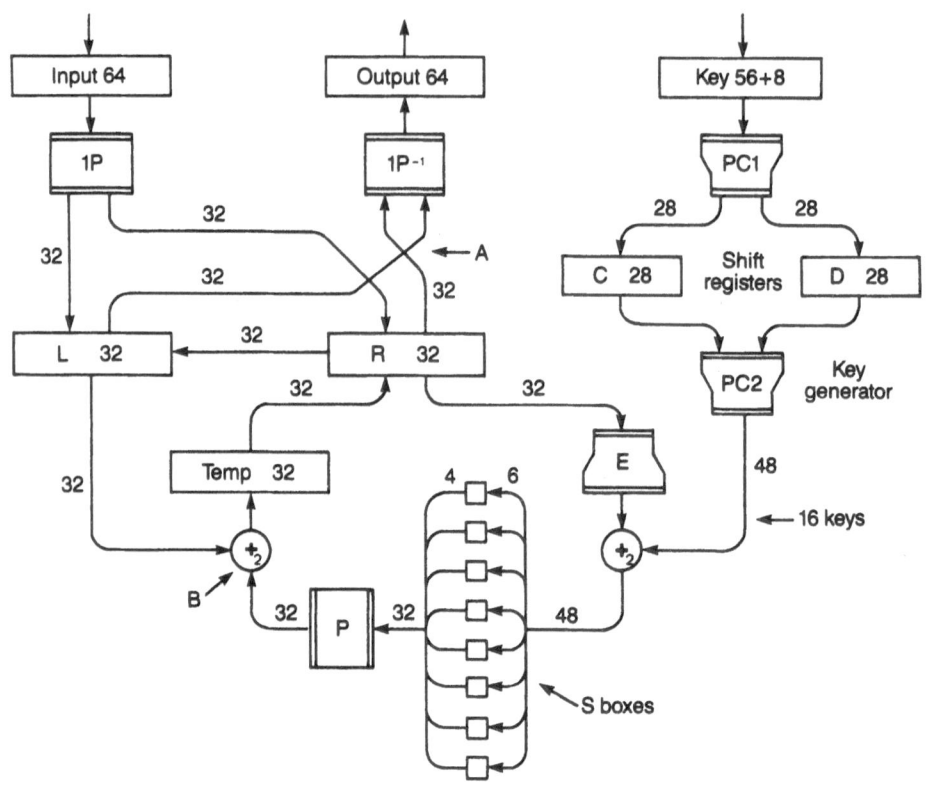

data encryption standard
Fig. 1. Logical structure.

TABLE 6
Key shifts for encipherment

Key	Number of shifts to the left
k_1	1
k_2	1
k_3	2
k_4	2
k_5	2
k_6	2
k_7	2
k_8	2
k_9	1
k_{10}	2
k_{11}	2
k_{12}	2
k_{13}	2
k_{14}	2
k_{15}	2
k_{16}	1

The process of decipherment is surprisingly straight forward and effectively repeats the encipherment action with the order of keys k_1, k_2 ...k_{16} reversed. The decipherment process can best be described in terms of the algebraic representation of the transformations.

Table 7
PC2

14	17	11	24	1	5
3	28	15	6	21	10
23	19	12	4	26	8
16	7	27	20	13	2
41	52	31	37	47	55
30	40	51	45	33	48
44	49	39	56	34	53
46	42	50	36	29	32

Let R_j, L_j, k_j represent the contents of registers L32, R32 and the 48 bit key (Fig 1) in the jth round. During encipherment:

$$L_j = R_{j-1} \qquad \text{eqn. 1}$$
$$R_j = L_{j-1} +_2 F(R_{j-1}, k_j) \qquad \text{eqn. 2}$$

where $F(R_{j-1}, k_j)$ is the output of the P box in the jth round and $+_2$ represents exclusive - or operation. These equations may be rewritten:

$$R_{j-1} = L_j$$

$$R_j +_2 F(R_{j-1}, k_j) = L_{j-1} +_2 F(R_{j-1}, k_j)$$
$$+_2 F(R_{j-1}, k_j)$$

Now $\qquad A +_2 A = 0$

Hence $\qquad R_{j-1} = L_j \qquad$ eqn. 3

and
$$L_{j-1} = R_j +_2 F(R_{j-1}, k_j) \quad \text{eqn. 4}$$

Substituting L_j for R_{j-1} in eqn. 4 gives

$$L_{j-1} = R_j +_2 F(L_j, k_j) \quad \text{eqn. 5}$$

The encipherment and decipherment process are illustrated in Fig. 3. At the first stage of encipherment:

$$R_2 = L_1 +_2 F(R_1, k_1)$$

$$L_2 = R_1$$

If we now follow the process from L16, R16; L16 is transposed by IP_{-1} to become the right hand half of the ciphertext block, at the decipherment stage it is undergoes the inverse transform and is then passed to the R0 register. Hence at the first stage of decipherment R0 contains L16, similarly L0 contains R16. Now from eqns. 3 and 5:

$$R_{15} = L_{16} \qquad \text{eqn. 3}$$
and
$$L_{15} = R_{16} +_2 F(L_{16}, k_{16}) \quad \text{eqn. 4}$$

Hence the encipherment action on the contents of L0 (=R16) and R0 (=L16) with key k_{16} has the effect of transferring the values L15 and R15 into the registers R1 and L1 respectively. Continuing in this manner results in the original plaintext at the end of the decipherment process.

These equations indicate that decipherment is performed by effectively performing the encipherment process with the order of the 16 keys, k_1, k_2...k_{16}, reversed. The production of the keys in reverse order for decipherment is undertaken by the key generator. During encipherment the contents of the 28 bit shift registers C and D are moved to the right a total of 28 times, thus the first key for decipherment k_{D1} corresponds to k_{16}. The subsequent set of shifts for C and D during decipherment are given in Table 8.

The processes of encipherment and decipherment depend upon the sequence of keys produced by the key generator. If for a particular key $k_1 = k_{16}$, $k_2 = k_{15}$ etc. then the same sequence is generated in the encipherment and decipherment processes; in this case double encryption will produce the original plaintext message; such keys are termed weak keys.

Table 8
Key shifts for decipherment

Key	Number of shifts to the right
k_1	0
k_2	1
k_3	2
k_4	2
k_5	2
k_6	2
k_7	2
k_8	2
k_9	1
k_{10}	2
k_{11}	2
k_{12}	2
k_{13}	2
k_{14}	2
k_{15}	2
k_{16}	1

A similar situation arises in the case of pairs of keys A, B with the property $A_1 = B_{16}$, $A_2 = B_{15}$... In this case encryp-

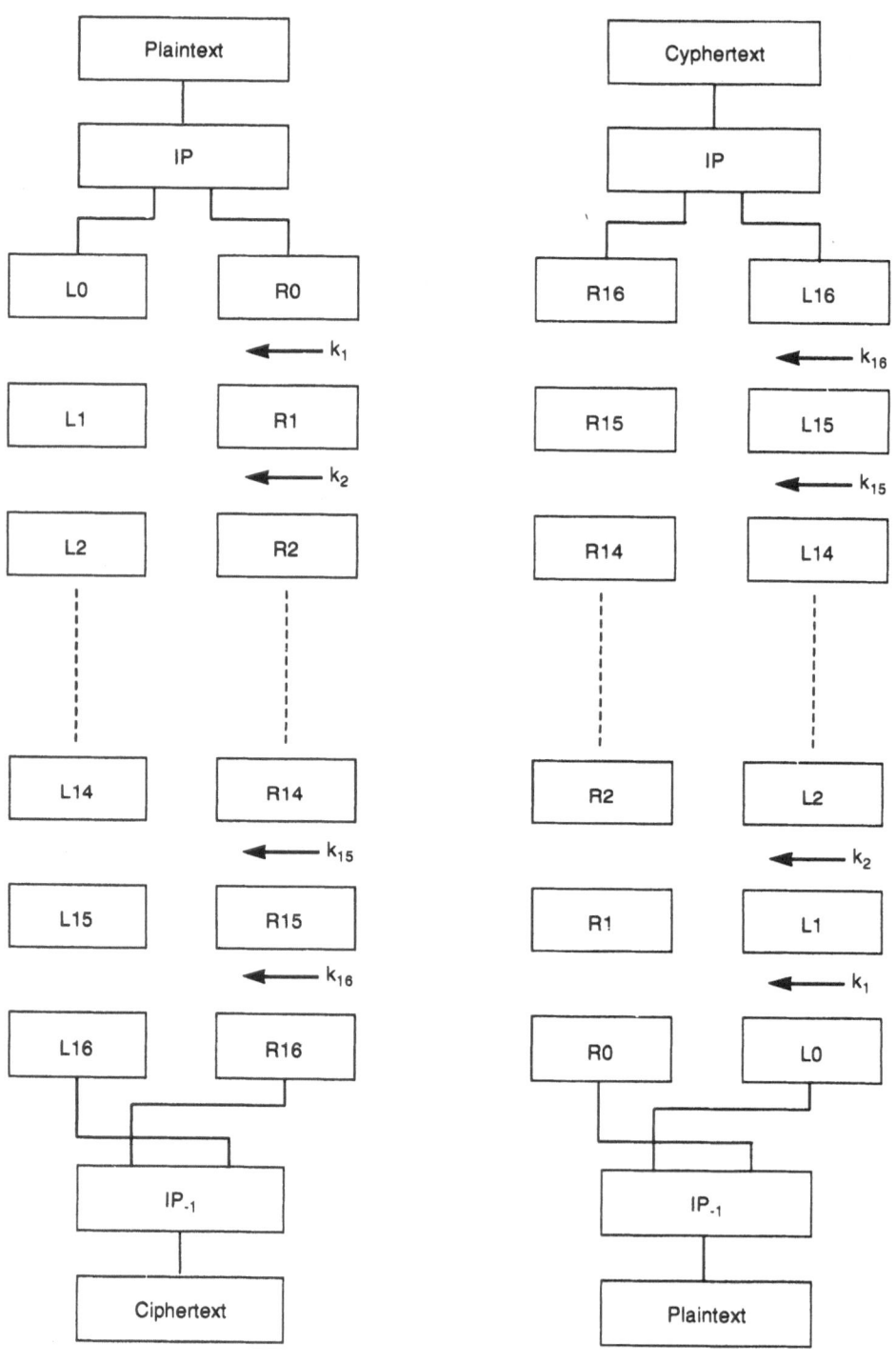

data encryption standard
Fig. 2. Ladder diagram

tion by one key followed by encryption with the second again produces the original plaintext; such key pairs are termed semiweak keys.

The security of DES has been the subject of considerable debate and a U.S. Senate investigation. The debate centered on the length of the DES key and upon the possibility that secret trapdoor functions were designed into the S boxes, no documentation on the design and reasons for the structure of the S boxes has ever been released. The effective length of the DES key is 56 bits and the possibility of a special purpose DES machine, with multiple parallel processors, which could search through all possible keys, has been debated but the conclusion of the Senate Select Committee was that the security of DES was adequate for its proposed field of use within its planned timespan.

The effective length of DES keys can be increased by multiple encipherment and this technique is employed for key-encrypting keys in some key management schemes. DES effectively transforms a 64 bit plaintext block into a 64 bit ciphertext block using a 56 bit key. It has the advantage of no message expansion and a comparatively short key. In effect, for a given key, DES may be considered as a codebook with 2^{64} entries. Thus the conventional DES mode is actually termed electronic codebook and it has a cryptographic weakness if highly formatted messages are enciphered with the same key. An attacker can detect the presence of commonly occurring ciphertext blocks and probably deduce plaintext-ciphertext pairs or at least gain some information on the nature of the traffic.

Other modes of DES operation, i.e. cipher block chaining, cipher feedback and output feedback can overcome these deficiencies of electronic codebook operation. DES may be implemented in software or hardware, LSI implementations can provide computation times of the order of microseconds thus provid-

ing high data rates for secure communication channels. *See* CIPHERTEXT, CRYPTOGRAPHIC KEY, ELECTRONIC CODEBOOK, EXCLUSIVE OR, FIPS, LUCIFER, MULTIPLE DES ENCIPHERMENT, PARITY BIT, P BOX, PLAINTEXT, PRODUCT CIPHER, S BOX, SEMIWEAK KEY, SUBSTITUTION CIPHER, TRANSPOSITION CIPHER, TRAPDOOR, WEAK KEY.

data exchange. In information security, functions to ensure the security of data during transmission over communication channels. *See* INFORMATION TECHNOLOGY SECURITY EVALUATION CRITERIA.

data flow analysis. In computer security, a method of static analysis that checks patterns of data used in the program, searching for: reference to variables not defined or set, variables set but not defined, variables set and not used etc. *See* STATIC ANALYSIS.

data flow control. *See* INFORMATION FLOW CONTROL.

data frame. In data communications, a packet of data transmitted over a network representing the whole or part of a message. *Compare* ACKNOWLEDGEMENT FRAME. *See* FRAME.

datagram. In data communications, a self contained packet, in a packet switching system, that contains sufficient routing information to enable it to reach its required destination. *See* DATAGRAM SERVICE, PACKET.

datagram service. In data communications, a connectionless service in which there is no acknowledgement of the arrival of individual datagrams. *Compare* CONNECTIONLESS SERVICE. *See* DATAGRAM.

data haven. In legislation, a region that is not subject to data protection legislation. *See* DATA PROTECTION.

data independence. In databases, pertaining to the structure of data that removes the close coupling with user programs, so that the logical or physical structure of the database may be changed without affecting the application programmer's view of the data. *See* LOGICAL DATA INDEPENDENCE, PHYSICAL DATA INDEPENDENCE.

data input voice answerback. In data communications, a system in which a user sends input to a computer using a terminal, e.g. a touchtone telephone, and receives a voice answerback from the computer that may be either actual recorded or synthesized human voice. *See* SPEECH SYNTHESIZER.

data integrity. (1) In data security, the property that data has not been altered or destroyed in an unauthorized manner. (ISO). *Compare* DATA CONFIDENTIALITY. (2) In data security, the state that exists when computerized data is the same as that in the source documents and has not been exposed to accidental or malicious alteration or destruction. (FIPS). *Compare* DATA CONFIDENTIALITY.

data in voice. In data communications, the type of transmission in which digital data displaces voice circuits in a microwave channel. *Compare* DATA UNDER VOICE, DATA ABOVE VOICE.

data item. In databases, the smallest unit of data that has independent meaning, e.g. an employee's name in a personnel record. *See* FIELD, RECORD. *Synonymous with* DATA ELEMENT.

data keeper. In legislation, a person with a responsibility for ensuring that regular checks are performed on the accuracy and relevance of personal data. *See* DATA PROTECTION.

data key. In key management, a key used to encrypt and decrypt, or to au-

thenticate data. (ANSI). *Compare* KEY ENCRYPTING KEY. *See* CRYPTOGRAPHIC KEY.

data leakage. In data security, the accidental flow of privileged information otherwise presumed to be secure to a person or persons. *Synonymous with* SEEPAGE.

data level. In data security, (a) Level I. Classified data. (b) Level II. Unclassified data requiring special protection; for example Privacy Act, For Official Use Only, technical documents restricted to limited distribution. (c) Level III. All other unclassified data. (OPNAVINST).

data link. (1) In data communications, a physical means of connecting two locations, e.g. a telephone wire. (2) In data communications, the physical medium of transmission, the protocol and the associated devices and programs that together enables data to be transferred from a data source to a data sink. *See* DATA LINK LAYER, DATA SOURCE, DATA SINK.

data link control. *See* PROTOCOL.

data link control standard. In data communications, a set of conventions for sending and receiving data to and from a data network.

data link encryption. In data security, encryption of data over the physical circuit. With this form of encryption the data enters the intermediate and final nodes in plaintext. *Compare* END-TO-END ENCRYPTION, NODE ENCRYPTION. *See* OSI SECURITY, PLAINTEXT. *Synonymous with* LINK ENCRYPTION, LINK TO LINK ENCRYPTION.

data link layer. In data communications, a layer in the ISO open systems interconnection model. The function of this layer is to convert an unreliable transmission channel into a reliable one for use by the layer above it, i.e. the network layer. The raw data bit stream is organized into frames each containing a checksum for detecting errors. *Compare* APPLICATION LAYER, NETWORK LAYER, PHYSICAL LAYER, PRESENTATION LAYER, SESSION LAYER, TRANSPORT LAYER. *See* BIT STREAM, CHECKSUM, FRAME, OPEN SYSTEMS INTERCONNECTION.

DataLock. In computer security, a virus that terminates and stays resident, infects COMMAND.COM, COM, EXE and OVL files, affects run time operation, corrupts program and OVL files. *See* VIRUS NAMES.

data management. In databases, pertaining to the organization and performance of functions that provide for the creation of stored data, access to it, regulation of input output devices and the enforcement of data storage conventions.

data manipulation language. In databases, a language used by a programmer to manipulate the transfer of data between the database and the application program.

data mining. In legislation, searching databases for personal data that may be used for marketing activities, etc. *See* DATA PROTECTION.

data modelling. In databases, pertaining to the identification of the fundamental groups of data and their interrelationships.

data modification. In data security, altering data in an unauthorized and undetectable manner. (ANSI).

data origination. In computing, the translation of information from its original form into machine readable form or directly into electrical signals.

data origin authentication. (1) In authentication, the corroboration that the source of data received is as claimed. (ISO). (2) In authentication, the positive identification of the source or sender of data received.

data owner. In data security, the statutory authority responsible for a particular type or category of information. Or, the individual or organization responsible for the actual data contained therein. (DODD). *See* OWNERSHIP.

dataplex. In data communications, a generic term used in the U.K. for services that involve multiplexing. *See* MULTIPLEXING.

dataplug. In communications, a proprietary name for a device that enables both telephone conversations and data to be multiplexed on a twisted pair cable connected to PABX. *See* MULTIPLEXING.

data processing. In applications, the systematic performance of operations on data to achieve a desired objective. These operations can include the handling, merging, sorting and computing of data. *See* AUTOMATIC DATA PROCESSING SYSTEM.

data protection. In legislation, procedures adopted to minimize the misuse of personal data. Concerns surrounding the protection of personal data have been an active area of debate since the 1960's.

It was soon recognized that computer systems, storing personal data, represented a potential threat to the individual. Whilst the legislation or constitution of individual states may not recognize the right of privacy per se, the ability to store and process vast amounts of data, concerning individual members of the population, has presented considerable dangers for a significant part of this century.

Throughout history, governments have sought to identify members of the population who were considered to be a threat on the basis of religious or political beliefs, or their ethnic backgrounds, etc. Such governments have either set up their own massive manual or automated databases of personal data, or exploited databases that were originally developed for legitimate purposes.

The potential power of such databases has undergone a phenomenal increase due to advances in computer and communication systems. A mass of individual data items, each collected for a limited purpose, can be assembled over international communication systems and correlated on large databases. Artificial intelligence techniques, such as neural networks or expert systems, can search such databases for patterns that are symptomatic of perceived 'undesirable' traits: misusers of welfare schemes, tax dodgers, illegal immigrants, drug dealers, failure to register for military service etc.

There are significant dangers to the individual recorded on such databases. The greatest danger is that the recorded data is inaccurate, due to poor data capture or miskeying, or simply outdated. Such inaccurate data can have a deleterious impact on the individual, e.g. refused a bank loan, denied employment or insurance cover, and the person affected will often have no means of rectifying, or even being aware of, the data error behind the decision.

Computer matching provides the users of disjoint databases with the opportunity to cross reference personal data, e.g. checking lifestyle against tax returns. The use of artificial intelligence techniques can provide for even more sophisticated searches, e.g. medical practitioners who make uncharacteristically high use of pathology services, travel patterns and behavior symptomatic of drug dealers. In many cases it may not even be possible to query why the system has identified a particular person, and the person would have little opportunity to appeal.

The private sector has often sought to exploit a mass of personal data for marketing purposes, or for protection against misuse of credit facilities. Data apparently collected for one purpose, e.g. application for a credit card, may be sold to marketing organizations, e.g. for junk mailing lists.

The Organization for Economic Cooperation and Development recognized the implications of transborder transfers of personal data in 1969 and its Data Bank panel examined the privacy issues of computer data. In 1980 the OECD adopted its Guidelines on the Protection of Privacy and Transborder Flows of Personal Data. These guidelines are advisory and not legally binding on any member state.

The Council of Europe adopted the Convention for the Protection of Individuals With Regard to Automatic Processing of Personal Data in 1981. The Convention is legally binding on any member state that ratifies it, and ratification requires the member state to adopt its own national data protection law.

Europe led the way in the adoption of data protection laws and there was a knock-on effect. Countries that did not adopt effective laws, could find that their organizations were prevented from transferring personal data with countries that had, and such prohibitions could impact upon commercial activities.

Data protection legislation varies considerably from country to country. Moreover, there are wide variations within countries, due to laws passed by constituent states or local authorities. Almost all such laws cover automated personal data files processed by central, or federal government agencies; some laws also apply to manual systems storing personal data. In many cases the private sector is not included in the legislation.

In most cases the laws give exemption to law enforcement agencies and data held for national security. However, countries in Eastern Europe have expressed the view that legislation should give protection against the potential for abuse from such files.

In many, but not all, cases the data protection law has set up a body to supervise the operation of effective data protection regulations. This body is seen to be most effective when it does not belong to the normal government bureaucracy but can report directly to the parliament or equivalent body.

There exists an obvious temptation, for organizations in countries with effective data protection legislation, to export personal data to countries that do not impose restrictions on its storage and processing. These potential data havens may, however, discover that the lack of data protection laws could result in the prohibition of export of personal data from countries that have adopted such laws. Such restrictions on transborder data flows could have a significant impact upon small countries that have set out to attract offshore banking systems etc.

The worldwide situation in regard to data protection legislation is confused and dynamic. In general most countries in Western Europe, North America, Australia, New Zealand, Israel and Japan have adopted some form of data protection legislation, although there is considerable variation amongst this legislation. Compare FREEDOM OF INFORMATION. See COMPUTER MATCHING, DATA HAVEN, DATA PROTECTION - AUSTRALIA, DATA PROTECTION - AUSTRIA, DATA PROTECTION - BELGIUM, DATA PROTECTION - CANADA, DATA PROTECTION - COUNCIL OF EUROPE, DATA PROTECTION - CYPRUS, DATA PROTECTION - DENMARK, DATA PROTECTION - EC, DATA PROTECTION - FINLAND, DATA PROTECTION - FRANCE, DATA PROTECTION - GERMANY, DATA PROTECTION - GREECE, DATA PROTECTION - GUERNSEY, DATA PROTECTION - ICELAND, DATA PROTECTION - IRELAND, DATA PROTECTION - ISLE OF MAN, DATA PROTECTION - ISRAEL, DATA PROTECTION - JAPAN, DATA PROTECTION - JERSEY, DATA PROTECTION - LUXEMBOURG, DATA PROTECTION - NETHERLANDS, DATA PROTECTION - NEW ZEALAND, DATA PROTECTION - NORWAY, DATA PROTECTION - OECD, DATA PROTECTION - PORTUGAL, DATA PROTECTION - SLOVENIA, DATA PROTECTION - SPAIN, DATA PROTECTION - SWEDEN, DATA PROTECTION - U.K., DATA PROTECTION - U.S.A.

data protection - Australia. In legislation, the Australian Privacy Act, 1988 is a federal law controlling the collection, storage, security and use of personal data by federal government agencies. Under the terms of this legislation federal government agencies must annually inform the Privacy Commissioner, formed by the act, of the extent, purpose and contents of personal data contained in their systems. The Privacy Amendment Act of 1990 extended the Privacy Commissioner's responsibilities to include the credit reference industry. Three states in Australia: Queensland, New South Wales and Victoria have also taken action to adopt data protection laws. See DATA PROTECTION.

data protection - Austria. In legislation, the Austrian Data Protection Act was enacted in 1978 and applies to natural and legal persons. The legislation requires the notification and registration of procedures relating to the handling of personal data See DATA PROTECTION.

data protection - Belgium. In legislation, draft data protection legislation was submitted to the Council of State in 1990. This legislation applies to both automated and manual systems handling personal data. It also applies to personal data on Belgian citizens processed abroad and accessible from systems in Belgium. See DATA PROTECTION.

data protection - Canada. In legislation, the Canadian Human Rights Act, 1977, created the post of Privacy Commissioner, and hence gave citizens the right to gain access to personal data held by government agencies. The subsequent Canadian Banking Act, 1980, placed restrictions on the transborder data flow of personal financial data. In 1982 the Privacy Act was passed, dealing both with privacy and freedom of access to information. The Privacy Act strengthened the powers of the Privacy Commissioner; the legislation only applies to Federal government bodies and agencies. However, Federal government computer systems annually provide detailed information on the nature of personal files processed. Data protection legislation has also been passed by the provinces of Quebec and Ontario. *See* DATA PROTECTION.

data protection - Council of Europe. In legislation, in 1981 the Council of Europe adopted the Convention of Protection of Individuals with Regard to Automatic Processing of Personal Data. This convention is legally binding on any member state that ratifies it. The convention required the ratification of each member state and to permit ratification, each member state had to adopt its own data protection laws. *See* DATA PROTECTION.

data protection - Cyprus. In legislation, in 1986 Cyprus signed the Council of Europe Convention on the Protection of Individuals with Regard to Automatic Processing of Personal Data. *See* DATA PROTECTION, DATA PROTECTION - COUNCIL OF EUROPE.

data protection - Denmark. In legislation, in 1978 the Danish parliament passed two data protection laws: the Danish Public Authorities Registers Act and the Danish Private Registers Act, dealing with the public and private sectors respectively. The Danish Private

Registers Act invokes relatively stringent restrictions on transborder data flows of personal data. These acts were amended in 1988 to include a mandatory requirement for the registration of all data files containing sensitive data plus stronger regulation over the credit industry. *See* DATA PROTECTION, TRANSBORDER DATA FLOW.

data protection - EC. In legislation, in July 1990 the European Community issued a proposal for the protection of personal data. The EC Directive applies to the processing of manual and automated personal data files, and to private sector and public sector systems. *See* DATA PROTECTION, DATA PROTECTION - COUNCIL OF EUROPE.

data protection engineering. In data security, the methodology and tools used for designing and implementing data protection mechanisms. (FIPS). *See* DATA PROTECTION.

data protection - Finland. In legislation, in 1987 Finland passed its Personal Data File Act that became law in 1988. The act extends to both public and private sectors, manual and automated files. Data users must inform the Data Protection Ombudsman of the establishment of a file of personal data. *See* DATA PROTECTION.

data protection - France. In legislation, in 1978 France passed its Law on Informatics and Freedoms. A data protection agency - the National Commission on Data Processing and Freedoms (CNIL) was established. The CNIL calls for registration of declarations in regard to personal data processed by the private sector. The CNIL also receives requests for its opinions on personal data processing by the public sector. Unlike the legislation in many countries police files are not exempt from the data protection law. *See* DATA PROTECTION.

data protection - Germany. In legislation, the Federal Law for the Protection Against Misuse of Personal Data was passed in 1977 and came into force in 1978. The law created the post of Federal Data Protection Commissioner. Only natural persons, not legal or corporate persons are protected by the law; moreover the law only applies to Federal authorities and administrations. The public authorities come under the jurisdiction of each State, or Land, that have their own data protection laws; these laws also cover the use of personal data in the private sector. *See* DATA PROTECTION.

data protection - Greece. In legislation, a draft bill, the Data Protection Law was submitted to the Greek parliament in 1987. The law applies to private and public sectors and to automated and manual personal data files. The draft bill creates a Data Protection Commission to oversee compliance with the law. *See* DATA PROTECTION.

data protection - Guernsey. In legislation, the Data Protection (Bailiwick of Guernsey) Law was adopted in 1986. The law is substantially similar to the U.K. Data Protection Act. *See* DATA PROTECTION, DATA PROTECTION - JERSEY, DATA PROTECTION - U.K.

data protection - Iceland. In legislation, the latest Data Protection law was passed in 1989. This law continues to provide for a Data Protection Commission to oversee compliance. The law applies to both public and private sectors, manual and automated files, natural and legal persons. *See* DATA PROTECTION.

data protection - Ireland. In legislation, Ireland's Data Protection Act was passed in 1988 and amended by the Data Protection (Access Modification) (Health) Regulations in 1989. The act has similarities with the U.K. Data Protection Act but it has a more restricted definition of personal data. A Data Protection Commission was established to enforce compliance with the law. The act does not apply to manual files nor to data subjects who are legal persons. *See* DATA PROTECTION, DATA PROTECTION - U.K.

data protection - Isle of Man. In legislation, the Data Protection Act, that is substantially similar to the U.K. Data Protection Act, was passed in 1988. *See* DATA PROTECTION, DATA PROTECTION - U.K.

data protection - Israel. In legislation, the Privacy Law that was has similarities with European legislation, was passed in 1981. *See* DATA PROTECTION.

data protection - Japan. In legislation, the Japanese Diet passed the Act for the Protection of Computer Processed Personal Data in 1988. This act applies to automated files processed by national government agencies. The Director General of the Management and Coordination Agency has responsibility for the management of the government compliance with the act. A number of prefectures and municipalities have adopted data protection ordinances. *See* DATA PROTECTION.

data protection - Jersey. In legislation, the Data Protection (Jersey) Law was passed in 1987. It addresses automated but not manual files of personal data, and it does not apply to data subjects who are legal or corporate persons. *See* DATA PROTECTION, DATA PROTECTION - GUERNSEY, DATA PROTECTION - U.K.

data protection - Luxembourg. In legislation, the Luxembourg Law Concerning the Use of Name-Linked Data in Computer Processing was passed in 1979. This law covers both the public and private sector. *See* DATA PROTECTION.

data protection - Netherlands. In legislation, the Netherlands Data Protection Act came into force in 1989. The act covers both automated and manual files containing personal data. A Registration Chamber was created by this law and the Chamber establishes rules for industry regulation of personal data systems. *See* DATA PROTECTION.

data protection - New Zealand. In legislation, data protection matters have been included in legislation such as the Companies Act, 1955, the Health Act, 1956, the Wanganui Computer Centre Act, 1976, the Area Health Boards Act, 1983 and the Adult Adoption Act, 1985. The New Zealand Human Rights Commission Act, 1977, granted the Human Rights Commission responsibilities to oversee privacy matters including personal data privacy. *See* DATA PROTECTION.

data protection - Norway. In legislation, Norway's Personal Data Registers Act of 1978 became law in 1980 and was amended in 1987. The law covers manual and automated files of personal data, public and private sector. The Data Inspectorate was established by the law. The 1987 amendment included references to credit reporting, direct marketing and telemarketing activities. *See* DATA PROTECTION.

data protection - OECD. In legislation, in 1980 the Council of the Organization for Economic Cooperation and Development adopted Guidelines for the Protection of Privacy and Transborder Data Flows of Personal Data. *See* DATA PROTECTION, TRANSBORDER DATAFLOW.

data protection - Portugal. In legislation, Portugal's National Assembly passed the Law on the Protection of Computerized Personal Data in 1991. The law applies to public or private sector automated personal files, for natural persons. The National Commission for the Protection of Automated Personal Data (CNPDPI) was created by this law. *See* DATA PROTECTION.

data protection - Slovenia. In legislation, Slovenia passed its Data Protection Act in 1990. The Act adopts the basic principles of the OECD Guidelines on the Protection of Privacy and Transborder Data Flows of Personal Data and the Council of Europe Convention on personal data. *See* DATA PROTECTION. DATA PROTECTION - OECD, DATA PROTECTION - COUNCIL OF EUROPE.

data protection - Spain. In legislation, the Spanish constitution has a provision that guarantees a citizen's right to privacy, including prevention of the misuse of personal information *See* DATA PROTECTION.

data protection - Sweden. In legislation, the first data protection act ever was passed in Sweden in 1973. This act covered both the public and private sectors. The Data Inspection Board was formed to oversee the quite strict requirements of this act. Particular attention was paid to the export of personal data since it was feared that organizations might simply bypass the Board and export data for processing elsewhere. The procedures associated with registration and export licenses were so burdensome that the act was amended in 1982 to make the procedures less cumbersome. *See* DATA PROTECTION.

data protection - UK In legislation, debate on data protection in the UK has been active since the early 1970's. This matter was considered by the Younger Committee (1972), two White Papers (1975) and the Lindop Committee (1976). Concern was expressed in the early 1980's at the failure to ratify the Council of Europe Convention. There was a danger that government agencies, and private sector companies, would no longer be permitted to transfer sensitive personal data to and from European countries that had adopted data protection laws.

The U.K. Data Protection Act was passed in 1984 and is based on eight Data Protection principles broadly in line with the recommendations of the Council of Europe Convention for the Protection of Individuals with regard to the automatic processing of personal data. The eight principles are:

- the information to be contained in personal data shall be obtained, and personal data shall be processed, fairly and lawfully;
- personal data shall be held only for one or more specified and lawful purposes;
- personal data held for any purpose or purposes shall not be used or disclosed in any manner incompatible with that purpose or those purposes;
- personal data held for any purpose or purposes shall be adequate, relevant and not excessive in relation to that purpose or those purposes;.
- personal data shall be accurate and, where necessary, kept up to date;
- personal data held for any purpose or purposes shall not be kept for longer than is necessary for that purpose or those purposes;
- a data subject shall be entitled:

to have access at reasonable intervals and without undue delay or expense to personal data of which he or she is the subject;

where appropriate, to have such data corrected or erased;

- appropriate security measures shall be taken against unauthorized access to, or alteration, disclosure or destruction of personal data and against accidental loss or destruction of personal data.

In addition, the act established a new office of Data Registrar, a national position, and a Data Protection Tribunal. It is the responsibility of the Registrar to set up and maintain a register of data users and persons carrying on computer bureaux services. The Tribunal hears appeals on behalf of users against decisions of, or actions by, the Registrar. The act requires that all users of automated personal data, in the public and private sector, register their systems with the Registrar, and comply with the principles except in specified exempted categories as listed below.

- personal data held by an individual in connection with domestic uses, such as personal, family or recreational purposes;
- personal data that the law requires to be made public, such as automated list of voters maintained by the Electoral Registration Officer;
- personal data used only for calculating and paying wages and pensions, keeping accounts or maintaining records of purchases and sales in order to ensure that payments are made;
- personal data used for distributing articles or information to data subjects and only if a very small amount of data is maintained, if the data subject objects to this data being maintained then the exemption does not apply;
- personal data held by an unincorporated club, all data subjects must be members of the club and if they object to the information being maintained the exemption does not apply;
- information which is only processed for the preparation of text, e.g. word processing;
- personal data which are kept for reasons of national security;
- other areas include taxation, health and social work, regulation of financial service, judicial appoint-

ments, legal professional privilege, personal data made public and backup data.

The Consumer Credit Act, 1974, gave a data subject right of access to personal data by consumer credit reporting agencies and such data is therefore also exempt from the Data Protection Act.

Under the Data Protection Act it is an offence to process or exchange automated personal data:

- while not being registered as a user;
- while being prevented by order of the Registrar from so doing;
- for purposes or exchanges which have not been registered.

The person who is the subject of information contained in a computer file is given the right to check that information, to receive a copy of the record and to take actions against loss where data is inaccurate or has been misused. Effective security procedures must be undertaken by bodies processing personal data to guard against unauthorized access. In addition the Computer Misuse Act, 1990, renders it illegal for to access computer systems in an unauthorized manner and modify data in any fashion. *See* COMPUTER MISUSE ACT - 1990, DATA PROTECTION, LINDOP COMMITTEE, PRIVACY, YOUNGER COMMITTEE.

data protection - USA In legislation, data protection legislation has been enacted at a Federal and State level within the USA but such legislation is less stringent than that currently in force in a number of European countries.

The Fair Credit Reporting Act, 1970 required credit bureaux to make their records available to data subjects, and limits disclosure of credit information to authorized bodies. The act also provides procedures for the correction of errors in personal data. However, it does not give data subjects any control on the disclosure of such personal data.

The Privacy Act of 1974 relates only to personal data processed by Federal agencies. It requires such Federal agencies to give notice of new proposed use of personal data, so that interested parties could make submissions. However, individuals so affected may experience difficulty in accessing such notices.

The Privacy Act set up a Privacy Protection Study Commission, but this was not a permanent body. The Commission reported its findings, including a recommendation that the Privacy Act should not be extended to the private sector, in 1977. The CIA and law enforcement agencies are exempted under the Privacy Act, but the Crime Control Act, 1973 required that state criminal justice information systems, produced under Federal funds, implemented measures to ensure privacy and security.

The Family Educational Rights and Privacy Act, 1974 provided data protection in respect to personal data held by schools and universities. This Act grants parents and students access to student records, right to challenge incorrect data and sets restrictions on the disclosure of such personal data.

The Freedom of Information Act, 1978 in a sense has a contrary purpose to that of the Privacy Act, inasmuch as it is directed to the disclosure of government information. It is therefore possible that personal data may be released by the Freedom of Information Act in contravention of the Privacy Act.

Data protection legislation, in relation to specific application areas, has been provided by the Right to Financial Privacy Act 1978, the Privacy Protection of Rape Victims Act. 1978, Electronic Funds Transfer Act, 1978, Privacy Protection Act, 1990, Paperwork Reduction Act, 1980, Debt Collection Act, 1982, Cable Communications Policy Act, 1984, Video Privacy Protection Act 1988 and the Federal Managers Financial Integrity Act.

There has been concern in the U.S.A. on the implications of computer matching techniques, on large databases, for personal data protection. The Computer Matching and Privacy Protection Act, 1988 provides baseline procedures for Federal agencies conducting such computer matches.

The Computer Security Act 1987 has implications for data protection, inasmuch as it was concerned with the level of data security of Federal computer systems. This was followed by the Computer Security Act, 1988 that formed the Computer System Security and Privacy Board. Three states Minnesota, New York and Hawaii have implemented data protection laws with some similarity to those enacted in Europe. *See* COMPUTER MATCHING, DATA PROTECTION.

data rate. (1) In data communications, the amount of data transferred per unit time on a data link, usually expressed in bits per second. (2) In computing, the rate, usually expressed in terms of bytes or word per second, at which data is transferred between the units of a computer system.

data reduction. In computing, the process of transforming raw data into a useful simplified form. This often involves such operations as adjusting, scaling, smoothing, compacting, and editing of data.

data retrieval. *See* INFORMATION RETRIEVAL.

Data Seal. In authentication, a proprietary, unpublished authentication algorithm.

data security. (1) The protection of data from accidental or malicious modification, destruction, or disclosure. (FIPS). (2) The science and study of methods of protecting data in computer and communications systems against unauthorized disclosure, transfer, modifications or destruction whether accidental or intentional. It involves four kinds of control: cryptographic control, access control, information flow control and inference control. *See* ACCESS CONTROL, COMPUTER SECURITY, CRYPTOGRAPHIC CONTROL, INFERENCE CONTROL, INFORMATION FLOW CONTROL. *Synonymous with* INFORMATION ASSET SECURITY, INFORMATION SECURITY.

data security architecture. In data security, the structure of an integrated data security system, designed to provide the appropriate level of security assurance.

The top level of the architecture may be considered to comprise the security policy of the organization, the next level the procedural security, that in turn is supported by the physical and logical security mechanisms. The facets of the architecture at each level should not only be compatible and complementary but should also provide defence in depth. Particular attention must be paid to the interfaces of the system to ensure that they maintain security integrity.

A well developed architecture will provide management with an overview of the total set of security countermeasures within the organization. Technical staff will have a well defined infrastructure within which current systems may be operated and new systems may be securely implemented. The well defined interfaces will provide a clear definition of security responsibilities. *See* DIGITAL DISTRIBUTED SYSTEM SECURITY ARCHITECTURE, SECURITY POLICY.

data security officer. In computer security, the person charged with the responsibility for protecting computing systems and their data against misuse.

data security package. In computer security, a software package that controls access to stored data. *See* ACF2, RACF, SMF, UCC1.

data set. (1) In databases, a named collection of data items, bearing a logical relation to each other and ordered in a prescribed manner, it may also contain data for accessing the data, e.g. indices. (2) In data communications, a modem. *Synonymous with* MODEM.

data set ready. In data communications, a signal used in modems to indicate that the power is on and that the modem is ready to receive data for transmission. It is also used for flow control; for example, if a printer is connected to a computer then the printer must ensure that the computer does not send characters faster than they can be printed. *See* DATA SET, MODEM, RS-232C.

data signalling rate. In data communications, the aggregate rate at which binary digits are transmitted over a circuit, expressed in bits per second. *Compare* DATA TRANSFER RATE. *See* BIT.

data signalling rate selector. In data communications, a signal employed when a modem allows switching between two transmission speeds. If the modem at the calling end sets the speed for the connection then the calling computer uses the data signalling rate selector (DTE source) to determine the line speed. The calling modem signals the speed to the answering modem, that informs the called computer by setting the data signalling rate selector (DCE) source to the appropriate value. *See* RS-232C, DCE, DTE, MODEM.

data sink. In data communications, that part of a data terminal device that receives data. *Compare* DATA SOURCE. *Synonymous with* SINK.

data source. In data communications, that part of a data terminal device that inputs data into a link. *Compare* DATA SINK.

data station. In data communications, the assembly of equipment that includes the data terminal equipment and data circuit terminating equipment. *See* DATA CIRCUIT TERMINATING EQUIPMENT, DATA TERMINAL EQUIPMENT.

data stream. (1) In cryptography, the plaintext or the ciphertext considered as a sequence of cryptographic characters in a stream cipher. *See* CIPHERTEXT, PLAINTEXT. (2) In data communications, a continuous stream of serial data being transmitted in character or binary digit form through a channel. The data stream may contain control and format information.

data structure. In computing, a system of relationships between items of data. Well designed high level languages permit the programmer to define and manipulate appropriate data structures that greatly reduce the complexity of programs. *See* ARRAY, HIGH LEVEL LANGUAGE, LIST, QUEUE, STACK.

data subject. In legislation, as defined by the U.K. Data Protection Act 1984, an individual who is the subject of personal data. *See* DATA PROTECTION, PERSONAL DATA.

data switching exchange. In data communications, equipment installed at a single location used to switch data traffic. *Compare* PACKET SWITCHING. *See* MESSAGE SWITCHING.

data terminal equipment. In data communications, any piece of equipment at which a communication path begins or ends, e.g. a VDU. *Compare* DATA CIRCUIT TERMINATING EQUIPMENT.

data terminal ready. In data communications, a signal used in conjunction with an auto-answer modem to indicate that it is ready to receive a call. *See* AUTOMATIC ANSWERING, RS-232C.

data transfer rate. In data communications, the average number of bits or bytes that pass between devices per unit time. The average disk transfer rate from a device, e.g. magnetic disk drive, will depend upon the electrical and mechanical properties of that device but the upper limit of the instantaneous rate may be a function of the interface or transmission path. *Compare* DATA SIGNALLING RATE. *See* BIT, BYTE, MAGNETIC DISK.

data transmission. *See* DATA COMMUNICATIONS.

data transparency. In data communications, a technique whereby any pattern of bits, including those normally reserved for control purposes, may be transmitted as a block. *See* TRANSPARENT.

data transport system. *See* WIDE AREA NETWORK.

data type. *See* ABSTRACT DATA TYPE, TYPE.

data under voice. In data communications, a transmission system that carries digital data on a portion of the microwave radio spectrum below the frequency used for voice transmission. *Compare* DATA ABOVE VOICE, DATA IN VOICE.

data user. In legislation, as defined by the U.K. Data Protection Act 1984, a person who holds data. A person holds data if:

- the data forms part of a collection of data processed or intended to be processed by, or on behalf of, that person;
- that person (either alone or jointly or in common with other persons)

controls the contents and use of the data comprised in the collection;
- the data are in the form in which they have been, or are intended to be, processed as mentioned above or (though not for the time being in that form) in a form into which they have been converted after being so processed and with a view to being further so processed on a subsequent occasion.

See DATA PROTECTION, PERSONAL DATA.

data validation. In computing, the act of checking that data fits certain defined criteria.

data word. In computing, an item of data stored as a single word. *See* WORD.

data word size. In computing, the length of a data word, in bits, that a particular CPU is designed to handle. *See* CPU, DATA WORD.

date of message origination. In authentication, the date on which the sender computed the MAC. This date is used to synchronize the authentication process through the selection of the proper key. (ANSI) *See* MAC, SENDER.

date/time stamp. In authentication, a field in a message giving the time and date of origination. It is used to protect against replay attacks. *See* REPLAY.

Day-Night switch. *Synonymous with* AUTHORIZED ACCESS CONTROL SWITCH.

db. *See* DECIBEL.

DBA. *See* DATABASE ADMINISTRATOR.

Dbase. In computer security, a virus that terminates and stays resident, infects COM files, corrupts data files, affects run-time operation, corrupts program and OVL files. *See* VIRUS NAMES.

DBMS. *See* DATABASE MANAGEMENT SYSTEM.

DC1. In codes, an ASCII control code corresponding to XON. *Compare* DC4. *See* ASCII, XON-XOFF PROTOCOL.

DC4. In codes, an ASCII control code corresponding to XOFF. *Compare* DC1. *See* ASCII, XON-XOFF PROTOCOL.

DCD. *See* DATA CARRIER DETECT.

DCE. *See* DATA CIRCUIT TERMINATING EQUIPMENT.

DCID. U.S. Director Central Intelligence Directive.

DDL. (1) Data Description Language. *See* data description language. (2) Document Description Language.

DDN. In data communications, Defense Data Network. *See* APRPANET.

DDP. In computing, distributed data processing.

DDS. In data communications, Direct Digital Service. *See* ISDN.

DEA. *See* DATA ENCRYPTION ALGORITHM.

DEA 1. In cryptography, ISO terminology for DES. *Compare* DEA 2. *See* DEA, DES, ISO.

DEA 2. In cryptography, ISO terminology for RSA. *Compare* DEA 1. *See* ISO, RSA.

DEA device. In cryptography, the electronic hardware part or subassembly that implements only the DEA as specified in ANSI X3.92-1981, and that is validated by the National Bureau of Standards. (ANSI). *See* ANSI X3.92-1981, DATA ENCRYPTION STANDARD.

deadlock. (1) In data communications, a situation in which a protocol can make no further progress either because there is no possible transition, or there is no possible transition which will cause forward progress. *See* PROTOCOL. (2) In operations, an error condition in which processing cannot continue because each of two elements of the process are waiting for an action from the other.

dead zone. In access control, an area within a protection pattern in which the sensor is non-effective.

deal. In banking, a transaction used in the context of specific products. *See* PRODUCT.

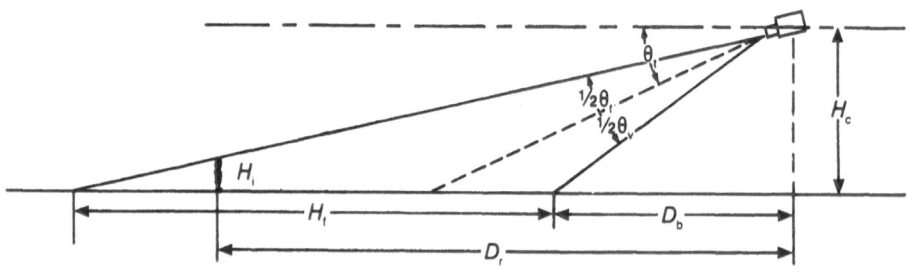

D_r = Distance, camera to object.
H_t = Vertical field of view.
θ_t = Angle of depression.
D_p = Dead zone.
H_c = Height of camera.
θ_v = Vertical angle of lens.

all dimensions in metres

dead zone.

debit advice. In banking, advice by the account servicing bank of a debit to the account of receiver (account owner). (ANSI). *See* ACCOUNT SERVICING BANK.

debit card. In banking, a card that enables the subscriber to purchase goods or services from a variety of outlets and give authority to debit the subscriber's nominated bank account. *Compare* CREDIT CARD.

debit party. In banking, the source of funds on the receiving bank's books. (ANSI). *Compare* BENEFICIARY, CREDIT PARTY.

debit transfer. In banking, an instruction where the sender with authorization specifies a debit party other than himself. (ANSI). *See* DEBIT PARTY. *Synonymous with* DIRECT DEBIT.

debug. In computing, the detection, isolation and correction of a mistake in a computer program or the computer system itself. *See* BUG, DEBUGGER.

debugger. In computing, a program to assist in testing and tracing errors in an application program. The debugger allows the user to step through a low level language program, one instruction at a time, providing details of register contents, etc. after each execution. *See* APPLICATION PROGRAM, DEBUG, LOW LEVEL LANGUAGE.

decentralized computer network. In data communications, a computer network where some of the functions that control the network are distributed over several network nodes. *See* NODE.

decibel. In electronics and communications, one tenth of a bel, a measure of signal strength relative to a given reference level. A decibel is ten times the common logarithm (base 10) of that ratio. *See* BEL, LOGARITHM.

decimalization table. In banking, a table used to translate hexadecimal characters into decimal characters. If it is required to derive decimal numbers from a string of binary digits, then the string may be divided into a series of 4 bit nibbles. Each nibble represents a hexadecimal value 0 - 9, A - F. The decimalization table allows a decimal number to be arbitrarily associated with each hexadecimal value. This procedure may be used to derive a PIN verification value from the ciphertext derived by encrypting identifying account data etc. *See* CIPHERTEXT, HEXADECIMAL, PIN VERIFICATION VALUE.

decipher. In cryptology, to convert, by use of the appropriate key, enciphered text into its equivalent plaintext. (FIPS). *Compare* ENCIPHER. *See* DECRYPT, KEY, PLAINTEXT.

decipherment. In cryptography, the reversal of a corresponding reversible encipherment. (ISO). *Compare* ENCIPHERMENT. *See* REVERSIBLE ENCRYPTION.

decision support system. In applications, an information processing system used to aid decision making, usually within a given organization. *See* DATABASE, KNOWLEDGE BASE.

declarative language. *Synonymous with* NONPROCEDURAL LANGUAGE.

declassification of magnetic storage media. In data security, a procedure that will totally remove all of the classified or sensitive information stored on magnetic media followed by a review of the procedure performed. A decision can then be made for (or against) actual removal of the classification level of the media. Declassification allows release of the media from the controlled environment if approved by the appropriate authorities. (DOD).

decode. To translate or determine the meaning of coded information. *Compare* DECIPHER, ENCODE. *See* DECODER.

decoder. In hardware, a logic device designed to convert data from one number system to another, e.g. from binary to decimal.

decoupling key. (1) In banking, the key used, together with the current contents of the key register to construct the current transaction key. In a card based mode of operation, decoupling keys are derived from information stored on the card holder's card. Alternative methods of generating the parameter are necessary for non-card based modes of operation. Essentially, at least one of the decoupling keys in a transaction is a function of some information, derivable by either the acquirer or card issuer and terminal that is however, not transmitted. (SAA). *See* ACQUIRER, CARD BASED MODE, CARD HOLDER, CARD ISSUER, KEY MANAGEMENT, KEY REGISTER, TRANSACTION KEY SYSTEM. (2) In key management, an item of information known to the host computer and terminal in an EFTPOS network, but not transmitted between them, and used in the formation of an authorization parameter. *See* TRANSACTION KEY SYSTEM.

decrypt. In cryptology, to convert, by use of the appropriate key, encrypted (encoded or enciphered) text into its equivalent plaintext. (FIPS). *Compare* ENCRYPT. *See* DECIPHER, ENCODE, KEY, PLAINTEXT.

decryption. *Synonymous with* DECIPHERMENT.

dedicated. A term indicating equipment reserved for one user or type of application. For example, a dedicated word processor may be reserved for the use of specific individuals or word processing technical reports.

dedicated access. In data communications, a permanent connection between a terminal and a service network or computer.

dedicated channel. In data communications, a circuit or channel that has been reserved or committed for a specific use or application, e.g. for emergency purposes.

dedicated mode. In computer security, the operation of an ADP system such that the central computer facility, the connected peripheral devices, the communications facilities, and all remote terminals are used and controlled exclusively by specific users or groups of users for the processing of particular types and categories of information. (FIPS). *See* DEDICATED SECURITY MODE.

dedicated security mode. (1) In computer security, the mode of operation in which all users have the appropriate clearance and need-to-know for all data in the system. The system is specifically and exclusively dedicated to and controlled for the processing of one particular type or classification of information either for full-time operation or for a specified period of time. (AFR). *Compare* MULTILEVEL SECURITY MODE, SYSTEM HIGH SECURITY MODE. *See* CLASSIFICATION, NEED TO KNOW. (2) In computer security, a mode of operation wherein all users have the clearance, formal access approval, and need to know for all data handled by the AIS. In the dedicated mode, an AIS may handle a single classification level and/or category of information or a range of classification levels and/or categories. (DODD). *See* AIS, CLASSIFICATION, NEED TO KNOW. (3) In computer security, the operation of an ADP system such that the central computer facility, the connected peripheral devices, the communications facilities, and all remote terminals are used and controlled exclusively by specific users or groups of users for the processing of particular types and categories of information. (FIPS).

DEE. Data Encryption Equipment.

default. In computing and operating systems, pertaining to the choice selected in the absence of specific instructions by the user. Default passwords are commonly exploited by hackers.

default classification. In data security, a temporary classification, reflecting the highest classification being processed in an automated system. The default classification is included in the safeguard statement affixed to the product. (AR). *See* CLASSIFICATION.

default to denial of access. In access control, pertaining to the design of a system in which access authorizations are mandatory and objects lacking those authorizations are locked out. *See* ACCESS AUTHORIZATION.

defeat. In physical security, pertaining to the successful bypassing of an alarm system or sensor permitting an intruder to effect an undetected entry.

Defense Data Network. *See* ARPANET.

defense industry information. Technical planning, requirements, and acquisition information provided to industry through various programs to enable industry to meet defense weapons and support systems needs. The programs include DOD IACs, potential contractor programs of DOD components, advanced planning briefings for industry, technical meetings on special topics, and similar services initiated by the OUSDR&E and other DOD components. (DODD). *See* IAC, OUSDR&E.

defensive depth. In computer security, a principle of design that attackers should be compelled to overcome a series of safeguards to achieve their objectives, e.g. access to a highly sensitive area, should require passage through the maximum number of controlled areas, and violation of one control point should initiate an alerting and reinforcing of all adjacent control points.

degauss. (1) In computer security, to apply a variable, alternating current (AC) field for the purpose of demagnetizing magnetic recording media, usually tapes. The process involves increasing the AC field gradually from zero to some maximum value and back to zero, that leaves a very low residue of magnetic induction on the media. (FIPS). (2) Loosely, to erase. (FIPS)

degausser. In electronics, an electrical device (AC or DC) or a hand-held magnet assembly that can generate coercive magnetic force for the purpose of degaussing magnetic storage media or other magnetic material. (DOD). *See* COERCIVE FORCE, DEGAUSS.

degradation. In data communications, a deterioration in the characteristics of a signal for whatever reason.

degree of trust. The level of confidence that can be placed in security mechanisms to correctly enforce the security policy. (AFR). *See* SECURITY POLICY.

DEK. *See* DATA-ENCRYPTING KEY.

DEL. *See* DELETE CHARACTER.

delay circuit. In physical security, a circuit in an alarm system that permits entry or exit within a given time period, thus allowing authorized personnel sufficient time to enter or exit before arming or disarming the system.

delay/denial of service. In communications security, pertaining to attacks undertaken to prevent messages from reaching their destinations within an acceptable time. This effect can be achieved by active wiretapping, Trojan Horse, message transmission or misrouting of messages. Active wiretapping can be used to remove or delay messages in the network. A Trojan Horse can receive coded signals from an attacker to initiate a system disruption. Unauthorized message transmissions can be used to flood the network so as to diminish the network performance, while misrouting of messages can prevent them from attaining their intended destinations either, at all, or within acceptable time periods.

The detection of delay/denial of service attacks is complicated if the attack is initiated in a quiescent traffic state. The transmitter then attempting to establish communication will discover that the service is denied or delayed by the lack, or delay, of acknowledgements from the receiver. On the other hand the receiver will be unaware of the attack. A request response mechanism provides warning of delay/denial attacks at a cost of a reduced effective bandwidth of the network. *See* ACTIVE WIRETAPPING, BANDWIDTH, BANKING NETWORKS, DENIAL OF SERVICE, REQUEST RESPONSE, TROJAN HORSE.

delay distortion. In data communications, a distortion caused by different propagation speeds of signals in a transmission medium arising from differences in their frequencies. This type of distortion does not affect voice but can have a serious effect on some data transmission.

delay equalizer. In communications, a corrective network used to render the phase delay, or the rate of change of phase shift with frequency, of a system, substantially constant over the desired frequency range. *See* PHASE DELAY.

delay line. In electronics, a device that causes a time delay in the transmission of a pulse.

delay vector. In data communications, a list of the estimated transit times for a packet from one node to every other node in a packet switching network. Used in adaptive routing systems. *See* ADAPTIVE ROUTING, PACKET SWITCHING.

delegate. In access control, to authorize one subject to exercise some of the authority of another. *See* SUBJECT.

delete character. In codes, a control character used to delete an erroneous or unwanted character, for example a character transmitted down a communications circuit.

deliberate threat. In computer security, a threat of a person or persons to consciously and willingly damage the computer system. *Compare* ACCIDENTAL THREAT, ACTIVE THREAT, LOGICAL THREAT, PASSIVE THREAT, PHYSICAL THREAT. *See* THREAT.

delimiter. In computing, a specified character used to denote the end of a field. *See* FIELD.

deliverable. In information security, an item or resource produced or used during development of a target of evaluation that is required to be made available to the evaluators for the purpose of evaluation. *See* INFORMATION TECHNOLOGY SECURITY EVALUATION CRITERIA, INFORMATION TECHNOLOGY SECURITY EVALUATION MANUAL.

delivery assurance. In data security, pertaining to the level of damage associated with the delay or denial of messages. Delivery assurance is concerned, not only with the loss of messages, but also with preventing the addition or replay of messages. *See*

DELAY/DENIAL OF SERVICE, END TO END ASSURANCE, REPLAY, SOURCE AUTHORIZATION.

delta modulation. In data communications, a form of differential PCM in which only 1 bit for each sample is used. *See* DIFFERENTIAL PCM.

delta routing. In data communications, a method of routing, in a packet switching network, in which a central routing controller receives information from nodes and issues routing instructions, but leaves a degree of discretion to individual nodes. *Compare* ADAPTIVE ROUTING, CENTRALIZED ADAPTIVE ROUTING, DIRECTORY ROUTING, FIXED ROUTING, HOT POTATO ROUTING. *See* NODE, PACKET SWITCHING NETWORK, ROUTING.

demand multiplexing. In data communications, a form of TDM in which time slots are allocated according to demand. *See* TDM.

demarcation strip. In data communications, a terminal board that acts as a physical interface between a business machine and the common carrier. *See* COMMON CARRIER.

democratic network. In data communications, a synchronized network in which no one clock has priority over any other. *Compare* DESPOTIC NETWORK, HIERARCHICAL NETWORK.

demodulation. In communications, the process by which an original modulating signal is recovered from a modulated wave. *Compare* MODULATION.

demodulator. In communications, a device that performs the function of demodulation on a data transmission circuit. It is usually found in conjunction with the device performing the modulation, together forming a modem. *See* DEMODULATION, MODEM.

demon. (1) In software protection, a program used to break some software protection schemes. The demon is used initially to intercept and monitor all disk requests made by the protected program. If a copy of the protected program is made with a bit copier (say) the demon will emulate the fingerprint used by the source program, and so be able to bypass the software protection scheme. The demon is not effective against programs that address the disk controller directly, rather than via the operating system. *Compare* DAEMON. *See* BIT COPIER, EXECUTE PROTECTION, FINGERPRINT, OPERATING SYSTEM.

demultiplexing. In data communications, the dividing of one or more information streams into a larger number of streams. *Compare* MULTIPLEXING.

denial. In communications, a condition that occurs in a network when no circuits are available and a busy tone is returned to the calling party.

denial of message service. In communications security, an attack on PDU's in a message stream that either discards PDU's in transit or delays PDU's going in one or both directions. *Compare* MESSAGE STREAM MODIFICATION, SPURIOUS ASSOCIATION INITIATION. *See* DENIAL OF SERVICE, PDU.

denial of service. (1) In data security, the prevention of authorized access to system assets or services, or the delaying of time critical operations (TNI). *See* DENIAL OF MESSAGE SERVICE. (2) In computer security, action or actions that prevent any part of an AIS from functioning in accordance with its intended purpose. This includes any action that causes the unauthorized destruction, modification, or delay of service. *See* DELAY/DENIAL OF SERVICE.

dense index. In databases, an index that contains an entry for every record to be searched. *Compare* NONDENSE INDEX. *See* INDEX, RECORD.

Den Zuk. In computer security, a virus that terminates and stays resident, infects floppy disk boot sector, affects run time operation and corrupts boot sector. *See* VIRUS NAMES.

dependability. In reliability, pertaining to the degree of certainty that a system will operate correctly.

dependence. The existence of a relationship in which the subject may not work properly unless the object (possibly another subject) behaves properly.

derived PIN. In banking, a PIN that is generated from some information related to the customer's account number or identity. The PIN is derived by an algorithm involving a secret key. Such PINs may be verified at any location, with access to the secret key used in the algorithm, without requiring storage of the PIN at the location. *See* PIN, PIN MANAGEMENT AND SECURITY, PIN OFFSET.

DES. *See* DATA ENCRYPTION STANDARD.

descriptive top-level specification. A Top-Level Specification that is written in a natural language (e.g. English), an informal program design notation, or a combination of the two. (DOD). *Compare* FORMAL TOP-LEVEL SPECIFICATION. *See* TOP-LEVEL SPECIFICATION.

descriptor. In computing, stored information that contains details on how other information is stored. A program can thus refer to the descriptor, of say a file, and then correctly interpret the data referred to. *See* FILE DESCRIPTOR.

designated approving authority. (1) In computer security, a designated official who approves the operation of automated systems at the computer facilities under his or her jurisdiction for processing of information or for critical processing. (AFR). *See* CRITICAL PROCESSING. (2) In computer security, a senior policy official who has the authority and the responsibility to make the management decision to accept or not accept the security safeguards prescribed for an AIS; the official who may be responsible for issuing an accreditation statement that records the decision to accept those safeguards. (DODD). *See* AIS, ACCREDITATION. (3) In computer security, an official assigned responsibility to accredit ADP elements, activities, and networks under the official's jurisdiction. (OPNAVINST).

design standard. Specific design criteria defining both result and method of performance per a standard. (ANSI). *Compare* PERFORMANCE STANDARD.

design verification. In computer security, the use of verification techniques, usually computer-assisted, to demonstrate a mathematical correspondence between an abstract (security) model and a formal system specification. (MTR). *See* SECURITY MODEL, VERIFICATION.

desk checking. In computing, the manual process in which representative data is traced through program logic to determine that the logical processing is as intended.

despotic network. In data communications, a synchronized network in which a single master clock controls all other clocks in the network. *Compare* DEMOCRATIC NETWORK. *See* HIERARCHICAL NETWORK.

destruction. In computer security, the physical alteration of ADP system media or ADP system components such that they can no longer be used for storage or retrieval of information. (DOE). *See* ADP.

destructive readout. In computing, pertaining to a reading action of stored data that necessarily erases the data held. *Compare* NONDESTRUCTIVE READOUT.

Destructor. In computer security, a virus that terminates and stays resident, infects COMMAND.COM, COM, EXE and OVL files, affects run time operation, corrupts program and OVL files. *See* VIRUS NAMES.

detector. In physical security, a device employed to detect an alarm condition requiring immediate action, e.g. intrusion, fire, smoke, unsafe equipment operation, equipment malfunction.

deterrent. In physical security, a device that inhibits unauthorized action. Locked doors are an example of physical deterrents whilst a surveillance camera can effect a psychological deterrence.

development center. In computing, a department that commits the necessary hardware and software to application development. *See* INFORMATION CENTER.

device assignment. In operating systems, pertaining to a facility of logical to physical assignments that allow peripheral devices to be operated as required, by an application program, without the requirement for physical disconnection and connection. *See* LOGICAL.

device control. In data communications, a character in a data transmission code available for controlling a device, e.g. turning it on or off.

Devil's Dance. In computer security, a computer virus that terminates and stays resident, infects COM files, affects runtime operation, corrupts program, OVL and data files and file linkage. *See* VIRUS NAMES.

DFT scrambler. *See* DISCRETE FOURIER TRANSFORM SCRAMBLER.

DGP. (1) In physical security, Data Gathering Panel, a control unit that receives, displays and stores alarm information. (2) In physical security, a transponder receiving a number of alarm signals for interfacing to an alarm processor.

DGT. Director Generale des Telecommunications.

DG XIII. Directorate General Section XIII of the Commission of European Communities that deals with the information market and innovation.

diagnostic code. In physical security, an alphanumeric display describing a system condition such as a malfunction. The code may be self explanatory or it may refer to a condition explained in detail in a manual or operator guide.

diagnostics. In operations, programs and techniques used to detect and isolate faults in a system, component or program. A diagnostic program will usually produce a printout containing an analysis of the operation being checked in order to assist with fault finding and correction. *Compare* DEBUGGER.

dial access. In data communications, the connection through the public switched telephone network, from a terminal to a service, network or computer.

dial back. *See* CALL BACK.

dialer. *Synonymous with* TELEPHONE DIALER.

dial-up control. In computer security, a security system to deal with misuse of computer systems by hackers. Such misuse can cause problems from illegal access and corruption of files to simple tying up the telephone line. Some dial-up systems require user identification, and verification, before the modem tone is transmitted, this process thwarts the hacker who dials telephone numbers in a sequence until a modem tone is received. Other security precautions include reactions to successive user failure to input the correct password, in some systems such calls are automatically diverted to a security officer who, unbeknown to the caller, initiates a trace of the calling telephone number. Call back systems require the users to identify themselves and then hang up. The authorized telephone number for that user is then called back, and after input of an identification code by the legitimate user, the connection is made. *See* CALL BACK, MODEM, TELEPHONE INTRUSION.

DIANE. Direct Information Access Network for Europe. Refers to information services offered over the Euronet system. *See* EURONET.

dibit. In data communications, a group of two bits. The four possible states of a dibit are 00, 01, 10, 11. *Compare* TRIBIT. *See* BIT.

dictionary attack. In access control, a technique to gain knowledge of passwords. A large dictionary of potential passwords is used to guess passwords. Such attacks may be detected by on-line monitoring of password entries. In some systems passwords are irreversibly encrypted and stored in a password file. The encryption technique may not involve a secret key, e.g. the password itself may be used as the key to encrypt a fixed data block. In this case the dictionary attack may be undertaken off-line, if the attacker can retrieve the password file. The attacker encrypts each entry in the dictionary and checks the result against the list of stored encrypted passwords. *See* HANOVER HACKER, MORRIS WORM, PASSWORD.

differential PCM. In data communications, a version of pulse code modulation in which the difference in value between a sample and the previous sample is encoded. Because fewer bits are required for transmission than under PCM, this technique is used in satellite communications. *See* PULSE CODE MODULATION, SAMPLING.

Diffie-Hellman technique. In cryptography, a public key method of key distribution. Two parties Alice and Bob exchange information that enables each of them to determine the same secret key, but it would be computationally infeasible for an eavesdropper to determine the key on the basis of the information exchanged.

Alice and Bob agree upon two integers α and prime p. Alice selects an integer a and calculates y_a:

$$y_a = \alpha^a \bmod p$$

Bob similarly selects an integer b and calculates y_b:

$$y_b = \alpha^b \bmod p$$

Alice and Bob exchange the computed values y_a and y_b; they then employ them to compute the secret key K:

$$K = (\alpha)^{ab} \bmod p.$$

Alice's computer uses the received value y_a and secret number a to compute:

$$K = (y_b)^a \bmod p$$

Similarly Bob's computer uses the received value y_a and secret number b to compute:

$$K = (y_a)^b \bmod p$$

The computational effort for each party is equivalent to some $2.\log_2 (p)$ multiplications of mod p. However an eavesdropper needs to calculate either a or b, to determine K, where:

$$a = \log_\alpha y_a \bmod p$$

The computation of integer a requires approximately $p^{1/2}$ calculations. If p is slightly less than 2^{200} then the communicating parties perform 400 multiplications mod p but an attacker must undertake 2^{100}, i.e. approximately 10^{30} computations to determine K.

A spoofer can, however, exploit this technique if it is possible to intercept communications between the communicating parties. The spoofer produces an integer c and computes:

$$y_c = \alpha^c \bmod p$$

The transmitted y_a is intercepted from Alice and the spoofer transmits y_c in its place to Bob. Similarly y_b from Bob is intercepted and is again replaced by y_c and forwarded to Alice. Alice computes a key based upon y_c and integer a, whilst Bob computes a key based upon y_c and b. The attacker likewise computes both keys. Subsequently Alice and Bob transmit encrypted data that can be decrypted, and re-encrypted for onward transmission, by the spoofer.

The Diffie-Hellman technique is covered by patents. *Compare* KEYLESS CRYPTOGRAPHY. *See* CRYPTOGRAPHIC KEY, ELGAMAL CIPHER.

diffuse risk from adversarial sources. In risk management, a situation common in computer security, where the nature of the risk, and the objects of the risk are diffuse, and the source of the risk could be a malevolent adversary. *See* RISK ANALYSIS, RISK ASSESSMENT.

diffusion. (1) In cryptography, a technique of increasing the strength of a cipher system by spreading the statistics of the message space into a statistical structure that involves long combinations of characters in the ciphertext. This effectively increases the length of the ciphertext required for any statistical analysis by a cryptanalyst. *Compare* CONFUSION. *See* CIPHERTEXT, CRYPTA-

NALYSIS, STRENGTH. (2) In cryptography, a characteristic of ciphering algorithms that conceal the statistical properties of the plaintext by diluting them in the ciphertext.

digital. Pertaining to digits or the representation of data or physical quantities by digits. *Compare* ANALOG.

digital bit pipe. In data communications, a conceptual channel between an end user and a carrier for the transmission of binary data.

digital communicator. In physical security, a device that automatically dials a central station, upon receipt of an alarm signal, and transmits a coded message containing details of the subscriber identity and nature of the alarm. Normally the digital communicator awaits an acknowledgement signal from the central station before shutting off. *See* CENTRAL STATION. *Synonymous with* DIGITAL DIALER.

digital dialer. *Synonymous with* DIGITAL COMMUNICATOR.

digital distributed system security architecture. In computer security, the security architecture developed for Digital Equipment Corporation distributed computer systems.

Overview
The architecture provides a framework, for a general purpose computing environment of heterogeneous systems, in which there are no central authorities or controls, and no global trust. The architecture covers user and system authentication, mandatory and discretionary access control, secure initialization and loading, and delegation.

A distributed system will have no single reference monitor enforcing a single security policy. Each system within the distributed system will have its own reference monitor enforcing its own policy. When an access request for a local object is received from a remote source, the local reference monitor must ensure that: the appropriate subject authentication has occurred, the remote system has been authorized by the subject to make that request and there is compatibility between the security policy of the remote subject and the local object, so that the access rights can be evaluated. There must also be some level of mutual trust between the reference monitors.

The architecture makes extensive use of MACs (Message Authentication Codes) to ensure the integrity of messages. The architecture also employs non-cryptographic MACs such that users may check the MAC of a message, without requiring access to a cryptographic key, but are unable to produce a message which will produce a predetermined MAC. Such non-cryptographic MACs must be distributed with guaranteed integrity, e.g. widely published by a trusted source. Such MACs may, for example, be used to evaluate the integrity of widely used software.

A secure channel may be provided by either a protected physical path, e.g. a wire, or an encrypted logical path. Such a secure channel provides either authentication or confidentiality or both, whereas an insecure channel provides neither. A secure physical channel is identified by a hardware address, e.g. an I/O port number on a computer, whereas an encryption channel is identified by a cryptographic key. Symmetric ciphers are employed for confidentiality of encryption channels and public key cryptography, with the use of certificates, are used for secure channels providing authentication.

Physical channels may be treated as objects and protected by access control but such access control is not appropriate for an encrypted logical path since use of the channel depends upon knowledge of the appropriate cryptographic keys.

Integrity of Loaded Software

The security of a computer system is critically dependent upon the integrity of loaded software. There are, however, effectively layers of software in a computer system. Boot software, resident in hardware or firmware, loads an operating system; the operating system may then load a system such as a DBMS which, in turn, loads a particular application program. Moreover computer processes, which effectively represent software in action, increasingly communicate with other processes over a network, and such processes should be in a position to undertake mutual authentication.

Software integrity may be checked in a similar manner to that used for transmitted messages, i.e. with MACs. The conventional MAC however is used between a given sender/receiver pair holding a secret symmetric cipher key. In the case of software integrity, to be checked by a population of receiving systems, certificates are used.

A boot software image is supplied with a secret/public key pair and a certificate containing the MAC of the operating system. When the operating system is loaded the boot image checks the MAC of the loaded software with that contained in the certificate. In the case of a successful check, the boot image creates a secret key/public key pair for the loaded software, signs a certificate for the MAC, and created public key, with the boot image secret key, erases boot secret information from any memory location that could be accessed by the operating system, and then executes the operating system.

The operating system can authenticate itself, to other processes, with the secret key and certificate supplied by the boot image. This whole process may be repeated as the next level of software is loaded; thus providing assurance on the loaded software integrity and a means for processes to authenticate each other in a distributed system.

Access Control

A consistent naming convention is essential for a distributed security architecture, remote subjects must be able to identify themselves to objects. Objects must have the capacity to correlate a subject with its stored access rights. In DSSA a hierarchical system of directories, and subjects, provides a means of providing a pathname for subjects. A unique userID is stored in the directory entry located by its pathname.

Access control rights are stored in access control lists, ACLs, of the objects, i.e. a subject's name and access rights are stored in the corresponding object's ACL. The ACL may contain names of subjects, groups of subjects and the names of subjects or groups which are denied access. A subject or group may be included in a denied access list, even if the subject is contained in a group granted access, or the group is the subgroup of such a group granted access.

Each ACL is in effect a file which itself is subject to access control, and thus has its own ACL. The potential infinite list of ACLs may be terminated by an ACL, acting as its own ACL.

Authentication

Subjects and systems may mutually authenticate each other using public key cryptography and challenge response techniques. The subject identifies itself to the system by first claiming a userID, and the system responds with a random number. The subject encrypts the random number with its secret key and returns the result to the system, which retrieves the public key, corresponding to the claimed userID, and uses it to decrypt the response from the subject. If the decrypted response corresponds to the original random number, the subject has successfully authenticated itself to the system. Similarly the user can enter into a challenge/response dialogue to authenticate the system. Smart cards with inbuilt public key cryptography

algorithms, and stored secret keys, provide users with a convenient mechanism to undertake such challenge/response procedures.

When user and system have authenticated each other; one may generate a secret symmetric cipher key, encrypt it under the other party's public key, and forward it for use in subsequent authentication, e.g. for encrypted MACs.

Authentication can be achieved without use of public key cryptography, if a trusted key distribution centre is used. Each party trusts the centre to develop information for authentication.

Certification authorities (CA) in the architecture are systems that are trusted to certify public keys, the MACs used to verify software integrity and that a given software image may be loaded into a particular computer system. The certificates provided by the CA relieve each system from having to record the public key of all subjects, against that subject identity. The CAs are therefore trusted to ensure that a subject correctly identifies itself to the CA when it supplies its public key. The certificate linking user ID and public key is signed with the secret key of the CA.

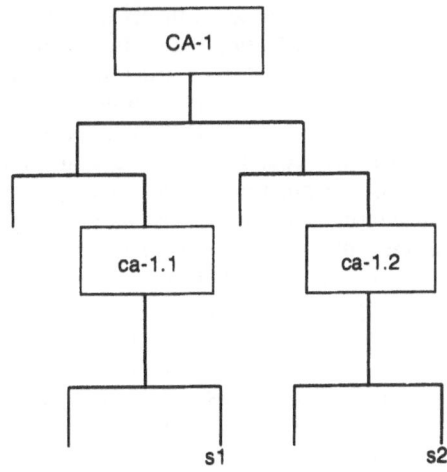

digital distributed system security architecture
Fig. 1. Hierarchy of CA's

Distributed systems are likely to have a number of CAs since it is unlikely that all subjects would be able to verify their identity and public key to a single CA. In these circumstances a hierarchy of CAs will exist, and the certificate issued by one CA, may be accompanied by another certifying the public key of the CA itself. The naming convention, mentioned above, employs a hierarchy of directories and subjects and CAs may be associated with particular directories. A CA located at a particular directory will certify other CAs immediately above, and below, it in the hierarchy. When one system receives a certificate from another, there will be an associated set of certificates representing a path up the hierarchy, until a common parent CA, is attained and then down the other side of the hierarchy to the CA of the second party.

For example in the hierarchy illustrated in Fig. 1, S1 would supply certificates issued by CA-1.1 for S1, by CA-1 for CA-1.1, and by CA-1.2 for CA-1. S2 would trust such certificates because they included one from CA-1.2 which is trusted by S2, and a chain of certificates which lead to S1.

Delegated Access Rights
Subjects do not access objects directly in a distributed system, but rather employ intermediaries that they trust to act on their behalf. The object system must however assure itself that an intermediary has the requisite delegated authority from the originating subject, and indeed the intermediary itself must assure itself of the authenticity of the subject. This assurance is provided in the architecture by delegation certificates. For example users authenticate themselves to a workstation and then issue a delegation certificate to that workstation. The workstation in turn may authenticate itself to a server and then produce the user's delegation certificate with an access request. The server checks the access

request against the user's name in the ACL of the file to be accessed.

There is no guarantee that the workstation will not issue subsequent requests that have not been authorized by the user, and there must be therefore some mechanism for ending the period of delegation. The user may erase the secret key used to sign the delegation certificate, and inform all systems that certificates signed with that key are no longer valid. The delegation certificates must, in any case, have a limited life, as specified by an expiry time/date, to minimize any compromise arising from system malfunction or compromise.

A user may wish to delegate only a limited set of rights, e.g. access to a particular set of files. Such limitation may best be achieved by users adopting a series of UserIDs corresponding to the set of rights to be delegated at any one time. The object system then simply checks the requested access against the particular UserID contained in the delegation certificate.

Revocation of Access Rights
Most security systems concentrate on the mechanisms which deal with the initial granting or denial of access, but what assurance exists for the mechanisms that revoke such rights? Thus how does the system respond to the situations: a name is to be withdrawn from an access list, a user has withdrawn from a group, a certificate for authentication or delegation is to be withdrawn or an authenticated session is no longer valid.

Immediate revocation of rights represents a difficult problem because systems hold current rights in a local store and it is impractical to reliably and immediately inform all systems that access control information has changed. Thus a system may parse an access control list, expanding all groups into userIDs. If a userID is withdrawn from a group then this information will not affect accesses in progress.

The architecture allows for slow, rather than immediate, revocation. Applications will decide when revocation decisions will be made, e.g. when a file is opened. Care must be exercised, however, to ensure that applications are not operated for extensive periods without checks on revocations. Certificates may be withdrawn before the expiry date, due to suspected compromise of the secret key, it is important that certificates are only retrieved from trusted stores that will report such revocations.

Authentication cannot be revoked; once a pair of systems have authenticated each other for a session there is no mechanism to withdraw such authentication. It is important therefore that sessions be of a limited duration, with new authentication sessions at intervals commensurate with the processes for checking trusted sources for certificates.

Mandatory Access Control
The architecture allows for mandatory as well as discretionary access control. Even though commercial systems will tend not to enforce mandatory access control, they should be compatible with systems that adopt such methods. An access request emanating from a remote system, enforcing mandatory access control, will be accompanied by label, specified by the remote reference monitor, corresponding to the access class of the subject initiating the request. Additionally certificates specifying the policy domain and set of access classes of the remote reference monitor will be supplied. The local monitor will only grant access on the basis of the supplied information, which may include details related to the level of assurance of the remote reference monitor, and the access class of the object. The revocation problem is more severe in the case of mandatory access control since any change in mandatory access control attributes must impact immediately. *See* ACCESS CONTROL LIST, CERTIFICATE, CERTIFICATION AUTHORITY, CHAL-

LENGE/RESPONSE, DIRECTORY, DISCRETIONARY ACCESS CONTROL, KEY DISTRIBUTION CENTER, LABEL, MANDATORY ACCESS CONTROL, MESSAGE AUTHENTICATION CODE, OBJECT, PUBLIC KEY CRYPTOGRAPHY, REFERENCE MONITOR, SECURE CHANNEL, SUBJECT, SYMMETRIC CIPHER.

digital enveloping. In cryptography, a technique in which anyone can seal a message, in such a way that only the intended recipient can open the sealed message. Typically the sender selects a random secret symmetric key and uses it to encrypt the message. The symmetric key is then itself encrypted with the recipient's public key, the encrypted key and encrypted message is then transmitted. *See* PUBLIC KEY, SYMMETRIC KEY SYSTEM.

digital keypad. In physical security, a keypad with numerical pushbuttons used to enter access control information for entry to, or exit from, a controlled area. The access control procedures may require that the appropriate code be entered within a specific time interval after depression of the first key. The system may include duress signals and system lockout if incorrect codes are entered. The keypad may also be used in conjunction with a card reader. *See* CARD READER, DURESS ALARM.

digital multiplex switching system. In data communications, the use of PCM and TDM systems over circuit switched lines. *See* CIRCUIT SWITCHING, PCM, TDM.

digital signal. A discrete or discontinuous electric signal, one whose various states are at discrete intervals apart. *Compare* ANALOG SIGNAL.

digital signalling. In data communications, the use of a digital transmission channel for the setting up, control and release of calls.

digital signature. (1) In authentication, data appended to, or a cryptographic transformation of, a data unit that allows a recipient of the data unit to prove the source and integrity of the data unit and protect against forgery, e.g. by the recipient. (ANSI). (2) In authentication, a data block appended to a message, or a complete encrypted message, such that the recipient can authenticate the message contents and/or prove that it could only have originated with the purported sender.

Overview

The digital signature is a function of:

- the message, transaction or document, to be signed;
- secret information known only to the sender;
- public information employed in the validation process.

Message Authentication Codes enable the receiver of a message to ensure that the contents cannot be undetectably changed accidentally, or deliberately by a third party. However, since both the sender and the receiver share the same secret information there is no method of resolving disputes. The receiver can compute the authenticator and could therefore change a message, or forge a new message, develop the authenticator and claim that it was transmitted by the sender sharing the same secret key for authentication. Conversely the sender could disown an authenticated message and claim that the receiver produced a forged message using the common secret key.

The essence of a digital signature is that the receiver must be able to prove that a message originated with a given sender, but must not be able to construct the signed message. Thus the sender requires secret information to construct the signed message and the receiver must be able to access public information to use in the validation of the message. In the case of a dispute the receiver must be in a position to supply non secret information to a judge, i.e. the signed message and the publicly available information, in order to prove the authentication and origin of the message.

Digital signatures may be broadly categorized as universal and arbitrated. Universal signatures may be validated by anyone with access to publicly available validation parameters, whilst arbitrated signatures require the services of a trusted arbiter who signs the message for the sender and validates it for the receiver.

Universal Signatures - Asymmetric Ciphers

Universal signatures can be provided with:

- public key cryptography;
- conventional algorithms and symmetric ciphers operated in a manner that effectively provides public key cryptography facilities.

RSA provides an extremely elegant and effective method of producing digital signatures. The essential features of this technique is that the message is initially enciphered with the sender's private key and the receiver obtains the original message by deciphering the signed message with the sender's public key. Thus

Sender develops

$$C = ek_s(M)$$

Receiver produces

$$M^R = dk_p(C)$$
$$= dk_p(ek_s(M)) = M$$

Where k_p is the sender's public key and k_s is the sender's private key.

In the conventional use of RSA the plaintext message is revealed by decipherment with the private key, of ciphertext produced by encipherment of the message with the receiver's public key, i.e. :

$$M = dk_s(ek_p(M))$$

The nature of RSA enables the two operations of encipherment and decipherment to be reversed, in terms of the keys used, and yet still produce the original message. This is because both operations involve exponentiation. The receiver of the signed message is assured that the message originated with the purported sender since only the sender had access to the secret key k_s.

There are, however, a number of additional precautions required in the implementation of this signature technique. Firstly, the message must contain a degree of redundancy, secondly it must guard against resequencing of message blocks and thirdly, additional encipherment is required to maintain secrecy.

The essence of the receiver's case, that only the sender could have originated the message, is that no third party could produce ciphertext, that would be transformed to a meaningful message by decipherment with the sender's public key.

The requirement that the received plaintext be meaningful implies that it contains a high degree of redundancy. If the nature of the message is such that it contains a low level of redundancy, e.g. a random collection of bits produced by a monitoring instrument, then an authenticator must be employed. The authenticator may be included as an integral part of the signed message, or signed individually and appended as a signature.

If a complete message is signed, then an attack is possible by simply re-

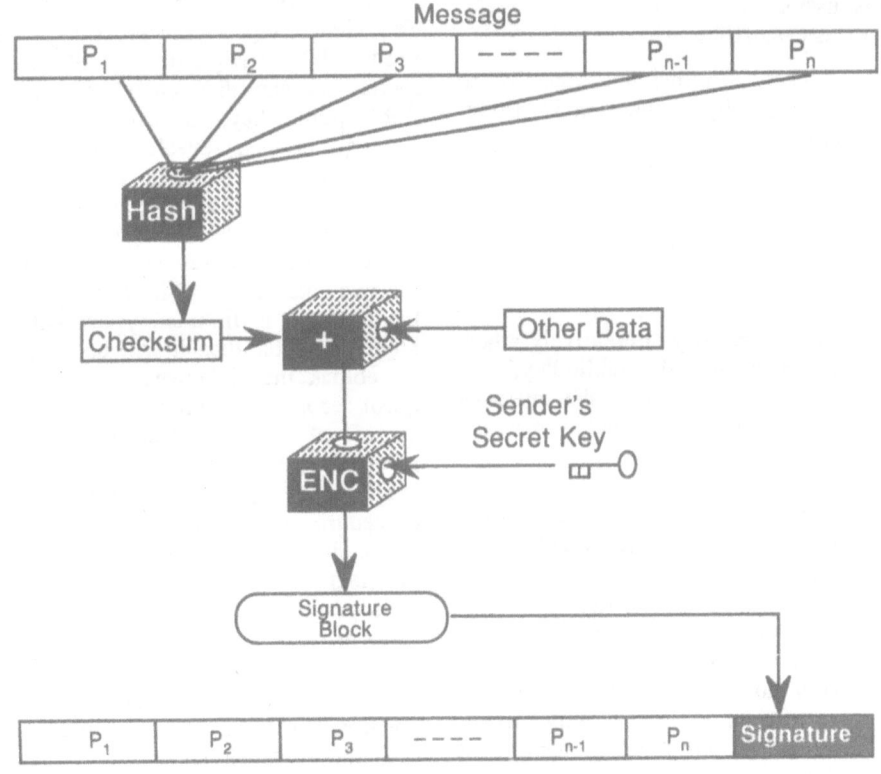

Signed Message (to Receiver)

Digital signature

sequencing the constituent RSA blocks. Such resequencing could still produce a meaningful message apparently signed by the sender. Such an attack can be thwarted by the inclusion of a sequence number in each block, or by the use of an authenticator sensitive to the ordering of message components.

An alternative approach is to produce a shorter 'signature block' by the use of hash, or message digest function, that has the property that it is computationally infeasible to determine a second message which will have the same message digest as that of the original. The message digest should of a length such that it can be computed as a single block in RSA. The message digest is then signed with the sender's secret key and attached to the plaintext message for transmission.

In this case Alice:

- subjects original message M to message digest function H producing message digest H(M);
- encrypts H(M) with secret RSA key to produce the signature block $ek_s(H(M))$;
- transmits M, $ek_s(H(M))$ and Alice identifying information to allow receiver to select Alice's public key, Alice may alternatively attach a certificate of the public key;
- Bob first computes the message digest of the received message M^R, i.e. $H(M^R)$;
- Bob then retrieves Alice's public key k_p, computes $dk_p(ek_s(H(M)))$ and compares the result with $H(M^R)$;
- if they are equal Bob accepts the message but also retains it together with the signature block and Alice's identifying information, or certificate, in case a judge is required to arbitrate a subsequent dispute.

A message signed with a secret RSA key can be transformed to plaintext with the corresponding public key. Such

messages can therefore be revealed by an attacker. If secrecy of signed messages is required then two cryptographic operations are required at both the sending and receiving ends. If message (M) is to be signed by Alice and enciphered for secure transmission to Bob then the transmitted message (C) is produced by:

$$C = ek_{pB}(ek_{sA}(M)) \ ,$$

Where k_{pB} is Bob's public key and k_{sA} is Alice's private key.

Thus the message is enciphered with Alice's secret key and then re-enciphered with Bob's public key. The inverse operations are performed by Bob.

Thus

$$M = dk_{pA}(dk_{sB}(ek_{pB}(ek_{sA}(M))))$$

The signed ciphertext message is first produced by encipherment with Alice's secret key and then encipherment with Bob's public key; the original plaintext message is then revealed by decipherment with Alice's public key and decipherment with Bob's secret key. This technique can lead to complications because the modulus corresponding to the two sets of keys will be different. If the message is first encrypted with the higher modulus then it will be necessary to reblock the ciphertext for the subsequent second encryption operation. If the process of signing and encipherment are reversed to avoid this problem then the judge is faced with a more complex procedure in checking the signature.

If a signature block is appended to the plaintext message then this plaintext message may be enciphered with the receiver's public key to protect its confidentiality.

An alternative to use of the RSA algorithm has been proposed and in this case the ElGamal algorithm is employed.

Knapsack ciphers do not provide the same facilities for digital signatures as RSA because they produce message expansion in the ciphering process. This means that encipherment, with knapsack ciphers, is not a bijection and thus the operations of encipherment and decipherment cannot be reversed for signing operations. A form of knapsack cipher modified for digital signature applications was proposed by Shamir. Both Rabin and Lamport-Diffie have proposed digital signature techniques involving public keys with conventional algorithms but these methods necessitate considerable message expansion, a large number of public keys and moreover the keys must be changed for each signature. They therefore involve major overheads in terms of public registry facilities and communications.

The authenticity of a public key registry is essential in digital signature applications. If an attacker can replace Alice's public key with one of his own, then Bob can be persuaded to accept messages, generated by the attacker, apparently signed by Alice. Similarly Alice may disavow messages by claiming that her secret key has been stolen and used to forge messages. Certificates may be employed to overcome this problem but it is still necessary to have some system of informing users of the withdrawal of certificates and the possible compromise of the secret key used to sign the certificates.

Universal Signatures - Symmetric Ciphers

Symmetric ciphers are unsuitable for digital signatures since the same key is used by the sender and receiver. However symmetric ciphers can be implemented so as to provide encipher-only and decipher-only keys. The essence of this technique is a cryptographic facility in which a master key, or an interchange key, is held in a tamper resistant module store. The messages between sender and receiver are encrypted under a data key but the users only have access to this data key when it is encrypted under the key-encrypting key. Using techniques similar to key notarization it is possible to ensure that the sender is provided with an encryption only facility, in relation to a specific receiver, whilst the receiver can decrypt but not encrypt such received messages. This is similar to a system of public and private keys; however the users of this system are restricted to those with access to the requisite cryptographic facility containing the interchange keys for specific pairs of users.

Arbitrated Signatures

Arbitrated signatures can be implemented with symmetric ciphers, such as DES, and effectively involve an authenticated message from a sender to an arbiter, and separate authenticated message from the arbiter to the receiver. Each user shares an individual secret key with the arbiter but the receiver and sender do not have knowledge of each others secret keys. In a typical arbitrated signature system the sender, Alice, shares a secret key (k_A) with the arbiter. The sender wishes to send a signed message of text (T) to Bob, and this will be the i th in sequence. A message (ID_A, ID_B, i, T) is formed by the sender, encrypted under k_A and an authenticator (AC), that is a function of k_A, is appended to it.

This total message, accompanied with Alice's identifier ID_A in clear, is forwarded to the arbiter. The identifier ID_A enables the arbiter to select the key k_A from a secure store; the message is then decrypted with this key, the identifier ID_A is extracted from the encrypted message and compared with the aforementioned cleartext value. If they are unequal the purported sender is informed and the procedure halts. Otherwise the authenticator is checked and the arbiter forms a codeword for genuine, or not genuine, depending upon the result. The arbiter then develops a message comprising (ID_A, ID_B, i, T, AC) plus the codeword for 'genuine' or 'not genuine'. Bob's identifier ID_B is then used by the arbiter to select Bob's secret key k_B from store. The arbiter encrypts the message under this key, appends an authenticator, also formed using k_B, and the resultant message is forwarded to Bob.

Bob decrypts the message, checks that it contains the codeword for 'genuine', that the arbiter's authenticator is consistent with the message and the authentication algorithm. Bob also retains the authenticator (AC) and the received message text for evidence in a dispute. A judge can ask the arbiter to compute the authenticator of the message, with key k_A, and compare the result with AC. Bob could not have computed AC since it involves a knowledge of the secret key k_A.

The arbitrated signature technique can be used with conventional symmetric ciphers and it does not require a special cryptographic facility with stored master keys. On the other hand it does demand the services of a trusted arbiter; it is therefore more appropriate for users within a closely knit association.

A dynamic password system can also be used to sign a message. Here, the message is first processed to form a checksum, that could be the MAC. This checksum is entered as a seven digit challenge into a special hand held device to produce a response; this is equivalent to the signature and is sent together with the message. The hand held device contains a secret key known only within a particular computer network; the network is thus able to confirm the authenticity of the signature. The use of automated electronic signatures in banking cash management schemes can potentially save a lot of back office overhead in the clerical checking of handwritten signatures. *See* ARBITRATED SIGNATURE, AUTHENTICATOR, BACK OFFICE, CERTIFICATE, DES, DSS, DYNAMIC PASSWORD, ELECTRONIC SIGNATURE, ELGAMAL DIGITAL SIGNATURE, INTERCHANGE KEY, KEY ENCRYPTING KEY, KEY NOTARIZATION, KNAPSACK CIPHER, LAMPORT-DIFFIE SIGNATURE, MAC, MESSAGE AUTHENTICATION, MODULO ARITHMETIC, PUBLIC KEY CRYPTOGRAPHY, RABIN SIGNATURE, RSA, TAMPER RESISTANT MODULE, UNIVERSAL SIGNATURE.

digital signature standard. In cryptography, a standard for digital signatures proposed by NIST.

In this standard a number of parameters are defined:

- p = a prime modulus such that $2^{511} < p < 2^{512}$;
- q = a prime divisor of p-1 where $2^{159} < q < 2^{160}$;
- $g = h^{(p-1)/q} \bmod p$, where h is any integer with $0 < h < p$ such that $h^{(p-1)/q} \bmod p > 1$;
- x = an integer such that $0 < x < q$;
- $y = g^x \bmod p$;
- m = the message to be signed and transmitted;
- k = random integer such that $0 < k < q$;
- H = a one-way hash function.

The parameters may be grouped:

- p, q and g are public knowledge and common to a group of users;
- x and k are secret to the person signing the message and k must be changed for each message;
- y is the signer's public key;
- H is not defined in the standard but it must be such that it is computationally infeasible to create a message corresponding to a given hash function or to find two messages with the same hash function.

When the sender wishes to sign message m a random number k is chosen and the sender computes:

- $r = (g^k \bmod p) \bmod q$;
- $s = (k^{-1} (H(m)) + xr)) \bmod q$.

The signature comprises r and s which is transmitted with the message m.

The recipient of the message receives m', s' and r' and wishes to confirm that s' and r' represent a valid signature for received message m'. The checks conducted are:

- $0 < r' < q$ and $0 < s' < q$, if either of these tests fail the signature is invalid and the message rejected otherwise the following checks are undertaken:
- $w = (s')^{-1} \bmod q$ is computed;
- $u1 = ((H(m'))w) \bmod q$ is computed;
- $u2 = ((r')w) \bmod q$ is computed;
- $v = (((g)^{u1} (y)^{u2}) \bmod p) \bmod q$ is computed;
- if $v = r'$ then the signature block may be accepted with a high level of confidence.

See DIGITAL SIGNATURE, ELGAMAL DIGITAL SIGNATURE.

digital switching. In communications, a process in which connections are established by operations on digital signals without their first being converted to analog signals. *See* DIGITAL SIGNAL.

digital transmission system. In data communications, a network in which analog information is digitized via a modulation technique and transmitted in a discrete form as a series of pulses. At the receiving station, the analog data is reconstituted from the digitized signals. Digital transmission systems support high data rates, error detection and minimize effects due to noise.

DIN. Deutsche Industrie Norm, the German standards organization.

diplex operation. In communications, the use of a single circuit, carrier or antenna for the simultaneous transmission or reception of two signals. *Compare* DUPLEX. *See* CARRIER.

direct access. In database security, a form of threat in which a user requests information at a higher security classification than that of the user and the system supplies that information. *Compare* INDIRECT ACCESS, TROJAN HORSE DIRECT RELEASE, TROJAN HORSE LEAKAGE.

direct data access arrangement. In data communications, a unit containing an isolation transformer, for interconnecting user equipment to a telephone network. It is designed to prevent harmful voltages or signals entering the network.

direct debit. *Synonymous with* DEBIT TRANSFER.

directly connected transaction. In banking, a transaction characterized by the condition that the card issuer (or its agent) with whom the acquirer communicates, has complete knowledge of the card holder's card and is therefore able to construct the card key. (SAA). *Compare* INDIRECTLY CONNECTED TRANSACTION. *See* ACQUIRER, CARD HOLDER, CARD ISSUER, CARD KEY, KEY MANAGEMENT.

direct memory access. In computing, a technique that allows a peripheral device to gain direct access to the main memory of the computer.

directory. (1) In databases, a file that stores relationships between records in other files. The directory contains an overview of the data held, and since it occupies less storage space than the data files, searches and operations performed on the directory are more efficient than those performed on the data files themselves. *Compare* DATA DICTIONARY, TREE STRUCTURED DIRECTORY. (2) In data communications, a table containing routing information. *See* DIRECTORY ROUTING.

directory routing. In data communications, a routing method that uses a directory at each node. The directory contains details of the preferred, and possibly second preference, outgoing link for each destination. *Compare* ADAPTIVE ROUTING, CENTRALIZED ADAPTIVE ROUTING, DELTA ROUTING, FIXED ROUTING, HOT POTATO ROUTING. *See* ROUTING.

Dir-Vir. In computer security, a stealth virus that terminates and stays resident, infects COMMAND.COM and COM files, affects run time operation, corrupts program, OVL and data files. *See* VIRUS NAMES.

DIS. In standards, ISO Draft International Standard. *See* ISO.

disaster. In risk management, a condition in which an organization is deemed to be unable to function due to an accidental or malicious occurrence.

disassembler. In data communications, a device that extracts the message content from packets. *See* PACKET SWITCHING, PACKET ASSEMBLER/DISASSEMBLER.

disaster plan. *See* CONTINGENCY PLANS, DISASTER RECOVERY PLAN.

disaster planning. In risk management, planning for any event that causes significant disruption to operations thereby threatening the business survival. *See* BUSINESS RESUMPTION PLANNING, DISASTER RECOVERY PLAN.

disaster recovery manual. In computer security, the documentation of a disaster recovery plan, including a description of activities to be performed, with supporting documents and checklists. *See* DISASTER RECOVERY PLAN.

disaster recovery plan. In computer security, the planned sequence of events that allows for the recovery of a computer facility and/or the applications

processed there. *See* CONTINGENCY PLANS.

disclosing. In legislation, as defined by the U.K. Data Protection Act 1984, pertaining to disclosing in relation to data, includes disclosing information extracted from that data; and, where the identification of the individual who is the subject of personal data depends partly on the information constituting the data and partly on other information in the possession of the data user, the data shall not be regarded as disclosed or transferred unless the other information is also disclosed or transferred. *See* DATA, DATA PROTECTION, PERSONAL DATA.

disclosure. In data security, the unauthorized acquisition of information. *See* MASQUERADING.

disclosure risk. In database security, the risk that information concerning an individual can be deduced by queries on a statistical database. *See* INFERENCE CONTROL, STATISTICAL DATABASE.

disconnect service message. In key management, an optional message to disconnect keys. *See* ANSI X9.17 - 1985.

discrepancy reports. In computer security, a listing of items that have violated some detective control and require further investigation.

discrete Fourier transform scrambler. In communications security, a voice scrambling technique in which the speech signal is digitized and split into frames. The signals for each frame are subjected to a discrete Fourier transform and the resulting frequency domain components are permuted. The resulting signal is then subjected to the inverse Fourier transform and transmitted. *Compare* TWO-DIMENSIONAL SCRAMBLER.

See VOICE SCRAMBLING. *Synonymous with* DFT SCRAMBLER.

discrete logarithm problem. In cryptography, a problem which states that a pair of integers g,s belong to a Galois Field GF(N), where N is prime; it is required to determine a positive integer x ($0 \leq x \leq N$) such that: $x = \log_g s$ (mod N). *See* GALOIS FIELD.

discretionary access control. In access control, a means of restricting access to objects based on the identity of subjects and/or groups to which they belong. The controls are discretionary in the sense that a subject with a certain access permission is capable of passing that permission (perhaps indirectly) on to any other subject. (DOD). *Compare* MANDATORY ACCESS CONTROL. *See* OBJECT, SUBJECT.

discretionary processing. In computer security, the activities that may be interrupted for some period of time. A loss of ability to process such applications for some period of time will not seriously affect the well-being of the organization. *Compare* CRITICAL PROCESSING.

discretionary protection. Access control that identifies individual users and their need-to-know and limits users to the information that they are allowed to see. It is used on systems that process information with the same level of sensitivity. (AFR). *Compare* DISCRETIONARY SECURITY. *See* DISCRETIONARY ACCESS CONTROL, NEED TO KNOW.

discretionary security. (1) In computer security, security measures initiated by the entities themselves. (2) In computer security, those aspects of a security policy that involve the provision of security services as a result of a request by an entity requiring an instance of communication. *Compare* MANDATORY SECURITY, NON-DISCRETIONARY SECURITY.

discretionary security policy. In access control, an access control policy in which a system administrator, or some other authorized person e.g. data owner, may make arbitrary decisions on which users may undertake specific access modes to a given set of data. *Compare* MANDATORY SECURITY POLICY. *See* DATA OWNER, DISCRETIONARY SECURITY.

disgruntled employee. *See* SECURITY THREATS.

dishonest employee. *See* SECURITY THREATS.

disjoint. Having no common areas.

disk crash. (1) In computing, a read/write head making destructive contact with a hard disk surface. (2) In computing, any hardware or software malfunction producing inaccessibility of disk data. *See* HARD DISK, MAGNETIC DISK.

disk drive. In computing, a mechanism for rotating a disk pack or a magnetic disk and controlling its movements. *See* DISK PACK, HARD DISK.

diskette. *Synonymous with* FLOPPY DISK.

Disk killer. In computer security, a virus that terminates and stays resident, infects floppy and hard disk boot sector, corrupts boot sector, affects run time operation, corrupts program, OVL and data files, formats or overwrites all or part of disk. *See* VIRUS NAMES.

disk pack. In computing, a set of disks on a common spindle, handled as a single unit.

disk server. In computing, a hard disk system providing backing storage to a number of networked microcomputer users. *See* FILE SERVER.

dissemination. *See* SPECIAL MARKINGS.

distortion. In data communications, any undesired change in waveform. The principal sources of distortion of waveforms are: non-linear relationship between input and output, non-uniform transmission at different frequencies and a phase shift not proportional to frequency. *See* INTERMODULATION DISTORTION.

distributed adaptive routing. In data communications, a method of routing in which the decisions are made on the basis of exchange of information between the nodes of a network. *See* ADAPTIVE ROUTING.

distributed database. In databases, a database that is located on a number of different computers that are often in different geographic locations. The database may have been designed as a single entity, e.g. to serve branches of a large organization, or it may have arisen as the result of a merger of a number of originally isolated systems.

distributed data processing. (1) In data communications, the distribution of processing functions and data throughout an organization to the locations they are needed. *See* COOPERATIVE PROCESSING, END USER COMPUTING, SYSTEM NETWORK ARCHITECTURE. *Synonymous with* DISTRIBUTED PROCESSING. (2) In computing, a collection of processes interconnected so as to decentralize resources and provide an environment for execution of application programs. *See* APPLICATION PROGRAM, DISTRIBUTED NETWORK, PROCESSOR.

distributed function. In data communications, the use of programmable terminals and other devices employed to carry out operations that were previously performed by the central processing unit, e.g. network management and data formatting. *See* NETWORK MANAGEMENT.

distributed network. In computing, any combination of loosely and tightly coupled systems. A typical configuration is illustrated in the diagram. The master comprises a tightly coupled multiprocessor with a large memory shared by two CPU's. The I/O arbiter allows both processors to access all I/O devices. If one CPU develops hardware problems the remaining processor can continue to run all programs albeit at a slower rate. The workstations can be complete processors with memory, disk and I/O devices. Each can run in a standalone mode; when a user requests services not available locally the workstation can request assistance from the master. Distributed networks can have very flexible architectures, e.g. star networks with all the workstations directly connected to the master or ring networks with cables daisy chaining from one office to the next. *See* CPU, DAISY CHAIN, WORKSTATION.

distributed processing. *Synonymous with* DISTRIBUTED DATA PROCESSING.

distributive law. In mathematics, two binary operations, satisfy the distributive law if:

$x + (y * z) = (x + y) * (x + z)$

$x * (y + z) = (x * y) + (x * z)$ where x, y and z are the variables and *, + represents the binary operations. *Compare* ASSOCIATIVE LAW, COMMUTATIVE LAW. *See* GALOIS FIELD.

DIV. *See* DATA IN VOICE.

DIVA. *See* DATA INPUT VOICE ANSWERBACK.

division. In databases, an operation in relational databases. If a relation A has two attributes X, Y and relation B has one attribute Z; with Y and Z defined over the same domain then the operation 'Divide A by B over Y and Z' produces a quotient defined on the same domain as X. The quotient contains tuples X;

the dividend (A) contains tuples (X,Y) and the divisor (B) contains tuples Z. The value X appears only if A contains pairs (X,Y) for all values of Y in B. *Compare* JOIN, PROJECTION, SELECTION. *See* ATTRIBUTE, DOMAIN, RELATIONAL DATABASE, TUPLE.

Division A. In information security, a division in the TCSEC criteria, systems in this division have been evaluated for all the functionality of Division B, Class B3 but have also satisfied stringent conditions of formal verification. It comprises one class: A1. *Compare* DIVISION B, DIVISION C, DIVISION D. *See* FORMAL VERIFICATION, ORANGE BOOK, TCSEC.

Division B. In information security, a division in the TCSEC criteria, systems in this division have been evaluated for discretionary access control. It comprises three classes: B1, B2 and B3, with B3 specifying more stringent conditions than B1. *Compare* DIVISION A, DIVISION C, DIVISION D. *See* DISCRETIONARY ACCESS CONTROL, MANDATORY ACCESS CONTROL, ORANGE BOOK, TCSEC.

Division C. In information security, a division in the TCSEC criteria, systems in this division have been evaluated for discretionary access control. It comprises two classes: C1 and C2, with C2 specifying more stringent conditions than C1. *Compare* DIVISION A, DIVISION B, DIVISION D. *See* DISCRETIONARY ACCESS CONTROL, ORANGE BOOK, TCSEC.

Division D. In information security, a division in the TCSEC criteria, systems in this division have been evaluated but failed to satisfy the criteria of any higher class. *Compare* DIVISION A, DIVISION B, DIVISION C. *See* ORANGE BOOK, TCSEC.

DMA. *See* DIRECT MEMORY ACCESS.

DML. *See* DATA MANIPULATION LANGUAGE.

DMS. *See* DIGITAL MULTIPLEX SWITCHING SYSTEM.

document cycle. *Synonymous with* BANKING CYCLE.

DOD. U.S. Department of Defense.

DODCSC. Department of Defense Computer Security Center. *See* NATIONAL COMPUTER SECURITY CENTER.

DODD. U.S. Department of Defense Directive.

DOD Information Analysis Center. An activity that acquires, digests, analyzes, evaluates, synthesizes, stores, publishes, and provides advisory and other user services concerning available worldwide scientific and technical information and engineering data in a clearly defined, specialized field or subject area of significant DOD interest or concern. IACs are distinguished from technical information centers and libraries whose functions are primarily concerned with providing reference or access to the documents themselves rather than the STI information contained in the documents. (DODD).

DOD security criteria. *See* ORANGE BOOK.

DOD Technology Transfer. Programs to promote military-civilian technology transfer and cooperative development on a systematic basis, including appropriate transfer of technology developed by the DOD to the U.S. civilian sector where such technology can be utilized profitably, and identification of new technologies of both military and civilian interest. (DODD).

DOD 5200.28-STD. Department of Defense Trusted Computer System

Evaluation Criteria, a standard declared in December 1985. *See* ORANGE BOOK, TCSEC.

DOE. U.S. Department of Energy.

domain. (1) In mathematics, the set of input values of a function. *Compare* RANGE. (2) In computer security, the set of objects that a subject has the ability to access. (DOD). *See* ACCESS, OBJECT, SUBJECT.

dominate. In computer security, a security level S_1 is said to dominate security level S_2 if the hierarchical classification of S_1 is greater than or equal to that of S_2 and the non-hierarchical categories of S_1 include all those of S_2 as a subset. (DOD). *See* BELL LAPADULA MODEL, SECURITY LEVEL.

DON. U.S. Department of the Navy.

dongle. In software protection, a small hardware device, supplied by a software producer, and inserted in the serial port of a microcomputer. The software package is designed to run only if the device is present. Dongles are not popular, partly because they tie up a microcomputer port, and in any case there are more effective software techniques for protection purposes. *See* EXECUTE PROTECTION.

Do-Nothing. In computer security, a virus that terminates and stays resident, infects COM files, corrupts program and OVL files. *See* VIRUS NAMES.

Doom2. In computer security, a virus that terminates and stays resident, infects COM and EXE files, affects run time operation, corrupts program, OVL and data files and file linkage. *See* VIRUS NAMES.

Dot killer. In computer security, a virus that terminates and stays resident, infects COMMAND.COM and COM files, affects run time operation, corrupts program and OVL files. *See* VIRUS NAMES.

double circuiting. In physical security, pertaining to the use of redundant wiring between sensors and the alarm system. *See* DOUBLE DROP.

double drop. (1) In physical security, a technique of transmitting an alarm signal using both a cross alarm and break alarm. *See* BREAK ALARM, CROSS ALARM. (2) In physical security, a means of providing redundancy in alarm wiring by using two telephone lines entering the building at different locations. *See* DOUBLE CIRCUITING.

double-supervised system. In physical security, an alarm system that initiates a warning signal in the event of trouble power inputs or power failure. *See* TROUBLE CONDITION.

down line load. In computing, the process sending programs or files from a host computer to a remote computer.

download. *Synonymous with* DOWN LINE LOAD.

downtime. In computing, the time during which a device is inoperable due to a fault. *See* MTBF.

DP. In standards, ISO Draft Proposal. *See* ISO.

DQDB. In data communications, distributed dual queue bus, a MAC protocol developed for use in municipal area networks. *See* MAC, MUNICIPAL AREA NETWORK.

DR/AS. *See* DIFFUSE RISK FROM ADVERSARIAL SOURCES.

draw down. In banking, an instruction to reduce the balance of the sender's account serviced by the receiver by a payment to the sender's account at another financial institution. (ANSI).

drop. In communications, that portion of outside telephone plant that extends from the telephone distribution cable to the subscriber's premises.

DSA. (1) In banking, Decimal Shift and Add, a proposed technique for computing an authenticator. It uses two secret 10 decimal digit keys and is based upon decimal arithmetic. *See* AUTHENTICATOR. (2) Digital Signature Algorithm. *See* DIGITAL SIGNATURE STANDARD.

DSE. *See* DATA SWITCHING EXCHANGE.

DSM. *See* ANSI X9.17 - 1985, DISCONNECT SERVICE MESSAGE.

DSO. *See* DATA SECURITY OFFICER.

DSR. *See* DATA SET READY.

DSS. *See* DECISION SUPPORT SYSTEM, DIGITAL SIGNATURE STANDARD.

DSV. *See* DYNAMIC SIGNATURE VERIFICATION.

DTE. *See* DATA TERMINAL EQUIPMENT.

DTI. U.K. Department of Trade and Industry.

DTLS. *See* DESCRIPTIVE TOP-LEVEL SPECIFICATION.

dual control. In key management, a process of utilizing two or more separate entities (usually persons), operating in concert, to protect sensitive functions or information. Both entities are equally responsible for the physical protection of materials involved in vulnerable transactions. No single person shall be able to access or to utilize the materials (e.g. cryptographic key). For manual key generation, conveyance, loading, storage and retrieval, dual control requires split

knowledge of keys among the entities. (ANSI). *See* CRYPTOGRAPHIC KEY, SPLIT KNOWLEDGE.

dual key. In cryptography, a term covering both weak keys and semiweak keys. *See* SEMIWEAK KEY, WEAK KEY.

dual redundancy. In reliability, a form of modular redundancy using two replicated units. One unit may be a standby spare that replaces the active unit when a fault is detected. Alternatively the two units are operated synchronously and their outputs compared. When a mismatch occurs an interrupt is raised and a fault recognition program is employed to identify and isolate the faulty module. *Compare* NMR, TRIPLE MODULAR REDUNDANCY. *See* MODULAR REDUNDANCY.

dual use system. In computer security, a system with both military and civilian use.

dumb device. In computing, a device, usually a terminal, that can only transmit or receive data to or from a servicing computer. *Compare* INTELLIGENT DEVICE, DUMB TERMINAL.

dumb terminal. In computing, a terminal (or computer using dumb terminal software) that allows communications with other computers, but does not enhance the data exchanged, or provide additional features such as upload/download. *See* CONFIGURABLY DUMB TERMINAL, DUMB DEVICE.

dump. (1) In computing, a bulk transfer of data from one medium to another, e.g. the transfer of the contents of a part of main memory to a line printer. *See* MAIN MEMORY. (2) In databases, pertaining to the regular backup of a database for security purposes.

dumpster diving. In computer security, a method of obtaining confidential information by examining the contents of legitimate users' waste paper baskets, trash cans etc.

duplex. *Synonymous with* FULL DUPLEX.

duplex circuit. In communications, a circuit used for transmission of signals in both directions at the same time. *See* FULL DUPLEX, HALF DUPLEX.

duress alarm. In physical security, a system that enables an individual to give an indication of a duress situation without unnecessarily endangering the individual. The alarm is operated by an unobtrusive sensor. *See* AMBUSH CODE.

DUV. *See* DATA UNDER VOICE.

dwell time. In physical security, the interval during which a single scene is displayed on a CCTV camera. *See* CCTV, VIDEO SWITCHER.

dynamic analysis. In computer security, a class of software tools for software analysis. Such tools analyze the compiled code by instrumenting and executing it. *Compare* STATIC ANALYSIS, DYNAMIC TESTING. *See* SOFTWARE ANALYSIS, SOFTWARE TOOL.

dynamic password. In access control, a system which effectively produces a new user password for each log-in. Some systems employ a token with an inbuilt clock, synchronized to a clock in the host computer. The user logs in and the dynamic password is indicated on the LCD display. The device may require the entry of a PIN before it provides the required dynamic password. Challenge response systems also effectively provide dynamic passwords. *See* CHALLENGE/RESPONSE, DES, LCD, PHOTOSENSOR, PIN, REPLAY, WATCHWORD.

dynamic signature verification. In access control, a signature verification technique based upon the manner in which the signature is written, rather than the two dimensional image of the signature. *See* BIOMETRICS, SIGNATURE ANALYSIS.

dynamic testing. In computer security, the testing of an application system by executing it with test data and comparing actual results with expected or known results. The techniques of dynamic testing include: program analyzers and the flaw hypothesis method. *Compare* STATIC EVALUATION. *See* DYNAMIC ANALYSIS, FLAW HYPOTHESIS, PROGRAM ANALYZER.

E

E0. In information security, the lowest level of assurance in ITSEC, corresponding to Division D in TCSEC. *Compare* DIVISION D, E1, E2, E3, E4, E5, E6. *See* ITSEC, TCSEC.

E1. In information security, a level of assurance in ITSEC. *Compare* E0, E2, E3, E4, E5, E6. *See* ITSEC.

E2. In information security, a level of assurance in ITSEC. *Compare* E0, E1, E3, E4, E5, E6. *See* ITSEC.

E3. In information security, a level of assurance in ITSEC. *Compare* E0, E1, E2, E4, E5, E6. *See* ITSEC.

E³. *See* END-TO-END ENCRYPTION.

E4. In information security, a level of assurance in ITSEC. *Compare* E0, E1, E2, E3, E5, E6. *See* ITSEC.

E5. In information security, a level of assurance in ITSEC. *Compare* E0, E1, E2, E3, E4, E6. *See* ITSEC.

E6. In information security, the highest level of assurance in ITSEC. *Compare* E0, E1, E2, E3, E4, E5. *See* ITSEC.

EAPROM. In computing, Electrically Alterable Programmable Read Only Memory. *Synonymous with* EPROM.

EAROM. *See* ELECTRICALLY ALTERABLE ROM.

eavesdropping. In data security, the unauthorized interception of information-bearing emanations through the use of methods other than wiretapping.

(FIPS). *Compare* WIRETAPPING. *See* COMPROMISING EMANATIONS, ELECTRONIC COUNTERMEASURES SWEEPING, PASSIVE ATTACK.

EBCDIC code. In codes, Extended Binary Coded Decimal Interchange Code (pronounced ip-sa-dik), one of two international data codes used in IBM equipment. This 8 bit code gives 256 combinations to represent a selection of graphic (printing) and nongraphic (control) codes. Used by IBM for representing characters and control values on large computers. *Compare* ASCII, ISO7.

ECB. *See* ELECTRONIC CODEBOOK.

ECC. *See* ERROR CORRECTION CODE.

ECCM. Electronic counter-countermeasures.

echocheck. *See* ECHOPLEX.

echoplex. In data communications, a method employing an echo of received data for error checking. A computer, receiving data from a communication link operating in a full duplex mode, returns the received data to the transmitter thus allowing it to verify that data was correctly received. *Compare* LOCAL ECHO. *See* FULL DUPLEX.

echo suppressor. In data communications, conventional telephone networks have echo suppressors to inhibit annoying echoes during telephone conversations. These devices detect the presence of a voice signal in one direction and inhibit signal flow in the opposite direction. These devices prevent full duplex data communications and must therefore be suppressed for data transfer. *See* FULL DUPLEX.

ECM. Electronic countermeasures.

ECMA. European Computer Manufacturers Association.

ECOMA. European Computer Measurement Association.

economic assessment. A detailed study of security measures, their operational and technical feasibility, and their costs and benefits. Economic assessment aids in planning and selecting security measures. (AFR). *See* RISK ANALYSIS.

economy of mechanism. In computer security, the principle of maintaining security design as simple as possible. *See* PRINCIPLES OF SECURE SYSTEMS.

ECSA. European Computer Services Association.

EDAC. In data communications, Error Detection And Correction. *See* FORWARD ERROR CORRECTION.

EDI. *See* ELECTRONIC DATA INTERCHANGE.

EDIFACT. In standards, EDI For Administration Commerce and Transport, a United Nations standard for EDI messages. The data to be transmitted is embedded in segments within messages, which also contain information about the receiver and a time stamp. Messages of the same type may also be grouped into functional groups, an interchange is a collection of messages or functional groups to a particular receiver. Compare ANSI X.12. *See* ELECTRONIC DATA INTERCHANGE, EDI SECURITY.

EDI security. In data security, security in electronic data interchange systems must provide users with the degree of security that has been associated with the traditional document and postal system, that it is intended to replace, i.e. user authentication, message authentication, proof of origin, non-repudiation and confidentiality. Moreover these services must be provided in a manner that does not involve the development of complicated individual protocols established between the trading partners, and they must be compatible with the legal system in which the trading partners operate.

User authentication implies that when Alice establishes communication with Bob, she must be able to verify that Bob is an existing user of the system, registered with specified credentials, e.g. user ID, user privileges etc. EDI messages are not normally exchanged in an interactive manner and therefore user authentication procedures which demand an information exchange between the parties, e.g. challenge\responses are not normally appropriate.

Message authentication implies that when Bob receives a message from Alice then he must be able to assure himself that the message originated from Alice, that the message has not been modified, or replayed.

Bob will require a proof of origin with an EDI message, received from Alice, such that any third party can verify that the message could only have been sent by Alice, i.e. it was not sent by another party and Bob could not have forged the message claiming that Alice was the originator. The proof of origin must also preclude the possibility that the message is simply a replay of an earlier message, e.g. an attempt to create a double payment authorization.

Non-repudiation in EDI systems appertains to receipts of messages such that if Alice has sent a receipt, a third party can verify that the receipt could only have been produced by Alice. The receipt must contain sufficient information to uniquely identify the original message in question. However, the receipt must be clearly designated as such and there must be no manner in which it could be confused with an original message.

Confidentiality is an important consideration at least for certain fields in EDI messages. Information on special pricing arrangements, the quantities, or types of goods ordered, may often be of commercial value.

These security requirements can be satisfied by cryptographic systems. Both symmetric and asymmetric cipher systems have been recommended for EDI applications, but the latter provide more elegant solutions particularly for those issues involving proof of origin.

The security primitives required in EDI security include message authentication codes, message detection codes, digital signatures, message encryption, filtering and key management.

Message authentication codes (MAC) are derived from the message to be authenticated, and a secret key, known only to the sender and recipient. They are appended to the message so that the recipient can be assured that the message originated with the purported sender and has not been subsequently modified.

Message detection codes (MDC) are similar to message authentication codes but do not use a secret key. Such codes have the property that it is not feasible to determine two messages which give rise to the same MDC.

Public key cryptography may be employed to provide a digital signature of the message, thus providing an assurance both of message integrity and proof of origin, such that a third party may subsequently verify that only the purported sender could have produced the message. Commonly an MDC of the message is encrypted with the secret key of the sender. The recipient may be assured of the authenticity of the sender's public key by the inclusion of the sender's certificate with the message.

A form of signature using symmetric ciphers is feasible if the sender and recipient are provided with special hardware systems, both containing the same secret key. The sender's system has only the facility to develop a MAC and the receiver's only the facility to verify the MAC. In this manner the recipient may be assured of the authenticity of a message, in terms of its originator and contents, but lacking the means of developing the MAC ensures that the origin may be verified by a third party in case of dispute.

Encryption of messages to ensure confidentiality involve both some form of key management and filtering. If symmetric ciphers, such as DES, are employed then a key management scheme, normally involving master-session keys, is employed. In the case of public cryptography the message may be encrypted with the recipient's public key. More commonly, however, a symmetric cipher is employed for the text encryption; the symmetric key employed is then itself encrypted with the recipient's public key and the encrypted key included with the encrypted message.

EDI systems have strict rules on the character sets to be employed in messages. However, the ciphertext produced by encryption of message text comprise random bit streams incompatible with such rules. Some form of filtering is thus required to add redundant information which allows the bit stream to be transmitted in a form containing only legitimate characters. The receiver then applies an inverse form of filtering to produce the original ciphertext bit stream prior to decryption.

The messages must contain sufficient embedded security information to enable the recipient to apply the appropriate processes of authentication checking, text decryption etc. Such information is commonly included in the form of security headers and trailers at appropriate places in the message.

Unlike point to point systems, EDI communications will involve a community of users and it is essential that a recipient is provided with a set of security protocols, and security relevant data embedded in the message. Standards which describe the manner in which security is to be employed are thus essential in EDI systems. ANSI X.12 has a section dealing with security and the TEDIS program has included security studies for EDIFACT systems. *See* ANSI X.12 - 1983, ASYMMETRIC CIPHER, CERTIFICATE, CIPHERTEXT, DIGITAL SIGNATURE, FILTERING, DES, ELECTRONIC DATA INTERCHANGE, EDIFACT, KEY MANAGEMENT, MAC, MDC, PUBLIC KEY CRYPTOGRAPHY, SYMMETRIC CIPHER.

edit. In computing, a procedure used to change or modify the form of data input to the system. This may involve testing input for correct format and adding or deleting characters.

editing run. In computing, a program run that will check new data for validity against a series of predefined rules and identify any errors for correction and resubmission. Typical tests include checking that dates and numbers fall within expected ranges, verification of check digits etc.

EDP. Electronic Data Processing. *See* DATA PROCESSING.

EDP auditor. In auditing, an auditor with responsibility for checking and verifying software controls of a computer system, identifying potential errors and security vulnerabilities. *Compare* EXTERNAL AUDITOR, INTERNAL AUDITOR. *See* EDP CONTROLS.

EDP controls. In auditing, the controls applied in an EDP system normally comprise:

- application controls;
- EDP installation controls;
- system development and maintenance controls.

Application controls, which include input, processing and output controls, are designed to ensure that valid transactions are processed and recorded completely, accurately, only once and in the correct timescale. EDP installation controls include, segregation of duties, supervision and monitoring of activities, access control to buildings, hardware and software, controls over data and program libraries etc.

System development and maintenance controls are designed to ensure that an implemented system is properly authorized and secure, as such they include:

- a project performance and management methodology;
- reviews of deliverables against agreed objectives;
- formal quality assurance procedures;
- effective stage testing;
- detailed implementation planning throughout the project;
- application change control procedures.

See EDP AUDITOR.

EDV. In computer security, a stealth virus that terminates and stays resident, infects floppy and hard disk boot sector, and hard disk partition table, corrupts boot sector, affects run-time operation. *See* VIRUS NAMES.

EEFI. *See* ESSENTIAL ELEMENTS OF FRIENDLY INFORMATION.

EEPROM. In computing, Electrically Erasable Programmable Read Only Memory. *Compare* EPROM. *See* PROM.

EEPROM security. In computer security, software stored on EEPROMs (Electrically Erasable PROM) provide a higher degree of security against unauthorized reading, than software stored on conventional ROM, since it is impossible to read the stored data with an optical or scanning electron microscope. *See* EEPROM, PROM, ROM.

EEROM. *See* ELECTRICALLY ERASABLE ROM, KEEPROM.

EFF. *See* ELECTRONIC FRONTIER FOUNDATION.

effectiveness. In information security, the extent to which a system satisfies its criteria. *See* INFORMATION TECHNOLOGY SECURITY EVALUATION CRITERIA.

E field. In physical security, a trade name for an electrostatic field sensor. *See* ELECTROSTATIC FIELD SENSOR.

EFT. *See* ELECTRONIC FUNDS TRANSFER.

EFTPOS. *See* ELECTRONIC FUNDS TRANSFER POINT OF SALE.

EFTS. Electronic Funds Transfer System. *See* ELECTRONIC FUNDS TRANSFER.

EIA. Electronic Industries Association.

EIN. *See* EUROPEAN INFORMATICS NETWORK.

electrically alterable ROM. In computing, a read only memory that can be programmed by applying a voltage to selected pins and erased either by exposure to ultraviolet light or by reversing the polarity used in writing. *Compare* EPROM. *See* ROM. *Synonymous with* EEROM, ELECTRICALLY ERASABLE ROM, EROM.

electrically erasable ROM. *Synonymous with* ELECTRICALLY ALTERABLE ROM.

electrically programmable read only memory. In computing, a read only memory that can be programmed by applying a voltage to selected pins. The term is applied both to devices that may, and may not, be reprogrammed. *See* ELECTRICALLY ALTERABLE ROM, PROM.

electrical metallic tubing. In communications security, a form of conduit providing some physical and electrical protection for cables.

electric field sensor. In physical security, a sensor comprising a wire charged with an alternating current voltage, one or more parallel sensing wires, an amplifier and a signal processor. The presence of an intruder produces variations in the electric field that are detected by the sensing wires, analyzed by the signal processor and cause activation of the alarm. *Compare* MAGNETIC SENSOR. *See* ELECTROSTATIC FIELD SENSOR.

electromagnetic emanations. In computer security, signals transmitted as radiation through the air and through conductors, particularly through power supply leads and printer cables. *See* COMPROMISING EMANATIONS, VAN ECK PHENOMENON. *Synonymous with* ELECTROMAGNETIC EMISSIONS, RADIO FREQUENCY EMISSIONS.

electromagnetic emissions. *Synonymous with* ELECTROMAGNETIC EMANATIONS.

electromagnetic interference. In computer security, a source of error conditions in computers caused by the pickup of stray electromagnetic radiation. *Compare* ELECTROMAGNETIC EMANATIONS. *Synonymous with* RADIO FREQUENCY INTERFERENCE.

electronic blackboard. In data communications, a system for sending handwriting, and hand drawn graphics, over a telephone line. The sender may use either a light pen or digitizing tablet, and the appropriate image will appear on a television monitor at the remote location.

electronic codebook. *Synonymous with* NATIVE MODE.

electronic coin. In banking, a cash token, of similar size to a coin, in the form of a contactless smart card, used as an electronic purse for vending machines, payphones etc. *Compare* ELECTRONIC PURSE. *See* CONTACTLESS SMART CARD.

electronic countermeasures sweeping. In communications security, the process of identifying and removing electronic listening devices from an area or piece of communication equipment. *See* ELECTRONIC LISTENING DEVICE.

electronic data interchange. In computing and communications, the transmission of documents from one computer to another over a network. If all trading parties have computer systems in which a standard has been agreed for electronic data interchange, such as X.400, then there are substantial benefits. Paper work is eliminated, suppliers can respond more rapidly to production requirements and the manufacturer does not have to re-key supplier invoice details. This eliminates transcription errors and reduces handling costs, particularly if the participants are multinational organizations using a global network. *See* EDIFACT, EDI SECURITY, ODETTE, X.400.

electronic data processing. In computing, data processing performed largely by electronic, as compared with manual or mechanical, techniques; usually involving company wide transactions.

electronic digital computer. In computing, in its simplest form a device, with a CPU, that accepts a set of instructions and data, performs computations or manipulations upon that data according to the instructions and delivers the results. The basic computer comprises an input device, a memory, a control and arithmetic unit and an output device.

electronic eavesdropping. In data security, the interception of wireless transmissions, e.g. radio or microwave transmissions, or information bearing electromagnetic energy emanating from electronic devices. *Compare* ACOUSTIC EAVESDROPPING. *See* COMPROMISING EMANATIONS, EAVESDROPPING, TEMPEST, VAN ECK PHENOMENON.

electronic filing. In computing, an aspect of office automation that is concerned with the filing of typical office records, e.g. memoranda, reports, diagrams, on magnetic tape or disk. In some cases microfilm techniques will be used for the storage of bulky objects and the system will normally allow for the recording of a catalog of paper objects that cannot conveniently be read into the computer system. *See* MAGNETIC DISK, MAGNETIC TAPE.

electronic frontier foundation. In legislation, a U.S. foundation formed to protect the civil rights of hackers who do not break into computer systems illegally. *See* HACKER.

electronic funds transfer. In banking, an automated system for transferring funds from one bank account to another using electronic equipment and data communications rather than paper media, e.g. checks, and the postal system. *Compare* EFTPOS. *See* BANKING NETWORKS, ELECTRONIC FUNDS TRANSFER POINT OF SALE, KEY MANAGEMENT, MESSAGE AUTHENTICATION, PIN MANAGEMENT AND SECURITY.

electronic funds transfer point of sale. In banking, pertaining to a point of sale terminal that is connected by communication line to a financial institution's computer. The terminal will normally read and transmit the information recorded on the magnetic stripe of a credit card and provide for the input of transaction details via a keyboard. *See* AS 2805, ELECTRONIC FUNDS TRANSFER, POINT OF SALE.

Electronic Industries Association. A standards organization specializing in the electrical and functional characteristics of interface equipment.

electronic listening device. In communications security, a device used to collect

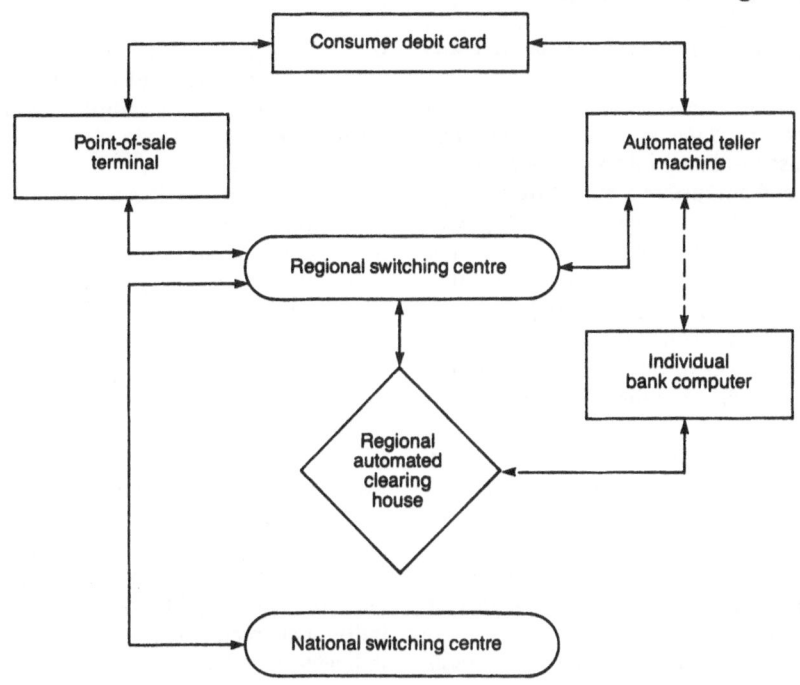

electronic funds transfer
EFT financial services and the supporting technology

	EFT TECHNOLOGIES				
FINANCIAL SERVICES	POS	ATM	Telephone banking	Automated clearing house	Wire transfer systems
Consumer-oriented EFT services					
EFT services which facilitate the transfer of information					
Check authorization	X	–	–	–	–
Check verification	X	–	–	–	–
Check guarantee	X	–	–	–	–
File look-up (balance inquiry)	–	X	X	–	–
EFT services which involve direct money transfers					
Deposit	–	X	–	–	–
Cash withdrawal	–	X	–	–	–
Bill or loan payment	–	–	X	–	–
Purchase	X	–	X	–	–
Interaccount transfer	–	X	X	–	–
Debit with overdraft privileges	X	X	–	–	–
Credit purchase	X	–	–	–	–
Cash advance	–	X	–	–	–
Corporate-oriented EFT services					
Wire transfers	–	–	–	–	–
Direct deposit of payroll	–	–	–	X	–
Pre-authorized debit services	–	–	–	X	X
Corporate cash management (including interbank and intrabank wire transfers)	–	–	–	X	X

and transmit information to an eavesd-ropper.

Such devices may be secreted in a room or connected to telephone equipment. The bug is used to listen into a conversation in a room and comprises a miniature microphone, amplifier, transmitter and power source. It will transmit the conversation in the form of a radio frequency signal that can be received as far as 10 kilometers away, depending upon the radio frequency used, the power of the transmitter and the density of the buildings in the transmission path.

Such devices can be as small as a low denomination coin and easily inserted into pens, ashtrays, staplers, clocks, light fittings etc. The presence of bugs can be detected by a wide frequency range radio receiver connected to an audio device or oscilloscope.

Telephone taps are similar to bugs excepts that they do not contain a microphone, or power source, and are connected in series or parallel with a telephone line. Since they require no power source they can remain in operation indefinitely and need not be inserted into a secure area such as an office.

The telephone tap can be connected to the appropriate telephone line at various points, e.g. at distribution frames located on the same floor, in the basement or outside the office building. Such taps may be used to eavesdrop on conversations, facsimile, telex or computer data. The presence of telephone taps may be detected by inserting a signal on the line and checking for echoes from interception points, checking variations in line voltage or resistance from the normal value, or physical inspection.

Protection against room bugs includes the use of a modulated ultrasonic sound transmission that will blanket the audio signals in the receiver. Protection against telephone bugs includes voice scrambling devices and transmitted masking tones, but such techniques require equipment at both the receiving and transmitting ends, e.g. an unscrambler, or filter to remove the masking tone, is required at the receiver. *See* VOICE SCRAMBLING, ELECTRONIC COUNTERMEASURES SWEEPING. *Synonymous with* BUG.

electronic mail. In data communications, a facility enabling users to exchange information addressed to a particular individual, or a group, using computer communication facilities. The options typically available in various systems can be classified as Send, Receive, File Options and Addressing Options.

The Send Options include Carbon Copy, Blind Copy, Reply Requested, Express, Registered and Delayed Delivery. The Carbon Copy option sends a copy of messages to all designated users, whilst Blind Copy performs a similar function without indicating the distribution list to individual recipients. Reply Requested indicates that the correspondence should be responded to. Express will receive some type of special handling on receipt, e.g. alerting the workstation. Registered option will give an indication of delivery to the intended recipient and Delayed Delivery arranges for the mail to be delivered at a specified time/date.

The Receive Options include Forward, Reply, Save, Delete and Scan. The Forward option sends the message to another user, with comments as appropriate, not on the original address list. Reply allows an immediate reply to the message whether requested or not. The Save option retains the message in an existing or new file for later editing, merging, review etc. Delete disposes of a message after reading and Scan allows a browse through pending mail looking only at originators, subject headings, etc.

The File Options available are Editing and Merging. The former allows reading of messages selected by date interval, search by keyword, originator, etc. Editing provides an off- or on-line edit capability, whilst Merging provides the user with the option to insert preformatted information into a message during preparation.

The Addressing Options comprise Group Addressing, Standard Distribution, Hidden Distribution and Account Number-/Name association. Group Addressing provides for the use of multiple user account numbers in the address list. Standard Distribution provides for prestored distribution lists whilst Hidden Distribution is similar to Blind Copy, i.e. no addressee sees the distribution list. The Account number/Name Association permits address by name rather than by user number. *See* ELECTRONIC MAIL SECURITY. *Synonymous with* COMPUTER BASED MESSAGE SYSTEM.

electronic mailbox. *See* ELECTRONIC MAIL.

electronic mail security. In communications security, security in electronic mail systems may be introduced to ensure the confidentiality and/or integrity of the electronic mail messages now widely used in commercial and research environments.

Electronic mail systems often involve complex networks with a wide variety of host systems and workstations; many of the participants may not require security services. In these circumstances such security services are best supplied on an end-to-end basis, thus avoiding the requirement to add security components to the multifarious systems forming the total network.

Senders must have some mechanism of ensuring that the recipient can engage in a secure exchange, prior to transmitting the message. Such end-to-end security can, however, provide no traffic flow security.

Encryption is required to ensure the confidentiality of whole messages, or of sensitive components of messages. Message integrity codes (MIC) may be employed as a form of checksum to provide a warning of message corruption. The functions producing the message integrity codes may involve cryptographic keys, or the MICs may be formed without the use of secret keys. The MICs themselves may be encrypted as a defence against malicious modification of messages.

The entire secure electronic mail message will require at least three sections: normal message headers, message headers related to security and the message text. The normal message headers, required by the electronic mail system, cannot be protected and will provide identification of the sender, recipient, subject heading etc. The subject heading contained in this message header will not be encrypted; if it comprises sensitive information then it should be treated as a dummy field (e.g. Encrypted Message No...), and the sensitive subject heading included in the encrypted portion of the message.

The message headers related to security will contain details of the senders and recipients, encryption algorithms (e.g. DES, RSA) and modes (e.g. electronic code book, cipher block chaining) used, cryptographic parameters, e.g. initialization vectors, identification of interchange keys, data keys encrypted under interchange keys, MICs, public key certificates if asymmetric ciphers are employed etc.

Electronic mail systems usually encompass a wide range of user workstation types, each type employing its own coding systems for message text, e.g. EBCDIC, ASCII, and local conventions for handling escape characters, carriage return, line feed etc. Thus the bit streams, representing the same message text at sender and receiver workstations, may exhibit significant differences. Such discrepancies can cause problems in the computation of MICs so that an uncorrupted message would produce a different MIC at the receiver, to that produced and transmitted by the sender. A similar problem can arise with the transmission of ciphertext.

The ciphertext produced by the encryption algorithm will comprise essentially an arbitrary bit stream. This stream will be encoded by the transmitting workstation and it is possible that some of the characters produced will have a particular significance to the transmission system, e.g.

a certain sequence may signify end of message, carriage return-line feed sequences may be transformed etc.

The abovementioned coding problems require special prior encoding of protected message text, and of the corresponding ciphertext. A canonical form of the message text is produced prior to the development of MICs. The bit stream representing the encrypted text must likewise be encoded, prior to transmission, in such a way that it will not be transformed by the network.

If symmetric ciphers are employed then the sender and recipient must be in possession of the same secret key, usually termed an interchange key (IK). This key may be exchanged by a secure channel, e.g. postal system, or provided to each party by a key server. In the latter case the two parties would each require independent secret keys for communication with such a key server. The interchange key is used to encrypt a data encrypting key (DEK) employed for the encryption of the text of a particular message. The DEK, encrypted by the IK, would be included in the message headers related to security, together with sufficient information for the recipient to identify the IK employed by the sender.

The recipient will hold a number of IKs, corresponding to e-mail users with whom the recipient undertakes secure communications; moreover a sender-recipient pair may store a number of IKs with various expiry dates. The DEK may be employed in the computation of the MIC, and the MIC itself may be encrypted with the IK.

If a message is distributed to a mailing list then the IKs may be identified separately for each recipient in the list, or a single IK may be used for all members of the list. The message headers related to security must identify each individual IK, for each individual recipient, in the former case. If a common IK is used for all members of the list then users will be dependent upon the security procedures adopted by all members of the mailing list to protect the IK. Moreover an attacker, who is a member of the mailing list, would be able to exploit the system and masquerade as any other member.

Asymmetric ciphers provide significant advantages for electronic mail systems. The asymmetric cipher will be employed to encrypt DEKs, the message text itself is still encrypted with a symmetric cipher. In this case the IK, used to encrypt the DEK, is the public asymmetric key of the recipient. The IK encrypting the MIC of the message is the secret key of the sender, thus providing a means of non-repudiation, in addition to a guarantee of message integrity. If asymmetric ciphers are employed then certificates should be provided to provide users with a guarantee of the authenticity of the public keys received.

A message, with an MIC encrypted by the sender's secret asymmetric cipher key, should include the certificate guaranteeing the authenticity of the public key to be used in verifying the signature. Similarly the public key employed to encrypt the DEK should be derived from a certificate contained in an earlier message from the intended recipient.

A single certification authority may not be appropriate in a large e-mail network because all members of the network, using security services, would require communication with that certification authority for each public key supplied. A hierarchy of certification authorities may-be more appropriate for large networks. In this case a user's public key is supplied in conjunction with a local certification authority public key. A certificate for that local certification authority's public key, signed by a higher order certification authority trusted to both sender and recipient, is also included in the senders message headers. *See* ASCII, ASYMMETRIC CIPHER, CERTIFICATE, CHECKSUM, CIPHER BLOCK CHAINING, DEK, DES, EBCDIC CODE, ELECTRONIC CODEBOOK, END--TO-END ENCRYPTION, ESCAPE CHARACTER, IK, INITIALIZATION VECTOR, MIC, PRIVACY ENHANCED MAIL, PUBLIC KEY,

RSA, SECRET KEY, SYMMETRIC CIPHER, TRAFFIC FLOW SECURITY.

electronic messaging. *See* BULLETIN BOARD.

electronic piggybacking. In computer security, the illicit insertion of messages through an unattended active terminal. *See* PIGGYBACK.

electronic publishing. In applications, a generic term for the distribution of information on electronic media, e.g. videotex. *See* VIDEOTEX.

electronic purse. In banking, a smart card application in which the smart card is charged with a specified value. The user can undertake transactions and the value of the transaction is debited from the card. *Compare* ELECTRONIC COIN. *See* SMART CARD. *Synonymous with* ELECTRONIC WALLET.

electronic signature. *Synonymous with* DIGITAL SIGNATURE.

electronic system for payments. In banking, an arrangement for the transfer of value and associated management of accounts by electronic means. *See* ELECTRONIC FUNDS TRANSFER.

electronic token. *See* SMART CARD.

electronic vaulting. In computer security, the realtime transmission of data from a data center to a vaulting facility.

electronic vibration detector. In physical security, a sensitive detection device employing a contact microphone.

electronic wallet. *Synonymous with* ELECTRONIC PURSE.

electrostatic field sensor. In physical security, a form of passive field sensor that detects the presence of an intruder by a disturbance in an ambient electric field. *See* ELECTRIC FIELD SENSOR.

element. In mathematics, an object, entity or concept having the properties that define the set. *See* SET.

ElGamal cipher. In cryptography, a public key cipher algorithm based upon the Diffie-Hellman key distribution scheme.

Alice and Bob each agree upon a large prime number p, such that p-1 has at least one large factor, and a second integer α less than p. Alice holds a secret integer number a and similarly Bob has a secret integer b. Alice computes:

$$y_a = \alpha^a \bmod p$$

and Bob computes

$$y_b = \alpha^b \bmod p$$

The numbers y_a and y_b may be considered as a form of public key for Alice and Bob respectively, and made available in a public directory together with α and p.

Alice wishes to send message represented by integer m < p-1 to Bob. First she chooses a number k in the range 0 - (p-1), obtains y_b from the public directory and computes:

$$K = y_b^k \bmod p$$

The ciphertext message comprises the two numbers c_1 and c_2 where:

$$c_1 = \alpha^k \bmod p \qquad c_2 = Km \bmod p.$$

Note that the ciphertext is double the length of the plaintext message m.

Bob can decrypt the message by first using the secret number b to compute K from c_1.

$$K = y_b^k \bmod p$$
$$= (\alpha^k)^b \bmod p$$
$$= (c_1)^b \bmod p$$

The second stage is to divide Km mod p by K to recover the message m.

Compare ELGAMAL DIGITAL SIGNATURE. *See* CIPHERTEXT, DIFFIE-HELLMAN TECHNIQUE, MODULO ARITHMETIC, PLAINTEXT.

ElGamal digital signature. In cryptography, an algorithm for producing a digital signature.

Alice and Bob each agree upon a large prime number p, such that p-1 has at least one large factor, and a second integer α less than p. Alice holds a secret integer number a, similarly Bob holds a secret integer b. Alice computes:

$$y_a = \alpha^a \bmod p$$

and Bob computes

$$y_b = \alpha^b \bmod p$$

The numbers y_a and y_b may be considered as a form of public key for Alice and Bob respectively, and made available in a public directory together, with α and p.

The process of signing a message m, where $0 < m < (p-1)$ by Alice comprises three steps.

- Alice chooses a random number k, uniformly between 0 and p-1 such that k and p-1 are coprime.
- Alice computes:

$$r = \alpha^k \bmod p$$

- Alice determines a value s, s < p-1, such that:

$$m = (a.r + k.s) \bmod (p-1).$$

The pair (r,s) comprises the signature for the message m. The recipient checks the signature by computing:

- $\alpha^m \bmod p$ and $(y_a)^r . r^s \bmod p$
- and checking that

$$\alpha^m \bmod p = (y_a)^r . r^s \bmod p$$

Note that Alice, unlike Bob, has access to the secret values a and k, whilst Bob has access to the public or transmitted values y_a, and r. Bob can therefore verify the signature but lacks the means of constructing it. . *Compare* ELGAMAL CIPHER. *See* DIGITAL SIGNATURE, COPRIME, DIFFIE-HELLMAN TECHNIQUE, MODULO ARITHMETIC.

emanation. In communications security, a signal emitted by a system that is not explicitly allowed by its specification. *See* COMPROMISING EMANATIONS, ELECTROMAGNETIC EMANATIONS, TEMPEST, VAN ECK PHENOMENON.

emanation security. In computer security, the protection that results from all measures designed to deny unauthorized persons information of value that might be derived from intercept and analysis of compromising emanations. (FIPS). *See* COMPROMISING EMANATIONS, TEMPEST, VAN ECK PHENOMENON.

embedded audit. In physical security, the use of security logs built into a computer system to provide for continual monitoring.

embedded system. An embedded system is one that performs or controls a function, either in whole or in part, as an integral element of a larger system or subsystem. For example, ground support equipment, flight simulators, engine test stands, or fire control systems.(DODD).

embezzlement. In legislation, an offense involving the theft of property by a person to whom the property has been entrusted.

embossed card. In access control, a form of access control card in which the coded information is embossed as a pattern on the surface of the card. *Compare* MAGNETIC STRIPE CARD. *See* CARD READER.

emergency plan. *See* CONTINGENCY PLANS.

emergency response. In risk management, pertaining to the immediate action taken to protect hardware and magnetic media in the event of a natural disaster, fire, power failure, equipment malfunction, vandalism, theft, tampering etc. *See* CONTINGENCY PLANS, EMERGENCY RESPONSE PLAN.

emergency response plan. In risk management, a plan that provides procedures to respond promptly and effectively to a potential disruption, so as to limit the damage. *See* CONTINGENCY PLANS, EMERGENCY RESPONSE.

EMI/RF radiation. In communications security, ElectroMagnetidnterference/Radio Frequency radiation. Unwanted signals produced from sources such as motors, generators, car ignitions and radio broadcasts. *See* CONDUCTIVE SHIELDING, EMI/RF SHIELD.

EMI/RF shield. In computer security, a specially designed metal shield to prevent the undesired transmission of radiated and conducted electromagnetic signals. *See* EMI/RF RADIATION, EMISSION SECURITY, ENCAPSULATION, TEMPEST, VAN ECK PHENOMENON.

emission security. In computer security, a component of COMSEC that results from all measures to deny unauthorized persons information of value that might be derived from intercept and analysis of compromising emanations from electrically operated classified information processing equipment and systems. (AR). *See* COMPROMISING EMANATIONS, TEMPEST, VAN ECK PHENOMENON.

Empire. In computer security, a virus that encrypts itself, terminates and stays resident, infects floppy or hard disk boot sector, affects run-time operation, corrupts program and OVL files. *See* VIRUS NAMES.

employee monitoring. In legislation, pertaining to systems that monitor employee keystrokes, errors, idle terminal time, keystroke dynamics etc. Such information may be used for employee profiling and job performance.

empty slot. In data communications, a packet that continually circulates around a ring network. Whenever a node on the circuit wants to send information it waits for an empty slot and then fills it with data and address information. *See* CAMBRIDGE RING, PACKET SWITCHING.

EMS. Electronic Mail Service. *See* ELECTRONIC MAIL.

EMT. *See* ELECTRICAL METALLIC TUBING.

emulator. (1) In computing, a combination of hardware and software that permits programs written for one computer to be run on another computer. In computer security terminology, the emulator is the portion of the system responsible for creating an operating system-compatible environment out of the environment provided by the kernel. In KSOS, the emulator maps the kernel environment into the Unix environment. (MTR). *See* KSOS, UNIX. (2) In computing, special purpose hardware or software that enables one system to act as if it were another. It is used, for example, to minimize reprogramming effort when a new computer replaces an existing one.

encapsulation. In communications security, the use of RF filtering techniques and high integrity RF shielding to contain all emanations within the equipment housing. *Compare* SOURCE SUPPRESSION. *See* COMPROMISING EMANATIONS, EMISSION SECURITY, TEMPEST PROOFING, VAN ECK PHENOMENON.

encipher. In cryptography, to convert plaintext into unintelligible form by means of a cipher system. (FIPS). *Compare* ENCODE, DECIPHER. *See* CIPHER SYSTEM. *Synonymous with* ENCRYPT.

encipherment. In cryptography, the cryptographic transformation of data to produce ciphertext. *Compare* DECIPHER-

MENT. *See* CIPHERTEXT. *Synonymous with* ENCRYPTION.

encode. (1) In cryptography, to convert plaintext into unintelligible form by means of a code system. (FIPS). *Compare* ENCIPHER. *See* CODE SYSTEM. (2) In data communications, to convert data, by means of a code, in such a way that it may be subsequently reconverted to its original form. (3) In data communications, to convert from one system of communication to another. *Compare* DECODE. *See* CODE.

encrypt. In cryptography, to convert plaintext into unintelligible form by means of a cryptographic system.(FIPS). *Compare* DECRYPT. *See* CRYPTOGRAPHIC SYSTEM. *Synonymous with* ENCIPHER.

encryption. In cryptography, the process of transforming data to an unintelligible form in such a way that the original data either cannot be obtained (one-way encryption) or cannot be obtained without using the inverse decryption process (two-way encryption). (FIPS). *See* ENCRYPT, END-TO-END ENCRYPTION, LINK ENCRYPTION. *Synonymous with* ENCIPHERMENT.

encryption algorithm. (1) In cryptography, an algorithm realized either in firmware or software and used in conjunction with a secret key for encrypting plaintext and decrypting ciphertext. *See* ALGORITHM, ENCRYPTION. (2) In cryptography, a set of mathematically expressed rules for rendering information unintelligible by effecting a series of transformations through the use of variable elements controlled by the application of a key to the normal representation of the information. (FIPS). *See* KEY. *Synonymous with* PRIVACY TRANSFORMATION.

encryptor board. In cryptography, an expansion board for a personal computer which provides encryption services, usually data encrypt and decrypt, gen-

eration and checking of MACs. The boards commonly provide for the secure storage of cryptographic keys and use a DES chip for fast, secure encryption and decryption. *See* CRYPTOGRAPHIC KEY, DES, EXPANSION BOARD, MAC, PERSONAL COMPUTER SECURITY.

end of address. In data communications, a control character that indicates to the receiver that the last character of the address has been transmitted and successive characters relate to the message.

end of block. In data communications, a control character that indicates to the receiver that the last character of a block has been transmitted. *See* BLOCK.

end of file. In data structures, a character indicating that the last record of a file has been read. *See* FILE, RECORD.

end-of-line resistor. In physical security, a device used to terminate an electrically supervised line. It renders the line electrically continuous and provides a fixed current and/or resistance reference point for measuring changes that produce alarm signals. *See* SUPERVISED LINE.

end-of-line supervision. In physical security, an alarm circuit that detects attempts to connect an electrical bypass.

end of message. In data communications, a control character that indicates an end of message; used to separate messages in a multimessage stream. *See* END OF TEXT.

end of text. In data communications, a control character that indicates to the receiver that the previous character was the last in a message text. *Compare* START OF TEXT.

end of transmission. In data communications, a control character that indicates to the receiver that transmission has been completed.

Endorsed Tempest Products List. In computer security, a U.S. list of computers, components and telecommunications equipment that conform to current guidelines for Tempest products. *Compare* EVALUATED PRODUCTS LIST, PREFERRED PRODUCTS LIST. *See* TEMPEST.

endorsement. In data processing, the marking of a form or document so as to direct or to restrict its further use in processing.

end-to-end assurance. In data security, the provision of assurance to the sender of a message that it was, or will be, correctly received. *See* DELIVERY ASSURANCE.

end-to-end control. In data communications, a technique for ensuring that information transferred between two data terminals is not lost or corrupted. *See* DATA TERMINAL EQUIPMENT, HANDSHAKING.

end-to-end encipherment. In communications security, encipherment of data within or at the source end system, with the corresponding decipherment occurring only within or at the destination end system. (ISO). *Compare* LINK ENCRYPTION. *See* DECIPHERMENT, ENCIPHERMENT. *Synonymous with* END-TO-END ENCRYPTION.

end-to-end encryption. In communications security, encryption of information at the origin within a communications network and postponing decryption to the final destination point. (FIPS). *Compare* LINK ENCRYPTION, NODE ENCRYPTION. *See* ENCRYPT, OSI SECURITY. *Synonymous with* END-TO-END ENCIPHERMENT.

end user. In communications, the source or destination of information flowing through a system.

end user computing. In computing, personal computing performed by an end user, including program development, via a personal computer or terminal linked to a mainframe. *See* FOURTH GENERATION LANGUAGE, INFORMATION CENTER, PERSONAL COMPUTING.

end user device. In computing, a device, e.g. a VDU, that provides the final output of an operation without need for further processing. *See* VDU.

enhanced services. In communications, a service that uses the basic facilities supplied by a common carrier to provide additional, different or restructured benefits. In the U.S. enhanced services are not regulated by the FCC. *See* BASIC SERVICE, COMPUTER INQUIRY 1980, VALUE ADDED NETWORK SERVICE.

Enigma. In computer security, a virus that encrypts itself, terminates and stays resident, infects EXE and OVL files, affects run-time operation, corrupts program and OVL files. *See* VIRUS NAMES.

Enigma machine. In cryptography, a multiple rotor type cipher machine used by Germany and its allies in the second world war.

ENQ. *See* ENQUIRY CHARACTER.

enquiry character. In data communications, a control character used to request a response from a remote station. The response may include station identification and the type of equipment in service.

enrolment. In access control, the procedure employed in biometric access control systems to capture and enter the biometric template for a new user into the access control storage system. *See* BIOMETRICS.

entity. In databases, an object or event about which information is stored in a database. *Compare* ATTRIBUTE, RELATIONSHIP.

entity identifier. In databases, a key that uniquely identifies an entity. *See* KEY.

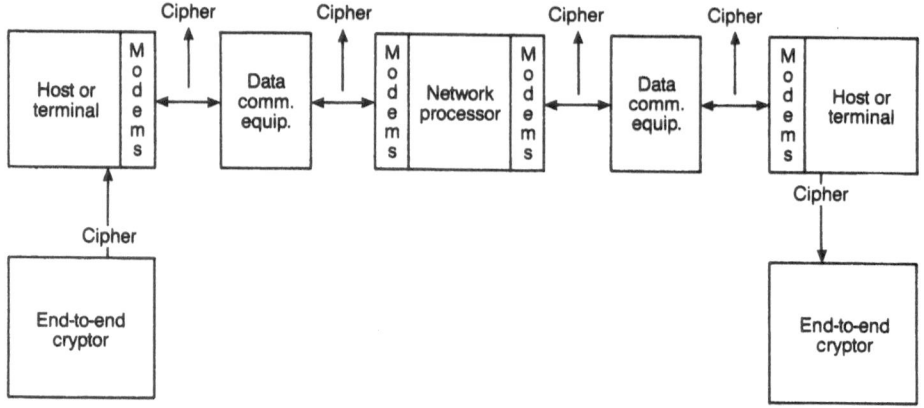

end-to-end encryption
With end-to-end encryption, only a node that either originates encrypted messages or is the final destination for encrypted messages, requires cryptographic capability. Routing information must be made a available to each intermediary node through which the message passes, consequently this approach is susceptible to traffic analysis.

entrance delay. *See* DELAY CIRCUIT.

entrapment. (1) In computer security, the deliberate planting of apparent flaws in a system for the purpose of detecting attempted penetrations or confusing an intruder about which flaws to exploit. (FIPS). (2) In access control, a technique in which certain vulnerabilities are made attractive to a potential attacker. These vulnerabilities are then heavily instrumented to detect and record any attacks. This technique has the disadvantage that intentional efforts to attract a user to attempt an attack may be of doubtful legality. *See* PSEUDO-FLAW, VULNERABILITY.

entropy. In mathematics, the mean value of the measure of information conveyed by the occurrence of any one of a finite number of mutually exclusive events. The entropy H(x) for event x with a probability of occurrence of p(x) is given by H(x) = -p(x) log p(x). *See* INFORMATION THEORY.

entry. *See* BETWEEN-THE-LINES ENTRY.

entry date. In banking, the date on which entries are made in the records of an account. (ANSI). *Synonymous with* POSTING DATE.

envelope. (1) In communications, the amplitude variations of an amplitude modulated carrier wave. *See* AMPLITUDE MODULATION. (2) In data communications, a byte to which a number of additional bits have been added for control and checking purposes.

environment. (1) The aggregate of external circumstances, conditions, and objects that affect the development, operation, and maintenance of a system. (DOD). (2) In computer security, those factors, both internal and external, of an ADP system that help to define the risks associated with its operation, e.g. the interfaces within the ADP system, the associated software, the type and level of information contained within the ADP system, the access control mechanisms used to restrict access, and the physical characteristics of the operational area. (DOE). *See* ACCESS CONTROL, ADP, PHYSICAL SECURITY.

EOA. *See* END OF ADDRESS.

EOB. *See* END OF BLOCK.

EOF. *See* END OF FILE.

EOM. *See* END OF MESSAGE.

EOT. *See* END OF TRANSMISSION.

EPL. *See* EVALUATED PRODUCTS LIST.

EPOS. Electronic Point of Sale. *See* EFTPOS, POINT OF SALE.

EPROM. (1) In computing, Erasable Programmed Read Only Memory. (2) In computing, Electrically Programmable Read Only Memory. *See* ELECTRICALLY PROGRAMMABLE READ ONLY MEMORY, ERASABLE PROGRAMMED READ ONLY MEMORY. *Synonymous with* EAPROM.

equal error rate. In access control, pertaining to a biometric device with equal false rejection rates and false acceptance rates. *See* BIOMETRICS, FALSE ACCEPTANCE RATE, FALSE REJECTION RATE.

equalization. In communications, a general term for a system designed to compensate for some form of deficiency in frequency response. *See* LOADING.

equipment check. In computer security, inbuilt equipment in a computer system to check the accuracy of processed, transmitted or stored data.

equivocation. In information theory, a conditional entropy. If a message X is conditional upon event Y then the equivocation of X given Y is given by:

$$H_Y(X) = -\Sigma_Y P(Y) \, \Sigma_Y P_Y (X) \, \log_2 (P_Y)(X))$$

Where $P(Y)$ = Probability of event Y, and $P_Y(X)$ = Probability of event X given

that event Y occurred. *See* ENTROPY, KEY EQUIVOCATION.

erasable programmed read only memory. *See* PROM. **erasable storage.** (1) In computing, a storage device whose data may be altered during the course of computation. (2) In computing, an area of storage used for temporary purposes. (3) In computing, a storage medium that can be erased and reused repeatedly, e.g. magnetic disk storage.

erasure. (1) In computer security, a security model rule stating that objects must be purged before being activated or reassigned. This ensures that no information is retained within an object when it is reassigned to a subject at a differing security level. (MTR). *See* OBJECT, OBJECT REUSE, SUBJECT. (2) In computer security, a process by which a signal recorded on magnetic media is removed (i.e. degaussed). Erasure may be accomplished in two ways: in AC erasure the media are degaussed by applying an alternating field that is reduced in amplitude from an initial high value (i.e. AC powered); in DC erasure, the media are saturated by applying a unidirectional field (i.e. DC powered or by employing a permanent magnet). (DOD). *See* DEGAUSS.

EROM. In computing, Erasable Read Only Memory. *Synonymous with* ELECTRICALLY ALTERABLE ROM.

error. (1) In mathematics, a discrepancy between a computed, or measured, value and some objective standard. *See* ERROR CONDITION. (2) In information security, a violation with respect to correct refinement. *See* CORRECT REFINEMENT.

error burst. In data communications, a series of consecutive errors. It is not unusual for errors to occur in groups or clusters.

error condition. In computing, a state

that results from an attempt to execute invalid instructions or operate on invalid data. *See* INSTRUCTION.

error correction code. In codes, a code designed to detect an error, in a word or character, identify the incorrect bit or bits and replace them with the correct ones. The number of incorrect bits that can be corrected depends upon the number of redundant bits used in the code. *Compare* ERROR DETECTION CODE. *See* HAMMING CODE, REDUNDANCY. *Synonymous with* SELF CORRECTING CODE.

error detection code. In codes, a code designed to detect, but not correct, an error in a word or character. The number of incorrect bits that can be detected depends upon the number of redundant bits in the code. *Compare* ERROR CORRECTION CODE. *See* PARITY CHECKING.

error extension. In cryptography, an effect that arises when noisy communication channels produce errors, or an attacker introduces changes, in transmitted ciphertext, and such errors result in even lengthier errors in the subsequent received plaintext. For example, in cipher block chaining a single bit error in the ciphertext will produce a garbled 64 bit plaintext block and a single one bit error on the succeeding plaintext block. *See* CIPHER BLOCK CHAIN-ING, CIPHER FEEDBACK. *Synonymous with* ERROR PROPAGATION, GARBLE EXTENSION.

error message. In computing, a statement indicating that the computer has detected an error in the translation or execution phase of a program.

error propagation. *Synonymous with* ERROR EXTENSION, GARBLE EXTENSION.

error rate. In data communications, the frequency of occurrence of errors, defined as the ratio of the number of bits incorrectly received to the total number of bits received.

error recovery service message. *See* ANSI X9.17 - 1985.

error service message. In key management, a message sent to report an error in a cryptographic service message. *See* ANSI X9.17 - 1985, CRYPTOGRAPHIC SERVICE MESSAGE.

error source statistics. In auditing, an accumulation of information on the type and origin of errors, used to assist in the formulation of remedial measures to reduce such errors.

ERS. *See* ERROR RECOVERY SERVICE MESSAGE.

ESC. *See* ESCAPE CODE.

escape character. *See* ESCAPE CODE.

escape code. In codes, a code combination that causes a device to recognize all subsequent code combinations as having an alternate meaning to their normal representation. Escape codes are used for indicating a sequence of control messages in ASCII. *See* ASCII. *Synonymous with* FLAG CODE.

escorts. In physical security, duly designated personnel who have appropriate clearances and access authorizations for the material contained in the system and are sufficiently knowledgeable to understand the security implications of and to control the activities and access of the individual being escorted. (OPNAVINST).

escrow agent. In software protection, an honest broker who is used to resolve disagreements between a software supplier and a licensee. A supplier deposits the source code with the agent for safekeeping, and a licensee will have rights to use it in the event of liquidation of the supplier or failure to give adequate support. *See* SOURCE CODE.

ESM. *See* ANSI X9.17 - 1985, ERROR SERVICE MESSAGE.

espionage. In legislation, the illegal gathering of proprietary or secret information by any means.

essential elements of friendly information. Information concerning a plan, project, or activity that, if acquired by hostile interests by any means, might jeopardize the successful execution of an operation. (AFR).

essentiality. In risk management, pertaining to data that has a high degree of importance for a user such that, if it is lost through unintentional modification or theft it can be recovered only at high expense.

Estelle State Transition Language. In data communications, a protocol specification language. *See* PROTOCOL.

Ethernet. In data communications, a trademark for a specific product that implements the IEEE 802.3 for local area networks. It was developed by Xerox. *Compare* CAMBRIDGE RING. *See* IEEE 802.3, LOCAL AREA NETWORK.

ETPL. *See* ENDORSED TEMPEST PRODUCTS LIST.

ETR. *See* EVALUATION TECHNICAL REPORT.

ETX. *See* END OF TEXT.

Euclid's algorithm. In number theory, a method of determining the greatest common divisor of two integers. Consider the two numbers 42 and 27 the method is illustrated below:

$$42/27 = 1 + 15/27$$
$$27/15 = 1 + 12/15$$
$$15/12 = 1 + 3/12$$
$$12/3 = 4 + 0$$

The greatest common divisor is the denominator of the quotient that has no remainder, i.e. 3. The algorithm has applications in public key cryptography where it is necessary to determine an inverse in modulo arithmetic, i.e. $w.w^{-1} = 1 \pmod n$, where w is coprime with n and it is required to determine w^{-1}. The problem is equivalent to determining two integers w^{-1} and k such that $w.w^{-1} = k.n + 1$. *See* COPRIME, GREATEST COMMON DIVISOR, KNAPSACK CIPHER.

Euler's Generalization. In number theory, for every integer b and n such that the greatest common divisor of b and n is 1 then:

$$b^{\phi(n)} \pmod n \equiv 1.$$

Where $\phi(n)$ is the Euler totient function. *See* COPRIME, EULER TOTIENT FUNCTION, FERMAT'S THEOREM, GREATEST COMMON DIVISOR, KNAPSACK CIPHER, MOD N.

Euler totient function. In number theory, the number of elements in the reduced set of residues for a given integer n, usually designated by $\phi(n)$. It is equal to the number of positive integers less than n that are relatively prime to n. *See* RELATIVELY PRIME, REDUCED SET OF RESIDUES, RSA.

Euronet. The data transmission network provided for the European Economic Community by the telecommunication authorities of member countries. Users on Euronet are able to access specialized scientific, technical and economic information via a packet switched network, which in turn is connected to the public telephone system of member countries. *See* PACKET SWITCHING.

European Informatics Network. In data communications, a European project established to coordinate research into networks and to promote agreement on standards. Its first task was to construct a packet switched subnet that became operational in 1976. *See* PACKET SWITCHING.

Evaluated Products List. A documented inventory of commercially available trusted computer hardware and software that has been evaluated against the Department of Defense Trusted Computer System Evaluation Criteria by the National Computer Security Center. (AFR). *Compare* ENDORSED TEMPEST PRODUCTS LIST, PREFERRED PRODUCTS LIST.

evaluation. In computer security, the evaluator's report to the Designated Approving Authority describing the investigative and test procedures used in the analysis of the ADP system security features with a description and results of tests used to support or refute specific system weaknesses that would permit the acquisition of identifiable classified material from secure or protected data files. (DODD). *See* ADP, DESIGNATED APPROVING AUTHORITY.

evaluation technical report. In information security, a report produced by an information technology security evaluation facility and submitted to the certification body detailing the findings of an evaluation and forming the basis of the certification phase of the evaluation of a target of evaluation. *See* CERTIFICATION BODY, INFORMATION TECHNOLOGY SECURITY EVALUATION CRITERIA, INFORMATION TECHNOLOGY SECURITY EVALUATION FACILITY, TARGET OF EVALUATION.

evaluator. In computer security, personnel specifically designated to participate in the test team review, analysis, testing, and evaluation of the security features of an automated system. (AR). *See* EVALUATION.

EVD. *See* ELECTRONIC VIBRATION DETECTOR.

even parity. *See* PARITY.

event code. In physical security, a signal generated by a digital communicator indicating the nature of the alarm. *See* DIGITAL COMMUNICATOR.

event sequence analysis. *See* STATIC ANALYSIS.

exchangeable disk storage. In computing, one or more disk units with disk packs that can be replaced by an operator. *See* DISK PACK.

EXCLUSIVE OR. A logical operation, A EXCLUSIVE OR B is true if either, but not both, A or B is true. The corresponding truth table is:

A	B	A EXCLUSIVE OR B
0	0	0
1	0	1
0	1	1
1	1	0

See DATA ENCRYPTION STANDARD.

execute protection. In software protection, the use of protection measures to prevent a program from being executed after it has been copied.

Most protection schemes depend upon the source diskette being uniquely defined by a fingerprint that cannot be copied across to another diskette. When the protected program starts execution it checks for the presence of the fingerprint, such as burn mark or weak bits. If it is present the execution will proceed, if not it will terminate.

The fingerprint must have three attributes: it must unique, uncopyable and detectable. The disadvantage of such protection schemes is that they prevent the legitimate taking of backup copies of software and the protected program usually cannot work on a hard disk.

In general, because most copy protection schemes require a test for the presence of a fingerprint, they can be bypassed by a patch. Given the current generation of debugging tools, the task is not too difficult for an expert.

A sufficiently smart copy program can

copy almost any characteristic. What cannot be copied with a copy program can usually be made to work with other tools. *See* BIT COPIER, BURN MARK, DEBUGGER, DEMON, DISKETTE, DONGLE, FINGERPRINT, INSTALL-DEINSTALL, PATCH, WEAK BITS.

executive state. In computer security, one of two generally possible states in which an ADP system may operate, and in which only certain privileged instructions may be executed; such privileged instructions may not be executed when the system is operating in the other, the user state. *See* ADP. *Synonymous with* SUPERVISOR STATE.

exhaustive attack. (1) In data security, attack aimed at discovering secret data by trying all possibilities and checking for correctness. (2) In cryptanalysis, a technique in which attempts are made to acquire plaintext or the cryptographic key by direct search methods. *Compare* ANALYTICAL ATTACK. *See* CRYPTOGRAPHIC KEY, KEY EXHAUSTION, MESSAGE EXHAUSTION, PLAINTEXT.

exit button. (1) In physical security, a button used to effect an exit from a controlled area when the card reader is only employed for entry. *See* CARD READER. (2) In physical security, a method of momentarily bypassing an alarm circuit to allow exit.

expander board. *Synonymous with* EXPANSION CARD.

expansion board. *Synonymous with* EXPANSION CARD.

expansion card. In hardware, a card added to the system in order to mount additional chips or circuits so as to extend the system capability, e.g. modem, additional RAM. In a microcomputer an expansion card normally connects directly to the system bus. *See* ADD-IN, BUS, ENCRYPTOR BOARD, MICROCOMPUTER, MODEM, RAM.

expert systems. In applications, a computer system that reflects the decision-making processes of a human specialist. It embodies organized knowledge concerning

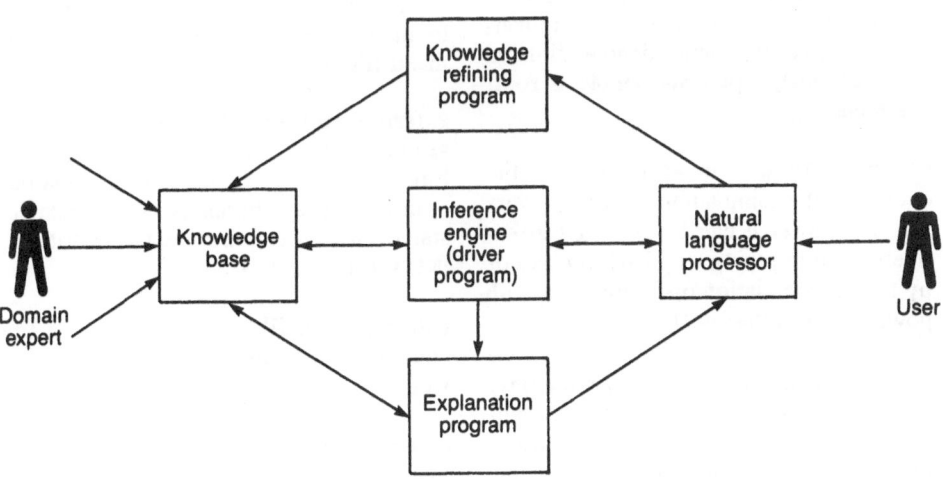

Expert system

a defined area of expertise and is intended to operate as a skilful, cost effective consultant. *See* artificial intelligence.

expired password. In access control, a password that must be changed by the user before log in may be completed. (DOD). *See* LOG IN, PASSWORD.

Exploitable channel. In computer security, any channel that is usable or detectable by subjects external to the Trusted Computing Base. (DOD). *See* SUBJECT, TRUSTED COMPUTING BASE.

exploitable vulnerability. In information security, a vulnerability that can be exploited in practice to defeat a security objective of a target of evaluation. *Compare* CONSTRUCTION VULNERABILITY, OPERATIONAL VULNERABILITY, POTENTIAL VULNERABILITY. *See* INFORMATION TECHNOLOGY SECURITY EVALUATION CRITERIA, TARGET OF EVALUATION, VULNERABILITY..

exponent. In mathematics, a number indicating how many times another number, the base, is to be repeated as a factor. Positive exponents denote multiplication, negative exponents denote division and fractional exponents denote a root. *See* BASE.

exponentiation. In mathematics, the operation of raising a number to a power; x to the power n can be achieved effectively by multiplying x by itself n times or by the exponentiation operation on x with power n. *See* EXPONENT.

exponentiation cipher. In cryptography, a cipher in which the encryption/decryption processes involve raising plaintext/ciphertext messages to specified powers, i.e. exponentiation, in modulo arithmetic. *See* DIFFIE-HELLMAN TECHNIQUE, EXPONENTIATION, MENTAL POKER, MODULO ARITHMETIC, POHLIG-HELLMAN CIPHER, RSA.

Export Administration Act of 1979. In legislation, U.S. legislation that limited the sale of equipment which had implications for national security, e.g. microchips, computer hardware and software, to the USSR and Soviet Bloc countries.

exportation. In data communications, the process that causes data to flow from one network component to an adjacent network component.

exposure. In computer security, the degree of relative availability of data in the environment in which it is used. Exposure is a major aspect of system vulnerability. *See* ACCESS, USAGE, VULNERABILITY.

expression. (1) A mathematical identity or relationship. (2) In computing, a source language combination of one or more operations. (3) In computing, a notation, within a program, that represents a value.

extension. In computing, a part of a file description. Commonly a file description takes the form - diskdrive: filename: extension - and the extension is employed to indicate the class of file: text, command file, etc.

external auditor. In auditing, a representative of a public accounting firm hired to provide an objective, impartial opinion on an organization's financial statements. *Compare* EDP AUDITOR, INTERNAL AUDITOR.

external data file. In computing, a file containing data that is stored separately from the program that processes it.

external interrupt. In computing, an interrupt not caused by an event in the instruction sequence that is interrupted; one caused by a device external to the processor, e.g. a peripheral. *Compare* SOFTWARE INTERRUPT. *See* INTERRUPT, PERIPHERAL.

external label. In computing, an identification label attached to the outside of a file medium holder, e.g. a sticky label attached to the case of a magnetic disk.

external schema. *Synonymous with* SUB-SCHEMA.

external security audit. In computer security, a security audit conducted by an organization independent of the one being audited. (FIPS). *Compare* INTERNAL SECURITY AUDIT. *See* AUDIT, SECURITY AUDIT.

external timing. In data communications, an option on some modems in which the clock or synchronizing bits are externally generated, normally by the data terminal to which the modem is connected. *See* MODEM.

eye retina analysis. In access control, a biometric technique based upon the fact that blood vessel patterns of the eye are unique to users, as discovered in 1935 by Dr. Robert Hill.

In the enrolment phase users place their heads squarely over the device, keeping their eye about half an inch above the lens, and concentrate on a visual alignment pattern. The user then presses a button to initiate the eye retinal scan; a low intensity light source scans the circular area of the retina in a 450 degree arc, some 320 data point readings are taken. A 40 byte template is produced by this operation for later access requests. The enrolment phase takes approximately one minute.

When requesting access the user simply places the eye against an eyepiece and the recognition period is less than 2 seconds. This is a simple, convenient and secure biometric system that seems to be increasingly favored in the access control field. The only potential disadvantages can arise for disadvantaged users, e.g. those in a wheelchair may not be able to reach the scanner. Some members of the general public may also express concerns that the scanning rays could damage their eyes, although it is claimed that any such fears are unfounded. *See* BIOMETRICS.

F

facilities management. In computing, the use of an independent service organization to manage and operate a computing installation.

facility. In data communications, a transmission path between two or more locations without terminating or signalling equipment.

facility code. In access control, a code that identifies the customer or location of equipment in an access control or alarm system.

facility line. In banking, the individual facility extended to a customer, of a predefined facility type. *See* FACILITY TYPE.

facility type. In banking, the name given to a facility, e.g. loan insurance, umbrella. *See* FACILITY LINE. *Synonymous with* PRODUCT TYPE, SERVICE TYPE.

facsimile. In communications, pertaining to the transmission of images over communication links that have a lower bandwidth than that necessary for video signals. The image is scanned by a light beam and a signal representing the brightness, of the section of the image under the scanning beam, is transmitted over the link in the form of a modulated analog or digital signal. At the receiving station the signal drives an energy source to reproduce the image by photographic, thermal or xerographic techniques.

factor. In mathematics, any of the numbers or quantities that are the oper-

ands in a multiplication operation. *See* OPERAND.

factoring. (1) In banking, the deposit of large numbers of fraudulent handwritten sales drafts through collusive, low volume, borderline merchants. (2) In data security, the security of the RSA cryptography system depends on the computational infeasibility of factoring a large product of two prime numbers each of about 100 digits. Such attacks have been attempted using spare computer power on networks. *See* CRYPTOGRAPHY, PRIME NUMBER, RSA.

fail safe. (1) In computer security, automatic termination and protection of programs and/or processing systems when a hardware or software failure is detected in an automated information system. (FIPS). *Compare* FAIL SOFT. *See* PRINCIPLES OF SECURE SYSTEMS. (2) In physical security, a condition in which a system failure causes lock equipment to revert to the open condition, e.g. to allow personnel to vacate a protected area. *Compare* FAIL SECURE. (3) In physical security, a system that initiates an alarm in the event of power or system failure. *Compare* FAIL SECURE.

fail secure. In physical security, pertaining to a condition in which a system failure causes lock equipment to revert to the locked condition. *Compare* FAIL SAFE.

fail soft. (1) In computer security, the selective termination of affected nonessential processing when a hardware or software failure is detected in an automated system. (FIPS). *Compare* FAIL SAFE. (2) In reliability, pertaining to a system that continues to operate, albeit in a degraded manner, even when a part of the system has failed.

failure access. In computer security, an unauthorized and usually inadvertent access to data resulting from a hardware or software failure in the ADP system. (FIPS). *See* ACCESS CONTROL, ADP

failure control. In computer security, the methodology used to detect and provide fail-safe or fail-soft recovery from hardware and software failures in an ADP system. (FIPS). *See* ADP, FAIL SAFE, FAIL SOFT.

fall back. In computing, backup procedures to be used in the event of a services or machine failure. These procedures may be manual or involve the use of other computers and databases.

false acceptance rate. In access control, the probability that a Type 2 error will occur. *Compare* FALSE REJECTION RATE. *See* TYPE 2 ERROR.

false rejection rate. In access control, the probability that a Type 1 error will occur. *Compare* FALSE ACCEPTANCE RATE. *See* TYPE 1 ERROR.

false solution. *Synonymous with* SPURIOUS KEY DECIPHERMENT.

family. In computing, a manufacturer's range of processors marketed to enable a customer to upgrade an installation with a more powerful unit without having to change the rest of the installation or programs.

FAR. *See* FALSE ACCEPTANCE RATE.

fast connect circuit switching. In data communications, a , form of circuit switching in which a terminal dials up the host computer, when one line has

been entered at the keyboard, the data is transmitted and the terminal disconnects the call. *Compare* CIRCUIT SWITCHING.

fast data encipherment algorithm. In cryptography, a block cipher algorithm designed by researchers at the Nippon Telegraph and Telephone Company as a replacement for the data encryption algorithm.

The cipher employs a 64 bit key and a 64 bit plaintext block; the component ciphers are designated FEAL-N where N is the number of rounds of iteration.

- FEAL-4 is to be employed for message authentication, cipher communications using the CBC mode and 64 bit hash functions;
- FEAL-8 is to be employed for cipher communications with the CBC mode;
- FEAL-16 is to be employed for peer entity authentication, cipher communication with the ECB mode;
- FEAL-32 is to be employed for applications where high security is required in a hostile environment subject to a variety of cryptanalytic attacks.

Chosen plaintext attacks on FEAL-4 and FEAL-8 have been reported. *See* BLOCK CIPHER, CBC, CHOSEN PLAINTEXT, DATA ENCRYPTION STANDARD, ECB.

Father Christmas. In computer security, a virus that infects COMMAND.COM and COM files, affects run time operation, corrupts program and OVL files. *See* VIRUS NAMES.

father file. In computing, a method used in the updating of disk or magnetic tape files so that, in the event of a serious corruption or loss of data, the master file can be reconstituted. When a new file is created, as a result of updates to a current file, the old master file is termed the 'father file'. The new, updated file is called the 'son file', whilst the file originally used to create the father file becomes the 'grandfather file'. *See* FILE.

fault. In risk management, a condition that causes a device or system component to fail to perform in a required manner (such as, a short circuit, broken wire, or an intermittent connection). (AR). *Synonymous with* LOOPHOLE.

fault diagnosis. In reliability, an activity that strives to locate a fault and to confine its damage.

fault tolerance. In risk reliability, the capability of a system to function correctly according to its design specifications despite the presence of transient or permanent faults.

fault trace. In computing, a record of faults and the circumstances of their occurrence as determined by a specially designed monitor system.

fault tree. In computing, a tree diagram for maintenance engineers that guides them to observations to be made, subsequent moves to be taken depending upon those observations and eventually remedial actions. *See* TREE.

F-AV. In information security, a functionality class defined in ITSEC, specified for systems which set high requirements for the availability of a complete system or special functions of a system. Such high availability requirements are significant in application areas such as process control systems. *See* ITSEC, TCSEC.

F-B1. In information security, a functionality class defined in ITSEC, which specifies mandatory access control, derived from Class B1 of TCSEC. *Compare* B1. *See* MANDATORY ACCESS CONTROL, ITSEC, TCSEC.

F-B2. In information security, a functionality class defined in ITSEC, which specifies mandatory access control, derived from Class B2 of TCSEC. *Compare* B2. *See* MANDATORY ACCESS CONTROL, ITSEC, TCSEC.

F-B3. In information security, a functionality class defined in ITSEC, which specifies mandatory access control, derived from Class B3 of TCSEC. *Compare* B3. *See* MANDATORY ACCESS CONTROL, ITSEC, TCSEC.

FC. *See* FC-FIPS.

F-C1. In information security, a functionality class defined in ITSEC, which specifies discretionary access control, derived from Class C1 of TCSEC. *Compare* C1. *See* DISCRETIONARY ACCESS CONTROL, ITSEC, TCSEC.

F-C2. In information security, a functionality class defined in ITSEC, which specifies discretionary access control, derived from Class C2 of TCSEC. *Compare* C2. *See* DISCRETIONARY ACCESS CONTROL, ITSEC, TCSEC.

FCAP. *See* FORTRAN COMPLEXITY ANALYSIS PROGRAM.

FCC. *See* FEDERAL COMMUNICATIONS COMMISSION.

FC-FIPS. In computer security, a joint National Institute of Standards and Technology, and National Security Agency project to produce a Federal Information Processing Standard that will replace the TCSEC.

This project will develop a series of FIPS and other documents that will provide criteria and guidance on security in operating systems and other information technology areas such as networks, data bases and applications. The FC-FIPS are intended to be useful to a broad base of users including the private, civil government and national defense communities.

The first project deals with the security functionality requirements for general purpose multi-user operating systems. *See* INFORMATION TECHNOLOGY SECURITY EVALUATION CRITERIA, MFSR, ORANGE BOOK, TCSEC.

FD. *See* FULL DUPLEX.

F-DC. In information security, a functionality class defined in ITSEC, specified for systems with high demands on the confidentiality of data during data exchange. An example candidate for this class is a cryptographic device. *See* CRYPTOGRAPHY, ITSEC, TCSEC.

F-DI. In information security, a functionality class defined in ITSEC, specified for systems which set high requirements with regard to the safeguarding of data integrity during data exchange. *See* ITSEC, TCSEC.

FDM. *See* FREQUENCY DIVISION MULTIPLEXING.

FDX. *See* FULL DUPLEX.

F-DX. In information security, a functionality class defined in ITSEC, specified for networks with high demands on the confidentiality and integrity of the information to be exchanged. For example this can be the case when sensitive information has to be exchanged via an insecure network. *See* ITSEC, TCSEC.

FDDI. *See* FIBER DISTRIBUTED DATA INTERFACE.

FEAL. *See* FAST DATA ENCIPHERMENT ALGORITHM.

FEC. *See* FORWARD ERROR CORRECTION.

Federal Communications Commission. The independent regulatory agency, established by Congress in the Communications Act of 1934 and empowered by that Act to regulate interstate and foreign radio and wire communications services originating in the United States.

Federal Criteria. *See* FC-FIPS.

federal funds. In banking, United States dollars on deposit at a Federal Reserve Bank in the United States. (ANSI).

Federal State Joint Board. In communications, a board established by the FCC and composed of commissioners representing state and federal jurisdictions. *See* FEDERAL COMMUNICATIONS COMMISSION.

FedWire. In banking, a payment service operated by the United States Federal Reserve System as a private wire network for transfers between financial institutions having accounts at the Federal Reserve Bank. (ANSI). *See* BANKING NETWORKS.

Feistel cipher. In cryptography, a class of block ciphers with the properties:

- the block size m is even, i.e. m = 2L, hence a plaintext block comprises two sections each of length L, thus $P = (x_0, x_1)$
- each key defines a set of subkeys $k_1, k_2 .. k_h$;
- for each subkey k_i there corresponds a transformation F_i defined on blocks of length L;
- the plaintext block P is encrypted in h steps as follows:

  Round 1: $(x_0, x_1) \rightarrow (x_1, x_2)$
  Round i: $(x_{i-1}, x_i) \rightarrow (x_i, x_{i+1})$
  Round h: $(x_{h-1}, x_h) \rightarrow (x_h, x_{h+1})$;

  Where $x_{i+1} = x_{i-1} +_2 F_i(x_i)$

- the ciphertext block C is given by (x_h, x_{h+1});
- prior to the decryption process the two halves of C are reversed and

the keys are supplied in reverse order:

Round 1: $(x_{h+1}, x_h) \rightarrow (x_h, x_{h-1})$
Round h: $(x_2, x_1) \rightarrow (x_1, x_0)$;
Where $x_{i-1} = x_{i+1} +_2 F_i(x_i)$

See BLOCK CIPHER, DATA ENCRYPTION STANDARD.

Fellowship. In computer security, a virus that terminates and stays resident, infects EXE files, affects run time operation, corrupts program, OVL and data files and file linkage. *See* VIRUS NAMES.

FEP. *See* FRONT END PROCESSOR.

Fermat prime. In mathematics, a prime number of the form

$F_n = 2^m + 1$

where $m = 2^n$

F_0, F_1, F_2, F_3 and F_4 are primes but $F_5 = 4294967297$ is not.

Compare MERSENNE PRIME.

Fermat's Theorem. In mathematics, if p is a prime number then for every integer b such that the greatest common denominator of b and p is 1 then:

$b^{p-1} \pmod{p} \equiv 1$

See EULER'S GENERALIZATION, GREATEST COMMON DIVISOR, MOD N.

fetch protection. In computer security, a system-provided restriction to prevent a program from accessing data in another user's segment of storage. (FIPS). *See* ACCESS, BOUNDS CHECKING.

Fiat Shamir algorithm. In cryptography, a zero knowledge proof algorithm which may be employed by Alice to prove her identity to Bob, without revealing sufficient information to permit Bob to subsequently masquerade as Alice. One form of the implementation of the algorithm is described below.

- An authentication service develops two large prime numbers, p and q and publishes the product n = p.q whilst retaining the secrecy of p and q. All subsequent operations are performed modulo n.
- Alice obtains from the service center a user identification number (ID) based upon (say) name, address etc. A number QR is then developed which is a function of ID and a variable V. With a knowledge of p and q it is possible to deduce a V and QR such that the latter has a square root modulo n, and to compute that square root.
- Alice has the task of proving to Bob that she knows the square root of QR, without actually revealing its value.
- Alice sends ID and V to Bob;
- Bob knows the procedure to compute QR from ID and V;
- Bob creates a random sequence of 1's and 0's and the following steps are performed until Bob is convinced that Alice knows the square root of QR.

  - Alice selects a number x, computes $t = x^2 \bmod n$, and sends the value of t to Bob;
  - Bob selects the next 1 or 0 in the random sequence and sends it to Alice;
  - If Alice receives a 1 then she forwards the product of x.sqrt(QR) mod n (i.e. sqrt(t.QR) mod n) to Bob, otherwise she forwards x.
  - Bob squares the number received from Alice and checks it against t.QR mod n (if a 1 were sent to Alice) or against t (otherwise).

From Bob's viewpoint if Alice knew the sequence of 0's and 1's to be sent then she could develop the required response without knowing the square-root of QR, i.e. Alice could be masquerading as the true owner of identity ID. If Alice were required to send both responses then she could not cheat but Bob would have sufficient information to compute the square root of QR. *See* MODULO ARITHMETIC, ZERO KNOWLEDGE PROOF.

fiber cross-talk. In communications, exchange of light wave energy between a core and the cladding of a fiber optic cable, the cladding and the ambient surrounding or between differently indexed layers. The cross-talk is deliberately reduced by making the cladding lossy. *See* CORE, FIBER OPTICS.

fiber distributed data interface. In data communications, a high performance token ring architecture employing fiber optics, operating over distances of up to 200 kilometers at 100 Mbps. The cabling comprises two rings, one transmitting in a clockwise direction and the other anticlockwise. If a cable break occurs, bypass relays in neighboring stations activate, joining the two rings on either side of the break and producing a single ring twice as long as the original individual rings. *See* TOKEN RING.

fiber optics. In communications, a technique that deals with the communication of signals by the transmission of light through extremely pure fibers of glass or plastic.

A fiber optic cable comprises a plastic or glass core surrounded by a layer of plastic or glass cladding that in turn is surrounded by a plastic jacket to protect the core from moisture and abrasion. The diameter of the core varies, with the type of fiber, from 2 to 200 microns. Light signals are inserted from LED's or injection lasers, propagated by refraction or internal reflection and are collected by light detectors at the receiving end.

The propagation along the cable is either reflective or refractive depending upon the type of cable - stepped index monomode, stepped index multimode or graded index multimode. Here the term index refers to refractive index and, as the names suggests, the refractive index of stepped index fibers is constant throughout the core and changes sharply at the core-cladding interface, whereas in the case of multimode graded index fibers, the index falls off gradually from the center of the core to its outer edges.

In monomode cables the core diameter is very low (2-10 microns) and there is only one path - along the center of the core - for the light signals. With stepped index multimode fibers the light rays travel at varying angles to the axis and are internally reflected at the core-cladding interface. In this case rays will travel along paths of different lengths and thus signal pulses are spread out and distorted.

In the graded index fiber light rays will travel faster near the outer edge of the core, than along the axis, because the refractive index is lower. This effect tends to reduce the dispersion because rays travelling along the longer paths tend to travel faster.

The light signals are produced either by LED's or injection lasers. The comparative advantage of the injection laser over the LED are higher power output and a narrow beam but they tend to be more expensive and have shorter working lives. The transmitted light is normally in the infrared bandwidth, the signal attenuation is very sensitive to wavelength, tending to decrease with increased wavelength.

The advantages of fiber optic cables, over conventional coaxial, are immunity from electromagnetic interference, high data carrying capacity, low signal attenuation, security, raw material cost, chemical stability and freedom from co-channel interference. From a data security viewpoint fiber optic cables

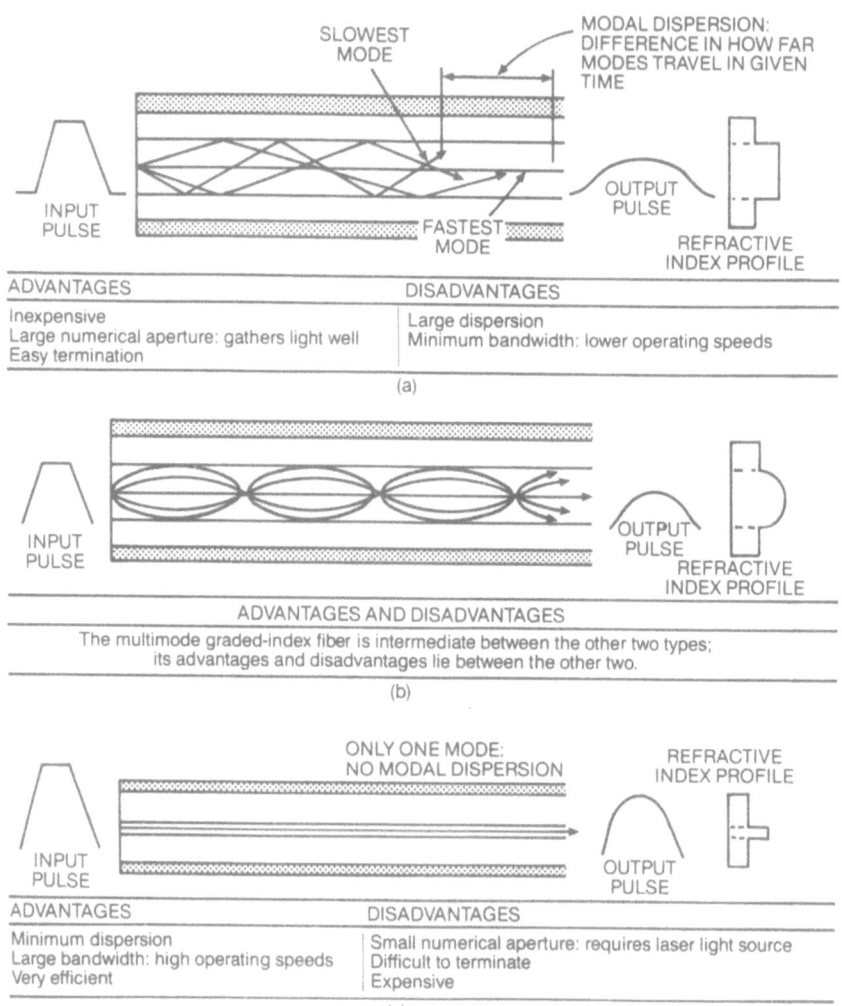

SLOWEST MODE

MODAL DISPERSION: DIFFERENCE IN HOW FAR MODES TRAVEL IN GIVEN TIME

INPUT PULSE

OUTPUT PULSE

FASTEST MODE

REFRACTIVE INDEX PROFILE

ADVANTAGES	DISADVANTAGES
Inexpensive Large numerical aperture: gathers light well Easy termination	Large dispersion Minimum bandwidth: lower operating speeds

(a)

INPUT PULSE

OUTPUT PULSE

REFRACTIVE INDEX PROFILE

ADVANTAGES AND DISADVANTAGES

The multimode graded-index fiber is intermediate between the other two types; its advantages and disadvantages lie between the other two.

(b)

ONLY ONE MODE: NO MODAL DISPERSION

REFRACTIVE INDEX PROFILE

INPUT PULSE

OUTPUT PULSE

ADVANTAGES	DISADVANTAGES
Minimum dispersion Large bandwidth: high operating speeds Very efficient	Small numerical aperture: requires laser light source Difficult to terminate Expensive

(c)

fiber optics

have the advantage that they do not emit radiating signals and are relatively difficult to tap although they can be subject to an active wiretap with a rogue fiber. *See* COMPROMISING EMANATIONS, ROGUE FIBER, TEMPEST PROOFING, WIRETAP.

field. In mathematics, a set of integers for which addition, subtraction, multiplication, division (except by 0) are defined and the commutative, associative- and distributive laws apply. A complete residue system, that is modulo a prime, forms a field. The concept of a field is closely related to modulo arithmetic. Consider a field comprising the digits 1, 2, 3..7., the addition and multiplication operations can be defined so that the results are members of the field, e.g.:

$4 + 6 = 3$
$3 \times 5 = 1$ etc.

Alternatively this can be expressed in terms of modulo 7 arithmetic $(4 + 6) \equiv 3 \pmod 7$, $(3 \times 5) \equiv 1 \pmod 7$. *See* ASSOCIATIVE LAW, COMMUTATIVE LAW, COMPLETE SET OF RESIDUES, DISTRIBUTIVE LAW, GALOIS FIELD, MODULO ARITHMETIC. (2) In data processing, a physical space on a data recording medium that is reserved for one or more related data elements. (3) In computing, an element of a record. *See* RECORD.

field data code. In codes, a standardized military data transmission code consisting of 7 data bits plus one parity bit. *See* BIT, PARITY.

field separator. In codes, a character that may be used to delimit fields or other items of data in the storage, transfer or transmission of data. *See* FIELD.

field tag. In authentication, a unique string of characters used in formatted messages that identifies the meaning and location of the associated data field. (ANSI). *See* FIELD.

FIFO. *See* FIRST IN FIRST OUT.

file. In computing, a collection of records that are logically related to each other and handled as a unit, for example, by giving them a single name. A file may exist on magnetic tape, disk, etc. *See* MAGNETIC DISK, MAGNETIC TAPE, RECORD.

file access. In data security, access control procedures that determine the files that may be accessed by an authorized computer user and the operations that may be performed using those files.

Computer files are allocated to directories and such directories may be organized in a tree structure. A potential user of a file must therefore be in possession of the file name, directory name and, possibly, names of parent directories. Access to the file may then be controlled by file passwords and/or access tables. File passwords provide similar protection to computer passwords.

The mapping that relates a user, file and file privilege are stored in access tables; alternatively the files may be partitioned into discrete segments and an access matrix relates the privileges granted to users, from one segment, when accessing files from another. For example, the files of a college may be partitioned into administrative, teaching and research; the partition matrix then indicates the file privileges granted to research staff when accessing administrative files.

Typical types of file privileges are: read, modify, bestow, write, amend and execute. Read allows the user to view the contents of a file but not to modify or use it, e.g. execute a program file. Modify is an all-encompassing term for the changes that can be made to a file. Bestow allows a user to grant access privileges to another user, but such privileges must not be in excess of those held by the bestower. Write privileges include saving, deleting, replacing, creating a file, changing the file contents and possibly creating or deleting a sub-directory. Append allows the user to add further information to a file without modifying existing data, e.g. a number of users can enter data from a statistical survey but not change the data entered by another, and execute enables the file to be executed as a program. File privileges may be granted to groups of users as well as individuals. *See* ACCESS CONTROL, DATABASE SECURITY, DIRECTORY, FILE PROTECTION, LOCKWORD, TREE STRUCTURED DIRECTORY.

file authentication code. In database security, a code produced in a manner similar to MAC that can be employed to provide assurance that data held in a file has not been deleted or modified. *See* MAC.

file cleanup. In computing, the removal of superfluous data from a file. *Synonymous with* FILE TIDYING.

file conversion. In computing, the process of changing the file medium or structure, often because of the requirements of a new program or change of hardware. *See* FILE, HARDWARE.

file descriptor. In computing, information normally stored as a header record on magnetic disk, or tape, giving details of the file name, generation number, expiry date, date of last access and structure of records. *See* DESCRIPTOR.

file layout. In computing, the arrangement and structure of data in a file, including the order and field size of each element. *See* FIELD, FILE. *Synonymous with* FILE ORGANIZATION.

file lock. In computing, a facility to deny access to a file. It is used in multi-user systems to prevent two users from simultaneously writing to the same file. *Compare* RECORD LOCK.

file maintenance. In computing, the activity of keeping a file up to date by adding, changing, or deleting data, e.g. the addition of new programs to a program library on magnetic disks. *See* FILE MANAGEMENT, FILE ORGANIZATION.

file management. In computing, a procedure or set of processes for creating and maintaining files. *See* FILE, FILE MAINTENANCE, FILE ORGANIZATION.

filename. In computing, a character string that uniquely identifies a file. Files can be identified by two names, external and internal. The external filename is that used by the operating system and comprises all the higher level owners of a file in a tree structured directory plus the extension. An internal filename can be allocated to a file within a program. The open file instruction will relate the internal and external filenames and in subsequent read or write instructions the internal filename is used. *See* EXTENSION, FILE, OPEN, OPERATING SYSTEM, PATH, TREE STRUCTURED DIRECTORY.

file organization. *Synonymous with* FILE LAYOUT.

file processing. In computing, the periodic updating of master files to reflect the effects of current data, e.g. a monthly stock run updating the master stock file.

file protection. (1) In computer security, the aggregate of all processes and procedures established in an ADP system and designed to inhibit unauthorized access, contamination, or elimination of a file. (FIPS). *See* FILE ACCESS, DATA CONTAMINATION, KEY MANAGEMENT. (2) In computing, a method of protecting files against unauthorized access by another user. If a common directory is employed the directory entries will contain a tag indicating the owner and type of protection required. Several levels of protection may be provided, e.g. allow write, allow read, allow execute and allow append. The latter level of protection permits users to write records at the end of the file but not read or modify existing records; a useful facility for gathering statistics from a variety of users. *Compare* MEMORY PROTECTION. *See* DIRECTORY, FILE, FILE ACCESS, RECORD.

file protect ring. In computing, a ring that when removed from a magnetic tape reel will prevent data from being written to the tape. *See* FILE PROTECTION.

file restructuring. In computing, a technique employed to optimize the location of data on a magnetic disk. During file operations the storage of data items depends upon the order in which they are received; in the long term this can lead to degradation of system performance. File restructuring is sometimes performed during systematic backup operations.

file security. In data security, the arrangements for ensuring the privacy or inaccessibility of files from unauthorized users. *See* DATA SECURITY, FILE ACCESS, FILE PROTECTION.

file server. In computing, a sophisticated form of disk server that maintains a complete logical file system. Networked microcomputer users can access information in the same directory areas and the file server mechanisms will deal with the problems of unauthorized access, concurrent accesses etc. A heterogeneous mix of microcomputers can also be accommodated by software, that resides in the microcomputers and converts operating system requests into equivalent file server requests. *See* DISK SERVER, FILE, SERVER.

file storage. In computing, peripherals that can store a mass of data. These include magnetic disk units, magnetic tape units etc.

file system check. In computing, a Unix command to check the file system integrity. If a damaged file is discovered the operator is asked for permission to repair it but such action may result in the loss of data. *See* FILE, UNIX.

file tidying. *Synonymous with* FILE CLEANUP.

file transfer, access and management. In data communications, the processes required when files are accessed remotely or transferred over a network.

file updating. In computing, one of the most common operations in data and transaction processing. The contents of a file are changed without altering the fundamental structure.

fill character. In computing, a character, usually a space, added to a set of characters to make the set a given length.

filter. In database security, a security kernel responsible for enforcing the requirements of multilevel security. *Synonymous with* GUARD.

filtering. In cryptography, a technique employed to transform ciphertext, which normally comprises a random bit stream, into a stream of characters permitted by a given transmission protocol. For example the bit stream may be divided into 4 bit groups and each group represented as a hexadecimal character 1 - 9, A - F, these characters may then be converted into 1 byte ASCII characters and transmitted. Such a technique adds redundancy to the transmitted stream and hence increases the number of bits in the transmitted stream. *See* ANSI - X.12.

FIMAS. In banking, Financial Institution Message Authentication Standard. *Synonymous with* ANSI X9.9 - 1986.

F-IN. In information security, a functionality class defined in ITSEC, specified for systems with high integrity for data and programs. Such requirements are significant for database systems. *See* INTEGRITY, ITSEC, TCSEC.

financial institution. In banking, an establishment responsible for the custody, loan, exchange or issue of money; for the extension of credit; and for facilitating transmission of funds. (ANSI).

financial message. In banking, a communication containing instructions that have financial implications. (ANSI).

fingerprint. (1) In software protection, a method of giving a unique mark, or signature, to a floppy disk, that cannot be duplicated. A special test routine detects if a signature is present, and if it is not found the protected program will be disabled. *Compare* DONGLE. *See* BURN MARK, EXECUTE PROTECTION, WEAK BITS. *Synonymous with* SIGNATURE, UNIQUE IDENTIFICATION. (2) In access control, a unique identifying attribute of an individual. *See* FINGERPRINT ANALYSIS.

fingerprint analysis. In access control, a biometric technique based upon measurement of the user's fingerprint. In 1897, the Metropolitan Police Commissioner, Sir Edward Henry, devised a method for the classification of fingerprints that was subsequently widely used by police forces.

The fingerprint is a ridge pattern on the skin of finger tips and this pattern displays three major features, whorls, loops and arches, plus more detailed characteristics termed fingerprint minutiae. Whorls are ridge patterns with spiral characteristics, loops are closed ridge patterns whilst arches are curvatures in the patterns that are not closed. The location and orientation of fingerprint minutiae play an important role in fingerprint identification; such minutiae include inter alia ridge branches where two ridges merge into a single ridge, and ridge endings where an individual ridge terminates.

Fingerprint scanning devices normally record two fingerprints to guard against denial of access due to injury to one finger. The finger is placed upon a small platen, often with a guide to assist in the consistent placement and orientation of the finger. Typical claimed Type 1 and Type 2 error rates are a false rejection rate of 2 % and a false acceptance probability of 0.0001 %.

Fingerprint images are normally read by the total internal reflection of the image on the glass platen. The image is affected by a variety of factors including skin oil residue, orientation, finger pressure etc. Some systems provide the user with feedback information such as an image of the fingerprint, or measurement of finger pressure in order to assist in the development of consistent images for scanning.

In some systems the administrator may be able to customize the access control parameters by setting parameters, on the acceptable degree of consistency in the enrolment phase and acceptable degree of match for an access attempt. The higher the degree of consistency in the enrolment phase implies that the only sample scans accepted for enrolment have a high degree of match with each other, thus ensuring that a high quality stored fingerprint template. If a low quality template is employed then it is more probable that the user will be subsequently falsely rejected. The match parameter, controls the degree of match between the template presented and that stored, that is considered adequate for a positive identification. If this is set to a low value then it will reduce Type 1 errors but has the associated danger of an increased possibility of registering a false acceptance.

Fingerprint scanners have many technical advantages for access control applications, and the price of such systems is likely to prove attractive in the future.

The disadvantage of these scanners can lie in the sensitivity of the public, since such techniques are commonly associated with forensic work. *See* BIOMETRICS, TYPE 1 ERROR, TYPE 2 ERROR.

FINS. In banking, Financial Institution Numbering System. *See* ANSI X9.5 - 1988.

FIPS. Federal Information Processing Standards.

FIPS PUB. Federal Information Processing Standard Publication.

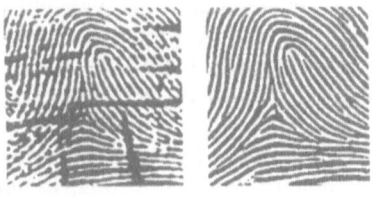

fingerprint analysis
Because no two individuals have the same fingerprint details, this method of access control relies on 'something owned' as the primary means of establishing personal identity.

FIPS Pub 65. A FIPS Pub dealing with risk analysis. *See* FIPS PUB, QUANTIFIED RISK ANALYSIS.

fire walls. In physical security, walls that have been sufficiently fireproofed to prevent the spread of fires.

firmware. (1) In computing, software that is permanently stored in a hardware device that allows reading of the software but not writing or modifying. The most common device for firmware is read-only memory. (AFR). *See* ROM. (2) In computing, computer programs recorded in a permanent or semipermanent physical medium incorporated in the computer equipment. (AR). (3) In computing, a program or data that has been permanently stored in a computer memory, i.e. a ROM, PROM, EROM, or EPROM. This method of implementing software contrasts with programs held on magnetic media and that must first be loaded into the RAM memory of the computer before they can be used. *See* EPROM, EROM, PROM, RAM, ROM.

first in first out. In computing, a method of storing and retrieving items

from a structure such that the first element stored is the first one retrieved. *Compare* LIFO. *See* QUEUE.

first normal form. In databases, a property of a relation, in a relational database. A relation is in first normal form if it does not have any repeating groups, i.e. the data can be expressed in the form of a flat file. *Compare* SECOND NORMAL FORM, THIRD NORMAL FORM. *See* FLAT FILE, NORMAL FORMS, RELATIONAL DATABASE, REPEATING GROUP.

Fish-6. In computer security, a stealth virus that encrypts itself, terminates and stays resident, infects COMMAND.COM, COM, EXE and OVL files, affects run time operation, corrupts program and OVL files and file linkage. *See* VIRUS NAMES.

FIU. U.S. Federation of Information Users.

fixed and exchangeable disk storage. In computing, a magnetic disk unit in which some disks are fixed and others may be exchanged by an operator. *See* EXCHANGEABLE DISK STORAGE, FIXED DISK STORAGE.

fixed disk storage. In computing, storage on non exchangeable magnetic disks. *Compare* EXCHANGEABLE DISK STORAGE.

fixed head disk. In computing, a disk system with a dedicated magnetic head fixed over each track. In the more common type of disk unit, the head is located on an arm and so there is a delay whilst the head is positioned to seek the data. By eliminating the head positioning delay, this method provides very high speed access.

fixed length record. In computing, a record that always has the same length as all other records with which it is logically or physically associated. *Com-*

pare VARIABLE LENGTH RECORD. *See* RECORD.

fixed point. In cryptography, a plain-text block which is not altered by a cryptographic transformation. In DES, if a weak key is employed, then there are 2^{32} fixed points. *Compare* ANTI-FIXED POINT. *See* DATA ENCRYPTION STANDARD, PLAINTEXT, WEAK KEY.

fixed routing. In data communications, a method of routing messages in which the behavior of the network is predetermined, taking no account of changes in traffic or network components. *Compare* ADAPTIVE ROUTING, DELTA ROUTING, DIRECTORY ROUTING, HOT POTATO ROUTING. *See* ROUTING.

flag. (1) In data communications, a character, typically consisting of eight bits, used to mark the start of a frame in a packet. *See* FRAME, PACKET SWITCHING. (2) In computing, a signal set up to indicate that a specific condition has occurred. For example, when a buffer is full.

flag bit. *See* FLAG.

flag code. *Synonymous with* ESCAPE CODE.

flag sequence. In data communications, a sequence of bits used to identify the beginning and end of a frame. *See* FLAG, FRAME, PACKET SWITCHING.

Flash. In computer security, a virus that terminates and stays resident, infects COMMAND.COM, COM and EXE files, affects run time operation, corrupts program, OVL and data files and file linkage. *See* VIRUS NAMES.

flat file. In databases, a file comprising a collection of records of the same type that do not contain repeating groups. A flat file can be represented by a two-dimensional array of data items. A relational database comprises a set of well structured flat files. *See* RECORD, RELATIONAL DATABASE, REPEATING GROUP.

flaw. In computer security, an error of commission, omission, or oversight in a system that allows protection mechanisms to be bypassed. (DOD). *See* PSEUDO-FLAW. *Synonymous with* LOOPHOLE.

flaw hypothesis. In computer security, a technique of dynamic testing, in which flaws are hypothesized on the basis of analogous flaws detected in other systems and then tested for existence in the system under study. *Compare* PROGRAM ANALYZER. *See* DYNAMIC TESTING, FLAW HYPOTHESIS METHODOLOGY.

flaw hypothesis methodology. In computer security, a system analysis and penetration technique where specifications and documentation for the system are analyzed and then flaws in the system are hypothesized. The list of hypothesized flaws is then prioritized on the basis of the estimated probability that a flaw actually exists and, assuming a flaw does exist, on the ease of exploiting it and on the extent of control or compromise it would provide. The prioritized list is used to direct the actual testing of the system. (DOD). *See* FLAW.

flexibility. In computing, the effort required to modify an operational program.

Flip. In computer security, a virus that encrypts itself, terminates and stays resident, infects COMMAND.COM, COM, EXE and OVL files, affects run time operation, corrupts program, OVL and data files and file linkage. *See* VIRUS NAMES.

flooding. In data communications, a routing method in which each node replicates incoming packets and sends copies to its neighbors, thus ensuring that the actual destination is reached quickly and with certainty, though with considerable use of transmission capacity. *See* NODE, PACKET SWITCHING, ROUTING.

flood testing. In computing, a method of testing the overall throughput of a system when all the terminals in a network are in use. *See* COMPUTER NETWORK.

floor sensor. *Synonymous with* AREA MAT.

floppy. In computing, an abbreviation for floppy disk or a floppy disk drive.

floppy disk. In computing, a thin flexible magnetic coated disk contained in a rigid or semi-rigid protective jacket. The floppy disk provides microcomputer users with a cheap, high capacity, direct access backing store. The floppy disk is contained within an envelope that is coated in its exterior to provide a cleaning action. The envelope has a number of apertures for the drive spindle, index hole to signal the start of a sector and a write inhibit notch. *See* PERSONAL COMPUTER SECURITY.

floppy disk drive. In computing, a drive mechanism for a floppy disk. The essential components of the drive are an electric motor and spindle to rotate the disk, one or more read/write heads, a head positioning system and, for many systems, a light source plus photo-detector to detect the start of sectors. The speed of rotation is low compared with hard disk drives because the read/write head is in contact with the disk and the speeds typically range from 300-600 r.p.m.

flops. In computing, floating point operations per second, a measure of computer performance. *Compare* LIPS, MIPS.

flow analysis. *See* INFORMATION FLOW ANALYSIS, TRAFFIC ANALYSIS.

flow control. In computer security, a strategy for protecting the contents of information objects from being transferred to objects at improper security levels. It is more restrictive than access control. (MTR). *See* INFORMATION FLOW CONTROL, OBJECT, SUBJECT. (2) In data communications, the control of data flow to prevent overspill of queues or buffers or loss of data because the intended receiver is unable to accept it. *See* BUFFER.

flying dutchman. In computer security, a form of malicious code, often developed as a student prank. It remained dormant until attempts were made by systems programmers to read the code, the program would then relocate itself and print a screen message, such as 'I was here, but now I've gone'. *See* MALICIOUS CODE.

flywheeling. In key management, a technique for the transmission of key updates in stream cipher systems. Key updates may be sent to the receiver during message transmission to enable the transmitter to change the cryptographic bit stream and maintain synchronism. The key update information is deciphered by the receiver and used to set the cryptographic bit stream generator to its updated setting. If, however, synchronization information is lost, due to a noisy channel or jamming, then the receiver is unable to continue decipherment. Flywheeling overcomes this problem by developing the key updates from a pseudorandom number generator. In this case if the receiver misses a key update then it can obtain it from the pseudorandom generator and use it to reset the cryptographic bit stream generator. *See* CRYPTOGRAPHIC BIT STREAM,

PSEUDORANDOM NUMBER, STREAM CIPHER.

FM. *See* FREQUENCY MODULATION.

FNF. *See* FIRST NORMAL FORM.

FNP. *See* FRONT END NETWORK PROCESSOR.

FOI. Freedom Of Information. Information or activities related to the U.S. Freedom of Information Act.

foil. In physical security, an electrically conductive ribbon used to detect intruders opening windows etc. It is connected into an electrical circuit and an alarm is activated if it is broken.

forbidden combination. In computing, a combination of bits that is not valid according to the criteria set by the programmer or system designer.

foreground program. In computing, a program that has a high priority and takes precedence over other programs that are running concurrently in a multi-programming environment. *Compare* BACKGROUND JOB.

Foreign Government Information. Information that is: (a) Provided to the United States by a foreign government or governments, an international organization of governments, or any element thereof with the expectation either expressed or implied, that the information or the source of information, or both be held in confidence. (b) Produced by the United States following or as a result of a joint arrangement with a foreign government or governments or an international organization of governments or any element thereof, requiring that the information or the arrangement or both be held in confidence. Information described in subparagraphs above and in the possession of the DOD is classified information in accordance with DOD 5200.1-R. (DODD).

forgery. In legislation, the fabrication of information by one party and the claim that such information was received in a communication from another party. *See* DIGITAL SIGNATURE.

Form. In computer security, a virus that terminates and stays resident, infects floppy disk boot sector, infects hard disk boot sector, corrupts boot sector, affects run time operation and corrupts data files. *See* VIRUS NAMES.

formal. Pertaining to rigorous respect for form, that is a mathematical or logical basis.

formal access approval. In data security, documented approval by a data owner to allow access to a particular type or category of information. (DODD). *See* DATA OWNER.

formal language. In computing, a formal language defines a set of symbols, the alphabet, and a set of strings of those symbols. The significance of formal languages in programming is that a given program may be considered as a string of a formal language, i.e. the programming language. The program is produced by writing expressions according to the syntax of the language, this is equivalent to using productions of a corresponding grammar. The translator checks if the program is one of the strings of the language and reports syntax errors if it is not. *See* GRAMMAR.

formal proof. In computer security, a complete and convincing mathematical argument, presenting the full logical justification for each proof step, for the truth of a theorem or set of theorems. The formal verification process uses formal proofs to show the truth of certain properties of formal specification and for showing that computer programs satisfy their specifications. (DOD). *See* FORMAL VERIFICATION, PROOF OF PROGRAM CORRECTNESS.

formal security policy model. In computer security, a mathematically precise statement of a security policy. To be adequately precise, such a model must represent the initial state of a system, the way in which the system progresses from one state to another, and a definition of a 'secure' state of the system. To be acceptable as a basis for a TCB, the model must be supported by a formal proof that if the initial state of the system satisfies the definition of a 'secure' state and if all assumptions required by the model hold, then all future states of the system will be secure. Some formal modeling techniques include: state transition models, temporal logic models, denotational semantics models, algebraic specification models. (DOD). *See* BELL-LA PADULA MODEL, SECURITY POLICY.

formal top-level specification. In computer security, a top-level specification that is written in a formal mathematical language to allow theorems showing the correspondence of the system specification to its formal requirements to be hypothesized and formally proven. (DOD). *Compare* DESCRIPTIVE TOP-LEVEL SPECIFICATION. *See* FORMAL SECURITY POLICY MODEL, TOP-LEVEL SPECIFICATION.

formal verification. In computer security, the process of using formal proofs to demonstrate the consistency (design verification) between a formal specification of a system and a formal security policy model or (implementation verification) between the formal specification and its program implementation. (DOD). *See* PROOF OF PROGRAM CORRECTNESS, SECURITY POLICY.

formant. In communications security, pertaining to a resonant frequency of the vocal tract. *See* VOICE SCRAMBLING.

format. (1) In computing, the predetermined mandatory order, organization or position of symbols in a computer instruction, data or word, data transmission message, etc. The order is mandatory so that the computer can understand and interpret the information. *See* INSTRUCTION, WORD, DATA TRANSMISSION. (2) In computing, a command to format a disk. *See* FORMATTING.

formatted dump. In computing, a dump in which certain data areas are isolated and identified. *See* DUMP.

formatting. In computing, an operation that initializes blank disks; initiating data is written so that the tracks are divided into sectors. No files can be written to the disk until this operation is performed.

form mode terminal. In data communications, an intelligent terminal that can download a form to the terminal. The form may contain read-only fields for information to the operator together with other fields for the receipt of input data via keystrokes. *Compare* PAGE MODE TERMINAL, SCROLL MODE TERMINAL. *See* FIELD, INTELLIGENT TERMINAL.

formulary. In computer security, a technique for permitting the decision to grant or deny access to be determined dynamically at access time, rather than at the time of creation of the access list. (FIPS). *See* ACCESS LIST.

For Official Use Only Data. In data security, data that is unclassified official information of a sensitive, proprietary or personal nature that must be protected-against unauthorized public release. (AFR). *See* UNCLASSIFIED INFORMATION.

FORTRAN. In computing, FORmula TRANslation. Fortran is a compiled general purpose high level language providing very efficient execution, especially for number crunching operations.

FORTRAN Complexity Analysis Program. In computer security, a complexity analysis program for Fortran programs that determines measures based upon the number of control paths in modules, and the length of programs or modules. *See* COMPLEXITY ANALYSIS, FORTRAN.

forward channel. In data communications, a transmission channel in which the direction of transmission coincides with that in which the user information is being transferred. *Compare* BACKWARD CHANNEL.

forward error correction. In codes, a method using a redundant code that enables both error detection and some error correction without retransmission. *See* ERROR CORRECTION CODE, ERROR DETECTION CODE, HAMMING CODE.

forward supervision. In data communications, use of supervisory sequences sent from the primary to a secondary station or node. *See* NODE, SUPERVISORY SEQUENCE, PRIMARY STATION, SECONDARY STATION.

FOUO. *See* FOR OFFICIAL USE ONLY DATA.

four eyes. In data security, pertaining to security measures that require transactions to be endorsed by a second employee.

fourth generation language. In computing, a user friendly language that enables one to obtain the desired information with less effort than that associated with conventional procedural languages. *See* DATABASE MANAGEMENT SYSTEM, DATA DICTIONARY, DATA PROCESSING, END USER, NONPROCEDURAL LANGUAGE, PROCEDURAL LANGUAGE, RELATIONAL DATABASE, SYNTAX.

four-wire circuit. In communications, a two-way circuit where the signals simultaneously follow separate and distinct paths in opposite directions in the transmission medium. A telephone circuit carries voice signals both ways and in the local loop this is achieved over two wires because the waveforms travelling each way can be distinguished. In the trunk network where amplifiers and multiplexers are used, the two directions of transmission have to be physically separated. It is called a four-wire circuit because, in its primitive form, it uses a pair of wires for each direction. *Compare* TWO-WIRE CIRCUIT. *See* TRUNK.

frame. (1) In computing, the array of bits across the width of magnetic tape. *See* BIT. (2) In data communications, a complete sequence of bits identified by an opening synchronization character, and usually including a field containing the user's data.

frame relay. In data communications, frame relay is one of a set of communications protocols specified by the CCITT as part of the overall concept of an Integrated Services Digital Network (ISDN). Frame relay (CCITT Recommendations I.122 and Q.922) is designed to provide a vehicle for high-speed information transfer between two network applications using an ISDN.
The initial step in the frame relay process is for a connection to be established between the communicating parties using the ISDN D channel call procedures (CCITT Recommendation I.451) (Fig. 1). Once a connection is established the information to be transferred is segmented with each information segment encapsulated in a suitable frame envelope (Fig. 2). The frames are then transferred between the communicating parties using the ISDN B channel (or other higher speed ISDN channel e.g. the H channel) (Fig. 3). The high rate of data transfer is achieved essentially by minimizing the

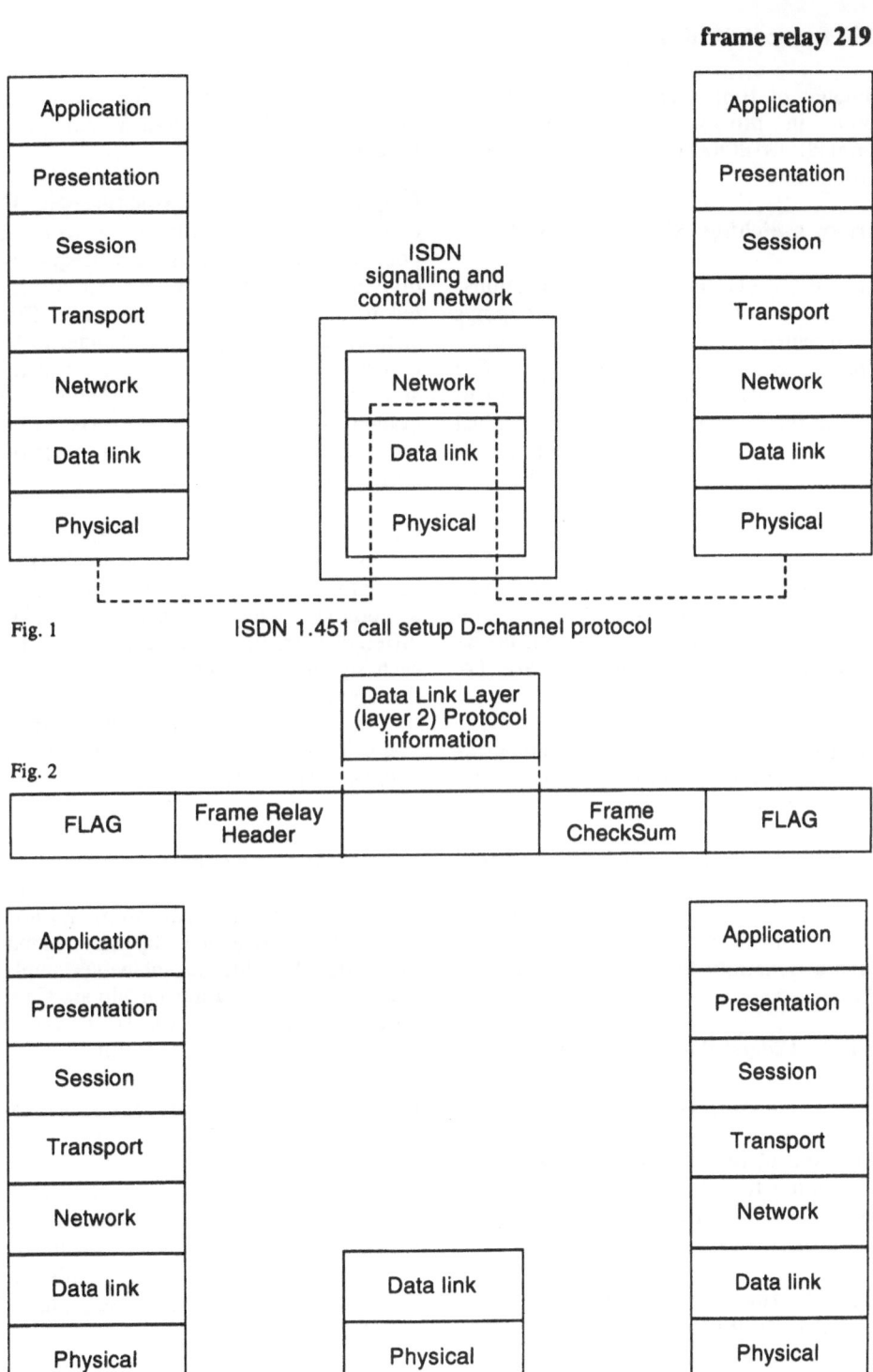

Fig. 1   ISDN 1.451 call setup D-channel protocol

Fig. 2

Fig. 3
frame relay   LAP-D frame transfer on the ISDN B-channel

amount of time spent by each network node in processing the frame. *See* FRAME, INTEGRATED SERVICES DIGITAL NETWORK.

frame switching. See FRAME RELAY.

framing. (1) In data communications, the process of selecting the bit groupings represented by one or more characters from a continuous stream of bits. *See* FRAMING BIT. (2) In data communications, the method by which individual frames, in a time division multiplexing system, are recognized so that the time slots can be correctly identified. *See* TIME DIVISION MULTIPLEXING.

framing bit. In data communications, bits used to make possible the separation of characters in a bit stream, but otherwise carrying no information. *See* BIT STREAM.

framing pattern. In data communications, a unique pattern of framing bits. *See* FRAMING BIT.

fraudulent retailer. In banking, a person who poses as an EFTPOS merchant, using a real, stolen or fake merchant number, and enters one or more invalid transactions into the system. *See* EFTPOS.

FRC. Federal Radio Commission.

FRD. Formerly Restricted Data.

freedom of information. In legislation, pertaining to the right of individuals to gain access to official information. *Compare* DATA PROTECTION.

French roundoff. *Synonymous with* SALAMI TECHNIQUE.

frequency agility. In communications security, a technique to counteract jamming in which the transmitted frequency is varied according to some sequence, known only to the transmitter and legitimate receiver, during transmission. *See* JAMMING.

frequency division multiple access. In communications, a technique in which a pool of frequency bands, in a frequency division multiplexing system, are allocated to users according to demand. This enables the capacity of the channel to be dynamically switched according to demand, as compared with a fixed allocation system. *Compare* TIME DIVISION MULTIPLE ACCESS. *See* FREQUENCY DIVISION MULTIPLEXING.

frequency division multiplexing. In communications, a process whereby two or more signals may be transmitted over a common wideband path, by using different parts of the frequency band for each signal. At the other end of the line the signals are separated and identified by selective filters that demultiplex them. *Compare* TIME DIVISION MULTIPLEXING. *See* FILTER.

frequency modulation. In communications, a form of modulation in which the instantaneous frequency of a carrier wave is caused to depart from the normal carrier frequency by an amount proportional to the instantaneous amplitude of the modulating envelope. *Compare* AMPLITUDE MODULATION, PHASE MODULATION. *See* MODULATION.

frequency multiplexing. *See* FREQUENCY DIVISION MULTIPLEXING.

frequency shift keying. In data communications, a method of signalling in which a carrier is frequency modulated by a signal that has a fixed number of discrete values. *See* FREQUENCY MODULATION.

frequent buyer. In legislation, a discount scheme, operated by supermarkets, in which consumers provide personal details in an application for the scheme. The supermarkets record individual purchases, by means of the bar codes on the goods, and can hence develop valuable marketing information, relating sales to consumer characteristics. *See* DATA PROTECTION.

Frere Jacques. In computer security, a virus that terminates and stays resident, infects COM, EXE and OVL files, affects run time operation and corrupts program and OVL files. *See* VIRUS NAMES.

Friday 13th. In computer security, a virus that infects COM files, corrupts program and OVL files. *See* VIRUS NAMES.

Frogs. In computer security, a virus that terminates and stays resident, infects COMMAND.COM and COM files, affects run time operation, corrupts program and OVL files. *See* VIRUS NAMES.

front end network processor. In computing, a front end processor that handles the interface functions between a computer and a data network. *See* FRONT END PROCESSOR.

front end processor. In computing, a small computer used to handle communication interfacing, e.g. polling, multiplexing, error detection for another computer. *See* MULTIPLEXING, POLLING.

front end security filter. In computer security, a process that is invoked to process data according to a specified security policy prior to releasing the data outside the processing environment or upon receiving data from an external source. (DODD).

front office. In banking, the location where direct dealing operations are conducted. *Compare* BACK OFFICE.

FRR. *See* FALSE REJECTION RATE.

FS. *See* FIELD SEPARATOR.

fsck. *See* FILE SYSTEM CHECK.

FSK. *See* FREQUENCY SHIFT KEYING.

FTAM. *See* FILE TRANSFER, ACCESS AND MANAGEMENT.

FTLS. *See* FORMAL TOP-LEVEL SPECIFICATION.

FTP. File Transfer Program. *See* FILE TRANSFER.

full duplex. In data communications, a mode of information transmission in which data is transferred in both directions simultaneously. *Compare* HALF DUPLEX, SIMPLEX. *Synonymous with* DUPLEX.

fully connected network. In data communications, a network in which each node is directly connected with every other node. *See* NODE.

fully distributed costs. In communications, a system for determining the costs of different services provided by a common carrier. In the U.S. the total allowable operating expenses and rate base are apportioned among the various services in accordance with fixed procedures established by the FCC. *See* FCC.

fully functional dependent. In databases, a collection of attributes A of a relation R is fully functionally dependent on another collection of attributes, B, of relation R if A is functionally dependent on the whole of B but not on any subset of B. Suppose a relation contains employee name, employee number and department, and every employee in a particular department has a unique number. Then the employee name is fully functionally dependent upon the employee number and department, because two employees in different departments may have the same number. *See* ATTRIBUTE,

FUNCTIONAL DEPENDENCE, RELATION, NORMAL FORMS.

Fu Manchu. In computer security, a virus that terminates and stays resident, infects COM, EXE and OVL files, affects run time operation, corrupts program and OVL files. *See* VIRUS NAMES.

functional dependence. In databases, an indication of the interrelationships of attributes in a relation. Attribute A of a relation R is functionally dependent of attribute B of relation R if, at every instant of time, each value of B has no more than one value of A associated with it. Suppose a relation contains employee name, employee number and department, if every employee has a unique number then the employee name is functionally dependent upon the employee number. Note that the employee number is not functionally dependent upon the employee name since two employees may have identical names. *See* ATTRIBUTE, FULLY FUNCTIONAL DEPENDENT, NORMAL FORMS, RELATION.

functional group. *See* ANSI - X.12, EDIFACT.

functional testing. In computer security, the portion of security testing in which the advertized features of a system are tested for correct operation. (DOD). **funds transfer.** In banking, a complete movement of funds directly between the originator and the beneficiary. A funds transfer may consist of one or more funds transfer transactions. (ANSI). *See* FUNDS TRANSFER TRANSACTION. *Synonymous with* TRANSFER.

funds transfer transaction. In banking, movement of funds directly between two parties involving no intermediaries other than a payment or communications service. (ANSI). *Synonymous with* TRANSFER.

funds type. In banking, characteristics of funds within a given currency, pertaining to availability and mobility, usage or exchange regulation, e.g. in the United States, 'same day funds' and 'next day funds'; in Belgium 'convertible francs' and 'financial francs'. (ANSI).

fuzzy sector technique. *Synonymous with* WEAK BITS.

F-Word. In computer security, a virus that terminates and stays resident, infects COMMAND.COM and COM files, affects run time operation, corrupts program, OVL and data files. *See* VIRUS NAMES.

G

G. *See* GIGA.

galactic. In databases, pertaining to data that is extensive and accessible from many places and by many applications.

Galois field. In cryptography, a Galois Field GF(p), where p is prime, is a mathematical system with a finite set of elements and two operations: addition and multiplication modulo p, each operation has an identity element, 0 for addition and 1 for multiplication. There are unique inverses for each element and the associative, distributive and commutative laws hold.

In cryptography GF(2^n) is employed. A binomial polynomial f(x) of degree n, i.e.

$$f(x) = x^n + a_{n-1} x^{n-1} + \dots. a_1 x + a_0$$

where the coefficients a_{n-1} etc. are binary digits, is used to define a number z such that f(z) = 0. The Galois Field GF(2^n) is the set of binomial polynomials $\{a_{n-1} z^{n-1} + \dots. a_1 z + a_0\}$. For example, for GF($2^3$) the binomial polynomial f(z) = $z^3 + z + 1 = 0$, defines a number z, and GF(2^3) comprises the elements $\{0, 1, z, 1+z, z^2, 1+z^2, z+z^2, 1+z+z^2\}$.

The operations permissible are addition and multiplication of the binomial polynomials. Hence

$$(z^2+1) + z^2 = 1,$$

Since the coefficients are added modulo 2, note that $z^3 + z + 1 = 0$.

$$(z^2+1) . z^2 = z^4 + z^2$$
$$= z . (z^3 + z + 1) + z$$
$$= z$$

The elements of the Galois Field may be written in binary notation, hence $a_{n-1} z^{n-1} + \dots. a_1 z + a_0$ can be represented by a binary number:

$$a_{n-1}, a_{n-2} .., a_1, a_0$$

Hence $z^2 + 1$ can be represented by 101. *See* FIELD.

GAO. U.S. General Accounting Office.

garbage. In computing, data and programs in store that are no longer required.

garbage collection. (1) In computing, an expression for cleaning dead records from a file. (2) In computing, the removal of items marked deleted from main memory to provide space for new programs or data. *See* FILE, MAIN MEMORY.

garbage in garbage out. In computing, an adage reflecting the fact that the quality of the output of a computer is dependent on the quality of the input.

garble extension. *Synonymous with* ERROR EXTENSION, ERROR PROPAGATION.

gateway. (1) In data communications, equipment used to interface networks so that a terminal can communicate with a terminal or computer on another network. *Synonymous with* COMMUNICATION SERVER. (2) In banking, an EFTPOS network in which a retailer is directly connected to one access provider that then redirects the transactions to the financial institutions of the customer and the retailer. *Compare* open system.

Gaussian distribution. In mathematics, a probability distribution derived by Gauss for the distribution of errors in experimental measurement. In communications, it is used to determine the probability that the amplitude of signal carrying information will exceed the amplitude of random noise on the channel. *Compare* POISSON DISTRIBUTION.

GCD. *See* GREATEST COMMON DIVISOR.

general purpose. A system that can be applied to a wide variety of tasks without essential modification. *Compare* SPECIAL PURPOSE.

general purpose computer. In computing, a digital computer designed to operate upon a wide variety of applications. It may be contrasted with a dedicated computer that would have special hardware and/or software for a specific purpose, such as the control of an industrial process. *Compare* SPECIAL PURPOSE.

General Services Administration. A U.S. federal government regulatory agency with responsibility for control of purchase of equipment, supplies and services by federal government departments and offices.

generation. (1) In computing, a measure of the remoteness of a file from the original file. *See* FATHER FILE. (2) In computing, pertaining to the class of facilities offered in programming languages. *See* FOURTH GENERATION LANGUAGE.

genuine. In cryptography, a cipher that is not an identity, i.e. the plaintext is not identical with the ciphertext. *Compare* IDENTITY.

geophone. In physical security, a form of seismic detector, designed to be buried underground, that senses fre-

quencies transmitted through the earth resulting from activity below ground or on the surface. *See* SEISMIC SENSOR.

GF(p). *See* GALOIS FIELD.

Ghost Boot. In computer security, a virus that terminates and stays resident, infects floppy and hard disk boot sector, corrupts boot sector, affects run time operation. *See* VIRUS NAMES.

Ghost COM. In computer security, a virus that infects COM files, corrupts boot sector, program and OVL files. *See* VIRUS NAMES.

GHz. Gigahertz. *See* GIGA.

GIDEP. U.S. Government Industry Data Exchange Program.

giga. A thousand million, i.e. 10^9.

GIGO. *See* GARBAGE IN GARBAGE OUT.

GISA. German Information Security Agency. *See* ZSI.

global. In computing, a variable whose value is accessible throughout the program. *Compare* LOCAL.

GMT. *See* GREENWICH MEAN TIME. *Synonymous with* CO-ORDINATED UNIVERSAL TIME.

go back n. In data communications, a protocol employed in a pipelining system. When a corrupted frame arrives, or a frame fails to arrive, the receiver discards all subsequent frames until the corrupted or lost frame is retransmitted and received correctly. *Compare* SELECTIVE REPEAT. *See* FRAME, PIPELINING.

good value. In banking, an expression used to request the application of a defined retroactive value date to a transaction. (ANSI).

GOSIP. In standards, Government OSI Profile, specifies standards and options within standards that are suitable for U.S. government use. GOSIP provides detailed implementation guidelines for OSI systems to ensure interoperability amongst products from different vendors.
See OPEN SYSTEMS INTERCONNECTION.

graceful degradation. *See* FAIL SOFT.

grade A central station. In physical security, one of the Underwriter's Laboratories categories of central stations. The categorization depends upon degree of protection provided, and criteria for equipment, personnel, procedures, records and maintenance. *Compare* GRADE AA CENTRAL STATION, GRADE B CENTRAL STATION. *See* CENTRAL STATION, UNDERWRITER'S LABORATORY.

grade AA central station. In physical security, one of the Underwriter's Laboratories categories of central stations. The categorization depends upon degree of protection provided, and criteria for equipment, personnel, procedures, records and maintenance. *Compare* GRADE A CENTRAL STATION, GRADE B CENTRAL STATION. *See* CENTRAL STATION, UNDERWRITER'S LABORATORY.

grade B central station. In physical security, one of the Underwriter's Laboratories categories of central stations. The categorization depends upon degree of protection provided, and criteria for equipment, personnel, procedures, records and maintenance. *Compare* GRADE A CENTRAL STATION, GRADE AA CENTRAL STATION. *See* CENTRAL STATION, UNDERWRITER'S LABORATORY.

grade of service. In communications, a measure of the quality of the service in terms of the availability of circuits when calls are to be made. Grade of service is measured during the busiest hour of the day and is usually expressed as the fraction of calls likely to fail at the first attempt owing to equipment limitations.

Graham-Shamir knapsack cipher. In public key cryptography, a form of knapsack cipher that it is claimed is safer, faster and easier to implement than the original Merkle-Hellmam knapsack. The 'easy' knapsack vector is represented as a matrix of binary digits. Each row of the matrix represents one of the integers of the knapsack vector $(a_1, a_2....a_n)$. An individual row a_j is represented by a row of binary digits (R_j, I_j, O_j, S_j) where:

R_j = long random bit stream.
I_j = n bits that are all zero except the jth.
O_j = a string of 0 bits.
S_j = a second random bit stream.

e.g.

		R	I	O	S
a_1	=	0101	1000	000	1010
a_2	=	1110	0100	000	1110
a_3	=	1011	0010	000	0110
a_4	=	1101	0001	000	0010

If a plaintext message 1100 were encrypted with this vector then the bit strings a_1 and a_2 would be added to form the message

		R	I	O	S
C	=	10011	1100	001	1000

This message does not hide the original plaintext because:

- the I block corresponds to the original message;
- the sum of digits in the S block is prevented from affecting the I block because any carries from the S block are caught within the O block, that must be long enough for this purpose.

The easy knapsack vector can be converted into a hard knapsack, for encipherment, in a similar manner to the Merkle-Hellman knapsack. Thus two integers w and m are selected and the rows of the matrix are multiplied by (mod m). This matrix is the public encrypting key and the message is enciphered as in the Merkle-Hellman cipher, the rows of the matrix corresponding to the knapsack vector $(a_1, a_2....a_n)$. At the receiving end the enciphered message is multiplied by w^{-1} (mod m) and the bits representing the original plaintext message are extracted from the I block. *Compare* RSA. *See* KNAPSACK CIPHER, MERKLE-HELLMAN KNAPSACK CIPHER, MODULO ARITHMETIC, SUPERINCREASING SERIES.

grammar. In computing, a method of specifying a formal language. A grammar comprises a set of rules, or productions, a set of terminal symbols, a set of nonterminal symbols and a starting symbol. The rules provide for the production of one string of symbols from another; nonterminal symbols may be converted into strings containing terminal and/or nonterminal symbols. The starting string must be the specified starting symbol for the grammar and applicable productions may be applied successively until the resultant string contains only terminal symbols, this final string will then be a legal string in the corresponding language. *See* FORMAL LANGUAGE.

grandfather file. *See* FATHER FILE.

granularity. (1) In computer security, the relative fineness or coarseness by which a mechanism can be adjusted. The phrase 'the granularity of a single user' means the access control mechanism can be adjusted to include or exclude any single user. (DODD). (2) In computer security, the extent of isolation with which a particular instance of a security service or mechanism is invoked. *See* ISOLATION.

graphic annunciator. In physical security, a mimic board with a map of the facility and locations of sensors or alarm zones. The state of sensors and alarms is presented visually. *See* ANNUNCIATOR.

Gray code. In codes, a binary code in which sequential numbers are represented by binary expressions, each of which differs from the preceding expression in only one place:

DECIMAL	BINARY	GRAY
0	000	000
1	001	001
2	010	011
3	011	010
4	100	110
5	101	111

greatest common divisor. In mathematics, the largest integer that exactly divides into two specified integers, e.g. the greatest common divisor of 8 and 12 is 4. *Compare* LEAST COMMON MULTIPLE. *See* RELATIVELY PRIME.

Greenwich Mean Time. *Synonymous with* CO-ORDINATED UNIVERSAL TIME.

grid sensor. *Synonymous with* BURGLAR ALARM PAD.

group. (1) In communications, an assembly of 12 telephone channels forming a 48kHz frequency band of a carrier transmission system. *See* CHANNEL. (2) In computing, a set of related records that have the same value for a particular field in all of the records. *See* FIELD, RECORD.

grouping. In database security, a form of cell restriction in which attribute value groups are combined so that no cell contains data from a limited number of records. For example if salary ranges 10,000 - 11,000 and age ranges 64 - 65 provide sensitive statistics then the salary range 10,000 - 12,000 and age range 63 - 65 may be used. *Compare* AUDIT EXPERT, CELL SUPPRESSION, IMPLIED QUERIES CONTROL, OVERLAP CONTROL, QUERY SET SIZE CONTROL. *See* CELL RESTRICTION. *Synonymous with* rolling up.

GSA. *See* GENERAL SERVICES ADMINISTRATION.

GSIS. U.S. Group for the Standardization of Information Services.

guard. In database security. *Synonymous with* FILTER.

guard band. (1) In computing, the blank portion of a magnetic tape that separates two tracks of information, thus preventing signal interference. (2) In communications, a narrow band of unused frequencies between allocated channels, intended to minimize the possibility of mutual interference.

guarding. The function of preventing the false operation of a device.

Guardwire. In physical security, a trade name for an intrusion detection system. Guardwire is a cable, threaded into a security fence, and it detects vibrations caused by intruders scaling the fence etc. The cable comprises two strands of ferrite based material that act as the poles of a permanent magnet; between theses poles are a pair of conductor wires, together with two inductor wires that are free to move in a one millimeter air gap. When the cable moves a current is produced in the inductor wires. The system is very sensitive and the signals produced by cable movement may be processed to minimize spurious alarms.

Guillou-Quisquater. In cryptography, an algorithm used to produce digital signatures. *See* DIGITAL SIGNATURE.

Guppy. In computer security, a virus that terminates and stays resident, infects COMMAND.COM and COM files, affects run time operation, corrupts program and OVL files. *See* VIRUS NAMES.

Gypsy. In computer security, a combined formal program specification language and a verifiable high order language, developed at the University of Texas, and designed in conjunction with a complete verification system. (MTR). *See* AFFIRM, HIERARCHICAL DEVELOPMENT METHODOLOGY, INA JO FORMAL METHODOLOGY.

H

hacker. (1) In computing, a computing enthusiast. The term is normally applied to people who take a delight in experimenting with system hardware, software and communication systems. *See* CRACKER. (2) In data security, an unauthorized user who tries to gain entry to a computer network by defeating the system's access controls. *See* ACCESS CONTROL, CRASHER, PHRACKER, TELEPHONE INTRUSION. *Synonymous with* TERMINAL THIEF.

hack hack. *Synonymous with* SCANNING.

half duplex. In data communications, transmission that takes place one way at a time on a two-way circuit. *Compare* FULL DUPLEX. *See* DUPLEX.

halon system. In physical security, a fire suppression system with the advantage, compared with water sprinklers, that it does not damage equipment, nor does it harm humans. It's use is however restricted by various treaties due to its environmental impact. *See* BROMOCHLORODIFLUOROMETHANE.

Hamming code. In codes, a forward error detection code capable of detecting and correcting single bit errors, and detecting but not correcting most multiple bit errors. *See* FORWARD ERROR CORRECTION.

hand geometry analysis. In access control, a biometric technique based upon measurements of the user's hand. This technique is particularly appropriate for controlled access at a point of entry, where a high throughput rate is re-

quired. The device may scan data related to hand size, bone structure, finger span and/or pattern of lines on the palm. A three-dimensional image can be gathered by a video camera. Typical equal Type 1 and Type 2 error rates of 1% have been reported. *See* BIOMETRICS, TYPE 1 ERROR, TYPE 2 ERROR.

handled by. In computer security, the activities performed on data in an AIS, such as collecting, processing, transferring, storing, retrieving, sorting, transmitting, disseminating and controlling. (DODD). *See* AIS.

handler. In computing, a program under the control of the operating system that controls a specific peripheral such as a disk or printer and also handles interrupts. *See* INTERRUPT.

handling caveats. *See* SPECIAL MARKINGS.

handling restrictions. *See* SPECIAL MARKINGS.

Hanover Hacker. In computer security, Markus Hess a hacker who penetrated Arpanet and Milnet from Germany and was traced by Clifford Stoll as reported in his book 'The Cuckoos Nest'. *See* CHAOS CLUB.

handshaking. (1) In data communications, the exchange of predetermined signals when a connection is first made across an interface, in order to confirm it is working satisfactorily and to prevent data loss. *See* INTERFACE, PROTOCOL. (2) In authentication, a procedure

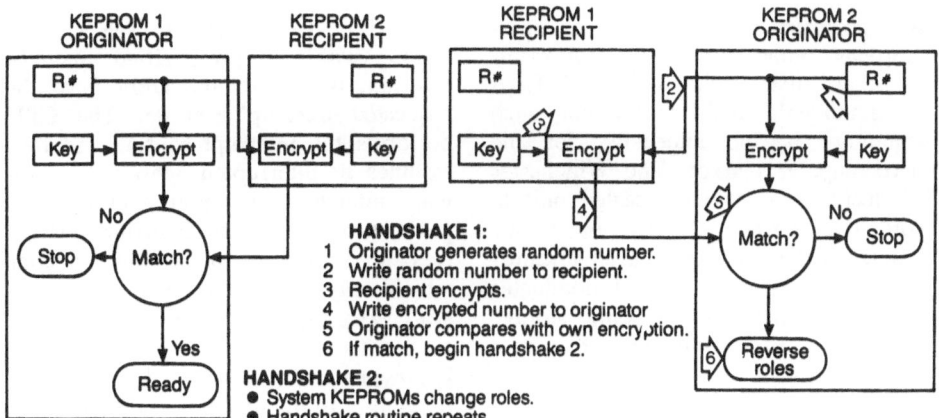

KEPROM 1 ORIGINATOR
KEPROM 2 RECIPIENT
KEPROM 1 RECIPIENT
KEPROM 2 ORIGINATOR

HANDSHAKE 1:
1 Originator generates random number.
2 Write random number to recipient.
3 Recipient encrypts.
4 Write encrypted number to originator
5 Originator compares with own encry,ption.
6 If match, begin handshake 2.

HANDSHAKE 2:
● System KEPROMs change roles.
● Handshake routine repeats.

handshaking
The authentication handshake sequence involves the generation and encryption (according to a secret key) of random numbers by two identically keyed Intel 27916 EPROMs. The two EPROMs compare the encrypted numbers, then swap roles and repeat the sequence. A mismatch results in the inability to gain access to the computer system or the EPROMs' contents. Courtesy of Intel Corp.

to ensure that communication has been established between two genuine nodes in a communications network. Handshaking procedures ensure that an attacker cannot masquerade as a genuine fake node. One method of handshaking relies upon two genuine nodes sharing a secret key. When node A establishes communication with node B then node A generates a random number (RN), encrypts it under the secret key, shared with node B, and transmits the encrypted message to B. At node B the random number is revealed by decryption. This random number is subjected to a non secret algorithm, the result (f(RN)) is encrypted with the same shared key and transmitted back to node A. At node A the message is decrypted and compared with the value f(RN) produced by subjecting the original random number to the algorithm f. *See* CRYPTOGRAPHIC KEY, HANDSHAKING PROCEDURE, MASQUERADING, MIDNIGHT ATTACK.

handshaking procedure. In computer security, a dialogue between a user and a computer, a computer and another computer, a program and another pro-

gram for the purpose of identifying a user and authenticating his identity, through a sequence of questions and answers based on information either previously stored in the computer or supplied to the computer by the initiator of dialogue. (FIPS). *See* HANDSHAKING. *Synonymous with* PASSWORD DIALOGUE.

Happy Day. In computer security, a virus that infects COMMAND.COM and COM files, affects run time operation, corrupts program and OVL files. *See* VIRUS NAMES.

Happy New Year. In computer security, a virus that terminates and stays resident, infects COMMAND.COM, COM, EXE and OVL files, affects run time operation, corrupts program and OVL files. *See* VIRUS NAMES.

hard disk. In computing, a direct access storage device with a rigid magnetic disk. High packing densities and data rates demand that the disk rotates at high speed with the read/write heads of the order of 1 micron above the disk surface. These requirements demand exacting engineering and an ultra clean operating environment. Conventional mainframe hard disk systems offer both fixed and removable disk packs but such technology is too expensive for the microcomputer market. The Winchester disk technology, using a sealed unit to avoid the ingress of dust or smoke particles that could cause head crashes, is relatively inexpensive and dominates the high performance backing storage market for microcomputers. *Compare* FLOPPY DISK.

hard error. In computing, an error in reading data from a magnetic disk that cannot be corrected. The loss of data is considered to be irrecoverable. *Compare* SOFT ERROR. *See* MAGNETIC DISK.

hardware. In computing, pertaining to physical equipment, e.g. disk drive, processor or printer, as opposed to programs, procedures, and associated documentation. *Compare* SOFTWARE.

hardware handshaking. In data communications, the passing of control characters between two devices, such as ACK, NAK, XON, XOFF for the purpose of controlling the flow of information between the devices. (AFR). *See* ACK, HANDSHAKING, XON-XOFF PROTOCOL.

hardware interrupt. In computing, an interrupt activated by a peripheral or some other external device. In a typical hardware interrupt operation the external device sends a signal, on an interrupt request line, to the CPU. If the CPU can respond to the interrupt it acknowledges the request and the external device places a byte on the data bus indicating the type of interrupt action requested. The CPU saves the details of its current states, registers, flags, pointer to return address, etc. on a stack. The byte, on the data bus, from the

external device is used to select a location, within a prespecified memory position, that holds the address of the requested interrupt routine. The CPU performs the interrupt routine and then resumes its interrupted operation. Hardware interrupts are significant in computer viruses since an interrupt guarantees invocation of a section of code which may contain a virus. *Compare* SOFTWARE INTERRUPT. *See* VIRUS.

hardware redundancy. In reliability, pertaining to the use of extra circuitry or equipment to provide a degree of fault tolerance. *See* DUAL REDUNDANCY, HYBRID REDUNDANCY, MODULAR REDUNDANCY, NMR, SELF-CHECKING CIRCUIT, STRUCTURAL REDUNDANCY, TRIPLE MODULAR REDUNDANCY.

hardware security. In physical security, computer equipment features or devices used in a data processing system to preclude unauthorized access to data or system resources.

hardwired. In computing, the implementation of a facility using logic circuits (hardware) rather than by using software. *See* HARDWARE, LOGIC CIRCUIT.

harmful event. In risk management, an instance of a threat acting upon a system vulnerability, in which the system is adversely affected. This may include physical damage to elements of the system or may be manifested in: denial of service, unauthorized use of data or system resources, unauthorized manipulation of data or programs for fraudulent purposes or unauthorized disclosure of information. *See* THREAT, VULNERABILITY.

harmonized criteria. *See* INFORMATION TECHNOLOGY SECURITY EVALUATION CRITERIA.

hartley. In information theory, a unit of information based on a scale of 10, i.e. the amount of information that can be derived from the knowledge of the occurrence of one random event out of 10 equiprobable events. *See* INFORMATION CONTENT.

hash function. In mathematics, a function which accepts any input number and produces an output of fixed length. The function effectively accepts input numbers from a large domain and produces an output in a limited range. *See* HASHING, ONE-WAY FUNCTION.

hashing. In computing, a method of allocating storage locations to records of a file. An algorithm is applied to the record key to produce the location address. With suitably designed algorithms this method provides for a more uniform distribution of memory locations than if a simple linear relationship were employed, particularly if the keys have a very large range and the records are clustered in certain bands. *See* FILE, KEY, RECORD.

hash total. In computing, a figure obtained by some operations upon all the items in a collection of data and used for control purposes. A recalculation of the hash total, and comparison with a previous computed value, provides a check on the loss or corruption of the data. *Compare* CHECKSUM, MAC.

hat box. *Synonymous with* SHRINK WRAPPED LICENSE.

Hayes. In data communications, a U.S. industry modem standard for call setup and flow control procedures. The Hayes' modem commands can be initiated by a program in a PC, e.g. for auto dial, or auto answer. Most asynchronous PC communication software will con-form to the Hayes protocols. *See* AUTO DIAL, AUTO ANSWER, ASYNCHRONOUS.

hazard. In risk management, an element or condition possessing the capability to inflict harm. *See* THREAT.

HD. *See* HALF DUPLEX.

HDLC. *See* HIGH-LEVEL DATA LINK CONTROL.

HDM. *See* HIERARCHICAL DEVELOPMENT METHODOLOGY.

HDX. *See* HALF DUPLEX.

head crash. In computing, a failure in a disk drive in which the head touches the rapidly rotating surface of a hard disk resulting in physical damage and data corruption.

header. (1) In data communications, the first part of a message or packet that contains information essential for handling the packet or message but that is not part of the text of the message, e.g. routing, destination information. *See* PACKET SWITCHING. (2) In computing, coded information giving details of a collection of data, e.g. length, but that is not part of the data itself. *See* HEADER LABEL.

header label. In computing, a label that precedes data records of a file and contains descriptive information about the file, e.g. file name, reel number, retention period etc. *See* FILE, HEADER.

heap. In computing, an area of storage used for the allocation of data structures; unlike the stack there are no restrictions on modes of access to the stored data. *See* STACK.

heat detector. In physical security, a

device that detects either a condition in which a fixed temperature is attained or in which the rate of change of temperature exceeds some predetermined value.

help. In computing, a facility provided by some software packages that enables a user to obtain information on certain aspects of the package during operation. *See* SOFTWARE PACKAGE.

hertz. In communications, the unit of frequency, one cycle per second. Abbreviated Hz.

heterogeneous computer network. In computer networks, a network of dissimilar host computers, such as those produced by different manufacturers. *Compare* HOMOGENEOUS COMPUTER NETWORK. *See* HOST COMPUTER.

heterogeneous multiplex. In data communications, a multiplex structure in which the information-bearing channels are not transmitting at the same data signalling rate. *Compare* HOMOGENEOUS MULTIPLEX. *See* DATA SIGNALLING RATE.

heuristic. In mathematics, a trial and error approach involving successive evaluations at each step made in the process of reaching the final result. In contrast, an algorithm represents a consistent approach in arriving at an optimal result. *See* ALGORITHM.

hex. *See* HEXADECIMAL.

hexadecimal. In mathematics, a numbering system with a radix of 16. This system is used because a byte, comprising 8 bits, can be conveniently expressed as 2 hexadecimal digits. Digits between decimal 10 and 15 are represented by the letters A to F respectively, e.g. the decimal number 26 can be represent-

ed as hexadecimal 1A. *See* BYTE, RADIX.

hico. *Synonymous with* HIGH COERCIVITY. *See* HIGH COERCIVITY CARD.

hidden files. In computing, a file that is not revealed by a normal directory search. Such files are normally part of the operating system and will be reported by a check disk command.

hidden object. *See* PERSISTENT OBJECT.

hidden sections. In computer security, menu options, or entire sub-menus, not visible or accessible to a user due to lack of adequate authorization.

hierarchical computer network. In computer networks, a network in which operations relating to control and processing are performed at several levels by computers specially suited for the tasks they have to execute.

hierarchical database. A database that allows records to be related to one another on a 1 to n mapping, e.g., an employee's record may point to a number of dependent's records. The records are thus interrelated by a tree structure. *Compare* NETWORK DATABASE, RELATIONAL DATABASE. *See* TREE STRUCTURE.

hierarchical decomposition. The ordered, structured reduction of a system or a component to primitives (TNI).

hierarchical development methodology. In computer security, a formal specification and verification methodology developed at SRI International. HDM is based on a nonprocedural, state-transition specification language, Special, and provides a security flow analysis tool, MLS, for verifying the multilevel security properties of a user-interface specification. (MTR). *See* AFFIRM, GYPSY, INA JO FORMAL DEVELOPMENT METHODOLOGY, MLS, SECURITY FLOW ANALYSIS, SPECIAL.

hierarchical directory. *Synonymous with* TREE STRUCTURED DIRECTORY.

hierarchical network. In data communications, a network that is synchronized through the use of clocks, where some clocks exert more control than others. Thus the operating rate of the network is a weighted average of the rates of all the clocks. *Compare* DEMOCRATIC NETWORK.

high coercivity. In access control, a term used for magnetic stripe cards in which the magnetic material has a coercivity greater than 2500 oersted. *Compare* LOW COERCIVITY. *See* COERCIVITY, HIGH COERCIVITY CARD, OERSTED.

high coercivity card. In access control, a magnetic stripe card employing a magnetic stripe with high coercivity material. The coercivity of the magnetic stripe material relates to the magnitude of the magnetic field necessary to delete or modify the recorded data on the stripe. In conventional bank cards with low coercivity material, of the order of 300 oersted, is used. The data on such cards may be deleted with a conventional magnet, and modified by a standard magnetic stripe read/write units. In some application areas cards with high coercivity material are employed, i.e. coercivity in excess of 2500 oersted. Such cards are less prone to accidental corruption and an attacker would require more expensive, specialist equipment to modify the data. The coercivity of the material relates to the magnetic force required to change the magnetism of the card. However, low

and high coercivity material can have the same remanence, thus the signal produced by the magnetic stripe data in a reader can be the same for low and high coercivity material. A magnetic stripe reader may therefore accept both low and high coercivity cards. If the card accepting unit also writes to the card, e.g. an ATM that writes an offset, then a unit that accepts low coercivity cards could read, but not write to a high coercivity card. *See* ATM, COERCIVITY, HIGH COERCIVITY, LOW COERCIVITY, MAGNETIC STRIPE CARD, OERSTED, REMANENCE.

high energy media. *Synonymous with* TYPE 2 MAGNETIC MEDIA.

high-level data link control. In data communications, a standard data link layer protocol defined by the ISO. It has a data format that is virtually identical with SDLC. *See* ISO, PROTOCOL, SYNCHRONOUS DATA LINK CONTROL.

high-level language. In computing, a language that enables programmers to specify a set of instructions in a form geared to the nature of the problem rather than the detailed operation of the computer. *Compare* LOW LEVEL LANGUAGE.

high-level protocol. In data communications, a protocol that enables users to carry out functions at a higher level than merely transporting streams or blocks of data. *See* PROTOCOL.

high-speed. In data communications, transmission speeds in excess of those normally attainable over voice grade channels, i.e. in excess of 9600 bits per second. *See* MEDIUM SPEED, NARROW BAND.

high-speed multiplex link. In data communications, a high-speed link over which many signals are combined and subsequently separated at the far end of the circuit. *See* MULTIPLEXING.

hit. (1) In databases, a comparison of two items of data in which specified conditions are satisfied. (2) In data communications, a momentary line disturbance that could result in the corruption of characters being transmitted. *See* HIT ON THE LINE.

hit on the line. In communications, a general term used to describe short-term disturbances caused by external interferences such as impulse noise produced by lightning or man-made interference. *See* HIT, NOISE.

Holocaust. In computer security, a stealth virus that terminates and stays resident, infects COMMAND.COM and COM files, affects run time operation, corrupts program, data and OVL files and file linkage. *See* VIRUS NAMES.

hologram. In access control, a three-dimensional image produced through a combination of photography and laser beams. Diffracted laser light from a subject is used to capture a two-dimensional interference pattern in photographic film. Holograms are used on credit cards since they are relatively difficult to counterfeit. *See* MAGNETIC STRIPE CARD.

home banking. In banking, the use of a domestic communications terminal, usually viewdata, to conduct transactions on the user's bank account. *Compare* SELF-BANKING. *See* HOME BANKING SECURITY, VIEWDATA.

home banking security. In banking, a banking service in which the customer conducts transactions with a terminal located at home and connected to the

bank over a public telephone network.

The data security systems adopted for home banking are affected by the acceptable cost of the home terminal, the use of an insecure public telephone network and the limits of usage complexity that would be tolerated by bank clients. Moreover the creditability of the system must not be adversely affected by incidents that pose no real danger to actual transactions but which could, nevertheless, cause clients to lose confidence in the system, e.g. crossed telephone lines causing a screenful of one client's transactions to appear on another's terminal.

A severe form of attack could arise from a direct interference with a telephone cable. An interposed personal computer could be used to masquerade as the bank to the user, and the user to the bank; enabling the transfer of funds from the client's account to the attacker's. *See* MASQUERADING, VANS SECURITY.

homerun. In physical security, a method of wiring in which each sensor is individually connected to the alarm system or annunciator, i.e. no multiplexing is employed. *Compare* MULTIPLEX. *See* ANNUNCIATOR.

homing sequential switcher. In physical security, a video switcher facility for automatically switching a monitor between specified CCTV cameras. The dwell times may be varied and cameras removed from the sequence or selected for extended viewing by manual commands. *See* CCTV, DWELL TIME, SEQUENTIAL SWITCHER, VIDEO SWITCHER.

homogeneous computer network. In computer networks, a network of similar host computers, such as those of one model of one manufacturer. *Compare* HETEROGENEOUS COMPUTER NETWORK.

homogeneous multiplex. In data communications, a multiplex structure in which the information-bearing channels are transmitting at the same data signalling rate. *Compare* HETEROGENEOUS MULTIPLEX. *See* DATA SIGNALLING RATE.

horizontal parity. *See* LONGITUDINAL REDUNDANCY CHECK.

host. In data communications, any computer based system connected to the network and containing the necessary protocol interpreter software to initiate network access and carry out information exchange across the communications network. This definition encompasses typical mainframe hosts, generic terminal support machines (e.g. ARPANET, TAC, DoDIIS, NTC) and workstations connected directly to the communications subnetwork and executing the intercomputer networking protocols. A terminal is not a host because it does not contain the protocol software needed to perform information exchange; a workstation is a host because it does have such capability (TNI).

host access control. In communications security, a means of restricting access at the ISO protocol level 3 based on the identity of hosts and/or groups to which they belong. *See* OPEN SYSTEMS INTERCONNECTION.

host computer. *See* HOST.

hostile threat environment. In physical security, an area that contains known threats and possesses little or no control over the surrounding area such as experienced by some diplomatic facilities. (AFR). *See* THREAT.

hot card list. In banking, a central file, containing details of cards denied pay-

ment privileges, that is accessed when payment is requested through an ATM. *See* ATM. *Synonymous with* BLACKLIST, HOT FILE, NEGATIVE FILE.

hot file. *Synonymous with* HOT CARD LIST.

hot mode. In communications security, a technique in which each terminal is required to continuously generate messages or dummy messages if necessary, any lack of communication from a terminal then indicates a system failure. *See* BANKING NETWORKS, DELAY/DENIAL OF SERVICE.

hot potato routing. In data communications, a method of routing in which a packet of data is transmitted from a node as soon as possible; even though the line chosen may not be optimal from a routing viewpoint. *Compare* ADAPTIVE ROUTING, CENTRALIZED ADAPTIVE ROUTING, DELTA ROUTING, DIRECTORY ROUTING, FIXED ROUTING. *See* PACKET SWITCHING.

hot site. In risk management, a fully equipped center that provides an alternative computing capability in the event of a computer disaster, e.g. flood or fire. A hot site typically includes computers, tape drives, disk storage and various peripherals. The computer facilities will be compatible with those of the original center to ensure that changeover problems are minimized. Membership of an organization providing the hot site will be limited as will the length of time of use of such sites. *Compare* COLD SITE. *See* CLOSED HOT SITE, CONTINGENCY PLANS, OPEN HOT SITE.

hot standby. In reliability, a method of hardware backup that is automatically switched into operation when a system failure is detected. *Compare* COLD

STANDBY, WARM STANDBY.

housekeeping. In computing, supporting operations that are secondary to the main processing objectives. For example, initialization, file creation and maintenance activities.

housekeeping information. In data communications, signals that are added to information signals but intended only for the receiving equipment so that it may function properly.

hub polling. In data communications, a method of polling on multidrop lines that reduces the time lost in line turnaround. The controller first polls the terminal furthest from it. The addressed terminal turns the line around, i.e. arranges for the signal to be sent in the opposite direction; the line turnaround may take hundreds of milliseconds on a telephone network with echo suppressors. If the terminal has data to transmit it sends it to the controller, however, if it has no data it forwards a polling message to its nearest neighbor. If this terminal has no data it, in turn, forwards a polling message to the nearest neighbor on the controller side. In conventional polling the controller addresses each terminal directly and each terminal must turn the line around to send a 'no data' message. *Compare* ROLL CALL POLLING. *See* ECHO SUPPRESSOR, MULTIDROP CIRCUIT, POLLING.

Huffman code. In codes, a code in which frequently occurring characters are assigned fewer symbols than less frequently occurring characters.

human interface functions. In computer security, TCB operations that require human intervention or judgement. Untrusted processes would not be able to invoke them. (MTR). *See* TCB.

Hybrid. In computer security, a virus that infects COMMAND.COM and COM files, affects run time operation, corrupts program and OVL files and file linkage. *See* VIRUS NAMES.

hybrid redundancy. In reliability, a form of modular redundancy combining the concepts of NMR and standby spare. When the voting system detects a faulty unit that unit is switched out and replaced by a standby spare. If three active and two standby spares are employed then the system will continue to function after three modules have failed. An NMR system with five modules can only tolerate a failure in two units. *See* MODULAR REDUNDANCY, NMR.

Hymn. In computer security, a virus that terminates and stays resident, infects COMMAND.COM, COM, EXE and OVL files, affects run time operation, corrupts program, OVL and data files. *See* VIRUS NAMES.

Hymn-2. In computer security, a virus that terminates and stays resident, infects COMMAND.COM, COM, EXE and OVL files, affects run time operation, corrupts program and OVL files and file linkage. *See* VIRUS NAMES. 11

Hz. *See* HERTZ.

I

I-4. *See* INTERNATIONAL INFORMATION INTEGRITY INSTITUTE.

I&A. In information security, Identification and Authentication. *See* INFORMATION TECHNOLOGY SECURITY EVALUATION CRITERIA.

IA5. *See* INTERNATIONAL ALPHABET NUMBER 5.

IAC. *See* DOD INFORMATION ANALYSIS CENTER.

IBAC. *See* IDENTITY BASED ACCESS CONTROL.

IC. *See* INTEGRATED CIRCUIT.

Icelandic. In computer security, a virus that terminates and stays resident, infects EXE files, affects run-time operation, corrupts program and OVL files. *See* VIRUS NAMES.

ICV. *See* INTEGRITY CHECK VALUE.

ID. *See* IDENTIFICATION CHARACTER.

IDA. In banking, IDentity of key for Authentication, identification of the cryptographic key used in performing message authentication. (ANSI). *Compare* IDE, MID. *Synonymous with* KEY IDENTIFIER.

IDE. In banking, IDentity of key for Encryption, identification of the cryptographic key used in performing message encryption. (ANSI). *Compare* IDA.

identification. (1) In access control, the process that enables, generally by the use of unique machine-readable names, recognition of users or resources as identical to those previously described to an ADP system. (FIPS). *See* ACCESS, ADP, RESOURCE. (2) In access control, the process of associating a unique characteristic to an individual. (ANSI). (3) In data communications, the procedure carried out by a host computer in verifying the identity of an individual line, device, subscriber, etc. requiring access. *See* HOST COMPUTER.

identification and authentication. In information security, functions to establish and verify the claimed identity of a user. *See* INFORMATION TECHNOLOGY SECURITY EVALUATION CRITERIA.

identification character. In data communications, a character that identifies a remote data station to the central station. *See* IDENTIFICATION.

identification risk. *See* DISCLOSURE RISK.

identifier. (1) In computing, a character or group of characters used to identify, indicate or name a body of data. (2) In computing, a name or string of characters employed to identify a variable, procedure, data structure or some other element of a program. *See* DATA STRUCTURE, PROCEDURE.

identifier code. In banking, a code that unambiguously identifies a party to a bank. (ANSI).

identity. In cryptography, a cipher in which the plaintext and ciphertext are identical. *Compare* GENUINE.

identity authentication. In access control, a set of manual or automated procedures that verify that users requesting access are who they claim to be.

identity based access control. In access control, an access control mechanism based only on the identity of the subject and object. *Compare* RULE BASED ACCESS CONTROL. *See* DISCRETIONARY ACCESS CONTROL, OBJECT, SUBJECT.

identity based security policy. In data security, a security policy based upon the identities and/or attributes of users, a group of users, or entities acting on behalf of the users and the resources/objects being accessed. (ISO) *Compare* RULE BASED SECURITY POLICY. *See* IDENTITY BASED ACCESS CONTROL.

identity token. In access control, a smart card, a metal key, or some other physical token carried by a system's user that allows user identity validation. *See* CARD READER, INTELLIGENT TOKEN, SMART CARD.

identity validation. In access control, the performance of tests, such as the checking of a password, that enables an information system to recognize users or resources as identical to those previously described to the system. *See* AUTHENTICATION.

IDES. In access control, Intrusion Detection Expert System, a proposed method for automatically detecting intrusion into computer systems by analysis of audit records. *See* AUDIT DATA, INTRUSION DETECTION.

idle character. In data communications, a control character transmitted on a telecommunication line when there is no information to be transmitted. The character will not be displayed, printed or punched by the accepting terminal.

idle time. In computing, operable time during which some or all of a computer system is not being used. *Compare* OPERATING TIME.

IDS. *See* INTRUDER DETECTOR SYSTEM.

IDU. *See* INTERFACE DATA UNIT.

IEC. International Electrotechnical Commission, a body responsible for electrical standardization, including standards for materials, components and methods of measurement. Some of the IEC's work relates to telecommunications applications in the fields of wires, cables, waveguides and CATV systems.

IEE. U.K. Institution of Electrical Engineers.

IEEE. U.S. Institute of Electrical and Electronics Engineering.

IEEE 802. *See* IEEE 802.3, IEEE 802.4, IEEE 802.5, IEEE 802.6.

IEEE 802.3. In data communications, a standard dealing with the physical and data link layers for CSMA-CD local area networks. *Compare* IEEE 802.4, IEEE 802.5, IEEE 802.6. *See* CSMA-CD, DATA LINK LAYER, ETHERNET, LOCAL AREA NETWORK, PHYSICAL LAYER.

IEEE 802.4. In data communications, a standard for a token bus local area network. *Compare* IEEE 802.3, IEEE 802.5, IEEE 802.6. *See* TOKEN BUS.

IEEE 802.5. In data communications, a standard for a token ring local area network. *Compare* IEEE 802.3, IEEE 802.4, IEEE 802.6. *See* LOCAL AREA NETWORK, TOKEN RING.

IEEE 802.6. In standards, a standard for municipal area networks (MAN). *Compare* IEEE 802.3, IEEE 802.4,

IEEE 802.5. *See* MUNICIPAL AREA NETWORK.

IERE. U.K. Institution of Electronic and Radio Engineers.

IFIP. The International Federation for Information Processing, a federation of professional and technical societies concerned with information processing. One society is admitted from each participating country. IFIP has a number of technical committees; IFIP TC 11 is the technical committee concerned with security and protection of information processing systems. *See* TC 11.

I Inf Sc. U.S. Institute of Information Scientists.

IIS. *See* I INF SC.

IK. *See* INTERCHANGE KEY.

IKV528. In computer security, a virus that infects COMMAND.COM and COM files, affects run-time operation, corrupts program and OVL files. *See* VIRUS NAMES.

illegal character. In computing, a character or combination of bits not valid according to some predetermined criteria, e.g. with respect to a specified alphabet for which that character is not a member. *Compare* FORBIDDEN COMBINATION.

immediate funds. In banking, same day funds in which settlement is simultaneous with the execution of the transaction. (ANSI).

IMP. *See* INTERFACE MESSAGE PROCESSOR.

impact. In computer security, the damage to an organization resulting from a harmful event. It is usually measured in monetary terms per occurrence, in more complex cases it may be measured qualitatively, e.g low to high, or by comparison. *See* HARMFUL EVENT, LOSS, MATRIX METHODOLOGY.

impact analysis. In computer security, the measure of loss from a harmful event. *See* HARMFUL EVENT, IMPACT, LOSS.

impartiality. In information security, a requirement that a security evaluation is free from unfair bias towards achieving any particular result. *See* INFORMATION TECHNOLOGY SECURITY EVALUATION CRITERIA.

impersonation. In computer security, an attempt to gain access to a system by posing as an authorized user. (FIPS). *See* ACCESS. *Synonymous with* MASQUERADING, MIMICKING.

implementation. In computing, the process of installing a computer system or an enhancement to an existing system. It represents the last stage of a series of steps prior to daily operation, including some or all of the following: feasibility study, outline system definition, detailed system specification, programming, integration tests and acceptance tests. In parallel with these activities, the user may be involved in equipment selection, staff training and establishing computer control policies. In very large computer projects, the industrial relations aspects of commissioning a new system may have to be thoroughly explored and agreed. *See* SYSTEMS ANALYSIS.

implementation verification. In computer security, the use of verification techniques, usually computer-assisted, to demonstrate a mathematical correspondence between a formal specification and its implementation in program code. (MTR). *See* FORMAL VERIFICATION.

implied queries control. In database security, a form of cell restriction control aimed at thwarting tracker attacks. At the time the query is posed the control attempts to determine all the query sets that can be deduced from the query and other permitted statistics. *Compare* AUDIT EXPERT, CELL SUPPRESSION, GROUPING, OVERLAP CONTROL, QUERY SET SIZE CONTROL. *See* CELL RESTRICTION, INFERENCE CONTROL, QUERY SET, TRACKER.

impulsive noise. In communications, interference characterized by short duration disturbances separated by quiescent intervals. For example, the interference with radio reception caused by the ignition system on a car.

inadvertent disclosure. In data security, accidental exposure of sensitive defense information to a person not authorized access. This may result in a compromise or a need to know violation. (AR). *See* NEED TO KNOW.

Ina Jo Formal Development Methodology. In computer security, System Development Corporation's specification and verification methodology, based on a nonprocedural state-transition specification language, Ina Jo. The Ina Jo methodology incorporated user-supplied invariants to produce a formal demonstration that security properties are met. (MTR). *See* AFFIRM, GYPSY, HDM.

in band signalling. In communications, a technique used in conventional telephone systems in which certain frequencies in the audio band are used to transmit signalling information. *See* SIGNALLING.

incoming message. In data communications, a message transmitted from a station to the computer. *See* STATION.

incoming traffic. In data communications, traffic passing through a network and having its origin in another network. *See* TRAFFIC.

incomplete parameter checking. In computer security, a system fault that exists when all parameters have not been fully checked for correctness and consistency by the operating system, thus making the system vulnerable to penetration. (FIPS). *See* OPERATING SYSTEM, PENETRATION.

Independent Verification and Validation. In computer security, the process of determining whether or not the products of a given phase of the software development cycle fulfil the requirements established during the previous phase, and the process of evaluating software at the end of the software development process to ensure compliance with software requirements.

index. (1) In mathematics, the index of k modulo n is the smallest integer t such that $g^t \equiv k \pmod{n}$, where g is a primitive root of n. *See* MODULO ARITHMETIC, PRIMITIVE ROOT. (2) In computing, a subscript of integer value that identifies the location of an item of data with respect to some other data item. (3) In databases, a list of the contents of a file, or document, with keys or references for locating the contents.

index build. In databases, the automatic process of creating an alternate index based on results obtained from using the current access methods.

indexed file. In computing, a file with an associated index that contains pointers to individual records, or groups of records, in the file. *See* FILE, INDEX, POINTER.

indirect access. In database security, a form of threat in which the user requests authorized data but the data returned is a function of unauthorized, i.e. higher security classified, data and under these circumstances an attacker may infer unauthorized information from that supplied. *Compare* DIRECT ACCESS,

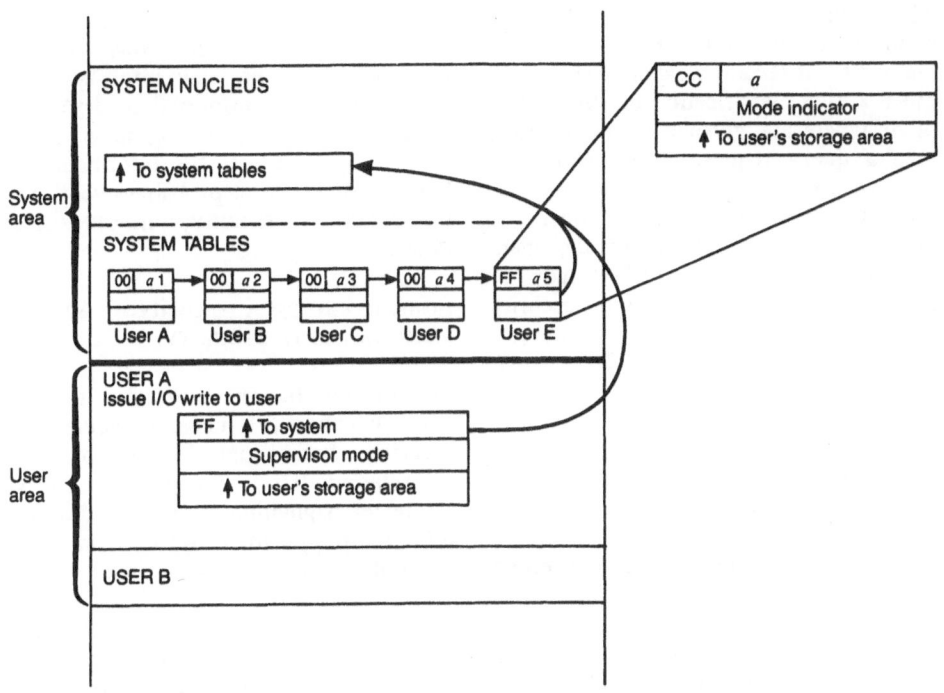

incomplete parameter checking
Users call operating system functions in a manner similar to subroutine calls, using many parameters. By supplying addresses outside the space allocated to that user's program, it is possible for control to be returned to the users in supervisor state. Reproduced with permission of IBM corp.

TROJAN HORSE DIRECT RELEASE, TRO-JAN HORSE LEAKAGE. *See* INFERENCE CONTROL.

indirectly connected transaction. In banking, a transaction characterized by the condition that neither the acquirer nor card issuer (or the agent of the card issuer) with whom the acquirer communicates has knowledge of the card holder's card. (SAA). *Compare* DIRECT-LY CONNECTED TRANSACTION. *See* ACQUIRER, CARD HOLDER, CARD ISSU-ER, KEY MANAGEMENT.

individual accountability. In access control, pertaining to measures to posi-tively associate the identity of a users with their access to machines, material, data etc. and the time, method and de-gree of access.

induced interference. In communica-tions, noise induced in a circuit as a result of electromagnetic coupling with an external source. *See* NOISE.

inertia sensor. In physical security, a sensor that activates an alarm when it is subject to a change in movement.

inference. In database security, the deduction of confidential information relating to an individual by correlation of statistical evidence relating to a group of individuals. *See* INFERENCE CON-TROL.

inference control. In database security, a control employed to prevent an enquirer from using data in a statistical database to obtain information concern-ing an individual. Inference controls are also required in relational databases where attributes may be given different security classifications. For example if the names of certain weapon systems are given a high classification but the names of designers are given a lower priority, then a query requesting the names of high security weapon systems may be refused. On the other hand a query of the form 'request names of designers responsible for system ZEUS' may be answered because the high security information, i.e. name of the system, was not actually released. *See* MULTI-LEVEL DATABASE SECURITY, STATISTICAL DATABASE.

infinity. In mathematics, a quantity greater than any assignable number.

informatics. (1) The science concerned with the collection, transmission, storage, processing and display of information. (2) Translation of the French term informatique that is normally considered to be equivalent to data processing.

information. (1) Any communication or reception of knowledge such as facts, data, or opinions, including numerical, graphic, or narrative forms, whether oral or maintained in any medium, including computerized data bases, paper, microform, or magnetic tape. (DODD). (2) The terms 'data,' 'information,' 'material,' 'documents,' and 'matter' are considered synonymous and used interchangeably in this Order. They refer to all data regardless of its physical form (e.g., data on paper printouts, tapes, disks or disk packs, in memory chips, random access memory (RAM), in read only memory (ROM), microfilm or microfiche, on communication lines, and on display terminals). (DOE). *See* RAM, ROM. (3) Knowledge that was unknown to the receiver prior to its receipt. Information can only be derived from data that is accurate, timely, relevant and unexpected. (4) The meanings

assigned to data by the agreed conventions used in its representation. If the content of a message is known prior to its receipt then no new information is conveyed. The information $I(x)$ for event x of probability $p(x)$ is given by $I(x) = -\log p(x)$, i.e. the information is highest for the least probable event. *See* INFORMATION THEORY, INFORMATION CONTENT.

information asset security. *Synonymous with* DATA SECURITY.

information bearer channel. In data communications, a channel capable of carrying both control and message information. It may therefore operate at a greater signalling rate than that required solely for user's data. *See* BEARER.

information center. In computing, a service strategy as well as an organization within a data processing department that provides a direct interface to, and supports services for, end user computing. *See* END USER COMPUTING, FOURTH GENERATION LANGUAGE.

information content. In information theory, a measure of the information conveyed by the occurrence of a symbol emitted by a source, measured in hartleys or shannons. Defined as the negative of the logarithm of the probability that this particular symbol will be emitted. If logarithms to the base 2 are used, the unit is the shannon, if base 10 is chosen, the unit is the hartley. In practice, the probability of a particular symbol being emitted may be conditional on the symbols that preceded it. Each successive result of tossing a coin would have an information content of 1 shannon. *See* HARTLEY, INFORMATION THEORY, SHANNON.

information flow analysis. In data security, the tracing of the flow of specific information types through an information system to determine whether the controls applied to the information are appropriate.

information flow control. (1) In data security, control on the flow of information within a computer system and as it leaves the computer system. (2) In data security, controls concerned with the right of dissemination of information, irrespective of what object holds the information. Whilst access controls regulate the accessing of objects, information flow control addresses what subjects might do with the information contained in them. *See* ACCESS CONTROL, LEAKAGE, OBJECT, SUBJECT.

information hiding. In computing, a principle in the design of program modules. Only the information essential to the user of the module, i.e. the interface, should be made available; details of how the module is implemented are hidden. This principle facilitates the development of large programs by independent programmers. The designer of a module is free to change its implementation details provided that the interface is not affected and the user can opt to use a different module with the same function and interface.

information integrity. *Synonymous with* DATA INTEGRITY.

information loss. In database security, a failure to provide the correct response to a legitimate query due to the form of inference control employed. Information loss may take the form of an unnecessary restriction on the provision of tables of statistics or the amount of noise injected in permitted statistics. *See* INFERENCE CONTROL, PERTURBATION.

information management. The use of Information Technology in the decision-making process. Managers have

increasingly to take decisions in decreasing periods of time on increasing amounts of information. This pressure is in part due to the pervasive nature of today's communications and computing; the remedy lies in the more efficient use of information technology itself. *See* INFORMATION TECHNOLOGY.

information networks. In databases, the interconnection of a physically dispersed group of databases linked via telecommunications so that the total information resource may be shared by a larger population of users.

information rate. In data communications, the number of symbols emitted by a source per second multiplied by the average information content per symbol. *See* INFORMATION CONTENT.

information redundancy. In reliability, pertaining to the use of additional bits in a digital signal to enable the validity of the representation to be checked. *See* ERROR CORRECTION CODE, ERROR DETECTION CODE, REDUNDANCY.

information resources management. The planning, budgeting, organizing, directing, training, and control associated with government information. The term encompasses both information itself and the related resources, such as personnel, equipment, funds, and technology. (OMBC). *Compare* INFORMATION MANAGEMENT.

information retrieval. In computing, pertaining to the techniques for storing and searching large quantities of data and making selected data available.

information security. (1) The sum of computer security and network security. *See* COMPUTER SECURITY, NETWORK SECURITY. (2) The result of any system of policies and procedures for identifying, controlling, and protecting from unauthorized disclosure, information whose protection is authorized by executive order or statute. (DOD). (3) The protection against the unauthorized disclosure, manipulation, destruction or alteration of information. Disclosure refers to the disclosure of protected information such as classified or proprietary information, or information subject to data protection legislation. Manipulation is concerned with changing some attribute of the information such as file ownership, security classification, data destination etc. Data can be destroyed quickly and efficiently, without leaving a trace, in electronic or magnetic storage devices; degaussing, removing the power from volatile storage or over-writing, are effective methods of destroying data. Data alteration involves making changes in the stored data itself, e.g. financial amounts, measured values or system control parameters. *Synonymous with* DATA SECURITY.

information system. The organized collection, processing, transmission, and dissemination of information in accordance with defined procedures, whether automated or manual. (DODD).

information system abuse. In data security, wilful or negligent activity that affects the availability, confidentiality, or integrity of information systems resources. Includes fraud, embezzlement, theft, malicious damage, unauthorized use, denial of service, and misappropriation. (AFR). *Compare* COMPUTER ABUSE. *See* INFORMATION SECURITY.

information systems director. The expanded role of the data processing manager to reflect the strategic importance of information systems in the corporate environment. *See* INFORMATION CENTER.

information systems security. In data security, the protection afforded to information systems in order to preserve the availability, integrity, and confidentiality of the systems and information contained within the systems. Such protection is the application of the combination of all security disciplines that will, at a minimum, include COMSEC, TEMPEST, computer security, OPSEC, information security, personnel security, industrial security, resource protection, and physical security. (AFR). *See* COMPUTER SECURITY, COMSEC, OPSEC, PHYSICAL SECURITY, PERSONNEL SECURITY, TEMPEST.

information technology. The acquisition, processing, storage and dissemination of vocal, pictorial, textual and numerical information by a microelectronics based combination of computing, telecommunications and video. Information technology has arisen as a separate technology by the convergence of computing, telecommunications and video techniques; computing providing the capability for processing and storing information, telecommunications is the vehicle for communicating it and video provides high quality display of images. This convergence has been catalyzed by the availability of complex, reliable and cost-effective microelectronic components and equipment. Global developments in electronics have also stimulated the search for common international standards, particularly in computing and telecommunications, that are paving the way for wide-scale applications of IT.

information technology facility. An organizationally defined set of personnel, hardware, software, and physical facilities, a primary function of which is the operation of information technology. (OMBC). *See* INFORMATION TECHNOLOGY.

information technology security evaluation criteria. In information security, a set of criteria developed for the evaluation of secure systems and products by the European Commission. The criteria are based upon earlier work undertaken by the U.K., German, French and Dutch governments.

Rationale
The criteria were developed because:

- much experience had been accumulated in the various countries and there would be much to gain by jointly building on that experience;
- industry did not want different criteria in the different countries;
- the basic concepts and approaches were the same, across countries and even across commercial, government and defence applications.

A draft document, Information Security Evaluation Criteria (ITSEC), was published in 1990 and the Commission of the European Community sponsored a consultative conference in September 1990 in Brussels. A revised document was produced in 1991.

The ITSEC scheme subsumes much of TCSEC document but it is broader in the range of security matters considered. Moreover, unlike the Orange Book, ITSEC separates out the evaluation of functionality and the level of assurance. Thus there are seven levels of assurance ranging from E0 to E6 and 10 functionality levels.

In the TCSEC criteria progression from Class D to Class A, involves simultaneously an increase in functionality, i.e. through discretionary access control to both mandatory and discretionary access control, and an increase in the level of assurance associated with the security functionality.

Target of Evaluation.
ITSEC deals with the security evaluation of both systems and products; the term Target of Evaluation (TOE) is used to cover both the product or system to be evaluated. The TOE will comprise components, some of which will be relevant to security, whilst others will not. The evaluation will concentrate on those components that are stated to be security relevant, but the other components will also be considered and shown not to be security relevant.

The essential difference between a product, and a system, in terms of security evaluation, is that the environment in which the system operates is known at the time of evaluation. Thus the security threats in that environment, and the security objectives of the system, can be described at the time of evaluation for a system.

In the case of product, the vendor can only provide a rationale for the security features, based upon some general assumptions on the environment and security objectives. The subsequent purchaser must then ensure that such assumptions are compatible, with the actual environment in which the product is to be deployed.

The precise specification of the security features of the TOE are described in a set of documents, termed the security target. The terms security objectives, security functions and security mechanisms appear frequently in the documentation and these may be categorized as:

- security objectives - why the functionality is required;
- security functions - what is actually done;
- security mechanisms - how it is done.

The security target might include, for example:

- security objectives;
- statements about a system environment or assumptions about a product environment;
- security functions;
- rationale for security functions;
- required security mechanisms;
- required evaluation level;
- claimed minimum strength of mechanism.

Security Functions

The ITSEC proposals are broader than those of TCSEC, the Orange Book, inasmuch as the sponsor, i.e. the body submitting the TOE for evaluation, may specify a broad range of security functionality. There is no restriction on the functionality that may be specified in a security target, in ITSEC, but it is recommended that the functionality be described under eight generic headings:

- identification and authentication - functions to establish and verify the claimed identity of a user;
- access control - functions to control the flow of information between, and the use of resources by, users, processes, and objects, including the administration and verification of access rights;
- accountability - functions to record the exercising of rights to perform security relevant actions;
- audit - functions to detect and investigate events that might represent a threat to security;
- object reuse - functions to control the reuse of data objects;
- accuracy - functions to ensure the correctness and consistency of security relevant information;

- reliability of service - functions to ensure consistency and availability of service;
- data exchange - functions to ensure the security of data during transmission over communication channels.

The functionality may also be stated in terms of predefined function classes, or as some combination of such classes. Ten such classes: FC1, FC2, FB1, FB2, FB3, FIN, FAV, FDI, FDC and FDX are defined in ITSEC. The first five classes are derived from the classes C1, C2, B1, B2 and B3 of TCSEC.

Thus the classes may be specified:

- FC1 - discretionary access control, equivalent to Class C1 of TCSEC;
- FC2 - discretionary access control, equivalent to Class C2 of TCSEC;
- FB1 - mandatory and discretionary access control, equivalent to Class B1 of TCSEC;
- FB2 - mandatory and discretionary access control, equivalent to Class B2 of TCSEC;
- FB3 - mandatory and discretionary access control, equivalent to Class B3 of TCSEC;
- FIN - for systems with high integrity

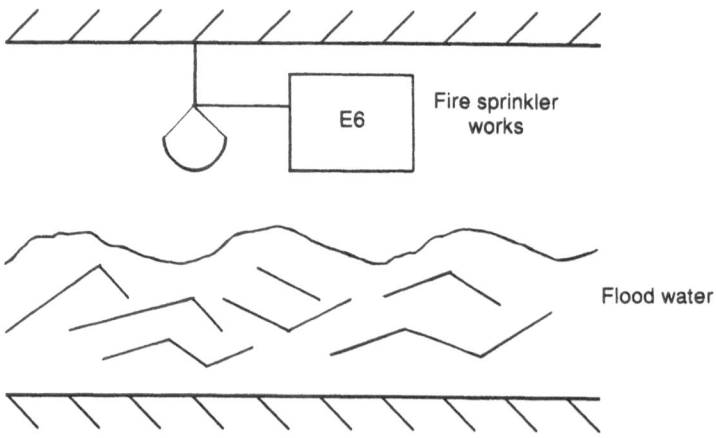

information technology security evaluation criteria
Does the countermeasure meet the threats of a hostile environment.

for data and programs. Such requirements are significant, for example, for database systems:

- FAV - sets high requirements for the availability of a complete system or special functions of a system. Such requirements are significant for process control systems, for example;
- FDI - sets high requirements with regard to the safeguarding of data integrity during data exchange;
- FDC - is intended for systems with high demands on the confidentiality of data during data exchange. An example candidate for this class is a cryptographic device;
- FDX - is intended for networks with high demands on the confidentiality and integrity of the information to be exchanged. For example this can be case when sensitive information has to be exchanged via an insecure network.

The functionality may be expressed in informal, semi-formal or formal forms, or a combination of such forms. Informal specifications using natural languages are the easiest to understand, but they may contain ambiguities. Semi-formal specifications use a restricted syntax that reduces the probability of such ambiguities. One such language, the Claims Language, was proposed by the U.K. DTI draft criteria, and requires the sponsor to specify security functionality using a series of templates. Writing specifications in the Claims Language is rather like producing computer programs in the restricted syntax of (say) Pascal.

Formal specifications are written in a mathematical notation based upon well established mathematical concepts. Such specifications are unambiguous and can be tested for consistency. It is also possible to demonstrate that a similarly specified design corresponds with the specification; such specification languages, e.g. Z, require however, special training even to read the specification.

The particular form of specification employed will depend upon the level of assurance that is claimed by the security target. The higher levels of assurance demanding more formal specifications, in general a combination of formal and informal specification may be employed to maximize the ease of understanding and to minimize the probability of ambiguity.

ITSEC, like TCSEC, is concerned with some measurement of the level of security provided. The functionality specifications are formed to meet the security objectives of the Target of Evaluation (TOE), and to counter the threats faced by the system in its environment, or the threats that it is assumed a product will face. This functionality is, however, only a statement of how the security is achieved. It does not deal with the assurance that such functionality is correctly implemented and effective.

Evaluation Levels

Seven evaluation levels are described, ranging from E0, representing inadequate assurance, rather like Division D of TCSEC, to the highest level E6 that demands formal descriptions of security architecture and consistency with the formal model of the security policy.

The evaluation is performed both in terms of correctness and effectiveness. The correctness criteria are applied first, but in the subsequent effectiveness evaluation some degree of iteration with the correctness criteria may well be required. In evaluating the correctness of security functions for a TOE, increasingly stringent criteria are applied to aspects of the development process, development environment, operational documentation and operational procedures for the evaluation levels E1 to E6.

The development process is considered to comprise the following number of sequential phases:

- Requirements - the identification and description of the security target for the TOE;
- Architectural Design - the overall top level definition and design of the TOE, identifying the basic structure, its external interfaces and its separation into major software and hardware components;
- Detailed Design - the refinement of the architectural design to a level of detail that can be used as a basis for programming and hardware construction;
- Implementation - the translation of the detailed design into actual hardware and software, and the testing of this implementation of the TOE against its specifications.

Factors contributing to the development of confidence are identified in the criteria for each of the above phases. In many cases the documentation required, for evaluation, will be identical to those employed in the normal development process produced in accordance with good software engineering practice. The criteria for the development environment place emphasis on topics such as configuration tools, choice of programming languages and tools, internal security measures adopted by the developer etc. This aspect of the criteria thus addresses the working practice of the developer. The operational documentation indicates the information provided by the developer to the client, whereas the operational procedures are those actually employed when the system is in use. In the case of the evaluation of a system, it is possible to assess the security implications of the procedures employed, in other cases the evaluator can only consider the proposed procedures as formulated by the developer or user.

For each of the six levels E1 to E6 the evaluation criteria specify the requirements for the defined development phases and operation. The documentation required, its contents and presenta-

tion or the procedures and standards it must define, are given for each level. There are normally three parties involved in the evaluation:

- the sponsor - the person or organization requesting the evaluation;
- the developer of the system or product;
- the evaluator.

Except at level E1, the burden for the provision of evidence is placed on the sponsor, who must then seek the necessary information from the developer. The evidence is then audited or checked by the evaluator. The evaluator is only required to generate evidence where such independent production is considered necessary to provide the necessary level of confidence in its conclusions.

The evaluation of the criteria for effectiveness is conducted after that for the evaluation of correctness. The correctness evaluation proves that the black box does indeed perform as promised, the next question is 'how effective is this black box in a hostile world?'. The effectiveness evaluation differs from the correctness evaluation in two important aspects, firstly they are not broken down by evaluation level, or by the phases of the construction and operation. Secondly most of the work undertaken in this phase of the evaluation is performed directly by the evaluators, although much of the evidence required will have been obtained in the previous correctness evaluation.

The following aspects of the TOE are considered in the evaluation of effectiveness: Suitability of Functionality, Binding of Functionality, Vulnerability Assessment: Construction, Strength of Mechanisms, Ease of Use, Vulnerability Assessment: Operational.

Suitability of Functionality - in evaluating the suitability of functionality the security target is examined and it is determined whether or not the security functions and mechanisms will counter the identified threats to the TOE. In the case of product employing one or more predefined functionality classes, without extension or omission, the TOE is assumed to be suitable for its intended purposes.

Binding of Functionality - although security functions may be suitable for their individual purposes it is possible that certain combinations of functions or mechanisms may interfere or conflict with each other. In evaluating the binding of functionality a study is undertaken of the interrelationships of security functions, and mechanisms, to ensure that they are mutually supportive and provide an effective and integrated whole.

Vulnerability Assessment: Construction - in the assessment of construction vulnerabilities the security weaknesses, that may have been identified during the correctness evaluation, are considered to determine whether or not they would actually compromise the security of the TOE as specified in the security target. It is possible that the threats identified may not exist in practice, or they may be countered by other security mechanisms in the TOE, or by means external to the TOE.

Strength of Security Mechanisms - in any security system certain assumptions are made about the inherent security of the underlying mechanisms and algorithms. For example, if the DES algorithm is used then it is normally assumed that no attacker could test for all possible DES keys. In considering the strength of the underlying mechanisms the level of resources, that would be necessary for an attacker to mount a direct attack on the system, are considered. A critical mechanism is defined as one that is not protected from attack by another stronger mechanism, and whose failure would cause a vulnerability. The objective of

the evaluation, of the strength of mechanisms, is to confirm the claimed minimum strength ratings for the critical mechanisms of the TOE.

The ratings for the minimum strength of TOE mechanisms are categorized:

- basic - all critical mechanisms provide protection against random accidental subversion, although they may be capable of being defeated by knowledgeable attackers;
- medium - all critical mechanisms provide protection against attackers with limited opportunities or resources;
- high - all critical mechanisms could only be defeated by attackers possessing a high level of expertise, opportunity and resources, a successful attack is judged to be beyond the normal practicality.

Ease of Use - the secure operation of any system depends upon the people and procedures in its operational environment. If these procedures are excessively demanding, or obscure, then there exists the danger that they will not be properly implemented. The external security measures such as procedural, physical and personnel controls, required to support the security functions and mechanisms of the TOE must be examined from this viewpoint. The evaluation of the ease of use provides an analysis of all possible modes of failure (the possible causes of failures and their consequences) due to human and other types of operational error. This analysis must show that any human or other errors in operation that has potential security implications shall be easily detectable.

Vulnerability Assessment: Operational - this phase of the evaluation is similar to that described above for construction vulnerability except that the vulnerabilities associated with the operational environment, e.g. configuration, startup, distribution of the TOE are examined.

Relation with TCSEC
The ITSEC and TCSEC criteria have a degree of interrelationship, for example the correspondence between classification levels may be roughly equated to:

ITSEC	TCSEC
E0	D
FC1,E1	C1
FC2,E2	C2
FB1,E3	B1
FB2,E4	B2
FB3,E5	B3
FB3,E6	A1

The development of ITSEC may be considered as a logical development of TCSEC, extending the range of classification to include considerations more applicable to the commercial and government sector. The problems of evaluation are, however, significant; the TCSEC criteria involve only 6 levels of detailed evaluation but problems of developing evaluation teams with expertise and experience in this field have been reported. There are 1344 potential ratings in ITSEC. Even though a number of these ratings are unlikely to arise there still exists the danger that the plethora of ratings combinations will cause confusion in the marketplace and create difficulties in developing adequate teams of skilled evaluators. *See* FC-FIPS, INFORMATION TECHNOLOGY SECURITY EVALUATION FACILITY, INFORMATION TECHNOLOGY SECURITY EVALUATION MANUAL, OBJECT REUSE, ORANGE BOOK, TCSEC.

information technology security evaluation facility. In information security, an organization accredited and licensed to perform ITSEC security evaluations. *Compare* CERTIFICATION BODY. *See* INFORMATION TECHNOLOGY SECURITY EVALUATION CRITERIA.

information technology security evaluation manual. In information security, a manual that builds upon ITSEC describing how a target of evaluation will be evaluated according to the criteria. *See* INFORMATION TECHNOLOGY SECURITY EVALUATION CRITERIA, TARGET OF EVALUATION.

information theory. (1) In mathematics, the theory concerned with the information rate, channel capacity, noise and other factors affecting information transmission. Initially developed for electrical communications, it is now applied to business systems and other areas concerned with information units and the flow of information in networks. *See* INFORMATION CONTENT, SHANNON'S LAW. (2) In cryptology, useful theoretical concepts of cryptography were developed within an information theory context by Shannon. There is an analogy between the detection of messages that have been corrupted with noise and the decryption of messages by a cryptanalyst. In both cases the receiver of the message attempts to recover the original message using the information contained in the received message, that has been modified by noise or encryption.

Cryptography may be considered to comprise the mapping of a set of plaintext messages to a set of ciphertext messages by a set of cryptographic keys. Consider the case in which one plaintext message, from a set of 26 such messages, can be encrypted with a key, from a set of 26 possible keys, to produce one of 26 possible ciphertext messages. Assume moreover that any one ciphertext message can be produced from any of the 26 plaintext messages if the appropriate key is employed.

The cryptanalyst upon receiving the ciphertext message has no information on the original plaintext message because any one of them could have been transmitted, to produce the ciphertext, depending upon the key chosen. In other words the conditional probability that the plaintext message (M) was sent, given that ciphertext (C) was received (i.e. $P_C(M)$), is equal to the unconditional probability $(P(M))$ that the message M was sent. This is a condition for perfect secrecy. The perfect secrecy arises because there are as many keys as there are plaintext, and ciphertext, messages and each plaintext message can generate each ciphertext message.

In many cryptographic systems, however, the range of possible keys is much smaller than the possible number of plaintext messages. Moreover, a proportion of the plaintext messages can be ruled out as meaningless garble; the cryptanalyst is thus aided by the degree of redundancy in natural language.

Consider the previous example of 26 plaintext/ciphertext messages and keys, and let each ciphertext message correspond to a letter of the alphabet. Thus the cryptographer is using a simple substitution cipher, replacing each plaintext letter with a corresponding ciphertext letter; 26 tables of substitutions are available corresponding to the 26 keys. If a meaningful English phrase is now transmitted the cryptanalyst gains information with each new character of the ciphertext message. The first character could be any one of 26 but with the second character certain bigrams can be discarded, e.g. QK, ZD etc., and thus the range of candidate keys is reduced with each such discard. If a phrase of 20 characters is sent then there will be a total range of 26^{20} possible messages, however, for any one ciphertext message there are only 26 candidate plaintext messages, i.e. one for each key. If the cryptanalyst examines the 26 possible plaintext messages, corresponding to the 26 keys, then it is extremely unlikely that more than one of these candidate plaintext messages will correspond to a meaningful English expression.

The redundancy of a language can be expressed mathematically in terms of its rate and absolute rate. The absolute rate of a language is defined in terms of the number of bits required to encode each character assuming that all characters have the same probability of occurrence. If each character of the English alphabet were equally likely to occur then the entropy of one character of a message would be given by:

$$H = \Sigma_{26} -(1/26) \log_2 (1/26)$$

$$= \log_2 (26) = 4.7$$

i.e. each character would require 4.7 bits for optimal encoding and the absolute rate of English message is thus 4.7 bits per character. The redundancy of a language severely reduces the amount of information conveyed with each character and the rate of a language is defined as the average number of bits of information contained in each character of a message, i.e. H(X)/N where N is the number of characters in the message. The rate for English messages ranges from 1 to 1.5 bits per character. The redundancy of a language is defined as the difference between the absolute rate and the rate of the language; thus the redundancy of English ranges between 3.2 and 3.7 bits per character.

The determination of a plaintext message, given the corresponding ciphertext, is equivalent to determining the key employed. The secrecy of a cipher can therefore be measured in terms of the key equivocation defined by:

$$H_C(K) = -\Sigma P(C) \Sigma P_C(K) \log_2 (P_C(K))$$

where

$P(C)$ = probability that ciphertext C is received.

$P_C(K)$ = probability that key used was K given that ciphertext C was received.

The key equivocation is a measure of the uncertainty of the key given that a certain ciphertext is received; a key equivocation of zero means that the ciphertext contains sufficient information to uniquely identify the key. If the key length is independent of the message length then the key equivocation will decrease with the length of the plaintext message.

The unicity distance is defined as the lowest message length such that the key equivocation is close to zero. If the rate and absolute rate of a language are r and R respectively then the ratio of meaningful and possible messages of length N is given by:

$$v = 2^{rN}/2^{RN} = 2^{-DN}$$

where

$$D = R\text{-}r \text{ is the redundancy.}$$

If $H(K)$ is the key entropy, i.e. the number of bits required to encode the key, then for a given ciphertext message there are $2^{H(K)}$ potential corresponding plaintext messages, all except one being false solutions. The proportion of these false solutions that correspond to meaningful messages is given by:

$$M = (2^{H(K)} - 1)v = (2^{H(K)} - 1)2^{-DN}$$

Since 2^{-DN} approaches zero for large N (provided $D > 0$) the number of false solutions is approximately given by $2^{H(K)\text{-}DN}$. Thus the unicity distance can be calculated:

$$H(K) - DN = 0, \text{ i.e. } N = H(K)/D.$$

In the case of DES the independent length of the key is 56 bits and thus $H(K) = 56$; using a value of 3.2 bits per character as the redundancy of English gives a unicity distance of $56/3.2 = 17.5$ characters, i.e. approximately two blocks of a DES message. The fact that a DES plaintext message can be derived from 2 blocks of ciphertext appears, at first sight, to be rather startling. It must be remembered, however, that this merely indicates that, theoretically, a cryptanalyst has sufficient information to determine the plaintext; in fact the actual determination is computationally infeasible because it involves more than 2^{57} DES decryptions.

Shannon's work was undertaken in the 1940's when the complexity of ciphers was limited by the computational power of electromechanical cipher machines.

Perfect secrecy can be ensured if the length of the secret key is equal to the length of the plaintext message and each key transforms the same plaintext message into a different ciphertext message. In modern practice, however, shorter keys can be employed provided that the cryptanalyst only has the option of an exhaustive search of all possible keys, and the size of the key space renders this computationally infeasible. *See* ABSOLUTE RATE, CRYPTANALYSIS, CRYPTOGRAPHIC KEY, ENTROPY, EQUIVOCATION, KEY EQUIVOCATION, KEY SPACE, NOISE, RATE, REDUNDANCY, SUBSTITUTION CIPHER, REASONABLENESS CHECK.

INFOSEC. Information Security *Compare* COMPUSEC, COMSEC.

infra red motion detector. In physical security, an intrusion detection device that senses changes in ambient temperature due to the movement of a body.

initialization vector. (1) In cryptography, a number used as a starting point for encryption of a data sequence to increase security by introducing additional cryptographic variance and to synchronize cryptographic equipment. (ANSI). (2) In cryptography, the content of the shift register in stream ciphers, or block ciphers with chaining, immediately prior to the encryption or decryption of the input stream. *See* BLOCK CIPHER CHAINING, CIPHER BLOCK CHAINING, CIPHER FEEDBACK, OUTPUT FEEDBACK, STREAM CIPHER. *Synonymous with* INITIALIZING VARIABLE.

initializing variable. *Synonymous with* INITIALIZATION VECTOR.

initial program load. In computing, a procedure to load the operating system into computer memory to start a normal period of processing or following a system malfunction.

initial synchronization. In communications security, a technique of voice scrambling in which the synchronization information, necessary for decryption of the received signal, is only transmitted at the beginning of the message. *Compare* CONTINUOUS SYNCHRONIZATION. *See* VOICE SCRAMBLING.

initiator. *Synonymous with* ORIGINATOR.

input data validation. In computing, a control technique used to detect inaccurate or incomplete input data. This may include format checks, completeness checks, reasonableness checks and limit checks.

input device. *Synonymous with* INPUT UNIT.

input output channel. *See* CHANNEL.

input output device. In computing, a device designed to communicate with a computer. The role of input output units is to convert the signals of the processor to, and from, data flows that can be interpreted by people, other devices or networks. *See* MODEM, SPEECH RECOGNIZER, SPEECH SYNTHESIZER, TERMINAL.

input output interface. In computing, an interface that will transmit an interrupt signal from a peripheral device to the CPU. *See* INTERFACE, INTERRUPT, CPU.

input output statement. In computing, any instruction that results in a transfer of data between main storage and input output devices.

input output unit. *See* INPUT OUTPUT DEVICE.

input unit. In computing, a device by which data can be entered into a computer system. *Synonymous with* INPUT DEVICE.

inquiry/response. In applications, a method of transaction handling in which a user interrogates the computer via a terminal and obtains a response almost immediately.

insertion loss. In communications, the power that is absorbed by the insertion of a passive element into a channel or electronic device. Insertion loss commonly usually occurs when a filter or equalizer is added to a communications channel. *See* CHANNEL, EQUALIZATION, FILTER.

inside perimeter. In physical security, pertaining to a line of protection, next to a protected area, passing through possible entry points, e.g. doors, windows, tunnels, skylights.

installation time. In computing, the time that is spent in the installation, testing and acceptance of hardware and software.

install-deinstall. In software protection, an execute protection method on a floppy disk that can be carried across to a hard disk. When installed on a hard disk, the protected software marks the hard disk in some manner, and at the same time the floppy disk is deactivated so it cannot be copied to another hard disk. If the user wishes to change machines, the program must be de-installed, thereby reactivating the floppy and deactivating the hard disk copy. *See* EXECUTE PROTECTION, FLOPPY DISK, HARD DISK.

instructing bank. In banking, the bank that instructs the sender to execute the transaction. (ANSI).

instructing party. In banking, the party instructing the sender to execute the transaction. (ANSI).

instruction. (1) In computing, a basic directive made by a programmer in a form that the computer can accept and execute. (2) In computing, a statement that specifies what operation is to be performed and the value or location of the operands. (3) In banking, a communication or that part of a communication that contains the authorization and required details for a transfer. (ANSI).

instruction format. In computing, the allocation of the bits of a machine code instruction to the operation code, operands etc. *See* INSTRUCTION SET, MACHINE CODE INSTRUCTION, OPERAND, OPERATION CODE.

instruction repertoire. *Synonymous with* INSTRUCTION SET.

instruction set. In computing, the complete list of machine code instruction types that can be decoded and executed by a given type of CPU. The instructions comprise an operation code and one or more operands that will employ one of the addressing modes available to the set. *See* COPROCESSOR, CPU, MACHINE CODE INSTRUCTION, MAIN MEMORY, SOFTWARE INTERRUPT. *Synonymous with* INSTRUCTION REPERTOIRE.

INTAMIC. *See* INTERNATIONAL ASSOCIATION FOR MICROCIRCUIT CARDS.

integer. In computing, a signed whole number. In binary notation special conventions are required to represent negative integers and the most common form is the two's complement. In this notation the first bit is a sign bit (1 for negative, 0 for positive). The two's complement of a negative number is obtained by reversing the 0 and 1 digits and then adding 1 to the least significant position. One byte can thus represent numbers in the range -128 to +127 and 16 bits can represent -32,768 to 32,767. *Compare* ORDINAL.

integral controller. In data communications, a communication unit built into a mini- or mainframe computer. *Compare* FRONT END PROCESSOR, CLUSTER CONTROL UNIT.

integrated circuit. In electronics, a combination of interconnected circuit elements inseparably associated on or within a continuous substrate. An integrated circuit may contain anywhere from a few to many thousands of transistors, resistors, diodes, capacitors.

integrated database. A database that has been consolidated to eliminate redundant data. *See* DATABASE.

integrated digital network. In data communications, a network in which digital transmission and digital switching are used. *See* DIGITAL SWITCHING, DIGITAL TRANSMISSION SYSTEM.

integrated modem. In data communications, a modem that is an integral part of the device with which it operates. *See* MODEM.

integrated optical circuit. In communications, the optical equivalent of a microelectronic circuit. It acts on the light in a lightwave system to carry out communications functions; generating, detecting, switching and transmitting light.

integrated services digital network. In data communications, an integrated digital network in which the same digital switches and digital paths are used to establish communications for different services, for example, telephony and data.

The ISDN concept represents a logical development in the provision of public communication services, recognizing the economies made possible by the advent of digital technologies, the increasing demands for a wide range of communication services and the need to provide the customer with a single interface to which can be connected a wide variety of user communication devices: voice, facsimile, data, alarm sensors etc.

The public telephone networks throughout the world expanded rapidly in terms of volume and user facilities in the last three decades. The analog technology of the voice network was, however, ill-suited to demands of computer data communications which first arose in the sixties, and exploded in the following decades. The necessary conversion of digital data, to a form compatible with voice signals, demanded expensive modems at each end of the communication link and severely limited data rates; low cost devices operated at a few hundred bits per second and the expensive end of the modem range could only provide data rates of a few thousand bits per second.

Data communications requirements for organizations concerned with large scale data transfers were thus met with separate, dedicated high speed data communication channels. However, a wide range of users looked to the telephone system to provide a variety of services: electronic mail, facsimile, telemetry, bulletin board connections etc., and to enhance the provision of voice communications in terms of quality and services. If these services were to be conducted within a voice service then it was logical that voice signals should be made to conform with data signals rather than vice versa.

Use of PCM, which converts voice signals to binary pulse trains, allows the communication link to concern itself with only one type of signal for all

transmissions: voice, data, facsimile etc. The signalling aspects of telephony, i.e. the control signals which set up and close down calls, had already been converted from analog to digital form, in most advanced countries, to benefit from the advances in microelectronics and digital technology.

Thus the concept of a communications system which concerned itself only with the transmission of digital data, and used digital signals for signalling purposes, originally proposed in the 1960's, has excited the communications world for nearly three decades. The success of such a venture is, however, inextricably linked with the economic realities of communication traffic, the development of international standards, the national and international politics of communications, the marketing policies of manufacturers and readiness of consumers to adapt to new ideas, and to pay for them.

An organization that installs an ISDN PABX will provide its users with interfaces illustrated in Fig. 1. At the users' side of the PABX the interfaces will support analog telephones, digital telephones, facsimile, computer terminals, personal computers, multifunctional workstations, and gateways to local area networks. Clearly such interfaces will also support alarm systems, electronic mail and even slow scan video systems for monitoring or alarm purposes. The actual interface types are analog telephone, terminal equipment designed to interwork with public ISDN, and Terminal Adaptors which are employed to connect equipment, not conforming to ISDN standard interfaces (Fig. 2).

ISDN defines three reference points R, S and T. The R interface is for those existing devices (TE2 equipment) not designed to interface with ISDN networks, and which therefore require a Terminal Adaptor. The S interface allows a wide variety of devices (TE1 equipment), which have been designed with ISDN interfaces, to be directly connected to the ISDN system; thus providing the user with a guaranteed common connection facility for a wide range of office or home equipment. The T reference point is the interface between the Network Terminator 2 (NT2), which includes switching and multiplexing functions, and Network Terminator 1 (NT1) which provides ISDN line termination functions at the user end.

The facilities which can be connected directly to the PABX include digital telephone, facsimile, multifunctional workstations and local area networks. Digital telephones may have a range of features including those listed below.

- Alphanumeric display for: indication of called numbers, internal calling numbers and names, external calling number, time and date, reminder messages, call processing information, mailbox messages, call failure indication, call alerting information and user prompts.
- User programmable keys, and single function keys for call transfer, automatic call back, call forwarding and last number redial.
- Hand free operation.
- Security feature, e.g. card reader for access control.

The facsimile devices connected to the system; both existing analog and Group 4 facsimile connected directly to an S interface may be used. A particular feature of the ISDN environment is likely to be the multifunctional workstation capable of integrating voice, text, image and data with a wide variety of features including:

- access to mailboxes;
- enhanced voice features similar to those of the digital telephone;
- terminal emulation for dialogues with a remote host computer;
- teletex functions;
- access to private and public databases, e.g. videotex;
- exchange and display of docu-ments between two or more terminals;
- personal computing functions, word processing, spreadsheets etc.;
- telephone directories;
- pointing device facilities, e.g. light pen, mouse.

Local area networks may have gateways to the ISDN network allowing LANs to be interconnected and thus providing users with the combined advantages of LANs, i.e. communication of bursts of high speed data transfers between local users, and PABX systems which are mainly switch oriented and related to voice communication traffic. LANs operated in different sites of an organization, linked via ISDN, will therefore provide the appearance of a large integrated network.

The PABX in an ISDN system will not be restricted to merely switching and information transport functions. Facilities for the storage and processing of information, as performed in the application processors (see Fig. 1) will provide functions such as facsimile mail, text mail and voice mail.

Current facsimile facilities have proved a boon to organizational communications but they suffer from the same disadvantages as the conventional telephone system. Communication has to be established with the receiving party, communication must take place at the time the user establishes the connection, and with multiple addresses a new connection has to be established for each receiving party. Facsimile mail may provide features such as:

- timed delivery of documents;
- broadcast facility;
- message wait indication;
- confidential mail;
- text to facsimile conversion;
- teletex to facsimile conversion.

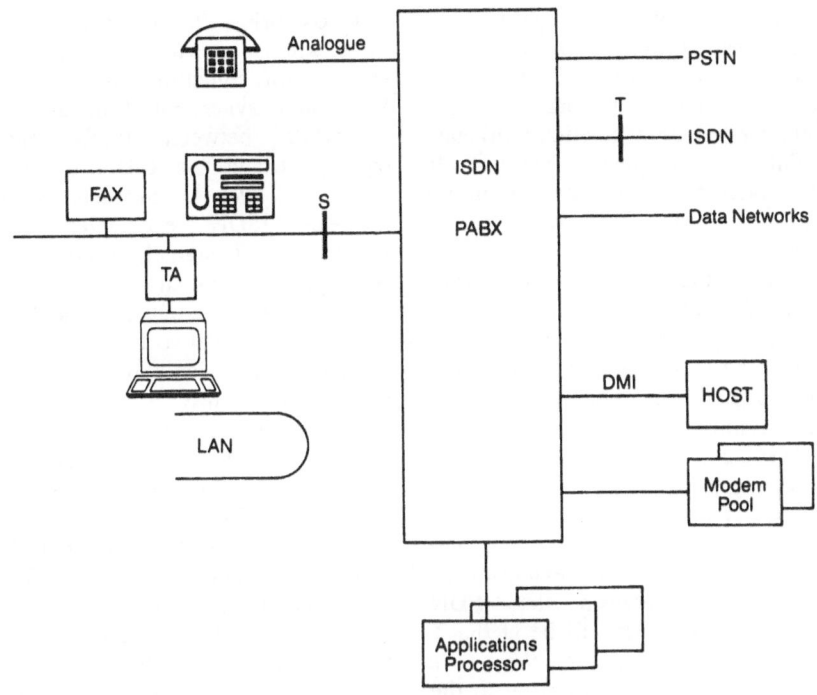

integrated services digital network
Fig. 1. ISDN PABX interfaces.

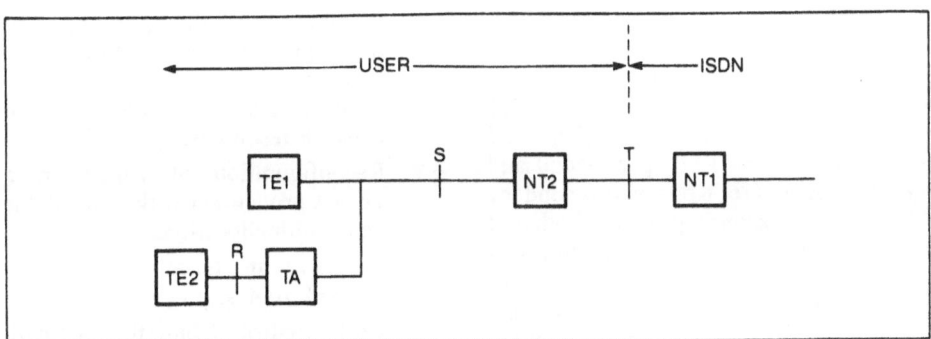

Definitions:
NT1   —   Network Terminator 1, which includes transmission functions.
NT2   —   Network Terminator 2, which includes switching and multiplexing functions
R   —   ISDN R reference point.
S   —   ISDN S reference point.
T   —   ISDN T reference point.
TA   —   Terminal Adapter.
TE1   —   Terminal Equipment Type 1, a type of terminal equipment which conforms to the standard interface at the S reference point.
TE2   —   Terminal Equipment Type 2, a type of terminal equipment which does not conform to the standard interface at the S reference point.

integrated services digital network
Fig. 2. CCITT ISDN reference configuration (user part).

Text mail facilities are similar to electronic mail provided by computer networks but with the added advantages that the mail may be delivered via digital telephones or multifunction workstations. Future developments could well include conversion services providing 'text to voice' and 'text to facsimile' delivery services.

Voice mail employs store and forward techniques for voice communications, allowing messages to be delivered on demand to the recipient. Individual users may be assigned a mailbox and access to it will normally be controlled by password. Messages may be transmitted for timed delivery, broadcast to selected groups and 'text to mail' facilities will allow recipients to receive text originated messages from telephone extensions.

The interface between the ISDN PABX and the network will be at the T interface (see Figs. 1 and 2); the user's Network Terminator 2 connecting to the networks NT1, at one end of the communication line and the line terminator (LT) interfaces with the ISDN exchange at the other end of the link. The interfaces to the ISDN network may be provided at the basic rate and primary access rate. There are two classes of channel in ISDN. The B channel is used for messages at 64 Kbits per second and the D channel (16 Kbits per second or 64 Kbits per second) provides both out of band common channel signalling and for auxiliary message services, e.g. alarm systems monitoring. Basic rate access (2B + D) comprises 2 B channels and 1 D (16 Kbits per sec) channel giving a total capacity of 144 Kbits per second. If connection to the ISDN network is via a PABX the terminals will be connected to the PABX using basic rate access either individually or as clusters of terminals sharing the channel. The primary rate access comprises 32 x 64 Kbit per sec channels in Europe and Australia; in North America and Japan it comprises 24 x 64 Kbits per sec channels. The European Primary Access Rate comprises 30 B channels for user information, one 64 Kbits per sec D channel for signalling and one channel for system synchronization and alarms. Signalling between ISDN customer equipment and the ISDN exchange is conducted over D channels; signalling between ISDN exchanges employs CCITT No 7 signalling and X.25 or X.75 protocols are used for connections between ISDN exchanges and Public Data Switched Networks.

International standards are of paramount importance in integrated, and international communication systems. The CCITT set up a special study group as early as 1968 to consider all questions related to PCM; in 1984 the I series of recommendations were adopted. In this series of recommendation I.100 serves as a general introduction to the concepts of ISDN, I.200 is concerned with services, I.300 with network aspects and I.400 with user network interfaces.

The user advantages of ISDN are summarized below.

- Flexibility in the allocation of bandwidth to applications and specific routes.
- Control over the allocation of network resources.
- Reconfiguration of routes in a virtual private network, and of the bandwidth allocations.
- Diversity in terms of alternate network routes.
- Cost control from the network management information which facilitates reconfiguration and network development processes.
- Integrated network interfaces for a range of telecommunication types of service thus reducing the proliferation of modems etc.
- User signalling capability which facilitates in house applications development to provide for integrated services, e.g. encryption, telemetering, surveillance, etc.

● Opportunities of value added services, voice prompts, database access, electronic mail etc.

See BAUD, BULLETIN BOARD, CCITT, ELECTRONIC MAIL, FACSIMILE, FACSIMILE MAIL, DIGITAL TELEPHONE, LOCAL AREA NETWORK, MODEM, PABX, PCM, PRIMARY RATE ACCESS, OPEN SYSTEMS INTERCONNECTION STORE AND FORWARD, TELEMETERING, VIDEOTEX, VOICE MAIL X.25, X.75.

integrity. (1) In data security, that computer security characteristic that ensures that computer resources operate correctly and that the data in the databases are correct. This characteristic protects against deliberate or inadvertent unauthorized manipulation of the system and ensures and maintains the security of entities of a computer system under all conditions. (AFR). (2) In data security, the quality or state of being unimpaired; soundness. (a) In data security, the capability of an automated system to perform its intended function in an unimpaired manner, free from deliberate or inadvertent unauthorized manipulation of the system. (b) In data security, inherent quality of protection that ensures and maintains the security of entities of a computer system under all conditions. (AR). (3) In computer security, the assurance, under all conditions, that a system will reflect the logical correctness and reliability of the operating system; the logical completeness of the hardware and software that implement the protection mechanisms; and the consistency of the data structures and accuracy of the stored data. In a formal security model, integrity is interpreted more narrowly to mean protection against unauthorized modification or destruction of information. (MTR). *See* DATA INTEGRITY, SYSTEM INTEGRITY. (4) In data security, the process of preventing undetected alteration of data. This term is preferred to authentication because the latter is commonly used in data communications to refer to peer entity verification. *See* AUTHENTICATION, DATA INTEGRITY, SYSTEM INTEGRITY. (5) In computing, the preservation of files for their intended purpose. *See* DATA INTEGRITY.

integrity check value. In communications security, a message authentication code or cryptographic checksum attached to a packet in an IEEE 802 based local area network for integrity checking. *See* MESSAGE AUTHENTICATION CODE, IEEE 802.

integrity level. In access control, a level of trustworthiness associated with a subject or object. *See* BIBA MODEL, TRUSTWORTHINESS.

integrity locking. *Synonymous with* SPRAY PAINT.

integrity policy. In data security, a security policy to prevent unauthorized users from modifying, i.e. writing, sensitive information (TNI). *Compare* SECRECY POLICY. *See* BIBA MODEL, SECURITY POLICY.

integrity validation procedure. In formal models, a term used in the Clark-Wilson model for a procedure required to check that the set of constrained data items correspond to a secure state. *See* CLARK-WILSON MODEL, CONSTRAINED DATA ITEM.

intelligence. (1) The product resulting from the collection, evaluation, analysis, integration and interpretation of all information concerning one or more aspects of foreign countries or areas, that is immediately or potentially significant to the development and execution of plans, policies, and operations. (DODD). (2) In computing, a property of a device containing local processing power. *See* INTELLIGENT DEVICE. (3) The definition of natural intelligence is of increasing importance in the discussion of the performance of artificial intelligence systems. Suggested definitions include, (a) a concept related to comprehensive invention, direction and criticism or judgement, (b) the aggregate or global capacity of individuals to act purposefully, to think rationally and deal effectively with their environments and (c) the general capacity of individuals consciously to adjust their thinking to new requirements and a general adaptability to new problems and conditions. *See* ARTIFICIAL INTELLIGENCE.

intelligent card reader. In access control, a card reader that compares the data, read from an access control card, with preprogrammed parameters. *Compare* ON LINE CARD READER. *See* CARD READER. *Synonymous with* OFF LINE CARD READER.

intelligent device. In computing, any device or peripheral that can be programmed. *Compare* DUMB DEVICE. *See* INTELLIGENT TERMINAL.

intelligent disk server. In computing, a disk server that provides a simple mechanism for networked microcomputers to request and gain access to centralized peripherals and disk volumes. The system can manage the efficient sharing of printers, tape drives, plotters etc. and also provide a degree of security by controlling individual user access to facilities. *See* DISK SERVER, FILE SERVER.

intelligent knowledge based system. *See* EXPERT SYSTEMS.

intelligent terminal. In computing, a device with a VDU, keyboard, processor memory and local software connected to a host computer. The terminal has sufficient processing capability to provide user prompts, editing capabilities etc. and can continue to operate in a limited mode for a certain time without communication with the host computer. Intelligent terminals are commonly employed in retail stores, banks, industrial data collection etc. *Compare* DUMB TERMINAL. *See* HOST COMPUTER, INTELLIGENCE, TERMINAL.

intelligent token. *Synonymous with* SUPERSMART CARD.

intelligible cross talk. In communications, pertaining to cross talk that has a reasonable degree of intelligibility. *See* CROSS TALK.

interactive. In architecture, a conversational type system in which a continuous dialogue can take place between a user and the computer. *See* INQUIRY/RESPONSE.

interactive computing. In computing, use of the computer such that the user is in control and may enter data or make other demands on the system that responds by the immediate processing of user requests and returning appropriate replies to these requests. (FIPS).

interactive videotex. *See* VIDEOTEX. *Synonymous with* VIEWDATA.

intercept. In communications security, pertaining to the targeting of a communications source and the subsequent acquisition of the transmitted information.

interceptability. In communications security, the vulnerability of a communications system to intercept. *See* INTERCEPT.

interchange. (1) In banking, the mutual acceptance and exchange of data messages between financial institutions, (ANSI). (2) In banking, a system in which card issuer and acquirer are not the same bodies. *Compare* LOCAL NETWORK. *See* ACQUIRER, ISSUER.

interchange group. *See* ANSI - X.12, EDIFACT.

interchange key. (1) In key management, a key used by two parties in an end-to-end encryption scheme as a key-encrypting key. *See* ELECTRONIC MAIL SECURITY, END-TO-END ENCRYPTION, KEY-ENCRYPTING KEY. (2) In key management, a secondary used as the basis of a key-encrypting key in a key notarization scheme. The interchange key is associated with a node, or a pair of nodes. It is combined with identifiers of users to form a notarized key that, in turn, is used to encrypt data-encrypting keys. *See* DATA-ENCRYPTING KEY, KEY-ENCRYPTING KEY, KEY NOTARIZATION, SECONDARY KEY.

interchange transaction. In banking, a transaction in circumstances in which the ATM, or EFTPOS terminal, is not controlled by the financial institution that issues the card. *Compare* LOCAL TRANSACTION. *See* EFTPOS, PIN MANAGEMENT AND SECURITY.

interdiction. In computer security, the act of impeding or denying the use of system resources to user. (FIPS). *See* DELAY/DENIAL OF SERVICE, DENIAL OF SERVICE, RESOURCE.

interface. (1) The common boundary between independent systems or modules, where communications takes place. (MTR). (2) In data communications, a shared boundary between two related devices or components defined for the purpose of specifying the type and form of signals passing between them. For example, the EIA RS-232C interface represents a standard set of signal characteristics (time, duration, voltage and current) specified by the Electronic Industries Association for use in communications terminals. It also includes a standard plug/socket connector arrangement. *See* RS-232C. (3) In computing, a specification of the communication

between modules of a program. *See* INFORMATION HIDING.

interface data unit. In data communications, the message passed from one layer to another in the Open Systems Interconnection Reference Model. The interface data unit comprises the service data unit plus control information. *Compare* PROTOCOL DATA UNIT, SERVICE DATA UNIT. *See* OPEN SYSTEMS INTERCONNECTION.

interface message processor. In data communications, a term originating in the ARPA network to describe a packet switching computer. *See* ARPA, DATA COMMUNICATIONS, INTERFACE PROCESSOR, PACKET SWITCH NODE.

interface processor. In data communications, a processor that acts as the interface between another processor or terminal, and a network or a processor controlling data flow in a network. *See* INTERFACE.

interference. In communications, any unwanted signals appearing in a channel at a level sufficient to impair the performance of the channel to a significant extent. Interference may be a result of natural or man made noises and signals. *See* EMI/RF RADIATION.

interim approval. In computer security, the temporary authorization granted an information system to process sensitive or critical information in its operational environment based on preliminary results of a comprehensive security evaluation of the information system. (AFR).

interlock. To prevent a machine or device from commencing further operations until the current one is completed.

intermediary bank. In banking, a bank, or banks, between the receiving bank and the beneficiary's bank through which the transfer must pass if specified by the sending bank. In such cases, this is the receiving bank's credit party. (ANSI). *See* CREDIT PARTY.

intermediate text block. In data communications, a control character used to end an intermediate block of characters. *See* END OF TEXT.

intermittent error. An error that occurs intermittently in a random way, is extremely difficult to reproduce and therefore to correct.

intermodulation distortion. In communications, a distortion resulting from the interaction of two or more frequencies when there is a nonlinear relationship between input and output signals.

internal audit. In auditing, the audit of a system conducted by a designated employee rather than by an external auditor. *Compare* EXTERNAL AUDIT. *See* INTERNAL SECURITY AUDIT.

internal auditor. In auditing, an employee of an organization with the responsibility for ensuring that organizational policies, standards and procedures are followed by employees.

The responsibilities of the internal auditor have been described by the Institute of Internal Auditors as 'an independent appraisal activity..' and as 'a control which functions by examining and evaluating the adequacy and effectiveness of other controls'.

Internal auditing is concerned with the evaluation and monitoring of systems and mechanisms of internal control. Such systems and mechanisms would normally include those which:

- ensured adherence to external regulations and management policies;
- safeguarded assets and ensured the propriety of liabilities;

- ensured the accuracy and reliability of records, financial statements and management information;
- confirmed that the results of corporate activities were consistent with their objectives.

Compare EXTERNAL AUDITOR. *See* INTERNAL AUDIT.

internal control documentation. Written policies, organization charts, procedural write-ups, manuals, memoranda, flow charts, decision tables, completed questionnaires, software, and related written materials used to describe the internal control methods and measures, to communicate responsibilities and authorities for operating such methods and measures, and to serve as a reference for persons reviewing the internal controls and their functioning. (DODD). *See* INTERNAL CONTROLS.

internal control review. A detailed examination of internal control to determine whether adequate control measures exist and are implemented to prevent or detect the occurrence of potential risks in a cost-effective manner. (DODD). *See* INTERNAL CONTROLS.

internal controls. The plan of organization and all of the methods and measures adopted within an agency to safeguard its resources, assure the accuracy and reliability of its information, assure adherence to applicable laws, regulations and policies, and promote operational economy and efficiency. (DODD).

internal reciprocal. In risk management, a disaster recovery strategy, adopted within an organization, employing mutual backup arrangements amongst installations in the organization. *Compare* RECIPROCAL.

internal security audit. In computer security, a security audit conducted by personnel responsible to the management of the organization being audited.(FIPS). *Compare* EXTERNAL SECURITY AUDIT. *See* AUDIT, SECURITY AUDIT.

internal security controls. In computer security, hardware, firmware, and software features within an automated system that restrict access to resources (hardware, software, and data) to only authorized subjects (persons, programs, or devices). Controls will also provide limit checks, reasonability checks, and so forth. (AFR). *See* FIRMWARE, REASONABLENESS CHECK, SUBJECT.

internal subject. In computer security, a subject that is not acting as a direct surrogate for a user. A process that is not associated with any user but performs system wide functions such as packet switching, line printer spooling, and so on (TNI). *See* SUBJECT. *Synonymous with* DAEMON, SERVICE MACHINE.

internal use. In data security, a security classification that requires no protection against disclosure in the organization. *See* CLASSIFICATION.

international alphabet number 5. In codes, a subset of ISO-7 in which characters for national use are either specified or not used. *See* ISO-7.

International Association for Microcircuit Cards. An organization of financial institutions created to study the microcircuit card and to investigate its application in financial fields. It was formed in 1981 with a membership of banks in seven countries: Belgium, France, Germany, Ireland, Luxembourg, The Netherlands and the U.K.. By 1985 the membership had expanded to include Sweden, Chase Manhattan Bank (USA), Norway, New Zealand, Bank of America and Denmark. The objectives of INTAMIC are: (a) The creation of

minimum standards for the use of microcircuit cards as a financial instrument and for international payments. (b) The joint study of the likely cost, security and operational capabilities of microcircuit cards. *See* MICROCIRCUIT CARD.

International Information Integrity Institute. An institute formed by SRI International and dedicated to the integrity and security of information as a business asset of the private sector throughout the world.

International Information Systems Security Certification Consortium. In information security, a consortium formed in 1990 by six computer industry associations to achieve certification of security experts.

International Network Working Group. A forum for discussing network standards and protocols. It is a working group within IFIP with the title 'International Packet Switching for Computer Sharing'. *See* IFIP.

International Packet Switched Service. In data communications, a packet switching system operated between Europe and the U.S.

International Standards Organization. An agency of the United Nations concerned with international standardization across a broad field of industrial products. *See* PROTOCOL STANDARDS.

International Telecommunications Union. A body that promotes international collaboration in telecommunications with a view to improving the efficiency of world services. It is a specialized agency of the United Nations and has three permanent committees, the IFRB (International Frequency Registration Board), the CCIR and the CCITT. Its regulations have the status of formal treaties between the participating countries and are binding on signatories who have acceded to them. *See* CCIR, CCITT, PROTOCOL STANDARDS.

Internet. In data communications, a U.S. network conduit comprising three networks: Arpanet, Milnet and NSFnet (National Science Foundation Network). It is used for research conducted for the U.S. Department of Defense by various government agencies, research centers and universities. *See* ARPANET MORRIS WORM.

Internet protocol. In data communications, a connectionless network protocol designed to handle the interconnection of LAN and WAN networks in ARPA Internet. *See* ARPANET, NETWORK LAYER, TCP/IP.

internetworking. In data communications, the process of connecting together several computer networks, that may have different protocols. The junctions between the networks are termed gateways and these junctions are responsible for ensuring that messages passing into another network conform to the necessary protocols of that network. *See* GATEWAY, PROTOCOL.

interoperability. (1) In communications security, the ability and extent to which one system can exchange information with another. (2) In key management, the ability to exchange cryptographic keys, whether manually or in an automated environment, with any other party. (ISO) *See* CRYPTOGRAPHIC KEY. (3) In key management, the ability to exchange keys, both manually and in an automated environment, with any other party implementing this standard, providing that both implementations use compatible options of this standard and compatible communications facilities. (ANSI X9.17). *See* ANSI X9.17 - 1985, CRYPTOGRAPHIC KEY.

interprocess communication. In computer security, communication between two different processes using system-supplied constructs; for example, shared files. (MTR).

interrupt. (1) In computing, a facility that enables a CPU to handle concurrently a number of input output devices on a priority basis. An interrupt is sent from an I/O device to the CPU requesting action, e.g. to receive data. The CPU will suspend execution of the current task, transfer control to a specified location in memory that then calls a routine to deal with the interrupt. On completion, control is returned to the interrupted task. *Compare* DMA. *See* CPU, INPUT OUTPUT DEVICE, VIRUS. (2) In data communications, to take action at a receiving station that causes the transmitting station to terminate a transmission.

interrupt controlled I/O. In computing, a technique for controlling data transfer between the processor and input output devices. Each I/O device, or its controller, is connected to an interrupt line and whenever the device needs attention it generates a signal to interrupt the processor. *Compare* DMA, POLLING. *See* INTERRUPT.

intersymbol dependence. In cryptography, a property of a cipher in which every bit of a ciphertext block is a sufficiently complex function of every preceding bit in the input plaintext. Cipher block chaining exhibits intersymbol dependence. *Compare* STRONG INTERSYMBOL DEPENDENCE. *See* CIPHER BLOCK CHAINING.

intervention signal. In data communications, a control signal designed for the equipment at either end of a channel rather than for the channel itself.

intractable. In mathematics, pertaining to a problem that is not solvable in polynomial time. *Compare* TRACTABLE. *See* TIME AND SPACE REQUIREMENTS.

intruder. In data security, a person who seeks to make illegal use of a data communication system. The intruder may listen in and attempt to decipher a ciphertext message or seek to actively interfere with the messages. *See* AT-TACKER, CIPHERTEXT, TROJAN HORSE, WIRETAP.

intruder detector system. In physical security, a software package that alerts the security officer when an attacker is attempting to penetrate the system. *See* INTRUDER.

intrusion. In legislation, trespassing by any means upon private property or controlled public property.

intrusion detection. In access control, pertaining to techniques which attempt to detect intrusion into a computer or network by observations on security logs or audit data.

There is considerable interest in development of systems with sufficient intelligence to detect suspected illegal access into computer systems or networks by on line analysis of audit records or security logs. A system termed IDES (Intrusion Detection Expert System) reported by Denning is a widely quoted model of the intrusion detection approach, based upon observed deviations of audit records from some normal pattern.

Denning suggested that examples of abnormal behavior associated with attacks on the system include:

- attempted break in: high rate of password failure, either for a single user or the whole system;
- masquerade/successful breakin: variation from normal login time, login location, use of resources, type of commands executed;
- legitimate user penetration: variation from normal pattern of usage, high number of reported protection violations;

- leakage by legitimate user: unusual login times, output directed to unusual printers;
- inference by legitimate user: unusually high number of records retrieved;
- Trojan Horse: variation in CPU or I/O resource usage;
- virus: unusual number of executable programs rewritten, increases in storage demands by executable programs;
- denial of service: high resource activity by one user and abnormally low activity by all other users.

The IDES model has six main components:

- Subjects - initiators of activity in the system being monitored;
- Objects - resources managed by the system;
- Audit Records - generated by the system when subjects perform, or attempt to perform, actions on objects, login, file accesses etc;
- Profiles - data structures that characterize the manner in which subjects behave in respect to objects, e.g. average number of logins per day by a given user at a specified terminal;
- Anomaly Records - generated when audit data is considered abnormal by a profile;
- Activity Rules - action taken when a condition is satisfied.

The audit records provide information on the interaction between a subject and individual object; if more than one object is involved in a interaction then individual audit records are developed for each interaction. For example, a user who copies date from File_A to File_B will cause three audit records to be produced, corresponding to the execute action of the Copy program, read action on File_A and write action on File_B.

The audit record contains six fields: subject, action, object, exception_condition, resource_usage and time/date stamp. Hence a typical audit record would specify that 'Jones read 1500 records of File_B at 11.00.01.07 on 24th November 1990 and no exception condition was raised'.

Profiles are defined to identify abnormal behavior, that may be indicative of an intrusion in the system. The profiles may be of the granularity of a single user and a single object, providing some measure of 'normal behavior', such that a deviation from this norm would be a good indicator of an attack, e.g. average number of records that Smith accesses from a Census database in a day. A sharp and major increase in such accesses could indicate that Smith is mounting an inference attack on the database, by accumulating a vast amount of data.

Profiles may also be defined for classes of subjects and classes of objects; e.g. virus attacks are not associated with a particular user, or file, but they may manifest themselves as unusually high write access on a class of .EXE files. Moreover, by monitoring class behavior it is possible to compare a user's behavior with the average behavior of members of the same class.

Profiles can build up a pattern of 'normal activity' by storing some statistical measure of behavior, e.g. failed-logins, on a subject or class of subjects. Such a measure could indicate, for example, poor typing skills of a particular user.

Events occur in the system, either due to the creation of an audit record, or a clock signal indicating that specified time period has been completed. An audit record may update the statistical data in a profile, or such profile data may be updated by data collected over a specified period.

Audit record or clock signal events

also cause a check to be made of any abnormal situation as indicated by a deviation between a reported value and the corresponding profile datum. For example, if a class of terminals suffered an unusually high number of login failures, during a working day, it might indicate that an attacker was trying out a 'guessed' password for a large number of users. Such an attack would only produce one reported login failure for each user, and would therefore not be picked up, as an unusual event, by the audit records for each individual user.

Abnormal behavior reported either by an audit record, or the data collected over a specified period, causes an anomaly record to be generated. The anomaly record generated by an individual audit record will inform the security officer of the type of intrusion suspected, one generated at the end of period will generate a summary report.

The IDES approach provides for the development of statistical information on normal behavior, such that deviant behavior can be identified and reported. It does not therefore rely upon the postulation of attack scenarios, and the collection of data appropriate to such scenarios. It does, nevertheless, demand some preconception on the types of behavior that are associated with an attack, so that the appropriate profiles can be developed. If too many types of profiles are formed then the security officer will be subjected to warnings of deviant behavior which have nothing to do with security, if too few then attacks may proceed unannounced.

Another approach to intrusion detection has been proposed which places considerable emphasis on the provision of software tools and facilities for the security officer The ISOA (Information Security Officer's Assistant) provides a flexible environment for automated audit analysis and network security monitoring. This system emphasizes the use of tools for the security officer including text display of audit records, graphic display of network security status, event triggered alarms, audit record compression, audit data storage, profile manipulation etc. *See* AUDIT DATA, EXPERT SYSTEMS, INFERENCE, SECURITY LOG, TROJAN HORSE, VIRUS.

intrusion detector. *See* AREA MAT, BEAM BREAK, BISTATIC MICROWAVE SENSOR, BREAK ALARM, BURIED-LINE INTRUSION PAD, CORD TRAP, DURESS ALARM, ELECTRIC FIELD SENSOR, ELECTROSTATIC FIELD SENSOR, FOIL, GUARDWIRE, INFRA RED MOTION DETECTOR, LASER INTRUSION DETECTOR, LINE SENSOR, MICROWAVE SENSOR, MODULATED PHOTOELECTRIC SENSOR, POINT PROTECTION, RADAR SENSOR, ULTRASONIC MOTION DETECTOR, VOLUMETRIC SENSOR, VIDEO MOTION DETECTOR.

Invader. In computer security, a virus that encrypts itself, terminates and stays resident, infects COM ,EXE and OVL files, infects floppy and hard disk boot sector, corrupts boot sector, program, OVL and data files and file linkage, affects run-time operation. *See* VIRUS NAMES.

invariant. In mathematics, a property that remains true after a given transformation.

inversion. In mathematics, a complementation process in binary arithmetic where all the 1's in a binary number are changed to 0's and vice versa. *See* COMPLEMENT.

inverted file. In databases, a file structure that facilitates searches for attributes by the provision of special lists or indices, e.g. a personnel file uses an employee number as the primary key but an inverted file might provide a list in departmental order, with associated employee numbers. Thus all the employees in a given department could be accessed so that it does not involve an exhaustive search of the total personnel file.

investigation. In computer security, the review and analysis of system security features (e.g., the investigation of system control programs using flow charts, assembly listings, and related documentation) to determine the security provided by the operating system. (OPNAVINST). *See* OPERATING SYSTEM.

invitation. In data communications, the process in which a processor contacts a station in order to allow the station to transmit an available message. *See* POLLING.

INWG. *See* INTERNATIONAL NETWORK WORKING GROUP.

ionization smoke sensor. In physical security, a smoke sensor comprising one or more chambers each containing minute amounts of radioactive material and two charged electrodes. The radioactive material ionizes the air in the chamber and the ionized air produces a small current through the electrodes, smoke particles entering the chamber attach themselves to the ions, decreasing their mobility and hence reducing the current flow. Such systems are fail safe. *Compare* PHOTOELECTRIC BEAM SMOKE DETECTOR. *See* COMBINATION SMOKE DETECTOR, FAIL SAFE.

I/O. input output.

IP. *See* INTERNET PROTOCOL.

IPC. *See* INTERPROCESS COMMUNICATION.

IPL. *See* INITIAL PROGRAM LOAD.

IPSE. Integrated Project Support Environment.

IPSS. *See* INTERNATIONAL PACKET SWITCHED SERVICE.

IR. *See* INFORMATION RETRIEVAL.

Iraqi Warrior. In computer security, a virus that infects COMMAND.COM and COM files, affects run-time operation, corrupts program, OVL and data files and file linkage. *See* VIRUS NAMES.

IRE. U.S. Institute of Radio Engineers.

irreversible encryption. (1) In cryptography, a DEA transformation of cleartext in such a way that the encrypted text cannot be decrypted back to the original cleartext by other than exhaustive procedures. (ANSI). *Compare* REVERSIBLE ENCRYPTION. *See* CLEARTEXT, EXHAUSTIVE ATTACK, DEA, PIN MANAGEMENT AND SECURITY. (2) In cryptography, a cryptographic transformation of plaintext such that there is no corresponding decryption operation. This technique can be employed, for example, to store passwords in a secure manner. The password, subsequently entered by a user, is subject to the same encryption process and the result compared with the stored encrypted password.

isarithmic control. In data communications, the control of flow in a packet switched network so as to maintain the total number of packets in transit below a certain limit. *See* FLOW CONTROL, PACKET SWITCHING.

ISC². *See* INTERNATIONAL INFORMATION SYSTEMS SECURITY CERTIFICATION CONSORTIUM.

ISDN. *See* INTEGRATED SERVICES DIGITAL NETWORK.

ISN. In banking, Input Sequence Number, a consecutive sequence number that allows for input message control between the sending bank and the service. (ANSI). *Compare* OSN.

ISO. *See* INTERNATIONAL STANDARDS ORGANIZATION.

ISO-7. In codes, a 7 bit code with 128 characters that is identical with ASCII, that is the U.S. version of this code, with the exception that certain bit patterns can be optionally allocated to national characters. *See* ASCII, INTERNATIONAL ALPHABET NUMBER 5.

ISO 7498. In standards, an International Standards Organization standard for Open Systems Interconnection. *See* OPEN SYSTEMS INTERCONNECTION.

ISO 7810. In standards, an International Standards Organization standard for the physical characteristics of identification cards.

ISO 7811. In standards, an International Standards Organization standard for the recording techniques of identification cards. *See* MAGNETIC STRIPE CARD.

ISO 7816. In standards, an International Standards Organization standard for smart cards. *See* SMART CARD.

ISO 7982-1. In standards, an International Standards Organization standard, bank telecommunications - Funds transfer messages - Part 1: Vocabulary and data elements.

ISO 8372. In standards, an International Standards Organization standard, information processing- modes of operation for a 64 bit block cipher algorithm. *See* DATA ENCRYPTION STANDARD.

ISO 8583. In standards, an International Standards Organization standard, Financial Transaction Card Originated Messages - Interchange Message Specifications. *See* SMART CARD.

ISO 8730. In standards, an International Standards Organization standard, banking - requirements for message authentication (wholesale). *See* MESSAGE AUTHENTICATION.

ISO 8731. In standards, an International Standards Organization standard, banking - approved algorithms for message authentication. *See* MESSAGE AUTHENTICATION ALGORITHM.

ISO 8732. In standards, an International Standards Organization standard, banking - key management (wholesale). *See* ANSI X9.17-1985, KEY MANAGEMENT.

ISO 9564. In standards, an International Standards Organization standard, PIN management and security.

ISO 9735. In standards, an International Standards Organization standard for EDIFACT. *See* EDIFACT.

ISO 9992. In standards, an International Standards Organization standard for financial transaction cards - messages between the integrated circuit card and the card acceptor device. *See* SMART CARD.

ISO 9807. In standards, an International Standards Organization standard, banking - requirements for message authentication (retail). *See* MESSAGE AUTHENTICATION.

ISO 10126. In standards, an International Standards Organization standard, banking - encipherment of wholesale financial messages.

ISO 10202. In standards, an International Standards Organization

standard for financial transaction cards - security architecture of financial transaction systems using integrated circuit cards. *See* SMART CARD.

ISOA. In access control, Information Security Officer's Assistant, a set of tools and facilities to assist a security officer to detect suspected intrusions into a computer system or network. *See* INTRUSION DETECTION.

isochronous transmission. In data communications, a form of data transmission, similar to synchronous transmission, but where there can be gaps between transmitted characters provided that a character always commences in synchronism with the timing sequence. *Compare* ANISOCHRONOUS TRANSMISSION. *See* SYNCHRONOUS TRANSMISSION..

isolated adaptive routing. In data communications, a method of signal switching in which the routing decisions are made solely on the basis of information available in each node. *See* ADAPTIVE ROUTING.

isolation. (1) In computer security, the containment of users and resources in an ADP system in such a way that users and processes are separate from one another as well as from the protection controls of the operating system. (FIPS). *See* ADP, COMPARTMENTALIZATION, ISOLATION ENFORCEMENT, OPERATING SYSTEM. (2) In communications, methods employed to prevent high voltages being applied to common carrier networks. *See* COMMON CARRIER.

isolation enforcement. In data security, a technique to ensure that secure information is partitioned into disjoint sets so that it cannot be transmitted from one secure application to another, that does not have the necessary access privilege. The isolation can be achieved by physical, temporal, logical or cryptographic separation. Physical separation implies that information cannot flow between physically separated systems; transmission by unwanted radiation is prevented by appropriate measures. If communication lines interconnect the isolated physical units then the information flows are restricted to a few specified channels that can be supervised. Temporal separation implies that information is processed in a given system at a particular time and is then purged before the system is assigned to a different security compartment. Logical separation is achieved by the trusted algorithms implemented with a combination of hardware and software. Cryptographic separation employs different cryptographic keys to encrypt the data assigned to the various security compartments. *See* CRYPTOGRAPHY, PERIODS PROCESSING, TEMPEST PROOFING, TEMPORAL SEPARATION.

ISO OSI. *See* OPEN SYSTEMS INTERCONNECTION.

ISRD. Information System Requirements Document.

ISSA. Information Systems Security Agency.

ISSO. Information System Security Officer. *See* INFORMATION SYSTEMS SECURITY.

issuer. In banking, the institution within a transaction interchange network that issues and verifies identification and authentication information on a customer. (ANSI). *See* AUTHENTICATION, CUSTOMER, INTERCHANGE.

IT. *See* INFORMATION TECHNOLOGY.

ITAR. U.S. International Traffic in Arms Regulations. These regulations include cryptographic equipment in the auxiliary military equipment category and therefore control the export of such equipment from the United States.

ItaVir. In computer security, a virus that infects EXE files, affects run-time operation, corrupts program and OVL files, file linkage and boot sector. *See* VIRUS NAMES.

item. In computing, a group of related characters treated as a unit. For example, a record may comprise a number of items, that in turn may consist of other items. *See* RECORD.

Items of Intrinsic Military Utility. End items other than those identified in the DOD Militarily Critical Technologies List whose transfer to potential adversaries shall be controlled for the following reasons: (a) The end product in question could significantly enhance the recipient's military or war-making capability either because of its technology content or because of the quantity to be sold; or (b) The product could be analyzed to reveal U.S. system characteristics and thereby contribute to the development of countermeasures to equivalent U.S. equipment. (DODD). *See* MILITARY CRITICAL TECHNOLOGY.

iteration. In computing, a process that repeats the same series of processing steps until a predetermined state or branch condition is reached. *Compare* RECURSIVE ROUTINE. *See* LOOP.

ITSEC. *See* INFORMATION TECHNOLOGY SECURITY EVALUATION CRITERIA.

ITSEF. *See* INFORMATION TECHNOLOGY SECURITY EVALUATION FACILITY.

ITSEM. *See* INFORMATION TECHNOLOGY SECURITY EVALUATION MANUAL.

ITU. *See* INTERNATIONAL TELECOMMUNICATIONS UNION.

ITU. *See* INTERNATIONAL TELECOM-
MUNICATIONS UNION.

IV. *See* INITIALIZATION VECTOR.

IVP. *See* INTEGRITY VALIDATION PRO-
CEDURE.

IV&V. *See* INDEPENDENT VERIFICA-
TION AND VALIDATION.

J

jamming. In communications security, a deliberate form of radiation interference aimed at radio, microwave or satellite transmissions. The use of high energy transmitters forces the jammer to use more powerful, and hence more expensive, transmission systems. Spread spectrum bandwidth transmission is distributed over a band of frequencies thus also increasing the problem of the jammer whilst the frequency agility technique changes the transmitted frequency randomly over the spectrum during transmission. *See* EMI/RF RADIATION, FREQUENCY AGILITY.

Jeff. In computer security, a virus that infects COMMAND.COM and COM files, affects run time operation, corrupts program, OVL and data files, formats and overwrites all or part of disk. *See* VIRUS NAMES.

Jerusalem. In computer security, a virus that terminates and stays resident, infects COM, EXE and OVL files, affects run time operation, corrupts program and OVL files. *See* VIRUS NAMES.

job transfer and manipulation. In data communications, a protocol that is used for submitting batch processing jobs to mainframe computers over a network. *See* PROTOCOL.

join. In databases, an operator in relational algebra. A join operation on two relations that share a common data item type produces a combined relation with attributes specified in the join operation. *See* RELATIONAL ALGEBRA, RELATIONAL DATABASE.

JoJo. In computer security, a virus that terminates and stays resident, infects COM files, affects run time operation, corrupts program and OVL files. *See* VIRUS NAMES.

Joker. In computer security, a virus that terminates and stays resident, infects COMMAND.COM and COM files, affects run time operation, corrupts program and OVL files. *See* VIRUS NAMES.

Joshi. In computer security, a stealth virus that terminates and stays resident, infects floppy and hard disk boot sector, and hard disk partition table, corrupts boot sector and data files, affects run time operation. *See* VIRUS NAMES.

journal. (1) In operations, a chronological record of changes made to a set of data, often used for reconstructing a previous version of the set in the event of corruption. *See* CORRUPTION. (2) In database security, an audit trail of database activities. *See* AUDIT TRAIL.

JTM. *See* JOB TRANSFER AND MANIPULATION.

July 13th. In computer security, a virus that encrypts itself, infects EXE files, affects run time operation, corrupts program, OVL and data files and file linkage. *See* VIRUS NAMES.

jump out. In physical security, to bypass all or part of an alarm system.

June 16th. In computer security, a virus that infects COMMAND.COM and COM files, formats or overwrites all or part of disk, affects run time operation, corrupts program and OVL files and file linkage. *See* VIRUS NAMES.

Justice. In computer security, a virus that terminates and stays resident, infects COMMAND.COM and COM files, affects run time operation, corrupts program and OVL files. *See* VIRUS NAMES.

K

KDC. *See* KEY DISTRIBUTION CENTER.

KEEPROM. In computer security, an EPROM whose contents cannot be read unless a specific data value is given to it. *See* EEPROM.

Kennedy. In computer security, a virus that terminates and stays resident, infects COM files, affects run-time operation, corrupts program and OVL files. *See* VIRUS NAMES.

Kerberos. In authentication, an authentication service designed for open network systems. It was originally developed for the MIT Athena project.

The service provides for users to securely access servers in a client-server network. Clients, who may be users or processes, provide credentials to the server to prove their identity. The system employs private key encryption and the credentials comprise tickets or authenticators. A ticket contains the name of the client, the name of the server, the network address of the client, a time-date stamp, the lifetime of ticket validity, and a session key. The ticket is encrypted with a secret key known only by the server and Kerberos. The session key, for use between client and server, is acquired by the client in the ticket which is then passed to the server by the client.

An authenticator accompanies a ticket and provides proof that the request is generated by the client. The authenticator comprises client name, network address and timestamp, it is encrypted with the session key contained in the ticket.

Initially the user logs into a workstation and a request is sent to the Kerberos authentication server for a ticket, to be used with the ticket granting service. The authentication server, checks that the user is known, generates a random session key and develops a ticket whose contents include: session key, client's name, name of ticket granting server, current time, ticket lifetime and client's network address. This ticket is then encrypted with a private key known only to the ticket granting server and the authentication server. A message including the ticket and the session key is then encrypted with the client's private key, known only to the client and the authentication server. Thus the message from the authentication server to the client is in the form:

$eK_c(K_{c,tgs}, eK_{tgs}(T_{c,tgs}))$

K_c - private key of client

K_{tgs} - private key of ticket granting server

$K_{c,tgs}$ - session key for use by client and ticket granting server

$T_{c,tgs}$ - the ticket for presentation to the ticket granting service and contains client name, ticket granting server name, client network address, time stamp, ticket lifetime and session key $K_{c,tgs}$.

When the workstation receives the encrypted ticket from the authentication server, it requests the user password; the client's private key, K_c, is computed from the password and used to decrypt the response, $eK_c(K_{c,tgs}, eK_{tgs}(T_{c,tgs}))$, from the authentication server. The user password and private key are then erased from workstation memory. The session key and ticket received from the workstation are thereafter used to authenticate the user.

When the user requests access to a server the client sends a message comprising three components to the ticket granting server:

$$s, eK_{tgs}(T_{c,tgs}), eK_{c,tgs}(A_c).$$

The authenticator A_c comprises the client name, address and a timestamp. Since it is encrypted with the ticket's session key, the ticket granting service is satisfied that it originated from the client at the time indicated in the timestamp.

The ticket granting service now generates a ticket to be used by the client in order obtain services from a server. The process is identical to that described above in the case of the authenticator granting a ticket for the ticket granting server. The ticket contains a session key to be used between the client and server, is encrypted with a secret key known only by the server and ticket granting service, and a message comprising the encrypted ticket and client-server session key is encrypted with the session key shared between the client and ticket granting server.

A client may request mutual authentication from the server. In this case the server extracts the timestamp from the client's message, increments it by 1,[1] encrypts it with the session key and returns the result to the client. *See* AU-THENTICATOR, SERVER, SESSION KEY, TICKET.

kernel. (1) In computer security. *See* SECURITY KERNEL. (2) In operating systems, the lowest level of an operating system comprising rigorously tested routines responsible for the allocation of hardware resources to the operating system processes and the programs running under the operating system. *See* NUCLEUS.

kernelized. In computer security, pertaining to an operating system designed to partition classes of users so that they can only access those facilities for which they have authorization. Such systems give the impression that different computers are available to users of different kernels. *See* SECURITY KERNEL.

key. (1) In cryptography, a sequence of symbols that controls the operations of encipherment and decipherment. (ISO). *Synonymous with* CRYPTOGRAPHIC KEY. (2) In cryptography, a symbol or sequence of symbols (or electrical or mechanical correlates of symbols) that control the operations of encryption and decryption. *See* ENCRYPT, DECRYPT. (FIPS). (3) In databases, one or more characters used for identifying a set of data. *See* PRIMARY KEY, SECONDARY KEY.

key agreement. In key management, a method that enables two parties, without prior agreement, to exchange messages in such a manner that they can agree upon a secret key known only to them. *See* DIFFIE-HELLMAN TECHNIQUE.

key certification center. In key management, a facility operated by the certification authority that generates and returns certificates. (ISO). *See* CERTIFI-CATE, CERTIFICATION AUTHORITY, DIGITAL SIGNATURE.

key check value. *Synonymous with* KEY VERIFICATION CODE.

key ciphertext avalanche. In cryptography, a property of a cipher in which a one bit change in the key, for a given plaintext-ciphertext-tuple produces a radical change in the ciphertext. *Compare* CIPHERTEXT, PLAINTEXT, PLAINTEXT CIPHERTEXT AVALANCHE, CRYPTOGRAPHIC KEY.

key collision. In cryptography, a phenomenon that has been reported in relation to DES. There are instances in which encryption of a specific data blocks give the same ciphertext for two different keys. *See* CIPHERTEXT, CRYPTOGRAPHIC KEY, DATA ENCRYPTION STANDARD.

key component. In cryptography, one, of at least two, parameters having the format of a cryptographic key, that is exclusive-or'ed with one or more like parameters to form a cryptographic key. (ANSI). *Compare* THRESHOLD. *See* CRYPTOGRAPHIC KEY, EXCLUSIVE OR.

key crunching. In key management, a technique for converting an easily remembered character stream into a DES key. A DES key comprises 64 bits, 8 of which are parity bits, and thus the user only has a free choice of 56 bits, i.e. 7 bytes. Using 7 byte character streams of easily remembered alphanumeric characters severely restricts the range of potential keys. If key crunching is employed the user enters an easily remembered character stream which is substantially longer than 7 characters. The stream is encrypted with cipher block chaining and returns the rightmost 56 bits of the last block as the required key. *See* CIPHER BLOCK CHAINING, CRYPTOGRAPHIC KEY, DES, LONG KEY, NATIVE KEY, PARITY BIT.

key distribution and control. In key management, the processes involved in the distribution and control of keys include:

- appointment of cryptographic personnel;
- responsibilities of cryptographic personnel;
- shipment and receipt of keying material;
- storage of keying material and encryption/authentication device

- physical keys;
- use of keying material;
- destruction of keying material;
- archiving of keys.

Personnel responsible for key management should be appointed by senior management. No one person should have overall control of encryption material, and cryptographic keys, and at least two key custodians should be available at all operational times to perform planned, and unplanned key changes. Custodians may be supported by subsidiary staff for specific duties, e.g. key entry.

The responsibilities of custodians include the receipt, verification, storage, recording, entry, change and destruction of keying material and such sensitive operations should be under dual control. The shipment and receipt of keying material should also be under dual control using registered mail, or preferably an employee courier. The development of procedures dealing with the checking of packages, exchange of documents verifying safe, undamaged and untampered receipt of keying material etc. is essential, and the packaging employed should facilitate preliminary checks before packages are opened.

Keying material should be stored in a secure receptacle, located in a secure, supervised environment. Access to such material should require actions by two custodians, e.g. dual locks on secure boxes with each custodian in possession of only one key. All such accesses should be logged. Backup keys to the locks of the secure receptacle should also be located in a secure environment and access to such keys should require the presence of both custodians. If physical cryptographic keys are stored electronically then their storage should be protected against the effects of short-term power supply outages.

No keying material should be destroyed prior to explicit instructions to that effect. Alternate custodians should witness the destruction of such material without gaining sight of the contents. All keying material must be destroyed in such a manner that it cannot be reconstructed. All such destruction of keying material must be recorded, with sufficient details to identify the material destroyed and the date/time, custodian etc. of the destruction process. These records must also be maintained in a secure environment.

The storage requirements of archived keys depends upon the security life of the keying material. If it is essential to maintain the same degree of security as that for the current keys then the above-mentioned procedures for key storage should be employed, or the archived keys should be encrypted. In the latter case the key-encrypting key should be subject to the aforementioned security procedures. If secrecy of archived keys is not essential then such keys should be provided with the same degree of storage protection as the organization's vital records. *See* CRYPTOGRAPHIC KEY, DUAL CONTROL, KEY-ENCRYPTING KEY, KEYING MATERIAL, SECURITY LIFE.

key distribution center. In key management, a center established for the purpose of providing cryptographic keys to two parties that:

- wish to communicate securely but do not currently share keys;
- individually share a key-encrypting key, or key pair with the center;
- do not have the capability to generate keys.

The party that wishes to originate an encrypted message requests data keys from the center, providing the identity of the intended recipient. The center acquires, or generates, two sets of data keys, encrypts and forwards them to the originating party. One set of the data keys is encrypted under the key-encrypting key currently employed for key transfers between the originator and the center, the second set, together with identifying information to guard against

misuse of the keys, is likewise encrypted under the center-ultimate recipient key-encrypting key. The originator then sends the second set of keys and identifying information to the intended recipient. *Compare* KEY TRANSLATION CENTER, POINT TO POINT. *See* ANSI X9.17 - 1985, CRYPTOGRAPHIC KEY, DATA KEY, KEY-ENCRYPTING KEY, KEY-ENCRYPTING KEY PAIR.

key-encrypting key. In key management, a cryptographic key used for encrypting (and decrypting) data-encrypting keys or other key-encrypting keys. (FIPS). (2) In key management, a key used exclusively to encrypt and decrypt keys. (ANSI) *Compare* DATA KEY. *See* KEY-ENCRYPTING KEY PAIR. *Synonymous with* SECONDARY KEY.

key-encrypting key pair. In key management, two encrypting keys used together to encrypt other keys. *See* ANSI X9.17 - 1985, KEYENCRYPTING KEY, MULTIPLE DES ENCIPHERMENT.

key equivocation. In information theory, the equivocation of a key in relation to receipt of a given ciphertext, given by:

$$H_c(K) = -\Sigma \, P(C) \, \Sigma \, P_c(K) \log_2 (P_c(K))$$

where

$P(C)$ = Probability of receipt of ciphertext C,

$P_c(K)$ = Probability that the key K was employed given that ciphertext C was received.

If the key equivocation is zero then there is no uncertainty of the key employed. Key equivocation usually decreases as the length of the message is increased. *See* CRYPTOGRAPHIC KEY, EQUIVOCATION.

key exhaustion. In cryptanalysis, an exhaustive attack technique in which the attacker possesses a fragment of the plaintext, the corresponding ciphertext and has knowledge of the cryptographic algorithm. A trial key is selected, the plaintext is encrypted with this key and the result compared with the known ciphertext. Alternatively if only ciphertext is available then it is decrypted with the trial key and the resulting plaintext is inspected to see if it corresponds to a meaningful message. *Compare* MESSAGE FORM:EXHAUSTION. *See* CRYPTOGRAPHIC KEY, EXHAUSTIVE ATTACK, KNOWN PLAINTEXT.

key generation. In cryptography, the origination of a key or of a set of distinct keys. (FIPS). *See* KEY GENERATOR, KEY MANAGEMENT.

key generator. In cryptography, a device, including associated alarms and self tests, for generating cryptographic keys (and where needed, IV's). (ANSI) *See* CRYPTOGRAPHIC KEY, IV, KEY GENERATION, KEY MANAGEMENT, KEY STREAM GENERATOR.

key gun. In key management, a device for transporting electronically stored cryptographic keys. A typical key gun is the size of a pocket calculator and it has connectors to receive keys from a source, and to deliver them to the destination device, e.g. a terminal. Electrical or optical coupling may be employed for the device connection.

The key gun must have mechanisms to prevent:

- loading a key by an attacker;
- reading the loaded key by an attacker;
- loading the keys into an attacker's terminal.

Key gun passwords can ensure that only authorized key generators and destinations communicate with the gun; destruction of stored keys upon readout, and key gun tamper resistant modules, can effectively prevent an attacker from acquiring the keys. *Synonymous with* KEY LOADER, KEY TRANSPORT MODULE.

key hashing. *Synonymous with* KEY CRUNCHING.

key identifier. *Synonymous with* IDA.

keying material. In key management, the data (e.g. keys and IV's) necessary to establish and maintain cryptographic keying relationships. (ANSI). *See* CRYPTOGRAPHIC KEY, IV, KEY DISTRIBUTION AND CONTROL, KEYING RELATIONSHIP.

keying relationship. In key management, the state existing between a communicating pair during that time they share at least one data key or key-encrypting key. (ANSI). *See* COMMUNICATING PAIR, CRYPTOGRAPHIC KEY, DATA KEY, KEY-ENCRYPTING KEY.

keyless cryptography. In key management, a method of communicating cryptographic keys in which the messages exchanged, between the communicating parties to establish the cryptographic keys, are not secret but their originators are. The originators select the name for the key (say K) and then, independently, generate a binary number of 2n bits. Thus Alice A generates a number $A(1),A(2),A(3).....A(2n)$ and Bob generates a number $B(1),B(2),B(3).....B(2n)$.

Alice next produces 2n messages of the form:

Message K: my bit i is A(i).
Similarly for Bob.

The messages are exchanged in such a manner that a passive wiretapper is unable to determine the originator, although the messages themselves may be read. For example each party may employ a secure channel to a center, that then displays the messages whilst giving no clue as to the originators of each one.

In reading the pair of messages:

Message K: my bit 5 is 1.
Message K: my bit 5 is 0Bob knows that bit 5 generated by him was 1 (say) and thus Alice transmitted a 0 in the fifth bit. Unauthorized message recipients, however, have no knowledge of the fifth bit transmitted from Alice to Bob. However, if the bits have equal value then the attacker knows precisely the bit value. When Alice and Bob read the messages and find coincident bits then both parties remove those bits from the key producing a new, shorter key. For example:

| Alice initially sends | 01110110001 |
| Bob initially sends | 10111000010. |

| NEW Alice key | 0101101 |
| NEW Bob key | 1010010 |

If necessary the process is repeated to produce a longer key. By convention the transmitted key is that eventually produced by Alice, that is the complement of that eventually produced by Bob. *See* CRYPTOGRAPHIC KEY.

key library. In cryptography, a stored collection of cryptographic keys for use by an individual or designated group. Access to the library is controlled by a separate, secret key. *See* CRYPTO-GRAPHIC KEY.

key list. In cryptography, a document containing the cryptographic keys to be employed by a cryptosystem during a specific cryptoperiod. *See* CRYPTO-GRAPHIC KEY, CRYPTOPERIOD, CRYPTOSYSTEM.

key loader. In key management, an electronic, self-contained unit that is capable of storing at least one key and transferring that key, upon request, into cryptographic equipment. (ANSI). *See* CRYPTOGRAPHIC KEY, CRYPTOGRAPHIC EQUIPMENT. *Synonymous with* KEY GUN, KEY TRANSPORT MODULE.

key management. (1) In cryptography, the generation, storage, distribution, deletion, archiving and application of keys in accordance with a security policy. (ISO). *See* KEY. (2) In cryptography, the processes concerned with the generation, distribution, storage and destruction of cryptographic keys and related information, e.g. initialization vectors.

Encipherment effectively reduces the problem of ensuring the secrecy of a mass of data, to that of protecting the secrecy of a cryptographic key. The problems associated with the various aspects of key management depend upon the range of the cryptographic techniques, the environment and applications in which the cryptographic keys are employed.

Key Generation
Key generation must be undertaken in such a manner so as to ensure that:

- the result of the generation process is unpredictable;
- the range of keys that can be produced are equal to the full range of valid keys;
- there is no substantial skew in the probability distribution of the keys produced;
- an attacker cannot influence the generation process;
- an attacker cannot change the output from the generator;
- an attacker cannot monitor the generator output.

If the output from the generator is, to some degree, predictable then an attacker could independently produce the same key, or a set of keys, containing the generated key. If the range of key outputs is a subset of the valid range of keys, or if there is an increased probability that a certain subset of keys will be generated, then the strength of the generation process will be less than that of the cryptosystem.

Key Distribution - Overview

Key distribution is one of the most complex problems in modern cryptographic systems. If a limited number of keys are to be distributed by manual methods then strict administrative procedures are required to maintain the security of the keying material. In many instances, however, the number of keys employed in the system, the frequency of key changes and the large, diverse user population demand that a variety of automated key distribution techniques be employed. Symmetric ciphers, such as DES, require that both the encipher and decipher processes employ the same key, and thus the cryptographic key must be securely exchanged between any two communicating parties.

Public key cryptosystems impose much less rigorous key management conditions in terms of secrecy, since the encipher key may be freely publicized, but on the other hand it is imperative that the authenticity of public keys be guarded.

Key management in database systems could be tackled by distributing the keys, used to encrypt the records, to the users. For example such users could be provided with a plastic card with the key stored in a magnetic stripe; use of the card would also require the input of a password at the terminal to minimize the impact of lost cards. However, this method inevitably increases the danger of loss of database confidentiality arising from the compromise of user keys. A better approach is to store the keys within the database system and to rely upon access controls to ensure that only privileged users can gain access to the keys, and hence the deciphered records.

One technique is to store the database file key, encrypted with the user's individual private key, together with the encrypted data. When a user requests access to the system the key manager delivers the user's private key and accesses the record containing the file key encrypted with the user key; the file key

is produced by decryption with the user's key and the database records are then decrypted to plaintext.

Access to the database, without knowledge of a user key, could however enable an attacker to modify the ciphertext. This could be purely malicious, replacing data with random ciphertext that decrypted to unintelligible text, or in the case of known plaintext/ciphertext pairs the attacker could replace one ciphertext record, corresponding to known plaintext, with another. These attacks can be stopped by the use of a validation record that contains the file key, operated upon by a one-way function, and stored in the database with the corresponding file. The file key, produced by decryption with the user's key, is subjected to the same one-way function and compared with the validation record, before any update of the database is allowed. If a two-key system is employed, for file encryption, the users may be granted either read, write or read and write privileges.

Key management for terminal-host communication commonly employ session keys to encrypt the messages in transit. These session keys have a life span restricted to the messages transmitted in an individual user session. Such session keys are generated by the host computer, upon request from a user, and are both stored in the host and transmitted, encrypted under a key-encrypting key known as the terminal key, to the terminal. It is a principle of such systems that the session key is never revealed, outside system tamper resistant modules, in plaintext form. Thus key-encrypting keys, termed master keys, are stored at the host, whilst each terminal has its own terminal key. Typically two master keys, $km0$ and $km1$, are stored in tamper resistant modules at the host and the terminal key, kt, is similarly securely stored in the terminal.

A session key, ks, is generated and then stored in the form $ekm0(ks)$. i.e. ks

encrypted with km0, at the host. This encrypted session key is decrypted with km0, and re-encrypted with kt for transmission to the terminal, where it is decrypted and stored in a tamper resistant module as ks.

Messages are encrypted and decrypted at the host in a tamper resistant module containing the master key, km0. For encryption the plaintext message is sent to the module, that is switched to the encryption mode, together with the encrypted session key ekm0(ks). The session key is revealed within the module by decryption of ekm0(ks) with km0, and ks is then used to encrypt the data; the decryption of data is similarly performed in the module, switched to the decryption mode.

This technique enables a large number of session keys, encrypted with km0, to be held in host storage outside the tamper resistant modules and ensures that the plaintext version of the session keys are never available outside these secure modules. Similar arrangements for encryption and decryption are available in a tamper resistant module at the terminal that contains the terminal key kt.

File security key management can be provided on a similar basis to that for database systems, as described above, or as an extension of terminal-host communication systems. In the latter case a file key, kf, is employed to encipher/decipher a file and this key is encrypted by a secondary file key, kg, the result ekg(kf) is stored, often with the file header.

A group of files can then be transmitted and only the secondary file key, kg, need be provided to the intended recipient. The files can be enciphered and deciphered with the same encryption/decryption modules used for terminal host communication; it is necessary, however, to produce the key input for these encryption/decryption modules, i.e. ekm0(kf).

Key Distribution - Financial Networks

Financial networks such as EFTPOS pose particular problems of key management. The terminals will be located in retailers' premises, and there will be a large number of such terminals. The terminals must be not be expensive to manufacture, they will be unsupervised outside working hours, they will be operated by relatively unskilled personnel, the time to complete a transaction must be kept to a minimum and the terminals should accept a wide range of cards from various card issuers.

The network will probably include a variety of host computers, operated by various financial institutions. The financial institutions will undertake various functions in the network, e.g. acquirer, card issuer, and will effectively demand communication to every terminal, possibly through one or more intermediate node computers. The financial institutions will naturally demand that they are not required to reveal confidential information, e.g. PINs, to other users of the network and that a failure in security of one institution should not compromise the security of another.

The situation is further complicated by the following factors:

- the number of network transactions per unit time will be very high;
- the total time of a transaction, including communication delays and host computer processing, must be kept to a level acceptable to a queue of customers;
- system failures must not cause a retailer to stop trading;
- the network technology cannot be updated without a very high expenditure on retailers' terminals etc. but attackers can always exploit the latest technological developments;
- the financial returns on a successful mass attack will be sufficiently

high to attract the attention of organized crime.

There are a number of national and international standards governing Electronic Funds Transfer key management. The Australian Standards AS2805 include:

Part 6.1 Key Management Principles;
Part 6.2 Key Management - Transaction Keys;
Part 6.3 Key Management - Session Keys - Node to Node;
Part 6.4 Key Management - Session Keys - Terminal to Acquirer.

These standards effectively propose two approaches to key management:

- session keys;
- transaction keys.

In each case tamperproof modules must be provided for storage of certain keys and for cryptographic processing.

The session key system is similar to that described above for terminal host security. A hierarchy of keys is developed: master keys, key-encrypting keys and session keys.

Master keys are used to encrypt lower order keys for storage, key-encrypting keys ensure that cryptographic keys cannot be compromised during transmission over the network and session keys are employed for transaction data. In DES systems the higher order keys are commonly double length keys and employ the encrypt-decrypt-encrypt operation to secure lower order keys.

Normally there are three session keys: data key, MAC key and PIN encryption key. It is essential that there be cryptographic separation of keys to guard against an attacker replacing one key for another. For example, the data key is used to protect sensitive information such as transaction amount and this amount may be legitimately revealed at the receiving host. However, PINs may be checked within the tamperproof module and never revealed at the host.

It must not be possible for an attacker to perform a decrypt PIN operation using the decrypt data facilities.

Cryptographic separation is normally provided by use of key variants for key-encrypting and master keys so that effectively session keys are encrypted under different key-encrypting or master keys.

More sophisticated methods, of preventing keys intended for one purpose being used for another, have been developed. Tagged key systems use the parity bits of DES keys to identify their functions. Control vectors may be associated with keys, and coupled with the corresponding key-encrypting keys, to specify the permissible processing of the keys.

Session key systems necessarily involve the manual loading of the same key-encrypting key at each end of the link. Thereafter such keys are individually updated at each end according to some agreed protocol.

In the case of transaction key systems a set of session keys are used for only one transaction. The transaction messages are linked so that any modification, loss or addition of transactions is automatically detected. In essence the problem of key distribution is ameliorated by a technique that allows the session keys to be independently generated at the terminal and host computer.

Each terminal and host initially store the same initial value of the terminal key. Session keys are computed from this terminal key and a one-way function (OWF). MACs are produced for request and response messages and the corresponding MAC residues are stored. At completion of the transaction the terminal key itself is updated with the OWF using the current terminal keys, MAC residues of request and response messages. An essential feature of the transaction key system is 'Other Card Data', i.e. data stored on the customer's magnetic stripe card, which is read at the terminal but not transmitted. This data provides a decoupling key which prevents a wiretapper from injecting messages or determining PINs even if the terminal key is compromised.

Key Distribution - Key Notarization
Key distribution systems must not only guard against exposure of the keys by an attacker but also against the modification, insertion or replay of keys by an attacker.

Key notarization provides recipients with the guarantee that a data key originated at the communicating party, initiating the transfer, and was intended for the recipient, i.e. an attacker has not transmitted a key intended for use between other communicating pairs. For example, when Alice, at node i, initiates communication with Bob at node j, then a node interchange key-encrypting key IK_{ij} is selected. Alice and Bob have identifiers, for DES keys these will be 28 bit numbers. The two identifiers are concatenated and then added modulo 2 to the 56 bit key IK_{ij}; the parity bits are then added to convert the result to a valid 64 bit DES key. This key is then employed as a key-encrypting key for the transfer of a data key from user Alice to Bob.

Key Distribution - Public Key Cryptography
Public key cryptosystems have an inherent advantage over symmetric ciphers, such as DES, inasmuch as an enciphering key need not be transmitted by a secure channel.

Nevertheless the public distribution of enciphering keys leads to potential misuse of public key cryptosystems by attackers. For example, if Alice, whilst enciphering a message for transmission to Bob, can be persuaded that the enciphering key is E_t rather than E_b, where E_t and E_b are the enciphering keys of the attacker and Bob respectively, then the attacker can decipher messages intended for, and instead of, Bob. Certificates signed by trusted authority may be used to tackle this problem.

The security of the deciphering key, in a public key cryptosystem, is only the responsibility of one person, i.e. the recipient of enciphered messages. This situation has the advantage that the deciphering key need never be transmitted, after it has been received by the user from the key generator.

Key Distribution - Key Exchange
A number of ingenious schemes have been devised, e.g. Diffie-Hellman technique and keyless cryptography, that enable a communicating pair to exchange cryptographic keys without requiring a secure communication link for the transfer of the information. *See* ACQUIRER, ANSI X9.17 - 1985, AS 2805, CARD ISSUER, CONTROL VECTOR, CRYPTOGRAPHIC KEY, DATABASE SECURITY, DECOUPLING KEY, DES, DIFFIE-HELLMAN TECHNIQUE, DIGITAL SIGNATURE, EFTPOS, HOST COMPUTER, INITIALIZATION VECTOR, KEY DISTRIBUTION AND CONTROL, KEY-ENCRYPTING KEY, KEY GENERATION, KEY MANAGEMENT DEVICE, KEYING MATERIAL, KEYLESS CRYPTOGRAPHY, MAC, MAC RESIDUE, MENTAL POKER, ONE-WAY FUNCTION, PIN, PUBLIC KEY CRYPTOGRAPHY, SESSION KEY, STRENGTH, SYMMETRIC CRYPTOSYSTEM, TAGGED KEYS, TAMPER RESISTANT MODULE, TRANSACTION KEY, TWO KEY CRYPTOSYSTEM.

key management device. In key management, a unit that provides for secure electronic distribution of data encryption keys to authorized users. In the DES case, these keys are essentially 56 bits in a 64 bit block therefore, 64 bit blocks can be electronically distributed by a key management (trusted) center. (GAO) *See* DATA ENCRYPTION STANDARD, KEY MANAGEMENT FACILITY.

key management facility. In key management, the physically protected enclosure (e.g. room or device) and its contents where cryptographic elements (i.e. cryptographic hardware, software, firmware, keys or IVs) reside. (ANSI). *See* CRYPTOGRAPHIC KEY, FIRMWARE, KEY MANAGEMENT DEVICE, IV.

key notarization. (1) In key management, a method of applying additional security to a key utilizing the identities of the originator and the ultimate recipient. (ANSI). (2) In key management, key notarization is employed in conjunction with cryptographic facilities, termed key notarization facilities, at each node in a network to provide an assurance on the authenticity of exchanged keys.

Interchange keys are associated with each node and node pair in the network. Interchange key IK_{ii} forms the basis of a key-encrypting key used for the encipherment of local data-encrypting keys, whilst IK_{ij} is designated for the encipherment of data keys used in communications from node i to node j.

The actual key-encrypting keys, used for local and communication data encipherment, is a function of the appropriate interchange key and the identifiers of the user or users.

If DES encryption is used then a 64 bit interchange key IK_{ij} is allocated for communication from node i to node j. Alice and Bob, at nodes i and j respectively, are allocated 28 bit identifiers a and b. The 64 bit key-encrypting key for the encryption of data keys used in Alice to Bob communications are produced by a mathematical manipulation of IK_{ij} and identifiers a and b:

- the first 7 bits of the 28 bit identifier a are 'exclusive or-ed' with the first 7 bits of the interchange key IK_{ij};
- the 8th bit of the key IK_{ijab} is produced as a parity bit of the 7 bits thus produced;
- the next 7 bits of the identifier a are 'exclusive or-ed' with the bits 9 - 15 of IK_{ij};

- bit 16 of IK_{ijab} is developed as parity bit of the 7 bits thus produced;
- the process is repeated for the remaining 14 bits of identifier a and the 28 bits of identifier b. The result of these operations is 64 bit parity checked DES notarized key IK_{ijab}.

Bob at node j receives ciphertext, from Alice at node i, encrypted under data-encrypting key k_d. Bob also receives data-encrypting key k_d encrypted by notarized key IK_{ijab}. In order to recover the plaintext message, Bob identifies himself, to the key notarization facility, with password PW_b and enters the identity of the transmitter Alice, the ciphertext, encrypted data-encrypting key and a decryption command. Interchange key IK_{ij}, is stored in the key notarization facility and notarized key IK_{ijab} is then formed from the identifiers, a and b, by the mathematical algorithm described above. The data key k_d is recovered from $eIK_{ijab}(k_d)$ by decryption, with IK_{ijab}, within the tamper resistant key notarization facility; this key is then used to decipher the ciphertext.

Key notarization restricts the use of keys to specific users at specific nodes for specific purposes. Thus Bob can use the data key k_d, received under encryption with IK_{ijab}, to decipher messages from Alice at node i, the key can be used for no other purposes.

This restriction on the use of DES keys can be employed in digital signature schemes. Alice at node i identifies herself with an identity number ID_a and secret password PW_a. The password is held in secondary storage encrypted under the notarized key IK_{aa}. The password input by the user is thus similarly encrypted and compared with the stored value. Upon user authentication the facility is placed into an active state for the user and can thereafter perform encryption, decryption, authentication, decryption/re-encryption functions etc. Data keys, and initialization vectors, etc. are generated within the facility according to the requests of users.

The facility also contains interchange keys for communicating nodes, these keys are, however, required at both sending and receiving nodes and must therefore be loaded into the facility by authorized personnel under secure conditions. *See* CRYPTOGRAPHIC FACILITY, CRYPTOGRAPHIC KEY, DES, DIGITAL SIGNATURE, EXCLUSIVE OR, INITIAL-IZATION VECTOR, INTERCHANGE KEY, KEY MANAGEMENT, PARITY BIT.

key offset. In key management, the process of exclusive-or'ing a counter to a key. (ANSI). *See* ANSI X9.17 - 1985, CRYPTOGRAPHIC KEY, EXCLUSIVE OR. *Synonymous with* OFFSET.

key pair. In key management, a pair of keys used to encrypt data, or more commonly data keys. In the encryption process one key is used to encrypt the plaintext, the second key acts upon the encrypted block with the decryption algorithm and the first key is used to re-encrypt the result. This technique protects against 'meet in the middle' attacks and also ensures that the key pair system is compatible with a single key system. *See* ANSI X9.17 - 1985, DATA KEY, KEY-ENCRYPTING KEY, MULTIPLE DES ENCIPHERMENT.

key partitioning. In key management, the use of master keys and variants thereof to encipher secondary and primary keys. This technique ensures that keys defined to one cryptographic operation cannot be misused or manipulated by another cryptographic operation. Thus isolation and independence can be achieved between different applications, e.g. file security and communications. *See* KEY MANAGEMENT, KEY VARIANT, PRIMARY KEY, SECONDARY KEY.

Keypress. In computer security, a virus that terminates and stays resident, infects COMMAND.COM, COM and EXE files, affects run-time operation, corrupts program, OVL and data files. *See* VIRUS NAMES.

key register. In banking, the memory location in the terminal or acquirer that contains a value, known only to the terminal and the acquirer, that is used in the computation of a transaction key between the terminal and acquirer. (SAA). *See* ACQUIRER, KEY MANAGE-MENT, TRANSACTION KEY.

key service message. In key management, a message that transfers a key from an originator to a recipient. *See* ANSI X9.17 - 1985.

key space. In cryptography, the range of all possible values that a cryptographic key may assume. In a cipher system the key space must be large enough to thwart key exhaustion cryptanalytic attacks. *Compare* CRYPTOGRAM SPACE, MESSAGE SPACE. *See* KEY EXHAUSTION.

keystone equipment. Includes manufacturing, inspection, or test equipment and is the required equipment for the effective application of technical information and know-how. Keystone materials have the same significant application. (DODD). *See* KNOW HOW.

key stream. *Synonymous with* CRYPTOGRAPHIC BIT STREAM.

key stream generator. In cryptography, the generator that produces the cryptographic bit stream for a stream cipher. *See* KEY GENERATOR, CRYPTO-GRAPHIC BIT STREAM, STREAM CIPHER.

keystroke dynamics analysis. In access control, a biometric technique based the individual typing characteristics of users, e.g. roll over timings between certain groups of characters, represent a convenient biometric characteristic for users logging onto computer terminals.

Such systems can measure over 100 specific characteristics of user's typing. The enrolment period may require some 10,000 keystrokes, but this enrolment data may be captured from the user's normal keyboard activity. For online devices, where each keystroke is directly read into the computer, this technique may require no additional equipment, since the necessary timing mechanisms could be undertaken by the computer itself.

If the login is to be undertaken over a network, however, then a local timing mechanism would be required because transmission over the network will introduce delays between keystrokes. The access decision may be made on the basis of about a dozen keystrokes. *See* BIOMETRICS.

key tape. In cryptography, a magnetic tape storing cryptographic key values.

key translation center. In key management, a center that is operated in a system similar to that of a key distribution center except that the originating party has the capability to generate a data key. A data, or key-encrypting key, to be used for communication with the ultimate recipient is generated by the originator, encrypted with the current key-encrypting key, shared between the originator and center, and forwarded to the center. The key translation center decrypts the received key, re-encrypts it, using notarization, with the key-encrypting key shared between the center and the ultimate recipient and returns it to the originator. The originator then forwards the re-encrypted key to the ultimate recipient. *Compare* KEY DISTRIBUTION CENTER, POINT TO POINT. *See* CRYPTOGRAPHIC KEY, DATA KEY, KEY-ENCRYPTING KEY, KEY NOTARIZATION.

key transport module. *Synonymous with* KEY GUN.

key variant. In key management, a master key derived from another master key by a simple mathematical operation, e.g. inverting selected bits, adding a constant modulo 2 etc. This technique permits the use of a hierarchy of master keys whilst only demanding secure storage for one of them. *See* CRYPTOGRAPHIC KEY, KEY PARTITIONING, MASTER KEY.

key verification code. In cryptography, a number related to the value of a stored cryptographic DES key. The stored cryptographic key is used to encrypt a block of 64 binary 0's, and the key verification code is equal to the most significant 24 bits of the ciphertext. The stored value of the key may be checked by computing its key verification code, and comparing it with a recorded value, without revealing the value of the cryptographic key. *See* CIPHERTEXT, CRYPTOGRAPHIC KEY, DATA ENCRYPTION STANDARD. *Synonymous with* KEY CHECK VALUE.

keyword. In computer security. *Synonymous with* PASSWORD.

kiss off tone. In communications, a tone generated by a central station after it has identified the communicator code and received all inputs from a digital communicator. The digital communicator restores the telephone line for normal voice communications upon receipt of this tone. *See* CENTRAL STATION, DIGITAL COMMUNICATOR.

kiting. In banking, the process of drawing a cheque on one account at the end of a period and paying it into another. The second account would have been credited but the first would not have been debited. Therefore the amount of funds is overstated.

knapsack cipher. In public key cryptography, an early form of public key cryptosystem proposed by Merkle and Hellman in 1978. An alternative form of the knapsack cipher was proposed by Graham and Shamir. *Compare* RSA. *See* GRAHAM-SHAMIR KNAPSACK CIPHER, MERKLE-HELLMAN KNAPSACK CIPHER.

KNF. Key Notarization Facility. *See* KEY NOTARIZATION. **know how.** Includes both the know-how of design and manufacturing and the know-how and related technical information that is needed to achieve a significant development, production, or use. The term know-how includes services, processes, procedures, specifications, design data and criteria, and testing techniques. (DODD).

knowledge base. In programming, a database containing the codified knowledge of a human expert or experts. *See* EXPERT SYSTEMS.

knowledge engineering. In programming, the process of building expert systems. *See* EXPERT SYSTEMS.

known plaintext. In data security, pertaining to techniques employed in cryptanalysis when the cryptanalyst has matched plaintext and ciphertext available. *Compare* CHOSEN PLAINTEXT,

CIPHERTEXT ONLY. *See* CIPHERTEXT, CRYPTANALYSIS, PLAINTEXT.

KNS. Key Notarization System. *See* KEY NOTARIZATION.

Korea. In computer security, a virus that infects floppy and hard disk boot sector, corrupts boot sector, affects runtime operation. *See* VIRUS NAMES.

KSM. *See* KEY SERVICE MESSAGE.

KSOS. In computer security, Kernelized Secure Operating System. The project to strengthen the Unix operating system with a security kernel to make it suitable for multilevel operations. (MTR). *See* KERNELIZED, OPERATING SYSTEM, SECURITY KERNEL, UNIX.

Kukaturbo. In computer security, a virus that terminates and stays resident, infects COMMAND.COM and COM files. *See* VIRUS NAMES.

KVC. *See* KEY VERIFICATION CODE.

KVM/370. In computer security, Kernelized VM/370, the kernelized version of IBM's VM/370 for the S/370 series architecture, being built and verified by System Development Corporation. (MTR). *See* KERNELIZED, OPERATING SYSTEM, SECURITY KERNEL.

L

label. (1) In computer security, a piece of information that represents the security level of an object and that describes the sensitivity of the information in the object. (DOD). *See* OBJECT. (2) In data security, the marking of an item of information to reflect its classification and its set of categories that represent the sensitivity of the information.

(a) Internal Label. The marking of an item of information, to reflect the classification and sensitivity of the information within the confines of the medium containing the information.

(b) External Label. The visible marking on the outside of the medium or the cover of the medium that reflects the classification and sensitivity of the information resident within the medium. (DOE). (3) In computing, one or more characters or a symbol employed in order to identify a program statement, or the entry point of a subroutine. *See* STATEMENT, SUBROUTINE. (4) In computing, an identification record for a tape or disk file.

Label. In computer security, a virus that terminates and stays resident, infects COMMAND.COM and COM files. *See* VIRUS NAMES.

Lamport Diffie signature. In authentication, a method of generating a digital signature.

If a message of N bits is to be sent then the sender generates 2N binary numbers $(x_1, X_1, x_2, X_2 \ldots x_N, X_N)$, each of k bits. A one-way function (f) is used to produce a further 2N binary numbers $(y_1, Y_1, y_2, Y_2 \ldots y_N, Y_N)$, where $y_m = f(x_m)$ and $Y_m = f(X_m)$ for $m = 1$ to N.

The 2N numbers $(y_1, Y_1 \ldots y_n, Y_N)$ and the one-way function (f) form the public key. The message sent $(m_1, m_2 \ldots m_N)$ comprises N bits; the sender transmits x_p if $m_p = 0$ and X_p if $m_p = 1$.

The receiver checks the value of the pth bit by submitting the received number to the one-way function (f) and comparing the result with y_p ($m = 0$) and Y_p ($m = 1$).

Only the sender knows the value of x_p that produces the result y_p, as the output of the one-way function, and the message is therefore signed.

This technique, however, involves a very long public key, which must be changed for every message sent, and considerable message expansion. The size k of each number, in the public key, must be sufficiently high to obviate an attack by exhaustively testing one-way function input numbers to produce the corresponding public key numbers (y and Y). *Compare* DSS, ELGAMAL DIGITAL SIGNATURE, RABIN SIGNATURE. *See* DIGITAL SIGNATURE, ONE-WAY FUNCTION.

LAN. *See* LOCAL AREA NETWORK.

Landwehr's security model for military message systems. In formal models, a model developed for military message systems.

Message systems often involve users in dealing with messages and files such that the classification of one part of the file or message may differ from that of another. A user cleared to top secret might well wish to extract a paragraph labelled confidential, from a secret file, and transfer that paragraph to a file classified confidential. Landwehr's model of military messages systems provide for the automated processing of both formal messages, exchanged by military organizations, and informal messages exchanged by individuals. Such systems allow for the creation, editing and transmission of outgoing messages, display and printing of incoming messages and store and retrieval which allows messages to be organized, and retrieved, on the basis of message files.

From a security viewpoint, handling messages is unlike those conventional data processing applications, where a user processes data, at a single security level, for an extended period. An MMS user may well be concerned with a number of individual messages, each with a different security classification, during a session, e.g. scanning newly arrived messages and printing all those classified secret. Moreover the individual messages may comprise component parts with varying security classifications; such a multilevel information structure is of a type termed container.

The Landwehr model aimed to provide a single integrated security model, for military message systems, which is appropriate to the security policies that those system must enforce. The model is independent of the techniques or mechanisms used to implement the security policy.

In the military message system users login, with a UserID, and then authenticate themselves using passwords, tokens etc. The system will store details of the operations that specific users may undertake on given objects. After login the user then assumes a particular role, within the stored user authorizations, and undertakes operations on messages in accordance with that role. For example, the user may decide to scan incoming messages and print all those that are unclassified. Thus the user with a particular role will initiate certain operations on messages, the system will either permit, or prevent, the user from undertaking such operations according to the stored authorizations and the security policy.

The security of such a system depends upon the users and the security policy imposed by the system. It is important that the system security is such that users are fully aware of the security consequences of their actions. For example, the system should not seek confirmation for security relevant actions from users, when the users may not fully appreciate the significance of such authorizations.

The system cannot prevent a user from compromising information if the user has legitimate access to that information. A number of assumptions are therefore built into the model:

- the Systems Security Officer correctly assigns device security classifications, clearances and role sets;
- the user enters correct classifications when composing, editing and reclassifying information;
- within a classification the user addresses messages to those with a need to know;
- the user exercises discretion in moving information from containers marked CCR (see below) to containers not so marked.

A number of terms, such as clearance, classification, UserID, user, object, etc., have a definitions that are close to the conventional security terms; the definitions that are specific to this model are:

- Role - the job a user is performing, such as downgrader, releaser or distributor. A user is always associated with at least one role at any instant, and the user can change roles during a session. To act in a given role the user must be authorized for it. Some roles may be assumed by only one user at a time (e.g. distributor). With each role comes the ability to perform certain operations.

- Container - a multilevel information structure. A container has a classification and may contain objects (each with its own classification) and/or other containers. In most military message system devices e.g. printers, message files and messages are containers.
- Entity - object or container.
- Container clearance required (CCR) - an attribute of some containers where it is important to require minimum clearance, so that if a user does not have, at least, this clearance, that user cannot view any of the entities within the container. Such containers are marked with the attribute, container clearance required (CCR).
- Identifier - an ID names an entity without referring to other entities. For example, the name of a message file is an ID for that file. Some, but not necessarily all, entities can be named by identifiers. Entities may also be named in other ways, e.g. the current message's text field's third paragraph, this is an indirect reference, see below.
- Direct reference - a reference to an entity is direct if it is the entity's ID.
- Indirect reference - a reference to an entity is indirect if it is a sequence of two or more entity names (of which the first may be an ID), see ID above.
- Access set - a set of triples (user-ID or role, operation, operand index) that is associated with an entity. Some operations require more than one operand, in this case the operand index specifies the particular function of this entity in the operation. Thus if an operation requires two operands, and the operand index is 2, then

the entity, for this triple, would correspond to the second operand.

- Message - a particular type implemented by a military message system, in most MMS family members a message will be a container. A message will include To, From, Date-Time Group, Subject, Releaser and Text Field plus additional fields, e.g. a draft message also includes a Drafter field.

The significant concept, in this model, is that of a container. A message is of the type container, since it has various fields that may have different security classifications. The message text may itself be a container, with some paragraphs classified secret, others unclassified and so on. Devices such as disks, printers etc. will also be containers. The classification of the container itself will be at least equal to the highest classification of the entities within it. The container is unlike an object in the sense that it is based upon a type rather than the current contents, thus a message will be container even though a particular instance comprises only a single object.

In some cases it is permitted for an unclassified user to view the unclassified paragraphs of a message, that also contains secret paragraphs. On other occasions it may be decided that an unclassified user making an indirect reference to a message, e.g. requesting access to the third paragraph of message text of message 39AZ, should not be permitted to view even that unclassified part of a secret message.

The model handles this latter requirement by the use of container clearance required (CCR) classifications. Normally a user may access an entity in a container if the user's clearance is at least equal to the classification of the entity. However, if a container is marked CCR, then a user can only view any entity within it, if that user has a clearance that is at least equal to the security classification of the container itself.

A multilevel secure MMS will be subject to the following assertions listed below.

- 1. Authorization - a user can only invoke an operation on an entity if the user's userID or current role appears in the entity access set along with that operation and with an index value, corresponding to the operand position to which the entity is referred to in the requested operation.
- 2. Classification hierarchy - the classification of any container is always as least as high as the maximum classification of the entities it contains.
- 3. Changes to objects - information removed from an object inherits the classification of that object. Information inserted into an object must not have a classification higher than the classification of that object.
- 4. Viewing - a user can only view (on some output medium) an entity with a classification lower than or equal to the user's clearance and the classification of the output medium. (This assertion applies to entities referred to either directly or indirectly).
- 5. Access to CCR entities - a user can have access to an indirectly referenced entity within a container marked Container Clearance Required only if the user's clearance is greater than or equal to the classification of the container.
- 6. Translating indirect reference - a user can obtain the ID for an indirect entity only if he is authorized to view that entity via that reference.
- 7. Labelling requirement - any entity viewed by a user must be labelled with its classification.

- 8. Setting clearances, etc. - only a user with the role of Systems Security Officer can set the clearance and role set recorded for a userID or the classification assigned to a device. A user's current role set can be altered only by that user or by a user with the role of Systems Security Officer.
- 9. Downgrading - no classification marking can be downgraded except by a user with a role of downgrader who has invoked a downgrade operation.
- 10. Releasing - no draft message can be released except by a user with the role of releaser. The userID of the releaser must be recorded in the release field of the draft message.

The model deals with the problem of aggregation. On the one hand it may be quite permissible for an unclassified user to view unclassified objects in a classified container. On the other hand this action could permit a degree of data aggregation. The user may be able to collect together a mass of unclassified material, which if disclosed in its totality, represents a security hazard. The model handles this situation with the use of CCR marking and direct/indirect references (Assertions 4 and 5). Suppose a container is marked CCR and has a classification secret, whilst it contains a number of unclassified objects. An unclassified user, with the authorizations to invoke a view operation for the object, and who knows the ID of one of these unclassified objects can view it by direct reference (Assertion 4). However, if the user is attempting to glean information, by scanning through the contents of a container, then the CCR marking would prevent that same item being accessed by an indirect reference to the container (Assertion 5). . *Compare* BELL-LA PADULA MODEL. *See* AGGREGATION, CONTAINER, MULTILEVEL DEVICE, OBJECT.

language. In computing, a set of characters, conventions and rules used to convey information. A language may be formally considered to consist of pragmatics, semantics and syntax. *See* FORMAL LANGUAGE, GRAMMAR, PROGRAM LANGUAGE, SEMANTICS, SYNTAX.

LAN security. In communications security, local area networks were initially conceived as systems which would facilitate communication between a wide variety of users and workstations in a limited geographic area with, possibly, gateway connections to wide area networks. They have therefore the potential vulnerabilities of computer systems and wide area networks.

It may be argued that the nature of LAN's is such that they present fewer security problems than WANs:

- the equipment is installed in secure premises;
- the transmission paths are short and traffic is localized to a specific area;
- access protection is guaranteed by passwords;
- fiber optics cabling can be used to inhibit line taps.

In fact the security of a LAN can present quite specific problems namely:

- the network was designed to facilitate the connection of additional workstations and to interface with a variety of manufacturers' equipment;
- the network would typically operate in a broadcast mode so that every message is transmitted to every workstation, a listener at any location is thus guaranteed access to every message;
- a variety of signal types may be transmitted through the network, thus unauthorized users and messages may be difficult to detect;

- a high proportion of computer frauds are perpetrated by employees;
- the flexibility and ease of access to network facilities increases the range of options available to a technically competent, fraudulently inclined employee;
- radio frequency emissions both by the network, and at point of interconnection, unless special precautions are taken.

Deliberate misuse of LANs can arise both from illicit taps and subversion of users or workstations. Illicit taps can be facilitated by the provision of spare interface points incorporated to allow for a future expansion of the network. Use of such illicit taps is also simplified by the well publicized, user friendly protocols of LANs. Passive listening on LANs using personal computers is a major problem.

A illicit workstation connected to a LAN may be used to listen in to sensitive information, or to inject illegal messages. Such messages could be used to disrupt the network or to trigger the release of security relevant information, e.g. the workstation may masquerade as a host to persuade another workstation user to reveal passwords.

An illicit workstation may be prevented or discovered by sensible physical access controls but the attacker may well be a legitimate user of a workstation. In this case the subversion may involve the attacker using a terminal in one area to gain access to sensitive data from another office. The attacker may also subvert the workstation itself by modifying the hardware or software. This opens up the possibility that the workstation would continually monitor and store network data, for later use by the attacker, who would be relatively safe from detection.

LANs are vulnerable not only to deliberate attack but also to network malfunctions which can have serious effects upon the organization's operating efficiency. The problems can arise from:

- inadequate protection against interference from power surges and current spikes;
- network failures or inadequate performance arising from cable installation performed by inexperienced staff or with inadequate attention given to network specifications, poor cable connections (e.g. tap points) is a major source of LAN downtime;
- ring networks, unlike star networks, are particularly susceptible to workstation failure, unserviceable nodes can be bypassed but such failures may cause temporary corruption of network data and degraded network performance, in general there is limited experience in LAN operation and inadequate diagnostic tools are available.

The important security features of a LAN are listed below;

- integrity of transmission, i.e. all valid messages completely and correctly received and invalid messages, from unauthorized users, or modifications of genuine messages, and replays, are inhibited;
- confidentiality of messages, if necessary employing encryption;
- access control for data and resources, i.e. no unauthorized use of workstations, this is particularly important if the LAN has a gateway to a WAN;
- protection against covert use of the network, e.g. by coded signals;
- service availability when the attack is directed towards incapacitating the network or reducing its performance by message flooding.

The protection of LANs can be tackled, at one level, as a management problem. The level of security applied must be appropriate to the estimated losses from an attack or system failure.

LANs were primarily designed to facilitate information interchange among professional and office workers. The impact of security precautions, upon users, should be such that they recognize the purpose and importance of such measures. Over restrictive user procedures may simply discourage use of the network or lead to circumvention of security measures; there are common reports of elaborate passwords written on the side of terminals to serve as aide memoires to the users. Sensible access controls to workstations, protection of cables against illegal taps, monitoring of network traffic etc., can in many cases, provide an adequate level of security.

The network topology itself can be designed to enhance security. For example if the network is effectively divided into subnets then the traffic to and from sensitive areas can be supervised by controlled gateways.

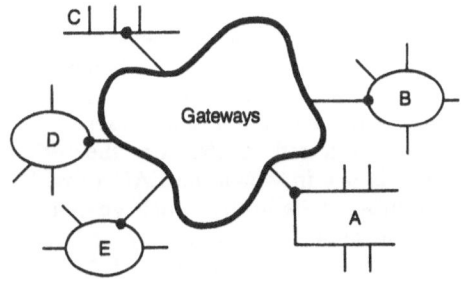

LAN security
LAN gateways

In those applications where security is a major factor the design of the network itself, or at least the interfaces to it, must be considered from a security point of view. A LAN may be designed as a distributed secure system if it is important to minimize the information flow from one security compartment to another. Other proposed security procedures for LANs are based upon the concept of unprotected and protected LANs.

The unprotected LAN security is based upon the assumption that the network is untrusted and unprotected, and the workstation itself may be subject to subversion, therefore security is a host function responsibility. A trusted unit, termed a Special Terminal Interface Unit (STIU), is interposed between the network interface and the workstation. The host will have a corresponding SHIU (Special Host Interface Unit) connected between the computer and the LAN interface. Sensitive messages will be encrypted on an end-to-end basis but the network control data must be sent in clear.

The host is assumed to be a trusted unit; the STIU and SHIU establish each others identities using installed cryptographic keys. The host then establishes the user's identity by requesting the user to input account number, and password, directly into the STIU, to obviate a subversive attack on the workstation. The account information will be sent in clear but the validation of passwords may involve messages encrypted by session keys, which are themselves functions of the password, and therefore only available to the host and user.

The protected LAN, on the other hand, is one in which the LAN provides a service, to its hosts, which guarantees authentication, mutual secrecy and message delivery. The protected LAN distrusts all hosts, workstations and users. Trusted Network Interface Units (TNIUs), which are tamper resistant and unforgeable, are built into the network.

Encryption may be employed for network communication but it is not essential if the physical installation is such that it renders the network impervious to illicit taps. Control of communication over the LAN is the responsibility of a Secure Authentication Server (SAS). In the quiescent state the TNIU can only communicate with the SAS. The user enters an account number, password and requests for resources, communication to other workstations etc. The TNIU transmits this information to the SAS which checks the user's identity, password, authorized privileges and requests. If these are valid the SAS sets up the requested connections and places the TNIU in a state which allows communications over these connections. When the user logs off the TNIU reverts to the quiescent state. *See* ELECTROMAGNETIC EMANATIONS, FIBER OPTICS, FLOODING, LOCAL AREA NETWORK, MASQUERADING, TAMPER RESISTANT MODULE, TRUSTED, VULNERABILITY, WAN, WIDE AREA NETWORK.

LAP. In data communications, Link Access Protocol, a data link layer protocol that is a subset of HDLC and is used in X.25-based networks. *See* DATA LINK LAYER, HDLC, PROTOCOL, X.25.

laser intrusion detector. In physical security, a device in which an alarm is activated when a low power laser beam is interrupted; its operation is similar to that of a photoelectric sensor. *See* PHOTOELECTRIC SENSOR.

last in first out. In computing, a system in which the next item to be selected is the one most recently added to the list. *Compare* FIRST IN FIRST OUT. *See* STACK.

lattice. In mathematics, a partially ordered set for which every pair of elements has a greatest lower bound and a least upper bound. *See* LATTICE MODEL.

lattice model. In database security, a model of the data in a statistical database useful for studying inference controls. The records contain common attributes, other than information directly identifying individuals, and with m attributes an m - dimensional table is formed. For example, with two attributes a 2-dimensional table is formed and the rows and columns are then divided into ranges of values for the attributes. Thus an age attribute may be divided into 10 columns representing ages 0 - 9, 10 - 19 etc. The entries in the individual cells of the table then represent a statistic, e.g. a count, over all records with attributes in the range represented by the cell. Thus in the 2-dimensional case a cell entry could represent the number of individuals in the 30 - 39 age range with 1 - 3 dependents. The m - dimensional table represents the most detailed set of statistics; m-1 dimensional tables are then formed containing corresponding coarser sets of statistics. Thus in the abovementioned 2-dimensional case one of the corresponding one dimensional tables would give counts of all individuals in the various age ranges, and the other a count of all individuals with various numbers of dependents. At the top level of the lattice a one cell table contains (say) the total number of individuals recorded. *See* DATABASE SECURITY, INFERENCE CONTROL, STATISTICAL DATABASE.

LAVA. In risk management, a risk analysis methodology. *See* RISK ANALYSIS METHODOLOGIES.

Law Enforcement Incident Reporting System. In legislation, a U.S. common database on criminal intelligence derived from the National Park Service, Bureau of Reclamation, Bureau of Land Management, Bureau of Indian Affairs and Fish and Wildlife Service. *See* DATA PROTECTION, DATA PROTECTION - U.S.A..

Lazy. In computer security, a virus that terminates and stays resident, infects COMMAND.COM and COM files, affects run-time operation, corrupts program and OVL files. *See* VIRUS NAMES.

LCD. *See* LIQUID CRYSTAL DISPLAY.

LCG. Linear Congruential Generator. *See* RANDOM NUMBERS.

LCM. *See* LEAST COMMON MULTIPLE.

LDDS. Limited distance data set. *See* LIMITED DISTANCE MODEM.

leaf. In computing, the node at the end of a path in a tree structure. *See* TREE STRUCTURE.

leakage. In data security, pertaining to unauthorized flow of information from a user, with access privileges, to a user lacking such privileges. *See* BELL-LA PADULA MODEL, INFORMATION FLOW CONTROL.

Leapfrog virus. In computer security, a virus that terminates and stays resident, infects COMMAND.COM and COM files, affects run-time operation, corrupts program, OVL and data files. *See* VIRUS NAMES.

leased circuit. In data communications, a circuit hired by subscribers for their exclusive and permanent use. It may be a point to point or multidrop connection. *See* MULTIDROP CIRCUIT, POINT TO POINT. *Synonymous with* NONSWITCHED LINE.

leased line. *See* LEASED CIRCUIT.

least common mechanism. In computer security, principle of least common mechanism, one of the principles of secure systems which states - the use of shared mechanisms amongst users should be minimized for their mutual security. *See* PRINCIPLES OF SECURE SYSTEMS.

least common multiple. In mathematics, the smallest integer that can be exactly divided by each of two specified integers, e.g. the least common multiple of 6 and 8 is 24. *Compare* GREATEST COMMON DIVISOR.

least cost network design. In data communications, a network of optimum design which meets the design specification at the least possible cost.

least privilege. In computer security, principle of least privilege, one of the principles of secure systems which states - every process should operate with the minimum level of privilege necessary to perform the requisite task. *See* PRINCIPLES OF SECURE SYSTEMS.

least significant bit. In computing, the bit which occupies the rightmost position in a binary number. *See* BIT.

least significant digit. In computing, the digit which occupies the rightmost position in a number and therefore has least weight.

Lehigh. In computer security, a virus that terminates and stays resident, infects COMMAND.COM, corrupts program and OVL files, formats or overwrites all or part of disk. *See* VIRUS NAMES.

LEIRS. *See* LAW ENFORCEMENT INCIDENT REPORTING SYSTEM.

Leprosy. In computer security, a virus that terminates and stays resident, infects COMMAND.COM, COM, EXE and OVL files. *See* VIRUS NAMES.

Leprosy-B. In computer security, a virus that infects COMMAND.COM, COM and EXE files. *See* VIRUS NAMES.

letter bomb. In computer security, a form of logic bomb, contained in electronic mail, that is triggered when the mail is read. *See* LOGIC BOMB, MALICIOUS CODE.

level. (1) In computer security. *See* SECURITY LEVEL, INTEGRITY LEVEL. (2) In communications, a general term for the magnitude of a signal, used for

voltage, current and power. (3) In data communications, the number of bits in each character of an information coding system. (4) In data communications, pertaining to the number of discrete signal elements that can be transmitted in a given modulation scheme. *See* MODULATION.

LFSR. *See* LINEAR FEEDBACK SHIFT REGISTER.

Liberty. In computer security, a virus that terminates and stays resident, infects COMMAND.COM, COM, EXE and OVL files, affects run time operation, corrupts program and OVL files. *See* VIRUS NAMES.

LIFO. *See* LAST IN FIRST OUT.

light conduit. In communications, an assembly of fibers, in a fiber optics cable, used for the transmission of light sources rather than encoded optical signals. *See* FIBER OPTICS.

light guide. *See* FIBER OPTICS.

LIMDIS. In data security, LIMited DIStribution. A handling caveat or special marking indicating limited distribution of the associated information. *See* HANDLING CAVEATS, SPECIAL MARKINGS.

limited access. In access control, limiting access to the resources of a system only to authorized personnel, users, programs, processes, or other systems, for instance computer networks. (AFR). *See* LIMITED ADP ACCESS SECURITY MODE.

limited ADP access security mode. In access control, an ADP system or network is operating in the limited access security mode when the type of data being processed is categorized as unclassified and requires the implementation of special access controls to restrict the access to the data only to individuals who by their job function have a need to access the data. (OPNAVINST). *See* LIMITED ACCESS.

limited distance modem. In data communications, a modem which does not apply a complex modulation scheme to the data before transmission but which applies the digital input (or a simple transformation of it) to the transmission channel. Used only for short distances of transmission. *See* MODEM. *Synonymous with* BASEBAND MODEM.

limited protection. In communications security, a form of short-term communications security applied to the electromagnetic 'or acoustic transmission of unclassified information which warrants protection against simple analysis and easy exploitation but does not require the level of protection needed for classified information. (AR).

Lindop Committee. A U.K. committee which considered the problems of data protection and privacy, and reported in 1976. *See* DATA PROTECTION, DATA PROTECTION - U.K., PRIVACY, YOUNGER COMMITTEE.

line. (1) In communications, a metallic conductor used for transmission purposes. (2) In data communications, a string of characters accepted by a central computer as a single block of input, e.g. all the characters entered prior to a carriage return command.

line adaptor unit. *See* MODEM.

linear complexity. In mathematics, the length of the shortest linear feedback shift register which can be used to generate a given sequence of binary digits; it is therefore a property of that sequence. *See* BINARY DIGIT, LINEAR FEEDBACK SHIFT REGISTER. *Synonymous with* LINEAR EQUIVALENCE, RECURSION LENGTH.

linear congruential generator. *See* RANDOM NUMBERS.

linear equivalence. *Synonymous with* LINEAR COMPLEXITY.

linear feedback shift register. In cryptography, a shift register in which the digit entered into the first stage is a linear function of current values in the other stages of the register. Such shift registers may be employed in the production of pseudorandom numbers or cryptographic bit streams for stream ciphers. *See* CRYPTOGRAPHIC BIT STREAM, LINEAR RECURRENCE RELATION, RANDOM NUMBERS, RECURSION ANALYSIS, SHIFT REGISTER, STREAM CIPHER.

linear function. In mathematics, a function which comprises the sum of terms, each of which is a constant multiplied by one, and only one, of the variables which are of first order only, e.g. $P = 5X + 10Y$.

linear query. In database security, a query in a statistical database which is a linear function of a particular nonkey field of a set of records. For example, if the salaries of employees in records 1, 2, 3 ... n are S_1, S_2,.... S_n then a linear query on these fields is: $c_1S_1 + c_2S_2 + ... + c_nS_n$ where c_i is an arbitrary real number selected by the enquirer. Linear queries can be used by attackers to obtain information concerning individuals from statistical databases unless appropriate inference controls are applied. *See* DATABASE SECURITY, INFERENCE CONTROL, STATISTICAL DATABASE.

linear recurrence relation. In cryptography, a relation of the form:

$$S_{r+n} = d_0S_r + d_1S_{r+1} + ... d_{n-1}S_{r+n-1}$$

where S is a sequence S_0, S_1, S_2 ...

Linear recurrence relationships are used to define the outputs of linear shift registers. If the linear shift register is used to produce a cryptographic bit stream for a stream cipher it is important that a cryptanalyst should be unable to deduce the linear recurrence relation from an available segment of the cryptographic bit stream. *See* CRYPTO-GRAPHIC BIT STREAM, LINEAR FEED-BACK SHIFT REGISTER, RECURSION ANALYSIS, STREAM CIPHER.

line communications. In communications, the transmission and reception of electric signals over a cable.

line control. In data communications, the sequence of signals used to control a channel. *See* CHANNEL.

line driver. In data communications, a hardware component that interfaces a device to a line, providing functions such as adding control characters to output data, interpreting control characters on incoming data, buffering incoming data, converting parallel to serial transmission etc. *See* PARALLEL TRANSMISSION, SERIAL TRANSMISSION.

line impedance. In communications, the impedance of a telecommunication line.

line level. (1) In data communications, the signal strength on a communications channel. (2) In data communications, a set of protocols concerned with the transmission and control of a transparent stream of bits along a communications channel. *See* DECIBEL, PROTOCOL, TRANSPARENT.

line load. In communications, the amount of traffic on a line, expressed as a percentage of its utilization to its total capacity. *See* TRAFFIC.

line protocol. *Synonymous with* LINK PROTOCOL.

line sensor. In physical security, a sensor with detection pattern within a narrow line between two or more points, e.g. a laser beam. *See* LASER INTRUSION DETECTOR, POINT PROTECTION.

line speed. In data communications, the rate at which signals may be transmitted over a given channel, measured in bauds. Effective speed varies with the capabilities of the equipment used and the amount of noise on the line. *See* BAUD, SHANNON's LAW.

line termination equipment. In data communications, data circuit terminating equipment, usually for a non telephone circuit. *See* DATA CIRCUIT TERMINATING EQUIPMENT.

line transient. In communications, an unwanted voltage pulse of very short duration, which can often produce errors in digital circuits not designed to minimize the effects of such interference.

link. (1) In communications, a transmission path of specified characteristics between two points, e.g. a telephone wire or a microwave beam. As well as the physical aspect of transmission, a link includes the protocol, associated devices and software, i.e. it can also be logical. *See* PROTOCOL, LOGICAL CHANNEL. (2) In computing, a routine that interfaces two separate programs, and through which control information is passed.

linkage. In computer security, the purposeful combination of data or information from one information system with that from another system in the hope of deriving additional information; in particular, the combination of computer files from two or more sources. (FIPS). *See* COMPUTER MATCHING.

link encryption. (1) In cryptography, end-to-end encryption within each link in a communications network. (FIPS). (2) In communications security, the application of online crypto-operations to a link of a communications system so that all information passing over the link is encrypted in its entirety. (FIPS). *See* ON LINE CRYPTO-OPERATION. *Compare* END-TO-END ENCRYPTION, NODE ENCRYPTION. *See* NETWORK ENCRYPTION, OSI SECURITY. *Synonymous with* DATA LINK ENCRYPTION, LINK TO LINK ENCRYPTION.

link protocol. In data communications, a protocol controlling the transfer of data over a communication line so that a meaningful exchange of information may take place. Link protocols deal with message formats, error recovery procedures, control characters, block lengths etc. *See* ADCCP, BISYNC, HDLC, PROTOCOL, SDLC. *Synonymous with* LINE PROTOCOL.

link to link encryption. *Synonymous with* DATA LINK ENCRYPTION, LINK ENCRYPTION.

liquid crystal display. In computing, a display device made of two glass plates sandwiched together with a special fluid. The liquid darkens when a voltage is applied.

Lisbon. In computer security, a computer virus that infects COM files, corrupts program and OVL files. *See* VIRUS NAMES.

list. (1) In computing, an ordered set of items of data. *Compare* STACK. (2) In computing, an action to print or display items of data that meet specific criteria. *Compare* WRITE.

Little Pieces. In computer security, a computer virus that terminates and stays resident, infects COM and EXE files, affects run time operation, corrupts program and OVL files. *See* VIRUS NAMES.

load. In computing, to enter data or a program into a computer memory from an auxiliary storage device.

loading. In communications, a method of improving the transmission characteristics of a telephone line by inserting a series of inductances along the line at regular intervals.

load life. In communications, the number of hours a device may dissipate power under specified operating conditions whilst remaining within its specified operational performance.

load sharing. In computer networks, a technique whereby computers on a network share work loads to attain a reasonably uniform distribution. This is achieved by the off-loading of jobs from a heavily loaded computer to one more lightly loaded. *See* JOB.

loan utilization. *Synonymous with* CURRENT UTILIZATION.

local alarm system. In physical security, a standalone alarm system designed to protect a user's premises, normally including an audible alarm device; it may, or may not, also be linked to a remote central station. *See* CENTRAL STATION.

local area network. In data communications, a high bandwidth bidirectional communications network which operates over a limited geographic area, typically an office building or a college campus.

The incentive for the development of LAN's arose from the proliferation of micro- and minicomputers in large organizations and the perceived trend to supply office workers with more communication devices - facsimile, communicating word processors, video and speech systems, etc. It is clearly desirable that a unified approach be adopted to the intercommunication of such varied devices. LAN's provide the computer user with the opportunity to communicate with other workers, to supply and access common data and share expensive peripherals, hard disk storage devices, sophisticated printers, etc.

The LAN comprises a cable network linking the constituent nodes. Each node corresponds to a user workstation equipped with a physical network interface device. The topology of the network may be ring, star or bus.

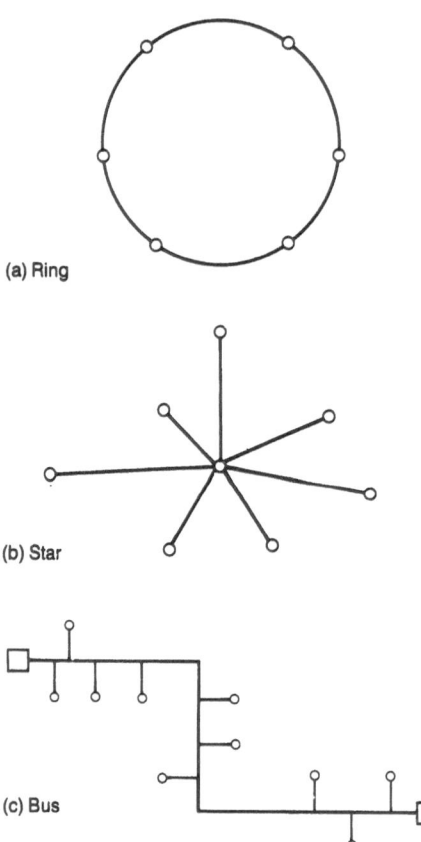

(a) Ring

(b) Star

(c) Bus

local area network

The star network is the logical successor to the traditional mainframe computer - multiterminal configuration but although it provides for a simple access protocol it has three disadvantages: network failure with central controller breakdown, low speed with controller bottlenecks and extensive wiring. The

current trends tend to favor bus and ring topologies.

The mode of transmission may be either baseband or broadband; the transmission medium may be twisted pair copper wire, coaxial cable or fiber optics. The access protocols available for bus and ring networks are CSMA-CD, control token or message slot. The success of LANs depended upon the confidence of users in the establishment of standards to guarantee trouble free interconnection and operation of a wide range of user devices.

Two common standards are Ethernet and Cambridge Ring. Other systems using CSMA-CD protocols often describe themselves as Ethernet type. IBM have also developed a LAN standard using a baseband ring and token passing protocol. The ECMA approved a LAN standard in 1982 which is compatible with Ethernet.

An important consideration to the LAN user is the interface card which connects the workstation to the network. The internal high speed bus structures of computers, facilitate the interconnection to the LAN and the interface card can be simply plugged into the backplane. The interface must also contain the software to handle data transfers. The ISO-OSI seven layer structure is significant in the design of LAN standards particularly where the LANs will require gateways to other LANs and wide area network. *Compare* METROPOLITAN AREA NETWORK, WIDE AREA NETWORK. *See* BACKPLANE, BANDWIDTH, BASEBAND, CAMBRIDGE RING, COAXIAL CABLE, CONTROL TOKEN, CSMA-CD, ECMA, ETHERNET, FACSIMILE, FIBER OPTICS, GATEWAY, ISO OSI, LAN SECURITY, MESSAGE SLOT, NODE, PROTOCOL, TOPOLOGY, TWISTED PAIR, VIDEOTEX.

local echo. In data communications, a technique in which the communications software, in a transmitting computer, displays the data transmitted into the communication link on the local terminal. *Compare* ECHOPLEX. *See* TERMI-NAL. *Synonymous with* LOCAL SOFT-WARE ECHO.

local fire alarm system. In physical security, an electrically operated system which produces alarm signals at one or more locations on the protected premises. *See* LOCAL ALARM SYSTEM.

local mode. In data communications, an internal operating state of a data terminal. In this condition a terminal is not able to accept incoming calls.

local network. In banking, a system in which the card issuer and acquirer are one and the same. *Compare* INTERCH-ANGE, LOCAL AREA NETWORK. *See* ACQUIRER, ISSUER.

local noninterfering coded station. In physical security, a fire alarm station that, on activation, transmits not less than four rounds of uninterrupted coded alarm signals. *See* CODED SYSTEM, ALARM STATION, POSITIVE NONINTER-FERING AND SUCCESSION CODED STAT-ION.

local software echo. *Synonymous with* LOCAL ECHO.

local transaction. In banking, a transaction between an ATM, or EFTPOS terminal, and the financial institution which both issues the card and controls the terminal. *Compare* INTERCHANGE TRANSACTION. *See* ATM, PIN MAN-AGEMENT AND SECURITY, EFTPOS.

lock. (1) In computing, mechanism for controlling multiple accesses to a common device such as a bus or memory. *See* BUS. (2) In computing. *See* FILE LOCK, RECORD LOCK.

lock-and-key protection system. In computer security, a protection system that involves matching a key or password with a specified access require-

ment. (FIPS). *See* ACCESS, KEY, PASS-WORD.

locking. In communications, a term used for the process of synchronizing a repetitive signal source with timing signals.

lockout. (1) In peripherals, a keyboard action which only registers the first key depression when a number of keys are depressed virtually simultaneously. (2) In databases, a technique in database systems designed to avoid update inconsistency. Only one user is allowed to access an item, for update or modification, at any one time. A disadvantage of this technique is that it can lead to a deadly embrace. If users Alice and Bob both wish to update a pair of records concurrently, X and Y, then lockout can produce the following undesirable sequence :

- Alice acquires X;
- Bob acquires Y;
- Alice requests Y but it is locked by Bob;
- Bob requests X but it is locked by Alice.

See RECORD, UPDATE INCONSISTENCY. (3) In communications, the inability of a subscriber on a circuit controlled by an echo suppressor to get through to a called party because of either excessive local noise or continuous speech from one party. *See* ECHO SUPPRESSOR. (4) In computing, a technique used to prevent access to critical data by two separate programs in a multiprogramming environment. *Compare* LOCK UP. *See* FILE LOCK, RECORD LOCK.

lock up. In computing, an unwanted state of a system from which it cannot escape, e.g. a deadly embrace in the claiming of common resources. *Compare* LOCKOUT.

lockword. In data security, a password

associated with a file or a data set. A file creator may specify a lockword for a file, or data set within a file, and thereafter users must input the lockword to gain access to the file or data set. If the lockword is revealed to another user then that user will normally only be allowed read access to the file, only the creator will have the unique combination of lockword knowledge and user identification, required for write access etc. *See* DATABASE SECURITY, DATA SET, FILE ACCESS, PASSWORD.

loco. *See* HIGH COERCIVITY CARD. *Synonymous with* LOW COERCIVITY.

log. In computing, a record or journal of a sequence of events of the jobs run through a computer.

logarithm. In mathematics, the logarithm of a number is the power to which the base must be raised to give that number. Thus in decimal arithmetic the logarithm (to base 10) of 100 is 2, since $10^2 = 100$. *See* BASE.

logging. In computer security, a record kept either manually or by the computer system to keep track of events that take place with respect to the system. *See* SECURITY LOG.

logic. In computing, the physical circuits which implement logical operations and functions. *See* LOGICAL OPERATOR.

logical. (1) Conceptual or virtual, as compared with physical or actual. (2) In computing, a two state quantity that can be stored as a single bit. Often used for such purposes as status flags. *See* BIT, FLAG.

logical access control. In access control, the use of procedures related to information and knowledge, e.g. passwords, rather than physical security. *Compare* PHYSICAL SECURITY.

logical channel. In data communications, a circuit that is used for packet switching operations between a terminal and a network node. The circuit may be a permanent virtual connection or one set up for the duration of the call. *See* PACKET SWITCHING, PERMANENT VIRTUAL CIRCUIT, VIRTUAL CIRCUIT.

logical completeness measure. In computer security, a means for assessing the effectiveness and degree to which a set of security and access control mechanisms meets the requirements of a set of security specifications. (FIPS). *See* ACCESS CONTROL MECHANISMS.

logical database. In databases, a database as viewed by its users. This structure of the data need not be the same as that of the physical database. *Compare* PHYSICAL DATABASE.

logical data independence. In databases, pertaining to the structure of the data that permits the schema to be changed without affecting the application programmer's view of the data. *Compare* PHYSICAL DATA INDEPENDENCE. *See* DATA INDEPENDENCE, SCHEMA.

logical expression. In mathematics, a statement that contains logical operators and operands and can be reduced to a value that may only be either true or false. For example, the boolean formulae for an EXCLUSIVE OR function Z = (A AND NOT B) OR (NOT A AND B) is a logical expression. *See* BOOLEAN ALGEBRA, EXCLUSIVE OR, LOGICAL OPERATOR.

logical operator. In computing, an operator that can be used in a logical expression to indicate the action to be performed on the terms in the expression. The logical operators are AND, OR, and NOT. All logic expressions can be written in terms of these three basic operations.

logical party. In key management, one or more physical parties that form one member of a communicating pair. (ANSI). *See* COMMUNICATING PAIR.

logical record. In computing, a record which is defined in terms of its functions rather than the physical manner in which it is stored. *Compare* PHYSICAL RECORD. *See* RECORD.

logical security. In data security, security provided by the operating system and basic software. *Compare* PHYSICAL SECURITY. *See* OPERATING SYSTEM.

logical threat. In computer security, a threat of the possibility of destruction or alteration of software or data. It would be realized by logical manipulation within the system rather than by a physical attack. For example, the threat could arise from an unauthorized user with dishonest motives, or from an unauthorized user who managed to access the system either on site or from a remote location through a network. *Compare* ACCIDENTAL THREAT, ACTIVE THREAT, DELIBERATE THREAT, PASSIVE THREAT, PHYSICAL THREAT. *See* THREAT.

logical unit. In data communications, a port through which a user gains access to the services of a network. *See* PORT.

logic bomb. In computer security, a form of Trojan Horse with a malicious action that is triggered by a specific event, e.g. number of times that a program is executed. *Compare* TIME BOMB. *See* MALICIOUS CODE, TROJAN HORSE.

logic circuit. In computing, a circuit comprising one or more gates or that performs a particular logic function.

logic path analysis program. In computing, a software utility that converts a source program into a structure chart or flow diagram. It may be used by audi-

tors to gain an understanding of the logic of the program. *See* COMPUTER AUDIT PACKAGES.

log in. *Synonymous with* LOG ON.

log off. In computing, an instruction to a computer system by a user that a session is to be terminated. *Compare* LOG ON. *Synonymous with* LOG OUT.

log on. (1) In access control, procedure used to establish the identity of the user, and the levels of authorization and access permitted. *Synonymous with* LOG IN, SIGN IN, SIGN ON. (2) In computing, a request by a user for access to a computer, usually a time sharing system. In initiating a connection, the user may have to supply identification such as an account number and password. *Compare* LOG OFF. *See* TIME SHARING, PASSWORD. *Synonymous with* LOG IN.

log out. *Synonymous with* LOG OFF.

long haul network. In data communications, networks that connect host computers in different cities using public telephone network, satellite communications etc. *See* HOST.

longitudinal parity check. (1) In computing, a parity check performed on a group of binary digits in a longitudinal direction for each track on a magnetic tape. (2) In data communications, a system of error checking performed at the receiving station after a block check character has been accumulated. *See* BLOCK CHARACTER CHECK, PARITY CHECKING.

longitudinal redundancy check. In codes, a redundancy code technique using one 8 bit check byte per transmitted block of data. The most significant bit of the check byte provides a parity check bit for the most significant bits of the characters in the block and so on for all other bit positions. *See* BIT, BYTE,

PARITY CHECKING, REDUNDANT CODE, X-MODEM.

long key. In cryptography, a character string used as a mnenomic form of a corresponding native key. *See* KEY CRUNCHING, NATIVE KEY.

loop. (1) In computing, a sequence of instructions which is repeated until some specific condition occurs. (2) In communications, a link or channel.

loopback test. In communications, a method of fault isolation on a local loop in which a signal is sent from a test point on a modem and returned to the modem. *See* MODEM.

loop checking. In data communications, a method of detecting transmission errors in which received data is returned to the sending station for comparison with the original data.

loophole. In computer security, an error of omission or oversight in software or hardware which permits circumventing the access control process. (FIPS). *See* ACCESS CONTROL. *Synonymous with* FAULT, FLAW.

loop network. In communications, a network configuration in which there is a single path between all nodes and the path is a closed circuit. *Compare* STAR. *See* NODE, RING.

loop plant. In communications, all the cables, ducts, joint boxes, cabinets, poles and ancillary equipment used to connect subscribers to their local office or exchange.

loro account. In banking, an account serviced by a bank on behalf of an account owner bank. (ANSI). *Synonymous with* VOSTRO ACCOUNT.

loss. (1) In risk management, the quantitative measure of expected deprivation due to a threat acting upon a vulnerable system resource. *See* ANNUAL LOSS EXPECTANCY, THREAT, VULNERABILITY. (2) In communications, a general term for the loss of signal energy during transmission along a circuit, expressed as the ratio of the signal power at the start of the circuit to the signal power at the receiver, usually expressed in decibels. *See* ATTENUATION, DECIBEL, SIGNAL.

low coercivity. In access control, a term used for magnetic stripe cards in which the magnetic material has a coercivity of about 300 oersted. *Compare* HIGH COERCIVITY. *See* COERCIVITY, HIGH COERCIVITY CARD, OERSTED.

low level language. In computing, a language that is closely related to the machine code language of a computer, i.e. one that is translated by an assembler. *Compare* HIGH LEVEL LANGUAGE.

low speed. In data communications, systems which operate at less than 2400 bits per second.

low water mark. In data security, pertaining to two or more security levels, the least of the hierarchical classifications, and the set intersection of the nonhierarchical categories. (DCID). *See* BELL-LA PADULA MODEL.

LRC. *See* LONGITUDINAL REDUNDANCY CHECK.

LTE. *See* LINE TERMINATION EQUIPMENT.

Lucifer. In cryptography, a product cipher developed by IBM which formed the basis for the development of the data encryption standard. It used 128 bit data blocks and a 128 bit key. *See* DATA ENCRYPTION STANDARD, PRODUCT CIPHER.

M

MAA. *See* MESSAGE AUTHENTICATION ALGORITHM.

MAB. *See* MESSAGE AUTHENTICATION BLOCK.

MAC. *See* MANDATORY ACCESS CONTROL, MEDIUM ACCESS CONTROL, MESSAGE AUTHENTICATION CODE. *Synonymous with* AC, DAC.

machine code instruction. In computing, an instruction expressed in the machine language for the particular processor. High and low level language instructions are eventually translated into corresponding machine code instructions before they are executed by the processor. *See* HIGH LEVEL LANGUAGE, LOW LEVEL LANGUAGE, MACHINE LANGUAGE.

machine independence. In computing, pertaining to a software design philosophy allowing programs written for one type of computer to be run without change on another type of computer. *See* PORTABILITY.

machine language. In computing, a language for programs that can be expressed directly in a binary format acceptable to the central processing unit. All other programming languages, e.g. low or high level, have to be translated into binary machine code before being executed in the central processing unit. *Compare* HIGH LEVEL LANGUAGE, LOW LEVEL LANGUAGE. *See* MACHINE CODE INSTRUCTION, TRANSLATOR.

MAC residue. In authentication, the 32 bits, of the 64 bit output checksum generated to form the MAC, that is not transmitted as part of the authentication block. *See* CHECKSUM, MAC, TRANSACTION KEY SYSTEM.

macrobend loss. In communications, the leakage of light when the optical cable is bent. *Compare* MICROBEND LOSS. *See* FIBER OPTICS.

magnetically encoded card. In access control and banking, a card that can be used for access control or for authority to initiate a transaction. The plastic card contains magnetically coded information on the surface, or embedded within it. The card may be of the magnetic spot, magnetic stripe or Wiegand effect type. *Compare* SMART CARD. *See* MAGNETIC SPOT CARD, MAGNETIC STRIPE CARD, WIEGAND EFFECT.

magnetic disk. In computing, a flat disk with a magnetizable surface layer on which data can be stored by magnetic recording. There are two main types of disk : hard and floppy, the former being rigid using a metal or glass base, the latter having a flexible, plastic base. The hard disk rotates at high speed (2400 rpm) so that data may be accessed without undue delay. A disk is logically formatted into tracks, with each track having a number of sectors. *See* FLOPPY DISK, HARD DISK.

magnetic field intensity. In electronics, the magnetic force required to produce a desired magnetic flux, given as the symbol H. (DOD). *See* OERSTED.

magnetic flux. In electronics, lines of force representing a magnetic field.

(DOD). *See* MAGNETIC FIELD INTENS-
ITY.

magnetic remanence. *See* REMAN-
ENCE.

magnetic saturation. In electronics,
the condition in which an increase in
magnetizing force will produce or result
in little or no increase in magnetic flux.
(DOD). *See* MAGNETIC FLUX.

magnetic sensor. In physical security,
a sensor that operates by detecting a
change in a magnetic field. *Compare*
ELECTRIC FIELD SENSOR.

magnetic spot card. In access control,
a card with magnetic spots embedded in
the laminated material to provide coding
of a unique identifier. *Compare*
MAGNETIC STRIPE CARD, WIEGAND
EFFECT. *See* MAGNETICALLY ENCODED
CARD.

magnetic stripe card. In access control
and banking, a plastic card with a narrow magnetic stripe that may be employed for access control or authority to
initiate a transaction. The data is normally encoded in three horizontal tracks
along the stripe. The magnetic fields
may be of low or high level intensity,
the former are employed for credit cards
whilst some high security access control
systems employ high intensity field
material because it provides greater
stability. Magnetic stripe cards can be
encoded or re-encoded with relatively
inexpensive equipment, special magnetic
stripes are therefore sometimes employed to inhibit the production of counterfeit cards. *Compare* MAGNETIC SPOT
CARD, WIEGAND EFFECT. *See* SAND-
WICH TAPE, WATERMARK TAPE. *Synonymous with* MAG STRIPE CARD.

magnetic tape. In computing, a
common storage medium for computer

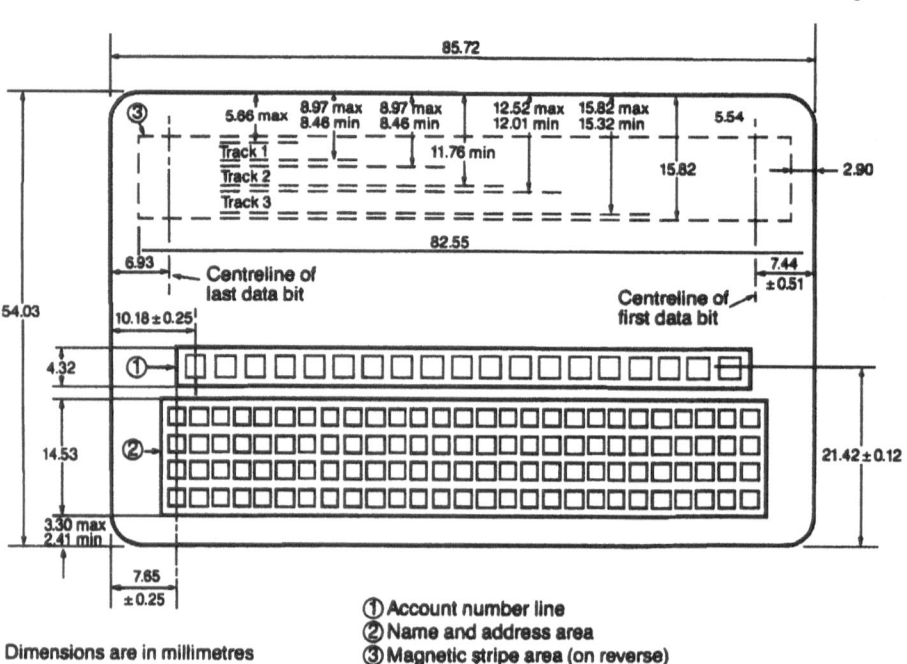

Dimensions are in millimetres

① Account number line
② Name and address area
③ Magnetic stripe area (on reverse)

magnetic stripe card

software and data. In personal computer applications the tape is 1/2 or 1/4 inch wide and comprises a magnetic coating of fine particles of ferric oxide suspended in an inert binder on a polyester backing. Magnetic tape is stored on reels, cassettes or cartridges. *Compare* MAGNETIC DISK.

mag stripe card. *Synonymous with* MAGNETIC STRIPE CARD.

mail box. *See* ELECTRONIC MAIL.

mainframe. In computing, a term normally applied to a large general purpose computer installation serving a major section of an organization or institution. *Compare* MICROCOMPUTER.

main memory. In computing, that part of a computer that holds data and programs, for random access by the central processing unit, in the form of binary digits. Storage and memory are synonymous. Main memory usually has a fast access but because it is relatively costly its size is usually restricted.

maintainability. In computing, the effort required to locate and fix an error in an operational program.

maintenance. (1) In reliability, any activity intended to keep a machine in a specified, operational condition, including preventive maintenance and corrective maintenance. *See* PREVENTIVE MAINTENANCE, CORRECTIVE MAINTENANCE. (2) In computing. *See* SOFTWARE MAINTENANCE.

make v. buy. In computing and data communications, the choice senior management face in either developing inhouse software or purchasing products/services from external suppliers.

malfunction. In computer security, a failure in the operation of system hardware.

malicious code. In computer security, software that is intentionally included in a system for the purpose of causing loss or harm (e.g. Trojan Horse). *See* BLOB, CHECK KITING, COOKIE MONSTER, FLYING DUTCHMAN, FRENCH ROUND-OFF, LOGIC BOMB, MALICIOUS LOGIC, MORRIS WORM, SALAMI TECHNIQUE, TIME BOMB, TRAPDOOR, TROJAN HORSE, VIRUS, WORM.

malicious logic. In computer security, hardware, software, or firmware that is intentionally included in a system for the purpose of causing loss or harm (e.g. Trojan Horse). (DOD). *See* MALICIOUS CODE, TROJAN HORSE.

malware. In computer security, software that contains malicious code. *See* MALICIOUS CODE. *Synonymous with* VANDALWARE.

MAN. *See* METROPOLITAN AREA NETWORK, MUNICIPAL AREA NETWORK.

managed data network. In communications, the use of one independent service organization to manage or operate a corporation's data communications. *Compare* VALUE ADDED NETWORK SERVICE.

manchester encoding. In data communications, a method of encoding binary data for transmission that ensures each bit, whether a 1 or a 0 produces a signal transition in each bit period. A 1 bit is encoded as signal high in the first half period and a signal low in the second, a 0 bit is encoded as a signal low followed by a signal high.

mandatory access control. In access control, a means of restricting access to objects based on the sensitivity (as represented by a label) of the information contained in the objects and the formal authorization (i.e. clearance) of subjects to access information of such sensitivity. (DOD). *Compare* DISCRETIONARY AC-

CESS CONTROL. *See* OBJECT, SENSITIV-
ITY LABEL, SUBJECT .

mandatory security. (1) In computer
security, the imposition of security
measures on entities. (2) In computer
security, the aspect of the security policy
insisted upon by system administrators,
that requires the provision of security
services for one or more instances of
communication. *Compare* DISCRETION-
ARY SECURITY.

mandatory security policy. In access
control, an access control policy in
which the right of a user to access a set
of data is determined on the basis of a
security clearance of the user and a
security classification of the data, e.g. a
user cleared to confidential would not be
allowed to read a file classified as
secret. *Compare* DISCRETIONARY ACCESS
CONTROL. *See* MANDATORY SECURITY.

manipulation detection. In data security, a mechanism which is used to detect
whether a data unit has been modified
(either accidentally or intentionally).
(ISO).

man-made noise. In communications,
interference caused by electrical machines, car ignition systems etc. *See*
INTERFERENCE.

man month. The amount of useful
work that an individual will contribute,
tackling a given task, within one month;
often used to assess the cost of writing a
program or designing a system.

manual alarm initiating device. In
physical security, a device that relays an
alarm signal when it is manually operated. *Compare* AUTOMATIC ALARM
INITIATING DEVICE.

manufacturing automation protocol.
In data communications, a protocol
developed for communications in a
factory automation environment. *Com-*

pare TECHNICAL AND OFFICE PROTO-
COL.

MAP. *See* MANUFACTURING AUTOMA-
TION PROTOCOL.

mapping. (1) In mathematics, a relationship between two or more quantities.
(2) In databases, the relationship between a given logical structure and its
physical representation on the computer.
See LOGICAL DATABASE, PHYSICAL
DATABASE.

Mardi Bros. In computer security, a
virus that terminates and stays resident,
infects floppy and hard disk boot sector,
corrupts boot sector, affects run-time
operation. *See* VIRUS NAMES.

Marion. In risk management, a risk
analysis methodology. *See* RISK
ANALYSIS METHODOLOGIES.

mark. In communications, an impulse
on a data circuit that corresponds to the
active condition of the receiving
apparatus. *Compare* SPACE. *See* BIT.

marking. In data security, the process
of placing a sensitivity designator (e.g.
'confidential') with data such that its
sensitivity is communicated. Such marking may be achieved by a rubber stamp
on a document, a header in a network
message, a special field in a database
record etc. *See* HEADER, LABEL, SPRAY
PAINT.

masking. In communications security,
pertaining to a technique in which transmitted information is hidden by the
addition of noise, music, tones etc.

masquerade. In authentication, the
pretence by an entity to be a different
entity. (ISO). *See* MASQUERADING.

masquerading. In data security, an
attempt to gain access to a system by
posing as an authorized user. (AR).

Compare SPOOFING. *Synonymous with* IMPERSONATION, MIMICKING.

mass storage device. In computing, a device having a large storage capacity, e.g. magnetic disk, magnetic drum. *See* MAGNETIC DISK, MASS STORAGE.

master code card. (1) In access control, an access control card used to set the codes, in a card reader, required by subsequent cards to gain access. (2) In access control, a universal access control card that grants entry or exit when entered in any card reader in the system. *See* CARD READER.

master coded system. In physical security, a configuration in which a common coded alarm signal is relayed for at least four rounds; thereafter it may be silenced manually or automatically. *See* CODED SYSTEM.

master file. In computing, a file containing relatively permanent information that is used as a source of reference and is updated periodically. *See* FILE.

master key. (1) In key management, a key-encrypting key. In a hierarchy of key-encrypting keys the master key will be the top level key-encrypting key. *See* KEY-ENCRYPTING KEY, KEY MANAGEMENT, THREE-LAYER ARCHITECTURE, TWO-LAYER ARCHITECTURE. (2) In cryptography, a long life key to a cryptographic function, used to encrypt long term data or other cryptographic keys.

master station. In data communications, a station that has accepted an invitation to pass data to one or more slave stations. At any one time, there can only be one master station on a link. *See* STATION, SLAVE.

matching. In computing, pertaining to the matching of items from the processing stream of an application with others developed independently so as to identify items unprocessed through either of the parallel systems.

matching network. In physical security, the necessary equipment and circuit arrangement to connect an audio signal to an alarm line. *See* ALARM LINE.

material. In data security, data processed, stored, or used in, and information produced by, an ADP system regardless of form or medium, e.g., programs, reports, data sets or files, records, and data elements. (DODD).

materiality. In auditing, pertaining to the minimum amount of money that should be detected in examinations by audit procedures.

mathematical model. A formal statement of the mathematical relationship between the elements of a system that are of particular interest. Mathematical models usually represent a simplified form of reality and are often used for prediction.

matrix. (1) In mathematics, a multidimensional array of quantities, manipulated in accordance with the rules of matrix algebra. (2) In computing, a logic network whose configuration is an array of intersections of its input/output leads, with logic circuits connected at some of these intersections. The network usually functions as an encoder or decoder.

matrix methodology. In risk analysis, a relatively straightforward technique for analyzing system security and for evaluating the level of risk.

Matrix methodology is particularly relevant to electronic payment systems. The following account is based on a paper published by the central banks of the Group of Ten Countries under the aegis of the Bank for International Settlements.

Introduction.

The elements of the methodology consist of a description of the security requirements, and a set of recommended safeguards. On the basis of this approach, the methodology identifies successively:

- the critical processing/communications functions;
- the threats that apply to each function;
- the vulnerabilities that apply to each threat;
- the safeguards corresponding to each vulnerability.

By this means a succession of matrices are logically developed: a function-threats matrix, a threats - vulnerabilities matrix, a vulnerabilities - safeguards matrix. The logical product of these three matrices is the final functions - safeguards matrix, that, as will be explained later, is the matrix that is of interest to the system management and users.

The functions of a system are automated macro-functions that characterize an operational aspect of the system and which, in some cases, may even be identical with the system itself. Examples of functions are: transfer of funds, automated clearing house, administrative message system, etc.

The threats that apply to each function are defined as events that might disrupt the system or diminish confidence in the system. Different generic threats could be identified, that could be grouped together for example in the following three categories:

- unauthorized disclosure of information (by insiders or outsiders);
- unauthorized modification of data (accidental or deliberate, by insiders or outsiders) and non-delivery of transactions;
- denial of service (short or long-term).

These threats are of a generic nature and can be considered to be typical of an electronic payment system. Vulnerabilities are defined as the means through which threats can occur, e.g. eavesdropping, unauthorized use of terminals, application software failures, etc.

Using this methodology, one could expect to detect thirty to forty vulnerabilities. In one application of this methodology vulnerabilities were identified relating to communications, software, personnel, physical facilities, kinds of data and ways of getting to data.

Finally, the safeguards are the protective measures corresponding to each vulnerability. Obviously the safeguards are very numerous; in one study, over 100 were identified, organized into different categories, relating to technical safeguards, physical safeguards and to procedures and policy.

The matrices.

The operational key to the methodology consists in the development and use of matrices based on the elements, viz. functions, threats, vulnerabilities and safeguards. These matrices in question are progressively more complex. Starting with the three basic matrices:

- functions - threats;
- threats - vulnerabilities;
- vulnerabilities - safeguards;

other matrices are derived by multiplying these, the most important derived matrix being functions - safeguards.

Two considerations are of basic importance for the effective application of the methodology. Firstly, careful judgement must be exercised when determining the value of cells of the matrices, and this becomes increasingly difficult as the number of elements increases, creating problems of consistency.

Secondly, for this reason and because of the inherent complexity of the matrices, it is necessary to automate the methodology, e.g. by using a personal computer. The complexity of the matrices usually results in some thousands of decisions having to be taken relating to the cells of the matrices. Consequently it is vital, both in effecting matrix multiplication and in identifying inconsistencies, to be able to perform an iterative process that enables one to determine the most precise values for the cells of the matrices - revising them in the light of inconsistencies - while constantly exercising careful judgement.

General considerations.
The value of the matrix methodology lies in the fact that it could employ an automated technique based on a set of independent basic elements and on the use of intercorrelated matrices, but is nevertheless mainly based on judgement: the approach does not substitute mechanics for judgement. Indeed, the person carrying out the investigation makes an evaluation on several levels:

- in initially assigning values to the cells of the matrices;
- in examining the inconsistencies that arise with the derived matrices;
- in evaluating the series of safeguards that constitute the minimum set of the security architecture.

In fact, the calculation yields for the vulnerabilities - safeguards matrix the number of times that each safeguard is required.

It is implicit that the safeguards most often selected are to be deemed - subject to verification-indispensable; thus, while some safeguards need to be added to cover vulnerabilities for which the selected safeguards provide no protection, unnecessary safeguards can be removed.

Use of the evaluation mechanism results in two sub-sets of safeguards, a main sub-set of 'above the line' safeguards and a secondary sub-set of 'below the line' safeguards.

A further characteristic of the methodology is that there are several matri-

ces, some basic and some derived, each with its own significance valid for a particular evaluation. In particular, there are two matrices worthy of consideration, one of chief interest to technicians: the vulnerabilities - safeguards matrix, and the other of principal interest to management and users: the functions - safeguards matrix. This distinction seldom appears in other methodologies, and is of considerable importance in that starting with the same elements, two different situations are highlighted, each addressed to a different sector.

This emphasizes the point that when the architecture of a network is being designed the corrections to the matrices for the iteration can come from different sources: management, technicians and users. Furthermore, from a management viewpoint, on-the-spot checks effected during the running of the system can be carried out by the three sectors independently and possibly in opposition to each other: the ensuing management instrument is definitely more effective than conventional ones for the checking of security.

A variation of the above methodology could be in choosing safeguards for categories of personnel. Indeed, in view of the fact that many jobs (console operations, programmers, systems analysts, etc.) are of considerable sensitivity from the security angle, a special job classification safeguards matrix can be defined, and clearly these safeguards differ from those already defined for the other matrices. A value of high, medium or low is assigned to each cell in the matrix.

Example.
Consider a bank teleprocessing system connecting the bank's EDP center to about 200 branches and customer installations; the system deals mainly with wire transfer and accounting messages.

The functions to be examined, therefore, are the following three:

312 matrix methodology

matrix methodology
Table 1.   Functions – threats matrix.

FUNCTIONS	THREATS					
	Unauthorized disclosure by outsider	Unauthorized modification by insider	Unauthorized modification by outsider	Inadvertent modification	Non-delivery of messages	Long-term denial of service
Wire transfer messages	L	H	H	M	M	H
Accounting messages	L	H	M	M	M	M
Sensitive administration messages	H	M	M	M	M	M

H = high importance; L = low importance; M = medium importance.

matrix methodology
Table 2.   Threats – vulnerabilities matrix.

Unauthorized disclosure by outsider	Unauthorized modification by insider	Unauthorized modification by outsider	Inadvertent modification	Non-delivery of messages	Long-term denial of service	Number of threats per vulnerability	VULNERABILITIES
–	Y	Y	–	–	–	2	C1 Message insertion through wiretapping
–	Y	Y	–	–	–	2	C2 Message modification through wiretapping
Y	–	–	–	–	–	1	C3 Eavesdropping
Y	Y	Y	–	–	–	3	C4 Visual eavesdropping
Y	Y	Y	–	–	–	3	C5 Authorized terminals
–	–	–	Y	–	–	1	C6 Transmission errors
–	–	–	Y	–	–	1	C7 Operator's console capabilities
Y	Y	Y	Y	Y	–	5	S1 Application software design/development
–	Y	–	–	–	–	1	S2 Application software maintenance
–	–	–	Y	Y	–	2	S3 Software conversions
–	–	–	Y	Y	–	2	S4 Environmental software failure
–	–	–	Y	Y	–	2	S5 Application software failure
–	–	–	Y	Y	–	2	S6 Production data
–	Y	–	–	–	–	1	S7 Source programs
–	Y	–	Y	–	–	2	S8 System libraries
–	–	–	–	Y	–	1	S9 Intelligent terminals used for message entry
Y	–	Y	–	–	–	2	S10 Security data
–	Y	–	–	–	–	1	S11 Maintenance/diagnostic facilities
–	Y	–	Y	–	–	2	S12 Data management facilities
Y	Y	Y	Y	Y	Y	6	P1 Transaction entry procedures
–	–	Y	–	–	–	1	P2 Intercept/supervisory terminals
–	Y	–	–	–	–	1	P3 Abnormal operating conditions
–	–	–	Y	Y	–	2	F1 Hardware failure
–	–	–	–	Y	Y	2	F2 Utility failure
–	–	–	Y	Y	Y	3	F3 Communication line failure
–	–	–	Y	Y	Y	3	F4 Natural/manmade disaster
6	12	8	13	11	4	–	Total threats

Y = realistic threat for the given vulnerability.

matrix methodology
Table 3.   Communications vulnerabilities – safeguards matrix.

VULNERABILITIES

C1 Insertion — wiretapping	C2 Modification — wiretapping	C3 Eavesdropping	C4 Visual eavesdropping	C5 Authorized terminals	C6 Transmission errors	C7 Operator's console	SAFEGUARDS
Y	–	–	–	–	–	–	1.1 Serial number messages
–	–	–	–	–	Y	–	1.2 End-to-end acknowledgement
Y	Y	–	–	Y	Y	Y	1.3 Reconciliation
Y	Y	–	–	–	Y	Y	2.1 Message authentication code
Y	Y	Y	–	–	Y	–	2.2 Encryption
–	–	–	–	–	–	–	3 System software
–	–	–	–	Y	Y	Y	4.1 General identification/authentication/ access control
–	–	–	–	–	–	Y	4.2 Password for access to sensitive objects
–	–	–	–	–	–	Y	4.3 Encryption of sensitive objects
–	–	–	–	–	–	Y	4.4 Establishment of closed user groups
–	–	–	–	–	–	Y	4.5 Operator's console control
–	–	–	–	–	–	–	5.1 Written back-up/recovery procedures
–	–	–	–	–	–	Y	5.2 Test of recovery/restart procedures in application programs
–	–	–	–	–	–	Y	5.3 Recovery/restart facilities in environmental software
–	–	–	–	–	–	Y	5.4 Back-up copies of data, software, procedures
–	–	–	–	–	–	Y	6.1 Control consoles log
–	–	–	–	–	–	–	6.2 Log of changes in security table
–	–	–	Y	–	–	–	6.3 Unauthorized attempt reports
–	–	–	Y	–	–	–	6.4 Terminate log-on failures and report
–	–	–	–	–	–	–	6.5 Log system dumps
–	–	–	–	–	–	–	6.6 Trace capability
–	–	–	–	–	–	–	6.7 Audit trails
–	–	–	–	Y	–	–	7.1 Lock communications facilities
Y	Y	Y	–	–	–	–	7.2 Control circuit test equipment
–	–	–	Y	–	–	–	7.3 Restrict visual access
Y	Y	Y	Y	Y	–	Y	7.4 Control unauthorized/vendor access
–	–	–	–	–	–	–	7.5 Back-up facilities
–	–	–	–	–	–	–	7.6 Back-up power
–	–	–	–	–	Y	–	8.1 Prevent maintenance schedule
–	–	–	–	–	–	Y	8.2 Review console logs
–	–	–	–	–	–	–	8.3 Software security features
–	–	–	–	Y	–	–	8.4 Abort/log/alarm security violations
–	–	–	–	–	–	–	8.5 Control hardware monitors
–	–	–	–	–	–	–	8.6 Diagnostic facilities and programs
–	–	–	–	–	Y	–	8.7 Collect traffic/performance statistics
–	–	–	–	–	–	Y	8.8 Simple operator dialog
–	–	–	–	–	–	–	9.1 Up-to-date user manuals, run books, etc.
–	–	–	–	–	Y	–	9.2 Problem report/track procedures
–	–	–	–	Y	–	Y	9.3 Security violation reporting procedures
–	–	–	–	–	–	–	10 Security policy
4	3	1	–	4	5	11	Technical controls
2	2	2	2	2	–	1	Physical controls
–	–	–	–	2	3	3	Procedural controls
6	5	3	2	8	8	15	Total vulnerabilities

Y = realistic safeguard.

matrix methodology
Table 4. Functions – safeguards matrix.

	SAFEGUARDS	FUNCTIONS		
		Wire transfer messages	Accounting messages	Sensitive administration messages
1.1	Serial number messages	H	–	M
1.2	End-to-end acknowledgement	H	M	M
1.3	Reconciliation	H	H	H
2.1	Message authentication code	H	M	H
2.2	Encryption	H	M	H
3.1	Structured design	H	H	H
3.2	Library program	H	H	H
3.3	Application documentation	H	H	H
3.4	Application release procedures	H	H	H
3.5	Application testing	H	M	M
3.6	Emergency software modify procedure	H	H	H
3.7	Change control procedure	H	H	H
3.8	System documentation	H	H	H
3.9	System testing	M	M	M
3.10	Data dictionary	H	H	H
3.11	Data administrator	H	M	M
4.1	General identification/authentication/ access control	H	H	H
4.2	Password for access to sensitive objects	H	H	H
4.3	Encryption of sensitive objects	H	M	H
4.4	Establishment of closed user groups	H	–	M
4.5	Operator's co le control	H	I	M
5.1	Written back-up/recovery procedures	H	H	H
5.2	Test of recovery/restart procedures in application programs	H	H	H
5.3	Recovery/restart facilities in environmental software	M	M	M
5.4	Back-up copies of data, software, procedures	H	H	H
6.1	Control consoles log	H	H	M
6.2	Log of changes in security table	H	H	H
6.3	Unauthorized attempt reports	H	H	H
6.4	Terminate log-on failures and report	H	H	H
6.5	Log system dumps	M	–	M
6.6	Trace capability	M	M	M
6.7	Audit trails	H	M	M
7.1	Lock communication facilities	H	–	M
7.2	Control circuit test equipment	M	–	M
7.3	Restrict visual access	H	–	M
7.4	Control unauthorized/vendor access	H	M	H
7.5	Back-up facilities	H	M	M
7.6	Back-up power	H	M	M
8.1	Prevent maintenance schedule	M	M	M
8.2	Review console logs	H	H	H
8.3	Software security features	H	H	H
8.4	Abort/log/alarm security violations	H	H	H
8.5	Control hardware monitors	M	M	M
8.6	Diagnostic facilities and programs	M	M	M
8.7	Collect traffic/performance statistics	M	M	M
8.8	Simple operator dialog	M	M	M
9.1	Up-to-date user manuals, run books, etc.	H	H	H
9.2	Problem report/track procedures	M	M	M
9.3	Security violation reporting procedures	H	H	H
10.1	Security and privacy policy	H	M	H
10.2	Security administrator	H	M	H
10.3	Contingency plans	H	–	M
10.4	Audit sensitive areas	H	M	H

H = high importance, M = medium importance.

- wire transfer messages;
- accounting messages;
- sensitive administration messages.

Table 1 presents the functions - threats matrix. Six threats are identified:

- unauthorized disclosure of information by an outsider;
- authorized modification of data by an insider;
- unauthorized modification of data by an outsider;
- inadvertent modification of data;
- non-delivery of messages;
- long-term denial of service.

Table 2 presents the threats vulnerabilities matrix. Twenty-six vulnerabilities are identified (seven for communications, twelve for software, three for personnel/procedures, four for physical facilities).

Table 3 gives the vulnerabilities - safeguards matrix for communications; similar matrices can be developed for software and procedural/physical facilities.

Finally, Table 4 gives the functions - safeguards matrix, as derived from all the vulnerabilities-safeguards matrices. *See* RISK ANALYSIS.

MCC. *See* MISCELLANEOUS COMMON CARRIER.

McCulloh-type system. In physical security, a system comprising equipment and wiring that enable an alarm initiating system to operate despite an open and/or ground at the same time.

MC system. *See* MASTER CODED SYSTEM.

MDC. In authentication, Manipulation Detection Code or Modification Detection Code, a data block appended to a message, prior to encipherment, in order to provide a degree of redundancy that will reveal modifications in ciphertext. The MDC is produced as a function of the complete message. *Compare* MAC. *See* MESSAGE AUTHENTICATION.

MDF. In data security, modification detection code. *See* MESSAGE AUTHENTICATION.

MDN. *See* MANAGED DATA NETWORK.

mean life. In reliability, the average or expected life of a given item of equipment, normally a function of design parameters and usage. *Compare* MEAN TIME BETWEEN FAILURE.

mean time between failure. In reliability, for a given period in the life of a piece of equipment, the average of the periods of time between consecutive failures under stated conditions. *Compare* MEAN LIFE.

mean time to recover. In reliability, the average time required to bring up a system into operation after repair, e.g. this may include reprocessing from the last checkpoint. *See* CHECKPOINT.

mean time to repair. In reliability, the average time needed to repair, or to correctively maintain, a piece of equipment.

medium access control. In data communications, a sublayer in the Open Systems Interconnection Reference Model that is concerned with the process of allocating a broadcast channel to which there are contending users. *See* BROADCAST, CARRIER SENSE MULTIPLE ACCESS WITH COLLISION DETECTION, OPEN SYSTEMS INTERCONNECTION.

medium speed. In data communications, transmission rates between 2400 baud and the limit of a voice grade circuit, 9600 baud. *See* BAUD, VOICE GRADE CHANNEL.

meet in the middle. *See* MULTIPLE DES ENCIPHERMENT.

memo advice. In banking, advice to a third party by the account servicing bank of a debit or credit to the account owner, issued only with authorization by the account owner. (ANSI). *See* ACCOUNT SERVICING BANK.

memory bounds. In computer security, the limits in the range of storage addresses for a protected region in memory. (FIPS).

memory bounds checking. *Synonymous with* BOUNDS CHECKING.

memoryless control. In database security, a form of inference control in which the criteria for the authorization of a query do not depend upon a record of previous queries or a list of permitted statistics. *Compare* A PRIORI CONTROL, AUDIT BASED CONTROL. *See* CELL RESTRICTION, INFERENCE CONTROL, TABLE RESTRICTION.

memory protection. In computing, a hardware or software method of ensuring that an application program does not access data, or write, in a memory location allocated to another user or a system utility. When a task accesses a given block of memory a check is made to determine whether it has the right to do so and an interrupt is generated if unauthorized access is attempted. *Compare* FILE PROTECTION. *See* APPLICATION PROGRAM, BOUNDS CHECKING.

mental poker. In cryptography, a form of communication in which information can be concealed from individual parties exchanging data but which also ensures that the concealed information can be subsequently checked by all parties.

In its simplest form it involves Alice and Bob playing poker remotely over the telephone. Neither trusts the other to play fairly and the cryptographic system employed must meet the specifications listed below.

- Alice and Bob must receive poker hands that are: disjoint, concealed from the other player and are equally likely for each player.
- Any additional cards drawn during play must conform to the above requirements and a player must be able to reveal a card without compromising the security of other cards in the hand.
- At the end of the game the players must be able to confirm that the game was played fairly and no player cheated.

A solution to this problem can be provided with an exponentiation cipher. The enciphering/deciphering keys for Alice and Bob are E_1, D_1, E_2, D_2 respectively. The enciphering transformations must commute so that:

$$eE_1(eE_2(M)) = eE_2(eE_1(M))$$

The process of game playing is as follows:

- Each of the 52 cards are represented by 52 messages M_1, M_2.... M_{52}, e.g. M_1 = ace of clubs.
- Alice encrypts the 52 above-mentioned messages with enciphering key E_1 thus producing 52 encrypted messages $eE_1(M_1)$, $eE_1(M_2)$....$eE_1(M_{52})$. These encrypted messages are forwarded to Bob in a random order.
- Bob selects 5 messages and returns them to Alice who accepts them as her playing hand, Alice decrypts these messages with D_1.
- Bob then selects 5 messages for his own hand and encrypts them with E_2, thus forming 5 messages of the form $eE_2(eE_1(M_i))$. These 5 doubly encrypted messages are also returned to Alice.
- Alice deciphers the 5 doubly encrypted messages with D_1, i.e. $dD_1(eE_2(eE_1(M_i)) = dD_1(eE_1(eE_2(M_i)) = eE_2(M_i))$ since the encryption algorithm is commutative.

- The 5 messages decrypted by Alice are then returned to Bob who then reveals them, by decryption with D_2, and accepts them as the playing hand.
- The game is played with cards revealed by either player; new cards can be distributed using the same techniques as those described above.
- At the end of the game both players reveal their keys to enable the progress of the game to be checked.

Exponentiation ciphers provide the required commutative encryption qualities i.e.

$$eE(M) \equiv M^E \bmod n$$
$$M \equiv dD(eE(M))$$
$$\equiv (eE(M))^D \bmod n$$

where M is coprime with n and $E.D = 1 \pmod{\phi(n)}$; $\phi(n)$ is the Euler totient function.

The technique can be subjected to attack, i.e. the players can cheat, if any message M is a quadratic residue modulo n. If a message M is a quadratic residue modulo n then it will retain this property under encryption by exponentiation. This information can place Bob in an advantageous position.

At the outset Bob knows that the cards can be divided into two sets, i.e. those that are quadratic residues and those that are not. Upon receipt of the encrypted messages it is possible to separate them into these two classes and Bob then has some additional information to aid in the selection and subsequent play. For example, if Bob always selects quadratic residue messages for Alice then he knows that there are certain cards that Alice cannot hold. *See* DISJOINT, EULER'S GENERALIZATION, EULER TOTIENT FUNCTION, EXPONENTIATION CIPHER, MODULO ARITHMETIC, QUADRATIC RESIDUE, RSA.

meridional ray. In communications, a ray of light that passes through the axis of the fiber as a result of an internal reflection, and is confined to a single plane. *See* FIBER OPTICS.

Merkle-Hellman knapsack cipher. In cryptography, a public key system devised by Merkle and Hellman based upon the knapsack problem.

This problem derives its name from a cylindrical knapsack and a set of rods, of the same diameter as the knapsack. The rods are of various lengths and it is required to determine a subset of the rods that exactly fit the knapsack. In mathematical terms this can be expressed as a one-dimensional array of integers $(a_1, a_2.....a_n)$ and a given integer C. The problem is to determine a subset of those integers that exactly sums to C.

An exhaustive search involves 2^n computations and the computational effort thus rises exponentially with the number of integers n. The knapsack problem is an NP problem, i.e. it is easy to check a solution but it is difficult to find the correct one.

With a superincreasing series of integers, however, the solution is quite straightforward. In this case the integers $(a_1, a_2.....a_n)$ are ordered and any member of the set is greater than the sum of all preceding terms.

Consider the superincreasing series (1, 5, 10, 20, 40), if the length of the knapsack, C, is 26 then the subset of integers summing to C can be quickly determined by a well conducted search as described below.

- Commence with a decision on the presence or otherwise of the largest integer $a_5 = 40$. Since C = 26 then a_5 cannot be in the set.
- Next $a_4 = 20$ and C = 26. In this case a_4 is less than C and it must be in the set because the sum of all the lesser terms (1 + 5 + 10)

cannot exceed 20, by the definition of a superincreasing series.

- The problem can now be redefined in terms of a new length of knapsack 26 - 20 = 6 and the smaller set of integers (1, 5, 10).
- Proceeding as above it is found that 10 is not in the set, but 5 and 1 are.
- The subset of integers is thus 20 + 5 + 1 = 26.

The knapsack problem thus represents a trapdoor one-way function. It is a one-way function because, given a set of integers it is easy to determine their sum C; the reverse operation of determining the subset, given C, is however computationally infeasible for large n in the general case, that involves an exhaustive search of all 2^n possibilities.

The trapdoor arises because it is possible to convert the problem from the general case to an easy knapsack problem, with a superincreasing series, given certain secret information.

The process of encryption and decryption using a knapsack cipher is described below.

- A superincreasing sequence $(a_1, a_2.....a_n)$ is selected, with a sufficiently high value of n to render an exhaustive search computationally infeasible.
- Two large coprime numbers w and m are selected with $w < m$. The inverse w^{-1} is computed where $w.w^{-1} \equiv 1 \pmod{m}$. This calculation can be performed with a method based upon Euclid's algorithm.
- A new set of integers is computed on the basis: $b_i = a_i.w \pmod{m}$, for $i = 1 .. n$.
- The set $(b_1, b_2.....b_n)$ is then published as the public enciphering key. The values of b may be reordered to disguise the original superincreasing series; the values of w and m are kept secret.

- The data to be enciphered is expressed in terms of blocks of binary digits with n bits per block, e.g. $(d_1, d_2.....d_n)$ where $d_i = 0$ or 1.
- The n bit blocks are then enciphered by computing the scalar product $(d_1, d_2.....d_n).(b_1, b_2..... b_n)$

$$C = \sum_{i=1,n} b^i d_i$$

Thus b_i is included in the sum C only if $d_i = 1$.

- The encrypted message, comprising a series of integers C_j, (corresponding to the scalar product for block j), is transmitted.
- The receiver, in possession of the secret information w^{-1} and m, converts each value of C to P where, $P \equiv C.w^{-1} \pmod{m}$.
- The original data $(d_1, d_2.....d_n)$ is easily determined from P and the superincreasing series $(a_1, a_2..a_n)$ as described above.

The secret information w^{-1} and m provides the trapdoor information inasmuch as it converts the hard knapsack problem with series $(b_1, b_2.....b_n)$ into the easy knapsack problem $(a_1, a_2.....a_n)$. The conversion to the easy knapsack problem is illustrated below.

- $P \equiv Cw^{-1} \pmod{m}$

  $\equiv w^{-1} \sum^n (d_i.b_i) \pmod{m}$

  $\equiv \sum^n (a_i.d_i) \pmod{m}$

- The superincreasing series $(a_1, a_2.....a_n)$ allows $(d_1, d_2.....d_n)$ to be quickly determined from the integer P.

Knapsack ciphers have the advantage that the computational effort in the encryption/decryption processes is relatively low, as compared with RSA, since only a limited number of multiplication and addition operations are involved. However they suffer from two disadvantages. Firstly the key is several kilobits in length, this is compared with a key of a few hundred bits for RSA or 64 bits for DES. Secondly there is message expansion and the ciphertext is, on average, twice as long as the original plaintext.

Knapsack ciphers have been subjected to attack and it is reported that a fast algorithm has been developed for crypt-analytic attacks. Shamir produced a paper in 1982 on a successful knapsack attack. *Compare* RSA. *See* DES, EUCLID'S ALGORITHM, GRAHAM SHAMIR KNAPSACK CIPHER, MODULO ARITHMETIC, NP CLASS, SCALAR PRODUCT, SUPERINCREASING SERIES, TRAPDOOR ONE-WAY FUNCTION.

Mersenne prime. In mathematics, a prime number of the form $2^n - 1$. If for a given n, $2^n - 1$ is prime, then n must be a prime number, however the converse is not true, i.e. if n is prime then $2^n - 1$ is not necessarily prime. *Compare* FERMAT PRIME. *See* PRIME NUMBER.

mesh. In computer networks, a configuration in which there are two or more paths between any two nodes. *Compare* RING, STAR. *See* NODE.

p with $2^p - 1$ prime	Discoverer	Year
19	Cataldi	1588
31	Euler	1722
61	Pervushin	1883
89	Powers	1911
107	Powers	1914
127	Lucas	1876
521 607 1,279 2,203 2,281	Lehmer–Robinson	1952
3,217	Riesel	1957
4,253 4,423	Hurwitz–Selfridge	1961
9,689 9,941 11,213	Gillies	1963
19,937	Tuckerman	1971
21,701	Nickel–Noll	1978
23,209	Noll	1978
44,497	Slowinsky–Nelson	1979
86,243	Slowinsky	1982

Mersenne prime

message. (1) A communication containing one or more transactions or one or more items of related information. (ANSI). (2) In data communications, an arbitrary amount of information whose beginning and end are defined or implied. *See* MESSAGE FORMAT.

message authentication. (1) In banking, the technique used between the sender and receiver to validate the source and part or all of the text of a message. (ANSI). (2) In authentication, the processes undertaken to ensure that:

- the message originated with the purported sender;
- the message contents have not been accidentally or intentionally altered or rearranged;
- the message has been received in the sequence that it was sent by the originator;
- the message was received by the intended recipient.

Message authentication is therefore concerned with the identities of the sender and receiver, modifications to message contents and the problem of replay. It is assumed that undesirable changes may be wrought by accident, e.g. noisy communication lines, or by a malicious third party. The problem of disputes, where the sender accuses the receiver of message alteration, or attempts to revoke the message, lies within the realm of digital signatures.

The authentication of the message sender requires some method that allows the recipient, Bob, to confirm that the message could only have been formed by the purported sender, Alice. This may imply that Alice holds some secret information not available to a third party. Clearly such secret information cannot simply be included in the message, e.g. as a password, since an attacker could access that information. Nor is it sufficient to encrypt that secret information. Suppose that Alice has a secret password P and encrypts it with a secret key k for inclusion in messages to Bob. An attacker would be unable to derive P from ek(P); Bob in possession of k and P, would be able to confirm that decryption of ek(P) produces Alice's password P. However, if the same encryption key is used for a number of messages, the attacker could subsequently present a message containing the ciphertext ek(P), which in itself is not confidential, and have the message accepted by Bob as authentic. Clearly the secret information must be securely bound to the whole message.

If the message contains some degree of redundancy, encryption of the whole message with a secret key enables the Bob to check that a given meaningful message could only have been produced by Alice with knowledge of that key. This is under the proviso that the encryption processes does not permit ciphertext blocks to be re-arranged or blocks from other messages to be substituted. If Alice sends two messages using the DES electronic codebook mode, both encrypted with the same key, then an attacker might re-arrange blocks of the ciphertext message, or substitute blocks from one message into the other, and there is no guarantee that Bob would spot the changes in the subsequent plaintext.

An effective method of guaranteeing that a message was formed in its entirety by Alice, and not subsequently corrupted or modified deliberately, involves a function that maps the message into an authenticator block. A hashing algorithm accepts as input a message of any length and produces a fixed length output. Changing a bit, or character, in the input message must cause a change in the output of the hashing function; likewise interchanging bits or characters in the input message must impact upon the output.

Since the hashing function maps any length message into a fixed size authenticator block, then the fixed number of potential authenticator blocks is less than the number of possible input messages. Consider an authenticator block comprising only 3 bits. In effect there are 8 different authenticator blocks and all potential messages may be subdivided in 8 categories; all the messages in a given category hash to the same authenticator block.

Clearly it is imperative that input messages, mapping onto the same authenticator block, should be highly dissimilar; otherwise a small change in a message would not guarantee a change in the authenticator block. Hence the authenticator block must be of sufficient length to guarantee a high number of message categories, and the hashing algorithm should ensure that members of the same category are highly dissimilar. In financial circles the authenticator block (MAC) is 32 bits in length.

Alice may append an authenticator block, formed by a hashing function, to a message so as to provide Bob with a degree of assurance that the message has not been corrupted. On receipt of the message, Bob operates upon it with the same hashing algorithm and checks the result with the appended authenticator block; if they check out then Bob may be reasonably sure that the message has not been accidentally corrupted. With a well designed hashing function, it is extremely unlikely that the accidental corruption would modify the input message into a second message which mapped to the same authenticator block.

However, Bob may not be convinced that such a check is a guarantee against malicious action of an attacker. If the authenticator is transmitted by a secure channel, and the hashing function is such that it is computationally infeasible to produce a second message corresponding to a given authenticator block, then Bob may indeed have some confidence against malicious modification. This technique may, for example, be employed to guarantee that delivered software has not been maliciously changed. Bob receives the software and

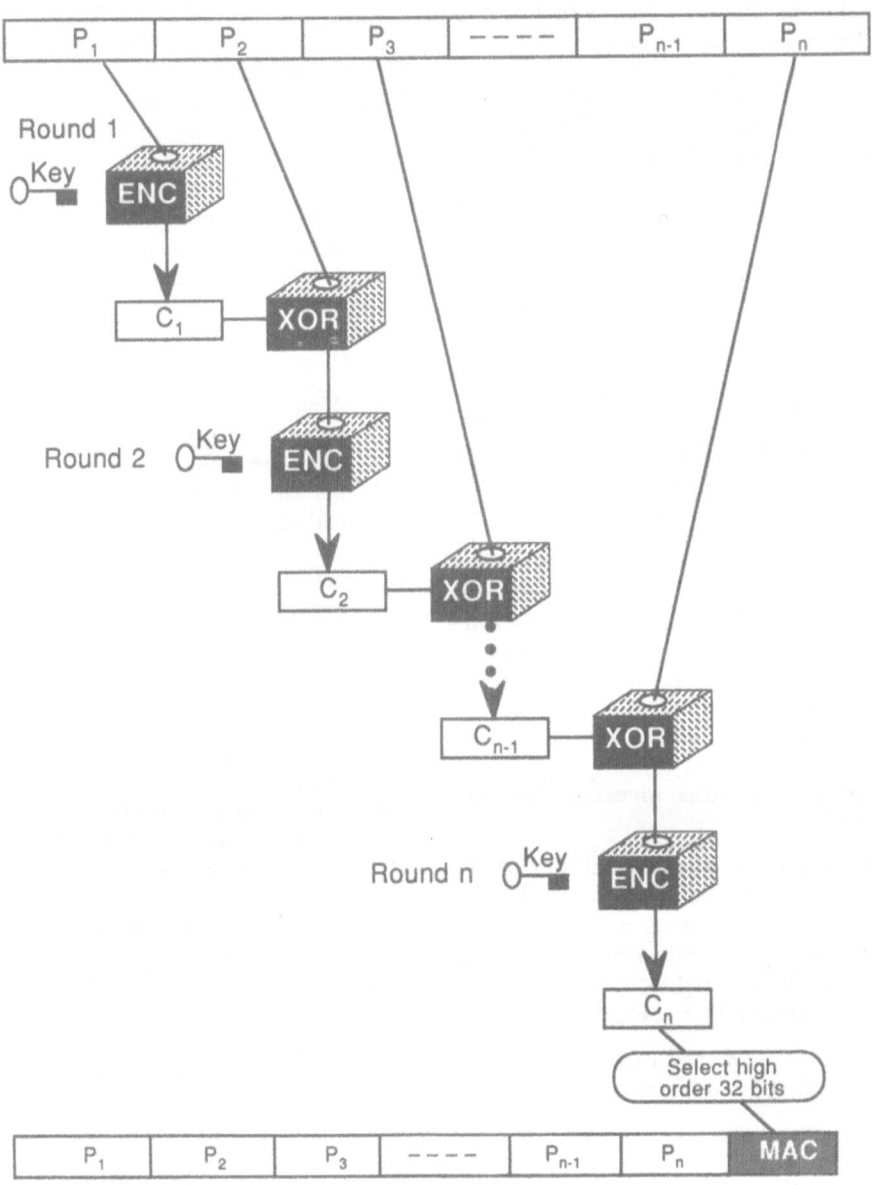

message authentication code

322 message authentication

can also obtain a guaranteed authenticator block, e.g. from the software manual provided by a trusted source. Bob can then check the integrity of the software by comparing the result of the hashing of the software, with the published authenticator block. If the message, or software, contains Alice's name then the authenticity of the source of the message or software is also provided.

If Alice and Bob exchange EDI messages over a public network, then they will not normally have access to a secure channel for the transmission of the authenticator block. If the authenticator block is simply appended to the message then Bob is faced with the possibility that an attacker produced the message, computed the corresponding authenticator block, and appended it to the message. In this case Alice must use some secret information, known only to Alice and possibly Bob, in conjunction with the authenticator block.

Alice might use a symmetric cipher, such as DES and a key k_a, known only by Alice and Bob, to encrypt the authenticator block. Similarly Bob uses a second secret key, k_b, for messages sent to Alice. Alternatively Alice might sign the authenticator block with the secret key of a suitable asymmetric cipher such as RSA. Thus Alice prepares a message M and

- computes an authenticator A by subjecting M to the hashing algorithm h, i.e. $A = h(M)$;
- encrypts A with her secret key k_a, producing $ek_a(A)$;
- transmits M and $ek_a(A)$ to Bob.

Bob receives M' and $ek_a(A')$ and checks the integrity of the message by:

- computing authenticator A'' = h(M');
- in the case of a symmetric cipher decrypts $ek_a(A')$ with k_a to give A', in the case of a public key cipher Bob employs Alice's public key to obtain A';

- Bob compares A'' with A', if they are the same, he is satisfied that the message originated from Alice and was not corrupted or deliberately modified in transmission.

The assurance that Bob experiences depends upon the inability of an attacker to encrypt the authenticator with Alice's secret key. However, the attacker may still have some tricks up his sleeve. Suppose that the hashing algorithm is comparatively simple such that the attacker could, in fact, produce a second message corresponding to a given authenticator A. In this case a potential attack is:

- Alice produces message M, computes $A = h(M)$ and transmits M, $ek_a(A)$ to Bob;
- the attacker captures a copy of M and $ek_a(A)$;
- attacker forms a fake message and massages it until he obtains a message M_1 such that $A_1 = h(M_1) = A = h(M)$, such massaging might be possible with a formatted financial message which has a large optional comment field;
- attacker transmits M_1 and $ek_a(A)$ to Bob;
- Bob computes $h(M_1) = A$, decrypts $ek_a(A)$ and accepts the message as genuine.

To obviate this attack Alice either uses a strong hash function, where the attacker is unable to determine an M_1, or alternatively combines the operation of hashing and encryption to form a message authentication code, as described in ANSI X9.9. In the latter case the message is subjected to cipher block chaining, using encryption key k_a, and the last block is retained, intermediate ciphertext blocks being discarded. The last block is termed the message authentication block. The leftmost 32 bits of the message authentication block are termed the message authentication code (MAC) and are transmitted in place of ek$_x$(A).

Another form of attack is replay, i.e. the attacker simply repeats a previous message complete with its authenticator; Bob accepts the replayed message since the authenticator block satisfies all the checks described above. To defend against replay attacks, Alice must include some field in the message to distinguish it from all previous messages, e.g. a time-date stamp, message sequence number. Some authentication systems provide for optional inclusion of fields within the authentication process; clearly the field used to make the message unique must be included amongst the authenticated fields.

If symmetric ciphers are employed then Alice and Bob must use different keys for their transmitted message, otherwise the attacker might simply replay one of Alice's message back to Alice, who accepts it as a message from Bob. This attack could succeed even if a time-date stamp or message sequence number were used, since Alice's replay defenses only apply to replays of Bob's messages.

Authenticated message sequence numbers also allow Bob to check that Alice's messages are handled in sequence. Alice may require a receipt from Bob, such receipts should be authenticated and contain sufficient information to uniquely identify Bob and the message to which the receipt refers. See ANSI X9.9 - 1986, ASYMMETRIC CIPHER, AUTHENTICATION, AUTHENTICATOR, BLOCK CIPHER, CBC, CIPHER BLOCK CHAINING, CIPHERTEXT, DIGITAL SIGNATURE, DES, ELECTRONIC CODEBOOK, HASH FUNCTION, KEY, MESSAGE AUTHENTICATION BLOCK, MESSAGE AUTHENTICATION CODE, MESSAGE SEQUENCE NUMBER, PUBLIC KEY CRYPTOGRAPHY, RSA, REPLAY, SYMMETRIC CIPHER, TIME-DATE STAMP.

message authentication algorithm. In banking, an algorithm to develop a number which is sent with a message so that the receiver can check that it has not been altered since it left the sender. ISO 8732 describes an algorithm which has been specifically designed where data volumes are high and efficient implementation by software is a desirable characteristic. The algorithm uses two 32 bit numbers as keys and the result of the algorithm is a 32 bit authenticator. *Compare* MESSAGE AUTHENTICATION CODE.

message authentication block. In banking, a block that is a cryptographic function of all data in a message or extended message generated under control of a transaction key. The MAB is split to form the message authentication code (MAC) and the message authentication code residue (MAC residue). (SAA). *See* MAC, MAC RESIDUE, MESSAGE AUTHENTICATION.

message authentication code. (1) In authentication, a number that is the result of passing a message through the authentication algorithm using a specific key. (2) In banking, a code in a message between the sender and receiver used to validate the source and part or all of the text of the message. The code is the result of an agreed calculation. (ANSI). *See* ANSI X9.9 - 1986. (3) In banking, a group of characters included with a message for the purpose of verifying that the message has not been fraudulently changed. The code is a cryptographic function of all data in the message, generated under control of a transaction key, and is therefore statistically unique to that message. The MAC is part of the message authentication block (MAB). (SAA). *Compare* MESSAGE AUTHENTICATION ALGORITHM. *See* MESSAGE AUTHENTICATION, MESSAGE AUTHENTICATION BLOCK, TRANSACTION KEY.

message certification. In authentication, a procedure in which a receiver

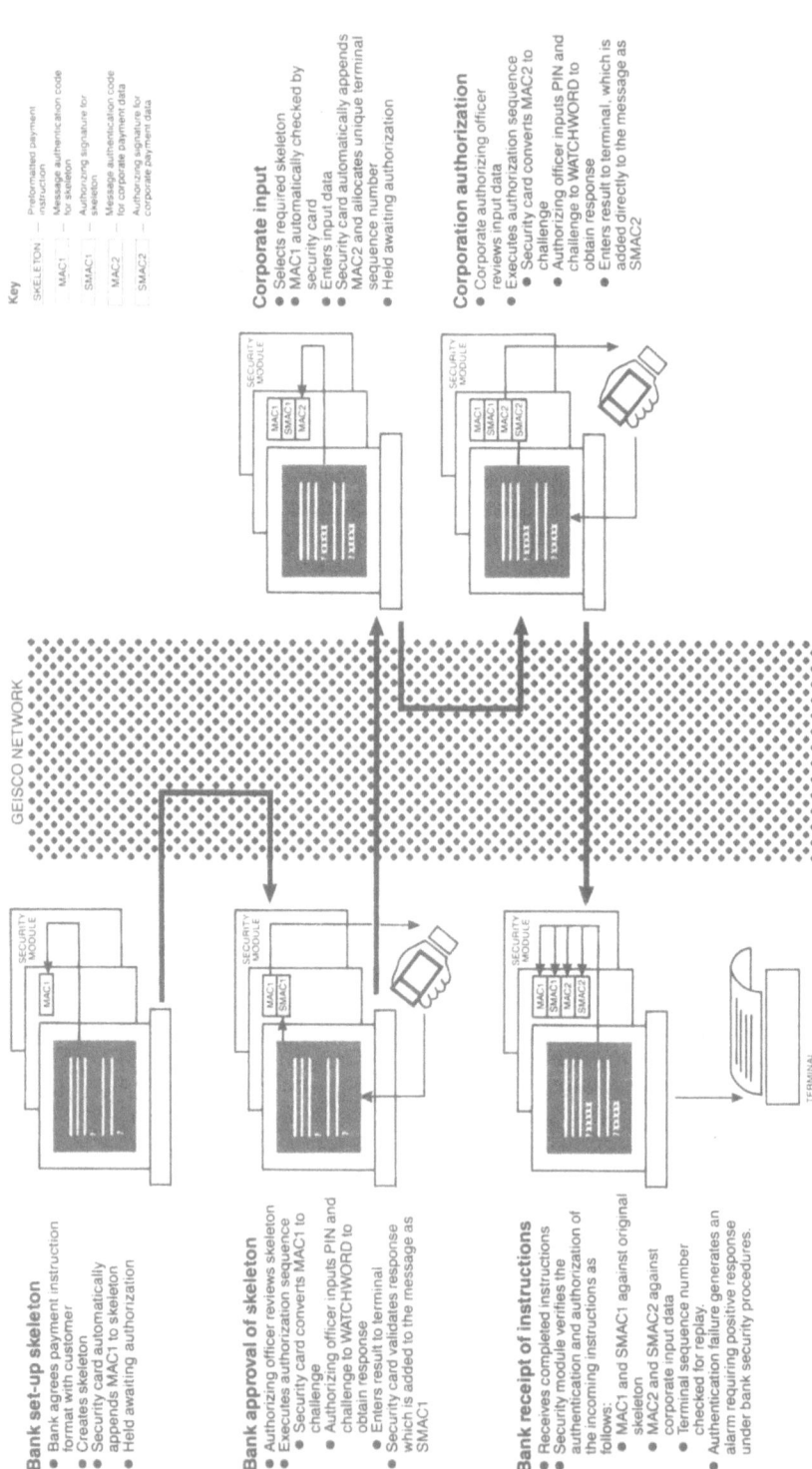

Key

SKELETON — Preformatted payment instruction

MAC1 — Message authentication code for skeleton

SMAC1 — Authorizing signature for skeleton

MAC2 — Message authentication code for corporate payment data

SMAC2 — Authorizing signature for corporate payment data

Corporate input

- Selects required skeleton
- MAC1 automatically checked by security card
- Enters input data
- Security card automatically appends MAC2 and allocates unique terminal sequence number
- Held awaiting authorization

Corporation authorization

- Corporate authorizing officer reviews input data
- Executes authorization sequence
- Security card converts MAC2 to challenge
- Authorizing officer inputs PIN and challenge to WATCHWORD to obtain response
- Enters result to terminal, which is added directly to the message as SMAC2

Bank set-up skeleton

- Bank agrees payment instruction format with customer
- Creates skeleton
- Security card automatically appends MAC1 to skeleton
- Held awaiting authorization

Bank approval of skeleton

- Authorizing officer reviews skeleton
- Executes authorization sequence
- Security card converts MAC1 to challenge
- Authorizing officer inputs PIN and challenge to WATCHWORD to obtain response
- Enters result to terminal
- Security card validates response which is added to the message as SMAC1

Bank receipt of instructions

- Receives completed instructions
- Security module verifies the authentication and authorization of the incoming instructions as follows:
  - MAC1 and SMAC1 against original skeleton
  - MAC2 and SMAC2 against corporate input data
  - Terminal sequence number checked for replay.
- Authentication failure generates an alarm requiring positive response under bank security procedures.

GEISCO NETWORK

SECURITY MODULE

TERMINAL PRINTER

message authentication

Authentication and authorization on GEISCO's Money Transfer System. The security solution developed by Racal–Guardata is a two-tier cryptographically based system using the DEA algorithm, firstly through the use of ANSI X9.9 and secondly by integrating personal authentication with message authentication. Together these two techniques provide a mechanism that ensures end-to-end message authentication and authorization that will identify the originating device and the authorizing officer. Courtesy of GEISCO & Racal-Guardata. *See* ANSI X9.9, BANKING NETWORKS, DIGITAL SIGNATURE.

provides proof to a sender that a particular message has been received. The acknowledgement from the receiver should be signed to ensure that it has not originated from an attacker. *See* DIGITAL SIGNATURE.

message digest. In authentication, a mathematical function which maps values from a large, possibly very large, domain into a smaller range. A good message digest is such that the results of applying the function to a large set of values in the domain will be evenly, and randomly, distributed over the range. (ANSI). *See* DOMAIN, RANGE.

message exhaustion. In cryptanalysis, a form of attack in which all possible plaintext combinations are encrypted and the corresponding ciphertext stored for future reference. In public key cryptography, the encrypting key is known by the cryptanalyst and thus the received ciphertext can be checked against the stored plaintext-ciphertext pairs. If the encryption key is not known then the process is conducted for all possible keys, if subsequently a fragment of plaintext and corresponding ciphertext is available then the stored plaintext-ciphertext pairs can be searched and the corresponding key determined. *Compare* KEY EXHAUSTION. *See* BLOCK CIPHER, BLOCKSIZE, CRYPTOGRAPHIC KEY, PUBLIC KEY CRYPTOGRAPHY.

message format. In data communications, rules for the placement of such portions of a message as the heading, address, text and end of the message. *See* ADDRESS, MESSAGE HEADING, MESSAGE TEXT.

message heading. In data communications, the leading part of a message that contains such information as the source or destination code of the message, the message priority, and the type of message. *Compare* MESSAGE TEXT.

message identifier. In authentication, a field of up to eight acceptable characters that may be used to identify a financial message or transaction. Typically, this field is a sequence number. (ANSI) *See* ANSI X9.9 -1986.

message integrity code. In authentication, a value developed, by a mathematical transformation of a message, that characterizes that message. Thus any minor change in the message, by substitution or transcription of a character (say) will result in a change in the message integrity code. The code may or may not be computed using some secret cryptographic key. *Compare* MESSAGE AUTHENTICATION CODE. *See* ELECTRONIC MAIL SECURITY.

message numbering. In data communications, a unique number given to each message in a system for identification purposes.

message oriented text exchange. In data communications, a protocol used for electronic mail; it is similar to X400. *See* ELECTRONIC MAIL, PROTOCOL, X.400.

message routing. In data communications, the process of selecting a route in a message switching system. *See* MESSAGE SWITCHING, ROUTING.

message sequence number. In authentication, a number used to uniquely identify a message and to ensure that messages are handled in sequence. *See* REPLAY.

message slot. In data communications, sequences of bits, sufficient to hold a full message, that are continually circulated around a ring local area network. A slot may be empty or full, and any node, on detecting an empty slot, may mark the slot as full and place a message in it. *Compare* DAISY CHAIN, CON-

TROL TOKEN. *See* CAMBRIDGE RING, LOCAL AREA NETWORK.

message space. In cryptography, the set of all possible messages that can be encrypted with a given cipher. *Compare* CRYPTOGRAM SPACE, KEY SPACE.

message specific random integer. In authentication, a random integer that is used with a specific message and is not intentionally reused for any other message. (ANSI).

message stream modification. In communications security, pertaining to attacks on the authenticity, integrity and /or ordering of the PDU's of the message stream. An attack on the authenticity can be made by modifying the protocol control information in PDU's so that they are sent to the wrong destination, or by inserting PDU's (created by the attacker or replayed from earlier messages) into the message stream. Similarly an attack on integrity will be directed to changing the data contained in the PDU. Ordering attacks will delete PDU's or modify sequencing information in the control portion of the PDU's. *Compare* DENIAL OF MESSAGE SERVICE, SPURIOUS ASSOCIATION INITIATION. *See* PDU.

message switching. In data communications, a technique for increasing the throughput of a network by the sequential switching of prestored messages. Unlike packet switching, messages are transmitted in their entirety and once in a network the system takes over responsibility for their delivery. *Compare* PACKET SWITCHING. *See* STORE AND FORWARD.

message switching center. In data communications, a center in which messages are routed according to information contained within the messages themselves. *Synonymous with* RELAY CENTER.

message text. In data communications, the part of a message that is relevant to the party receiving the message. The message text excludes the header and control information. *Compare* MESSAGE HEADING.

message transfer agent. In data communications, a component of electronic mail systems that relays the message from sender to receiver. If the message transfer agent receives a message from a user agent it checks the syntax and returns the message, together with an explanation, to the user agent if it is found to be invalid. If the message is valid then a message identifier and time-date stamp is affixed to it. The message is then processed in the same manner as messages received from other message transfer agents. If the message is intended for a local mailbox then it is delivered, queued for delivery or stored in the mailbox; otherwise it is passed to the next message transfer agent for onward transfer. *Compare* USER AGENT. *See* ELECTRONIC MAIL, USER AGENT, X.400.

metadata. (1) In computing, data referring to other data (such as data structures, indices, and pointers) that are used to instantiate an abstraction (such as 'process', 'task', 'segment', 'file', or 'pipe'). (2) In computing, a special database, also referred to as a data dictionary, containing descriptions of the elements (e.g., relations, domains, entities or relationships. (NCSC).

method of advice. In banking, a specified way of informing a party. (ANSI). *See* ADVICE.

metropolitan area network. In communications, a communications network that serves a city. *Compare* LOCAL AREA NETWORK. *Synonymous with* MUNICIPAL AREA NETWORK.

MF keypad. In communications, a keypad producing multifrequency signals that can be used with suitable types of telephone exchanges both for call set-up purposes and subsequently to transmit low speed data, i.e. less than 600 baud.

MGTU Virus. In computer security, a virus that infects COMMAND.COM and COM files, affects run-time operation, corrupts program, OVL and data files. *See* VIRUS NAMES.

MIC. *See* MESSAGE INTEGRITY CODE.

Michelangelo. In computer security, a standard boot sector virus loosely based upon the Stoned virus. It has a trigger date set to March 6, i.e. Michelangelo's birthday. *See* VIRUS, VIRUS NAMES.

MICR. Magnetic Ink Character Recognition, a technique for the identification of characters printed with ink that contain particles of a magnetic material. MICR is used in the banking industry to record transmitted codes and account numbers on checks for data processing. *Compare* OPTICAL CHARACTER RECOGNITION.

microbend loss. In communications, the leakage of light caused by minute sharp curves in the optical cable that may result from imperfections when the glass fiber meets the sheathing that covers it. *Compare* MACROBEND LOSS. *See* FIBER OPTICS.

Microbes. In computer security, a virus that terminates and stays resident, infects floppy and hard disk boot sector, corrupts boot sector, affects run-time operation, corrupts data files. *See* VIRUS NAMES.

microcircuit card. *Synonymous with* SMART CARD.

microcomputer. A term applied to desktop computers designed for hobbyists, small businesses or educational applications, as compared with a micro-

processor that is the central processing chip of the microcomputer.

microdata file. In database security, a file containing information on individuals, private households, enterprises etc. *See* INFERENCE CONTROL.

micro mainframe link. *See* COOPERATIVE PROCESSING.

microprocessor. In computing, a single chip containing a complete central processing unit consisting of an arithmetic logic unit, and a control unit. Various microprocessors are capable of accepting coded instructions for execution in 8, 16 or 32 bit word format and act as the central processor unit, or a coprocessor, in a microcomputer.

microprocessor card. *See* SMART CARD.

microwave motion detection. *See* MICROWAVE SENSOR.

microwave sensor. In physical security, an intrusion detection device that detects the movement of a person through a pattern of microwaves produced by a transmitter. The detection is effected by a Doppler effect or beam break principle. The Doppler effect is an apparent change in frequency as the speed between a source of radiation and the receiver changes. *See* BEAM BREAK.

MID. In banking, Message IDentifier, identification of a financial message or transaction that may be used in computation of a MAC, test or authenticator. (ANSI). *See* AUTHENTICATOR, MAC, TEST.

midnight attack. In key management, an attack in which a complex communication session, between a host and a terminal, including the transmission of the session key, encrypted under the terminal key, is wiretapped and recorded. Later, figuratively at midnight, the attacker gains access to the unattended terminal and inputs to it the recorded host-terminal traffic, thus masquerading as the host to the terminal. The terminal deciphers the recorded ciphertext using the recorded encrypted session key. This attack can be thwarted by handshaking. *See* HANDSHAKING, MASQUERADING, SESSION KEY, TERMINAL KEY.

migration. In databases, a technique in which the use of fast access store is optimized by moving the less frequently accessed items to a slower, low-cost storage device.

military critical technology. Goods accompanied by sophisticated operation, application, or maintenance know-how that would make a significant contribution to the military potential of any country or combination of countries and that may prove detrimental to the security of the United States. (DODD). *See* KNOW HOW.

Milnet. In data communications, Military Network. *See* INTERNET.

Milwauke 414. In computer security, a group of seven youths in the Milwauke, Wisconsin area who gained illegitimate access to computers spread across the U.S. and Canada in 1983. The group was named after the Milwauke's area telephone code. *See* HACKER, TELEPHONE INTRUSION.

mimicking. *Synonymous with* MASQUERADING.

minimal cover time. In cryptography, the shortest cover time for any conceivable attack. *See* COVER TIME.

minimum knowledge proof. *Synonymous with* ZERO KNOWLEDGE PROOF.

minimum weight routing.. In data communications, a method of optimizing

the transmission of a message by associating a weighting factor with each link in the network. The chosen route is the one that minimizes the sum of the weights of the lines it uses. If the weights chosen are the transit delays associated with lines, a minimum delay routing is obtained. *See* ADAPTIVE ROUTING, DIRECTORY ROUTING.

minor change to a system of records. In computing, a change that does not significantly change the system; that is, does not affect the character or purpose of the system and does not affect the ability of an individual to gain access to his or her record or to any information pertaining to him or her that is contained in the system; e.g. changing the title of the system manager. (OMBC).

MIPS. In computing, Million Instructions Per Second, a measure of computing power. *Compare* LIPS.

Mirror. In computer security, a virus that terminates and stays resident, infects EXE files, affects run-time operation, corrupts program and OVL files. *See* VIRUS NAMES.

miscellaneous common carrier. In communications, common carriers not engaged in providing telephone or telegraph services. Usually these carriers are responsible for radio and TV transmission services using terrestrial microwave links. *See* COMMON CARRIER.

MIX1. In computer security, a virus that terminates and stays resident, infects EXE files, affects run-time operation, corrupts program and OVL files. *See* VIRUS NAMES.

Mix2. In computer security, a virus that terminates and stays resident, infects COMMAND.COM, COM ,EXE and OVL files, affects run-time operation, corrupts program and OVL files. *See* VIRUS NAMES.

MLAT. *See* MUTUAL LEGAL ASSIST-ANCE TREATY.

MLS. (1) MultiLevel Security. *See* MULTILEVEL SECURE. (2) In computer security, the multilevel security formula generator, a flow analysis tool developed at SRI for use with HDM. (MTR). *See* HDM, SECURITY FLOW ANALYSIS.

MMS. Military Message System. *See* LANDWEHR'S SECURITY MODEL FOR MILITARY MESSAGE SYSTEMS.

mockingbird. In computer security, a computer program or process that mimics the legitimate behavior of a normal system feature (or other apparently useful function) but performs malicious activities once invoked by the user. *Compare* TROJAN HORSE, VIRUS.

MOD. In banking, Message Origination Date, the date on which the originator computed the MAC, test or authenticator. (ANSI) *See* AUTHENTICATOR, MAC.

mode. (1) In cryptography, pertaining to the manner in which a block cipher may be operated, e.g. electronic code-book, cipher block chaining etc. *See* BLOCK CIPHER, CIPHER BLOCK CHAIN-ING, ELECTRONIC CODEBOOK. (2) In computing, an option in a method of operation, e.g. binary mode, alphanu-meric mode etc. (3) In mathematics, the most frequently occurring value in a statistical sample. (4) In communica-tions, pertaining to the manner in which light rays travel along the fiber. *See* FIBER OPTICS, MODE DISPERSION, MONO-MODE FIBER, MULTIMODE FIBER.

mode dispersion. In communications, the dispersion that arises from the differ-ent paths traversed by the light rays in an optical fiber. This dispersion causes a distortion of the received pulse. *See* FIBER OPTICS, MODE, MONOMODE FIBER, MULTIMODE FIBER.

model. (1) In data security, an expres-sion of policy in a form that a system can enforce, or that analysis can use for reasoning about the policy and its en-forcement. (2) The representation of a particular system in a logical form, e.g. through software, to predict some future occurrence.

modeling. In legislation, use of a com-puter to plan a crime.

MODEM. In data communications, MOdulator-DEModulator, a device that modulates the transmitted signal and demodulates the received signal at a data station. For example, a modem is used to convert a digital signal from a com-puter into an analog signal for transmis-sion over a network and is commonly employed for the intercommunication of microcomputers over the telephone network. A modem may work in half duplex or full duplex mode over a two or four wire circuit. *See* FOUR WIRE CIRCUIT, FULL DUPLEX, HALF DUPLEX, MODULATION, LIMITED DISTANCE MO-DEM, SECURITY MODEM. *Synonymous with* DATA SET.

mode of attack. In information security, a sequence of actual attacks made on a specific attack path. This is done by performing a direct or indirect attack on a particular vulnerability of each countermeasure in that path *See* ATTACK PATH, INFORMATION TECHNOLOGY SECURITY EVALUATION CRITERIA, VUL-NERABILITY.

mod n. In mathematics, b (mod n) is the remainder resulting from the division of integer b by integer n, e.g. 7 (mod 3) is 1. *See* CONGRUENT, MODULO ARITH-METIC, RESIDUE.

modular redundancy. In reliability, a method of hardware redundancy in which a module is replicated and the multiple copies run in parallel. The outputs of the modules are compared and differences between them indicate the presence of a fault. *Compare* STRUCTURAL REDUNDANCY. *See* DUAL REDUNDANCY, HARDWARE REDUNDANCY, HYBRID REDUNDANCY, NMR, TRIPLE MODULAR REDUNDANCY.

modulated photoelectric sensor. In physical security, an intrusion detector that uses a modulated beam of, usually infra red, light. The receiver produces an alarm signal when there is no incident light modulated at the specified frequency. Thus the system reacts both to a beam break and also to bypass attempts using a beam of light directed to the receiver. *See* PHOTOELECTRIC SENSOR.

modulating signal. In communications, a signal that is impressed upon a carrier wave to vary it in some specified manner. *See* CARRIER, MODULATION.

modulation. In communications, a process by which information is impressed upon a carrier wave for transmission purposes. The term covers processes where some characteristic of a continuous wave, such as its frequency or amplitude, is varied in accordance with a modulating signal such as a speech, television or facsimile waveform. *See* AMPLITUDE MODULATION, FREQUENCY MODULATION, MODULATING SIGNAL, PHASE MODULATION, PULSE MODULATION.

modulation rate. In communications, the reciprocal of the shortest time interval between successive significant instances of the modulated signal. If this measure is expressed in seconds, the modulation rate is in bauds. *See* BAUD, MODULATION.

modulator. In communications, the equipment or apparatus that modifies some characteristic of a signal. *See* MODULATION.

module interface analysis. *See* STATIC ANALYSIS.

modulo arithmetic. In mathematics, a form of arithmetic in which only the remainders, after division by a specified integer, are used.

If b is divided by n giving remainder c this is written as: $b \equiv c \pmod{n}$ or b is congruent c modulo n; c is called the residue of b modulo n.

Addition and multiplication may be performed directly on the residues, i.e. If $b_1 \equiv c_1 \pmod{n}$ and $b_2 \equiv c_2 \pmod{n}$ then $b_1 + b_2 \equiv c_1 + c_2 \pmod{n}$.

Similarly with multiplication, for integers k_1, k_2:

$$b_1.b_2 = (k_1.n + c_1).(k_2.n + c_2)$$
$$= (k_1.k_2.n + c_1.k_2 + c_2.k_1).n + c_1.c_2$$

Hence

$$b_1.b_2 \equiv c_1.c_2 \pmod{n}.$$

A particularly useful modulo arithmetic technique arises in exponentiation. If a 200 digit number is to be raised to a high power in modulo arithmetic it is obviously useful if the power itself can be reduced by modulo arithmetic. There are two cases to be considered, firstly place a restriction that the n be a prime number and that b is not divisible by n. Fermat's Theorem gives the useful result:

$$b^{n-1} \equiv 1 \pmod{n} \text{ e.g.}$$

$$2^6 = 64 \equiv 1 \bmod (7)$$

Hence it is permissible, given the restrictions on b and n, to reduce the power of b modulo n-1. For example :

$2^{16} \equiv 2^6.2^6.2^4 \pmod 7 \equiv 1.1.2^4 \pmod 7 = 2$, hence in the computation of $2^{16} \pmod 7$ the exponent can be reduced from 16 to 4.

If n is not prime then Euler's Generalization must be used. In this case it is first necessary to define the Euler totient function written $\phi(n)$, this is equal to the number of integers coprime with n in the range 1.. n-1.., e.g. $\phi(10)$ = 4, (1 3 7 9). Euler's Generalization states that:

$$b^{\phi(n)} \equiv 1 \pmod{n}$$

provided that b is coprime with n. Thus with this proviso it is permissible to reduce the exponent modulo $\phi(n)$, e.g. $3^7 \pmod{10} \equiv 2187 \pmod{10} \equiv 7$, reducing the exponent $\phi(10) = 4 \pmod{n}$, gives $3^7 \pmod{10} \equiv 3^3 \pmod{10} \equiv 27 \pmod{10} \equiv 7 \pmod{10}$.

Modulo arithmetic is important in cryptography because it introduces a high degree of randomness into functions, rendering it difficult for a cryptanalyst to narrow down an area of search. Consider the cubic function y = x^3. If x is known to lie between 6 and 15 then y must lie in the range 216 to 3375. However if modulo 10 arithmetic is used then y could take on any of the values 6, 3, 2, 9, 0, 1, 8, 7, 4 or 5. Moreover the pattern of output changes unpredictably with variations in the input; a small change in x from 9 to 10 produces a variation in y from 9 to 0, i.e. from one extreme value, in the range of possible outputs, to the other. See CONGRUENT, COPRIME, EULER'S GENERALIZATION, FERMAT'S THEOREM, RSA.

modulo n. See CONGRUENT, MOD N, MODULO ARITHMETIC.

modulo N check. In computing, a means of checking the values of data whereby an operand is divided by a number N and the remainder used as a check digit. Often N is taken to be 11, thus 81 modulo 11 is 4. See OPERAND.

modulo 2. In mathematics, an operation equivalent to exclusive or, i.e. $0 + 0 = 0$, $0 + 1 = 1$ and $1 + 1 = 0$. It is significant in DES operations and is written $A +_2 B$. Note that $A +_2 A =$ 0. See DES, EXCLUSIVE OR, MODULO ARITHMETIC.

monitoring. In data security, the recording of relevant information about each operation by a subject on an object, maintained in an audit trail for subsequent analysis. Compare THREAT MONITORING. See AUDIT TRAIL, AUTOMATED SECURITY MONITORING, OBJECT, SUBJECT.

monitoring station. In physical security, a remote area at which guards can monitor security system annunciators or alarm receivers. Compare CENTRAL STATION.

monoalphabetic cipher. In data security, a substitution cipher in which each letter of the alphabet maps onto another letter with each individual pairing arbitrarily fixed by the cryptographer. Compare POLYALPHABETIC CIPHER. See CIPHER, CRYPTOGRAPHY, SUBSTITUTION CIPHER.

monolithic TCB. In computer security, a TCB that consists of a single TCB subset. (NCSC). See BLUE BOOK, TCB SUBSET.

monomode fiber. In communications, a fiber with a very narrow core (2-10 microns); the only path for transmission is along the axis, thus producing low dispersion. Compare MULTIMODE FIBER. See FIBER OPTICS, MODE, MODE DISPERSION.

Monxla. In computer security, a virus that infects COMMAND.COM and COM files, affects run-time operation, corrupts program and OVL files. See VIRUS NAMES.

Morris worm. In computer security, a worm produced by a graduate student Robert Tappan Morris that attacked the United States Internet in November 1988.

Internet is a logical network in the United States comprising many physical networks connecting some 60,000 academic, research and military computers. The Milnet network, in this system, was reserved for high security military communications but not the most classified military information.

Within a few hours the infestation spread throughout the network; by next morning several thousand computers were infected. The network suffered a major disruption and system administrators disconnected their computers from it, to avoid further damage.

The Worm was written in the C programming language and it attacked Sun Microsystem Sun 3 systems and Vax (Vax is a trademark of Digital Equipment Laboratory) computers running under variants of BSD 4 Unix (Unix is a trademark of AT&T Laboratories).

The Worm contained no code to perform malicious actions. Its deleterious effects arose from the overloading of network computers, infected by the Worm, from the time wasted in checking computers which might have been, but in fact were not, infected by it, and the massive efforts of computer scientists to analyze the Worm and to rectify its actions. Thus the Worm did not:

- affect system or user files;
- modify user programs to assist in its propagation;
- install Trojan Horses;
- record or transmit passwords revealed by the attack;
- attempt to gain system administrator, i.e. superuser, privileges.

The Worm was written in C and it comprised two components:

- A bootstrap program, also termed a vector program, comprising a 99 line source code program written in C.
- Two large relocatable object files containing Sun 3, and

Vax, versions respectively of the main body of the Worm.

The operation of the Worm may be divided into attack, defence and population control mechanisms. In the attack phase the Worm, having invaded an account in a host machine, sought to infect other machines by first:

- determining the address of remote hosts;
- inserting the bootstrap program onto one of those hosts;
- compiling and executing the bootstrap program on that host;
- employing the action of that bootstrap program to download the remainder of the Worm and then execute the Worm on the new host.

The defence mechanisms were designed to avoid detection and obviate counterattacks on the Worm, they made life difficult for those seeking to analyze the operation of the Worm from any captured code. The population control techniques sought to avoid a proliferation of Worm infection, on any one host, by a technique of identifying the presence of another Worm and then effectively throwing a die to determine which one of the pair should commit suicide.

As a first step, in the infection of a new host, the Worm obtained the address of such hosts, and names of accounts held on that host. This information was obtained from a variety of user readable files held on the host, already infected by the Worm. Remote hosts were then attacked by exploiting either one of two known software flaws, in Sendmail and finger programs, or poor user security discipline.

The Sendmail system is a very complex piece of software that provides electronic mail facilities for the network. A message sender, operating on one host, produces a message and appends the appropriate network address of the intended recipient. Sendmail transmits the message through the network, possibly using gateways that provide connections from one local network into another, and eventually Sendmail stores the message in the appropriate electronic mail file on the recipient's host computer.

Thus electronic mail must provide a mechanism to insert data into another computer on the network, when the sender may not have the necessary privileges to login to that computer. This, in itself, does not present a security problem. However, if the sender could, in some way, cause the insertion and execution of programs on the recipient computer then there exists a loophole for viruses and worms. This facility can be provided by the Sendmail package under certain circumstances. Normally mail is delivered to a mailbox file, however, Sendmail also allows an intended recipient to direct incoming mail to a process. For example, such a process could send a return message, informing the sender that the recipient is on vacation and therefore unavailable to read the mail.

A loophole in the Sendmail facility was provided by the debug routine. If the system administrator left the debug flag on, then the sender, rather than the addressee, could direct the mail to a process. This loophole was apparently developed for testing the operation of Sendmail in the network, but it provided a serious security loophole. An unauthorized user could invoke operations on remote computers linked to the network. The Worm sent a message, exploiting the debug loophole, which downloaded the bootstrap program, compiled and executed it.

A second loophole arose from a flaw in the fingerd daemon in the finger program. A daemon is a program which continually checks for certain conditions which, when satisfied, cause it to spring into action. The finger program allows a local user to obtain information about a user on the host machine, the fingerd daemon provides this facility for remote users. Thus it is possible to send a request asking if a particular user is currently logged in to the remote host. The finger program, in itself, posed no particular security hazard. However, the fingerd routine had a programming flaw, it stored received data into a stack, without checking if there was sufficient storage space allocated to accommodate it.

The Worm invoked the fingerd program with a specially constructed long message which overfilled the buffer, overwriting (i.e. corrupting) parts of the stack. On exit from the fingerd program control was passed to code which contained instructions supplied by the Worm. These inserted instructions were designed so as to cause the Worm bootstrap program to be compiled and executed.

The third path for infection did not rely upon software flaws but rather exploited lax security practices on the part of the users. The Worm had a sophisticated system of guessing passwords, when it had guessed a password then it had a means of logging into a user account on the local machine. Moreover this privilege could also allow the Worm to access the same user's accounts on other network machines.

Morris was found guilty of the attack on the Internet network, was fined $10,000, given three years probation and 400 hours of community work. *Compare* XMAS TREE. *See* DEBUG, INTERNET, LOOPHOLE, MALICIOUS CODE, VIRUS, WORM.

motion detector. In physical security, a system that detects movement within a protected area by comparing ambient energy fields, or detecting reflections or changes in successive energy transmissions. *See* INFRA RED MOTION DETECTOR, MICROWAVE SENSOR, ULTRASONIC MOTION DETECTOR. *Synonymous with* PRESENCE DETECTOR.

MOTIS. *See* MESSAGE ORIENTED TEXT EXCHANGE.

M out of N code. In codes, a transmission code with inbuilt error detection facilities. A specified number of bits (M), in a character of N bits, must be 1 bits. Any received character not containing a total of M 1 bits initiates an error procedure. *See* ERROR DETECTION CODE. *Synonymous with* CONSTANT RATIO CODE.

MSAR. In computer security, Minimum Security Assurance Requirements. *See* MFSR.

m-sequence. In mathematics, a sequence of binary digits that can be generated by applying linear feedback to a shift register of length n bits and which has a period of 2^{n-1} bits. An m-sequence has the maximum linear complexity for its period. *See* BIT, LINEAR COMPLEXITY, LINEAR FEEDBACK SHIFT REGISTER.

MSFR. In computer security, Minimum Security Functionality Requirements. A set of requirements for general purpose multi-user operating systems developed as part of the FC-FIPS project. These requirements build upon the previous work of both TCSEC and ITSEC. They define baseline requirements applicable to multi-user workstations, minicomputers and mainframes. They may be used as a set of guidelines to assist designers in constructing application specific requirements. The document identifies eight security enforcing functions, similar to the ITSEC approach:

- identification and authentication;
- access control;
- accountability;
- audit;
- object reuse;
- accuracy;
- reliability of service;

- data exchange.

In each case it gives quite detailed specifications labelled either (R) or (A). 'R' indicating a specification to satisfy the needs of a typical commercial enterprise or government organization. 'A' indicating a desirable specification that may be required by a typical commercial enterprise of government organization. It is recognized in the document that the presence of desired security features alone is not sufficient to establish the potential value of a computer product for protecting information. The requirements therefore constrain the product development and assessment procedures and specify the evidence to be produced as a result of assurance requirement processes. A minimum security assurance requirements (MSAR) will be included in the FC-FIPS for use with the MSFR. These assurance requirements will represent a convergence of TCSEC C2 and the ITSEC E2 level. *See* BASELINE, ITSEC, FC-FIPS, FIPS, ORANGE BOOK, TCSEC.

MSM. In authentication, Message Stream Modification. *See* MESSAGE AUTHENTICATION.

MTA. *See* MESSAGE TRANSFER AGENT.

MTBF. *See* MEAN TIME BETWEEN FAILURE.

MTS. In data communications, Message Transfer Service in the CCITT X.400 message handling standard. *Compare* MTA, UA. *See* X400.

multicast. In communications, the simultaneous transmission of data or signals to selected group of stations. *Compare* BROADCAST, POINT-TO-POINT.

multidrop circuit. In data communications, a circuit rented to a customer for the transmission of data between a central site, usually a computer, and a number of outstation terminals. Two-way transmission is possible between any terminal and the central site, but not directly between terminals. *Compare* POINT-TO-POINT. *See* CIRCUIT. *Synonymous with* MULTIPOINT CIRCUIT.

multilevel database security. In data security, the methods employed to protect the security of a database which contains data with various levels of security classification and serves a user population with various levels of security clearance. A legitimate user of the database must be provided with all the facilities of a conventional database containing information within that user's aegis of privilege. On the other hand, such legitimate user's must be prevented from gaining access to, or even inferring, information beyond their level of privilege.

The designer of the multilevel database system must also deal with security problems that can arise from covert channels, i.e. with the leakage of secure information by some form of cooperation between a user and malicious code embedded in the computer software. This is a severe problem because DBMS software is notoriously complex and defies currently available formal evaluation methods.

If a secure multilevel system is to be evaluated then there must be a statement on what is to be achieved in terms of security, i.e. an explicit security policy must be stated. In access control terms there are two forms of policy:

- discretionary access control;
- mandatory access control.

In database systems a user will formulate a query, which may well involve extensive selection criteria, applied to a mass of data items within many files. In these circumstances the problem of assigning a classification to the query's response is one of some complexity. It is, of course, always possible to play safe and give data a classification equal to that of the highest classified file accessed, thus denying access to many requests. However, the database must provide a service to users at all security clearances. At each level, a user should be granted read facilities as if the database contained only that data which had a security classification dominated by the users clearance.

Another serious concern is with database integrity; a large database will be subject to continual data insertion, update and deletion, in many cases such inputs will derive from a large population of users. Maintaining data integrity is of fundamental concern to database designers and administrators.

A third area of concern is the implementation of a reference monitor. Current databases have DBMS software that is extremely complex. If the security relevant features are to be designed into the DBMS then this will involve either:

- a redesign of the DBMS of an existing system

or
- the design of a new DBMS.

In either event, it will be extremely difficult to guarantee the efficacy of security features built into a very large, complex software package.

Three approaches to secure multilevel databases have been described:

- security compartments which effectively provide physically separate databases for each security classification level;
- integrity locking which enables a security filter to be retrofitted to an existing DBMS;
- Denning relational model.

Secure Compartment Systems.
Multilevel systems pose much more serious design problems, from a security viewpoint, than single level systems. In the latter case a user either does, or does not, have the necessary clearance

to use the system; the major security considerations are then related to physical access control.

It might appear, therefore, that the problem of secure multilevel database systems could be solved by the replication of the DBMS, and the stored data, for each security level. The system for the lowest security level containing only data at that level; the top classified database would contain data at all levels.

Clearly one of the major disadvantages of such a database system is that it negates the policy of minimizing data redundancy. If an item of data, with a low classification, is to be inserted, modified or deleted then all databases containing that item must be modified. Inevitably there will exist inconsistencies across the databases, since such updates are unlikely to occur simultaneously.

Froscher proposed the use of a parallel computer to develop a high performance trusted database management system. The proposed system is illustrated in Fig. 1. The disk systems hold all the data required by a user with a given clearance level. The unclassified disk holding only unclassified data; the top secret disk holding data of all classification levels etc. The DBMS is replicated for each disk system and each one is managed by a trusted node controller (TNC). Users interface with the DBMS through a Trusted Front End. Thus the security relevant features of the system are contained within two relatively small trusted systems and are not embedded within the complex DBMS.

The function of the Trusted Front End is to ensure that user requests are directed to the database subsystem corresponding to the classification level that the user logged in. A user may log in at any level up to that corresponding to the user's clearance. The Trusted Front End also ensures that data returned from the system is directed to the correct user. The Trusted Node Controller ensures, inter alia, that the correct user addresses are added to returned data.

The proposed architecture provides safeguards against the four forms of database attack, i.e. direct access, indirect access, Trojan Horse direct release and Trojan Horse leakage. In each case these attacks may only arise if data can be retrieved at a higher classification level than that of the user login.

The question of updates does, however, pose some complex problems. When a user logged in at a low level inserts, updates or deletes a data item, then all databases at, and above, that level must be updated. Such updates should be performed concurrently, to avoid data inconsistencies. The protocols and message passing must be carefully evaluated; the DBMS will require some mechanism to report error messages, and such error messages from the high classification systems could provide a form of covert channel.

The replication of data covers many of the problems of mandatory access control but it would be impracticable to use replication for discretionary access control. The Trusted Front End may be employed to store the access control lists, indicating which users are permitted to access a given relation. The Trusted Node Controller then only retrieves data from a disk if access to that relation has been approved by the Trusted Front End. However, the guarantee that the DBMS has no access to data, beyond the aegis of privilege of the user, does not apply in the case of discretionary access control. Thus the various forms of attack described above demand careful consideration in relation to the possibility that data may be leaked to a user which is in contravention to the discretionary access control rules at the time.

Integrity Locking.
An important question in the design of a secure multilevel database system is 'can security be retrofitted onto an existing database?'. Given the considerable design effort in producing even a single

level DBMS, it is clear that such an approach could well provide the only feasible solution to enhancing the security of an existing system.

One could propose the concept of a filter, interfacing the DBMS, which would serve a similar function to a reference monitor, mediating access between the user and the data retrieved by the DBMS. The integrity locking, or colloquially 'spray paint' technique, was proposed for this purpose (see Fig. 2.). The separation of database access, and security checking system, implies that the formal security verification need only be applied to the filter and thus need not extend to the complex software of the DBMS.

With integrity locking the filter applies a cryptographic checksum to each item of data that is to be labelled with a security classification. The checksum is effectively a MAC computed over the data item, and classification label, using a secret key known only to the filter. The data itself is stored in clear and can therefore be manipulated by the DBMS; any unauthorized attempt to modify stored data, or to change its security classification, will however be detected by the filter when it validates the checksum. This technique was nicknamed spray paint because each item of data is indelibly colored with its classification.

The function of the filter is to:

- compute checksums using a stored secret key for input data and associated security label, and append those checksums to the data;

- validate the checksums of data returned to it by the DBMS and the associated security label;

- detect and report any invalid checksum which would indicate illegal tampering with data or associated security

label, e.g. attempts to downgrade a security label;

- ensure that the security level of the response to queries lies within the user's security clearance.

The functions of the filter should be kept as simple as possible to facilitate the formal verification of its security. Thus the filter should not have the complex accessing and retrieval functions of the DBMS.

Denning Relational Model.
Denning's secure multilevel relational database model provides an extremely valuable insight into the nature of the problems associated with secure multilevel databases.

The model deals with both confidentiality and integrity classifications. In effect a classification of an object, and the clearance of a subject is described by a secrecy component (secrecy level, secrecy categories) and integrity component (integrity level, integrity categories). The major concern of the model relates to the assignment of classifications and it will simplify the discussion if the classification is considered to comprise a simple hierarchical secrecy level such as SECRET, etc.

Denning made extensive use of the concept of views in the model to deal with the problems arising from interrelationships in the data from a security viewpoint, and also as a mechanism to filter data presented to a user.

In the model a classification is associated with each element, i.e. table entry. The classification is not associated with the data per se, but rather with the position in the table. Thus an entry for nuclear.location indicating the location of a nuclear site may be secret but the actual value Littleborough would not.

Assigning a classification to each element does not imply that the classification need be stored with each element; in some cases the classification may be stored by tuple, attribute or even relation. Nor does the classification of data by element imply that it is possible to give every element a classification independently. In some cases the user is given the impression an item of data is stored, when in fact it is computed from stored items. In such a case the classification of those items must be used to determine the classification of the retrieved item.

The classification for returned data are derived by views. In other words a classification of returned data is determined by a view, which either has a fixed level of classification, or computes its classification on the basis of other data in the database. Thus all data, retrieved from the database, is classified according to a set of views, termed classification constraints. In effect the classification is accorded to the view, and the classification may be a constant, or a function of the data which forms the input to the view.

The advantage of this approach is that it can:

- allocate classifications on some constant or conditional basis;
- deal with the interrelationships which can arise between classifications of elements;
- sanitize data allowing it to have a classification lower than that which would be allocated by pure derivation rules;
- allocate a classification to aggregated data which may be higher than that which would be allocated by pure derivation rules.

Using this technique it is possible to declare, say, that all the items in a table dealing with location of military camps is confidential except when the camps are located in missile bases, in which case they are secret.

If the classification is applied to elements that are derived from other elements then the classification of the derived element must be equal to the greatest classification of the elements used in the derivation.

This use of all item classifications in the derivation rules provides protection against the Indirect Access attack. If highly classified data is used in some intermediate manner, in answering a low classification user query, then there exists the danger that the user may be able to infer that information from the query response.

In the case of sanitization it may be permissible to assign a classification lower than that of the data from which it was derived. For example the total wages bill for an organization could well be given a lower classification than that allocated to managers' salaries, even though the managers' salaries would be used in the summation.

In the case of classification constraints used for sanitization rules, the classification of the derived element must be no greater than the classification of all elements used in the retrieval, and no less than the classification of all elements that could be inferred from the retrieved data. In the case of the total wages bill the classification of the sum might be set to:

- the greatest classification of the individual wages if the number of salaries in question were less than one hundred;
- unclassified in all other cases.

The justification for the lower classification, in the second case, arises because it would be unlikely that an individual wage could be inferred from the sum.

On the other hand occasions arise in which an aggregation of data is more sensitive than the individual parts. Such aggregation may arise when two or more items of information may individually have a low classification, but which in combination become very sensitive. Such a situation could arise if

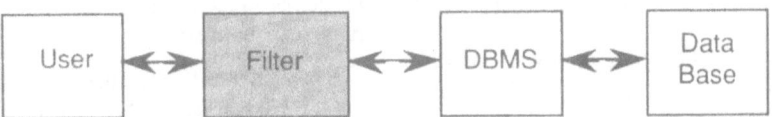

Multilevel database security
Fig. 1. Use of a filter to simulate a reference monitor.

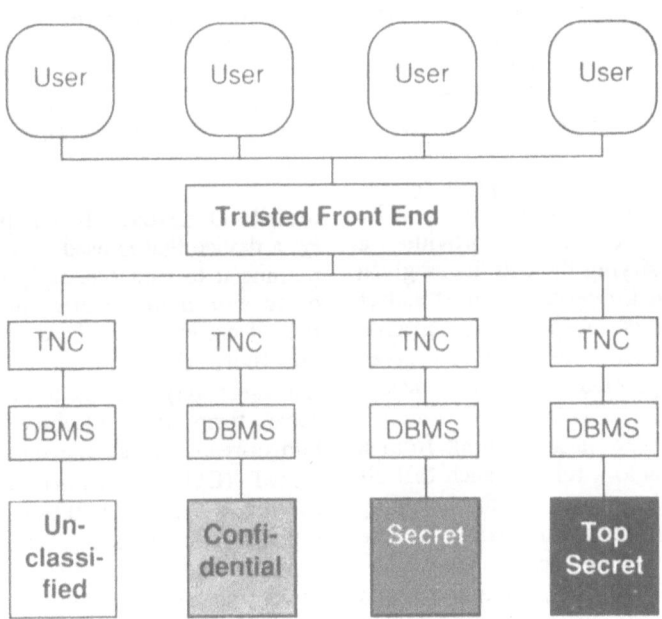

Multilevel database security
Fig. 2. Compartmented multiple level secure database.

a financial transaction is linked to the person who pays the money, and the person who receives the money. The individual pairs (username, transaction#) might be unclassified but the two pairs with the same transaction#, and payer and payee names could be very sensitive.

In general classification constraints can be defined for aggregates of data, similar to those for sanitized data, except that the classification for the view will be higher than that for the individual items of data, which act as a input to the view.

The set of classification constraints for a database, i.e. constant, derived, sanitized and aggregate must satisfy the conditions of completeness and consistency. The completeness requirement states that all data retrieved must be allocated a classification, by a classification constraint. The consistency condition is that the set of classification constraints only produce one classification for such retrieved data.

Classification constraints provide a mechanism for assigning a classification for the data in the target of the view; all the data in the target will have the same classification, i.e. that assigned by the classification constraint. The classification constraints provide a means of classifying the data items given in response to a query. The next aspect of the model is to specify the mechanisms by which a user with a given clearance is granted, or denied, access to data.

An access view is a mapping from a set of relations to a relation such that all the data in the source of the mapping has a classification dominated by the classification of the access view. The restriction on both the source and target data of the view ensures that no higher classified data can be inferred from the data returned in the view. In addition to a security classification the view also specifies the permitted form of access e.g. retrieve, insert, update etc.

A user may access the target data of an access view if the mandatory and discretionary access security rules are satisfied by the logged in security clearance and ID of the user, the classification of the access view and the mode of access. For example, a user may read data if:

- the user's security classification dominates that of the access view;
- the view permits the retrieve mode;
- the user has been granted discretionary read access to the view target data.

See AGGREGATION, ATTRIBUTE, BELL-LA PADULA MODEL, BIBA MODEL, BLUE BOOK, COVERT CHANNEL, DATABASE SECURITY, DBMS, DIRECT ACCESS, DISCRETIONARY ACCESS CONTROL, DOMINATE, INDIRECT ACCESS, INTEGRITY LOCKING, MANDATORY ACCESS CONTROL, MULTILEVEL SECURE, POLY-INSTANTIATION, REFERENCE MONITOR CONCEPT, RELATION, RELATIONAL DATABASE, TROJAN HORSE DIRECT RELEASE, TROJAN HORSE LEAKAGE, TUPLE, VIEW.

multilevel device. In computer security, a device that is used in a manner that permits it to simultaneously process data of two or more security levels without risk of compromise. To accomplish this, sensitivity labels are normally stored on the same physical medium and in the same form (i.e. machine-readable or human-readable) as the data being processed. (DOD). *Compare* SINGLE-LEVEL DEVICE. *See* MULTILEVEL NETWORK SUBJECT, MULTILEVEL SECURE, MULTILEVEL SECURITY MODE, SECURITY LEVEL, SENSITIVITY LABEL.

multilevel network subject. In communications security, a network subject that causes information to flow through the network at two or more security levels without risk of compromise. To accomplish this, sensitivity labels are transmitted with the data. *See* MULTI-LEVEL DEVICE, MULTILEVEL SECURE, MULTILEVEL SECURITY MODE, SECURITY LEVEL, SENSITIVITY LABEL, SUBJECT.

multilevel secure. In computer security, a class of system containing information with different sensitivities that simultaneously permits access by users with different security clearances and need-to-know, but prevents users from obtaining access to information for which they lack authorization. (DOD). *See* MULTILEVEL DEVICE, MULTILEVEL NETWORK SUBJECT, MULTILEVEL SE-CURE, MULTILEVEL SECURITY MODE, NEED TO KNOW.

multilevel security mode. (1) In computer security, a mode of operation that provides a capability for various levels and categories or compartments of data to be concurrently stored and processed in an automated system and permits selective access to such material concurrently by users who have differing security clearances and need-to-know. Internal controls, as well as personnel, physical, and administrative controls, separate users and data on the basis of security clearance. The internal security controls must be thoroughly demonstrated to be effective in preventing unauthorized access to information. (AFR). (2) In computer security, a mode of operation in effect when at least some users with access to the system do not have a security clearance or a need-to-know for all classified material in the information system. This mode provides the capability for the concurrent access to and use of the information system by uncleared users and users having different security clearances and need-to-know. The identification, segregation, and control of users and sensitive material on the basis of security clearance, and material classification category, and need-to-know must be essentially under automated control. Operation in this mode should be predicated on a comprehensive demonstration that the internal security controls can effectively prevent malicious attempts to bypass these controls. (AFR). (3) In computer security, a mode of operation under an operating system (supervisor or executive program) that provides a capability permitting various levels and categories or compartments of material to be concurrently stored and processed in an ADP system. In a remotely accessed resource-sharing system, the material can be selectively accessed and manipulated from variously controlled terminals by personnel having different security clearances and access approvals. This mode of operation can accommodate the concurrent processing and storage of (a) two or more levels of classified data, or (b) one or more levels of classified data with unclassified data depending upon the constraints placed on the system by the Designated Approving Authority. (DODD). *See* DESIGNATED APPROVING AUTHORITY, MULTILEVEL DEVICE, MULTILEVEL NETWORK SUBJECT, MULTILEVEL SECURE, NEED TO KNOW.

multilink. In data communications, a branch between two nodes consisting of two or more data links. *See* DATA LINK.

multimode fiber. In communications, a fiber having a core large enough to permit optical energy to propagate in a number of different modes. *Compare* MONOMODE FIBER. *See* FIBER OPTICS, MODE, MODE DISPERSION.

multipath. In communications, a pulse dispersal resulting from the fact that the light rays through a fiber have different velocities and paths. *See* MODE DISPERSION.

multiple access rights terminal. In access control, a terminal that may be used by more than one class of users; for example, users with different access rights to data. (FIPS). *See* ACCESS.

multiple categories. In access control, a Department of Defense clearance that may be required in addition to top secret clearance based on a current special background investigation. *Compare* CONFIDENTIAL CLEARANCE, ONE CATEGORY, SECRET CLEARANCE, UNCLASSIFIED INFORMATION, UNCLEARED. *See* CLEARANCE, TOP SECRET CLEARANCE.

multiple DES encipherment. In cryptography, the effective length of a DES key can be increased by multiple encipherment.

A simple double encipherment using two different keys does not, however, increase the effective key length from 56 to 112 bits.

If a known plaintext attack is mounted on doubly enciphered plaintext then one search is conducted by encipherment of the known plaintext, with a range of keys, and a second is conducted by corresponding decipherment of the ciphertext. The results of each of these searches is individually sorted and compared; a match then indicates a possible key pair. The search will produce a substantial number of candidate key pairs but a second search, using these candidate keys, with a different plaintext-ciphertext pair will normally reveal the key pair used in the original double encipherment. This technique is termed 'meet in the middle' and it indicates that double encipherment effectively only increases the key length from 56 to 57 bits, since the effort of finding a pair of keys is approximately twice that of determining a single key.

A form of triple key action involving encipherment with one key (k_1), decipherment with a second key (k_2) and re-encipherment with a third key (k_3) overcomes the danger of a meet in the middle attack. In some instances k_1 and k_3 are equal thus only requiring 2 keys. This technique has the advantage that it can be made compatible with single key encipherment $(k_1 = k_2 = k_3)$. However, it has been shown that such a scheme may be still susceptible to a form of meet in the middle attack and it is therefore recommended that three different keys be employed.

The whole question of multiple DES encipherment does however currently leave some unanswered questions. The meet in the middle attack involves sorting and storing 2^{56}, 64 bit numbers, and then checking entries in this list. This represents a massive data storage and retrieval task which could well be more expensive and time consuming than key exhaustion computations employing DES microchips. The statement that simple double encryption is only equivalent to increasing the effective key length by one bit ignores the abovementioned cost, time and effort involved in the storage aspect of the attack. *See* CRYPTOGRAPHIC KEY, DES, KEY-ENCRYPTING KEY, KEY MANAGEMENT, KNOWN PLAINTEXT.

multiple key retrieval. In databases, the technique of retrieving records based upon the value of several keys, some or all of which are secondary keys. *See* KEY, RECORD, SECONDARY KEY.

multiple routing. In data communications, a method of sending a message where more than one destination is specified in the header of the message. *See* MESSAGE HEADING, ROUTING.

multiplex. In physical security, pertaining to alarm systems that use multiplexed signals between the sensors and annunciator or alarm system. *See* ANNUNCIATOR. *Compare* HOMERUN.

multiplexer. In data communications, equipment that takes a number of channels and combines the signals into one common channel for transmission. At the remote end, a demultiplexer extracts each of the original signals. *See* MULTIPLEXING.

multiplexing. (1) In cryptography, a technique for generating random number sequences employed as cryptographic bit streams. Two linear feedback shift registers of length k and 2^k respectively are employed. The output of the shorter register is used to select the bit, of the longer register, that is to be output to the random sequence. *See* BIT, CRYPTO-GRAPHIC BIT STREAM, LINEAR FEEDBACK SHIFT REGISTER.

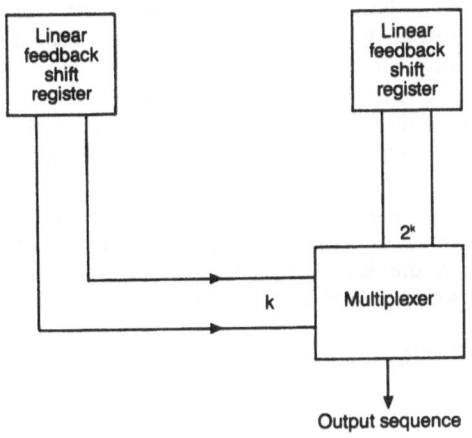

multiplexing
A method of generating random sequences for cryptographic bit stream.

(2) In communications, the process of combining a number of signals so that they can share a common transmission facility, thereby making more efficient use of the shared resource. *See* FREQUENCY DIVISION MULTIPLEXING, TIME DIVISION MULTIPLEXING.

multiplex mode. In data communications, a means of transferring data to, or from, low speed I/O devices on a multiplexer channel by interleaving bytes of data. *See* BYTE, INPUT OUTPUT DEVICE, MULTIPLEXER. *Synonymous with* BYTE MODE.

multipoint circuit. *Synonymous with* MULTIDROP CIRCUIT.

multipoint connection. In data communications, a communication link that joins three or more data stations, with the link going from one station to the next in sequence rather than a star arrangement. *See* STAR.

multi-user security mode of operation. In computer security, a mode of operation designed for systems that process sensitive unclassified information in which users may not have a need-to-know for all information processed in the system. This mode is also for microcomputers processing sensitive unclassified information that cannot meet the requirements of the stand-alone mode of operation. (AFR). *Compare* MULTILEVEL SECURITY MODE. *See* NEED TO KNOW.

municipal area network. In data communications, a network with the characteristics:

- physically large, compared with local area networks extending typically over 50 kms;
- readily interconnected allowing network operators to provide high speed data services nationally and internationally;
- supports many different user groups whilst maintaining data security between groups;
- intended principally for operation by public network operators, and has been designed to use the existing and future transmission paths of public networks.

Compare LOCAL AREA NETWORK, WIDE AREA NETWORK. *Synonymous with* METROPOLITAN AREA NETWORK.

Murphy. In computer security, a virus that terminates and stays resident, infects COMMAND.COM, COM, EXE and OVL files, affects run-time operation, corrupts program and OVL files. *See* VIRUS NAMES.

Music Bug. In computer security, a virus that terminates and stays resident, infects floppy disk boot sector and hard disk partition table, corrupts boot sector, affects run-time operation. *See* VIRUS NAMES.

mutual authentication. (1) In authentication, where both users communicating authenticate each other. (ANSI). (2) In data security, providing mutual assurance regarding the identity of subjects and/or objects. For example, a system needs to authenticate a user, and the user needs to authenticate that the system is genuine. *See* AUTHENTICATION, OBJECT, SUBJECT.

Mutual Legal Assistance Treaty. In legislation, a treaty that gives U.S. law enforcement and revenue officials access to confidential personal data and records in a country that has signed the treaty. *See* DATA PROTECTION.

mutually prime. *Synonymous with* COPRIME.

mutually suspicious. In computer security, pertaining to the state that exists between interactive processes (subsystems or programs) each of which contains sensitive data and is assumed to be designed so as to extract data from the other and to protect its own data. (FIPS).

mutual security. In communications security, pertaining to the testing of permutations used in time element scrambling. If two permutations are such that the result of one permutation, followed by the inversion of the second permutation, is close to the original sequence of segments then one of these permutations should not be used in the scrambling process. Mutual security testing checks each new permutation, to be used in the stored set of permutations, against each permutation already in the set. *See* TIME ELEMENT SCRAMBLER, VOICE SCRAMBLING.

MUX. *See* MULTIPLEXER.

MVS. In authentication, MAC Validation System, a system for testing the conformance of vendor devices to Federal and commercial data authentication standards. *See* MAC.

N

NAK. *See* NEGATIVE ACKNOWLEDGE-MENT.

NAK attack. In computer security, a penetration attack that capitalizes on a potential weakness in an operating system that does not handle asynchronous interrupts properly and thus leaves the system in an unprotected state during such interrupts. (FIPS). *See* INTERRUPT, OPERATING SYSTEM, PENETRATION.

narrow band. In data communications, pertaining to a channel with a bandwidth less than that of a voice grade channel. Normally used for communication speeds of less than 300 bits per second. *See* BANDWIDTH, VOICE GRADE CHANNEL.

NASA. *See* NATIONAL AERONAUTICS AND SPACE AGENCY.

National Aeronautics and Space Agency. A U.S. government agency that is responsible for administration of the communications satellite program.

National Commission on Data Processing and Freedoms. *See* DATA PROTECTION - FRANCE.

National Communications Security Directive 4. A U.S. directive entitled 'National Policy on Control of Compromising Emanation' dated 1981. It required federal agencies to protect classified information against compromising emanations. *See* COMPROMISING EMANATIONS.

National Computer Security Center. A center of the National Security Agency formed as a result of NSDD-145. The primary goal of the Center is to encourage the widespread availability of trusted computer systems in the U.S. It was formerly known as the Department of Defense Computer Security Center. *See* NSDD-145.

National Crime Information Center. In legislation, an FBI center concerned with crime intelligence. *See* DATA PROTECTION - U.S.A.

National Institute for Science and Technology. A U.S. body, originally called the National Bureau of Standards. It is an agency with responsibility for setting Federal standards for the effective and efficient use of computers systems.

National Security Agency/Central Security Service. The U.S. National Security Agency was established in 1952 as a separately organized agency within the Department of Defense, for the signals intelligence and communications security activities of the U.S. Government. It was charged with the additional mission of computer security in 1984. The Central Security Service was established in 1972 to provide a more unified cryptological organization within the Department of Defense. The three primary missions of the National Security Agency/Central Security Service are communications security, computer security and foreign intelligence information.

National Security Directive-42. In legislation, a directive that requires Federal agencies to adhere to the Computer Security Act. *See* COMPUTER SECURITY ACT OF 1987.

native key. In cryptography, a crypto-graphic key in the form of binary bits as required by the encryption or decryption algorithm. *Compare* LONG KEY.

native mode. In cryptography, a DES mode of operation in which one or more 64 bit input blocks produce corresponding 64 bit ciphertext blocks by successively presenting the input blocks for encipherment. For a given key DES effectively provides an electronic codebook with 2^{64} entries of plaintext-ciphertext pairs. If messages are highly formatted then certain ciphertext blocks are likely to recur and be of value to an attacker. *Compare* CIPHER BLOCK CHAINING, CIPHER FEEDBACK, OUTPUT FEEDBACK. *See* DATA ENCRYPTION STANDARD. *Synonymous with* ELECTRONIC CODEBOOK.

natural language. A language in which the rules reflect current usage without being specifically prescribed. The language employed by users in normal communication as compared with restricted language used for communication with computers, indexing documents etc. *Compare* PROGRAM LANGUAGE.

navigation. In databases, the process of moving through a database, following an explicit path from one data item to the next, until the required item is attained.

NCC. UK National Computing Center.

NCIC. *See* NATIONAL CRIME INFORMATION CENTER.

NCSC. *See* NATIONAL COMPUTER SECURITY CENTER.

necessary bandwidth. In communications, the width of bandwidth that is just sufficient to ensure that the transmission

of information is at the speed and of the quality required. *See* BANDWIDTH.

need to know. (1) In data security, a determination made by the processor of sensitive information that a prospective recipient, in the interest of national security, has a requirement for access to, knowledge of, or possession of the sensitive information in order to perform official tasks or services. (DOD). *See* NEED TO KNOW VIOLATION. (2) In data security, the necessity for access to, knowledge of, or possession of certain information required to carry out official duties. Responsibility for determining whether a person's duties require that possession of, or access, to such information and whether the individual is authorized to receive it rests upon the individual having current possession, knowledge, or control of the information involved and not upon the prospective recipient. (OPNAVINST). *See* NEED TO KNOW VIOLATION. (3) In data security, a policy that restricts access to classified information to personnel whose duties necessitate such access.

need to know violation. In data security, the disclosure of classified or other sensitive defense information to a person who is cleared, but has no requirement for such information to carry out assigned official duties. (AR). *See* NEED TO KNOW.

negative acknowledgement. In data communications, a signal sent from receiver to transmitter to indicate that a message with detectable errors has been received. The transmitter then repeats the message. *Compare* AFFIRMATIVE ACKNOWLEDGEMENT.

negative card. In banking, a card held by a legitimate user but for which facilities are to be restricted (e.g. a debit card held by a card holder with an unauthorized overdraft). *Compare* HOT CARD LIST. *See* DEBIT CARD.

negative disclosure. In database security, a form of personal disclosure in which it is possible to deduce that an individual does not have a particular attribute, e.g. does not suffer from a particular disease. *See* PERSONAL DISCLOSURE.

negative file. *Synonymous with* HOT CARD LIST.

negative safeguard. In computer security, a safeguard that is assumed to be functioning when, in fact, it is not.

netkey. In cryptography, a technique in which a single cryptographic key is used for all transmissions between terminals in a given network. *Compare* SESSION KEY.

network. (1) In data communications, two or more systems connected by a communications medium whose responsibility is the transference of information from one system to another. (AFR). (2) In data communications, a network is composed of a communications medium and all components attached to that medium whose responsibility is the transference of information. Such components may include AISs, packet switches, telecommunications controllers, key distribution centers, and technical control devices. (DODD). *See* AIS, KEY DISTRIBUTION CENTER, PACKET SWITCHING. (3) In data communications, the interconnection of two or more ADP central computer facilities that provides for the transfer or sharing of ADP resources. The ADP network consists of the central computer facilities, the remote terminals, the interconnecting communication links, the frontend processors, and the telecommunications systems. (OPNAVINST). *See* FRONT END PROCESSOR. (4) A series of interconnected points. (5) In communications, a system of interconnected communication facilities.

network architecture. In data communications, a set of layers and protocols (including formats and standards that different hardware/software must comply with to achieve stated objectives) that define a network (TNI). *See* OPEN SYSTEMS INTERCONNECTION, PROTOCOL.

network component. In data communications, a network subsystem that is evaluatable for compliance with the trusted network interpretations, relative to that policy induced on the component by the overall network policy (TNI). *See* COMPONENT.

network connection. In data communications, any logical or physical path from one host to another that makes possible the transmission of information from one host to the other. An example is the TCP connection. But also, when a host transmits an IP datagram employing only the services of its connectionless Internet Protocol interpreter, there is considered to be a connection between the source and the destination hosts for this transaction (TNI). *See* CONNECTIONLESS SERVICE, DATAGRAM, TCP/IP.

network control program. In computer networks, a part of the operating system of a host computer that establishes and breaks logical connections. It communicates with the user processes in the host computer on one hand, and the network on the other. *See* HOST COMPUTER, OPERATING SYSTEM.

network control station. In communications, a station that coordinates the use of a communications network.

network control system. In data communications, the computer system that provides the means of collecting and processing information concerning the status of a telecommunications network. (GAO)

network database. In databases, a structure that permits a linkage from any item to any other item. *Compare* HIER-ARCHICAL DATABASE, RELATIONAL DATABASE, TREE DATABASE.

network delay. In data communications, the transit time for a packet, in a packet switched network, defined as the interval between the time that the last bit, of the packet, leaves the entry node and the time at which the first bit enters the destination node. *See* COMPUTER NETWORK, PACKET SWITCHING.

network diagram. A diagram indicating the nodes, and their interconnections. *See* NODE.

network discretionary access control. In communications security, discretionary access control applied to network components at protocol level 3. *See* DISCRETIONARY ACCESS CONTROL, OSI SECURITY.

network encryption. In communications security, techniques employed to encrypt messages transmitted through a network. The provision of secure communications in a network is complicated by the presence of intermediate nodes that receive the messages and redirect them to appropriate output links.

There are three methods of dealing with encryption within networks, i.e. link encryption, node encryption and end-to-end encryption (see Fig. 1.).

Link encryption requires cryptographic devices at each end of the communication link, the messages are thus decrypted before they enter the node; they are re-encrypted, under a different key, after leaving the node and before entering the next communication link. Node encryption provides for the message decryption, and re-encryption under a different key for transmission to the next node, within secure modules in the node. End-to-end encryption involves no intermediate decryption and re-encryp-

tion; two users at each end of the communication path must therefore agree upon the cryptographic keys to be employed.

Link encryption is completely transparent to the user but the messages are passed through the nodes in clear. This situation may be unacceptable to some users with particularly sensitive data. Node encryption is also transparent to the user whilst end-to-end encryption may be under the complete control of the user, i.e. private cryptography, or it may be a facility provided by the system operator. It is also possible to combine end-to-end and node or link encryption thus producing a double encryption of the messages.

The cost of cryptographic devices is highest for link encryption, involving two such devices on every secure communication link. Node encryption allows all communication links, entering and leaving nodes, to share a node cryptographic unit. End-to-end encryption only requires cryptographic units at those end nodes demanding such facilities.

The Reference Model for Open Systems Interconnection (OSI) (Fig. 2) provides a useful framework for comparing end-to-end and link encryption in the context of communications network architectures. In the case of end-to-end encryption, the encryption and decryption processes must occur at one of the host resident layers i.e. the application, presentation, session, or transport layers. Once the encryption has been effected, protocol control information added to the message by subsequent (lower) layers is transmitted across the network in clear. Thus in the example of shown in Fig. 3, subversion of the intermediate network nodes or wiretapping of the communications links will reveal information for traffic analysis but not the actual content of the message. In the case of link encryption, the encryption and decryption processes are performed at the data link layer. In this case (Fig. 3) only the protocol control information

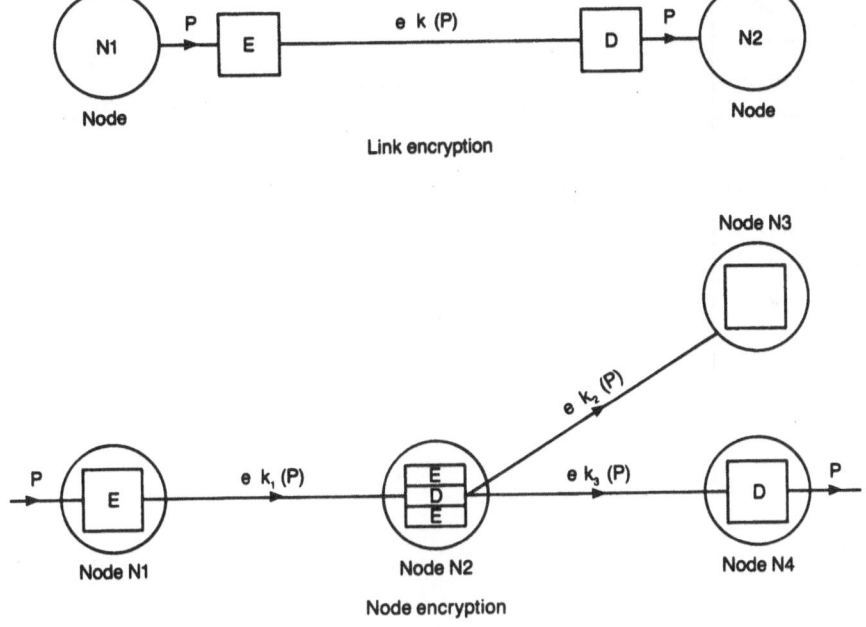

Link encryption

Node encryption

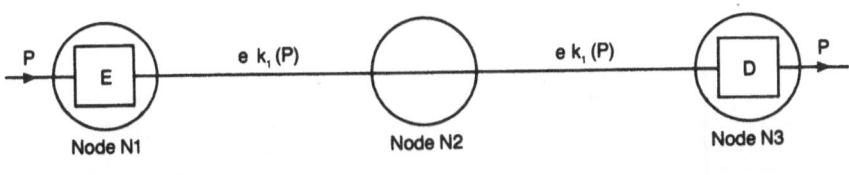

End-to-end encryption

network encryption
Fig. 1.

added to the message at the data link layer is transmitted across the link in clear. Hence the receiving node must be able to decrypt at least the protocol control information added by the network layer in order to determine to which node the message should be routed. See CRYPTOGRAPHIC EQUIPMENT, CRYPTOGRAPHIC KEY, END-TO-END ENCRYPTION, KEY MANAGEMENT, LINK ENCRYPTION, NODE ENCRYPTION, OSI SECURITY, PRIVATE CRYPTOGRAPHY, TRAFFIC ANALYSIS.

network guard. In communications security, a security system that performs

350 network guard

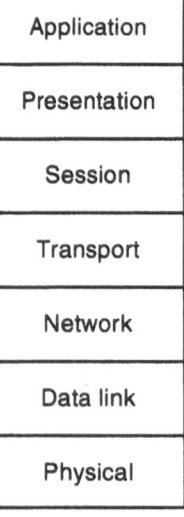

Application
Presentation
Session
Transport
Network
Data link
Physical

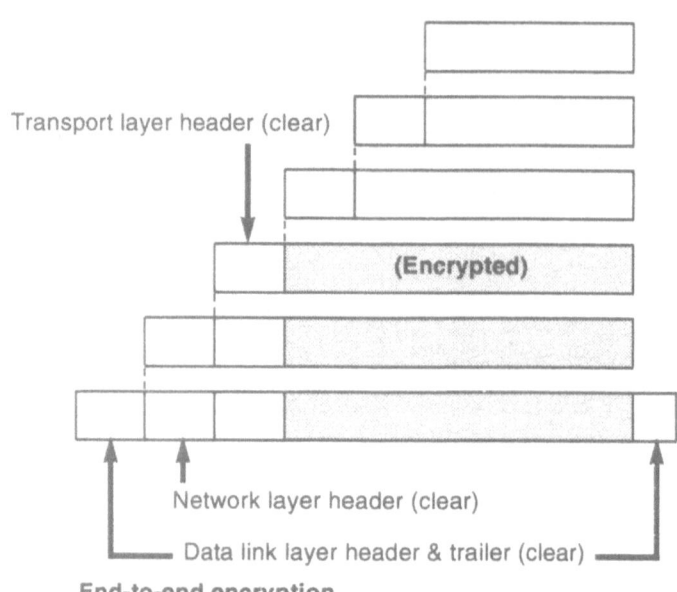

Transport layer header (clear)

(Encrypted)

Network layer header (clear)

Data link layer header & trailer (clear)

End-to-end encryption

network encryption
Fig. 2

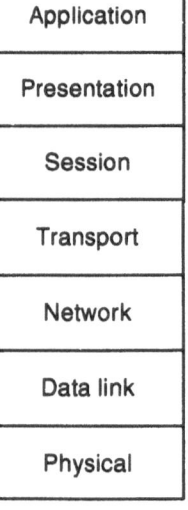

Application
Presentation
Session
Transport
Network
Data link
Physical

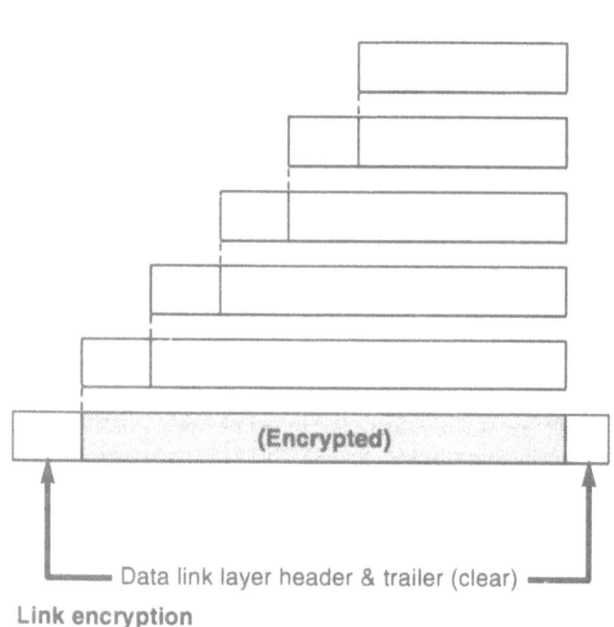

(Encrypted)

Data link layer header & trailer (clear)

Link encryption

network encryption
Fig. 3

access control between networks, where each network is operating in a separate security domain. The network guard may also control the directional flow of data between the networks according to a preprogrammed security policy, e.g. discretionary access control, mandatory access control etc.

network layer. In data communications, a layer in the ISO Open Systems Interconnection Reference model. This layer is responsible for control of the operation of the subnet. It is primarily concerned with routing techniques in a point-to-point system and the effects of poor routing, i.e. congestion. *Compare* APPLICATION LAYER, DATA LINK LAYER, PHYSICAL LAYER, PRESENTATION LAYER, SESSION LAYER, TRANSPORT LAYER. *See* OPEN SYSTEMS INTERCONNECTION, ROUTING.

network management. In data communications, the systematic procedures necessary to plan, organize and control an evolving communication network with optimum costs and performance.

network management system. In data communications, a system that enables the network supervisor to monitor the status of every communication line, modem and terminal in the network and to locate failures. Usually a controlling unit monitors the network via a low-speed secondary channel independent of the main data channel. *See* CHANNEL, MODEM.

network operating center. In data communications, an installation that facilitates reliable network operation by the monitoring of network status, supervision and coordination of network maintenance, collecting usage and accounting data etc.

network redundancy. In data communications, a property of networks that have more links than are strictly neces-

sary to connect the nodes, thus enabling the network to continue to function if certain links fail.

network reference monitor. In access control, a concept that refers to an abstract machine that mediates all access to objects within the network by subjects within the network (TNI). *See* REFERENCE MONITOR CONCEPT.

network security. In communications security, the protection of networks and their services from unauthorized modification, destruction or disclosure. Providing an assurance that the network performs its critical functions correctly and there are no harmful side effects. Includes providing for information accuracy (TNI).

network security architecture. In communications security, a subset of network architecture specifically addressing security relevant issues (TNI).

network security model. In communications security, a model implementing the concepts of the network security architecture. An extension of the OSI basic reference model covers security aspects that are general architectural elements of communications protocols. The general security-related architectural elements can be applied appropriately in the circumstances for which protection of communication between open systems is required. Existing standards may be improved or new standards developed, using the guidelines and constraints in the network security model. *See* NETWORK SECURITY ARCHITECTURE, OSI SECURITY.

network sponsor. In communications security, the individual or organization that is responsible for stating the security policy enforced by the network, for designing the network security architecture to properly enforce that policy and for ensuring that the network is implemented in such a way that the policy is enforced. For commercial, off-the-shelf systems, the sponsor will normally be the vendor. For a fielded network system the sponsor will normally be the project manager or system administrator (TNI).

network structure. In computing, a structure in which any node can be connected to any other node. *Compare* TREE STRUCTURE.

network system. In data communications, a system that is implemented with a collection of interconnected network components. A network system is based on a coherent security architecture and design (TNI). *See* NETWORK SECURITY ARCHITECTURE.

network termination unit. In data communications, the part of the network equipment that connects directly with the DTE, it operates between the local transmission lines and the subscribers' interface. *See* DTE.

network timing. In data communications, timing signals transferred from DCE to DTE to control the transmission of digits across the transmitted and received data circuits. *See* DCE, DTE.

network topology. In communications, the geometric arrangement of nodes and links in a network.

network trusted computing base. In communications security, the totality of protection mechanisms within a network system, including hardware, firmware and software, the combination of which is responsible for enforcing a security policy (TNI). *Compare* TRUSTED COMPUTING BASE. *See* SECURITY POLICY, TRUSTED COMPUTING BASE.

network user identification. In data communications, the identification code used by a customer on a public dial port

to identify himself for accounting purposes. *Compare* USER ID. *See* NETWORK USER IDENTITY, PACKET SWITCHING, PUBLIC DIAL PORT.

network user identity. In data communications, a code required for dial-up access to a data network. *Compare* USER ID. *See* NETWORK USER IDENTIFICATION.

network virtual terminal. In data communications, an abstract terminal used to enable systems with incompatible terminals to intercommunicate over a network. Each terminal is served by software which maps the functions of the network virtual terminal to the functions of that particular terminal type. *See* VIRTUAL TERMINAL.

network weaving. In communications security, a technique using different communication networks to gain access to an organization's system. For example, an attacker makes a call through AT&T, jumps over to Sprint, then to MCI, and then to Tymnet. The purpose is to avoid detection and trace-backs to the source of the call. *See* HACKER.

new hire orientation. In procedural security, pertaining to methods adopted to induct new employees into an organization's security procedures. *See* COMPUTER FRAUD CONTROL, PERSONNEL SECURITY.

New Sunday. In computer security, a virus that terminates and stays resident, infects COM, EXE and OVL files, affects run-time operation, corrupts program, data and OVL files and file linkage. *See* VIRUS NAMES.

next-day funds. In banking, funds immediately available for transfer in like funds and, subject to settlement, available the next business day for same-day funds transfer or withdrawal in cash. This funds type is only applicable to certain specific US dollar transactions.

(ANSI). *Compare* SAME-DAY FUNDS. *See* FUNDS TYPE.

nibble. In computing, a word comprising 4 bits. *Compare* BYTE. *See* BIT, WORD.

NIFTP. In data communications, Network Independent File Transfer Protocol. *See* FILE TRANSFER.

NIIT. National, International and Intercontinental Telecommunication network.

Nina. In computer security, a virus that terminates and stays resident, infects COMMAND.COM and COM files, affects run-time operation, corrupts program, OVL and data files. *See* VIRUS NAMES.

NIST. *See* NATIONAL INSTITUTE OF STANDARDS AND TECHNOLOGY.

NKSR. *See* NON-KERNEL SECURITY-RELATED SOFTWARE.

NMR. In reliability, a form of modular redundancy similar to triple modular redundancy except that N units, N being an odd number, are employed. *Compare* TRIPLE MODULAR REDUNDANCY. *See* MODULAR REDUNDANCY.

no contract. In data security, no contractor dissemination; indicates that the information contained in the document must not be released to contractors or consultants. (DOE).

node. (1) In data communications, a computer system that is connected to a communications network and participates in the routing of messages within that network. Networks are usually described as a collection of nodes that are connected by communications links. *See* NETWORK. (2) In data communications, a place that has significance for data routing, a point of interconnection to a network. (3) In computing, an entity on two or more access paths.

node computer. In data communications, a computer used to interconnect the host computers. The host computers are connected to the communications network via a node computer. *See* HOST COMPUTER.

node encryption. In communications security, a method of encryption of network data in which the data is decrypted within an intermediate node, and re-encrypted, under a different key, for onward transmission. The decryption and re-encryption is performed in secure modules and thus plaintext is not transmitted through the node. *Compare* END-TO-END ENCRYPTION, LINK ENCRYPTION. *See* NETWORK ENCRYPTION, PLAINTEXT.

NOFORN. In data security, NO FOReigN dissemination. The term indicates that the information contained in the document must not be released to foreign nationals. (DOE).

noise. (1) In communications, a random undesired signal. *See* THERMAL NOISE. (2) In key management, a random signal whose properties can be used for generating cryptographic session keys. *See* RANDOM NUMBERS, SESSION KEY. (3) In database security, random numbers added to data items in perturbation techniques. *See* INFERENCE CONTROL, PERTURBATION.

noise temperature. In electronics, the temperature of a thermal noise source producing the same output noise power, in the same bandwidth, as the device under consideration. *See* THERMAL NOISE.

nomenclature. A consistent method for assigning names to elements of a system.

Nomenclature. In computer security, a virus that terminates and stays resident, infects COMMAND.COM, COM, EXE and OVL files, affects run-time operation, corrupts program, OVL and data files. *See* VIRUS NAMES.

nonbreak glass station. In physical security, a manual fire alarm station that does not require the glass plate or rod to be broken in order to activate the alarm. *See* ALARM STATION.

nonce. In cryptography, a random number used in a request/response protocol. *See* REPLAY.

noncoded system. In physical security, a system in which a continuous alarm signal is relayed for a predetermined minimum period. Thereafter the fire alarm may be silenced either manually or automatically. *Compare* CODED SYSTEM.

noncompatibility. In computing, pertaining to a situation in which one system is unable to retrieve information stored in another or to run programs developed on another. *Compare* COMPATIBILITY.

nondense index. In databases, an index that provides information on the location of a group of records. Once the location is accessed the records must be scanned sequentially until the one corresponding to the appropriate key is found. *Compare* DENSE INDEX. *See* INDEX, RECORD, KEY.

nondestructive readout. In computing, pertaining to reading action that does not change the data held. *Compare* DESTRUCTIVE READOUT.

nondeterministic polynomial class. *See* NP CLASS.

non-discretionary security. In data security, the aspect of DOD security policy that restricts access on the basis of security levels. A security level is composed of a read level and a category set restriction. For read-access to an item of information, a user must have a clearance level greater than or equal to the classification of the information, and also have a category clearance that includes all of the access categories specified for the information. (MTR). *Compare* DISCRETIONARY SECURITY. *See* MANDATORY SECURITY.

noninvertibility. In cryptography, a property of a cryptographic algorithm. The algorithm is said to be noninvertible if it is computationally infeasible to determine the cryptographic key given the plaintext and corresponding ciphertext. *See* CIPHERTEXT, COMPUTATIONALLY INFEASIBLE, CRYPTOGRAPHIC ALGORITHM, CRYPTOGRAPHIC KEY, PLAINTEXT.

non-kernel security-related software. In computer security, security-relevant software which is executed in the environment provided by a security kernel, rather than as part of the kernel. Processes executing NKSR software may or may not require special privilege to override kernel-enforced security rules (MTR). *See* SECURITY KERNEL.

nonoverwriting virus. In computer security, a virus that appends itself to the infected program in such a way that the program may be successfully executed after the action of the virus code. *Compare* OVERWRITING VIRUS. *See* VIRUS.

nonprime attribute. In databases, an attribute that is not a prime attribute, i.e. it is not a member of a candidate key. *Compare* PRIME ATTRIBUTE. *See* CANDIDATE KEY, RELATIONAL DATABASE.

nonprocedural language. In computing, a language in which the user specifies the desired end result rather than the processes required to attain it. For example, having specified a family tree and defined grandson as the son of a grandparent's son or daughter then the user may input a request for the grandsons of a specified person. *Compare* PROCEDURAL LANGUAGE. *Synonymous with* DECLARATIVE LANGUAGE.

nonrepudiation. (1) In authentication, a service that provides proof of the integrity and origin of data, both in an unforgeable relationship, which can be verified by any third party at any time. (ANSI). (2) In authentication, an authentication that with high assurance can be asserted to be genuine, and that cannot subsequently be refuted. *Compare* REPUDIATION.

nonreturn to zero. In data communications, a method of data transmission in which a voltage of one polarity represents a 1 bit and the other polarity represents a 0 bit. The circuit carries data whenever it is enabled. It is a common method of data transfer between a computer and its peripherals.

nonsecret design. In data security, the principle that aspects of the design of a secure system need not be kept secret because the security lies in secret keys, parameters etc. For example the DES algorithm is public knowledge and the secrecy of the cipher depends upon the secret keys. This principle allows the system to be investigated by a wide variety of specialists searching for potential security design faults. On the other hand it can be argued that the openness increases the risk of discovering a design flaw, or trapdoor, in a system that has become widely used with, potentially, very serious consequences. *See* DES, TRAPDOOR.

nonstandard sector. In software protection, a floppy disk that has been formatted in a nonstandard way and so cannot be copied using operating system utilities. *See* EXECUTE PROTECTION, FLOPPY DISK, FORMATTING, OPERATING SYSTEM.

nonswitched line. *Synonymous with* LEASED CIRCUIT.

nontransparent mode. In data communications, transmission of characters in a defined format, e.g. ASCII, in which all defined control sequences and characters are recognized and treated. *Compare* CONTROL CHARACTER, TRANSPARENT DATA COMMUNICATION CODE. *See* ASCII.

nonvolatile storage. In computing, storage media that retain information when the power supply is removed. *Compare* VOLATILE STORAGE.

normal forms. In databases, a class of relations, in relational databases, with defined properties of interrelationship between the attributes. The use of normal forms in a database reduces problems in the manipulation and storage of data that can arise from inherent interrelationships between attributes. *See* RELATION, ATTRIBUTE, FIRST NORMAL FORM, RELATIONAL DATABASE, SECOND NORMAL FORM, THIRD NORMAL FORM.

nostro account. In banking, a record kept by an account owner bank of an account serviced on its behalf by an account servicing bank. (ANSI). *See* ACCOUNT SERVICING BANK.

notarization. (1) In authentication, the registration of data with a trusted third party that allows the later assurance of the accuracy of its characteristics such as content, origin, time and delivery. (ISO). (2) In cryptography, a method of applying additional security to a key utilizing the identities of the originator and the ultimate recipient. (ANSI). *See* CRYPTOGRAPHIC KEY. *Synonymous with* KEY NOTARIZATION.

NP Class. In mathematics, Nondeterministic Polynomial Class, a class of problems in which the time taken to determine a solution rises exponentially with the size of the problem, but the time taken to check a solution rises linearly or in polynomial time. *See* NP COMPLETE, PUBLIC KEY CRYPTOGRAPHY, TIME AND SPACE REQUIREMENTS.

NP complete. In mathematics, a class of NP problems that have the property that if any one of them has an easily implemented method for finding a general solution then all the NP problems would have such methods. *See* NP CLASS.

n-respondent, k%-dominance. In database security, a criterion of inference control used with census data. It defines a sensitive statistic as one in which n or fewer records constitute more than k% of the total. *See* INFERENCE CONTROL, SENSITIVE STATISTIC, STATISTICAL DATABASE.

NRZ. *See* NONRETURN TO ZERO.

NSA. U.S. National Security Agency. *See* NATIONAL SECURITY AGENCY/CENTRAL SECURITY SERVICE.

NSA COMSEC module. In cryptography, under the CCEP the NSA is endorsing two types of cryptographic products, Type I and Type II. A Type I product is intended for use in protecting classified U.S. government information and will only be used by the U.S. government and its contractors, it will not be available outside government control. A Type II product will also be used by the U.S. government and its contractors but it will also be available for the commercial private sector. Type I and Type II products cannot be exported. Type I and II products will contain one of three types of semiconductor chip modules supplied by NSA through a COMSEC module vendor. These modules embody a secret encryption algorithm in a sealed chip protected against reverse engineering. Each module includes essential security features and standard input and output format. The modules will be supplied to user end item vendors, as OEM devices, who will then manufacture secure communications equipment embodying these modules.

Both Type I and II modules will have three variants, that differ in size, cost and speed, designed for: single channel voice, computer data and high speed data. Modules within a single variant will be interoperable with each other. *Compare* DATA ENCRYPTION STANDARD. *See* CCEP, COMSEC, OEM, NSA, REVERSE ENGINEERING.

NSD-42. *See* NATIONAL SECURITY DIRECTIVE-42.

NSDD. U.S. National Security Decision Directive.

NSDD-145. National Security Directive 145. A Directive in which the US President recognized the security problem and susceptibility of private sector communications. As a result of this directive the NSA adapted its CCEP program to permit the private sector access to CCEP equipment. *See* CCEP, DES, NSA, NSA COMSEC MODULE.

NSI. U.S. National Security Information.

NTCB. *See* NETWORK TRUSTED COMPUTING BASE.

NTCB partition. In communications security, the totality of mechanisms within a single network component for enforcing the network policy, as allocated to that component; the part of the NTCB within a single network component (TNI). *See* NETWORK COMPONENT, NTCB, SECURITY POLICY.

NTISS. U.S. National Telecommunications and Information System Security.

NTISSC. U.S. National Telecommunications and Information System Security Committee.

NTISSD. U.S. National Telecommunications and Information System Security Directive.

NTISSP-200. U.S National Telecommunications and Information Systems Security Policy - 200, a U.S. policy dated 1987 that required all systems, acting on behalf of the government and accessed by users at various authority levels, to be evaluated to at least C2 level as defined by the Orange Book. *See* C2, ORANGE BOOK.

n-tuple. In mathematics, a collection of n elements, normally ordered. *See* TUPLE.

nucleus. In computing, that part of the operating system that is the center of all control and resource management activities; it handles resource allocation and access to I/O interfaces. It is often distinguished from the kernel by the mixture of normal programming and microcoding. *See* I/O, KERNEL.

NUI. *See* NETWORK USER IDENTIFICATION.

nuisance alarm. In physical security, an activation of an alarm by an equipment failure or similar fault.

null modem. In data communications, a device employed to connect two systems that normally communicate with modems. For example if two computers communicate directly using RS-232C interfaces both would transmit data on pin 2 and would expect to receive data on pin 3. In this case a null modem would simply comprise a plug-socket system to connect pin 2 on one computer and to pin 3 on the other and vice versa. *See* MODEM, RS-232C.

null string. In computing, a string that contains no characters. *See* STRING.

null suppression. In codes, the bypassing of null characters to be stored or transmitted to save transmission time or storage space. *See* DATA COMPRESSION.

number. A mathematical entity indicating a quantity or amount of units.

number crunching. In computing, pertaining to processing activities that involve a high proportion of mathematical operations on the data, usually arising in scientific applications. Such applications make heavy use of the CPU and involve comparatively few input-output operations. *See* CPU.

O

OA. Office Automation.

object. (1) In computer security, a passive entity that contains or receives information. Access to an object potentially implies access to the information it contains. Examples of objects are: records, blocks, pages, segments, files, directories, directory trees, and programs as well as bits, bytes, words, fields, processors, video displays, keyboards, clocks, printers, network nodes etc. (DOD). *Compare* SUBJECT. (2) In computing, an entity in computer memory that contains and protects a set of related data. Objects perform assigned tasks by communicating with each other. For example a processor object stores vital data for the processor, if another processor is added to the system it is merely necessary to add a corresponding object in memory.

object authentication. In authentication, the verification that objects, e.g. large programs, have not been altered during some period in which they were not under direct control.

object code. In computing, the code of a user's program after it has been translated. *Compare* SOURCE CODE.

objective of defense. In computer security, security defensive procedures are designed to achieve the objectives: (a) prevent occurrence of the exposure by the erection of barriers between any threat and the vulnerabilities to it, (b) minimize or contain the impact of damage, mainly through the use of successive layers of protection so that a threat agent is restricted in terms of what it can achieve, and (c) maximize recovery from damage. Provide for ways of circumventing the damage, e.g. use of backup and reconstruction of files. *See* DEFENSIVE DEPTH, THREAT, VULNERABILITY.

objectivity. In information security, a property of a test whereby the result is obtained with the minimum of subjective judgement or opinion. *See* INFORMATION TECHNOLOGY SECURITY EVALUATION CRITERIA, INFORMATION TECHNOLOGY SECURITY EVALUATION MANUAL.

object language. In computing, the output language of a translation process. *Compare* SOURCE LANGUAGE.

object program. In computing, a program in object code form. *See* OBJECT CODE.

object protection. (1) In access control, the controls employed to restrict access to an object. *See* OBJECT. (2) In physical security, the means employed to protect objects of value, e.g. safes, files, from the protected area.

object reuse. In computer security, the reassignment to some subject of a medium (e.g. page frame, disk sector, magnetic tape) that contained one or more objects. To be securely reassigned such media must contain no residual data from the previously contained object or objects. (DOD). *See* OBJECT, RESIDUE, SUBJECT. (2) In information security, functions to control the reuse of data objects. *See* INFORMATION TECHNOLOGY SECURITY EVALUATION CRITERIA.

358

OCD. In banking, Other Card Data, data recorded on the card that is not normally known to parties other than the card issuer or its agent. (SAA). *See* CARD KEY.

OCI. U.S. Office of Computer Information. An office of the Department of Commerce.

OCR. *See* OPTICAL CHARACTER RECOGNITION.

octal. In mathematics, pertaining to the number 8. Octal notation uses a base of 8 and is a convenient form of representing binary numbers, e.g. decimal 66 = octal 102 = binary 1 000 010. *Compare* HEXADECIMAL. *See* BINARY.

octet. In computing, a group of eight binary digits treated as an entity. *See* OCTAL.

odd even check. *Synonymous with* PARITY CHECKING.

odd parity. *See* PARITY.

odd prime. In mathematics, any prime number except 2. *See* PRIME NUMBER.

ODETTE. Organization for Data Exchange and TeleTransmission in Europe. A European body that sets standards for document layout so they can be sent over a data network and understood by the recipient. *See* ELECTRONIC DATA INTERCHANGE.

Oe. *See* OERSTED.

OEM. *See* ORIGINAL EQUIPMENT MANUFACTURER.

oersted. In electronics, a unit of measure of the magnetizing force necessary to produce a desired magnetic flux across a surface. (DOD). *See* MAGNETIC FLUX.

OFB. *See* OUTPUT FEEDBACK.

off line. In operations, pertaining to processing equipment that is not connected to a computer or network, or the operations performed on such equipment. *Compare* ON LINE.

off line card reader. In access control, an access control card reader that contains sufficient intelligence to make entry or exit decisions based upon the information read from the access card. *Compare* ON LINE CARD READER. *See* CARD READER. *Synonymous with* INTELLIGENT CARD READER.

off line crypto-operation. In communications security, encryption or decryption performed as a self-contained operation distinct from the transmission of the encrypted text, as by hand or by machines not electrically connected to a signal line. (FIPS). *Compare* ON LINE CRYPTO-OPERATION. *See* ENCRYPT, DECRYPT.

off line encryption. *See* OFF LINE CRYPTOSYSTEM.

offset. (1) In physical security, the distance on the ground surface where an intruder is able to avoid detection by crawling under a span sensor. *See* SPAN SENSOR. (2) In physical security, the overlapping of span beam coverage by staggering the transmitters and receivers to minimize gaps in beam coverage. (3) In banking, a number that mathematically relates a calculated identification code to a customer selected PIN. (ANSI). *See* PIN MANAGEMENT AND SECURITY. *Synonymous with* PIN OFFSET. (4) In key management. *Synonymous with* KEY OFFSET.

off site storage. In physical security, the technique of maintaining backup material in a secured area off premises. *See* BACKUP PROCEDURES.

Off Stealth. In computer security, a stealth virus that terminates and stays resident, infects COMMAND.COM, COM, EXE and OVL files, affects runtime operation, corrupts program, OVL and data files. *See* VIRUS NAMES.

OIS 21. In data security, a BSI committee for data security standards. *See* BSI, TC 97/SC20.

OMB. U.S. Office of Management and Budget.

OMR. *See* OPTICAL MARK RECOGNITION.

one category. In data security, a Department of Defense clearance that is required in addition to top secret clearance based on a current special background investigation. Authorization to access rights are granted by a responsible individual. *Compare* CONFIDENTIAL CLEARANCE, MULTIPLE CATEGORIES, SECRET CLEARANCE, UNCLASSIFIED INFORMATION, UNCLEARED. *See* CLEARANCE, TOP SECRET CLEARANCE.

one end device. In computer security, a protection device against telephone intrusion that is installed at either the host computer or the user end of the telephone link. *Compare* TWO END DEVICE. *See* PORT PROTECTION DEVICE, SECURITY MODEM, TELEPHONE INTRUSION.

one key cryptosystem. *Synonymous with* SYMMETRIC CRYPTOSYSTEM.

one-time pad. In cryptography, a cipher that uses a nonrepeating random key stream. One-time pads are the only ciphers that achieve perfect secrecy but the length of the key is equal to the length of the message. They are mainly used for diplomatic communications. *See* PERFECT SECRECY, STREAM CIPHER.

one-time passwords. In access control, passwords that are changed after each use and are useful when the password is not adequately protected from compromise during log in (e.g., the communication line is suspected of being tapped). (FIPS). *See* EXPIRED PASSWORD, LOG IN, PASSWORD.

one-way cipher. In cryptography, a cipher that is an irreversible function from plaintext to ciphertext, i.e. it is not computationally feasible to decipher the ciphertext. This technique can be used to store encrypted passwords in a computer system. When a user enters a password it is similarly encrypted and compared with the stored encrypted password. With this technique an attacker cannot determine the cleartext version of the passwords even if illegal access is gained to the computer memory. However, the attacker may gain a benefit from gaining access to the encrypted password file since a dictionary attack may be mounted offline. *See* COMPUTATIONALLY INFEASIBLE, DICTIONARY ATTACK, ONE-WAY FUNCTION. *Synonymous with* IRREVERSIBLE ENCRYPTION.

one-way function. In cryptography, a computation based upon two items of data K and D such that the output O is given by $O = dK(D) \oplus D$, where d denotes decryption using the DES algorithm.

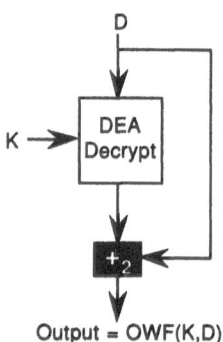

Output = OWF(K,D)

one-way function

Given one input (K or D) and O the determination of the other input requires an exhaustive search of all possible values.

In some cases one input may be a known value. In this case it should be used as the key input (K). If the output (O) and the input (D) are known then the attacker can easily compute dK(D) by the EXCLUSIVE OR operation on O and D.

The attacker must now exhaustively check values of K, but when a value (say) K' is found such that eK'(D) equals eK(D) then the search is ended. However, if the known value is used as the key then the attacker must exhaustively search all possible input data blocks. Moreover, even when a match is found there is a requirement to conduct further searches because it is the nature of the one-way function that a number of data blocks may map to the same output block for a given key. *Compare* ONE-WAY HASH FUNCTION. *See* TRANSACTION KEY SYSTEM. (2) In cryptography, a mathematical function f, which is easy to compute, but which for a general y in the range, it is computationally difficult to find a value x in the domain such that $f(x) = y$. There may be a few values y for which finding x is not computationally difficult. (ANSI). *See* DOMAIN, RANGE. (3) In cryptography, a function $f(x)$ such that it is easy to compute $f(x)$ given x, for any x in its domain, but that the inverse is computationally infeasible. In public key cryptography it is possible to multiply two large prime numbers but computationally infeasible to compute the factors of the product. *See* COMPUTATIONALLY INFEASIBLE, DOMAIN, PASSWORD.

one-way hash function. In cryptography, a function, $F(x)$, with the properties:

- F can be applied to any argument of any size.
- F produces a fixed length output.

- Given F and x it is easy to compute F(x).
- Given F it is computationally infeasible to find any pair of values, x and x', such that if $x <> x'$ and $F(x) = F(x')$.

Compare ONE-WAY FUNCTION.

onion skin architecture. In architecture and data communications, a layered structure that facilitates communication between processes at the same level, employing lower level processes in a manner that is largely transparent to the user process. In communication systems this approach facilitates the design and use of complex networks and systems. Processes receive messages from the layer above and pass them to corresponding processes at the same level by initially transmitting them to the layer below. These processes need only be concerned with the passage of messages through two layer interfaces although the total system may have many layers. *See* TRANSPARENT, ONION SKIN LANGUAGE, OPEN SYSTEMS INTERCONNECTION.

onion skin language. In databases, a computer language to manipulate a hierarchy of systems. A database system may be constructed as a set of systems of increasing complexity such that one system is a subset of the next. An onion skin language will manipulate the most complex system and subsets of the language will manipulate the successive system subsets. *See* ONION SKIN ARCHITECTURE.

on line. In operations, pertaining to data processing and communication equipment that is connected to a computer or communication channel. *Compare* OFF LINE.

on line card reader. In access control, a card reader connected to a central processor that accepts the access control

362 on line crypto-operation

card data and makes access/no access decisions. *Compare* INTELLIGENT CARD READER, OFF LINE CARD READER. *Synonymous with* SYSTEM CARD READER.

on line crypto-operation. In communications security, the use of crypto-equipment that is directly connected to a signal line, making single continuous processes of encryption and transmission or reception and decryption. (FIPS). *Compare* OFF LINE CRYPTO-OPERATION. *See* DECRYPT, ENCRYPT.

on line encryption. *See* ON LINE CRYPTO-OPERATION.

Ontario. In computer security, a virus that encrypts itself, terminates and stays resident, infects COMMAND.COM, COM and EXE files, affects run-time operation, corrupts program, OVL and data files. *See* VIRUS NAMES.

open hot site. In computer security, a hot site operated for profit and made available to companies that are not affiliated to the operator of the site. *Compare* CLOSED HOT SITE. *See* HOT SITE.

open position. In banking, the exposure to which the bank is placed when current aggregate assets and liabilities in a given currency are not balanced.

open security environment. In computer security, an environment that includes those systems in which one of the following conditions holds true: (a) Application developers (including maintainers) do not have sufficient clearance or authorization to provide an acceptable presumption that they have not introduced malicious logic. (b) Configuration control does not provide sufficient assurance that applications are protected against the introduction of malicious logic prior to and during the operation of system applications. (DOD). *See* CONFIGURATION CONTROL, MALICIOUS LOGIC.

open shop. In computing, a facility in which the end users can design, develop, test and run their own programs. *Compare* CLOSED SHOP.

open storage. In data security, the storage of classified information, not in GSA-approved secure containers, within an accredited facility while such facility is not occupied by authorized personnel. (AR).

open system. In banking, an EFTPOS network in which transactions are routed directly between the retailer and the financial institutions involved, crediting the retailer's account and debiting the customer's account. *Compare* GATEWAY. *See* EFTPOS.

open systems. In computing and communications, a term which is used to describe systems, usually derived from different vendors, that may exchange information, or use services, through standard interfaces operating to common standards, as opposed to a proprietary system which normally only permits easy connections amongst the vendor's subsystems. In general an open system should have properly defined interfaces, services and protocols and these definitions should be available to third parties.

open systems interconnection. In data communications, pertaining to an ISO reference model intended to coordinate the development of standards at all levels of communication. The objective is to allow purchasers of communication equipment much greater freedom in mixing and matching equipment as well as a greater degree of protection against obsolescence.

The model has seven layers - physical, data link, network, transport, session, presentation and application. These layers are illustrated in the figure.

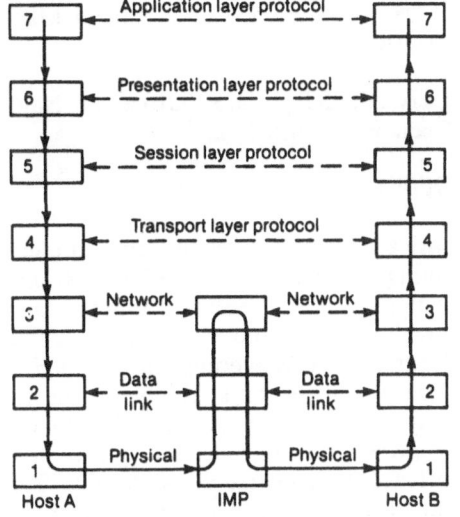

open systems interconnection
The seven layers provide independence for the various operations in communication.

The concept of the layers provides for a considerable degree of independence between the multifarious and complicated operations involved in data communications. A process operating at a level believes that it is communicating with its corresponding layer in the receiving host. It accepts messages from the layer vertically above it, adding control information to it and passing it on to the layer immediately below. At the receiving end the process is reversed, messages are received from the layer below it, control information is stripped off and the message passed up to the next level.

The concept can be illustrated by businesses communicating in different countries. Businessman A in Turin is only concerned to pass a business analysis to Businessman B in Tokyo. He passes on the analysis to a translator who only speaks Italian and English. The translator produces an English version of the business analysis and hands the result to a post office for transmission. The post office forwards the message by letter to Tokyo where it is handed to a local translator who con-

verts the text from English to Japanese and hands it up to Businessman B. The degree of independence is obvious, the translators could agree on a different common language and the post office could select a whole variety of message transmissions; the other layers are unaware and unaffected by the changes.

The physical layer is concerned with the transmission of a raw bit stream. The data link layer uses error detection codes and host to host control messages to convert an unreliable transmission channel into a reliable one. The network layer in a point-to-point network is primarily concerned with routing and congestion. The transport layer provides reliable host to host communication and hides the details of the communication network from the session layer.

The session layer, in turn, is responsible for setting up, managing and closing down process to process connections, whilst the presentation layer performs useful transformations in the text, e.g. text compression, and allows for dialogues with incompatible intelligent terminals.

The content of the application layer is left to the users and standard protocols for specific industries, e.g. banks. *Compare* SNA. *See* APPLICATION LAYER, BIT, DATA LINK LAYER, ERROR DETECTION CODE, HOST, OSI SECURITY, PHYSICAL LAYER, POINT-TO-POINT, PRESENTATION LAYER, ROUTING, SESSION LAYER, TEXT COMPRESSION, TRANSPORT LAYER.

operand. In mathematics, the quantity that is to be the subject of a mathematical operation. *Compare* OPERATOR.

operating system. In computing, a collection of software programs intended to directly control the hardware of a computer (e.g. input/output requests, resource allocation, data management), and on which all the other programs running on the computer generally depend. *See* UNIX.

operating time. In communications, the total time required for dialing the call, waiting for connection to be established and coordinating the subsequent transaction with the personnel or equipment at the receiving end.

operational data security. In data security, the protection of data from either accidental or unauthorized, intentional modification, destruction or disclosure during input, processing or output operations.

operational site security manual. The manual documents the operational requirements, security environment, hardware and software configurations and interfaces; all security procedures, measures, and features; and, for computer facilities, the contingency plans for continued support in case of a local disaster. (AFR). *See* CONTINGENCY PLANS.

operational vulnerability. In information security, a vulnerability that takes advantage of a weakness in non-technical countermeasures to violate the security of a target of evaluation. *Compare* CONSTRUCTION VULNERABILITY, EXPLOITABLE VULNERABILITY, POTENTIAL VULNERABILITY. *See* INFORMATION SECURITY EVALUATION CRITERIA, VULNERABILITY.

operations security indicators. In data security, actions or classified or unclassified information, obtainable by an (OPSEC) adversary, that would result in adversary appreciations, plans, and actions harmful to achieving friendly intentions and preserving friendly military capabilities. (AFR). *See* OPSEC.

operator. (1) A person charged to enable a piece of equipment to fulfil its function. (2) In mathematics, a character that designates a mathematical or logical operation, e.g. +.

OPM. U.S. Office of Personnel Management.

OPNAVINST. U.S. Office of Navy Operations Instruction.

OPSEC. OPerations SECurity.

optical character recognition. In computing, pertaining to techniques and equipment for reading printed, and possibly handwritten, characters on a document and converting them to digital code for input to a computer. In its simplest form light is beamed onto the character and the reflected light is projected onto a matrix of photocells. The output of the matrix is scanned and the received signal is read into a storage cell matrix where a match is sought with a set of stored character patterns. *Compare* OPTICAL MARK RECOGNITION.

optical density card. In access control, a form of access control card in which numerical information is encoded in translucent material of controlled varying density. The card is read by transmitting light through the encoded area. It is used for high security applications because the card is relatively difficult to counterfeit. *See* CARD READER. *Synonymous with* VARYING DENSITY HOLOGRAPHIC CARD.

optical digital disk. *See* OPTICAL DISK STORAGE.

optical disk. In video disk, a disk in which the information is etched on the surface as a series of pits and is read by a laser beam. *See* OPTICAL DISK STORAGE.

optical disk storage. In backing storage, the use of plastic and metal disks with minute pits, embedded into circular tracks, that represent the stored bits. The disk is read by a laser beam in the same manner as conventional video disks. The optical digital disk is similar to a video disk or audio compact disk except that it is used to store binary data rather than pictures or sound. The total storage capacity of optical disk systems is of the order of gigabytes and the cost per bit is currently only 10% of that of hard disk systems. The current disk players may be read only or write-once-only and read, and these systems do not, therefore, have the flexibility of the erasable magnetic disk units. Moreover, the write/read systems are very expensive compared with conventional microcomputer peripherals.

optical mark recognition. In computing, pertaining to techniques for recording marks on documents. The marks are usually short lines or filled-in squares on formatted documents, e.g. answers to multiple choice questions on examination papers, customer order documents. The document is positioned and scanned by a light beam, and transmitted, or reflected light, is collected by photocells. The significance of the data depends upon its coordinate position on the document and the signals from the photocells are input to a computer. *Compare* OPTICAL CHARACTER RECOGNITION.

optical memory. *See* OPTICAL DISK STORAGE.

optional. In standards, a feature not required by a particular standard or not required to meet an optional provision of the standard. (ANSI).

Orange Book. In computer security, a U.S. Department of Defense publication 'Department Of Defense Trusted Computer System Evaluation Criteria' issued in August 1983 and revised in March 1985.

Overview
In the document there are three main reasons for the development of the criteria.

- To provide users with a metric with which to evaluate the degree of trust that can be placed in computer systems for secure processing of classified and other sensitive information.
- To provide guidance to manufacturers as to what security features to build into their new and planned commercial products in order to provide widely available systems that satisfy trust requirements for sensitive applications.
- To provide a basis for specifying security requirements in acquisition specifications.

The Orange Book is divided into two Parts, the first dealing with the Criteria in detail and the second with the rationale and guidelines of those criteria. The book also has four appendices describing the Commercial Product Evaluation Process, Summary of the Criteria Divisions, Summary of the Evaluation Criteria Classes and the Requirement Directory. Finally there is a useful Glossary and List of References.

A multilevel computer system is designed to process a range of classified data, and serve a population of users with a range of security clearances. Such a computer might also contain maliciously coded software which could cause data of one classification to be leaked into a file of a lower classification; or cause the security of highly classified data to be maliciously downgraded and made available to a user with a low security clearance.

A trusted computer system is defined as: a system that employs sufficient hardware and software integrity measures to allow its use for processing simultaneously a range of sensitive or classified information.

The Orange Book is concerned with the evaluation of trusted computer systems, as defined above, and it uses the term trusted computing base to refer to the reference validation mechanism be it a security, kernel, front end security filter or the entire trusted computer system. The trusted computing base (TCB) is defined as: the totality of protection mechanisms within a computer system, including hardware, firmware and software, the combination of which is responsible for enforcing a security policy. It creates a basic protection environment and provides additional user services required for a trusted computer system. The ability of a trusted computing base to correctly enforce a security policy depends solely on the mechanisms within the TCB and the correct input by system administrative personnel of parameters (e.g. a user's clearance) related to the security policy.

The evaluation criteria require a statement of the security policy that is to be enforced, by the trusted computer system under evaluation. Moreover convincing arguments are to be presented that explain why the TCB satisfies the first two design requirement of the reference monitor, i.e. tamper proofing and a guarantee that the monitor is invoked for all accesses.

The criteria deal with discretionary and mandatory access control policies and the wording of the criteria for mandatory access control is related to the Bell LaPadula model.

The criteria define the statement of requirements of a secure computer system, i.e. secure systems will control through specific security features access to information such that only properly authorized individuals, or processes operating on their behalf, will have access to read, write, create or delete information.

Fundamental Requirements

Six fundamental requirements are derived from this basic objective and they are grouped under the headings: Policy, Accountability and Assurance. The requirements under the first two head-

ings are concerned with what is required to control and monitor access to the information, and those under the heading of Assurance, deal with how one can obtain credible assurances that the trusted system accomplishes the security objective.

Policy.

- There must be an explicit and well defined security policy enforced by the system.
- Access labels must be associated with objects.

Accountability.

- Individual subjects must be identified.
- Audit information must be selectively kept and protected so that actions affecting security can be traced to the responsible party.

Assurance.

- The computer system must contain hardware/software mechanisms that can be independently evaluated to provide sufficient assurance that the system enforces the four requirements stated above.
- The trusted mechanisms that enforce the basic requirements must be continuously protected against tampering and/or unauthorized change.

Divisions

The criteria categorize trusted computer systems into four divisions: A, B, C and D. The highest division, A, is reserved for the systems providing the most comprehensive and assured security. Each division represents a major improvement in the overall confidence, that can be placed in the system for the protection of sensitive information.

Two of the divisions, C and B, are further divided into classes: C1, C2, B1, B2 and B3, Class C2 represents a higher level of security than Class C1 etc.

The four divisions may be summarized as:

- Division D - Minimal Protection.
- Division C - Discretionary Access Control.
- Division B - Mandatory Access Control.
- Division A - Verified Protection.

Within each division and class the criteria are listed under the headings: policy, accountability, assurance and documentation.

Division D is characterized by minimal protection. It is reserved for systems that have been evaluated and fail to meet the criteria of any higher class.

Division C, Class C1 criteria relate to a discretionary access control system for a population of cooperating users. The subjects may be identified as individual users, members of specified groups or the general population of users, when authorized users specify permitted access modes to objects. The users of the system must be able to prove their identity, e.g. by passwords, and the identification information must be protected from unauthorized access. The mechanism that enforces the access control must be well defined and protected from tampering or external interference, and it must be possible to periodically check that this mechanism is working correctly.

The system is checked to ensure that it performs according to its documentation and that there are no obvious ways in which the security system can be bypassed.

The documentation requires inter alia a description of the protection mechanisms, how they are used and interact with each other. A statement is required on the manufacturer's protection philosophy, how this is translated into the TCB; advice on the operation of the secure system and test plans etc.

Class C2 is the highest evaluation class for systems that do not impose mandatory access control. It requires that the system may identify, control and audit the accesses of an individual user.

The object reuse requirement specifies that, for example, a sector on a disk must be purged of stored data before it is returned to a general pool for re-allocation.

The audit requirements are more stringent than those of Class C1 and the audit data must be protected from unauthorized disclosure. The testing procedures must seek flaws that would permit unauthorized access to data or audit data.

Division B, Class B1 introduces the requirement for mandatory access control, in addition to all the discretionary access control facilities of Class C2; it thus represents a major additional requirement to Division C systems. The mandatory access control demands that all stored files etc. be given a security classification, and labelled with that classification. If any information is received into the system then it must be correctly labelled by an authorized user and it must be possible to audit that action. Similarly when data is output from the system it must be correctly labelled.

The mandatory access control requires that security classification be based on both a security level and a set of categories. The Bell-La Padula requirements of simple security condition and *-property are imposed for read and write accesses respectively. The developer must provide the security model on which the TCB is based, and demonstrate that the reference monitor concept has been implemented.

The TCB is required to maintain data that identifies and authenticates each individual user and that user's security classification.

Extensive testing for security flaws is required and if any such flaws are found they must be effectively removed or neutralized, and the system retested. A convincing argument is required to demonstrate that the TCB enforces the security model.

Class B2 systems may be categorized as exhibiting structured protection. The TCB is based upon a clearly defined and documented formal security policy which requires that the mandatory and discretionary access control be extended to all subjects and objects in the ADP system. The system must provide a trusted path between the user and the TCB for login and authentication. This implies that no untrusted software can masquerade as the TCB to the user, e.g. for the purpose of collecting passwords. Covert channels are addressed, if the covert channel cannot be eliminated it is essential that any potential information leakage which cannot be audited is shown to be at an acceptably low rate. There are specific requirements on the design of the TCB which must be structured into protection critical and non-protection critical elements. The TCB interfaces with the user must be well defined and the TCB modularized so that it may be subjected to more thorough testing and rigorous review. The implementation must be shown to be consistent with the Descriptive Top Level Specification. The system must be relatively resistant to penetration and stringent configuration management control is demanded.

In B3 systems the developer is required to demonstrate conformity with the reference monitor concept, thus ensuring that it is tamperproof and small enough to permit extensive analysis and tests; thus the TCB should be structured so as to exclude code not essential for protection. The system is required to be highly resistant to penetration; the auditing requirements are expanded so that the administrator is informed if the number of security relevant events ex-ceeds some threshold value thus indicating an imminent violation of the security policy.

The most significant point about A1 systems is that they provide no more security functionality than Class B3 systems. They do, however, provide a much higher level of assurance that the system meets its security policy.

The production of the Orange Book was a significant milestone in the world of computer security, it provided, for the first time, a measure of the security provided by a computer system. This development was followed by the Information Technology Security Evaluation Criteria and FC-FIPS. *Compare* FC-FIPS, INFORMATION TECHNOLOGY SECURITY EVALUATION CRITERIA. *See* A1, BELL-LA PADULA MODEL, B1, B2, B3, COVERT CHANNEL, C1, C2, D, DESCRIPTIVE TOP-LEVEL SPECIFICATION, DISCRETIONARY ACCESS CONTROL, FORMAL SECURITY POLICY MODEL, FRONT-END SECURITY FILTER, MALICIOUS CODE, MANDATORY ACCESS CONTROL, MULTILEVEL DEVICE, OBJECT, OBJECT REUSE, REFERENCE MONITOR, SIMPLE SECURITY PROPERTY, STAR SECURITY PROPERTY, SECURITY KERNEL, SUBJECT, TAMPERPROOF, TRUSTED COMPUTER SYSTEM, TRUSTED COMPUTING BASE, TRUSTED PATH. *Synonymous with* TRUSTED COMPUTER SECURITY EVALUATION CRITERIA.

ORCON. In data security, ORiginator CONtrolled, an indication that documents bearing the marking are controlled by the originator. Reproduction or redistribution require the permission of the originator. (DOE).

order. In mathematics, a property of integers in modulo arithmetic. If an integer m is coprime with another n, in modulo n arithmetic, then the order of m is the lowest integer such that m^p (mod n) $\equiv$ 1. The maximum value of p is n-1, if p is less than n-1 then it must be a divisor of n-1. *See* COPRIME, FER-

MAT'S THEOREM, MODULO ARITHMETIC.

order control. In database security, a form of table restriction control that limits the level of tables in the lattice model that can be used to answer queries. If the threshold is set at d then a query involving more than d attributes would not be permitted. *See* LATTICE MODEL, TABLE RESTRICTION.

ordinal. In mathematics, an unsigned integer. When stored in 8 bits ordinals can assume values in the range 0-255, with 16 bits the range is 0-65,535. *Compare* INTEGER. *See* BIT.

orientation. In computer security, the formal and informal presentations and discussions with the authority responsible for the ADP system that supplements the information in the initial security testing and evaluation (ST&E) request and provides the system evaluators an introduction to the operating environment, the techniques used to provide system security, the identity and location of documentation describing the implementation of system security measures (e.g., O/S modifications, etc.), and the techniques available to demonstrate the effectiveness of such measures in meeting requirements of DOD Directive 5200.28. (DODD). *See* ST&E.

original equipment manufacturer. In computing, a manufacturer who purchases equipment, adds value to it, e.g. by enhancing its capabilities or making it suitable for a specific application area, and resells it.

originator. (1) In data communications, the person, institution or other entity that is responsible for and authorized to originate a message. (ANSI). *Compare* RECIPIENT. *See* MESSAGE. (2) In banking, the initiator of the transfer instructions. (ANSI). *Synonymous with* INITIATOR. (3) In banking, the party (logical or other) that is responsible for originating a cryptographic service message. (ISO). *Compare* RECIPIENT. *See* CRYPTOGRAPHIC SERVICE MESSAGE.

originator's bank. In banking, the bank acting for the originator of the transfer. (ANSI). *See* ORIGINATOR.

Oropax. In computer security, a virus that terminates and stays resident, infects COM files, corrupts program and OVL files, affects run-time operation. *See* VIRUS NAMES.

OSI. *See* OPEN SYSTEMS INTERCONNECTION.

OSI security. In communications security, open systems interconnection security provides tools for the secure internetworking of open systems.

Overview
The security standards in OSI are emerging rapidly (See Fig. 1). The security architecture is described in ISO 7498-2 - Information processing systems - Open Systems Interconnection - Basic Reference Model Part 2: Security Architecture, the CCITT will publish the Security Architecture as X.800 in 1992. This architecture will be supported by a number of frameworks, e.g. ISO 10181, currently in the process of development. An upper layer security model, will provide more detail on the provision of security services by protocols in layers 6 and 7, and a lower layer model is similarly proposed for layers 1-5. Some of the services provided by application layer protocols include:

- The Directory;
- Message Handling Systems;
- CASE Modules.

The ISO security architecture extends the field of application of ISO 7498 to cover secure communications between open systems. The standard is concerned with the visible aspects of a communica-

Reference model

Security architecture	7498-2

Frameworks

Overview	10181-1
Authentication	10181-2
Access control	10181-3
Non-repudiation	10181-4
Confidentiality	10181-5
Integrity	10181-6
Audit	10181-7
Key management	

Layer models/guides

Upper layer model 10745
Lower layer model/guide

Protocols and procedures

Directory security features
Message handling security features
ACSE authentication
Security exchange ASE
Transport layer security protocol
Network layer security protocol
Data link security protocols
Physical layer security protocol
Etc.

OSI security

tions path which permit end systems to achieve a secure transfer of information between them, but not with the security measures required in end systems, installations, and organizations, except when they have implications on the choice and position of security services in OSI.

Services and Mechanisms

The standard distinguishes between security services and the mechanisms required to implement those services. The security services considered are listed below.

Authentication:

- peer entity authentication;
- data origin authentication.

Access Control

Data Confidentiality:

- connection confidentiality;
- connectionless confidentiality;
- selective field confidentiality;
- traffic flow confidentiality.

Data Integrity:

- connection integrity with recovery;
- connection integrity without recovery;
- selective field connection integrity;
- connectionless integrity;
- selective field connectionless integrity.

Non-repudiation:

- non-repudiation with proof of origin;
- non-repudiation with proof of delivery.

Peer entity authentication is a service provided by an N layer, to a N+1 layer, to corroborate that the peer entity is the claimed N+1 layer entity. In the case of a connection, peer entity authentication at the start of the connection, combined with data integrity services for the life of the connection, can together provide assurance on the source of all data units transferred, the integrity of individual data units. Peer entity authentication may also, e.g. by the use of sequence numbers, guard against the duplication of data units.

In the case of connectionless integrity the N layer service informs the N+1 layer on any modification to a single connectionless Service Data Unit (SDU); in addition a limited form of detection on replay may be provided.

The selective field confidentiality and integrity services provide for the security services to be restricted to preselected data items within messages. Non-repudiation with proof of origin prevents a sender from latter reneging upon a message; similarly non-repudiation with proof of delivery prevents recipients from successfully denying the receipt of messages.

The security mechanisms to provide the abovementioned security services are categorized as specific and pervasive. The former are incorporated into the appropriate N layer to provide a security service, whilst pervasive mechanisms are not specific to any particular service or any particular layer. The security mechanisms are listed below.

Specific Security Mechanisms.

- encipherment;
- digital signature mechanisms;
- access control mechanisms;
- data integrity mechanisms;
- authentication exchange mechanism;
- traffic padding mechanism;
- routing control mechanism;
- notarization mechanism.

Pervasive Security Mechanisms:

- trusted functionality;
- security labels;
- event detection;
- security audit trail;
- security recovery.

Access control mechanisms may be applied at either end of the communications path, or at some intermediate point. If a connectionless data transfer is undertaken then the requirements for peer level access control mechanisms must be known, a priori, at the origin, and must be recorded in the Security Management Information Base.

The data integrity requirements differ if the mechanism is to be applied to a stream of data units, or fields within data units, although the first type of service cannot be provided without the second. The protection of a sequence of data units, e.g. against loss of order, duplication, loss, replay, insertion or modification requires some form of sequence numbering, time stamping, cryptographic chaining etc. In the case of a connectionless service, time stamping may be employed to provide limited protection against replay.

Authentication exchange mechanisms may be based upon authentication information, e.g. passwords, cryptographic techniques or characteristics/tokens possessed by the entity.

Routing control mechanisms may select routes dynamically, or by pre-arrangement, so as to employ only physically secure subnetworks, links or relays. Data with certain labels may be forbidden by the security policy from passing through certain subnetworks, links or relays. When a connection is established, or a connectionless data unit transmitted, the sender may also specify certain subnetworks, links or relays to be avoided.

Pervasive security mechanisms may be considered as aspects of security management. Security labels may be additional data associated with a data unit in transit, in which case they must be clearly identifiable so that they can be checked at appropriate stages; they must also be securely bound to their data unit. Labels may also be implied by the use of a specific cryptographic key, or by the context of the data such as its source or route.

Event recording of security relevant events such as specific security violations, specified selected events or overflow of a counter may be caused by one of the following actions:

- local reporting of an event;
- remote recording of an event;
- logging the event;
- recovery action.

Security recovery responds to requests from security mechanisms, e.g. event handling and management functions, and undertakes appropriate recovery actions which may be:

- immediate;
- temporary;
- long-term.

Immediate recovery may abort operations, e.g. by disconnection; temporary actions may create the temporary invalidation of an entity and long-term actions may place an entity in a black list or change a cryptographic key.

An illustrative relationship between security services and security mechanisms is given in Fig. 2.

SERVICE	MECHANISM
Peer Entity Authentication	E, DS, AE
Data Origin Authentication	E, DS
Access Control Service	AC
Connection Confidentiality	E, RC
Connectionless Confidentiality	E, RC
Selective Field Confidentiality	E
Traffic Flow Confidentiality	E, TP, RC
Connection Integrity with Recovery	E, DI
Connection Integrity without Recovery	E, DI
Selective Field Connection Integrity	E, DI
Connectionless Integrity	E, DS, DI
Selective Field Connectionless Integrity	E, DS, DI
Non-Repudiation, Origin	DS, DI, N
Non-Repudiation, Delivery	DS, DI, N

Where E - Encipherment, DS - Digital Signature, AC - Access Control, DI - Data Integrity, AE - Authentication Exchange, TP - Traffic Padding, RC - Routing Control, N - Notarization.

Location of Services in Layers
The decision on location of security services to layers and consequent placement of security mechanisms was based upon the principles listed below:

- the number of alternative ways of achieving a service should be minimized;
- it is acceptable to build secure systems by providing security services in more than one layer;
- additional functionality required for security should not unnecessarily duplicate existing OSI functions;
- violation of layer independence should be avoided;
- the amount of trusted functionality should be minimized;
- wherever an entity is dependent on a security mechanism provided by an entity in a lower layer, any intermediate layers should be constructed in such a way that security violation is impracticable;
- wherever possible, the additional security functions of a layer should be defined in such a way that implementation as self-contained modules is not precluded;
- the security architecture is assumed to apply to open systems consisting of end systems containing all seven layers, and to relay systems.

Security service requests may be sent from the N+1 layer to the N layer or may be provided by the N+1 layer itself. The establishment and operation of the service will differ for connection and connectionless communications. Calling and operating a security service involves a dialogue with a database containing appropriate security parameters for both parties to the connection, rules derived from security policies and information related to security management. This conceptual database is termed the Security Management Information Base (SMIB).

If the security services are provided by the N layer, for the N+1 layer, then the N layer will carry out a negotiation with the SMIB. The security services provided may result from an N+1 layer request, and such requests may be denied by the N-layer if they conflict with administratively imposed requirements, stored in the SMIB, for the N+1 layer. Alternatively the N layer may add to the requested protection any security services specified as mandatory, in the SMIB, for the N+1 layer. If the N+1 layer does not specify a target security protection, then the N layer may proceed with the communication using a default security protection as specified in the SMIB for the N+1 layer.

When the N layer has determined the requisite target protection it will attempt to provide it, either directly from the N layer or by passing a request to the N-1 layer. If the required target protection cannot be achieved then no communication will take place.

A layer may provide its own security services, as opposed to the relying upon the services of the layer immediately below it. In this case the layer communicates directly with the SMIB. Reports of active attacks will be provided if, for example, a data modification has been reported for a connection integrity without recovery service, i.e. the layer must decide upon its own recovery actions.

Not all the security services available on a connection oriented protocol are available in the connectionless protocols. For example, protection against replay, insertion and deletion must be provided by higher connection oriented layers. The originator of a connectionless SDU must ensure that it contains all the information to make it acceptable to the destination.

The placement of security services in the various layers is described below.

Physical Layer:

- connection confidentiality
- traffic flow confidentiality;

Data Link Layer:

- connection confidentiality;
- connectionless confidentiality;

Network Layer:

- peer entity authentication;
- data origin authentication;
- access control service;
- connection confidentiality;
- connectionless confidentiality;
- traffic flow confidentiality;
- connection integrity without recovery;
- connectionless integrity.

Transport Layer:

- peer entity authentication;
- data origin authentication;
- access control service;
- connection confidentiality;
- connectionless confidentiality;
- connection integrity with recovery;
- connection integrity without recovery;
- connectionless integrity.

Session Layer:

- No security services;

Presentation Layer:

facilities will be provided:

- connection confidentiality;
- connectionless confidentiality;
- selective field confidentiality.

facilities may be provided:

- traffic flow confidentiality;
- peer entity authentication;
- data origin authentication;

- connection integrity with recovery;
- connection integrity without recovery;
- selective field connection integrity;
- connectionless integrity;
- selective field connectionless integrity;
- non repudiation with proof of origin;
- non repudiation with proof of delivery.

Application Layer

- peer entity authentication;
- data origin authentication;
- access control service;
- connection confidentiality;
- connectionless confidentiality;
- selective field confidentiality;
- traffic flow confidentiality;
- connection integrity with recovery;
- connection integrity without recovery;
- selective field connection integrity;
- connectionless integrity;
- selective field connectionless integrity;
- non repudiation with proof of origin;
- non repudiation with proof of delivery.

Security Management

Security management in the standard is concerned with both the aspects of security management relative to OSI, and the security of OSI management. Management of OSI security services and mechanisms involves the distribution of management information to these services and mechanisms, plus the collection of information concerning the operation of these services and mechanisms. It is not, however, concerned with the passing of security relevant information in protocols, e.g. parameters in connection requests. The conceptual repository of this security relevant information is the Security Management Information Base (SMIB). Exchange of information between systems and the SMIB must be provided with security protection.

Various system administrators will need to exchange security relevant information to establish and extend the SMIB. Such communications may take place within or outside OSI communication paths.

The three categories of OSI security management are:

- system security management;
- security service management;
- security mechanism management.

The system security management is concerned with the management of security aspects of the overall OSI environment, including:

- overall security policy management, including updates and maintenance of consistency;
- interaction with other OSI management functions;
- interaction with security service management and security mechanism management;
- event handling management;
- security audit management;
- security recovery management.

Security service management is concerned with the management of particular security services. Typically: actions associated with determination and assignment of target security protection for the service, selection rules for specific security mechanisms to provide the requested service, negotiation of any mechanisms that require prior management agreements, invocation of specific security mechanisms and interaction with other security service and mechanism management functions.

Security mechanism management may typically include topics such as key management, encipherment management, digital signature management,

access control management, data integrity management, authentication management, traffic padding management, routing control management and notarization management.

In the security of OSI management appropriate security services and mechanisms will be invoked to ensure that OSI management protocols and information are adequately protected.

Security Frameworks
The security frameworks (See Fig. 1) provide the next level of detail for OSI security. They will comprise:

- Overview 10181-1;
- Authentication 10181-2;
- Access Control 10181-3;
- Non-Repudiation 10181-4;
- Confidentiality 10181-5;
- Integrity 10181-6;
- Audit 10181-7;
- Key Management.

These frameworks will describe the general purpose models, mechanisms, data elements and sequence of operations that can be used for specific security services.

An upper layer model will address protocol developments and supply more detail on the provision of security services in layers 6 and 7. A lower layer model will similarly address the same question for layers 1-5.

Users and user applications can provide their own security or use the security services provided by application layer protocols. Such services include the Directory, Message Handling Services and CASE modules.

The Directory described in CCITT X.500 and ISO 9594 currently provides simple and strong authentication for Directory accesses. Simple authentication is based upon passwords whilst strong authentication employs public key cryptography, digital signatures and certificates. Digital signature methods may also be used to protect the integrity of data exchanged with the Directory.

The Directory may also hold security relevant information, such as certificates, and may therefore be able to support security mechanisms of other applications.

Message Handling Systems are standardized in the CCITT X.400 series, and the closely aligned ISO 10021. The security services provided by the Message Handling System include:

- authentication of origin of messages, proof of delivery and peer entity authentication;
- non-repudiation of message origin, delivery or submission;
- content integrity and message sequence integrity;
- message and message flow confidentiality;
- message security labelling;
- management services to change credentials and register permissible security labels.

CASE (Common Application Service Elements) modules provide common services for applications such as MHS and Directory. Modules under development will allow for the exchange of information between two application entities to support authentication, access control, confidentiality, non repudiation, integrity etc. *See* APPLICATION LAYER, AUTHENTICATION, CERTIFICATE, CONNECTIONLESS SERVICE, DATA INTEGRITY, DATA LINK LAYER, ENCIPHERMENT, KEY, NETWORK LAYER, NOTARIZATION, OPEN SYSTEMS INTERCONNECTION, PERVASIVE SECURITY MECHANISM, PHYSICAL LAYER, PRESENTATION LAYER, RELAY, REPLAY, SDU, SECURITY AUDIT TRAIL, SESSION LAYER, SMIB, TIME STAMP, TRAFFIC PADDING, TRANSPORT LAYER, TRUSTED FUNCTIONALITY, X.400, X.500

OSN. In banking, Output Sequence Number, a consecutive sequence number that allows for output message control between the service and the receiving bank. (ANSI). *Compare* ISN.

other card data. In banking, a specified field on a bank customer magnetic stripe card used in transaction key systems. *See* TRANSACTION KEY SYSTEM.

OTP. In communications, Office of Telecommunications Policy, in the Executive office of the U.S. President. An agency that develops and recommends U.S. public policy in the area of telecommunications.

OUSDR&E. Office of the Under Secretary of Defense for Research and Engineering.

outage. In reliability, a period of system nonfunction due to a power supply failure.

output. In computer security, information that has been exported by a TCB. (DOD). *See* TCB.

output feedback. In cryptography, a stream cipher DES mode of operation. In the output feedback mode a cryptographic bit stream is 'exclusive or-ed' with the plaintext to produce the ciphertext at the transmitter. An identical system at the receiver, equipped with the same cryptographic key, produces the same cryptographic bit stream that is 'exclusive or-ed' with the ciphertext to reveal the original plaintext.

The cryptographic bit stream may produce 1 bit, 1 byte blocks etc., to be 'exclusive or-ed' with the corresponding blocks in the plaintext. The cryptographic bit stream block is also fed back to the shift register to form the input to the DES encryption unit, where it is encrypted to provide a 64 bit output, the leftmost segment of which is selected for the next cryptographic bit stream block.

The shift registers must be initialized with the same initialization vector, IV. This IV is transmitted in plaintext from the transmitter to the receiver as the preamble of the message. It is not necessary to transmit a full 64 bit block for

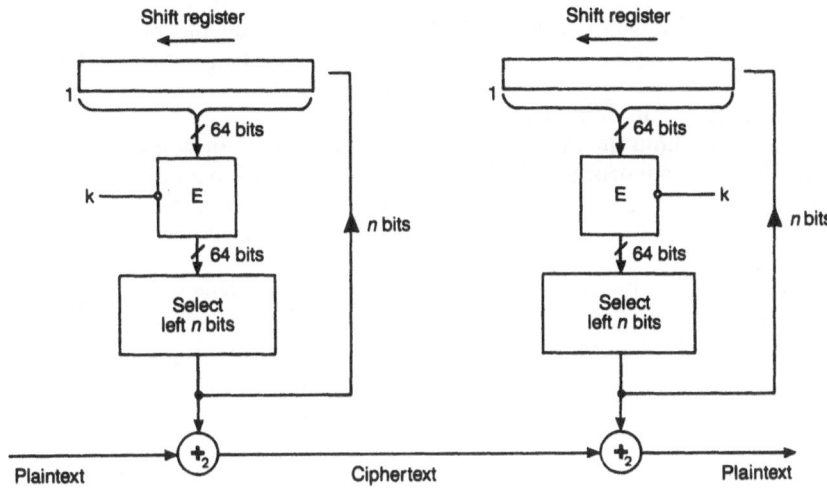

output feedback

this purpose; it may be arranged that both shift registers be initially set to zero and (say) 8 bits transmitted to set the IV. Short preambles may, however, be ill-advised if highly formatted messages are transmitted.

The major advantage of output feedback, as compared with cipher feedback, lies in its lack of error extension. A one bit error in the ciphertext will only produce a corresponding one bit error in the plaintext at the receiving end. This lack of error extension is advantageous in applications such as voice scrambling where the plaintext is highly redundant; a one bit error can be tolerated whereas a number of garbled blocks will produce an irritating output disturbance. On the other hand an absence of error extension allows an attacker to introduce planned and undetectable changes in the received plaintext. A loss, or spurious addition, of a block in the ciphertext stream will cause a loss of synchronism between the transmitting and receiving data streams and the received plaintext will thereafter be garbled. *Compare* CIPHER BLOCK CHAINING, CIPHER FEEDBACK, ELECTRONIC CODEBOOK. *See* CIPHERTEXT, CRYPTOGRAPHIC BIT STREAM, CRYPTOGRAPHIC KEY, DES, ERROR EXTENSION, PLAINTEXT, SHIFT REGISTER, STREAM EXCLUSIVE OR, IV, CIPHER.

output protection. In data security, pertaining to the procedures adopted for the security of information produced by an automated system.

outsourcing. In computing, the practice of procuring from external specialist sources rather than developing application systems, for example, within the organization itself.

overhead bit. In codes, a bit that transmits no information but is included for control or error checking purposes. *See* PARITY CHECKING.

overlap control. In database security, a form of cell restriction using an audit trail so that a limit may be set on the number of records in common over the query sets. *Compare* AUDIT EXPERT, CELL SUPPRESSION, IMPLIED QUERIES CONTROL, QUERY SET SIZE CONTROL. *See* AUDIT TRAIL, CELL RESTRICTION, QUERY SET.

overlay network. In communications, a network of transmission links and switching centers superimposed upon another network and interconnected with it at specific points.

other network and interconnected with it at specific points.

overt channel. In communications security, a path within the system that is designed for the authorized transfer of data. *Compare* COVERT CHANNEL.

overwrite cycle. In computer security, a method of securely removing data from electronic or magnetic storage. A one bit pattern, or character, is written into every addressable location then the complement of that pattern or character is written into every addressable location or sector. *See* OBJECT REUSE, OVER-WRITE PROCEDURE, RESIDUE.

overwrite procedure. In computer security, a procedure to remove or destroy data recorded on ADP magnetic storage media by recording patterns of unclassified data over or on top of the data stored on the media. (DOD). *See* OBJECT REUSE, OVERWRITE CYCLE, OVERWRITING.

overwriting. In computer security, the obliteration of recorded data by recording different data on the same surface. (FIPS). *See* OVERWRITE PROCEDURE.

overwriting virus. In computer security, a virus that overwrites the initial part of the infected program thus causing it to crash after execution of the virus. *Compare* NONOVERWRITING VIRUS. *See* VIRUS.

OWF. *See* ONE-WAY FUNCTION.

ownership. In data security, the right of users to dispense and revoke privileges for objects they own, e.g. access on programs and data sets. *See* ACCESS CONTROL, DATA SET.

P

P1. (1) In data communications, the relay protocol of the CCITT X.400 message handling standard. *Compare* P2, P3. *See* X.400. (2) In computer security, a virus that encrypts itself, terminates and stays resident, infects COM files, affects run-time operation, corrupts program, OVL and data files and file linkage. *See* VIRUS NAMES.

P2. In data communications, a protocol, of the CCITT X.400 message handling standard, which defines the message header and various parts of the message. *Compare* P1, P3. *See* X.400.

P3. In data communications, the submission protocol, of the CCITT X.400 message handling standard. *Compare* P1, P2. *See* X.400.

PABX. *See* PRIVATE AUTOMATIC BRANCH EXCHANGE.

pacing. In data communications, a method by which a receiving station controls the rate of transmission in order to avoid a loss of data.

packet. In data communications, a self-contained component of a message, comprising address, control and data signals, that can be transferred as an entity within a data network. *See* PACKET SWITCHING.

packet assembler/disassembler. In data communications, a unit installed by a network operator to interface a packet-switching network to a user terminal. The unit assembles character stream messages from the terminal into packets, for transmission over the network, and disassembles incoming packets from the network. *See* PACKET-SWITCHING NETWORK.

packet interleaving. In data communications, a form of multiplexing, in a packet-switching network, in which packets from various subchannels are interleaved onto a main channel. *See* MULTIPLEXING, PACKET, PACKET SWITCHING.

packet radio. In data communications, a network with radio links so that a packet may be received by more than one station. *See* PACKET SWITCHING.

packet sequencing. In data communications, a method of ensuring that packets arrive at the receiving station in the same sequential order that they were originally transmitted. *Compare* DATAGRAM SERVICE. *See* PACKET, PACKET SWITCHING.

packet switching. In data communications, a method of message transmission in which each complete message is assembled into one or more packets that can be sent through the network, collected and then reassembled into the original message at the destination. The individual packets need not even be sent by the same route. The communication channels are only occupied during the transmission of a packet as compared with a conventional circuit switching in which a connection is made and maintained for the duration of the complete message transmission. *Compare* CIRCUIT SWITCHING, MESSAGE SWITCHING. *See* COMPUTER NETWORK, DATAGRAM SERVICE, PACKET.

packet-switching exchange. In data communications, the computer system that provides the interface between users and the node to node packet-switching network. The functions of the exchange include network protocol, packet sequencing and routing. *See* PACKET, PACKET-SWITCHING NETWORK, PROTOCOL, ROUTING.

packet-switching network. In data communications, a network of devices that communicate between each other by transmitting packets addressed to particular destinations. *See* PACKET SWITCHING.

packet switch node. In data communications, a switching node in a packet-switching network. Packet switch nodes are more powerful computers that have tended to replace interface message processors, whilst preforming the same type of function. *See* INTERFACE MESSAGE PROCESSOR, PACKET-SWITCHING NETWORK.

packet terminal. In data communications, a terminal, in a packet-switching network, capable of forming its own packets and interacting with a network character terminal. *Compare* CHARACTER TERMINAL. *See* PACKET, PACKET SWITCHING.

packing density. In computing, the number of bits that may be stored per unit length on a recording medium, e.g. magnetic tape. *See* MAGNETIC TAPE.

PACX. In data communications, Private Automatic Computer Exchange, a switching and contention system which allows a range of terminals, with different speeds, to communicate, through a number of output ports, with several other devices such as computers. *See* CONTENTION, PORT.

PAD. *See* PACKET ASSEMBLER/DISASSEMBLER.

padding. In cryptography, the additional characters added to a plaintext message, to ensure that its length is an integral number of blocks for encryption by a block cipher. *See* BLOCK CIPHER, PADDING INDICATOR.

padding indicator. In cryptography, an indicator employed in cipher block chaining mode of DES operation. It is used to indicate the number of padding characters in the last 64 bit block of plaintext when the message stream does not comprise an integral number of 64 bit blocks. *See* CIPHER BLOCK CHAINING.

page. In computing, an area of storage space. *See* MEMORY ORGANIZATION.

page frame. In computing, an area of storage that can store a page. *See* PAGE.

page mode terminal. In data communications, a terminal that provides a page display, typically 25 lines of 80 characters, and allows the cursor to be moved over the screen to modify the display. *Compare* FORM MODE TERMINAL, SCROLL MODE TERMINAL.

palindromic key. In cryptography, a DES key in which sub-key 1 = sub-key 16, sub-key 2 = sub-key 15 etc. Only DES weak keys have this property. *Compare* ANTI-PALINDROMIC KEY. *See* CRYPTOGRAPHIC KEY, DATA ENCRYPTION STANDARD, SUB-KEY, WEAK KEY.

palmprint analysis. In access control, an identification technique; palmprints, like fingerprints, are unique to an individual. Creases, skin tone, and swirls can be detected by a video camera; the digitized output from the camera is compared with an image, corresponding to the user id, which is stored in an access control database. A fast access time can be provided, with a false reject rate of less than one percent and an extremely low false acceptance rate.

Compare FINGERPRINT ANALYSIS, HAND GEOMETRY ANALYSIS. *See* BIOMETRICS, USER ID.

PAM. *See* PULSE AMPLITUDE MODULATION.

PAN. *Compare* PIN. *See* PRIMARY ACCOUNT NUMBER.

parallel communication. *See* PARALLEL TRANSMISSION.

parallel computer. In computing, a computer with multiple logic or arithmetic units enabling it to perform parallel operations or parallel processing. *Compare* SERIAL COMPUTER. *See* PARALLEL PROCESSING.

parallel messages. In cryptography, messages enciphered with the same cryptographic bit stream. *See* CRYPTOGRAPHIC BIT STREAM.

parallel operation. The performance of simultaneous, and usually, similar actions, on a related set of inputs. *See* PARALLEL PROCESSING, PARALLEL TRANSMISSION.

parallel processing. In computing, pertaining to a system in which more than one process is active at a given instant. The term is often applied to systems that have more than one processor but where only one is active at any one time. *Compare* SERIAL COMPUTER.

parallel simulation. In auditing, a technique in which an auditor produces a simulation program to perform identical processing of an organization's program under review. *See* COMPUTER AUDIT PACKAGES.

parallel transmission. In data communications, the simultaneous transmission of elements constituting the same code, e.g. each bit of a word is sent simultaneously on an individual wire. It has a higher bit rate than corresponding serial transmission but requires 8 wires to convey individual bytes and is therefore mainly used for transmission over short distances, e.g. for buses within a computer. *Compare* SERIAL TRANSMISSION. *See* BIT RATE.

parameter. (1) A quantity that, individually, or as part of a set, specifies a system or process. (2) A specified variable of a system or process that temporarily assumes the properties of a constant.

parent. In computing, the element, in a hierarchical system, that is immediately superior to the element in question, e.g. in a tree structure the node that points to the particular node in question. *See* TREE STRUCTURE.

Paris. In computer security, a virus that infects COMMAND.COM, COM, EXE and OVL files, affects run-time operation, corrupts program, OVL and data files and file linkage. *See* VIRUS NAMES.

parity. In codes, pertaining to a condition in which the number of items in a group is odd or even. *See* PARITY CHECKING.

Parity. In computer security, a virus that infects COMMAND.COM and COM files, affects run-time operation, corrupts program, OVL and data files. *See* VIRUS NAMES.

parity bit. In codes, the bit added to a bit grouping, if necessary, in order to produce parity. *See* PARITY CHECKING, PARITY.

parity checking. In codes, a form of redundancy checking. The convention odd or even parity is selected, the number of 1 bits in a grouping is counted and a parity bit is set to 1 or 0 so to produce parity with the selected convention, i.e. an odd or even number of 1 bits. Upon receipt of the grouping the number of bits is checked and an error reported if the selected parity is not found. Parity checking detects the loss, or unwanted inclusion, of an odd number of bits. *See* PARITY, PARITY BIT, REDUNDANCY CHECKING. *Synonymous with* ODD EVEN CHECK.

passband. In communications, the range of signal frequencies that can be satisfactorily transmitted on a given channel, e.g. the passband on voice grade channels is 300-3000 Hz. *See* Hz.

passive. (1) In communications security, a property of an object or network object that it lacks logical or computational capability and is unable to change the information it contains (TNI). *See* OBJECT. (2) In communications security, those threats to the confidentiality of data which, if realized, would not result in any unauthorized change in the state of the intercommunicating systems (e.g. monitoring and/or recording of data) (TNI).

passive attack. In data security, an attack in which the intercepted data is recorded and later analyzed. *Compare* ACTIVE ATTACK. *See* MIDNIGHT ATTACK, PASSIVE WIRETAPPING.

passive electronic card. *See* PROXIMITY CARD READER.

passive sensor. In physical security, a sensor which does not generate or transmit a signal but which detects changes in radiation patterns produced by a disturbance in the ambient radiation or the introduction of a source of radiation.

passive threat. (1) In risk management, the threat of unauthorized disclosure of information without changing the state of the system. (ISO). *Compare* ACTIVE THREAT. *See* THREAT. (2) In computer security, a potential breach of security the occurrence of which would not change the state of the system. Hardware, software, data etc. would remain unaltered. Such a threat could arise from unauthorized reading of files, or use of the computer system for an unauthorized application. *Compare* ACCIDENTAL THREAT, ACTIVE THREAT, DELIBERATE THREAT, LOGICAL THREAT, PHYSICAL THREAT. *See* THREAT.

passive wiretapping. In computer security, the monitoring and/or recording of data while the data is being transmitted over a communications link. (FIPS). *Compare* ACTIVE WIRETAPPING. *See* PASSIVE ATTACK.

passphrase. In access control, a sequence of characters, longer than the acceptable length of a password, that is transformed by a password system into a virtual password of acceptable length. (FIPS). *See* PASSWORD, VIRTUAL PASSWORD.

password. (1) In authentication, confidential authentication information, usually composed of a string of characters. (ISO). (2) In access control, a private character string that is used to authenticate an identity. (DOD). *See* AUTHENTICATE. (3) In access control, a popular form of knowledge test for access control. A password is a string of alphanumeric data or a phrase that must be entered into a system to gain access to a physical area or a resource.

Normally the password is associated with a user identification, the user inputs the user id and then responds to the request for the password. The user id is usually transmitted in clear to the host computer but the password may be protected in transmission.

The use and misuse of passwords is now common and management must adopt sensible measures to ensure that they provide an appropriate degree of security. In particular the password robustness must be matched to the level of security required. The factors affecting password management are listed below.

- Users must be trained and motivated to ensure the effectiveness of the password access control. In particular they must be fully aware of the repercussions of failure to protect their passwords and ensure that measures are taken to detect a lack of password security, e.g. by monitoring accesses.
- Passwords should be easy to remember so that users need not make written records of them.
- Passwords should be changed regularly.
- System records of passwords should be protected, e.g. by encryption.
- The system must combat attempts to guess a password by successive log in attempts.
- Passwords must not be displayed at a terminal during log in.

The design of passwords to facilitate their use, without recourse to written records, can take one of several forms. In general the length of a password should be consistent with the level of security required; access to top secret information may reasonably demand a lengthy password but systems designed to reduce the incidence of computer game playing should not burden legitimate users with memorizing 20 digit numbers.

Some systems allow the users to select their own passwords; this enables users to select some easily remembered string of characters or digits but it has led to passwords that are too short, or easily derived from a knowledge of the names of the user's wife or daughter. Phrases are more easily remembered but they also substantially increase both the time taken to enter them at a keyboard, and the probability that a legitimate user will make a significant number of typing errors, and hence be mistaken for an attacker.

Phonetic passwords can be both short and easily remembered, e.g 'joglin' is easier to remember than 'zxdswv'. Phonetic password generators can generate such random passwords. The management of passwords must be designed to ensure that:

- They are disabled as soon they are known to have been compromised or as soon as an employee resigns, retires, is transferred and most particularly, if the owner's loyalty to the organization is known to have changed, e.g. an employee under notice of dismissal.
- Passwords must be changed periodically, such changes minimize the danger of compromise and also ensure the regular notification of changes in users.
- Users must be encouraged to change passwords if they believe that they may have been compromised or if they are difficult to remember.

See ACCESS CONTROL, DYNAMIC PASSWORD, EXPIRED PASSWORD, ONE-WAY FUNCTION, ONE-TIME PASSWORDS, PASSPHRASE, PERSONAL PASSWORD, TIME-DEPENDENT PASSWORD, USER ID, VALID PASSWORD, VIRTUAL PASSWORD. *Synonymous with* KEYWORD.

password based encryption algorithm. In cryptography, a secret key algorithm in which the key is derived from a user supplied password. *See* SECRET KEY ALGORITHM.

password dialogue. *Synonymous with* HANDSHAKING PROCEDURE.

password system. (1) In access control, a part of an ADP system that is used to authenticate a user's identity. Assurance of unequivocal identification is based on the user's ability to enter a private password that no one else should know. (DOD). *See* PASSWORD. (2) In access control, a system that uses a password or passphrase to authenticate a person's identity or to authorize a person's access to data and which consists of a means for performing one or more of the following password operations: generation, distribution, entry, storage, authentication, replacement, encryption and/or decryption of passwords. (FIPS). *See* PASSPHRASE, PASSWORD.

patch. *See* PROGRAM PATCH.

path. In computing, a method of specifying a file in a tree structured directory. The full specification of a file involves the names of all the subdirectories in the path from the root to the leaf containing the file e.g. \ADMIN \ACCOUNT \COMP-B \RESULTS. The file need only be specified in terms of the path from the current subdirectory e.g. if the current subdirectory is AC-COUNT then the file can be specified by \COMP-B\RESULTS. *See* DIRECTORY, TREE STRUCTURED DIRECTORY.

patrol scrutiny. In physical security, the use of security personnel to patrol work areas, particularly outside normal working hours, to detect intruders and unauthorized use of terminals, to check for security violations, e.g. classified documents or passwords, left on desks.

pattern directed analysis. In computer security, a method of static analysis in which certain patterns of instructions, associated with security flaws, are postulated and sought in the software. For example, routines that do not clear registers and data buffers after use. *See* STATIC ANALYSIS.

pattern sensitive fault. In reliability, a fault that occurs in response to a particular pattern of data.

pause retry. In data communications, a network control program option enabling a user to specify the number of times that a message should be transmitted in the event of transmission errors, and the time interval between each attempt.

pay date. In banking, the date on which the funds are to be available to the beneficiary for withdrawal in cash. (ANSI). *Compare* VALUE DATE. *See* BENEFICIARY.

Payday. In computer security, a virus that terminates and stays resident, infects COM, EXE and OVL files, corrupts program and OVL files. *See* VIRUS NAMES.

payment. In banking, a transfer of funds in any form between two parties. (ANSI).

payment cycle. *Synonymous with* BANKING CYCLE.

payment message. *See* TRANS-ACTION/PAYMENT MESSAGE.

payment order. In banking, an instruction that specifies a funds transfer. (ANSI).

payment service. In banking, a service that moves messages among subscribers and also effects settlement for those messages that constitute funds transfer transactions. (ANSI). *See* FUNDS TRANSFER TRANSACTION.

P box. In cryptography, permutation box, a component of an encryption algorithm which applies a transposition cipher on the input signal. *Compare* S BOX. *See* DATA ENCRYPTION STANDARD, TRANSPOSITION CIPHER.

PC. *See* PERSONAL COMPUTER.

P Class. In complexity theory, a class of problems that can be solved in polynomial time. *Compare* NP CLASS. *See* TIME AND SPACE REQUIREMENTS.

PCM. *See* PULSE CODE MODULATION.

PCS. *See* PHYSICAL CONTROL SPACE.

PDC. *See* PERMANENT DATA CALL.

PDM. *See* PULSE DURATION MODULATION.

PDN. *See* PUBLIC DATA NETWORK.

PDS. *See* PROTECTED DISTRIBUTION SYSTEM.

PDU. *See* PROTOCOL DATA UNIT.

peer entity. In data communications, an entity in a corresponding layer of the OSI seven layer model. *See* OPEN SYSTEMS INTERCONNECTION.

peer entity authentication. (1) In authentication, the corroboration that a peer entity in an association is the one claimed. (ISO). *See* PEER ENTITY. (2) In communications security, pertaining to the action of communicating parties seeking to verify each others identities. *See* AUTHENTICATION, MASQUERADING.

PEM. *See* PRIVACY ENHANCED MAIL.

penetration. (1) In computer security, a successful unauthorized access to an ADP system. (FIPS). *See* ACCESS. (2) In data security, an attack on the security of a computer system, undertaken to test the effectiveness of the security and to highlight any areas of weakness. *See* PENETRATION TESTING, THREAT TEAM. (3) In data security, the successful violation of a protected system (TNI).

penetration profile. In computer security, a delineation of the activities required to effect a penetration. (FIPS). *See* PENETRATION.

penetration signature. (1) In computer security, the description of a situation or set of conditions in which a penetration could occur. (FIPS). (2) The description of usual and unusual system events which in conjunction can indicate the occurrence of a penetration in progress. (FIPS). *See* PENETRATION.

penetration study. In computer security, a technique of static evaluation in which individuals are challenged to find unknown weaknesses in security controls. *Compare* CODE REVIEW, SOURCE CODE ANALYZER. *See* STATIC EVALUATION.

penetration testing. (1) In computer security, the portion of security testing in which the penetrators attempt to circumvent the security features of a system. The penetrators may be assumed to use all system design and implementation documentation, which may include listings of system source code, manuals, and circuit diagrams. The penetrators work under no constraints other than those that would be applied to ordinary users. (DOD). *See* TIGER TEAM. (2) In computer security, the employment of special programmer/analyst teams that attempt to penetrate a system for the purpose of identifying any security weaknesses. (FIPS). *See* PENETRATION, TIGER TEAM.

Pentagon. In computer security, a virus that infects floppy disk boot sector and corrupts boot sector. *See* VIRUS NAMES.

percentage supervision. In physical security, the ratio of the change in resistance or current to the normal operating resistance or current in a supervised line required to produce an alarm signal. *See* ALARM SIGNAL, SUPERVISED LINE.

percent denial. In communications, the average percentage of attempted calls, in the busy hour, that are blocked due to network loading. A measure of the grade of service in a dial access circuit group. *See* DIAL ACCESS.

perfect secrecy. In cryptology, a condition defined by the situation in which the conditional probability that the plaintext message P was sent, if ciphertext message C was received, is equal to the probability that plaintext message P was transmitted. Thus receipt of the ciphertext message provides no additional information, to an attacker, on the nature of the plaintext message. A necessary and sufficient condition for perfect secrecy is that for all plaintext messages P, the conditional probability that ciphertext C was received, given that P was transmitted, is equal to the unconditional probability that ciphertext C was received. *See* INFORMATION THEORY, KEY EQUIVOCATION.

performance standard. General design criteria defining the desired result without specifying the method of achieving that result. (ANSI). *Compare* DESIGN STANDARD.

Perfume. In computer security, a computer virus that infects COM files, corrupts program and OVL files. *See* VIRUS NAMES.

perimeter. In computer security, a boundary within which security controls are applied to protect assets. A security perimeter typically includes a security kernel, some trusted code facilities, hardware and possibly some communication channels. *See* CHANNEL, SECURITY KERNEL, TRUSTED.

perimeter barrier. In physical security, a physical barrier designed to supplement the protection of an inside or outside perimeter. *See* INSIDE PERIMETER, OUTSIDE PERIMETER.

periodic audit. In computing, a verification of a file or of a phase of processing intended to check for problems and encourage future compliance with control procedures.

periods processing. In computer security, intervals of time when security environments are temporarily established for processing information. For example, an automated system could process Top Secret in the dedicated security mode during one period, both Confidential and Secret in the controlled security mode in a second period, and only unclassified material in a third period. The system is purged of all information and brought to a secure state when transitioning from one period to the next. There will be users during the new period who do not have clearance and need-to-know for information processed during the previous period. (AFR). *Compare* MULTILEVEL SECURE. *See* CONTROLLED SECURITY MODE, DEDICATED SECURITY MODE, ISOLATION ENFORCEMENT, NEED TO KNOW. *Synonymous with* TEMPORAL SEPARATION.

peripheral. In computing, a device to perform an auxiliary action in the system, e.g. input/output, backing storage. *See* BACKING STORAGE.

permanent data call. *Synonymous with* PERMANENT VIRTUAL CIRCUIT.

permanent virtual circuit. In data communications, a special type of virtual call service in which the logical links between specific terminals are permanently set-up so that call set-up and release procedures are eliminated. *See* VIRTUAL CIRCUIT. *Synonymous with* PERMANENT DATA CALL.

permissions. In computer security, a description of the type of authorized interactions a subject can have with an object. Permissions include: read, write, execute, add, modify, and delete. (AFR). *Synonymous with* ACCESS MODE.

permutation. In mathematics, any one of the total possible number of positional arrangements in a group.

persistent object. In computer security, a technique in which a resource is given a secret name known only to the programs which can use it and reference to that resource is then made an inaccessible component of the executable objects which use the resource. For example, a file is given a name and that name is included in the source code of application programs that are allowed to access it. The application programs exist only in a compiled form on the computer and the name of the file is then removed. The resource is thus hidden from all programs except those which 'know' its secret name. *See* APPLICATION PROGRAM, SOURCE CODE.

personal authentication. *See* PERSONAL VERIFICATION.

personal computer. In computing, a microcomputer and peripherals designed to provide computing facilities for an individual user. *See* MICROCOMPUTER. *Synonymous with* HOME COMPUTER.

personal computer security. The protection of data stored and processed on a personal computer, against unauthorized disclosure or modification, and the protection of the hardware, and storage media, against loss, modification or damage.

Introduction.
Personal computers and other small systems have unique security problems that must be understood if effective security measures are to be implemented. Although personal computers provide essentially the same functionality as large systems, i.e. they permit the rapid manipulation and examination of large amounts of text and data, there are some characteristics that present special security problems. In general, the differences are in the following areas:

- physical accessibility;
- built-in security mechanisms;
- nature of the data;
- users.

Basic physical protection of a computer system is required to assure operational reliability and basic integrity of hardware and software. Other security mechanisms, e.g. those implemented in systems hardware and software, rely on this underlying level of protection.

With personal computers, physical accessibility is not as easily controlled, indeed, accessibility is inherent in the concept of a 'personal' computer. It is seldom feasible to build a protective 'shell' around an individual personal computer. This means that protection against damage, hardware modification, or unauthorized access presents particular difficulties.

Since many technical security mechanisms, e.g. access control software and cryptographic routines, are often dependent on the integrity of the underlying hardware and software, these security mechanisms may no longer provide the intended degree of protection.

A second security problem with most personal computers is the lack of built-in hardware mechanisms needed to isolate users from sensitive, security related, system functions. For example, the typical personal computer does not support the following important security mechanisms, that have long been available on larger systems:

- multiple processor states, enabling separate domains for users and system processes;
- privileged instructions, limiting access to certain functions, e.g. reading and writing to disk, to trusted system processes;
- memory protection features, preventing unauthorized access to sensitive parts of the system.

Without such hardware features it is impossible to prevent user programs from accessing or modifying parts of the

operating system and thereby circumventing intended security mechanisms.

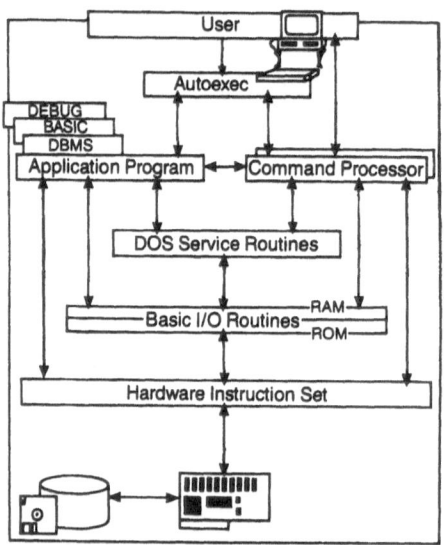

personal computer security
Fig. 1. Internal access paths within a personal
computer.

Figure 1 illustrates many of the internal
interfaces that exist within a personal
computer system. Effective security
within the computer itself requires that
the paths by which users may access
data and system functions be limited and
tightly controlled. The hardware mechanisms mentioned above are designed to
limit and control these paths.

It can be seen from the illustration that
control mechanisms implemented at a
given level, e.g. in an application program or even in the operating system,
can be circumvented by using one of the
alternate paths. Although it takes a
certain level of technical competence to
exploit such weaknesses, many experienced personal computer users acquire
such skills.

The information processed and stored
on personal computer systems may often
be more sensitive and accessible than
that found on larger, multi-user systems.
This situation arises because the
information on a given machine is often
associated with one person or a well
defined group. This information is likely
to be in the form of memoranda, reports, spreadsheets, or simple lists
which are readily accessible using software tools familiar to all personal computer users. Lastly, such data will tend
to be in a relatively 'final' form, rather
than a mass of unanalyzed or unprocessed data. All of this may make the
job of searching for specific information
easier than on a large system.

Hardware protection.
To prevent theft of PC's, and other
office equipment, several types of equipment lockdown devices are available.
These may be used to secure the equipment to a table or other fixed object;
some devices also prevent access to the
system power switch. It is becoming
increasingly important to prevent unauthorized access to the inside of the PC
equipment itself, to ensure component
theft protection and configuration control. Many systems contain valuable
expansion boards, e.g. additional memory, modems, graphics interfaces, which
have become a popular theft target.

In addition, system security mechanisms, e.g. cryptography, may be dependent on certain components, and the
integrity of such components must be
protected. Equipment lockdown devices
often provide additional protection
against access to the interior of the
equipment. Alternatively, devices are
available for some systems which simply
lock the equipment cover.

Personal computers are designed to
operate in the typical office environment, i.e. without special air conditioning, electrical power quality control, or
air contamination controls. In general, it
can be argued that 'if the people are
comfortable, the PCs will be comfortable'. Nevertheless, special attention
should be given to minimizing the environmental hazards to which such equipment is exposed.

Particular care should be given to the
protection of magnetic media. Not only

is it the primary repository of each user's information, it is perhaps the system component most vulnerable to damage. Fixed or hard disks are usually relatively well protected from environmental contaminants. However, care must be exercised when moving these units, because of the danger of damage to read/write heads or other internal components.

Virtually every personal computer system has at least one floppy disk drive. Flexible diskettes are the most prevalent medium for distributing software and data, and the handling of diskettes is an integral part of using almost any PC. The actual magnetic disk is contained within a protective jacket. However, there must be openings in the jacket for access by the read/write heads of the drive mechanism. These surfaces are particularly vulnerable to damage. Microfloppy disks employ a rigid plastic casing with a retractable access cover thus reducing the vulnerability to rough handling and contaminants. PC users are often quite careless in handling magnetic media, and management has the responsibility of providing proper training in this area.

Personal computer system and data access control.
There are three aspects to the issue of controlling access to systems and information:

- authorization - establishing the rules which determine who may access which systems and information;
- identification - of users and the systems or data which they are permitted to access;
- access control - enforcement of the specified authorization rules.

The process of access control implies that some rules exist to specify which users are authorized to access which system resources, normally programs or data. Such rules must be established by the 'owners' of the resources to be controlled. Authorization rules may consist of nothing more than a statement that only members of a given group or department are to have access to a given computer or application system. On the other hand, the rules may consist of formal definitions of information classifications and rules for accessing each. The type of authorization rules adopted will depend on the needs of each organization. It is important, however, that there be some type of authorization process.

For authorization rules to be enforced, it is necessary that users and resources, usually data, be identified. In a personal computer environment, user identification may be implicit or explicit. In a typical situation, a user establishes 'authority' to use the system simply by being able to turn it on. If such implied identification is to mean anything at all, the system must be a true 'personal', i.e. single user, system and there must be adequate physical controls to ensure that only legitimate users are able to gain access.

Locked offices or equipment enclosures can provide some degree of assurance in this area. If a system is shared, then such simple identification procedures may not be adequate.

For most situations in which PCs are shared, user identification should be authenticated in some manner. This requires an explicit interaction between the system and the user. This should be accomplished with some type of system 'log on' process in which the user provides a non secret identifier, e.g. name or account number, and some evidence to authenticate that claim, e.g. a password. User log on authentication should occur whenever the system is powered up, or a new user accesses the system. In addition to identifying the user, there must be some means of identifying the resources to be protected. These 'resources' are usually files containing data or programs.

It has long been accepted practice to label sensitive documents and other materials with clear external indicators. Typically, the front cover, and often each page, of such documents must have a standard marking to indicate classification and handling requirements. Although such labelling is not always as easy to accomplish with the various forms of magnetic media used with personal computers, it is not difficult for floppy disks, the most common form of data storage medium. Diskettes containing sensitive information can be marked with special labels or brightly colored jackets. This will enable personnel to identify readily those materials that require special protection. This also makes the sensitivity of materials obvious to a would-be thief, so it must be assumed that users will provide appropriate protection for all such materials.

Two basic approaches are available for protecting data. The first approach is to prevent unauthorized persons from gaining access; the second is to deny effective use of information even if access is gained. Logical access controls provide the first type of protection, cryptography provides the second. It is often appropriate to combine both types of protection.

The problems of controlling logical access are different for data stored on removable and those stored on fixed media. If the data is resident on removable media, then the simple lock-and-key approach will probably provide the most cost-effective solution. If diskettes containing sensitive data cannot be protected in this manner, e.g. during shipment, then encryption may be appropriate. If data resides on non-removable media, e.g. a hard disk, then controlling access to the data requires first controlling access to the machine itself, i.e. user identification, and then to the data available to the user.

Cryptography provides protection against unauthorized disclosure. It also can ensure the detection of unauthorized modifications of information, since any change to encrypted data, without the necessary cryptographic key, will be highlighted by the presence of garbled sections in the subsequent plaintext. It should be clear, however, that cryptography does not prevent modification or destruction; it simply ensures the detection of such events. Critical data, therefore, cannot be protected by encryption alone.

There are several commercially available software and hardware based products which provide personal computer users with cryptographic capabilities. These products, in general, enable the user to perform the following cryptographic functions:

- enter or change cryptographic keys;
- encrypt a block of data;
- decrypt a block of data.

In some cases, facilities are provided for the generation and management of keys. Usually, however, this is left to the user. Indeed, this can be one of the major problems in the effective use of cryptography, since the secrecy of keys are critical to the protection provided by cryptography.

The normal manner in which cryptography is used in a personal computer environment is to encrypt and decrypt entire files. Typically, a user prepares a file and then runs an encryption utility to produce a ciphertext version of the file. The original file should then be overwritten. The utility program must again be used to decrypt and produce a plaintext version of the file.

The user is usually responsible for selecting, entering, and remembering the key used for the encryption and decryption process. Commercial cryptographic products usually provide utility programs for bulk file encryption and decryption as well as a utility to overwrite old files.

Problems with bulk encryption and decryption of data files include general inconvenience, the need to overwrite plaintext files, and the personnel training necessary. An alternative to the above-mentioned file encryption process is the use of a cryptographic facility which is integral to the file input/output subsystem. Basically, each block of data to be written to disk is first encrypted, and each block read from disk is decrypted before it is passed to the requesting program. This makes the entire cryptographic process almost transparent to the user and eliminates the inconvenience and dangers associated with bulk file procedures. Users with sufficient technical expertise can implement such a capability themselves. In addition, there are some excellent commercial hardware and software products available.

Another aspect of access control, that often is overlooked, is that of data 'residue' left on disk or in memory. This is data that is stored in areas of disk or memory which have been released to reuse. Such information often can be read by subsequent users. A common example of the disk residue problem is associated with the erasing of disk files (e.g., with the Erase or Delete commands). This process usually results only in the setting of a file deleted indicator in the file directory, not the physical erasure or overwriting of the actual data. This problem can be solved by using a program to 'purge', i.e. overwrite, all file data as part of the deletion process. Although such programs are relatively easy to write, they are usually not provided as standard features of personal computer operating systems. Therefore, they must be acquired or written by the user.

Backup and contingency planning.
The problem of backup and contingency planning in a personal computer environment is essentially the same as for other data processing activities. Indeed, for organizations with both personal computers and large scale systems, the backup and contingency planning should

be an integrated process. However, there are special considerations for personal computers due primarily to the wide distribution of equipment and number of people involved.

Contingency planning consists of those activities undertaken in anticipation of potential events which could cause serious adverse effects. This, of course, could apply to individual users and their applications as well as to organizations. In a personal computer environment, one of the key elements in the contingency planning process is the individual user, since there is no central staff to perform many of the important functions.

Contingency plans should consist of emergency procedures, resource, i.e. hardware, software, data, backup preparations, and backup operation plans. In addition, comprehensive contingency plans will include recovery and test procedures. With a personal computer there is obviously a need to encourage regular and systematic backup of files, since such backup can no longer be performed centrally and systematically as is the case with a large scale system. The method and frequency of backup must be determined by each user, based on the storage media and the volatility of the data involved.

The most common backup medium is floppy disk, since virtually every personal computer has a floppy disk drive. For systems with hard disks, however, a full file backup may require more than 20 diskettes. Alternatives, such as streaming cassette backup systems should be considered if incremental backups to diskette are too difficult or time consuming.

It is important for users to understand the threats addressed by backup procedures. The obvious reason for backing up files is to enable recovery of data after loss due to media or hardware problems or accidents, e.g. unintentional erasure of files. This encourages users to store backup copies in a convenient, nearby location. The other threat of concern, however, is loss resulting from a fire, theft, flood etc., which might involve an entire office or building. In these situations, locally stored backup copies would be lost along with the originals. It is also wise to retain two backup copies. If the original data is lost then damage to the only backup copy during transit, or loading, would be disastrous.

Viruses

The personal computer has been attacked by a multifarious population of viruses. The complexity and impact of such viruses has increased significantly in recent years and viruses represent the single most significant factor in personal computer security. To some extent the virus danger has forced personal computer users to take personal computer security seriously and to adopt sensible procedures, e.g. backup.

There are a wide variety of software packages designed to assist users to protect their systems against viruses and many organizations have set-up centralized units to provide anti-viral defenses. In particular large organizations now implement procedures to minimize the danger of illicit use of personal computers, introduction of untested or illicit software etc.

Additional Factors

Operators of important applications, whether on small or large systems, will require reliable audit trails; organizations also may wish to monitor use of personal computers by employees. A single user personal computer may need special audit trail facilities both as an historical record and as an aid in recovery from errors. The placement and use of audit trails in personal computer systems, however, requires special considerations. Organizations with substantial investment in personal computer equipment may wish to monitor the usage of such equipment. Although this is not primarily a security concern,

effective monitoring can have security benefits.

The types of event that may be of interest include:

- system startup;
- user session initiation and completion;
- program initiation and completion;
- access to specific data files.

In most organizations, the personal computer is but one of several types of data processing devices used. Increasingly, there is a need to connect personal computers as terminal devices to larger host systems or to connect two or more personal computers in networks. The security issues in each of these situations are basically the same as have always existed in multi-user host systems and data communications networks. There are some unique issues, however, which should be addressed by managers.

When a personal computer is used as a terminal device to a host system, the basic requirements for security and access control remain with the host. As far as the host is concerned, it is just another terminal. It must be recognized, however, that the personal computer has the ability to upload, and download large amounts of data at rates often exceeding those possible with ordinary terminals.

Communications software for personal computers often provide the facility to store telephone numbers and log on sequences for frequently called host systems. A significant potential problem exists when users store passwords or other sensitive information in this manner. In effect, the security of the host is now dependent on the physical security provided over the personal computer and its files. Users should be instructed never to store host system passwords or other sensitive information in communication software control files. All electronic equipment emanates electromagnetic signals, (Fig. 2). For some equipment, e.g. computers, communication lines, data terminals, these emanations may carry information which can be detected by appropriately placed monitoring devices. Security measures intended to combat this problem are known as 'Tempest' controls. In the US, applications involving classified (National Security) data must normally be processed on equipment that has been specially shielded or modified to minimize emanations.

Management.
The preceding sections have described the nature of security exposures facing the users of personal computer systems and some of the specific control measures which can be used to reduce those exposures. This section provides a management perspective to the problem and an approach to managing information-security in a personal computer environment. There are three basic strategies for protecting information resources from the threats mentioned so far:

- prevent threats from striking;
- detect that threats have struck;
- recover from damaging effects.

Any given security measure will fall into one or more of these basic strategies. The objective of security management is to select cost-effective control measures which involve all of the above protection strategies. These strategies are not, in isolation, of value to a manager or user concerned with protecting information.

A systematic approach to identifying and implementing security requirements is needed. In general, such an approach should include the following activities:

- asset identification - identifying and classifying the information and other assets that require protection.
- risk assessment - identifying and evaluating the threats, specific vulnerabilities, and degree of exposure.
- control selection and implementation - selecting control measures which provide cost-effective reduction of exposure.
- audit and evaluation - ongoing activities to review the continued effectiveness and appropriateness of controls.

The underlying objective of these activities is the selection and implementation of cost-effective control measures. With unlimited resources, virtually any level of security could be achieved. However, no rational organization should commit resources in excess of the risks involved. The key, therefore, is risk management.

When analyzing risk, it is important to view the problem as an information security problem, not a computer security problem. This is particularly true as the personal computer becomes just another office tool such as the typewriter, dictating machine, or telephone. Risks are related primarily to information and only secondarily to the physical devices on which that information may be stored or processed.

Ideally there should be a formal assignment of authority and responsibility for information security management for the entire organization. This applies to information in any form, whether it be on a personal computer, a mainframe system, or on paper. However, the basic operational responsibility should be placed with the people who 'own' the information, have the incentive to protect it, and have the necessary authority and resources, i.e. the user organizations. Therefore, except for development of policy and guidance, a single point of responsibility for personal computer security is probably inappropriate.

Many security controls ultimately depend on trust in individuals. Therefore, there should be some process to screen personnel who are authorized to access sensitive information systems. Management should establish formal control procedures over the development and use of information systems. This is more easily done when such information systems are relatively well structured and distinct.

There should be periodic formal assessments of threats and of risk associated with sensitive information systems. This is required as a basis for selection of cost-effective control measures for those systems.

Systems, organizations, and environments change. This often results in changes in the risks facing an information system. There should be a program of regular audits and evaluations of sensitive systems to ensure the continued adequacy, effectiveness, and appropriateness of security measures.

The elements listed above do not, in themselves, assure appropriate protection. Rather, they provide a consistent framework within which to build an effective information security program.

As is the case for any security program, it is management's responsibility to provide the lead in assuring security for personal computer systems. This is all the more important due to the growing number of people in the organization who are or will soon be involved in the use of such systems. Management should focus on:

- protecting information, not computers;
- emphasizing the use of a risk management approach to make protection decisions;
- assigning responsibility and necessary authority for security to the actual 'owners' and users of the information resources.

(Acknowledgement is made to Dennis D Steinauer, 'Security of Personal Computer Systems: A Management Guide',

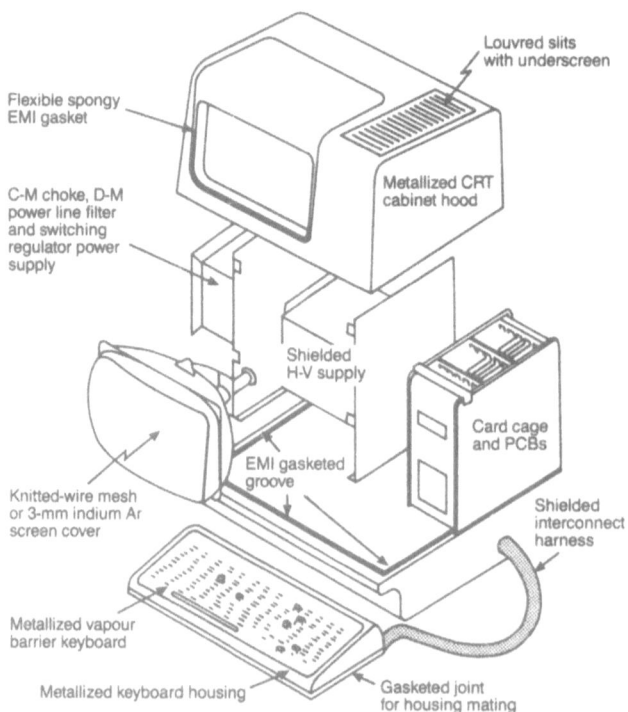

personal computer security
Fig. 2. Radiation control measures. Courtesy of Interference Control Technologies, Inc.

NBS Special Publication 500-120. National Bureau of Standards, 1985.) *See* ACCESS CONTROL, AUDIT TRAIL, BACK/UP RESTORE, CONTINGENCY PLANS, CRYPTOGRAPHIC KEY, CRYPTOGRAPHY, DIRECTORY, DOWNLOAD, FLOPPY DISK, HARD DISK, INFORMATION SECURITY, LOG ON, MODEM, OWNERSHIP, PASSWORD, PLAINTEXT, PURGING, RESIDUES PROBLEMS, RISK ANALYSIS, RISK MANAGEMENT, SOFTWARE PROTECTION, SOFTWARE TOOL, SPREADSHEET, TAPE STREAMER, TEMPEST PROOFING, VAN ECK PHENOMENON.

personal computing. In applications, computing performed by an end user on a personal computer, including machine operation and often involving word processing, spreadsheet and database applications. Personal computing is characterized by its informal approach, simplified procedures and on demand availability, in contrast to conventional electronic data processing. *See* DATABASE, END USER COMPUTING, ELECTRONIC DATA PROCESSING, SPREADSHEET.

personal data. (1) In legislation, any unique data used in the system of records to locate or retrieve an individual's record. Information subject to the Privacy Act of 1974. (AFR). (2) Data about an individual including, but not limited to, education financial transactions, medical history, qualifications, service data, criminal or employment history which ties the data to the individual's name, or an identifying number, symbols, or other identifying particular assigned to the individual, such as a finger or voice print or a photograph. (OPNAVINST). *See* FINGERPRINT, VOICE PRINT. (3) In legislation, as defined by the U.K. Data Protection Act 1984, data consisting of information which relates to a living individual who can be identified from that information (or from that and other information in the possession of the data user), including any expression of opinion about the individual but not any indication of the intentions of the data user in respect of that individual. *See* DATA, DATA PROTECTION.

personal disclosure. In database security, a situation in which a user can deduce a previously unknown sensitive statistic concerning an individual. Such disclosure can be approximate, positive or negative. *See* DATA PROTECTION, DISCLOSURE RISK, NEGATIVE DISCLOSURE, SENSITIVE STATISTIC. *Synonymous with* COMPROMISE.

personal identification. *See* PERSONAL VERIFICATION.

personal identification number. *See* PIN.

personal identifier. In data security, a data item associated with a specific individual which represents the identity of that individual and may be known by other individuals. (FIPS).

personal password. In access control, a password that is known by only one person and is used to authenticate that person's identity. (FIPS). *See* PASSWORD, VALID PASSWORD.

personal verification. In banking, the validation of secret quantities provided by a user to establish his authority to institute a transaction. *See* PIN VALIDATION.

personnel security. In computer security, the procedures established to insure that all personnel who have access to any sensitive information have the required authorities as well as all appropriate clearances. (FIPS). *See* ACCESS, SENSITIVE INFORMATION.

perturbation. In database security, a technique of inference control for statistical databases in which either:

- random data is added to individual items of retrieved data used in computing requested statistics;

or

- the computed and released statistic is based upon only a sample of all relevant records;

or

- the released statistics are rounded off.

The effect of the random data may be negligible in determining the statistic but can render inferred data highly inaccurate. For example, if an individual salary is to be inferred by requesting the total salary of all members of a large department and the total set of all non-immigrant members of the department, then the result could be used to deduce the salary of the only immigrant departmental employee.

Perturbation techniques which add random numbers to each sum would cause the deduced salary, the difference of 2 large numbers, to be completely inaccurate. *Compare* CELL RESTRICTION, TABLE RESTRICTION. *See* INFERENCE CONTROL, RECORD BASED PERTURBATION, RESULT BASED PERTURBATION, STATISTICAL DATABASE.

pervasive security mechanism. In communications security, a term used in OSI security. A pervasive security mechanism is not specific to a particular security services or associated with a particular layer. *See* OSI SECURITY.

Phantom. In computer security, a virus that terminates and stays resident, infects COMMAND.COM and COM files, affects run-time operation, corrupts program and OVL files. *See* VIRUS NAMES.

phase delay. In communications, the time delay represented by a change in the phase of a sinusoidal wave in passing through two points on a transmission path.

phase modulation. In communications, a method of modulation in which the phase of the sinusoidal carrier is varied in accordance with the modulating signal. *Compare* AMPLITUDE MODULATION, FREQUENCY MODULATION, PULSE MODULATION. *See* CARRIER.

phase shift keying. In data communications, a method of changing the phase of a sinusoidal signal to represent binary data. If only two discrete phases are employed then each phase corresponds to a binary 1 or 0. If four phase shifts are used then each one may correspond to a dibit. *See* DIBIT, PHASE MODULATION, QUADRATURE AMPLITUDE MODULATION.

phone phreaking. *See* PHREAK.

photoelectric beam smoke detector. In physical security, a smoke detector which is activated by the reduction in intensity of a received light beam due to the obscuration effects of the smoke between a light source and a photoelectric cell. *See* PHOTOELECTRIC SENSOR.

photoelectric sensor. In physical security, a sensor which uses a change in light intensity at a receiver to produce an electrical signal which activates an alarm. Photoelectric sensors may operate with visible light or infra red radiation.

photosensor. In physical security, a device that receives a light signal and produces a corresponding electrical signal.

phracker. In computer security, a person who combines phone 'PHReaking' with computer 'hACKing.' *See* HACKER, PHREAK.

phreak. In communications security, PHone frEAK, a person fascinated by the telephone system. Commonly, an individual who uses personal knowledge of the telephone system to make calls at the expense of another. *Compare* HACK-ER. *See* PHRACKER, TELEPHONE INTRUSION.

physical barrier. In physical security, any physical manifestation, e.g. fences, rivers, walls, cliffs, designed to delay or prevent intrusion into a protected area.

physical control space. In physical security, the spherical space surrounding electronic equipment used to process information which is under sufficient physical control to stop hostile intercept of compromising emanations. It is usually expressed in meters and can be controlled by fences, guards, patrols, walls, and so forth. The exact method of securing the PCS may vary depending upon resources available. (AFR). *See* COMPROMISING EMANATIONS, TEMPEST, VAN ECK PHENOMENON.

physical database. In databases, the form that the database is held in storage including any pointers that it may contain. A number of different logical databases may be based upon the same physical database. *Compare* LOGICAL DATABASE.

physical data independence. In databases, pertaining to the composition of databases that enables the physical storage structure to be changed without affecting the logical structure. *Compare* LOGICAL DATA INDEPENDENCE. *See* DATA INDEPENDENCE.

physical layer. In data communications, the bottom layer in the ISO Open Systems Interconnection Reference model. This layer is concerned with the transmission of the raw bit stream. *Compare* APPLICATION LAYER, DATA LINK LAYER, NETWORK LAYER, PRESENTATION LAYER, SESSION LAYER, TRANSPORT LAYER. *See* BIT STREAM, OPEN SYSTEMS INTERCONNECTION.

physical record. (1) In computing, a record associated with a specific area of physical storage. (2) In computing, the largest unit of data that can be transmitted in a single read or write operation. *Compare* LOGICAL RECORD.

physical security. (1) In risk management, the measures used to provide physical protection of resources against deliberate and accidental threats. (ISO). *Compare* LOGICAL SECURITY. (2) The use of locks, guards, badges, and similar administrative measures to control access to the computer and related equipment. (FIPS). *See* ACCESS. (3) In computer security, the measures required for the protection of the structures housing the computer, related equipment and their contents from damage by accident, fire and environmental hazards. (FIPS).

physical threat. In computer security, a threat potentially affecting the actual existence and physical condition of the computer facilities, e.g. theft of equipment, fire, terrorist attack. *Compare* ACCIDENTAL THREAT, ACTIVE THREAT, DELIBERATE THREAT, LOGICAL THREAT, PASSIVE THREAT. *See* THREAT.

PI. *See* PADDING INDICATOR.

PIC. In access control, Personal Identification Code, a unique alphanumeric code used to identify an individual, usually in combination with a physical token, such as a magnetic stripe card. The token is entered into an appropriate computer/communication terminal to effect a transaction. *See* MAGNETIC STRIPE CARD, PIN.

piezoelectric detector. In physical security, a detector which operates by the electric current generated when a piezoelectric crystal is subjected to mechanical stress.

piggyback. *See* BETWEEN-THE-LINES ENTRY, ELECTRONIC PIGGYBACKING, PIGGYBACK ENTRY, PIGGYBACKING.

piggyback entry. In access control, unauthorized access that is gained to an ADP system via another user's legitimate connection. (FIPS).

piggybacking. (1) In data communications, a method of sending acknowledgements with outgoing messages, e.g. in HDLC messages from A to B contain information on the frames received by A from B. *See* HDLC, ACKNOWLEDGMENT, FRAME. (2) In computer security. *Synonymous with* TAILGATING.

PIN. (1) In access control, Personal Identification Number, a unique, personal number that must be entered by a user before a remote terminal, or point of sale terminal, can be used to transfer information or complete a transaction. *Compare* PASSWORD. *See* POINT OF SALE TERMINAL, PIN MANAGEMENT AND SECURITY. (2) In banking, the 4 to 12 position alphanumeric code or password the customer possesses for authentication. (ANSI). *Compare* PAN. *See* PIN MANAGEMENT AND SECURITY.

PIN assignment. In banking, the process of establishing the relationship between customer authentication and identification data. (ANSI). *See* PIN, PIN MANAGEMENT AND SECURITY.

Ping Pong-B. In computer security, a virus that terminates and stays resident, infects floppy and hard disk boot sector, affects run-time operation, corrupts boot sector. *See* VIRUS NAMES.

PIN issuance. In banking, the act of conveying PIN information to a consumer. (ANSI). *See* PIN, PIN MANAGEMENT AND SECURITY.

PIN mailer. In banking, a document containing a PIN in clear form. The document must be printed under conditions of high security which ensure that an employee cannot open, read or closely examine the document. The mailer is often produced as a multi-part sealed form so that the PIN can only be read by unsealing the form. *See* PIN, PIN MANAGEMENT AND SECURITY.

PIN management and security. In banking and data security, the set of processes involved in the generation, assignment, delivery, issuance, storage, entry, verification, transmission, deactivation and destruction of PINs.

PINs may be employed in two types of environment:

- an organization where selected employees or members use PINs to gain access to the organization's facilities, e.g. computer systems, databases;
- an EFT or EFTPOS network serving one or more financial institutions and an extremely large, diffuse customer base.

The general principles of PIN management and security are common to both application areas but the number of users, the relationship between the user and the system and the potential damage resulting from inadequate PIN management and security, is quite different in the two cases. Since the magnitude of the task and the complexity of the environment is greater on the case of EFT and EFTPOS systems, PIN management and security will be considered from that viewpoint.

An EFT, or EFTPOS, system must guarantee the security of the customer's identification and the integrity of the customer's unique transaction, from customer to card issuer to customer, irrespective of the location of the terminal used by the customer. Such terminals will usually be unsupervised, and in the case of EFTPOS systems, they may be vulnerable to modification and misuse by dishonest retailers or retailers' employees.

The risks attendant upon the discovery of PINs, by unauthorized persons, can arise from:

- misuse of lost or stolen cards;
- mass fraud arising from the production and misuse of counterfeit cards.

The potential loss arising from the misuse of lost or stolen cards is limited by the time period between the loss and its reporting to the card issuer, and the maximum permitted value of daily transactions. Moreover many illegal acquirers of such cards will lack the ability to determine their PINs.

The mass fraud which could, however, be perpetrated if counterfeit cards were produced, and the corresponding PINs derived or obtained, is a major source of concern. The misuse of a card would not be reported to a card issuer until the customer had checked a monthly (say) statement and reported the fraudulent transaction. The card issuer would then be faced with the following problems:

- The major administrative costs of rectifying the effects of individual fraudulent transactions.
- The problem of customers reporting legitimate transactions as fraudulent because they had forgotten the transaction or were fraudulently exploiting the situation.
- The loss of customer confidence.

It is therefore important that the processes involved in the generation, assignment, delivery, issuance, storage, entry, verification, transmission, deactivation and destruction of PINs should obviate the possibility of PIN disclosure.

Generation of PINs

PINs may be employed in a transaction interchange system where customers enter their identification and authentication details, when initiating transactions, at terminals connected to the acquirer's network. The message details are transmitted to the card issuer who has the responsibility to authenticate the customer and authorize the transaction. PINs may also be employed in a private network where the authentication of customers and authorization of transactions are performed entirely within the network.

PINs may be generated as derived PINs, randomly generated PINs or customer selected PINs. A derived PIN is a function of the customer's account number or some other non secret identifying information; the derived PIN may therefore be verified by applying the same algorithm to the customer identifying information, used to derive the PIN, and comparing the result with the PIN value input by the customer at the terminal.

Clearly the ability to calculate the PIN must be restricted to the card issuer, e.g. DES encryption may be employed and the secrecy of the key maintained. The PIN may be verified at a terminal that has access to the key used in the derivation algorithm, without storing the PIN on the card. The PIN generation technique should be fully automated and the results printed on a PIN mailer to avoid employees gaining access to customers' PINs. Such derived PINs must be encrypted prior to storage.

The problem with derived PINs is that the PIN is defined by the account number or identifying information and the cryptographic key employed. Thus difficulties arise if the PIN is suspected of compromise, or it must be changed following loss of the customer bank or credit card. Similarly if the bank wishes to change the cryptographic key it must inform all customers of the new derived PINs.

PIN offsets may be employed to overcome these problems. The derived PIN is computed and then the customer PIN may be selected on a random basis; the

PIN offset is a number which relates the derived PIN to the actual PIN. For example the offset may be added to the actual PIN to produce the derived PIN. The PIN offset need not be a secret number and may therefore be included on the magnetic stripe data. The PIN may be checked locally, the terminal reads the account number or identifying data, and computes the derived PIN. The actual PIN is entered by the customer, the PIN offset is read from the card, added to the input PIN and compared with the derived PIN.

A randomly assigned PIN is produced by a random process such that a knowledge of any sequence of generated PINs will not enable the determination of any other PIN. The generated PINs must lie within the range of permissible PINs, in terms of character set and PIN length. Randomly assigned PINs may be difficult to remember and hence increase the danger that customers will make written records which could be lost or stolen with the card. Methods of generating sequences of characters, which are easier to remember, are available but this technique considerably reduces the range of assigned PINs, for a given PIN length, and hence requires rather longer PINs. The generation of such PINs demands strict security precautions to prevent card issuer employees gaining unauthorized access to PIN information combined with customer identification.

Customer-selected PINs are likely to be such that they are easily remembered but there exists the strong possibility that such PINs will bear a deducible relationship to the customer's personal details: names of children, birthdate, car registration numbers etc. Since customers will tend to reject a large number of possibilities, within the PIN range, the minimum PIN length must be sufficient to provide a wide range of PINs in use.

Local checking of customer-selected, and randomly assigned, PINs is possible using the PIN offset technique. The PIN offset is computed as the difference (say) of the PIN and derived PIN. It is important that the combination of PIN and PIN offset, equal to the derived PIN, is not disclosed. With such information an attacker may produce a fake card, including customer account data, select a random PIN, compute the PIN offset and store it on the fake card. Such a card and associated PIN will be accepted by local terminals, even though the PIN used by the customer, is not revealed.

An alternative technique employs PVVs (PIN verification values). The PVV is derived by encrypting a combination of account number and customer PIN; the 4 digit PVV is then derived from the 16 hex characters of the ciphertext, e.g. selecting those hex characters corresponding to decimal digits. Special routines are employed if there are fewer than four decimal digits in the ciphertext. The PVV is stored on the magnetic stripe card and used in PIN checking in a similar manner to PIN offsets. In this case the entered PIN is combined with account data and the PVV computed, the computed PVV is then compared with the stored value.

Delivery of PINs
The delivery mechanism for a PIN must be such that it does not appear in clear form where it can be linked to customer identification. PINs must not be mailed in the same envelope as the corresponding credit or bank cards and the return address on the envelope must be different to that used with the card. The PIN shall be printed in such a manner that it is only visible to the customer. If a customer has more than one card then the information accompanying the PIN must be sufficient for the customer to correlate the PIN with the appropriate card, but insufficient to compromise the PIN if it is intercepted. Card issuers must provide adequate security to protect the PINs in the handling of PIN documents, returned envelopes, waste material etc.

The reporting by a customer, of a customer-selected PIN, should not involve the revealing of that PIN to a card issuer's employee; if an employee is authorized to initiate the entry of a PIN, by a customer, then that employee's identity should be incorporated in the transaction record. Customers may inform the card issuer of their PINs in person, by mail or by telephone.

Input of a PIN by the customer, in person, requires that:

- the card issuer employee, authorized to initiate the input, must check the customer's identification;
- the employee's identity must be checked and authenticated by the system;
- the PIN entry process must be initiated by the employee and disabled immediately upon the PIN entry.

With mail or telephone entry of customer-selected PINs the procedures adopted must ensure that any person intercepting the customer's mail, or eavesdropping the telephone call, would be unable to relate the PIN to the customer's account information. In mailing, the customer needs to be informed that the returned form holding the PIN number, and the associated envelope, must not contain the customer's name, address or account identifying information. The form needs to contain a control number to enable the card issuer to correlate the PIN with the customer account number; this control number may, for example, be an encrypted form of the account number.

Telephone inputs must be to an audio response or recording system to avoid the possibility that the customer will accidentally, or in responding to an invitation to do so, reveal a name or address.

Once issued PINs may need to be changed or customers may need to be informed of forgotten PINs. The security arrangements in this case must be no less than those for the issuance and delivery of new PINs. Customers must be informed by mail that their PINs have been changed, this correspondence should not contain the PIN and it should contain instructions to inform the card issuer immediately if the change had not been requested by the customer. If the change is initiated by the customer at an unattended terminal, then the old PIN must be entered; some additional form of identification, e.g. a one-shot PIN change authorization card may also be required. Replacement of an exposed PIN may require special security arrangements, depending upon whether the PIN is derived, randomly assigned or customer-selected. For example, if a derived PIN is exposed then some data element employed in generating the PIN, e.g. the offset, must also be changed.

Storage of PINS

PINs must always be encrypted prior to storage, and such encryption may be either reversible or irreversible. Reversible encryption allows the original PINs to be recovered and re-encrypted with a new key. If the encryption key is compromised, however, it must be considered that all PINs encrypted under that key have been compromised and protection by re-encryption under a new key will be too late.

Irreversible encryption ensures that the original PINs cannot be revealed but PINs of limited length may be determined by an exhaustive search, i.e. every PIN in the limited range is subjected to the irreversible encryption algorithm and compared with the stored encrypted values. Irreversible keys cannot be decrypted and re-encrypted under new keys, however, this facility may be achieved by the reversible encryption, of irreversibly encrypted PINs, for storage. All PINs should be combined with information related to the customer account number, prior to encryption, to obviate the danger that stored PIN values are modified by an attacker. PINs written on the magnetic stripe of a customer card must be encrypted, reversibly or irreversibly. Again some account identifying information must be combined with the PIN, prior to encryption, in case an attacker has the facilities to erase and rewrite the contents of the stripe.

Customers and users are responsible for the secrecy of their PINs; after entry into the system, however, the card acceptor is responsible for PINs in transit, storage or processing. At the point of entry there is an overlap of customer and card acceptor responsibility. The customer should ensure that onlookers are unable to observe the sequence of key entry and the design of the terminal must preclude the visual display or printing of entered PINs.

Verification of PINs

The verification of PINs is the responsibility of the card issuer or delegated agent. PINs may be verified by comparison of received data and a PIN, retrieved from storage, which corresponds to the customer account number. The verification may involve an algorithm performed on an entered PIN and comparison with an encrypted value of the PIN stored on the card, or an algorithm performed on account data and compared with the entered PIN. Such algorithmic verification can be undertaken at a remote location, on- or offline, provided that the requisite encryption keys are available at that location.

A check digit may be included in a PIN, to check the reasonableness of the entered PIN, this facilitates an early detection of a miskeyed PIN but such check digits do not authenticate the PIN data.

PINs are encrypted both during transmission, and in storage, different cryptographic keys are used for these processes. Encryption for transmission is reversible but stored values may be reversibly or irreversibly encrypted. With reversible encryption employed, both for transmission and storage, the comparison may be performed by decryption, of both the transmitted and stored keys, and comparison of cleartext values. Such decryption comparisons must, of course, be performed in a secure environment. Alternatively one PIN may be decrypted and then re-encrypted with the second key for comparison of encrypted values. For reversible transmission, irreversible storage systems the transmitted PIN must be decrypted and then subjected to the irreversible encryption process for comparison with the stored value.

The protection of PINs in transmission may be achieved by physical security of the transmission medium or by encryption. Physical security of the transmission medium involves monitoring against unauthorized connections and possibly physical protection, e.g. a continuous metal conduit, pressure sensors in a pressurized conduit, etc. Such physical protection, which may also involve shielding electromagnetic radiation, tends to be both complex and expensive. Encryption techniques demand secure modules for the storage of master cryptographic keys and encryption/decryption processes.

PINs are deactivated when a customer account is closed or a PIN is compromised. Such intentional deactivation should involve the physical destruction of written records, erasure of electronic storage media, etc. Precautions must be taken against the accidental or deliberate destruction of stored PIN data and back-up copies held in a secure location must be subjected to the same level of encryption security as the original data. *See* ANSI X9.8 - 1982. DERIVED PIN, IRREVERSIBLE ENCRYPTION, PIN ASSIGNMENT, PIN ISSUANCE, PIN MAILER, PVV, OFFSET, REFERENCE PIN, SHOULDER SURFING.

PIN offset. In banking, a value that relates a derived PIN to actual PIN

PIN management and security

Trade-offs in alternative PIN generation techniques. Reprinted with permission of American Bankers' Association, all rights reserved. *American Standard X9.8 Personal Identification Number Management and Security* is published by the American Bankers' Association for the Accredited Standards Committee, X9 on Financial Services. The document is available for sale at a price of US$40 plus US$8 shipping charge to the UK by writing and including payment to ABA Order Processing Department, 44-B Industrial Park Circle, Waldorf, Maryland, USA 20601.

	Assigned derived PINs	Assigned random PINs	Customer-selected PINs
Memorization	⊖ More difficult to remember an arbitrary value	⊖ More difficult to remember an arbitrary value	⊕ Easy to remember
PIN number space utilization	⊕ If good derivation technique used, distribution will be flat over PIN number space	⊕ Values may be assigned to give flat distribution over PIN number space	⊖ If not discouraged, customer likely to select values easily guessed (e.g. birthdates and names) and distribution of values over PIN space is unlikely to be flat
Delivery	⊖ Requires delivery mechanism (usually PIN mailers)	⊖ Requires delivery mechanism (usually PIN mailers)	⊕ Requires attendance at ⊖ issuer's locations
Initial authentication	⊖ Mail delivery (if used) lacks initial in-person authentication	⊖ Mail delivery (if used) lacks initial in-person authentication	⊕ In-person selection permits manual authentication by issuer's personnel
Delivery vulnerability	⊖ Delivery leaves PIN vulnerable to interception	⊖ Delivery leaves PIN vulnerable to interception	⊕ No interception of PIN possible if customer enters selected value
Forgotten PINs	⊕ Same PIN value regeneratable for ease of customer memorization	⊖ Reassignment of same PIN value (for ease of customer memorization) requires reversibly encrypted PIN storage	⊖ Retrieval of same value if forgotten (probably less often than assigned PINs) requires reversibly encrypted PIN storage
Retrievability controls	⊖ Ability to regenerate same PIN value makes PIN retrievable to issuer personnel (adequate controls are critical)	⊕ PIN may be stored irreversibly encrypted, if desired, to impede retrievability	⊕ PIN may be stored irreversibly encrypted, if desired, to impede retrievability
PIN verification value storage	⊕ Does not require storage of PIN verification values	⊖ Requires storage of PIN verification values at issuer	⊖ Requires storage of PIN verification values at issuer
Off-issuer verification	⊕ Permits PIN verification by systems delegated by issuer's distribution of derivation key (provided that distribution, use and storage of key in non-issuer systems can be adequately safeguarded)	⊖ PIN verification at non-issuer systems requires transporting PIN verification values, which is usually prohibitive	⊖ PIN verification at non-issuer system requires transporting PIN verification values, which is usually prohibitive
Disclosed PINs	⊖ Believed disclosure of PIN requires reissuance or re-encoding of card PAN, and possible interim delay in card usability	⊖ Believed disclosure of PIN requires generation and delivery of a new value, deactivation of the old value, and interim delay in card usability	⊕ PIN is easily changeable in person at issuer location if believed disclosed. No delay in card usability
Card reissuance	⊖ Reissuance of card with new PAN (e.g., change of level of issuance) necessitates delivery of a new PIN	⊕ Reissuance of card with new PAN may retain same PIN (no PIN delivery required) if not irreversibly encrypted with PAN	⊕ Reissuance of card with new PAN may retain same PIN (customer need not re-select)
Key disclosure	⊖ Disclosure of the key used in PIN derivation exposes PINs for all cards, with no other data needed	⊕ Disclosure of both PIN storage encryption key and stored verification values is necessary for all PIN disclosure (this may be slightly further alleviated by use of irreversible encryption)	⊕ Disclosure of both PIN storage encryption key and stored verification values is necessary for all PIN disclosure (this may be slightly further alleviated by use of irreversible encryption)
Influencing PIN values	⊕ It is not possible to influence derived values and still have them function correctly	⊖ Tampering with the random number generator could cause the range of assigned values to be severely restricted and influenced. This may be difficult to detect.	⊕ User is free to choose own value ⊖ Issuer's personnel may make suggestions which severely affect the range and probability of his choices

⊕ relative advantage; ⊖ relative disadvantage

value. Derived PINs have the disadvantage that the PIN is effectively fixed by the customer account number and the cryptographic key used in the derived PIN computation. A PIN offset is an arbitrary value that relates the actual PIN to the derived PIN, thus the actual PIN may be changed by simply making a corresponding change to the offset. The offset value need not be secret and can thus be stored on customers' cards. The PIN entered by the customer is combined with the offset value read from the card and compared with the computed derived PIN value for local-PIN checking. *See* DERIVED PIN, PIN MANAGEMENT AND SECURITY. *Synonymous with* OFFSET.

PIN pad. In access control, a tamper resistant unit used for PIN entry at customer terminals. The PIN pad usually comprises a key pad and a display for instructions to the customer; it stores cryptographic keys for local encryption of the PINs. *See* CRYPTOGRAPHIC KEY, PIN.

PIN validation. In banking, personal verification based upon a PIN. *See* PERSONAL VERIFICATION, PIN.

PIN verification. In banking, verification of a customer's authenticity by the issuer. (ANSI). *See* ISSUER, PIN MANAGEMENT AND SECURITY.

PIN verification value. In access control, a decimal number related to the value of a PIN. A plaintext block, based upon a concatenation of the PIN and its corresponding account number, is DES encrypted with a secret double length key. Typically the first 4 bits of the ciphertext is examined, if this set corresponds to a decimal value 0-9, it is accepted, if it corresponds to hexadecimal value A-F it is rejected. This process is continued with successive 4 bit values until the requisite number of decimal digits is obtained. If this process does

not produce sufficient decimal digits then the scan is repeated and 10 is subtracted from hexadecimal values A - F. Alternatively a decimalization table may be employed. The PIN verification value can be used for checking the value of an entered PIN. If the PIN verification value is stored on a magnetic stripe card then the entered PIN can be checked offline by an ATM equipped with the double length key used in the determination of PIN verification value and a comparison of the stored and computed PVVs. Alternatively the PIN may be securely transmitted to a central location and then checked against stored PIN verification values, a process which involves fewer security risks than storing the PINs at the central location. *Compare* CARD VERIFICATION VALUE. *See* ATM, DATA ENCRYPTION STANDARD, DECIMALIZATION TABLE, MULTIPLE DES ENCIPHERMENT, PIN, PIN MANAGEMENT AND SECURITY.

pipeline cipher. In cryptography, a cipher that can exploit a pipeline computer architecture. One block of plaintext enters the processing unit and the first stage of encipherment is undertaken, when this is completed the second block of plaintext enters the processing unit and the first stage of encipherment is undertaken for this block whilst the first plaintext block is undergoing the second stage of encryption etc.

pipelining. In data communications, a technique employed in communication systems in which the sender requires an acknowledgement from the receiver of correct receipt of frames, and the transmission time is long. The sender transmits (say) n frames of data for a period, equal to the time required for a frame to reach the sender and an acknowledgement to reach the receiver. Thereafter the sender will transmit frame m whenever it has received acknowledgement for frame m-n. *See* FRAME, GO BACK N, SELECTIVE REPEAT.

PIR. In physical security, Passive Infra Red sensor. *See* INFRA RED MOTION DETECTOR, PASSIVE SENSOR.

piracy. In software, the illicit copying and distribution of software, usually for financial gain. *Compare* SOFTWARE CREEP.

PKC. *See* PUBLIC KEY CRYPTOGRAPHY.

Plague. In computer security, a virus that infects COM and EXE files. *See* VIRUS NAMES.

plaintext. (1) In cryptography, unenciphered information. (ISO). *Compare* CIPHERTEXT. (2) In cryptography, intelligible text or signals that have meaning and that can be read or acted upon without the application of any decryption. (FIPS). *See* DECRYPT. *Synonymous with* CLEAR DATA, CLEARTEXT.

plaintext ciphertext avalanche. In cryptography, a property of a cipher in which a one bit change in the plaintext produces a radical change in the corresponding ciphertext. *Compare* KEY CIPHERTEXT AVALANCHE. *See* CIPHERTEXT, CRYPTOGRAPHIC KEY, PLAINTEXT.

planted record. In database security, a type of attack in which plaintext records are added to a encrypted database and the subsequent changes in database contents provide details of plaintext-ciphertext pairs. *See* CHOSEN PLAINTEXT.

Plastique. In computer security, a virus that terminates and stays resident, infects COMMAND.COM, COM, EXE and OVL files, affects run-time operation, corrupts program, OVL and data files. *See* VIRUS NAMES.

plug compatible manufacturer. A manufacturer who produces equipment that can be operated in conjunction with another manufacturer's equipment when connected by plug and cable. A term commonly employed in connection with IBM equipment.

POB. Point of Banking. *Compare* POS.

pocket banking. *See* SUPERSMART CARD.

Pohlig-Hellman cipher. In cryptography, a cipher with a similarity to RSA but which is unsuitable for public key cryptography since the deciphering key can be easily computed from the enciphering key.

With this cipher a large prime n is selected and the arithmetic is performed in the Galois field GF(n). An encryption key E is selected which is less than n. Encryption is performed in a similar manner to RSA, i.e. the ciphertext C is produced by exponentiation of a block of plaintext message M thus:

$$C \equiv M^E \pmod{n}.$$

Compare RSA. *See* EULER'S GENERALIZATION, EULER TOTIENT FUNCTION, GALOIS FIELD, KNOWN PLAINTEXT, PRIME NUMBER, PUBLIC KEY CRYPTOGRAPHY.

pointer. In computing, a variable that holds the address of an item of data. In a simple chained list a pointer will hold the address of the next item in the list.

point of sale. In banking, a position where a customer pays for goods or services. *See* POINT-OF-SALE TERMINAL.

point-of-sale terminal. In banking, a terminal used at a location where customer transactions are performed, and designed for particular input functions. In many cases they will be operated by unskilled staff and have facilities for direct reading of data, e.g. automatic reading of coded tags or bar codes. More sophisticated terminals may be linked to the customer's bank for automatic account debiting. *See* ELECTRONIC FUNDS TRANSFER POINT OF SALE.

point protection. In physical security, pertaining to a sensor or group of sensors used to monitor, or detect, intrusion in a small area. *Compare* LINE SENSOR.

point-to-point. (1) In key management, an arrangement in which a communicating pair share a key encrypting key, or a key encrypting key pair, to enable the exchange of data keys or furtherkey-encrypting keys. At least one of the parties must have the capability to generate or acquire keys. *Compare* KEY DISTRIBUTION CENTER, KEY TRANSLATION CENTER. *See* ANSI X9.17 - 1985, COMMUNICATING PAIR, CRYPTOGRAPHIC KEY, DATA KEY, KEY ENCRYPTING KEY, KEY ENCRYPTING KEY PAIR, POINT-TO-POINT ENVIRONMENT. (2) In communications, pertaining to connection between two, and only two, terminal installations. The connection may include switching facilities. *Compare* BROADCAST, MULTICAST, MULTIDROP CIRCUIT.

point-to-point environment. In key management, a point-to-point environment exists when each member of a communicating pair has a public key with its associated secret key, and the certificate of this public key produced by a common certification authority, so that further symmetric data keys may be exchanged. At least one member of the communicating pair shall have the capability of generating or otherwise acquiring symmetric keys. (ISO). *See* CERTIFICATE, CERTIFICATION AUTHORITY, POINT-TO-POINT, PUBLIC KEY, SECRET KEY, SYMMETRIC KEY SYSTEM.

Poisson distribution. In mathematics, a probability distribution pertinent to traffic flows in computing and communication systems. It is used to estimate the size, and waiting times, of queues for service systems in which the arrival and service rates have certain specified statistical properties. *Compare* GAUSSIAN DISTRIBUTION.

polarized return to zero. In communications, a method of signalling with three states, positive and negative signals represent one each of the binary states and the line condition returns to zero voltage between the signals. *See* BIT.

police connect. In physical security, pertaining to an alarm reporting system connected to a police station. *See* CENTRAL STATION.

police station unit. In physical security, an alarm receiver that can be installed at a police station to receive alarm signals from a protected area. *See* POLICE CONNECT.

policy. In information security, an informal, generally natural language description of desired system behavior. Policies may be defined for particular requirements, such as security, integrity and availability. *Compare* CORPORATE SECURITY POLICY. *See* SECURITY POLICY.

Polimer. In computer security, a virus that infects COMMAND.COM and COM files, affects run-time operation, corrupts program, OVL and data files. *See* VIRUS NAMES.

Polish-2. In computer security, a virus that terminates and stays resident, infects COMMAND.COM and COM files, affects run-time operation, corrupts program, OVL and data files. *See* VIRUS NAMES.

Polish 217. In computer security, a virus that infects COMMAND.COM and COM files, affects run-time operation, corrupts program, OVL and data files. *See* VIRUS NAMES.

polling. In data communications, a method of controlling terminals on a multidrop or clustered data network where each terminal is interrogated in turn by the computer to determine whether it is ready to receive or transmit data. Data transmission is only initiated by the computer. *See* CLUSTER, HUB POLLING, MULTIDROP CIRCUIT, ROLL CALL POLLING.

polling list. In computing, a list specifying the sequence in which terminals are to be polled. *See* POLLING.

polling overhead. In computing, the time spent by the computer in the polling interrogation of terminals. *See* POLLING.

polyalphabetic cipher. In cryptography, a substitution cipher employing a cluster of monoalphabetic ciphers. A cryptographic key is repeatedly written above the plaintext and the key letter indicates which particular monoalphabetic cipher is to be employed to encrypt the corresponding plaintext letter. *Compare* MONOALPHABETIC CIPHER. *See* CIPHER, CRYPTOGRAPHY, SUBSTITUTION CIPHER.

polyinstantiation. In data security, the simultaneous existence of multiple data objects with the same name when the multiple instantiations are distinguished by their classification. Polyinstantiation can arise in multilevel relational databases. If an entry in a table has a Top Secret classification, and a user with a Confidential security clearance accesses that table, then the retrieved table will have a NULL entry against the Top Secret item. The user must have no way of distinguishing between a genuine NULL entry, and one arising from the presence of a higher classified entry. Thus if the user in question decides to insert an item classified Confidential into that position in the table, the entry must be accepted and on subsequent accesses retrieved by the user. A user with a Top Secret clearance will thereafter retrieve two items against that table entry, one classified Confidential and the other Top

Secret. *See* MULTILEVEL DATABASE SECURITY, RELATIONAL DATABASE.

polynomial code. In codes, an error detection code in which a mathematical operation is performed on the data to be sent and is repeated at the receiving end; a check is then performed to detect any data corruption in transmission or transfer. Typically the total obtained from the summation of the binary numbers, corresponding to the bit patterns of the transmitted characters, is divided by an constant specified for the code. The remainder is transmitted as the cyclic check character at the end of the message. At the receiving location the total is then performed as above with the cyclic check character added. If division by the same arbitrarily selected constant is performed and the remainder is zero, the message is accepted as uncorrupted. *See* CYCLIC REDUNDANCY CHECK, ERROR DETECTION CODE.

polynomial time. *See* TIME AND SPACE REQUIREMENTS.

port. In computing, a functional unit of a node through which data can leave or enter a data network or a computer. *See* NODE, PORT PROTECTION DEVICE.

portability. In computing, pertaining to programs in a form that enables them to be run on more than one computer system.

portable detector system. In physical security, a complete detection system that may be easily transported; normally has provisions for a local alarm device, alarm lines and automatic or manual resetting. *See* ALARM LINE.

portable duress sensor. In physical security, a sensor carried by an individual that is activated manually or automatically in an emergency or duress situation. The automatic action may be initiated by the sensor being in a horizontal position for more than a specified time period. The sensor carries a radio frequency or ultrasonic transmitter which signals a central alarm monitoring station via a local receiver. *See* DURESS ALARM.

portfolio. In banking, the group of products to any given counterparty or counterparty group, extended by the bank or division of the bank. *See* COUNTERPARTY, COUNTERPARTY GROUP, PRODUCT.

port protection device. In computer security, a device connected to the communications port of a host computer which has the function of authorizing user access to the port.

The PPD may operate between host and modem or between the modem and telephone set. The PPDs may have up to four typical features:

- password tables;
- call back to originator;
- camouflage;
- attack signalling and logging.

All PPDs require that users enter passwords in order to access the dial-up port. These passwords are in addition to those required for log on to the computer itself, PPDs limit the number of password attempts per telephone connection. With the callback to originator feature the user is required to enter the password, a PPD table is searched to locate the user's telephone number corresponding to the entered password, the call is disconnected and the PPD calls back the user. This facility can, however, be subject to attack; if the intruder can trick the PPD into falsely sensing a line disconnect then the call back is thwarted. Moreover if the PPD reserves a set of lines exclusively for call back, then an intruder may simply camp on one of them, with an appropriate ringing signal, and intercept a call back attempt intended for a valid user.

If the PPD is connected between the telephone set and modem then it can camouflage the computer by responding to calls with a synthesized human voice. For a PPD connected between the modem and computer the camouflage is produced by means of a screen display which is quite different from that of the computer display. Attack signalling and logging facilities provide warning signals and records of dial-up attack attempts. *See* ATTACK SIGNALLING, CALL BACK, TELEPHONE INTRUSION.

POS. *Compare* POB. *See* POINT-OF-SALE TERMINAL.

positive noninterfering and succession coded station. In physical security, a fire alarm station which when activated will transmit at least three rounds of coded alarm signals without interference from any other station on the circuit. One or more of these stations, if subsequently activated, will transmit at least three rounds of their coded signals without interference with each other or the first station activated. *See* CODED SYSTEM, ALARM STATION, LOCAL NON-INTERFERING CODED STATION.

positive response. In data communications, a response indicating that the message was received successfully. *See* ACKNOWLEDGEMENT.

postcondition. In computing, an assertion, expressed in terms of values of program variables, or relationships between them, which characterizes the state of a program immediately after the execution of a given set of statements. A program is said to be totally correct if it commences in a state corresponding to the precondition and terminates in a state corresponding to the postcondition. *Compare* PRECONDITION. *See* PROOF OF PROGRAM CORRECTNESS.

posting date. *Synonymous with* ENTRY DATE.

Post Telegraph and Telephone. A government operated common carrier outside the USA, *See* COMMON CARRIER.

postulated threat. In computer security, the means through which the hypothesized ability or intent, inferred from related conditions or evidence, threatens to adversely affect an automated system, facility, or operation. (AR). *See* THREAT.

potential vulnerability. In information security, a suspected vulnerability that may be used to defeat a security objective of a target of evaluation, but the exploitability or existence of which has not yet been demonstrated. *Compare* CONSTRUCTION VULNERABILITY, EXPLOITABLE VULNERABILITY, OPERATIONAL VULNERABILITY. *See* INFORMATION TECHNOLOGY SECURITY EVALUATION CRITERIA, VULNERABILITY.

power. In mathematics, the number of times that a quantity is multiplied by itself. *See* EXPONENT.

power restart. In reliability, a facility that detects a fall off in the supply voltage and initiates an interrupt routine enabling the computer to prepare itself for the power loss. The program can be resumed without error when power is restored.

PPD. *See* PORT PROTECTION DEVICE.

PPL. *See* PREFERRED PRODUCTS LIST.

PPM. *See* PULSE POSITION MODULATION.

pre-alarm. (1) In physical security, an audible alarm activated in systems with entry/exit delay circuits to warn the user that the alarm must be disarmed within a specified time period. If the alarm is not disarmed then a signal is sent to a central station. *See* DELAY CIRCUIT. (2) In computer security, an alarm that warns security staff of an equipment fault.

precondition. In computing, an assertion, expressed in terms of values of program variables, or relationships between them, which characterizes the state of a program immediately before the execution of a given set of statements. A program is said to be totally correct if it commences in a state corresponding to the precondition and terminates in a state corresponding to the postcondition. *Compare* POSTCONDITION. *See* PROOF OF PROGRAM CORRECTNESS.

predicate. (1) In mathematics, a logical statement made about some state, i.e. it can only assume the value true or false. (2) In databases, a term of a relational calculus expression that specifies the condition to be satisfied by the terms in the retrieved set. *See* RELATIONAL CALCULUS, RELATIONAL DATABASE.

predicate transformer. In computing, a set of statements which transform a precondition into a postcondition. *See* POSTCONDITION, PRECONDITION, PROOF OF PROGRAM CORRECTNESS.

Preferred Products List. A U.S. list telecommunications and information processing systems and equipment which conform to the previous form of measuring compliance to the national Tempest standard. *Compare* ENDORSED TEMPEST PRODUCTS LIST, EVALUATED PRODUCTS LIST. *See* TEMPEST.

prefix. In communications, a code at the beginning of a message.

presence detector. *Synonymous with* MOTION DETECTOR.

presentation layer. In data communications, a layer in the ISO Open Systems Interconnection Reference model.

Unlike lower layers this layer is concerned with the syntax and semantics of the messages handled. It will include services that are commonly required by a range of users and may therefore relieve such users from providing them individually. Thus it performs generally useful transformations such as text compression. *Compare* APPLICATION LAYER, DATA LINK LAYER, NETWORK LAYER, PHYSICAL LAYER, SESSION LAYER, TRANSPORT LAYER. *See* INTELLIGENT TERMINAL, OPEN SYSTEMS INTERCONNECTION, TEXT COMPRESSION.

presignal system. In physical security, a system in which key personnel are notified when first operation of a manual fire alarm station or an automatic detector activate only a prespecified group of alarm indicators. *See* CHIME, ALARM STATION.

preventive maintenance. In reliability, a regular routine of checking equipment and replacing substandard parts to minimize the possibility of equipment failure. *Compare* CORRECTIVE MAINTENANCE.

primary account information. In banking, data at a financial institution that serves to identify an individual and relate that individual to accounts. (ANSI). *See* FINANCIAL INSTITUTION, PRIMARY ACCOUNT NUMBER.

primary account number. In banking, the PAN consists of the issuer identification number, and it identifies the issuer to which the transaction is to be routed. The account number comes next. It identifies to whom the transaction is to be applied. The last element is the check digit. (ANSI X9.8).

primary key. (1) In databases, a key that uniquely identifies an entity. *Compare* SECONDARY KEY. *See* ENTITY, CANDIDATE KEY. (2) In key management, a key employed in the encipher-

ment/decipherment of data. *Compare* SECONDARY KEY. *Synonymous with* DATA-ENCRYPTING KEY.

primary station. In data communications, a station on a data link with the right to select a secondary station and transmit a message. There should only be one primary station on a data link at any one time. Primary status is temporary, allocated to a station so that it may transmit a message. *Compare* SECONDARY STATION.

prime attribute. In databases, an attribute of a relational database that is a member of at least one candidate key. *See* ATTRIBUTE, CANDIDATE KEY, RELATIONAL DATABASE.

prime number. In mathematics, a number that cannot be produced by multiplying integers (other than the number itself and 1). The study of prime numbers is extremely important in some aspects of public key cryptography. *See* PUBLIC KEY CRYPTOGRAPHY, RSA.

primitive. A basic or fundamental unit.

primitive root. In mathematics, an integer m, in modulo n arithmetic, such that the order of m is equal to n-1. *See* MODULO ARITHMETIC, ORDER.

principal. In information security, a person or system that can be authorized to access objects or can make statements affecting access control decisions. *Synonymous with* SUBJECT.

principle of closed environment. *See* CLOSED ENVIRONMENT, PRINCIPLES OF SECURE SYSTEMS.

principle of complete mediation. *See* PRINCIPLES OF SECURE SYSTEMS.

principle of least common mechanism. *See* PRINCIPLES OF SECURE SYSTEMS.

principle of least privilege. (1) In computer security, the principle requires that each subject in a system be granted the most restrictive set of privileges (or lowest clearance) needed for the performance of authorized tasks. The application of this principle limits the damage that can result from accident, error or unauthorized use. (DOD). *See* PRINCIPLES OF SECURE SYSTEMS, SUBJECT. (2) In computer security, the granting of the minimum access authorization necessary for the performance of required tasks. (FIPS). *See* ACCESS, AUTHORIZATION, NEED TO KNOW, PRINCIPLES OF SECURE SYSTEMS.

principles of secure systems. In computer security, Saltzer and Schroeder enunciated the following principles of secure systems listed below:

- Simplicity - the accuracy of security measures, incorporated in hardware and software, can be more readily checked if those measures are simple and small.
- Fail safe - accesses should require explicit authorization, i.e. the default situation is no access.
- Complete mediation - checking of access against access control information must be performed under all circumstances including normal operation, maintenance, recovery etc.
- Separation of privilege - a two-key philosophy, with each key located in a separate compartment, ensures that a single failure does not result in a security break.
- Least privilege - every process should operate with the minimum level of privilege necessary to perform the requisite task.
- Least common mechanism - the use of shared mechanisms amongst users should be minimized for their mutual security.
- User acceptability - security measures should not unduly interfere with the work of users whilst, of course, fulfilling all necessary security constraints.
- Public scrutiny - security measures should be available for review by experts, e.g. encryption algorithms can be widely publicized, with their security depending only on the secrecy of the cryptographic key.

See COMPLETE MEDIATION, CRYPTOGRAPHIC KEY, FAIL SAFE, LEAST COMMON MECHANISM, NONSECRET DESIGN, LEAST PRIVILEGE, SEPARATION OF PRIVILEGE, SIMPLICITY, USER ACCEPTABILITY.

printed circuit board. In computing, a plastic board upon which electronic components such as resistors, capacitors and integrated circuits are mounted and interconnected by plated or etched foil conducting paths. Printed circuit boards are used as plug-in modules in microcomputers. *See* EXPANSION CARD, INTEGRATED CIRCUIT. *Synonymous with* CIRCUIT BOARD.

Print Screen. In computer security, a virus that terminates and stays resident, infects floppy and hard disk boot sector, corrupts boot sector and data files, affects run-time operation. *See* VIRUS NAMES.

print suppress. In computer security, to eliminate the printing of characters in order to preserve their secrecy; for example, the characters of a password as it is keyed by a user at an input terminal. (FIPS) *See* PASSWORD.

priority. In computing, a rank assigned to a task that determines its precedence in receiving system resources.

priority processing. In computing, a method of operating a computer system so that the sequence in which programs are processed is fully determined by a system of priorities.

priority scheduler. In computing, a system that uses input and output queues in its job scheduling to improve overall performance.

privacy. (1) In legislation, the right of individuals to control or influence what information related to them may be collected and stored and by whom an to whom that information may be disclosed. (ISO). *See* DATA PROTECTION. (2) In data security, the right to insist on adequate security of, and to define authorized users of, information or systems (TNI). (3) The right of an individual to self-determination as to the degree to which the individual is willing to share with others information about himself that may be compromised by unauthorized exchange of such information among other individuals or organizations. (FIPS) *See* COMPROMISE, DATA PROTECTION. (5) The right of individuals and organizations to control the collection, storage, and dissemination of their information or information about themselves. (FIPS) (6) In data security, the right of an individual to exercise some form of control both over the information that is stored about him or her, and the personnel that are allowed to access such information. A cause of severe concern among many communities particularly when the developments of information technology facilitate the collection, correlation and distribution of sensitive personal information. The legislation governing such activities varies considerably from country to country. *See* DATA PROTECTION, PRIVACY PROTECTION.

Privacy Act 1974. In legislation, a U.S. act which provides individuals with a degree of control or influence on the collection, storage and dissemination of their personal data. *See* PERSONAL DATA.

privacy enhanced mail. In communications security, an optional confidentiality and integrity service for Internet electronic mail transfers. In terms of X.400 the service is part of the user agent (UA) and is transparent to the message transfer system (MTS). The PEM service involves the addition of a header to the user message which is treated as just another part of the message by the MTS. The PEM service incorporates automated key management and complete message integrity using symmetric or asymmetric ciphers and, optionally, selective encipherment using a symmetric cipher. *See* ASYMMETRIC CIPHER, ELECTRONIC MAIL SECURITY, KEY MANAGEMENT, SYMMETRIC CIPHER, USER AGENT, X.400.

privacy protection. In computer security, the establishment of appropriate administrative, technical, and physical safeguards to ensure the security and confidentiality of data records and to protect both security and confidentiality against any anticipated threats or hazards that could result in substantial harm, embarrassment, inconvenience, or unfairness to any individual about whom such information is maintained. (FIPS). *See* CONFIDENTIALITY, DATA PROTECTION, SECURITY.

privacy transformation. *Synonymous with* ENCRYPTION ALGORITHM.

private address space. In computing, a range of computer addresses assigned to a particular user. *See* ADDRESS.

private automatic branch exchange. In communications, an electronic private branch exchange.

private cryptography. In communications security, the provision of cryptography that is not transparent to the user. Link and node encryption is transparent to a user, end-to-end encryption may be transparent if it is automatically provided as system service. *See* END-TO-WENDENCRYPTION, LINK ENCRYPTION,

Action steps

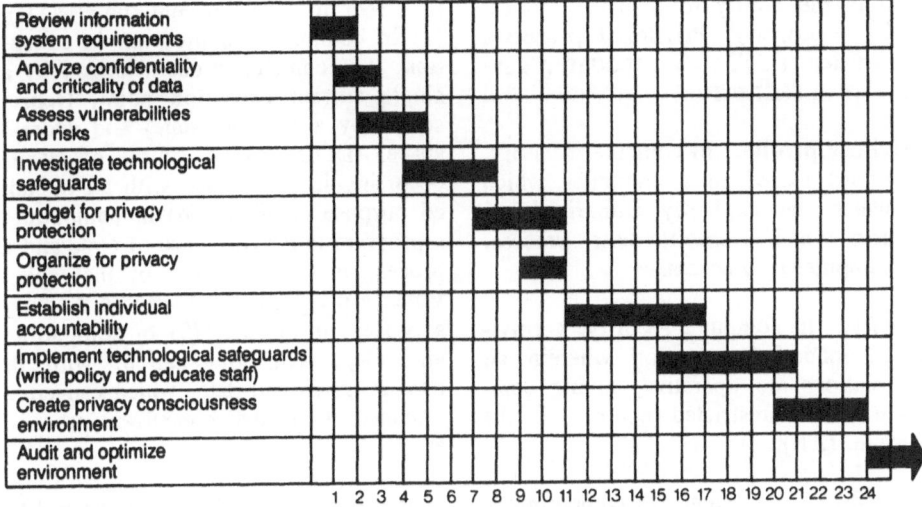

Action steps	1	2	3	4	5	6	7	8	9	10	11	12	13	14	15	16	17	18	19	20	21	22	23	24
Review information system requirements	▮																							
Analyze confidentiality and criticality of data		▮																						
Assess vulnerabilities and risks			▮																					
Investigate technological safeguards				▮▮																				
Budget for privacy protection						▮																		
Organize for privacy protection								▮																
Establish individual accountability										▮▮														
Implement technological safeguards (write policy and educate staff)														▮▮										
Create privacy consciousness environment																				▮				
Audit and optimize environment																								⟶

Time period (arbitrary units)

privacy protection
A generalized privacy protection plan. Like all organizational objectives, information privacy cannot be achieved without the commitment of top management to a well-defined plan of action supported by appropriate resources.

network encryption, node encryption, transparent.

private dial port. In data communications, a dial-in port, of a packet-switching network, providing an access port for one customer, with an unlisted telephone number. *Compare* PUBLIC DIAL PORT. *See* PACKET SWITCHING.

private key. In cryptography, the cryptographic key used to decipher, or sign, messages in public key cryptography. This key is kept secret by the owner of the key. *Compare* PUBLIC KEY. *See* CIPHERTEXT, CRYPTOGRAPHIC KEY, DIGITAL SIGNATURE, PUBLIC KEY CRYPTOGRAPHY.

private key encryption. *Synonymous with* SECRET KEY ENCRYPTION.

private line. *See* LEASED CIRCUIT.

privilege. In computing, pertaining to a program or user and characterizing the type of operation that can be performed.

Privileged users or programs can perform operations normally considered to be the domain of the operating system and which can affect the system performance. *See* OPERATING SYSTEM.

privileged data. In data security, data not subject to usual rules because of some special circumstance. For example, chaplain, legal, and medical files. (AFR).

privileged instructions. (1) In computer security, a set of instructions generally executable only when the ADP system is operating in the executive state; for example, the handling of interrupts. (FIPS) *See* EXECUTIVE STATE. (2) In computer security, special computer instructions designed to control the protection features of an ADP system ; for example, the storage protection features. (FIPS).

privileged process. In computer security, a process that is afforded (by the kernel) some privileges not afforded normal user processes. A typical privilege is the ability to override the security *-property. Privileged processes are trusted. (MTR). *See* SECURITY KERNEL, STAR PROPERTY.

privilege profile. In computer security, a record stored in a computer which indicates the explicitly authorized resources which a specific user, process, or computer may access.

privity. In computer security, a privileged mode of operation wherein all instructions are operative, giving complete and unrestricted control of the system. (AR).

procedural language. In computing, a conventional high-level language in which the programmer specifies the actions necessary to attain the desired result. *Compare* NONPROCEDURAL LANGUAGE.

procedural security. *Synonymous with* ADMINISTRATIVE SECURITY.

procedure. (1) In computing, the course taken for the solution of a problem. (2) In computing, a subroutine. *See* SUBROUTINE.

procedure oriented language. In computing, a high-level language oriented towards a given class of procedures.

procedures. *See* BACKUP PROCEDURES, HANDSHAKING PROCEDURE, RECOVERY PROCEDURES, SYSTEM INTEGRITY PROCEDURES.

process. (1) In computing, the active system entity through which programs run. The entity in a computer system to which authorizations are granted; thus the unit of accountability in a computer system. A process consists of a unique address space containing its accessible program code and data, a program location for the currently executing instruction, and periodic access to the processor in order to continue. (MTR). (2) In computing, a program in execution. It is completely characterized by a single current execution point, (represented by a machine state) and address space. (DOD). (3) A course of events occurring in accordance with an intended purpose or effect. (4) In computing, a program is a static piece of code and a process is the execution of that code. When a program is loaded into memory a process is created. (5) In computing, an independent computation, with its own program and data, which can communicate with other concurrent processes.

processing. In legislation, as defined by the U.K. Data Protection Act 1984, pertaining to the amending, augmenting, deleting or re-arranging of the data or extracting the information constituting the data and, in the case of personal data, processing means performing any of the abovementioned operations by reference to the data subject. *See* DATA, DATA SUBJECT, DATA PROTECTION ACT 1984, DATA PROTECTION - U.K., PERSONAL DATA.

processing priority. In banking, the level of urgency requested by the sender for the processing of the message by the receiver. (ANSI).

processor. In computing, a device or system capable of performing operations upon data. A central processing unit is a hardware processor, a compiler is a language processor. *See* CENTRAL PROCESSING UNIT, COMPILER, HARDWARE.

processor utilization. In computing, the proportion of processor time spent in performing useful and necessary tasks in relation to the total available time.

product. In banking, the name of the product offering by the bank, e.g. service or facility.

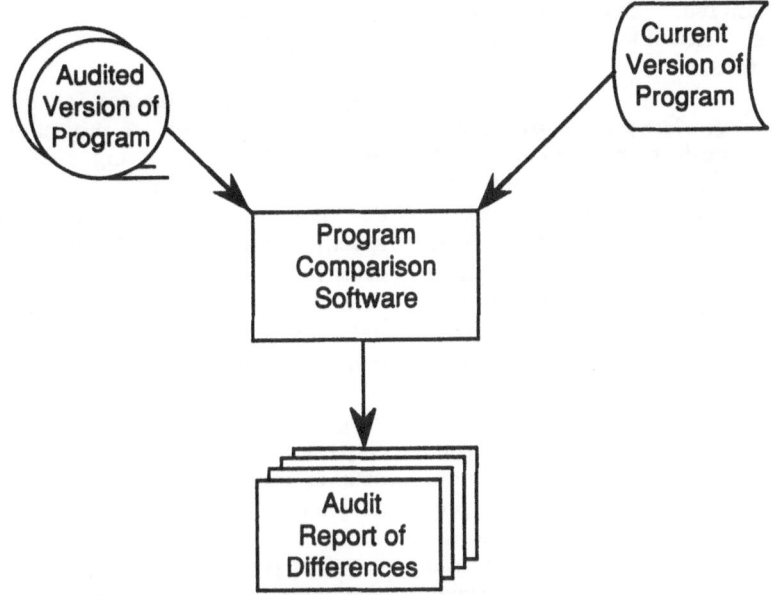

program comparison utilities

product cipher. In cryptography, a cipher produced by a composition of a number of substitution and transposition ciphers. *See* DES, FEISTEL CIPHER, SUBSTITUTION CIPHER, TRANSPOSITION CIPHER.

production run. In computing, a routine execution of a commonly used program, e.g. calculation of pay checks.

product type. *Synonymous with* FACILITY TYPE.

profile. In banking, the presentation of data over a time period as distinct from one particular time.

profiles. In computer security, a detailed security description of the physical structure, equipment components, equipment locations and relationships, and general operating environment of the automated system. (AR).

program. In computing, a complete series of definitions and instructions, conforming to the syntax of a given computer language, that when executed on a computer will perform a required task. *See* SOURCE PROGRAM, OBJECT PROGRAM, PROGRAMMING, SYNTAX.

program analyzer. In computer security, a software tool used in dynamic testing; the analyzer collects data in the program under test during its execution. The analyzer can be used to evaluate the degree to which test data has exercised the program and to identify extraneous code which might constitute an unauthorized modification. *Compare* FLAW HYPOTHESIS. *See* DYNAMIC TESTING.

program comparison utilities. In auditing, a software utility that allows an auditor to check a critical operational program against an authorized version. *See* COMPUTER AUDIT PACKAGES.

program language. In computing, a set of formal rules to define the manner in which data structures are formulated and the processing instructions are written and organized. *See* HIGH-LEVEL LANGUAGE, LOW-LEVEL LANGUAGE, PROGRAMMING.

programming. The process by which a computer is made to perform a specialized task. It involves the creation of a formalized sequence of instructions which can be recognized and implemented by the machine. These instructions (the program) are a static entity, but when executed they result in a useful information handling process. All programs are concerned, either directly or indirectly, with the flow of information. Data, whether stated explicitly or made an intrinsic component of the program, is used as an input which is then processed, or computed, to generate an output. All of the functions performed by a computer depend, at some stage, upon a program.

programming standards. In computing, a set of rules produced by an organization to impose a discipline on the production of programs. The rules may range from those dealing with the decomposition of large programs into individual modules, to the use of individual program constructs, e.g. loops. *See* LOOP.

program patch. (1) In computing, a section of software code inserted into a program to correct mistakes or to alter the program. (2) In computer security, a section of code added to object code and thus not affecting the source code. Such patches may therefore bypass normal control procedures and could be used for illegal program modification. *See* OBJECT CODE, SOURCE CODE.

program specification. In computing, a document providing complete details of a program, giving its function, files accessed, input/output requirements, etc.

program statement. In computing, an expression or a generalized instruction in a source language. *See* SOURCE LANGUAGE.

projection. In databases, an operation in relational algebra. A projection on a given relation, specifying attributes of that relation, produces a second relation containing only a set of tuples with the specified attributes, and with all duplicates removed. *Compare* DIVISION, JOIN, SELECTION. *See* RELATIONAL ALGEBRA, RELATIONAL DATABASE. PROM. In computing, Programmable Read Only Memory, a form of ROM that can be programmed by a user. Blank memory chips are purchased and the required data is input to the chip in a special device (PROM programmer). *See* ROM.

proof of program correctness. In programming, a formal mathematical demonstration that the semantics of the program are consistent with the specification for that program.

The traditional method of checking out programs by test data is unreliable, inefficient and provides no guidance on the development of error-free programs.

The result of test runs are unreliable because there is no rigorous method of selecting test data which will ensure that all possible paths through the program are checked. The method is inefficient both because large sets of test data are required and if the program fails, for any one set of data, then the program must be modified and the complete test run restarted, from the beginning, to ensure that no additional bugs were inserted with the modification.

The most serious shortcoming of this technique, however, is that it provides no disciplined approach to program development; in fact the successive modifications of the program to correct faults, indicated by the test data, can result in final programs that are extremely difficult to maintain or update.

Methods of formal proof of correctness depend, in the first instance, upon a mathematical statement, or assertion, which declares precisely and unambiguously the desired result of the program in terms of the input data and states. This would be a formidable task for substantial programs but it is interesting to note that this is the form of programming for nonprocedural languages. The assertion on the program output data or states is termed the postcondition. The precondition is an assertion on the input data or states prior to the execution of the program. A program is deemed to be correct if its execution, commencing with states corresponding to the precondition, produces a set of states which satisfy the postcondition. The proof of total program correctness requires both that the postcondition is true if the program terminates (known as the proof of partial correctness) and proof that the program does indeed terminate.

Proving that a given program will guarantee to terminate in the specified postcondition is a formidable task for large programs. The significance of these formal techniques, however, lies not in the post hoc proof of correctness but in the disciplined approach that they provide for the production of error-free programs.

Each module within a large program can be developed in an error-free manner by the successive use of pre- and postconditions; in a sequential program the postcondition of one segment becomes the precondition for the succeeding one. This approach can highlight typical potential bugs, e.g. division by zero, string operations on empty strings. Conditional jump statements within a program involve a number of possible paths and the preconditions must cover both the precondition states for each route and the condition required for that route to be selected.

Programs containing loops are the potential source of many bugs, typically endless loops arise in certain conditions or the loop does not terminate with the required set of output states. The formal techniques provide a disciplined approach, to the design of loops, which require the programmer to ensure that the loop commences with the necessary initial condition, that the loop will terminate and when it does the necessary postcondition is met. An important concept is that of a loop invariant which is a state which is true before and after each execution of the statements in the loop. The selection of the loop invariant provides a new insight into the behavior of program loops. The formal approach ensures that the loop terminates after a finite number of iterations and that the postcondition is satisfied upon termination. *See* BUG, LOOP, POSTCONDITION, PRECONDITION, PREDICATE TRANSFORMER.

PROPIN. In data security, Caution-Proprietary Information Involved. (DOD). *See* PROPRIETARY DATA.

proprietary data. Data that is created, used, marketed by individuals having exclusive legal rights. (AFR). *See* SOFTWARE PROTECTION.

proprietary fire alarm system. In physical security, a system including a central supervising station and equipment to enable operators to maintain, test and operate the system and to take requisite action upon receipt of an alarm signal.

protected distribution system. (1) In communications security, an approved telecommunications systems to which electromagnetic and physical safeguards have been applied to permit safe electric transmission of unencrypted sensitive information. (AR). (2) In communications security, a telecommunications system to which acoustical, electrical, electromagnetic and physical safeguards have been applied to permit its use for secure electrical or optical transmission of unencrypted classified information or sensitive unclassified information. (DOE). *See* FIBER OPTICS.

protected subsystem. (1) In communications security, user provided (layer 7) programs that control access to objects at a finer granularity than provided by the kernel. *See* KERNEL, OPEN SYSTEMS INTERCONNECTION. (2) In data security, a collection of procedures and data objects encapsulated in a domain of its own so that the internal structure of the data object is accessible only to the procedures of the protected subsystem. The procedures may be called only at the designated domain entry points and only by the designated subjects. *See* DOMAIN, SUBJECT. (3) In computer security, a program or subsystem that can act as a subject. *See* SUBJECT.

protected wireline distribution system. In data security, a telecommunications system which has been approved by a legally designated authority and to which electromagnetic and physical safeguards have been applied to permit safe electrical transmission of unencrypted sensitive information. (FIPS). *See* SENSITIVE INFORMATION. *Synonymous with* APPROVED CIRCUIT.

protection. In access control, pertaining to mechanisms and techniques that control access to stored information. *See* DATA-DEPENDENT PROTECTION, DATA PROTECTION, FETCH PROTECTION, LOCK-AND-KEY PROTECTION SYSTEM, PRIVACY PROTECTION.

protection-critical portions of the TCB. In computer security, those portions of the TCB whose normal function is to deal with the control of access between subjects and objects. (DOD). *See* ACCESS, OBJECT, SUBJECT, TCB.

protection pattern. In physical security, the area of protection covered by a sensing device.

protection philosophy. In computer security, an informal description of the overall design of a system that delineates each of the protection mechanisms employed. A combination (appropriate to the evaluation class) of formal and informal techniques is used to show that the mechanisms are adequate to enforce the security policy. (DOD). *See* SECURITY POLICY.

protection ring. In computer security, one of a hierarchy of privileged modes of an ADP system that gives certain access rights to the users, programs, and processes authorized to operate in a given mode. (FIPS).

protective redundancy. In reliability, the use or replicated modules in hardware or software, or the use of error correcting codes to render a system fault tolerant. *See* ERROR CORRECTION CODE, FAULT TOLERANCE, REDUNDANCY. *Synonymous with* SPACIAL REDUNDANCY.

protocol. (1) In data communications, a set of rules that determine the meaning and format of frames, packets or messages exchanged between peer entities in a layer of the Open Systems Interconnection Reference Model. *See* OPEN SYSTEMS INTERCONNECTION. (2) In data communications, a formally specified set of conventions governing the format and control of inputs and outputs between two communicating systems.

protocol converter. In data communications, a device that interfaces two communicating systems working to different protocols. For example, a protocol converter can interface to a microcomputer, via the asynchronous RS-232C serial port, and to an IBM SNA/SDLC synchronous network. All EBCDIC/ASCII code conversions are carried out, as well as cursor positioning, screen buffering and error handling. *Compare* SOFTWARE PROTOCOL CONVERTER. *See* ASCII, ASYNCHRONOUS TRANSMISSION, CODE CONVERSION,

EBCDIC CODE, PROTOCOL, RS-232C, SDLC, SNA.

protocol data unit. In data communications, a segment of a service data unit plus control header. When a layer in the Open Systems Interconnection Reference Model transfers a service data unit it may break it into segments and give each segment a header for transmission, thus forming a protocol data unit packet. *Compare* INTERFACE DATA UNIT, SERVICE DATA UNIT. *See* OPEN SYSTEMS INTERCONNECTION.

protocol standards. In data communications, defined protocols which facilitate communication amongst a wide and diverse body of users. Early protocols merely provided for the interconnection of similar devices and the Arpanet was an exception which permitted the interconnection of any two communicating systems. Some early protocols, e.g. BISYNC, became ad hoc standards since they were adopted by many other manufacturers. There are two international bodies concerned with protocol standards - CCITT and ISO. CCITT is responsible for standards in the field of public telecommunication services. It is a permanent committee of the ITU and its best known recommendations are the V- and X-series for analog and digital data transmission. ISO has a large number of member bodies, one of each participating country - BSI in the U.K., ANSI in U.S.A., AFNOR in France. Other bodies such as CCITT and ECMA are also represented. The European Conference of Post and Telecommunications Administrations undertake standardization in the field of telephony extending into other facilities provided by PTTs, e.g. digital data networks. National organizations such as IEEE promulgate standards, e.g. RS-232C, equivalent to CCITT V.24 and a local area network standard IEEE 802. *See* AFNOR, ANSI, ARPA, BISYNC, BSI, CCITT, ECMA, IEEE, IEEE 802, ISO, ITU LOCAL AREA NETWORK, PTT, RS-232C, V, X.

protocol suite. In communications security, a collection of protocol implementations properly (but in practice not always) based on a protocol reference model. *See* PROTOCOL.

provisions. In banking, items allowed against profits in relation to actual or anticipated default.

proximity card reader. In access control, a card reader which does not require insertion of the card into the reader. The card contains tuned radio frequency circuits which interact with signals generated by the reader. The subsequent frequency fluctuations are detected by the reader and interpreted by circuitry to determine the coding on the card. *See* CARD READER, SMART CARD, TRANSMITTER.

pseudo-flaw. In computer security, an apparent loophole deliberately implanted in an operating system program as a trap for intruders. (FIPS). *See* ENTRAPMENT, LOOPHOLE.

pseudorandom number. In computing, a number generated by a specific algorithm to approximate to a random number. Such algorithms are designed to produce numbers with specified statistical properties. *See* RANDOM NUMBERS.

PSK. *See* PHASE SHIFT KEYING.

PSN. *See* PACKET SWITCH NODE, PACKET-SWITCHING NETWORK.

PSOS. In computer security, Provably Secure Operating System. A capability-based operating system structured as a hierarchy of nested abstract machines. PSOS was designed at SRI and the system design utilizes SPECIAL and MLS. (MTR). *See* CAPABILITY, MLS, SPECIAL.

PTT. *See* POST TELEGRAPH AND TELE-
PHONE.

public data network. In data communications, a network to supply a data
transmission service to the public, provided by a public authority or recognized private operating agency.

public dial port. In data communications, a dial-in port providing access to a
packet switched network from a terminal
connected to the public telephone network. *Compare* PRIVATE DIAL PORT.

public domain. In legislation, material
which has not been copyrighted or for
which the copyright has expired. *See*
COPYRIGHT.

public key. In cryptography, the key
(in an asymmetric or public key cryptosystem) of a user's key set which is
known to other users. (ISO). *Compare*
SECRET KEY. *See* ASYMMETRIC ALGOR-
ITHM, PUBLIC KEY CRYPTOGRAPHY. (2)
In cryptography, the cryptographic key
used to encipher messages, or check
signatures in public key cryptography.
This key is made generally available by
the intended receiver of the ciphertext or
signature. *Compare* PRIVATE KEY. *See*
CIPHERTEXT, CRYPTOGRAPHIC KEY,
DIGITAL SIGNATURE, PUBLIC KEY CRYP-
TOGRAPHY.

public key cryptography. In cryptography, an asymmetric cryptosystem,
i.e. one in which the enciphering and
deciphering keys are different and it is
computationally infeasible to calculate
one from the other, given the enciphering algorithm. In public key cryptography the enciphering key is made public
but the deciphering key is kept secret; it
has advantages over symmetric ciphers,
such as DES, in the areas:

- security of messages, from a
  variety of sources, directed to an
  individual organization;

- key management;
- digital signatures.

If a number of individuals wish to send
secure information to a central organization then symmetric ciphers require
that initial arrangements be made for the
individual, and the organization, to share
a unique secret key. Public key cryptography on the other hand enables the
organization to publish a single enciphering key, possibly in a public
directory, and potential senders of the
messages need only access this directory, encipher their message using the
public key and agreed algorithm, and
transmit it to the organization. Such
senders will be unable to decipher messages, sent by other individuals using
the same key, because the deciphering
key is secret and held only by the organization in question.

The secrecy of the public key is not
required but it is essential that the integrity of the key in the public directory
be guaranteed. If an attacker could
replace an organization's public key,
with an enciphering key produced by the
attacker himself who would also hold
the corresponding deciphering key, then
secret information destined for the organization would be available to the
attacker.

It is important that users do not use
highly formatted messages because an
attacker has a completely free choice in
chosen plaintext attacks. Thus an attacker could take an intelligent guess at
the meaning of certain repeated blocks
in ciphertext messages, encrypted with a
given public key. Thereafter the attacker
would check out those guesses by enciphering them with the public key, and
comparing the results with the ciphertext
blocks.

Key management is another area in
which public key cryptography is likely
to make significant inroads. Since it is
no longer necessary to exchange a secret
key prior to establishing secure communications, public key cryptography

may be used for the transmission of key-encrypting keys and data keys. This technique has advantages, over the use of public key cryptography for the encipherment of the message data, inasmuch as symmetric ciphers, such as DES, are less computationally demanding than current public key cryptography methods.

Some public key cryptography algorithms provide elegant digital signature techniques. If the deciphering key can be used for encipherment, and vice versa, then the receiver can decipher a message, using the public key, and be sure that the received message could only have been enciphered by the holder of the secret 'deciphering' key.

Diffie and Hellman were the first to publish a paper introducing the concepts of public key cryptography and their work 'New Directions in Cryptography' appeared in 1976. The idea of a non-secret enciphering key was a major advance in cryptography; it implies that there is no requirement, at all, for a secure channel between the sender and receiver of messages. In the absence of cryptography a secure channel is essential to maintain the whole message secret from the enemy; with conventional cryptography the requirement for a secure channel is reduced to that for the transmission of the cryptographic key.

Public key cryptography enables a sender to access an enciphering key, e.g. from a public directory, encipher a message and send it to the recipient, who must hold the private deciphering key; at no stage is a secure channel required.

Cryptography may thus be considered to have developed in three phases. Originally the encryption algorithm and any associated keys, were kept secret. In the second phase the encryption algorithms were made publicly available but the encryption and decryption keys, which might or might not be identical, were not revealed. With public key cryptography both the method of encryption and the enciphering keys are made public, the secrecy of the cipher depends upon the security of the private deciphering key.

These three stages of development represent increasing demands upon the cryptographic algorithm, which can be represented by $C = f(M,E)$, where C is the ciphertext, M is the plaintext, E is the enciphering key and f is the encryption routine. If both the encryption algorithm (f) and the encryption key (E) are secret the cryptanalyst is provided with no information except that the ciphertext represents a meaningful message in a given natural language, the cryptographic routine may, in these circumstances, be a relatively simple operation. When the encrypting algorithm (f) is public knowledge and the encrypting key (E) is secret then the demands upon the cryptographic routine depend upon the length of the key.

If the key is random, and of the same length as the message, then the routine can again be relatively simple because the cryptanalyst has insufficient information to recover the plaintext message. If however the key is relatively short, compared with the message, then the techniques of information theory indicate that the redundancy of natural languages provides the cryptanalyst with sufficient information to decipher the ciphertext. In mathematical terms the cryptanalyst must attempt to compute an inverse function $E = h(M,C)$. The complexity of the encryption routine must be such that this process is computationally infeasible.

With public key cryptography the cryptanalyst is, in theory, provided with sufficient information to decipher the message without any recourse to a study of the redundancy of the plaintext language. Since both the encryption algorithm and the encryption key are publicly available, a mathematical analysis will indicate the relationship between the unknown deciphering key and the known enciphering key and algorithm. Thus the cryptographic algorithm must be such that it is computationally infeasible for a cryptanalyst to perform the inverse function $M = p(C,E)$. In mathematical terms this implies that the enciphering algorithm, f, must be a one-way function.

The public key cryptographer has, however, a much more demanding task than that of merely producing an efficient one-way function; whilst the cryptanalyst must be prevented from computing $M = p(C,E)$, it is clearly important that the legitimate recipient be able to obtain the plaintext message with reasonable computational efficiency. Thus the additional restriction on $f(M,E)$ is that it be a trapdoor one-way function, i.e. the legitimate user, armed with a private deciphering key (D), can easily compute the function $M = g(C,D)$.

Complexity theory provides a class of problems, known as nondeterministic polynomial, or NP problems, which are candidates for trapdoor one-way functions. NP problems have the property that the time taken to solve them increases exponentially with the size of the problem but the time taken to check a solution only increases as a polynomial function of size.

The requirements of public key cryptography may be listed below.

- There is a pair of encryption and decryption algorithm $C = f(M,E_k)$, $M = g(C,D_k)$ where the plaintext and ciphertext messages, M and C, are members of a finite set of messages.
- The algorithms, f and g, are easy to compute for all values of M, E_k, C, D_k.
- For every value of k it is computationally infeasible to compute D_k from E_k.
- For every value of k it is possible to compute inverse pairs, E_k and D_k.

Specific cryptosystems may place additional constraints on f and g. For example, digital signature applications require that for $C = f(M,D_k)$, $M = g(C,E_k)$.

One common class of public key cryptography is based upon exponentiation ciphers. The Diffie-Hellman technique, Pohlig-Hellman cipher, RSA and mental poker are all exponential ciphers, i.e. given M, E and n it is possible to compute M^E (mod n), where M, E and n can be numbers with hundreds of decimal digits. However it is computationally infeasible to compute M given M^E (mod n), E and n.

The Diffie-Hellman technique can be employed to exchange private keys over insecure channels, the Pohlig-Hellman cipher does not meet the crucial requirement of public key cryptography inasmuch as it is easy to compute the deciphering key from a knowledge of the enciphering key and algorithm. RSA is an exponentiation cipher based upon the computational infeasibility of factoring large products of primes. Mental poker is an exponentiation cipher which can be used, for example, by two parties playing poker over the telephone.

A second class of public key cryptography is based upon knapsack ciphers. The knapsack problem involves the selection of a subset of integers such that their sum equals a specified value. The vulnerability of knapsack ciphers has been the subject of considerable discussion and Shamir described a method of breaking the basic Merkle-Hellman knapsack in 1982.

A third technique for public key cryptography has been described which is based upon the technique of error correcting codes. In conventional data communications the message can be transformed with the addition of redundant error correcting bits; during transmission the total message, i.e. data and error correction bits, may be changed by noise. The receiver performs a transformation upon the message to extract the original data from the corrupted message. A public key cryptographic technique has been proposed in

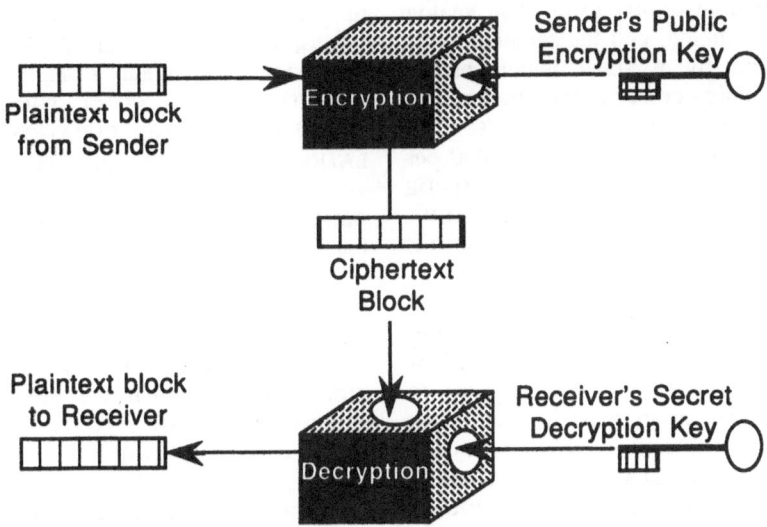

public key cryptography

which the message transformation matrix comprises a public enciphering key. The sender first transforms the message with this matrix, transforming and expanding the message with the addition of redundant data bits. A specified number of bits is then changed in a random manner. The receiver is in possession of a secret transformation matrix and recovers the original data; sufficient redundant bits having been added to the original message to allow the receiver to filter out the noise deliberately introduced by the sender. *See* ASYMMETRIC CRYPTOSYSTEM, AUTHENTICATION, DES, DIFFIE-HELLMAN TECHNIQUE, DIGITAL SIGNATURE, ELGAMAL CIPHER, ERROR CORRECTION CODE, INFORMATION THEORY, KEY MANAGEMENT, KNAPSACK CIPHER, MENTAL POKER, POHLIG-HELLMAN CIPHER, RSA, SYMMETRIC CRYPTOSYSTEM, TRAPDOOR ONE-WAY FUNCTION.

public key distribution. In cryptography, a method of exchanging secret keys between communicating parties which does not require a secure channel. *See* DIFFIE-HELLMAN TECHNIQUE, KEYLESS CRYPTOGRAPHY, KEY MANAGEMENT, PUBLIC KEY CRYPTOGRAPHY.

public switched network. In communications, a switching system that provides switching transmission facilities to customers.

pull station. In physical security, a manual alarm system, designed for use by members of the public, comprising a manual switch in a heavy duty equipment box. The subsequent alarm may be coded and transmitted to a central location.

pulse amplitude modulation. In communications, a method of pulse modulation in which the amplitude of a train of pulses is adjusted in accordance with the input signal amplitude. *Compare* PULSE CODE MODULATION, PULSE DURATION MODULATION, PULSE POSITION MODULATION. *See* MODULATION, PULSE MODULATION.

pulse code modulation. In communications, a technique for transmitting analog information in digital form. The analog signal is sampled, and the sampled value represented by a fixed length binary number. This number is then transmitted as a corresponding set of pulses. In telephony, the sampling rate is 8000 per second. *Compare* PULSE AMPLITUDE MODULATION, PULSE DURATION MODULATION, PULSE POSITION MODULATION. *See* SAMPLING, PULSE MODULATION.

pulse duration modulation. In communications, a pulse modulation technique in which the width of the pulse, in a pulse train, is adjusted in accordance with the input signal. *Compare* PULSE AMPLITUDE MODULATION, PULSE CODE MODULATION, PULSE POSITION MODULATION. *See* PULSE MODULATION. *Synonymous with* PULSE WIDTH MODULATION.

pulse modulation. In communications, a signal transmission system in which the information content is impressed upon a pulse train by adjusting either the pulse amplitude (PAM), pulse duration (PDM), pulse position (PPM) or by binary codes based upon the presence and absence of pulses (PCM). *See* PULSE AMPLITUDE MODULATION, PULSE DURATION MODULATION, PULSE POSITION MODULATION, PULSE CODE MODULATION.

pulse position modulation. In communications, a pulse modulation method in which the timing of the individual pulses, in a pulse train, depends upon the modulating signal. *Compare* PULSE AMPLITUDE MODULATION, PULSE CODE MODULATION, PULSE DURATION MODULATION. *See* PULSE MODULATION.

pulse repetition rate. In electronics, the number of pulses per unit time.

pulse train. In data communications, a series of pulses having similar characteristics. A method of conveying binary information in which the presence, or absence, of a pulse represents a binary one or zero respectively.

pulse width modulation. *Synonymous with* PULSE DURATION MODULATION.

purging. (1) In computing, the orderly review of storage and removal of inactive or obsolete data files. (FIPS). (2) In computer security, the removal of obsolete data by erasure, by overwriting of storage, or by resetting registers.(FIPS). *See* OVERWRITING, PERSONAL COMPUTER SECURITY.

PVC. *See* PERMANENT VIRTUAL CIRCUIT.

PVV. *See* PIN VERIFICATION VALUE.

Q

QAM. *See* QUADRATURE AMPLITUDE MODULATION.

quadratic residue. In mathematics, a property of some integers in a given modulo arithmetic. A number c is a quadratic residue modulo n if it is co-prime with n and there exists another number x such that: $x^2 \equiv c \pmod{n}$. In other words a quadratic residue has an integer square root modulo n. *See* CO-PRIME, MENTAL POKER, MODULO ARITH-METIC.

quadrature amplitude modulation. In data communications, a method of converting digital signals into analog signals for transmission over a telephone network. It combines both amplitude and phase modulation techniques. A 16 point signal structure, giving 16 carrier states, can be achieved by combining 12 phase angles and 4 phases with amplitude modulation. The 4 phases that have modulated amplitudes have two possible amplitude levels. *Compare* AMPLITUDE MODULATION, FREQUENCY SHIFT KEY-ING, PHASE MODULATION. *See* ANALOG SIGNAL, CARRIER, DIGITAL SIGNAL.

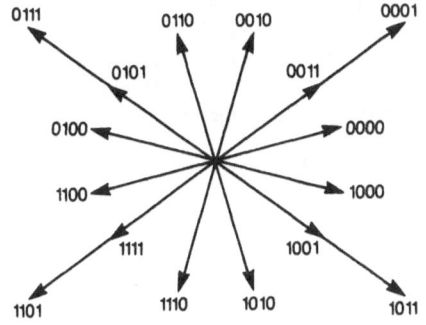

quadrature amplitude modulation

qualitative risk analysis. *Compare* QUANTITATIVE RISK ANALYSIS. *See* MATRIX METHODOLOGY, RISK ANALYSIS METHODOLOGIES.

quantitative risk analysis. In risk management, a risk analysis methodology which aims to quantify a risk score, normally in financial terms. The objective of such a methodology is to enable management to balance the cost of proposed security countermeasures against a realistic estimate of the risk impact.

The methodology comprises the basic steps: asset identification, risk calculation and countermeasure evaluation.

The asset identification phase is conducted to produce a realistic assessment of the probability and costs associated with identified threats to the system. It comprises three stages: assets, threats and security surveys.

The resources to be protected are first identified and valued. In computer security these resources will be, inter alia:

- equipment and supplies;
- intellectual property (data and programs);
- computer services and processes.

Financial values can be readily placed upon hardware and proprietary software. However the costs associated with the replacement of data and programs or the loss of a computer service may involve at least an estimate of the cost of recreating data from source documents or of temporarily transferring in house processes to an external bureau.

In general, however, enquiries directed to the allocation of a monetary value to the individual sets of data in a large

425

organization, are likely to produce responses which are highly subjective and treated with considerable skepticism.

The determination of estimates associated with threats are even more problematic even if a consistent, methodical and structured approach is employed to encourage staff to focus attention on specific issues and hence identify sensible ranges of values.

The common threats to a computer system may be listed:

- natural disasters;
- sabotage;
- vandalism;
- fraud;
- theft;
- public utility failure;
- hardware failure;
- human error.

Historical data is commonly employed in the insurance industry to aid such estimation but the relative youth, and massive diversity, of the information technology industry mitigates against this approach.

The threats represent those entities which inherently exist. The degree to which they will actually cause a harmful impact on the organization depends upon the organization's vulnerability to those threats. Thus any building is subject to a threat of fire; a wooden building in an industrial area is much more vulnerable to such a threat than a concrete building set in its own grounds. The estimate of the likelihood of a particular threat arising and then causing a serious impact in a particular environment is a complex issue.

The security survey conducted in the asset identification phase will therefore include consideration of the factors listed below.

- Existing hardware and software systems: documentation, access controls, operational availability.
- Data processing applications: standards, documentation.

- Operations: standards, information dissemination, procedures, libraries, contingency planning, document storage.
- Physical environment: reliability of public utilities, neighborhood, access control, security of building, maintenance procedures.
- Data communications: transmission circuits, cabling installations, message distribution and validation.
- Personnel: employment procedures, training, supervision, career development, vetting.

The asset identification phase is followed by the risk calculation that gives managers a concise set of data that will then be used to facilitate the evaluation of countermeasures. The threats are considered in terms of the estimated costs associated with their outcome (impact) and the frequency of occurrence. Such estimates can only be given in terms of orders of magnitude and hence a quantized set of values is specified for both the cost of the impact and frequency. It is more convenient to work in terms of i and f, see Table 1 than actual values and frequencies (See Table 1)

i	Impact (I)	f	Frequency (F)
1	10	1	Once in 300 years
2	100	2	Once in 30 years
3	1 000	3	Once in 3 years
4	10 000	4	Once in 100 days
5	100 000	5	Once in 10 days
6	1 000 000	6	Once a day.

TABLE 1.

The expected loss can be calculated from:

Expected Loss = Loss associated with event (I) x Probability of that event (F).

The logarithmic scales employed in the table provide associated variables $I = 10^i$ and $F = (10^{(f-3)}) / 3$ This leads to a calculation of the Annual Loss Expectancy (ALE):

$$ALE = I.F = (10^{(f+i-3)}) / 3.$$

For example, an estimated loss of $10,000 occurring with a frequency of once in 3 years produces an ALE of $3,000, rounded off to the nearest $1,000. The calculations of ALE is greatly simplified by the quantizing proposed above; a table of ALE for various values of i and f reduces the effort of the calculations. The pairing of impacts and frequencies must be conducted methodically; printed forms will aid the recording of data and the calculation of associated ALEs, and a number of software packages are also available for this purpose.

If a particular resource is subjected to a variety of threats then it must be paired with each appropriate threat and the ALE calculated accordingly. A running total of ALE for each resource affected by a specific threat should thus be developed.

The calculated ALEs provide management with a priority list of potential threats. The next phase of risk analysis is a consideration of the various security countermeasures available and their associated costs. The benefit of a countermeasure is estimated from the difference between the total appropriate threat ALE and the cost of the security measure.

If the management decide that the risk analysis has isolated an important threat and the security countermeasure cannot be implemented in the immediate future the risk analysis will have provided a realistic measure of the amount of insurance that should be taken out for the interim period. *Compare* QUALITATIVE RISK ANALYSIS. *See* FIPS PUB 65, RISK ANALYSIS, RISK ANALYSIS METHODOLOGIES.

quantize. In communications, to assign one of a fixed set of values to an analog signal as part of an analog to digital conversion process, e.g. in pulse code modulation, an analog signal is sampled, quantized and a corresponding set of binary pulses is produced. *See* PULSE CODE MODULATION.

quantizing noise. In communications, noise arising from the process of analog to digital and subsequent digital to analog conversion. The quantization process produces discrepancies in the input and output analog signals. *See* QUANTIZE.

query language. In databases, a part of the database management system that provides facilities for the interrogation of data. The complexity of the query facilities vary from language to language. Query languages usually also provide some facilities for database modification and updating. *See* DATABASE MANAGEMENT SYSTEM, RELATIONAL DATABASE.

query modification. In database security, a technique in which user queries are modified to conform to the user access rights. For example if a user were only permitted to access personnel records for a specific department, and the input query were for all females in the organization, then the query would be modified so that the information returned would only relate to females in the aforementioned department.

query set. In database security, a set of records selected by the selection criteria of a particular enquiry.

query set size control. In database security, a form of cell restriction that restricts queries based upon a very small or very large set of records. If a query is based upon few records it is possible that the statistics relating to an individual may be eventually deduced. If a very large set of records (P) is involved then the statistics released, coupled with the statistics for the total set of records (N), could be used to infer data on the small set (N-P) set of records. *Compare* AUDIT EXPERT, CELL SUPPRESSION, GROUPING, IMPLIED QUERIES CONTROL, OVERLAP CONTROL. *See* CELL RESTRICTION, INFERENCE CONTROL.

queue. (1) In data structures, a list in which items are added at one end and removed from the other. (2) In data structures, processes or items awaiting service on a FIFO principle. *Compare* STACK. *See* LIST, FIFO.

queuing time. In communications, the time spent in waiting to send, or receive, a message due to contention on the

R

Rabin signature. In authentication, a method of digital signatures using DES encipherment. The sender generates 36 DES keys $(k_1, k_2 \ldots k_{36})$ and 36 random numbers $(x_1, x_2 \ldots x_{36})$ which are each 64 bit input blocks for DES encipherment. A further 36 numbers $(y_1, y_2 \ldots y_{36})$ are produced by encipherment of the x values with the corresponding DES keys, i.e. $y_i = ek_i(x_i)$. The x and y values are then published as the public keys for the signature, together with a function (f).

The sender produces a signature of a message (M) by operating upon it with the algorithm (f) forming a 64 bit output. This output (f(M)) is used as the input for 36 DES operations with the keys $(k_1, k_2 \ldots k_{36})$. The 36 outputs of these encipherments $(S_1, S_2 \ldots S_{36})$, where $S_i = ek_i(f(M))$, form the digital signature of the message (M).

The receiver validates the signature by requesting 18 selected keys from the sender, i.e. the receiver randomly selects 18 integers in the range 1 to 36. The sender provides the requested keys and the receiver then checks for each:

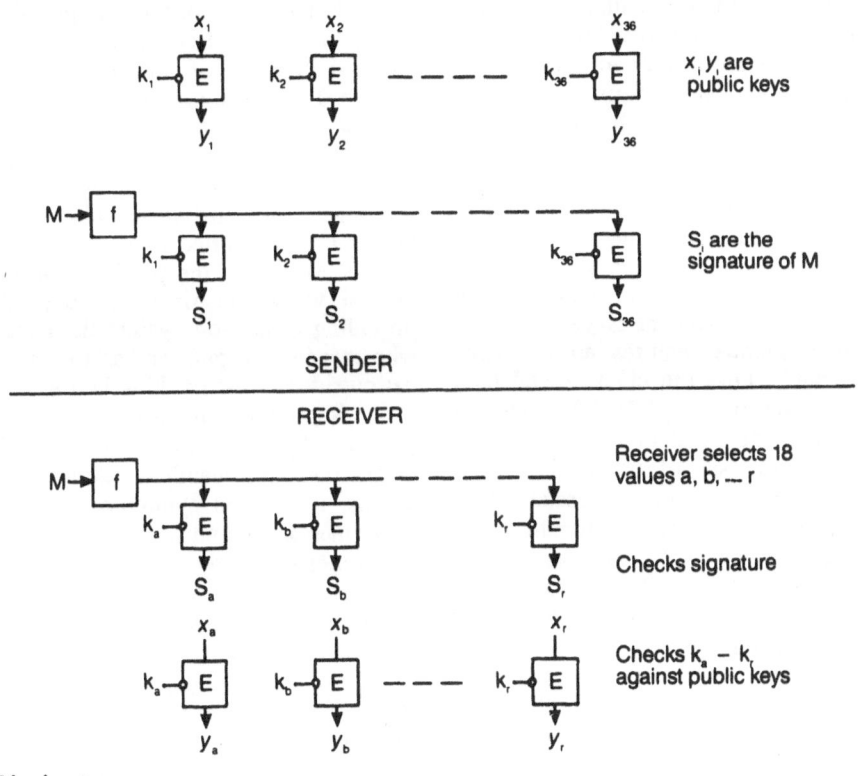

Rabin signature

$S_i = ek_i(f(M))$

In the case of a dispute the judge requests the 36 keys from the sender and checks them against the 36 published pairs $(x_1, y_1, \ldots x_{36}, y_{36})$, i.e. $y_i = ek_i(x_i)$ for $i = 1$ to 36. The judge then checks the 36 signatures $(S_i = k_i(f(M)))$, if 19 or more of these signatures check out then the judge declares the message valid, if 18 or less signatures check out then the message is declared a forgery.

Receivers who attempted to forge a message could do so and develop 18 valid signatures from the keys provided by the sender, however, they would be unable to produce the remaining 18 signatures which would conform with the published pairs (x_i, y_i). The sender could provide 18 genuine signatures and 18 false signatures. If by chance the receiver selected just those 18 keys corresponding to the genuine signatures the sender could disavow the message. However the probability of selecting 18 given numbers, at random, from 36 is of the order of 10^{-10}. In practice the receiver will select at least one of the false signatures, the checking procedure will fail in this case and the receiver will refuse to accept the message. Using substantially fewer than 36 keys increases the possibility that a sender would risk producing a false message.

This technique requires an extensive set of public keys (36 blocks of 64 bits) and the transmission of 18 DES keys, in addition to the 36 S blocks of 64 bits. Moreover the set of public keys can only be used for one message. This represents a very heavy communication overhead for the 64 bit signature. *Compare* ELGAMAL DIGITAL SIGNATURE, LAMPORT-DIFFIE SIGNATURE. *See* DIGITAL SIGNATURE.

RACF. In access control, Resource Access Control Facility, an IBM software security product that assists in the control of user access to application data sets, volumes, transactions and terminals.

RACF is a program product that functions with the IBM MVS and VM operating system to provide enhanced access control. It meets user and system security requirements by providing ability to:

- identify and verify users;
- authorize users to access the protected resources;
- control the means of access to resources;
- log and report various attempts of unauthorized access to protected resources;
- administer security to meet an installation's security goals.

User access can be granted according a 'something the user knows', or 'something the user has' principle. Users are identified with a unique name, i.e the user id, and are allocated a password. An operator identification card may also be used in place of, or in addition to, password verification for terminal processing.

Users are granted access to system resources according to their access privileges, such privileges also specify the type of permitted access, e.g. read, update. Moreover the privileges may be limited to certain time and day, thus providing protection against the attacker who manages to gain access to a terminal outside normal working hours.

The logging and reporting of accesses, provided by RACF, can alert management, both to unauthorized access attempts, a common symptom of attacker experimentation, and to variances from a user's normal pattern of accesses. Such variances can be an indication of an attacker successfully masquerading as a user, or conceivably a user undertaking unauthorized processing.

RACF provides a flexible access control which can be tailored to an installation's security requirements. The security administration is facilitated in RACF by the use of profiles, both for users and resources. A user may be identified as an individual or as a member of a group. Such profiles provide relevant security information on the user, e.g. user id, encrypted password, security classifications, user attributes (e.g. auditor privileges), profile owner, etc. The user attribute - revoke - prevents the user from entering the system, and thus provides an extremely simple mechanism to withdraw all access privileges at a stroke.

The security classification for the user is similar to the military type classifications, comprising a hierarchy and a set of categories. The hierarchy is expressed as security level, each installation may associate names for security levels, e.g. confidential, with a number; the higher the number, the higher the security level. A user is also granted a set of categories, such categories may relate to their job functions. For example an accountant concerned with the funding of building projects might be assigned the set of categories {BUILDING, FINANCE}. Protected resources are similarly allocated security classifications.

RACF rules of access according to security classifications are less sophisticated than those of Bell-La Padula. A user is allowed to access a resource if the security level of the user is equal or greater than that of the resource, and if the resource set of categories is a subset of those held by the user. Thus the abovementioned accountant would be permitted access to a data resource, with classification confidential and category set {BUILDING}, but not to a data with the same security level but the different category set {BUILDING, CONSTRUCTION}.

The administration of access control is greatly simplified if those users with a high degree of commonality, from the access viewpoint, are treated as a group. For example, a project team is likely to make considerable cooperative use of files associated with the project. In RACF all users belong to at least one group. The groups form a hierarchical structure with superior groups owning other groups lower in the tree. Information about groups is stored in the group profiles in the RACF database.

The security relevant features of protected resources are also described in resource profiles. In this case the information contained in the profile includes, resource name, profile owner, universal access authority, access list, security classification, auditing options, warning options and notification options.

The access to the resource are controlled firstly by the security classification; this security classification comprises a security level and a category set. If the user's security classification is lower than that of the resource then access is denied.

If the user's security classification is equal to, or above that, of the resource, see above, then a second check is made to determine if the user has the requisite discretionary access control privilege for the resource. The resource profile access list specifies the type of access e.g. update, read, execute that is permitted for a specific user or group; the privilege 'none' excludes a user or group from access. The universal access authority represents the default access authority; users or groups not specifically named in the access list may be granted access implicitly by the universal access authority.

Terminals are included in the set of protected resources; thus a legitimate user may be given access privileges only to a specific terminal. This provides additional security; even if an attacker gains knowledge of a user id, and password, then use of this information may only be of value if the attacker can access the system from the terminal allocated to the legitimate user, during the day/time periods specified for that user.

The user/group and resource profiles provide a straightforward mechanism for RACF to determine whether or not a user access request may be granted.

Such access is only granted if the user/group profile aligns with that of the requested, protected resource.

RACF facilitates the logging and reporting of security relevant events. A security log is written for detected, unauthorized attempts to enter the system, and optionally for detected authorized, or unauthorized, attempts to access protected resources, or to issue RACF commands.

The logging system also sends messages to a security console for detected, attempted security violations. Optionally immediate reports on detected unauthorized attempts to access protected resources, or modify the contents of the RACF database, can be made. In addition a user can request notification of an unauthorized attempt to access a resource. Statistical information such as time/date and number of times that a user enters a system, or accesses a specific resource can also be supplied.

RACF currently permits an MVS/XA installation to meet the U.S. Department of Defence Class C2 level. *See* ACCESS LIST, BELL-LA PADULA MODEL, C2, DISCRETIONARY ACCESS CONTROL, INTRUSION DETECTION, ORANGE BOOK, PASSWORD, SECURITY LEVEL, SOMETHING THE USER HAS, SOMETHING THE USER KNOWS, USER ID.

radar sensor. In physical security, an intrusion detector that measures changes in a received radar signal's frequency caused by the movement of a body through the beam. *See* INTRUSION DETECTION.

radio frequency emissions. *Synonymous with* COMPROMISING EMANATIONS.

radio frequency interference. *See* JAMMING. *Synonymous with* ELECTROMAGNETIC INTERFERENCE.

radio frequency motion detector. In physical security, an intrusion detection system in which the protected area is saturated with radio frequency waves and an alarm is initiated if the pattern is disturbed. *See* RADAR SENSOR.

radix. In mathematics, in a radix numeration system the total value of a numeral represented by a string of characters is the sum of each character multiplied by its weight. The ratio of the weight of one digit to the preceding one is the radix for the number system used, and is always a positive integer. Thus in a hexadecimal system the radix is 16 and the number 123 has the decimal value of 291 = ((1 x 16 x 16) + (2 x 16) + 3). *See* BASE.

Rainbow Series. In computer security, a set of standards related to computer security issued by the U.S. Department of Defense. The Orange Book deals with computer security evaluation, the Yellow Book deals with the means of determining the most appropriate security level required for a particular installation, the Red Book deals with network security and the Blue Book with secure databases. *See* BLUE BOOK, ORANGE BOOK, RED BOOK, YELLOW BOOK.

RAM. *See* RANDOM ACCESS MEMORY.

RAMP. *See* RATING MAINTENANCE PROGRAM.

random. In mathematics, a character set that has equal probability of being selected from the total population of possibilities, hence unpredictable. (ANSI).

random access. In computing, access to data such that the next location from which a word or byte is to be retrieved is independent of the location of a previously accessed word or byte. *Compare* DIRECT ACCESS, SEQUENTIAL ACCESS.

random access memory. (1) In computing, a memory chip used with microprocessors, information can be both read from, and written into, the memory but the contents are lost when the power supply is removed. (2) In computing, any form of storage in which the access time for any item of data is independent of the location of the data most recently obtained.

random cipher. In cryptography, a cipher in which, for a given ciphertext message and a given key, the decipherment process is as likely to produce one plaintext message as any other. The result of the decipherment process for a given key and a given ciphertext message is uniformly distributed over the complete range of meaningful and meaningless messages, of the given length, in the language. *See* CRYPTOGRAPHIC KEY, INFORMATION THEORY.

random data perturbation. In database security, a record based perturbation technique in which a random number is added to each data item, as it is extracted, and before it is used to compute the required statistic. *Compare* RANDOM SAMPLE QUERIES. *See* INFERENCE CONTROL, PERTURBATION, RECORD BASED PERTURBATION.

random line switching. In computer security, a technique to reduce the effect of compromising emanations from a VDU, using frequent random switching of signal patterns. The technique can, however, produce screen flicker and an eavesdropper may be able to decode the signals due to the low permutation capability. *Compare* WHITE NOISE EMITTER. *See* COMPROMISING EMANATIONS, VAN ECK PHENOMENON.

random numbers. In applications, numbers generated by a random process having the properties that each number is independent of its predecessors, and the probability distribution of the numbers conforms to a specified distribution, e.g. Gaussian, Poisson, uniform.

The application for random numbers arises when an input is required to be unpredictable, i.e. independent of previous inputs. True random numbers can only be produced by a genuine random process, e.g. the number of electrons emitted by a heated cathode in a small interval of time.

An approximation to random number sequences, known as pseudorandom numbers, can, however, be generated by mathematical techniques; pseudorandom number generators can be supplied as software routines or incorporated into the facilities of high-level languages. These pseudorandom numbers are generated by a deterministic procedure and do not therefore conform to the strict definition of a random number, but within their limitations they are suitable for a variety of applications.

Pseudorandom number sequences are generated with a specified input, or seed. One technique squares the previous number and extracts the middle digits to form the next number in the sequence; current routines, however, are usually based upon linear congruential generators (LCG). The numbers are generated by a formula:

$$x2 = \text{mod} (a * x1 + c, m).$$

where $x1$ = previous random number, $x2$ = current random number, a, c and m are integers selected for the generator, mod $(x, m) = x - \{x/m\} * m$ and $\{x/m\}$ = integer part of the quotient. The parameters a, c and m must be selected with care in order to provide pseudorandom number sequences with the desired randomness characteristics.

In particular c and m should have no factors in common, a must be greater than the square root of m, and m should be a prime number equal to or less than the largest integer that the programming language can handle.

The number generated by an LCG depends upon the previous number in the sequence. Thus if the sequence

random numbers
Schematic of an LCG, showing how the division of the number line into equal intervals, m, can produce pseudorandom numbers. The location of each number inside the corresponding intervals is haphazard. It results from using the modulus function and leads to a pseudorandom series.

always commences with the same seed then it will produce the same effect for each computer run. Moreover if a given number occurs at position m, and at position n, in the sequence then the sequence following the nth position will be identical to that following the mth.

Since the total set of possible pseudorandom integers is limited to those contained in the range 0 .. m-1 the LCG will eventually produce a number already delivered, earlier in the sequence, and thus very long runs will inevitably exhibit cyclic properties. The period of these cycles will be even less than m if c and m have factors in common. It is possible to extend the period for a given value of m by using 2 LCG's, with different values of m, in conjunction with each other.

The probability distribution of the LCG sequences are nominally uniform but these characteristics must also be checked if long sequences are employed. If random numbers with Gaussian or Poisson distributions are required the numbers must be subject to requisite transformations.

Encryption algorithms represent good pseudorandom generators since a minor change in plaintext will produce a major variation in the subsequent ciphertext. Cipher feedback and output feedback modes of operation of DES effectively use the algorithm to produce a pseudorandom sequence for the cryptographic bit streams used in stream cipher operation.

An application area for random numbers arises in the field of data security.

In some cases authentication between two communicating entities is estab-

lished by the generation of a random number, that is then concatenated with a message, encrypted with a secret key and transmitted by one party. The response to this message, also includes the same random number, or some function of it, giving the original sender an assurance that it is a genuine response to a particular message.

In this case it is essential that no attacker can deduce the subsequent stream of random numbers, if one of them is obtained. This can be achieved by feeding back the last generated random number into an encryption device, e.g. a DES chip, with another secret key, encrypting it and performing additional mathematical manipulations to produce the next random number.

An extremely important aspect of random number generation arises in the development of cryptographic bit streams for stream ciphers. *See* CRYPTOGRAPHIC BIT STREAM, CRYPTOGRAPHY, HIGH-LEVEL LANGUAGE, LCG, REPLAY, SEED, STREAM CIPHER.

random process. In mathematics, a process in which the output cannot be fully predetermined from a knowledge of the system variables. One in which the outcome depends upon one or more random events. *See* RANDOM NUMBERS.

random rounding. In database security, a form of result-based perturbation in which the statistic is randomly rounded either to the next higher or the next lower multiple of the rounding base. *Compare* CONTROLLED ROUNDING, SYSTEMATIC ROUNDING. *See* INFERENCE CONTROL, RESULT-BASED PERTURBA-

TION, PERTURBATION.

random sample queries. In database security, a record based perturbation technique in which a statistic is computed from a sample of the records, meeting the query criterion, rather than the whole set. *Compare* RANDOM DATA PERTURBATION. *See* INFERENCE CONTROL, PERTURBATION, RECORD BASED PERTURBATION.

range. In mathematics, the set of output values of a function. *Compare* DOMAIN.

rank. (1) In mathematics, to arrange in ascending or descending order according to some criterion. (2) In computing, a measure of the relative position in an array, group, series or classification. *See* ARRAY.

rate. In information theory, a measure of the average number of bits of information in each character of a message. Consider the set of messages of length N, for a given language, if the entropy of the messages is H then the rate for all sequences of the language of length N is given by H/N. *See* ABSOLUTE RATE, ENTROPY.

rating maintenance program. In computer security, an NCSC program to allow for the updating of security evaluation of computer systems, according to the Orange Book, as such systems undergo inevitable modifications in their life cycles. The Orange Book evaluation procedures are lengthy and it would be unrealistic to undertake such evaluations de nouveau each time that the system were modified. *See* ORANGE BOOK.

rational number. In mathematics, any number that can be expressed by the ratio of two integers where the divider is nonzero.

raw data. In computing, unprocessed

and nonreduced data.

RBAC. *See* RULE-BASED ACCESS CONTROL.

RD. Restricted Data.

RDC. *See* REMOTE DIAGNOSTIC CENTER.

read. (1) In computer security, a fundamental operation that results only in the flow of information from an object to a subject. (DOD). *Compare* WRITE. *See* OBJECT, SUBJECT. (2) In computing, the process of acquiring or interpreting data from an input device, store or some other medium.

read access. In computer security, permission to read information. (DOD). *Compare* WRITE ACCESS. *See* READ.

read-only memory. In computing, a storage device whose contents can only be changed by a particular user, by particular operating conditions or by a particular external process. Read-only storage can include storage media where the writing action is inhibited by the operating system or by some mechanical device, e.g. a tag on a diskette. The term ROM conventionally implies a storage device not designed to be modified by conventional write procedures and that is used to store permanent information in computers and microcomputers.

ready state. In data communications, a condition at the DTE/DCE interface that indicates the DTE is prepared to accept an incoming call and the DCE is ready to accept a call request. *See* DCE, DTE, CALL REQUEST.

real number. In mathematics, a number that may be represented by a finite or infinite number of digits in fixed radix numeration system. *See* RADIX.

realtime. In computing, pertaining to actions that are performed in conjunction with some external process or user and that are required to meet the time constraints imposed by that process or user, e.g. control of an aircraft guidance system, an on line information service. *See* REALTIME INPUT, REALTIME OUTPUT, REALTIME REACTION.

realtime input. In computing, input data received into the system within a time scale, or at instants of time, determined by some other system. *Compare* REALTIME OUTPUT. *See* REALTIME.

realtime operation. *See* REALTIME.

realtime output. In computing, output data that must be delivered within a time scale, or at instants of time, determined by some other system. *Compare* REALTIME INPUT. *See* REALTIME.

realtime reaction. In computer security, a response to a penetration attempt that is detected and diagnosed in time to prevent the actual penetration. (FIPS). *See* PENETRATION, REALTIME.

reasonableness check. In computing, a test for the existence of a gross error, e.g. by checking that a data value lies within a prespecified range.

received data. In data communications, a data path for received data. *Compare* TRANSMITTED DATA. *See* RS-232C.

received line signal detector. In data communications, a signal from a modem to a computer to inform it that some device is trying to make contact. It may be used to trigger the computer to generate a log on invitation. *See* LOG ON, MODEM, RS-232C. *Synonymous with* CARRIER DETECT.

receive only. In data communications, terminals or other equipment capable of receiving data or messages but lacking a keyboard or other input device.

receiver. (1) In data communications, a subject reading from a communication channel. *Compare* SENDER. *See* CHANNEL, SUBJECT. (2) The person, institution or other entity responsible for the receipt of a message. (ANSI). *Compare* SENDER.

receiver's correspondent bank. In banking, a bank receiving funds on behalf of the receiver from the sender or the sender's correspondent bank. (ANSI). *Compare* SENDER'S CORRESPONDENT BANK.

receiver signal element timing. In data communications, a signal used on synchronous modems. In the case of received data the modem provides this signal or the clock. *Compare* TRANSMITTER SIGNAL ELEMENT TIMING. *See* RS-232C, SYNCHRONOUS MODEM.

receiving bank. In banking, the bank to which the message is delivered. (ANSI).

recipient. (1) In banking, the party (logical or other) that is responsible for receiving a cryptographic service message. (ISO). *Compare* ORIGINATOR, SENDER. *See* CRYPTOGRAPHIC SERVICE MESSAGE. (2) In data communications, the person, institution or other entity that is responsible for and authorized to receive a message. (ANSI). *Compare* ORIGINATOR. *See* MESSAGE.

reciprocal. In risk management, a disaster recovery strategy, adopted within or between organizations, employing mutual backup arrangements amongst installations in the organizations. *Compare* INTERNAL RECIPROCAL.

reconciliation. In auditing, pertaining to the identification and analysis of detected differences between values contained in two substantially similar files or between a detail file and a control total.

record. (1) In computing, a collection of related data treated as a unit, e.g. details of name, address, age, occupation and department of an employee in a personnel file. *Compare* FIELD. *See* LOGICAL RECORD, PHYSICAL RECORD. (2) In computing, to store signals on a recording medium for later use.

record based perturbation. In database security, a form of perturbation applied to records as they are extracted and prior to their use in computing the required statistic. The perturbation may take the form of adding random numbers to the retrieved data items or selecting/rejecting data items so that the overall statistic is computed on the basis of only a sample of the retrieved data. *Compare* RESULT-BASED PERTURBATION. *See* INFERENCE, PERTURBATION, STATISTICAL DATABASE.

record layout. In computing, the manner in which the data is organized in the record, i.e. description and size of fields. *See* FIELD.

record length. In computing, the number of words or characters in a record. *See* WORD, RECORD.

record lock. In computing, a facility to deny access to a record in a file. It is used in multiuser systems to prevent two users from simultaneously updating the same record. *Compare* FILE LOCK. *See* RECORD.

record separator character. In computing, the indicator specifying the logical boundary between records. *See* RECORD.

recovery. In reliability, the activity of placing a system back into an error-free state from which normal operation can resume.

recovery procedures. (1) In computer security, the actions necessary to restore a system's computational capability and data files after a system failure or penetration. (FIPS). *See* PENETRATION. (2) In data communications, processes whereby specified stations attempt to resolve erroneous or conflicting conditions arising from some malfunction, or external situation, in the transfer of data.

recursion analysis. In cryptanalysis, a technique to determine the linear recurrence relationship of a linear shift register producing a cryptographic bit stream for a stream cipher. *See* CRYPTOGRAPHIC BIT STREAM, LINEAR RECURRENCE RELATION, LINEAR FEEDBACK SHIFT REGISTER, STREAM CIPHER.

recursion length. *Synonymous with* LINEAR COMPLEXITY.

recursive routine. In computing, a routine that may be used as a routine of itself, calling itself directly or being called by another routine, one that it itself has called. *Compare* ITERATION. *See* RECURSIVE SUBROUTINE.

recursive subroutine. In computing, a subroutine that calls itself. The state of the subroutine must be stored in each successive call and the data representing the state is often stored on a stack. *See* RECURSIVE ROUTINE, STACK, SUBROUTINE.

red. In communications security, refers to equipment and wire lines handling non-encrypted, classified information. (AFR). *Compare* BLACK.

red/black concept. In communications security, separation and routing control for red and black wire systems. *See* RED, BLACK.

Red Book. *Compare* BLUE BOOK, ORANGE BOOK, YELLOW BOOK. *See* RAINBOW SERIES. *Synonymous with*

TNI.

red tape operation. In computing, an operation on data that is necessary for internal purposes but does not contribute to the final answer.

reduced set of residues. In mathematics, a subset of residues for a given integer n where each member of the subset is relatively prime to n. For example, if n is 12 the reduced set of residues would be {1,5,7,11}. *See* REL-ATIVELY PRIME, RESIDUE.

redundancy. (1) In information theory, the difference between the absolute rate and the rate of a language. *See* ABSO-LUTE RATE, RATE. (2) In reliability, the use of additional system components to mitigate the effects of component malfunction. *See* HARDWARE REDUNDANCY, INFORMATION REDUNDANCY, SOFTWARE REDUNDANCY, TIME REDUNDANCY. (3) In communications, the fraction of the gross information content of a message that can be eliminated without losing any essential information. In computing and data communications, redundant characters, e.g. parity bits, are added to data to provide a method of detecting errors in transmission or processing. *See* PARI-TY CHECKING, REDUNDANCY CHECKING.

redundancy checking. In codes, the performance of a calculation on received data and comparison of results with redundant codes to check for certain processing or transmission errors. *See* ERROR CORRECTION CODE, ERROR DE-TECTION CODE, REDUNDANT CODE.

redundant code. In codes, additional bits added to characters for error checking purposes, e.g. parity bits and hamming codes. *See* REDUNDANCY CHECK-ING, HAMMING CODE, PARITY CHECK-ING.

redundant processing. In auditing, a repetition of processing and an accom-panying comparison of individual results for equality.

RedX. In computer security, a virus that infects COMMAND.COM and COM files, affects run-time operation, corrupts program and OVL files. *See* VIRUS NAMES.

re-encipher from master key. In key management, a facility provided in key management systems that employ session keys. Such session keys are encrypted under terminal, or cross-communication, key-encrypting keys during transmission, and stored under master keys whilst resident in host or node computers. Secure facilities must be provided to convert such encrypted session keys from encryption under one key-encrypt-ing key to the other. Re-encipher from master key is a facility that produces the session key by decryption with the master key and then re-encrypts it with the terminal or cross-communication key. Such functions are performed in tamper-resistant modules with stored master keys; thus none of the keys involved in the process are ever avail-able in cleartext form outside the mod-ule. *Compare* RE-ENCIPHER TO MASTER KEY. *See* KEY-ENCRYPTING KEY, SES-SION KEY.

re-encipher to master key. In key management, a facility similar to re-encipher from master key. In this case the encrypted session key is decrypted with the terminal, or cross-communi-cation, key-encrypting key and is re-encrypted with the master key. *Compare* RE-ENCIPHER FROM MASTER KEY. *See* KEY-ENCRYPTING KEY, SESSION KEY.

reference. In banking, a transaction identifier that is normally included as part of the information supplied with the transaction itself, and can subsequently be used to distinguish the transaction identified from other transactions, e.g. in nostro account reconciliation. (ANSI).

See NOSTRO ACCOUNT.

reference monitor. In access control, a security control concept in which an abstract machine mediates accesses to objects by subjects. In principle, a reference monitor should be complete (in that it mediated every access), isolated from modification by system entities, and verifiable. A security kernel is an implementation of a reference monitor for a given hardware base. (MTR). *See* COMPONENT REFERENCE MONITOR, OBJECT, REFERENCE MONITOR CONCEPT, SECURITY KERNEL, SUBJECT.

reference monitor concept. (1) In access control, an access control concept that refers to an abstract machine that mediates all accesses to objects by subjects. (DOD). *See* ACCESS, OBJECT, REFERENCE MONITOR, REFERENCE VALIDATION MECHANISM, SUBJECT. (2) In access control, an access control concept in which an abstract machine mediates all accesses to objects by subjects.

The computer system compels users, and processes, to submit all requests for access to the reference monitor; the user or process privileges, in regard to that object, are then checked for each access. In this way it may not be necessary to validate every piece of application program code for potential security violations.

If the process, under which the program is operating, does not have the requisite privileges then access to classified data will not be granted by the reference monitor. If the process has the requisite privileges, and the program contains some Trojan Horse to leak classified data to an unclassified file, then the reference monitor can detect and block the write access to the file. The reference monitor might not, however, detect the leakage of data by some more indirect information channel, i.e. by a covert channel.

If the reference monitor is to perform its security role then it must meet three design requirements:

- the reference monitor mechanism must be tamper-proof;
- the reference validation mechanism must always be invoked;
- the reference validation mechanism must be small enough to be subject to analysis and tests, the completeness of which can be assured.

See ORANGE BOOK.

reference monitor concept
Trojan Horse tries to pass data from secret file to confidential file but access file request has to be passed to Reference Monitor which blocks it. (Secret data must not be written to confidential file.)

reference PIN. In banking, the official version of the cardholder's PIN used for comparison against the PIN as entered in the PIN entry device. *See* PIN MANAGEMENT AND SECURITY.

reference validation mechanism. In computer security, an implementation of the reference monitor concept that validates each reference to data or programs by any user (program) against a list of authorized types of reference for that user. It must be tamper-proof, must always be invoked and must be small enough to be subject to analysis and tests, the completeness of which can be assured. (NCSC). *See* REFERENCE MONITOR CONCEPT.

regeneration. In communications, the process of producing a duplicate of a message or data from an unambiguously recognizable but distorted signal, e.g. a set of on-off pulses attenuated in transmission.

register. In computing, a memory device, usually high-speed, and of limited specified length, e.g. one byte, one word; used for special purposes, e.g. arithmetic computing.

register insertion. In data communications, pertaining to a technique in which a message to be transmitted, in a local area network, is first loaded into a shift register. The network loop is broken and the shift register inserted either when it is idle or at a point between two adjacent messages. The message to be sent is then shifted out to the network, any message arriving during this period is shifted into the register behind the transmitted message. *Compare* CONTROL TOKEN, DAISY CHAIN, MESSAGE SLOT. *See* LOCAL AREA NETWORK.

regrade. In data security, a determination that classified information requires a different degree of protection against unauthorized disclosure than currently

provided, together with a change of classification designation that reflects such different degree of protection. An 'upgrade' results in a higher classification; a 'downgrade' results in a lower classification. (MTR).

regulatory agency. In data communications, an agency controlling the specialized and common carrier tariffs. *See* COMMON CARRIER, SPECIALIZED COMMON CARRIER, TARIFF.

reimbursement bank. In banking, the bank providing cover for a payment order. (ANSI). *See* RECEIVER'S CORRESPONDENT BANK, SENDER'S CORRESPONDENT BANK.

reimbursement party. In banking, the party that is the source of funds to the receiver. (ANSI).

re-key. In physical security, pertaining to the action of modifying key locks or card readers to function with a new key set or access code. *See* CARD READER.

REL. Releasable only to those mentioned.

relation. In databases, a flat file. In a relational database the data is stored as entities, and attributes, of those entities in two-dimesional arrays, e.g. a relation might comprise employee name, employee number, department and salary. *See* RELATIONAL DATABASE, FLAT FILE.

relational algebra. In databases, a language that provides a set of operators for manipulating relations in a relational database, e.g. if there were two relations R1 (employee number, employee department) and R2 (employee number, project) and a user required to know that departments were involved with a given project then a set of operations would be specified and the resulting relation would comprise a table of departments associated with the project. *Compare*

RELATIONAL CALCULUS. *See* JOIN, PROJECTION, RELATIONAL DATABASE.

relational calculus. In databases, a language in which a user specifies the set of results required from the manipulation of the data in a relational database. Relational calculus provides a concise unambiguous mathematical notation for statements such as: take the two relations (employee number, project) and (employee number, department) and produce the relation (department) for project = DYNAMO. The result would be a list of departments whose employees were working on the DYNAMO project. The distinction between relational algebra and relational calculus is that the former specifies the actions to be performed and the latter specifies the nature of the desired result. *Compare* RELATIONAL ALGEBRA. *See* DATABASE SECURITY, RELATIONAL DATABASE.

relational database. In databases, a database in which the individual files, termed relations, hold data in the form of flat files, or tables. The restriction upon the form of these tables is given below.

- Within the relational system the table must contain only one type of record. Each record has a fixed number of fields, all of which are explicitly named.
- The fields within a table are distinct and repeating groups are not allowed.
- There are no duplicate records.
- There is no predetermined sequence of records.

The processing of data involves operations on whole tables, or relations, rather than upon individual records within a table. The result of such processing is new tables.

The table is rectangular, thus all entries must contain data and there are no repeating groups. If a record were to contain an employee's history and the variable number of training courses attended were to be recorded then a separate table would be constructed. This table would contain (say) four fields, employee's number, name of course, date commenced and result. The variable number of courses attended would thus be accommodated by a variable number of entries in the 'training course' relation.

All the values in a given column refer to the same class of attribute of the entries. These values must be drawn from some domain of possible values, e.g. a date.

The fundamental operations on a relational database are selection, projection, join and division; the latter is, however, not so commonly employed. Selection produces a new table containing the same number of columns as the original relation but the rows will contain those of the original relation that satisfy some specified criteria. For example if the table provided details of sales and salesmen then the selection might be on the basis of sales > 2000.

The projection operation on a table specifies columns to be selected. The resulting table thus contains only a subset of the columns of the original table, moreover it may only contain a subset of the original rows. This is because no duplicate records are permitted, in relational databases, and if two rows only differ in the columns deleted by the projection then only one record will be carried forward to the new relation.

The join operation combines information from two or more tables. A common field in two tables is used as the basis of the combination and records with equal values in the common field are concatenated in the resulting relation.

It is necessary to give careful consideration to the contents of relations and to the inherent relationships between attributes of a record, the inclusion of redundant information in a record can lead to problems and a process of normalization is essential in the construction of a relational database. *See* ATTRIBUTE, DIVISION, DOMAIN, FIELD, FLAT FILE, JOIN, NORMAL FORMS, PROJECTION, RECORD, RELATION, RELATIONAL ALGEBRA, RELATIONAL CALCULUS, REPEATING GROUP, SELECTION.

relational operator. In mathematics, a symbol used to compare two values, e.g. > (greater than), = (equals), < (less than).

relationship. In databases, a statement linking two entities, e.g. if a personnel database has entities: employee and department, then 'works in' would be a relationship linking these entities. *Compare* ATTRIBUTE, ENTITY. *See* RELATIONAL DATABASE.

relative error. In mathematics, ratio of the absolute error of a quantity to its true, theoretically correct or specified value.

relatively prime. In mathematics, pertaining to two integers with a greatest common divisor of 1, e.g. 8 and 21. *See* GREATEST COMMON DIVISOR, PRIME NUMBER. *Synonymous with* COPRIME.

relative table size control. In database security, a form of table restriction control known as s_m/N-criterion, employed in inference control. The value of s_m is the number of cells in a m-dimensional lattice model table, and N is the total number of records in the database. If the ratio of the number of cells to the total number of records exceeds some specified threshold then it is likely that some cells correspond to a low number of records and the table is not made available for user requests. *Compare* ORDER CONTROL. *See* INFERENCE CONTROL, LATTICE MODEL, RECORD, TABLE RESTRICTION.

relay. In communications, a point-to-point reception and retransmission system.

relay center. *Synonymous with* MESSAGE SWITCHING CENTER.

release time and date. In banking, the time and date the sender authorizes a service to forward the message to the receiver. (ANSI).

reliability. (1) The extent to which a system can be expected to perform its intended function with required precision (TNI). (2) The ability of a system to perform its function under specified conditions for a stated period of time. The overall reliability of a system is a function of the mean time between failure, the mean time to repair and the mean time to recover. *See* MEAN TIME BETWEEN FAILURE, MEAN TIME TO RECOVER, MEAN TIME TO REPAIR, REDUNDANCY.

reliability of service. In information security, functions to ensure consistency and availability of service. *See* INFORMATION TECHNOLOGY SECURITY EVALUATION CRITERIA.

remanence. (1) In computer security, a measure of the magnetic flux density remaining after removal of an applied magnetic force. Can also mean any data remaining on ADP storage media after removal of the power. (DOD). *See* RESIDUE. (2) In computer security, the residual magnetism that remains on magnetic storage media after degaussing. (FIPS). *See* DEGAUSS.

remitter. In banking, a general term indicating the source of funds in a payment order. (ANSI).

remote. (1) In data communications, pertaining to a system connected to a host system by a communication link. (2) In data communications, pertaining to a cluster control unit that is connected to a mainframe via a modem, as compared to a local controller that is directly wired. *See* CLUSTER CONTROL UNIT.

remote access. *See* REMOTE.

remote batch processing. *See* REMOTE JOB ENTRY.

remote detector panel. In physical security, a device located at a monitoring station rather than within the protected area that provides supervision of the inter-area lines. *See* MONITORING STATION, PROTECTED AREA.

remote diagnostic center. In computing, a center operated by an equipment supplier to reduce the number of on-site visits by maintenance engineers. These centers can pose security risks to computer systems. Sensitive files should be taken off-line before commencement of an RDC investigation and RDC connections should be not be undertaken unless specifically authorized by computer systems operations staff.

remote job entry. In operations, the submission of a job to a peripheral that is connected to the processor via a communication link.

remotely accessed resource-sharing computer system. A computer system that includes one or more central processing units, peripheral devices, remote terminals, and communications equipment or interconnection links, that allocates its resources to one or more users, and which can be entered from terminals located outside the central computer facility. (DODD). *See* RESOURCE SHARING COMPUTER SYSTEM.

remote station. (1) In data communications, a station that can call, or be called by, a central station in a point-to-point switched network. (2) In a multipoint network, a tributary station. *See* TRIBUTARY STATION, POINT-TO-POINT.

remote station fire alarm system. In physical security, a system of electrically supervised devices with direct circuit protection between control units, or alarm initiating equipment, in protected premises and signal indicating devices in a remote station. *See* REMOTE STATION SYSTEM.

remote station system. In physical security, a system in which a remote location, staffed and operated by an independent body, e.g. a police station, is used to receive alarm signals. *See* ALARM SIGNAL.

removable cartridge disk. In computing, a hard disk system in which disks, in a cartridge, may be removed and replaced.

repeatability. In information security, pertaining to a state in which a repeated evaluation of the same target of evaluation to the same security target by the same ITSEF yields the same overall verdict as the first evaluation. *See* INFORMATION TECHNOLOGY SECURITY EVALUATION CRITERIA, INFORMATION TECHNOLOGY SECURITY EVALUATION MANUAL, SECURITY TARGET, TARGET OF EVALUATION.

repeater. In data communications, a device that interconnects networks. The repeater simply forwards bits from one network to another, and thus effectively comprises the physical layer of the Open Systems Interconnection Reference Model. *Compare* BRIDGE, GATEWAY, ROUTER. *See* OPEN SYSTEMS INTERCONNECTION, PHYSICAL LAYER.

repeating group. In computing, a group in a record that can occur any number of times, e.g. the names of dependents in an employee's file. It is not possible to predetermine the number of fields to be allocated to such a group and records with repeating groups cannot fit into flat files. *See* RECORD, FIELD, FLAT FILE.

reperformance test. In auditing, a technique in which an auditor independently processes data and compares the results with those produced by the system under consideration.

replay. In authentication, a form of attack in which the message sequence is changed or a stored data item is replaced with a previously stored value.

This form of attack can succeed even if the message or stored data item is authenticated or encrypted. In its simplest form, an attacker can simply record a message, including its authenticator, and re-insert it into the communication link. Such a message could, for example, cause a financial transaction to be performed twice. Alternatively an item in a database may be updated by a legitimate user and then restored to its original value by an attacker.

Message sequence numbers

sent	rec'd	Messages in transit	rec'd	sent
n	$m-1$	M_1	$n-1$	m
		Message n A_1	?	
$n+1$	$m-1$	M_2	n	m
	?	Message m A_2		
$n+1$	m	M_3	n	$m+1$
		Message $n+1$ A_3	?	
$n+2$	m	Scope of authenticators A_i	$n+1$	$m+1$

replay
Fig. 1. Sequencing messages.

Replay of transmitted messages can be detected, in principle, by requiring that a message be different from all preceding messages using the same key. The techniques to obviate replay attacks are:

- sequence numbers;
- message chaining;
- random number exchanges;
- date/time stamps.

If two communicating parties insert sequence numbers in their messages, and include these numbers within the authentication computations then an attacker can neither replay an earlier message without detection, nor modify a message sequence number. The two communicating parties must keep a record of the last sequence number sent and received.

The use of message sequence numbers is complicated if the messages are transmitted over a network in which they may arrive out of sequence, or some messages may be lost. The receiver could decide to accept only messages with sequence numbers greater than the last one received, but this could well result in the rejection of legitimate but delayed messages. Thus if the last sequence number received were 24, and a message with sequence number 31 were received then the receiver would reject delayed messages 25 - 30.

Alternatively the receiver could record all received sequence numbers and simply check each incoming number against this record, such a system would involve a heavy overhead in a transactions processing environment.

A compromise solution is to use a sliding bit map (see Fig. 2).

A 1 entry in the bitmap indicates that a message has been received with the corresponding sequence number. If a message arrives with a sequence number less than that corresponding to the first entry (i.e. N in Fig. 2) then it is rejected because it is impossible to differentiate between a highly delayed message and a replay.

If the sequence number corresponds to one of the numbers of the bit map (e.g. N + 2), then the corresponding entry is

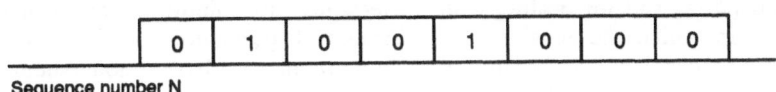

Sequence number N

Fig. 2 Sequence bit map.

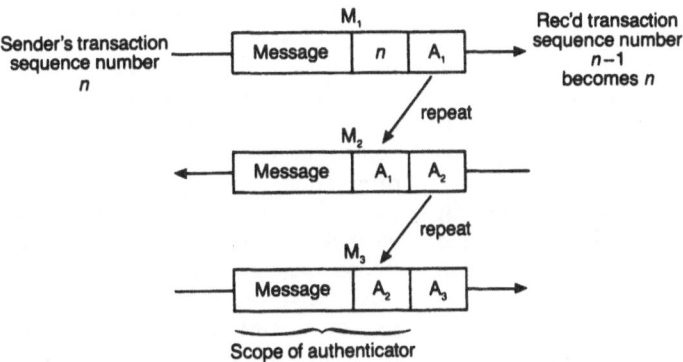

Fig. 3 Message chaining

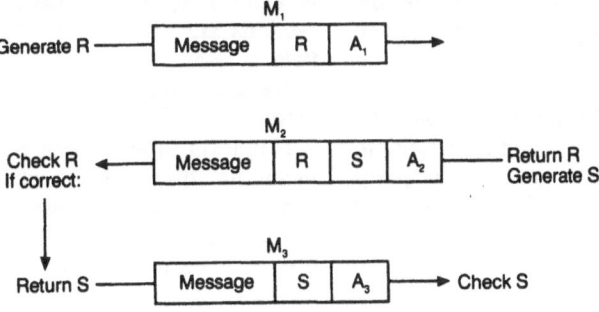

Fig. 4 Authentication with random numbers

replay

checked. A bit map entry of 0 allows the message to be accepted and the entry is updated to 1. If the entry is a 1 then the message is a replay and is rejected.

There are various strategies for moving up the window, and for dealing with the situation in which the received sequence number lies beyond the top of the window. For example, if the last accepted message sequence number corresponded to the first entry in the bit map, then the window is moved up so that the base number N corresponds to the first zero entry.

If the received message sequence number lies beyond the top of the window, then the window is moved up so that it enables the entry to be recorded, and the base number N corresponds to a zero entry.

Message chaining between parties A and B can be achieved by inserting a field from the last message received into the next message transmitted. For example, the authenticator A1 of the last message from Alice is included in the next message from Bob to Alice (see Fig. 3). The authenticator A2 of this message is computed in the basis of the message text plus the chaining field (A1).

An alternative method of chaining can be achieved with cipher block chaining, or cipher feedback, by using the last 64 bits of the ciphertext received as the initialization vector of the next message transmitted.

Random numbers may also be included in messages to provide protection against replay. Alice includes a random number (R1) in her message to party Bob, this random number is included with the message text (M1) in computing the authenticator (A1). In his response Bob includes the received random number (R1) and a second random number (R2), generated by Bob; the authenticator (A2) is computed over the second message text (M2), random numbers (R1 and R2). Alice checks the received random number R1 and inserts the received random number R2 in its response to Bob.

In using this technique the size of the random numbers must be sufficiently large, in comparison with the number of messages, to minimize the danger of accidental generation of duplicate random numbers. No action should be taken as a result of the intermediate messages until the third message has been received and checked by Bob.

Sequence numbers, chaining and random number techniques for defense against replay involve the communicating parties in overheads on maintaining records of sequence numbers, etc. If the time delays in communication are kept reasonably low then message fields, containing the time and date of message origination, can give single message protection against replay attack, provided that the time/date field is included in the message authentication.

A stored file in a database may have its own authenticator but individual items in such files are likely to be subject to frequent updates; each such update necessitates a recomputation of the authenticator for the whole file. If the file is partitioned, with each partition separately authenticated, then there exists the possibility of an attack by rearranging the order of sections, or restoring a section, and its individual authenticator, to an earlier value. If sections are accessed by their addresses then a re-arrangement of sections could cause users to be supplied with incorrect data.

This form of attack can be obviated by including the section address in the computation of the authenticator. The danger of restoration of previous sections can be met by including a version number, in each section, and maintaining a record of all version numbers in a separate authenticated file update record. The update record must itself be protected against restoration by the inclusion of a date/time stamp. *See* AUTHENTICATOR, CIPHER BLOCK CHAINING, CIPHER FEED-

BACK, CRYPTOGRAPHIC KEY, DATE/TIME STAMP, INITIALIZATION VECTOR, MESSAGE AUTHENTICATION.

replenishment deposit. In banking, a payment that increases the balance of the originator's account serviced by the receiver, e.g. the result of a bank transfer for its own account. (ANSI). *See* ORIGINATOR.

reporting line. *Synonymous with* ALARM LINE.

reproducibility . In information security, pertaining to a state in which a repeated evaluation of the same target of evaluation to the same security target by a different ITSEF yields the same overall verdict as the first ITSEF. *See* INFORMATION TECHNOLOGY SECURITY EVALUATION CRITERIA, INFORMATION TECHNOLOGY SECURITY EVALUATION MANUAL, SECURITY TARGET, TARGET OF EVALUATION.

repudiation. In communications security, denial by one of the entities involved in a communication of having participated in all or part of the communication. (ISO). *Compare* NONREPUDIATION. *See* DIGITAL SIGNATURE.

request for service message. In key management, a message that sends keys, intended for an ultimate recipient, to the key translation center for translation. *See* ANSI X9.17 - 1985, KEY TRANSLATION CENTER.

request reply service. In data communications, a connectionless service in which a sender sends a single datagram containing a request and the reply contains the answer. *See* CONNECTIONLESS SERVICE, DATAGRAM.

request response. In communications security, a technique to warn users that a delay/denial of service attack is in operation. If such attacks are initiated during a quiescent traffic state then intended receivers of messages will be unaware that messages are being blocked. Request response messages may be periodically sent between communicating parties to ensure that open communication paths exist. *See* DELAY/DENIAL OF SERVICE, HOT MODE, TRAFFIC ANALYSIS.

request service initiation. In key management, an optional message requesting the initiation of a new keying relationship. *See* ANSI X9.17 - 1985.

request to send. In data communications, a signal used in conjunction with another - clear to send - as a handshaking protocol in half duplex operation. The computer generates the request to send signal to the modem and awaits a clear to send signal before transmitting data. *Compare* CLEAR TO SEND. *See* HALF DUPLEX, HANDSHAKING, MODEM, RS-232C.

requirement. A statement of the system behavior needed to enforce a given policy. Requirements are used to derive the technical specification of a system. *See* POLICY, SPECIFICATION.

rescue dump. In computing, a complete dump of computer storage and states onto a peripheral device so that, in the event of a major system failure, e.g. loss of power supply, the program can be recommenced at the state of the last rescue dump. *See* DUMP.

Research in Secured Operating Systems. In computer security, a pattern directed analysis tool. *See* PATTERN DIRECTED ANALYSIS.

reset. (1) In program operation, to manually terminate a program on a microcomputer, (2) In program operation, to restore a register, storage location or storage device to its initial state.

resident software. In computing, any program held permanently in memory to provide a service to other programs, e.g. a resident compiler. *See* SOFTWARE, COMPILER.

residual error rate. In data communications, the ratio of the total number of bits, bytes or blocks incorrectly received but uncorrected or undetected by the error control device, to the total number of corresponding units transmitted.

residual intelligibility. In communications security, the proportion of a voice scrambled message that can be understood directly. *See* VOICE SCRAMBLING.

residual risk. In risk management, the portion of risk that remains after security measures have been applied. (AFR).

residue. (1) In mathematics, if b is congruent to c modulo n then b is a residue of c modulo n. *See* CONGRUENT. (2) In computer security, data left in storage after processing operations, and before degaussing or rewriting has taken place. (FIPS). *See* DEGAUSS. (3) In authentication. *See* MAC RESIDUE.

residues problems. In computer security, a class of security problems that can arise from information left in storage after processing. Such information may be unavailable to legitimate users but can be revealed by ingenious programmers, e.g. an erased file may remain on a disk and an erase flag prevents normal access via the operating system, however, the file can be resurrected by requisite programming. *See* OBJECT REUSE, PERSONAL COMPUTER SECURITY, RESIDUE.

resource. (1) In computer security, anything used or consumed while performing a function. The categories of resources are: time, information, objects (information containers), or processors (the ability to use information). Specific examples are: CPU time, terminal connect time, amount of directly addressable memory, disk space, number of I/O requests per minute etc. (DOD). *See* OBJECT. (2) In computer security, in an ADP system, any function, device, or data collection that may be allocated to users or programs. (FIPS).

resource sharing. (1) In computer operations, in an ADP system, the concurrent use of a resource by more than one user, job or program. (FIPS). *See* RESOURCE. (2) In computer networks, the joint use of resources available on a system, or network, by users or peripherals, e.g. microcomputer users in a local area network can share a hard disk drive or printer. *See* HARD DISK, LOCAL AREA NETWORK, SERVER.

resource sharing computer system. A computer system that uses its resources, including input/output (I/0) devices, storage, central processor (arithmetic and logic units), control units, and software processing capabilities, to enable one or more users to manipulate data and process coresident programs in an apparently simultaneous manner. The term includes systems with one or more of the capabilities commonly referred to as timesharing, multiprogramming, multiaccessing, multiprocessing or concurrent processing. (DODD).

responder. In communications, a device that automatically transmits a predetermined signal when activated by a received signal. *Compare* TRANSPONDER.

response service message. In key management, a message providing an authenticated response to a key service message. *See* ANSI X9.17 - 1985, KEY SERVICE MESSAGE.

response time. (1) The time taken by a system to attain a specified state or produce a specified output, after receiving an input. (2) In computing, the time between the generation of the last character at the terminal and receipt of the first character of the reply.

response to request service message. In key management, a message used in response to an RFS, ERS or RSI. *See* ANSI X9.17 - 1985, ERS, RFS, RSI.

restricted area. In physical security, any area to which access is subject to special restrictions or controls for reasons of security or safeguarding of property or material. (AR).

result-based perturbation. In database security, a form of perturbation in which the correct statistic is computed and the result itself is perturbed, typically by some form of rounding. *Compare* RECORD BASED PERTURBATION. *See* INFERENCE, PERTURBATION, STATISTICAL DATABASE.

retailer. In banking, the card acceptor in a retail EFTPOS system. (SAA). *See* CARD ACCEPTOR.

retention period. In data security, the length of time for which a file is to be kept before it is overwritten. The retention period and the date on which the file was written are used to calculate the earliest date on which the file expires. The date the file was written and the retention period or the expiry date will be written as part of the file label and will be used as a security precaution against the accidental destruction of a file.

retro target. In physical security, a transceiver sensor that employs a reflector to return the beam back to the receiver section of the transceiver. *See* TRANSCEIVER.

reusability. In computing, the extent to which a program can be used in other applications and is related to the packaging and scope of functions that the program performs.

reverse engineering. A process by which the design of a product is determined by a detailed study of the product itself, e.g. the software on a ROM can be determined by a microscopic study of the ROM chip. Such techniques have implications for manufacturers protecting product design. *See* ROM.

reverse funds transfer. In banking, a debit transfer in which the credit party is the sender. (ANSI). *See* DEBIT PARTY.

reverse interrupt. In data communications, a control character sequence sent by the receiving station, in a binary synchronous communications system, to request a premature termination of the transmission in progress. *See* BINARY SYNCHRONOUS COMMUNICATIONS.

reversible encryption. In cryptography, a DEA transformation of cleartext in such a way that the encrypted text can be decrypted back to the original cleartext. (ANSI). *Compare* IRREVERSIBLE ENCRYPTION. *See* DEA.

review and approval. In computer security, the process whereby information pertaining to the security and integrity of an ADP activity or network is collected, analyzed, and submitted to the appropriate DAA for accreditation of the activity or network. (OPNAVINST) *See* DAA.

RF. Radio Frequency.

RFE. *See* RADIO FREQUENCY EMISSIONS.

RFI. *See* RADIO FREQUENCY INTERFERENCE.

rfm. *See* RE-ENCIPHER FROM MASTER KEY.

rfmk. *See* RE-ENCIPHER FROM MASTER KEY.

RFS. *See* REQUEST FOR SERVICE MESSAGE.

ring. (1) In computing, a structure in which the last pointer of a chain list references the first element in the same list. (2) In data communications, a network topology in the form of a ring so that each node is connected only with two neighbors on each side. A break in the network affects all parties. *Compare* BUS, STAR. *See* LOCAL AREA NETWORK.

ring back. In data communications, a procedure that allows a telephone to be used both for computer connections and normal voice calls. Computer connections require two calls; the first, that is usually only one ring, alerts the modem that will not answer, however, unless the ringing stops for some period, typically 30 seconds. *Compare* CALL BACK, RING INDICATOR.

ring indicator. In data communications, a signal that indicates that a modem has received a new call. The ring indicator signal goes up and down as the telephone bell rings so that the computer can answer after a specified number of rings. *Compare* RING BACK. *See* MODEM, RS-232C.

risk. (1) In computer security, the loss potential that exists as the result of threat vulnerability pairs. Reducing either the threat or the vulnerability reduces the risk. (AFR). *See* THREAT, VULNERABILITY. (2) The uncertainty of loss expressed in terms of probability of such loss. (AR). *See* ALE. (3) In computer security, the probability or likelihood that a threat agent will successfully mount a specific attack against a particular system vulnerability. *Compare* SAFEGUARD. *See* MATRIX METHODOLOGY, RISK ANALYSIS, RISK ANALYSIS METHODOLOGIES, THREAT, VULNERABILITY.

risk analysis. (1) In risk management, a part of risk management that is used to minimize risk by effectively applying security measures commensurate with the relative threats, vulnerabilities, and values of the resources to be protected. The value of the resources includes impact on the organization the automated system supports, and the impact of the loss or unauthorized modification of data. Risk analysis consists of four modules: sensitivity assessment, risk assessment, economic assessment, and security test and evaluation. (AFR). *See* ECONOMIC ASSESSMENT, RISK ASSESSMENT, SECURITY TEST AND EVALUATION, SENSITIVITY ASSESSMENT. (2) In computer security, an analysis of system assets and vulnerabilities to establish an expected loss from certain events based on estimated probabilities of the occurrence of those events. (FIPS).

risk analysis methodologies. In risk management, a risk analysis can, in theory, provide management with the necessary data to implement information security procedures and systems in a cost-effective and consistent manner. However, in practice there is a wide divergence of views on the effectiveness of this approach and the methodology to be selected.

In the broadest sense the methodologies may be classified as:

- quantitative or qualitative;
- manual or automated.

Quantitative approaches, in the purest sense, aim to present a balance of costs of the security measure against the likely cost of not implementing the measure. An Annual Loss Expectancy (ALE) is based upon the concept, that in any one year there is a probability f, that an asset loss i will occur. Therefore the implied cost of taking no precautions is $ALE = f.i$. In these circumstances countermeasures with an annual cost of c will be cost-effective if they result in a reduced ALE, such that the reduction in

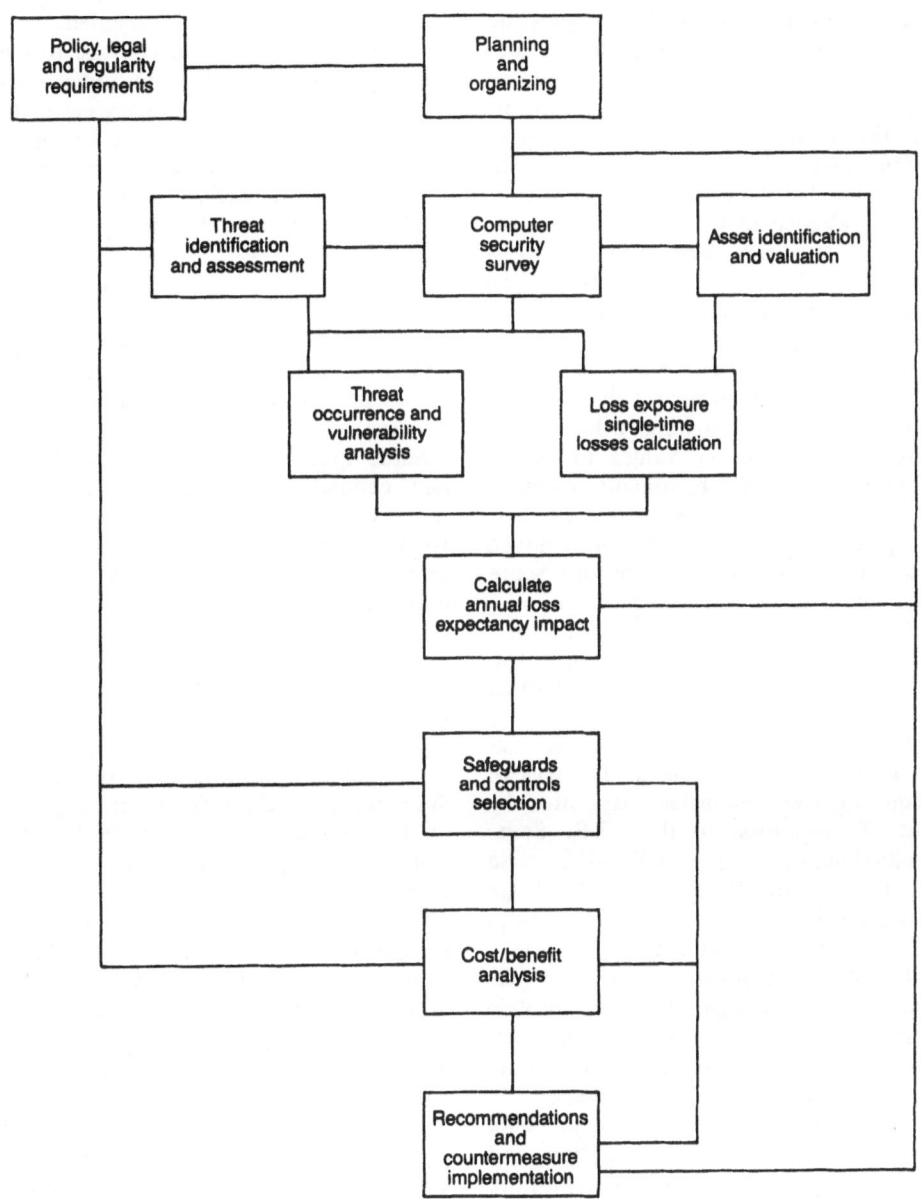

risk analysis
Risk assessment process Source: *System Security,* 1985 (London: Online Publications).

ALE is greater than c. In practice such calculations can often only be performed after extensive and expensive surveys, based upon inadequate and highly subjective data.

Other quantitative methodologies do not attempt such direct monetary calculations but aim at developing scores so that there can be some sensible prioritization in the implementation of countermeasures. It may be unrealistic to guarantee that the cost of security can be strictly aligned to the expected business loss. However, large organizations should have a means of ensuring that the security countermeasures are directed to the areas of greatest need.

Various methodologies such as CRAMM attempt to reduce the effect of subjectivity, by assigning value scores rather than monetary values to assets. Thus managers may be asked to estimate the likely effect of a loss of availability, integrity or confidentiality of a given data in operational terms, and to a score is assigned to the response.

Gaining an estimate of probability of a security incident impacting an organization, is even more problematic than that of asset valuation. Such estimations require considerable expertise and experience of risk assessment. The cost of acquiring such estimates may often be out of proportion to the ALE. Some methodologies e.g. CRAMM and MARION provide in-built knowledge bases so that some reasonable estimates may be achieved at an acceptable cost.

Qualitative approaches such as the matrix methodology aim to provide management with a concise picture of the risk situation without attempting to determine its financial implications.

Risk analyses involve a major data collection, collation, computation and reporting task. Many methodologies are supported by software packages to reduce the manual effort and paperwork. Nevertheless paper-based approaches have a number of advantages, particularly for initial risk studies which act as a

pilot for later and more detailed projects. Such approaches:

- require less initial training;
- provide considerable flexibility in the description of survey data;
- allow the survey to respond to the situation revealed in interviews etc. thus allowing interviewers to skip over questions that are obviously irrelevant to a particular section, to collect additional data that is clearly relevant etc.

Some computer based methodologies involve complex navigation through menus, may require intensive training, and complicate the task of recording and retrieving information for quite simple systems.

Some systems combine paper based and computer based approaches, e.g. using the computer to print out survey forms containing relevant local information etc. The sheer volume of data collected for a large survey presents problems of collation, report preparation etc. which can only be reasonably tackled by computer systems. Moreover there is often considerable potential duplication of effort in risk analyses, e.g. similar information processing systems used throughout an organization. Computer based methodologies can greatly facilitate the re-use of survey data for similar systems.

There is a potential disadvantage with computer based methodologies because some may encourage a black box approach, accepting input data and providing an internally computed response. The current state of the art of risk analysis is such that management need to be in a position to subject the whole process to critical study, to ensure that there are no hidden assumptions that are inappropriate to their organization. Audit trails which enable the results to be traced back to the survey data are important. In addition some systems provide 'what if' facilities which can, at least, enable management to explore the sensitivity of the results to local factors.

The black box problem is inherent in systems which contain an in-built knowledge base since the intellectual property of that base remains with the suppliers. The knowledge base may be updated by the suppliers but there is no opportunity for the organization to include its own evolving experience and expertise. *See* LAVA, CRAMM, MARION, MATRIX METHODOLOGY, QUANTITATIVE RISK ANALYSIS, RISK ANALYSIS, RISKCALC, THE BUDDY SYSTEM.

risk assessment. (1) In risk management, a study of the vulnerabilities, threats, likelihood, loss or impact, and theoretical effectiveness of security measures. Managers use the results of a risk assessment to develop security requirements and specifications. (AFR). *See* RISK ANALYSIS, THREAT, VULNERABILITY. (2) In computer security, an identification of a specific ADP Facility's assets, the threats to these assets, and the ADP Facility's vulnerability to those threats. (DOE). *See* RISK ANALYSIS, THREAT, VULNERABILITY. (3) In risk management, an analysis of system assets and vulnerabilities to establish an expected loss from certain events based on estimated probabilities of the occurrence of those events. The purpose of a risk assessment is to determine if countermeasures are adequate to reduce the probability of loss or the impact of loss to an acceptable level. (OPNAVINST). *See* RISK ANALYSIS, VULNERABILITY. (4) In risk management, the quantification of probability of an unfavorable outcome in the absence of any deliberate intervention. *See* MATRIX METHODOLOGY, RISK ANALYSIS.

RISKCALC. In risk management, a risk analysis methodology. *See* RISK ANALYSIS METHODOLOGIES.

risk index. In data security, the disparity between the minimum clearance or authorization of system users and the maximum sensitivity (e.g., classification and categories) of data processed by a system. (DOD). *See* ORANGE BOOK, SENSITIVITY.

risk management. (1) The total process to identify, control, and minimize the impact of uncertain events. The objective of the risk management program is to reduce risk and obtain and maintain DAA approval. The process facilitates the management of security risks by each level of management throughout the system life cycle. The approval process consists of three elements: risk analysis, certification, and approval. (AFR). *See* DAA, RISK ANALYSIS, RISK ASSESSMENT. (2) An element of managerial science concerned with the identification, measurement, control, and minimization of uncertain events. An effective risk management program encompasses the following four phases: (a) Risk assessment, as derived from an evaluation of threats and vulnerabilities. (b) Management decision. (c) Control implementation. (d) Effectiveness review. (AR). *See* RISK ANALYSIS, RISK ASSESSMENT. (3) A disciplined approach adopted to identify, measure and control uncertain events in order to minimize loss and optimize the return on the money invested for security purposes. The objective of risk management is to attain the most effective precautions against: destruction of assets, unauthorized modification or manipulation of company data, unauthorized disclosure of company data and denial of company assets and data processing services to unauthorized personnel. In the field of computer security, risk management encompasses risk analysis, management decision-making and implementation of security measures and reviews. *See* MATRIX METHODOLOGY, RISK ANALYSIS.

RISOS. *See* RESEARCH IN SECURED OPERATING SYSTEMS.

RJE. *See* REMOTE JOB ENTRY.

rogue fiber. In communications security, an active wiretap on a fiber optic cable which may be implemented by fusing a fiber onto the cable by the application of heat. *See* ACTIVE WIRE-TAPPING, FIBER OPTICS.

rollback. (1) In reliability, a technique of recovery from system failure. Recovery points are inserted at intervals in the program and when such a point is attained, in program operation, the total state of the system is stored in a protected standby memory. When a fault is detected a control unit switches over to standby memory, the status of the machine is restored and the program re-executed from the recovery point, the original memory now being used as standby. *See* TIME REDUNDANCY. (2) In databases, a technique employed to protect the database against incorrect user actions. The state of the database is preserved and subsequent transactions stored, if the user decides to implement the total set of transactions a commit command is issued, if the rollback command is employed the transactions are aborted and do not affect the database. *Compare* COMMIT.

roll call polling. In data communications, a method of polling in multidrop systems in which the controller sends messages addressed to each terminal in turn enquiring if they have any data to transmit. *Compare* HUB POLLING. *See* POLLING.

rolling up. *Synonymous with* GROUP-ING.

ROM. *See* READ ONLY MEMORY.

ROS. In communications security, a Swedish abbreviation for electromagnetic signals. *See* VAN ECK PHENOMENON.

rotation. In computer security, the policy of routinely moving files or their backup copies from the data center or tape library to locations outside the data center.

rotation of duties. In procedural security, a personnel policy in which staff are routinely moved to other duties after specified periods of time.

This policy prevents an individual from gaining a monopoly of knowledge and inhibits fraudulent activities. If one person remains in a post for an indefinite period then a situation can arise in which that individual becomes irreplaceable since he/she gains a monopoly of knowledge necessary to perform that task. This situation presents considerable difficulties if that person is unavoidably absent or cannot be contacted following a disaster.

A fraudulent operation may often require that the perpetrator is guaranteed supervision of a particular task over extended periods, such fraud is not uncommonly discovered when the perpetrator is unavoidably absent from the place of work. Rotation of duties reduces the opportunities for such fraudulent operations.

The disadvantages of rotation of duties include the operational disadvantages of breaking up effective working teams and retraining costs. Such rotation may also enable employees to gain a comprehensive knowledge of security arrangements in an organization. *Compare* SEPARATION OF DUTIES. *See* PERSONNEL SECURITY.

router. In data communications, a device that interconnects networks that use the same transport layer of the Open Systems Interconnection Reference Model but have different network layers. *Compare* GATEWAY, REPEATER, ROUTER. *See* NETWORK LAYER, OPEN SYSTEMS INTERCONNECTION, TRANSPORT LAYER.

routing. In data communications, the assignment of a path for a message or packet to attain its ultimate destination. *See* ADAPTIVE ROUTING, DATA COMMUNICATIONS, DIRECTORY ROUTING, HOT POTATO ROUTING.

routing control. (1) In communications security, a security service in open systems interconnection security that prevents data being transmitted over links, or through relays, that are not considered to provide an adequate level of security for the data in question. *See* OSI SECURITY, ROUTING. (2) In communications security, the application of rules during the process of routing so as to chose or avoid specific networks, links or relays. (ISO).

routing table. In data communications, a table, at a node of a message switching network, indicating the preferred, and sometimes second preference, outgoing line for each destination. *See* FIXED ROUTING, DIRECTORY ROUTING, ROUTING.

RS. In data communications, a prefix used by the Electronic Industries Association for widely used standards in North America. *Compare* V, X. *See* ELECTRONIC INDUSTRIES ASSOCIATION, RS-232C, RS-366, RS-423A, RS-449.

RS-232C. In data communications, an extremely popular standard employed in serial connections for computers. The official title is Interface between Data Terminal Equipment and Data Circuit Termination Equipment employing serial binary interface. The C in the prefix indicates that it has been revised.

The standard has four parts :

- electrical signal characteristics;
- interface mechanical characteristics;
- functional description of the signals;
- list of standard interface types.

The electrical signal characteristics define the voltages corresponding to the binary signal values. The mechanical characteristics describe the disposition and size of the plug pins. The functional description of the signals defines 21 signals and the list of standard subsets of these signals used in different types of modems.

The corresponding CCITT recommendations are V.24 and V.28. The RS-232C was designed for interconnection between a computer and modem at one end of a telephone connection, and a terminal and modem at the other end. It is also commonly employed for the interconnection of two DTE's but in this respect it has the disadvantage that transmission is limited to a maximum distance of 50 feet and maximum transmission rate of 19,200 bits per second. The RS-232C standard does not cover the protocol for answering calls and modem control for reversing direction in a half duplex link. *Compare* RS-366, RS-423A, RS-449. *See* CCITT, MODEM, NULL MODEM, V.24, V.28.

RS-232. *See* RS-232C.

RS-366. In data communications, an EIA standard that defines how the computer presents digits, to be dialed, to the autodialer, how the computer signals the end of the number and the actions taken when the autodialer cannot complete the call. *See* AUTODIALER, EIA, RS-232C, V.25.

RS-422A. In data communications, an EIA interface standard for high data rates, 100 kilobits per second over 40 feet or 1 kilobits per second over 4,000 feet. It uses two wires for each signal. Unlike the RS-232C standard it only comprises the electrical specifications. *Compare* RS-423A. *See* DATA RATE, EIA, RS-232C, V.11, X.27.

RS-423A. In data communications, an EIA interface standard using unbalanced transmissions for lower transmission rates than the RS-422A standard, 100,000 bits per second over 40 feet and 1000 bits per second over 4,000 feet. Like the RS-422A standard it only comprises electrical specifications. *Compare* RS-422A. *See* DATA RATE, EIA, RS-232C.

RS-449. In data communications, a standard designed to replace RS-232C. *See* RS-232C.

RSA. In cryptography, Rivest-Shamir-Adleman, an algorithm named after its designers that is of extreme importance in public key cryptography. It uses a trapdoor one-way function based upon the computational difficulty of factoring the product of large prime numbers (i.e. integers with several hundred decimal digits). Thus the computation involved in multiplying two large prime numbers p and q is minimal but it is computationally infeasible to derive the factors p and q from a product n consisting of several hundred decimal digits. However, there have been reports of successful attempts to factorize large products of primes by use of networked workstations. A large number of such workstations are employed with the factorizing algorithm operating in background mode, thus the cost of the operation is comparatively low, and the process usually takes several weeks.

The process of developing the keys and encrypting/decrypting the messages are described below.

- Two large prime numbers (p and q) are randomly selected and their product n is determined. This value of n is made public.
- The Euler totient function of n, i,e, the number of integers in the range 1...n-1 that are coprime with n, is determined. Since p and q are primes the Euler totient function is given by:
$\phi(n) = (p-1)(q-1)$, provided that p $<>$ q. This value is kept secret.
- Select an integer E in the range of 2...$\phi(n)$-1, such that E is coprime with p-1 and q-1. This is the public encrypting key.
- Calculate the private deciphering key D by:
$ED \equiv 1 \mod (\phi(n))$.
- D is the deciphering key and is kept secret, the values of E and n are made public, but the calculation of D demands a knowledge of $\phi(n)$ and computation of this function by an attacker involves the computationally infeasible factoring of n into p and q.
- The public encrypting key E, and n, are made publicly available, e.g. in a directory.
- For encryption the data is broken into blocks M_1, M_2,... with block lengths chosen so that the individual message blocks have a numerical value less than n. The blocks are then raised to the power E, modulo n, i.e. the ciphertext blocks C_1 etc. are calculated by:

$$C_1 \equiv (M_1)^E \mod n$$
$$C_2 \equiv (M_2)^E \mod n$$

- Decryption of the ciphertext message is performed by a similar operation, to that described above, except that the ciphertext blocks are raised to the power D, modulo n, i.e.:

$$M_i \equiv (C_i)^D \mod n \equiv (M_i)^{ED} \mod n$$

- The original message is recovered by the deciphering process since according to Euler's theorem

$$M \equiv M^x \mod n \text{ if}$$
$$x \equiv 1 \mod \phi(n).$$

This process can be illustrated by a simple example.

- Select p = 101, q = 103. Hence n = 101 x 103 = 10403.
- $\phi(n) = (p-1)(q-1) = 10200$.
- Select E to be coprime with 10200 and in the range 2 - 10119, let E = 97.
- Compute D using Euler's Generalization:
  $97.D = 1 \pmod{10200}$.

Compute $\phi(\phi(n))$, i.e. the number of integers in the range 1.. 10199 that are coprime with 10200, $\phi(\phi(10403)) = 2560$.

$$D \equiv E^{(\phi(\phi(n))-1)} \bmod (\phi(n))$$

$$\equiv 97^{(2559)} \bmod (10200)$$

$$= 8833$$

Note 97 x 8833 = 856801 (mod 10200) = 1 (mod 10200).

- E and n are published in a public directory as 97 and 10403 respectively.
- Sender wishes to send message M = 33. This is encrypted as C = $33^{97} \pmod{10403} = 4933$.
- The receiver decrypts this message using the secret key D:

$$D = 4933^{8833} \pmod{10403} = 33.$$

It would appear that an attacker could decrypt the message by repeated encryption thus raising the ciphertext message by successive powers modulo n, until plaintext was recovered. In practice, however, with encryption and decryption keys using 100 or more decimal digits the number of iterations would be excessive and this form of attack would be computationally infeasible.

There have been a number of studies on potential attacks on RSA, these have indicated that the integers p and q need to be selected with some care and both p-1 and q-1 should have one large factor each.

RSA is a major step forward in public key cryptography and it provides an elegant method of digital signature. The encryption/decryption processes are more computationally demanding than those of DES, and knapsack ciphers, and may therefore impact upon the maximum data rates for network encryption systems. The size of keys for RSA are also considerably greater than those for DES but are less than that required for knapsack ciphers.

In key management RSA could be employed to encipher the DES keys in a network thus removing the requirement of complex techniques to transmit key-encrypting keys; the traffic in key-encrypting keys is much lower than that of network data and the additional computational load of RSA encryption/decryption would not significantly affect the throughput. *Compare* KNAP-SACK CIPHER. *See* COPRIME, DES, EULER'S GENERALIZATION, EULER TOTIENT FUNCTION, KEY-ENCRYPTING KEY, MODULO ARITHMETIC, PRIME NUMBER, PUBLIC KEY CRYPTOGRAPHY, TRAPDOOR ONE-WAY FUNCTION.

RSI. *See* ANSI X9.17 - 1985, REQUEST SERVICE INITIATION.

RSM. *See* ANSI X9.17 - 1985, RESPONSE SERVICE MESSAGE.

RTM. *See* RE-ENCIPHER TO MASTER KEY.

rtmk. *See* RE-ENCIPHER TO MASTER KEY.

RTR. *See* ANSI X9.17 - 1985, RESPONSE TO REQUEST SERVICE MESSAGE.

rule. In computing, a statement in an expert system that enables the likelihood of an assertion, or the value of an object, to be established. A rule combines lower level assertions or objects to produce a value for a higher level assertion or object. *See* EXPERT SYSTEMS, OB-

JECT, RULE-BASED SYSTEM.

rule-based access control. In access control, access control based on the specific rules relating to the nature of the subject and object, beyond just their identities - such as security labels. *Compare* IDENTITY BASED ACCESS CONTROL. *See* MANDATORY ACCESS CONTROL.

rule based security policy. In data security, a security policy based upon global rules imposed for all users. These rules usually rely on a comparison of the sensitivity of the resources being accessed and the possession of corresponding attributes by users, a group of users or entities acting on their behalf. (ISO). *Compare* IDENTITY BASED SECURITY POLICY. *See* RULE BASED ACCESS CONTROL.

rule-based system. In computing, an expert system that consists of a set of antecedent-consequent rules, a database and an executive. The rules are conditional statements that describe how to modify the database when certain patterns are recognized in the data. The executive looks after pattern matching, monitoring database changes, deciding that rule should be executed next and performance of the execution. *See* DATABASE, EXPERT SYSTEMS.

running key. *Synonymous with* KEY STREAM.

run to run totals. In computing, the utilization of output control totals resulting from one process as input control totals over subsequent processing. The control totals are used as links in a chain to tie one process to another in a sequence of processes or one cycle to another over a period of time.

R/W. Read/Write.

S

S-847. In computer security, a virus that terminates and stays resident, infects COM files, affects run-time operation, corrupts program and OVL files. *See* VIRUS NAMES.

sabotage. In legislation, the premeditated destruction of personnel, property or physical plant in an effort to disrupt or terminate manufacturing or other operations by a government or by a private enterprise.

Saddam. In computer security, a virus that terminates and stays resident, infects COMMAND.COM and COM files, affects run-time operation, corrupts program, OVL and data files and file linkage. *See* VIRUS NAMES.

safeguard. In computer security, a protective measure to mitigate against the effect of system vulnerability. *See* MATRIX METHODOLOGY, VULNERABILITY.

safeguarding statement. In data security, a statement affixed to computer outputs which states the highest classification being processed in an automated system at the time the product was produced and requiring its control at that level until a responsible person can determine its true classification. (AR).

safe prime. In mathematics, a prime number of the form $2p + 1$, where p is an odd prime. Safe primes are significant in RSA because they provide greater protection against sophisticated factoring algorithms. *See* FACTORING, ODD PRIME, RSA.

safety. In physical security, the property that a system will satisfy certain criteria related to the preservation of personal and collective safety.

SAGITTAIRE. In banking, Systéme Automatique de Gestion Intégré par Télétransmission de Transaction Avec Imputation de Règlements Etrangers, an electronic interbank payment service operated by the Banque de France within France for SWIFT members and sub-members located in France and which handles French franc payments only. (ANSI). *See* BANKING NETWORKS, SWIFT.

SAISS. Subcommittee on Automated Information System Security.

salami technique. In computer security, a form of Trojan Horse which has the effect of adding small amounts to a fraudster's account over long periods. The fractions of lowest denomination coins, produced by arithmetic processing, are rounded off and then credited to the perpetrator's account. *Compare* CHECK KITING. *See* MALICIOUS CODE. *Synonymous with* FRENCH ROUNDOFF.

same day funds. In banking, signifies funds available for transfer today, subject to the settlement of the transaction through the payment mechanism used. (ANSI).

sampling. In database security. *See* RANDOM SAMPLE QUERIES.

sandwich tape. In access control, a material used for magnetic stripes which is designed to increase the difficulty of

459

manufacturing counterfeit magnetic stripe cards. The stripe material comprises a low coercivity material bonded above a high coercivity material. A high intensity field is used to encode the stripe such that both materials are magnetized. In the reader the stripe is first subject to a low intensity erase field which demagnetizes the low coercivity material. If a counterfeiter uses conventional magnetic material then the forged data will be removed by the erasing field. On the other hand a counterfeiter using the sandwich material must have access to expensive magnetic encoders capable of developing the high magnetic fields necessary to magnetize the high coercivity layer. *Compare* WATERMARK TAPE. *See* COERCIVITY, MAGNETIC STRIPE CARD.

sanitization. (1) In data security, a technique by which it is permissible to assign a security classification to a data item that is lower than that of the data from which it was derived. For example the total wages bill for an organization could well be given a lower classification than that allocated to managers' salaries, even though the managers' salaries would be used in the summation. *See* MULTILEVEL DATABASE SECURITY. (2) In data security, the elimination of classified information from magnetic media to permit the reuse of the media at a lower classification level or to permit the release to uncleared personnel or personnel without the proper information access authorizations. (DOE). *See* SANITIZING.

sanitizing. (1) In data security, to erase or alter sensitive data in order to reduce its sensitivity. *See* SENSITIVE INFORMATION. (2) In data security, the degaussing or overwriting of sensitive information in magnetic or other storage media. (FIPS). *Synonymous with* SCRUBBING. *See* SANITIZATION.

saturation testing. In data communica-tions, a technique of checking the performance of a communications network by means of a large bulk of messages. It is undertaken to check for system faults that only arise in exceptional circumstances, e.g. the simultaneous arrival of two messages. *Compare* FLOOD TESTING.

Saturday 14th. In computer security, a virus that terminates and stays resident, infects COM, EXE and OVL files, formats or overwrites all or part of disk, affects run-time operation, corrupts program and OVL files and file linkage. *See* VIRUS NAMES.

S box. In cryptography, substitution box, a component of an encryption algorithm which performs a substitution cipher on the input signal. *Compare* P BOX. *See* CRYPTOGRAPHY, DATA ENCRYPTION STANDARD, SUBSTITUTION CIPHER. *Synonymous with* SUBSTITUTION BOX.

scalar. In mathematics, a quantity that takes a single numerical value, e.g. height. *Compare* VECTOR.

scalar product. In mathematics, a method of multiplying two vectors to produce a scalar. The scalar product of vectors $(a_1, a_2.....a_n)$ and $(b_1, b_2.....b_n)$ is given by

$$S = \sum_n a_i.b_i.$$ *Synonymous with* DOT PRODUCT.

scan. In computing, a procedure to investigate every node in the structure. *See* NODE.

scanner. In communications security, a device used to intercept radio communications usually in the citizen band, cellular radio, police, fire, ambulance transmissions, etc. areas.

scanning. In computer security, searching for telephone numbers and passwords by successively trying various combinations of numbers and letters. *See* EXHAUSTIVE ATTACK, HACKER. *Synonymous with* HACK HACK.

scavenging. In computer security, searching through residue for the purpose of unauthorized data acquisition. (FIPS). *Compare* BROWSING. *See* RESIDUE.

scenario analysis. *Synonymous with* FLAW HYPOTHESIS METHODOLOGY.

scheduled circuits. In data communications, leased circuits provided by British Telecom specially conditioned for data use. *See* CONDITIONING.

schema. In databases, a map of the overall logical structure of a database.

schematic. A diagram of a system's components and their interconnections or interrelationships.

Schnorr cipher. In cryptography, a variation on RSA which has shorter signatures and faster signature generation. *See* DIGITAL SIGNATURE, RSA.

SCI. *See* SENSITIVE COMPARTMENTED INFORMATION.

scientific and technical information. Communicable knowledge or information resulting from or pertaining to the conduct and management of R&D efforts. STI is used by administrators, managers, scientists, and engineers engaged in scientific and technological efforts and is the basic intellectual resource for and result of such effort. (DODD).

SCOMP. In computer security, Secure COMmunications Processor. The name given to the Honeywell Level 6 minicomputer modified to increase its protection capability. Four protection rings were added along with user-initiated

input/output to direct-memory access devices. (MTR). *See* PROTECTION RING, SECURITY KERNEL.

Scott's Valley. In computer security, a computer virus that encrypts itself, terminates and stays resident, infects COM, EXE and OVL files, affects runtime operation, corrupts program, OVL and data files and file linkage. *See* VIRUS NAMES.

scrambler. (1) In communications, a coding device applied to communication links for security purposes or to avoid harmful repetitive patterns of digital data. Such repetitive patterns may arise in phase modulated systems and produce a zero phase shift over a comparatively long period, with a resultant loss in synchronization between the transmitter and receiver decoders. *See* PHASE MODULATION. (2) In communications security. *See* VOICE SCRAMBLING.

scrolling. In computing, the continuous horizontal or vertical movement of a screen display such that new data appears at one edge whilst old data disappears from another.

scroll mode terminal. In data communications, a terminal without local intelligence, keystrokes are displayed and transmitted individually and received characters are displayed as received. The displayed lines scroll upwards as they are filled by displayed characters. *Compare* FORM MODE TERMINAL, PAGE MODE TERMINAL.

scrubbing. *Synonymous with* SANITIZING.

SDLC. *See* SOFTWARE DEVELOPMENT LIFE CYCLE, SYNCHRONOUS DATA LINK CONTROL.

SDU. *See* SERVICE DATA UNIT.

search key. In databases, the data to be

compared with a specific part of each item in a search. *See* KEY.

SECDED. In codes, Single Error Correction Double Error Detection, an error correction and detection code which can detect and correct one bit errors and detect but not correct two bit errors. Simple parity checks can only detect but not correct one bit errors whilst two bit errors cannot even be detected. *See* BIT, ERROR CORRECTION CODE, ERROR DETECTION CODE, HAMMING CODE, PARITY CHECKING.

secondary channel. In data communications, a data channel derived from the same physical path as the main data channel but completely independent from it. It carries auxiliary information, at a low data rate, dealing with device control, diagnostics etc. *See* CHANNEL.

secondary destination. In data communications, any of the destinations specified in a message except the first.

secondary key. (1) In key management. *Compare* PRIMARY KEY. *Synonymous with* KEY-ENCRYPTING KEY. (2) In databases, a key that does not uniquely define a record. A key that contains the value of an attribute other than the unique identifier. *Compare* PRIMARY KEY. *See* ATTRIBUTE.

secondary station. In data communications, a station selected to receive information from a primary station. The designation of secondary status is only temporary, it is produced by the primary station for the duration of the message transmission. *See* PRIMARY STATION.

second normal form. In databases, a property of a relation in a relational database. A relation is in second normal form if it is in first normal form and every nonprime attribute of the relation is fully functional dependent upon each candidate key of the relation. An exam-

ple of a relation not in second normal form is EMPLOYEE-NUMBER, PROJECT-NUMBER, PROJECT-NAME, PROJECT-COMPLETION-DATE. The pair EMPLOYEE-NUMBER, PROJECT-NAME is a candidate key for the relation but PROJECT-COMPLETION-DATE is functionally dependent upon a subset of this key, i.e. PROJECT-NUMBER and is thus not fully functional dependent upon the candidate key. The disadvantage of this relation arises if only one employee is assigned to a project and that employee resigns. All records pertaining to the employee are deleted and details of the PROJECT-COMPLETION-DATE are lost even though the project may be live. *Compare* FIRST NORMAL FORM, THIRD NORMAL FORM. *See* CANDIDATE KEY, FULLY FUNCTIONAL DEPENDENT, NONPRIME ATTRIBUTE, NORMAL FORMS, RELATIONAL DATABASE.

second sourcing. (1) The licensing of rights for manufacturing electronic components, typically a microprocessor. (2) The securing of component supplies from two or more separate sources.

secrecy. *Synonymous with* CONFIDENTIALITY.

secrecy classification. In data security, an attribute of data or objects which expresses the relative potential damage arising if the data or object is compromised to an adversary. *See* COMPROMISE.

secrecy order. In legislation, a U.S. government order, normally related to patent applications, which forbids disclosure of information or an invention when it is ruled that such disclosure would be harmful to national security.

secrecy policy. In data security, a security policy to prevent unauthorized users from reading sensitive information (TNI). *Compare* INTEGRITY POLICY. *See*

SECURITY POLICY.

Secret. *See* CLASSIFICATION.

secret clearance. In access control, a U.S. Department of Defense clearance which typically requires a national agency check consisting of a search of U.S. Federal Bureau of Investigation fingerprint and investigative files and the Defense Central Index of Investigations. In some cases further investigation is required. *Compare* CONFIDENTIAL CLEARANCE, UNCLEARED, UNCLASSIFIED INFORMATION, TOP SECRET CLEARANCE, ONE CATEGORY, MULTIPLE CATEGORIES. *See* CLEARANCE.

secret key. In cryptography, the key (in an asymmetric or public key cryptosystem) of a user's key set which may be known only by that user. (ISO). *Compare* PUBLIC KEY. *See* ASYMMETRIC ALGORITHM, PUBLIC KEY CRYPTOGRAPHY.

secret key algorithm. *Synonymous with* SYMMETRIC CRYPTOSYSTEM.

secret key encryption. In cryptography, an encryption algorithm that only uses secret keys. *Compare* PUBLIC KEY CRYPTOGRAPHY. *See* ENCRYPTION ALGORITHM. *Synonymous with* PRIVATE KEY ENCRYPTION.

secret sharing scheme. In cryptography, a technique which enables a group of n people to share knowledge of a secret key, and for the key to be later derived from their shared knowledge if some of the members are subsequently unavailable. With an appropriate secret sharing technique, for some given value t (t < n), any subgroup of t members have sufficient information to derive the key, but it is infeasible for any smaller subgroup to do so. Such techniques may be used to distribute a master key amongst a group of trusted managers. *See* THRESHOLD.

sector. In computing, a portion of a rotational magnetic storage device that can be accessed by the magnetic heads in the course of a particular rotation. Magnetic disks are divided into circular tracks and each track is then subdivided into sectors holding a block of data. A sector is the smallest element of disk store that can be addressed by the computer.

secure channel. In communications security, an information path in which the set of all possible senders can be known to the receivers, or the set of all possible receivers can be known to the senders, or both. *See* RECEIVER, SENDER.

secure configuration management. In computer security, the use of procedures appropriate for controlling changes to a system's hardware and software structure for the purpose of insuring that such changes will not lead to a decreased data security. (FIPS). *See* DATA SECURITY.

secure management information base. In communications security, a conceptual database proposed for open systems interconnection security which will hold security relevant information required by end users in open systems. *See* OSI SECURITY.

secure module. *Synonymous with* TAMPER RESISTANT MODULE.

secure operating system. In computer security, an operating system that effectively controls hardware and software functions in order to provide the level of protection appropriate to the value of the data and resources managed by the operating system. (FIPS). *See* BELL-LA PADULA MODEL, OPERATING SYSTEM, RESOURCE.

secure path. *Synonymous with* TRUSTED PATH.

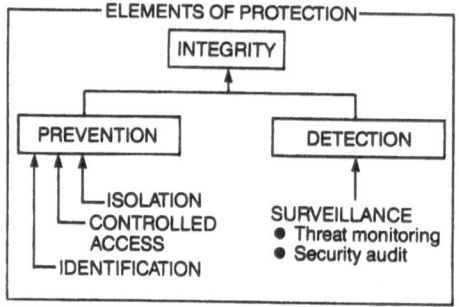

ELEMENTS OF PROTECTION

INTEGRITY

PREVENTION   DETECTION

ISOLATION
CONTROLLED
ACCESS
IDENTIFICATION

SURVEILLANCE
● Threat monitoring
● Security audit

secure operating system
Structure for developing secure operating system requirements. Prevention represents the passive line of defense, while detection implies not only discovering attempts, but also initiating effective reaction. Integrity is the assurance that the system works as intended, that all access attempts are mediated, that security control is maintained at all times, and that there are no unknown operational modes. Reproduced with permission of IBM Corp.

secure state. In computer security, a known, intended condition through the use of protected or trusted software. In periods processing, the secure state may be reached by booting the controlled copy of the operating system at the beginning of each session. (AFR). *See* PERIODS PROCESSING, TRUSTED SOFTWARE.

secure telephone system. In computer security, a telephone system in which the security of the communications is enforced by voice scrambling and/or online supervision circuitry. *See* VOICE SCRAMBLING.

secure working area. In data security, an accredited facility which is used for handling, discussing, or processing sensitive defense information. (AR). *See* SENSITIVE DEFENSE INFORMATION.

security. The quality or state of being cost-effectively protected from undue losses (e.g., loss of goodwill, monetary loss, loss of ability to continue operations, etc.). *See* ADD-ON SECURITY, ADMINISTRATIVE SECURITY, COMMUNICATIONS SECURITY, COMPUTER SECURITY, DATA SECURITY, EMANATION SECURITY, PERSONNEL SECURITY, PHYSICAL SECURITY, PROCEDURAL SECURITY, TELEPROCESSING SECURITY, TRAFFIC FLOW SECURITY.

security architecture. In computer security and communications security, the subset of computer architecture dealing with the security of the computer or network system (TNI). *See* NETWORK ARCHITECTURE.

security area. In physical security, a physically defined space containing classified matter (documents or material) subject to physical protection and personnel access controls. (DOE). *See* RESTRICTED AREA.

security audit. (1) In data security, an examination of data security procedures and measures for the purpose of evaluating their adequacy and compliance with established policy. (FIPS). (2) In data security, an independent review and examination of system records and activities in order to test for adequacy of system controls, to ensure compliance with established policy and operational procedures and to recommend any indicated changes in controls, policies and procedures. (ISO).

security audit trail. In data security, data collected and potentially used to facilitate a security audit. (ISO). *See* SECURITY AUDIT.

security breach. In data security, a violation of security controls producing the danger of loss of system components or compromise of information.

security compliant channel. In communications security, a channel in which the enforcement of the network policy depends only upon the characteristics of the channel either (a) included in the evaluation, or (b) assumed as an installation constraint and clearly documented in Trusted Facility Manual (TNI).

security critical mechanisms. In computer security, those security mechanisms whose correct operation is necessary to ensure the security policy is enforced. The mechanisms may or may not be part of the TCB. (AFR). *See* SECURITY POLICY, TCB.

security feasibility study. In computer security, a study to determine if controls are available to meet the security objectives, the extent to which they will satisfy the objectives, whether the controls should be recuperative, preventive or detective and the optimum mix of administrative, physical and technical controls. *See* RISK ANALYSIS.

security filter. (1) In computer security, a set of software routines and techniques employed in ADP systems to prevent automatic forwarding of specified data over unprotected links or to unauthorized persons. (FIPS). *See* SECURITY KERNEL. (2) In database security. *See* FILTER.

security flow analysis. In computer security, a type of security analysis performed on a nonprocedural formal system specification which locates potential flows of information between system variables. By assigning security levels to system variables, many indirect information channels can be identified.

Security flow analysis defines a security model similar to the access control model (Bell-La Padula) but with a finer protection granularity. (MTR). *See* BELL-LA PADULA MODEL, GRANULARITY.

security function. In information security, a statement on the type of security implemented to meet a security objective. *Compare* SECURITY MECHANISM, SECURITY OBJECTIVE. *See* INFORMATION TECHNOLOGY SECURITY EVALUATION CRITERIA.

security incident. In data security, any act or circumstance that involves classified information that deviates from the requirements of governing security publications, for example, compromise, possible compromise, inadvertent disclosure, and deviation. (AFR).

security inspection. In computer security, an examination of an ADP system to determine compliance with ADP security policy, procedures, and practices. (OPNAVINST).

security kernel. (1) In computer security, a localized mechanism, composed of hardware and software, that controls the access of users (and processes executing on their behalf) to repositories of information resident in or connected to the system. The correct operation of the kernel along with any associated trusted processes should be sufficient to guarantee enforcement of the constraints on access. TCBs have

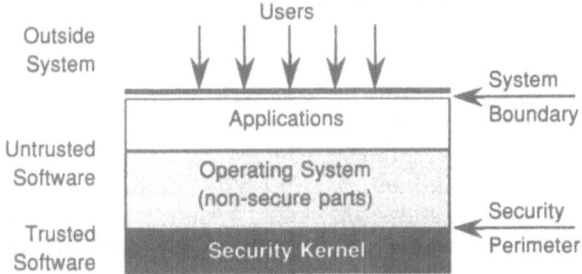

security kernel

been implemented using security kernels along with trusted processes. (MTR). *See* TCB. (2) In computer security, the hardware, firmware, and software elements of a TCB that implement the reference monitor concept. It must mediate all accesses, be protected from modification, and be verifiable as correct. (DOD). *See* REFERENCE MONITOR CONCEPT, TCB. (3) In computer security, the central part of a computer system (software and hardware) that implements the fundamental security procedures for controlling access to system resources. (FIPS). *See* ACCESS CONTROL, FILTER, RESOURCE.

security label. (1) In access control, the marking bound to a resource (which may be a data unit) that names or designates the security attributes of that resource. (ISO). (2) In data security, a sensitivity indicator which is permanently associated with protected data, processes and or other resources and which may be used in enforcing security policy. *See* SPRAY PAINT. (3) *Synonymous with* SENSITIVITY LABEL.

security level. In computer security, the combination of hierarchical classification and a set of non-hierarchical categories that represent the sensitivity of information. (DOD). *See* SENSITIVITY.

security life. In cryptography, the time span over which cryptographically protected data has value. (ANSI).

security line. *Synonymous with* ALARM LINE.

security log. In computer security, a record of all computer events that are considered to be security relevant, and maintained for intrusion detection or post hoc investigations of suspected computer misuse. *See* INTRUSION DETECTION.

security loop. *Synonymous with* ALARM LINE.

security management. *See* OSI SECURITY.

security measures. In computer security, elements of software, firmware, hardware, or procedures that are included in the system for the satisfaction of security specifications. (AFR). *See* FIRMWARE.

security mechanism. In information security, the means employed to implement a security function. *Compare* SECURITY FUNCTION, SECURITY OBJECTIVE. *See* INFORMATION TECHNOLOGY SECURITY EVALUATION CRITERIA.

security model. In computer security, a model that defines the system enforced security rules. It specifies the access controls on the use of information and how information will be allowed to flow through the system. It also provides the mechanism for specifying how to change access controls and interfaces dynamically without compromising system security.

security modem. In computer security, a modem installed in a user terminal with integrated security functions. Such modems incorporate outbound call-screening security to control host access from the user end. The user enters a password for a given host computer, the security modem checks the password against host computer telephone numbers and if a match is found the modem dials up the computer and initiates log on procedures. *Compare* PORT PROTECTION DEVICE. *See* MODEM, TELEPHONE INTRUSION.

security module. A module employed for secure cryptographic processing. *Synonymous with* TAMPER RESISTANT MODULE.

security monitor. In physical security, a device which provides supervision of an alarm line and associated equipment. *See* ALARM LINE.

security objective. In information security, a statement on the rationale of security requirements, such objectives are required to specify the requisite security functions and mechanisms. *Compare* SECURITY FUNCTION, SECURITY MECHANISM. *See* INFORMATION TECHNOLOGY SECURITY EVALUATION CRITERIA.

security parameter. *See* CRYPTOGRAPHIC KEY, INITIALIZATION VECTOR, PASSWORD.

security perimeter. *Synonymous with* CONTROL ZONE.

security peripheral. *Synonymous with* CRYPTOGRAPHIC FACILITY.

security policy. (1) In data security, the set of criteria for the provision of security services. (ISO). *See* IDENTITY BASED SECURITY POLICY, RULE BASED SECURITY POLICY, SECURITY SERVICE. (2) In computer security, the set of laws, rules, and practices that regulate how an organization manages, protects, and distributes sensitive information. (DOD). *See* SENSITIVE INFORMATION. (3) In communications security, the statement of the rules for the provision of security services for one or more instances of communication. A security policy is based upon those security services required and enforced by the appropriate system administration and also other security services requested by an entity wishing to communicate with the system. *See* DISCRETIONARY SECURITY, MANDATORY SECURITY. (4) In information security, a security policy is a course or general plan of action to be adopted by an organization to ensure that the information assets are protected in terms of confidentiality, authenticity and availability.

Overview
An organizational policy defines the security requirements, responsibilities and control for the organization. The security policy will define the main security objectives to be achieved and will encompass the organizational view on risk, and the security framework to achieve the business objectives. It is important that the security policy requirements relate to the business impact of security incidents, to provide a reasonable prioritization of security measures. The policy will assign responsibilities for security activities and indicate the degree of accountability and authority of staff members, a member of senior management should have overall responsibility for security. The policy will also contain an indication of the controls that will be included in the maintenance of security.

Security Policy Contents
The typical contents of a security policy include:

● the responsibilities of owners, users, custodians and specific departments such as data security;
● risk management, risk assessment and data classification/valuation;
● contingency planning and resilience;
● security during systems development and implementation;
● access to data and systems, and storage control;
● telecommunications security;
● personal computer security;
● physical security;
● environment and access control;
● legal requirements;
● personnel policies.

Creation of a security policy
The development of a security policy may be undertaken by a corporate or information security department, or by external consultants. However, ownership and approval of the policy is the

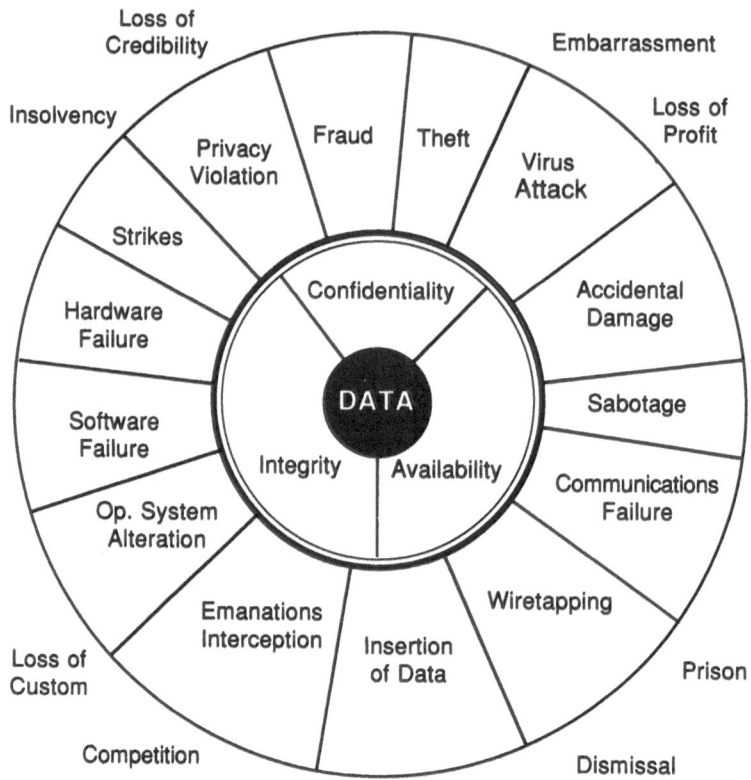

security policy *Impacts resulting from security breaches. The Security Policy (thick line) will determine the balance of the controls*

responsibility of senior management, a security depends upon authority and promulgation. The policy must be backed by the authority of top management and clear responsibilities established for its maintenance. At all level employees must be fully aware of the outcomes, including disciplinary outcomes, of violation of the policy.

Promulgation of the policy needs to be tackled at a number of levels. Contracts of employment should clearly indicate individual responsibilities and potential disciplinary actions resulting from security breaches. Similarly when an employee terminates a contract any ongoing responsibilities should be clearly stated. Training programs, posters, logon screens, organizational publications, e.g. newsletters, should also be

used to maintain an appropriate level of awareness.

security policy model. In computer security, an informal presentation of a formal security policy model. *See* FORMAL SECURITY POLICY MODEL.

security relevant event. In computer security, any event that attempts to change the security state of the system (e.g., change discretionary access controls, change the security level of the subject, change user password, etc.). Also, any event that attempts to violate the security policy of the system, (e.g., too many attempts to log in, attempts to violate the mandatory access control limits of a device, attempts to downgrade a file, etc.). (DODD). *See* DIS-

CRETIONARY ACCESS CONTROL, LOG IN, MANDATORY ACCESS CONTROL, PASSWORD.

security requirements. In computer security, the types and levels of protection necessary for equipment, data, information, applications, and facilities. (AFR).

security safeguards. In computer security, the protective measures and controls that are prescribed to meet the security requirements specified for an AIS. Those safeguards may include but are not necessarily limited to: hardware and software security features, operations procedures, accountability procedures, access and distribution controls, management constraints, personnel security, physical structures, areas, and devices. (DODD).

security service. (1) In communications security, a service, provided by a layer of communicating open systems, which ensures adequate security of the systems or of data transfers. (ISO) *See* OSI SECURITY. (2) In communications security, a service, provided by a layer of communicating open systems, which ensures adequate security of the system or of data transfers. (ANSI). *See* OSI SECURITY.

security specifications. (1) In data security, a detailed description of the safeguards required to protect a sensitive application. (OMBC). (2) In computer security, a detailed description of the countermeasures required to protect an ADP activity or network from unauthorized (accidental or unintentional) disclosure, modification, and destruction of data, or denial of service. (OPNAVINST). *See* DENIAL OF SERVICE.

security target. In information security, a specification of the security objectives of the target of evaluation. *See*

INFORMATION TECHNOLOGY SECURITY EVALUATION CRITERIA, SECURITY OBJECTIVE, TARGET OF EVALUATION.

security test and evaluation. (1) In data security, the process to determine that the system's administrative, technical, and physical security measures are adequate for the system; to document and report test findings to appropriate authorities; and to make recommendations based on test results. Managers may choose to conduct the ST&E as an integral part of other tests and evaluations. They must ensure changes made to correct one problem do not adversely affect other previously tested security measures. (AFR). (2) In computer security, an examination and analysis of the security safeguards of an AIS as they have been applied in an operational environment to determine the security posture of the AIS. (DODD). *See* AIS, SECURITY TEST.

security testing. In computer security, a process used to determine that the security features of a system are implemented as designed and that they are adequate for a proposed application's environment. This process includes hands-on functional testing, penetration testing and verification. (DOD). *See* FUNCTIONAL TESTING, PENETRATION TESTING, SECURITY TEST AND EVALUATION, TIGER TEAM, VERIFICATION.

security threats. In risk management, the source of security threats may be listed:

- errors and omissions caused by honest employees;
- dishonest employees who take advantage of some missing control or misuse their authority and seek to conceal their actions;
- fire and natural disasters;
- disgruntled employees or ex-employees who want to cause harm to the management, unlike dishonest

employees they do not seek to conceal the results of their actions;

- water damage;
- external threats e.g. terrorism, hackers, riots.

See HACKER.

security violation. In computer security, an incident in which a person defeats or bypasses security controls in order to gain unauthorized access to information, to make unauthorized use of system resources or to illegally remove system components.

seed. In mathematics, a number supplied to a random number generator to commence the sequence. *See* RANDOM NUMBERS.

seepage. In computer security, the accidental flow, to unauthorized individuals, of data or information access to which is presumed to be controlled by computer security safeguards. (FIPS). *Synonymous with* DATA LEAKAGE.

segment. (1) In computing, a self-contained portion of a computer program that can be executed without the entire program necessarily resident in the internal store at any one time. (2) In communications, a section of a message that can be held in a buffer. *See* BUFFER.

seismic sensor. In physical security, a sensor designed for earthquake detection or detection of subterranean vibrations. They include piezoelectric sensors, buried geophones or balanced pressure sensors. *See* PIEZOELECTRIC DETECTOR.

seize. In data communications, to gain control of a channel in order to transmit a message.

selection. In databases, an operation on a relational database in which a new relation is formed by selecting records, from the original relation, according to specified criteria on fields. *Compare* DIVISION, JOIN, PROJECTION. *See* FIELD, RECORD, RELATIONAL DATABASE.

selective calling. (1) In data communications, a system where remote stations may be called in for transmissions of messages when required, excluding all other stations on the circuit. (2) In data communications, the facility of a transmitter to select the stations, on the same line, that are to receive the message.

selective coded system. In physical security, a configuration in which each manual fire alarm station and each group of automatic detectors is associated with an individual one-, two-, three or four digit code. It sounds on all alarm-indicating devices when the manual station or automatic detector is activated. *See* ALARM STATION.

selective dump. In computing, a dump of one or more selected areas of storage. *See* DUMP.

selective field protection. In communications security, the protection of specific fields within a message which is to be transmitted. (ISO). *See* FIELD.

selective repeat. In data communications, a protocol employed in a pipelining system. When after a corrupted frame arrives, or a frame fails to arrive, the receiver buffers all subsequent frames until the corrupted or lost frame is transmitted and correctly received. The receiver then passes on the retransmitted frame, followed by the frames in the buffer, and acknowledges highest numbered frame. *See* FRAME.

selector channel. In data communications, a channel designed to operate with only one input/output device at any one time. After selection of the input/output device the whole message is transmitted byte by byte. *See* BYTE.

self-banking. In banking, the use of automatic tellers machines, cash dispensers and communication terminals by individual clients to perform banking transactions. The equipment may be located in a bank, place of work etc. *Compare* HOME BANKING. *See* AUTOMATIC TELLER MACHINE, CASH DISPENSER.

self-checking circuit. In reliability, a form of hardware and information redundancy in which circuits are able to detect failures in themselves and fail in a predicted safe manner. *See* FAIL SAFE, HARDWARE REDUNDANCY, INFORMATION REDUNDANCY.

self-correcting code. *Synonymous with* ERROR CORRECTION CODE.

self-synchronizing. In cryptography, a property of a cipher which provides for an automatic recovery after an error has occurred. Suppose a plaintext stream is input into two cryptographic devices, which produce identical output for identical inputs. If an error occurs in the ciphering process of one of the devices then the outputs will differ, however, if the process is self-synchronizing then the outputs will become equal again after some recovery period. *See* BLOCK CIPHER CHAINING, STREAM CIPHER CHAINING. *Synonymous with* SELF-SYN-CHRONOUS.

self-synchronous. *Synonymous with* SELF-SYNCHRONIZING.

semantics. The study or science of the relationship between symbols and their meaning.

semiweak key. In cryptography, a pair of DES keys with the property that decipherment with one key of the pair corresponds to encipherment with the other and vice versa. In other words if plaintext is enciphered with one key and the resulting ciphertext is enciphered with the second key then the original ciphertext is obtained. The semiweak key pairs for DES are:

```
01FE01FE01FE01FE and FE01FE01FE01FE01
1FE01FE00EF10EF1 and E01FE01FF10EF10E
01E001E001F101F1 and E001E001F101F101
1FFE1FFE0EFE0EFE and FE1FFE1FFE0EFE0E
011F011F010E010E and 1F011F010E010E01
E0FEE0FEF1FEF1FE and FEE0FEE0FEF1FEF1
```

Compare WEAK KEY. *See* DES.

sender. (1) In data communications, an implementation encoding a data value for transfer. *Compare* RECIPIENT. (2) In data communications, a subject writing to a channel. *Compare* RECEIVER. *See* CHANNEL, SUBJECT. (3) In data communications, the person, institution or other entity responsible for and authorized to originate a message. Here, the concept of responsibility, e.g. financial responsibility, is paramount. (ANSI). *Compare* RECEIVER.

sender's correspondent bank. In banking, a bank providing funds on behalf of the sender to the receiver direct or though the receiver's correspondent bank. (ANSI). *See* RECEIVER'S CORRESPONDENT BANK.

sending bank. In banking, a bank that inputs messages to a service. (ANSI).

sensitive application. In data security, an application of information technology that requires protection because it processes sensitive data, or because of the risk and magnitude of loss or harm that could result from improper operation or deliberate manipulation of the application. (OMBC).

sensitive business data. In data security, data which requires protection under Title 18, USC 1905, and other data which by its nature requires controlled distribution or access for reasons other than that it is classified or personal data. Sensitive business data is recognized in the following categories:

(a) For Official Use Only - Requiring confidentiality of information derived from Inspector General, authority, or other investigative activity.

(b) Financial - Requiring protection to ensure the integrity of funds or other fiscal assets.

(c) Sensitive Management - Requiring protection to defend against the loss of property, material, or supplies or to defend against the disruption of operations or normal management practices, etc.

(d) Proprietary - Requiring protection to protect data or information in conformance with a limited rights agreement or which is the exclusive property of a civilian corporation or individual and which is on loan to the Government for evaluation or for its proper use in adjudicating contracts.

(e) Privileged - Requiring protection for conformance with business standards or as required by law. (Example: Government developed information involving the award of a contract.) (OPNAVINST).

Compare SENSITIVE DEFENSE INFORMATION, SENSITIVE COMPARTMENTED INFORMATION. *See* SENSITIVE DATA, SENSITIVE INFORMATION.

sensitive compartmented information. (1) Intelligence information requiring special controls indicating restricted handling. (DODD). (2) All information and materials requiring special Community controls indicating restricted handling within present and future Community intelligence collection programs and their end products. These special Community controls are formal systems of restricted access established to protect the sensitive aspects of intelligence sources and methods and analytical procedures of foreign intelligence programs. The term does not include

Restricted Data as defined in Section II, Public Law 585, Atomic Energy Act of 1954, as amended. (DCID). *Compare* SENSITIVE BUSINESS DATA, SENSITIVE DEFENSE INFORMATION. *See* SENSITIVE DATA, SENSITIVE INFORMATION.

sensitive data. (1) In data security, data that require protection due to the risk and magnitude of loss or harm that could result from inadvertent or deliberate disclosure, alteration, destruction of the data. The term includes data whose improper use or disclosure could adversely affect the ability to accomplish a mission, proprietary data, records about individuals requiring protection under the Privacy Act, and data not releasable under the Freedom of Information Act. (OMBC). (2) In data security, data that, as determined by a competent authority, must be protected because its unauthorized disclosure, alteration, loss, or destruction will cause perceivable damage to someone or something. (AFR). *See* SENSITIVE BUSINESS DATA, SENSITIVE COMPARTMENTED INFORMATION, SENSITIVE DEFENSE INFORMATION, SENSITIVE INFORMATION, SENSITIVITY.

sensitive defense information. In data security, any information which requires a degree of protection and which should not be made generally available. This type of information includes, but is not limited to, that information which must be safeguarded as to:

(a) Prevent damage to national defense and which usually bears a security classification.

(b) Assure the individual privacy of U.S. citizens as provided by the Privacy Act of 1974.

(c) Maintain the confidentiality for FOUO information derived from the Inspector General, an audit, or other investigative activities such as medical or other jurisprudence or disciplinary information derived from records of doctor/patient or lawyer/client relationships.

(d) Protect funds, supplies, and material from theft, fraud, misappropriation, or misuse. This includes asset or resource accounting or systems or operations which are involved in the control and distribution of funds or the processing of information which offers the opportunity to divert economically valuable resources.

(e) Protect proprietary information which is the exclusive property of an individual or corporation. This proprietary information may be on loan, leased, or purchased by the Government or made available to the Government for its proper use, to include evaluating or adjudicating contracts.

(f) Protect Government-developed privileged information involving the award of contracts.

(g) Protect information which the commander considers essential for mission accomplishment. (AR).

Compare SENSITIVE BUSINESS DATA, SENSITIVE COMPARTMENTED INFORMATION. *See* FOUO, PROPRIETARY DATA, SENSITIVE DATA, SENSITIVE INFORMATION.

sensitive information. (1) In data security, information contained in the Military Critical Technologies List, information which could be useful to a hostile agent in the development of countermeasures, information which could involve new or high technology, information which could involve key indicators of operational capabilities which could be used by hostile agents to determine operational capabilities, weaknesses, and wartime missions, (AFR). *See* MILITARY CRITICAL TECHNOLOGY. (2) In data security, information that, as determined by a competent authority, must be protected because its unauthorized disclosure, alteration, loss, or destruction will at least cause perceivable damage to someone or something. (DOD). (3) In data security, any information which requires a degree of protection and which should not be made generally available. (FIPS). *See* SENSITIVE BUSINESS DATA, SENSITIVE COMPARTMENTED INFORMATION, SENSITIVE DATA, SENSITIVE DEFENSE INFORMATION. (4) In legislation, information which if lost, misused, accessed or modified without authorization could adversely affect the privacy of individuals and be in violation of the U.S. Privacy Act. *See* DATA PROTECTION, DATA PROTECTION - U.S.A, PRIVACY PROTECTION.

sensitive software. In computer security, any data processing software that could bypass, penetrate, or damage data processing security controls. (AR).

sensitive statistic. In database security, a statistic from a statistical database that can be used to reveal information about an individual. *See* INFERENCE CONTROL, N-RESPONDENT, K%-DOMINANCE, STATISTICAL DATABASE.

sensitive systems. In computer security, a system which processes sensitive data or performs a sensitive function. The categories of sensitive systems, in increasing order of sensitivity are listed below.

- Applications providing general processing support, e.g. engineering calculations used in aircraft design.
- Funds disbursement, accounting, asset management systems, e.g. payroll.
- General purpose information systems, e.g. generalized data management systems.
- Automated decision-making systems, e.g. fully automated funds disbursement and accounting systems.
- Real time control systems, e.g. air

traffic control.
- Systems affecting national security or wellbeing, e.g. integrated electronic funds transfer.

sensitivity. (1) In data security, the characteristic of a resource which implies its value or importance, and may include its vulnerability. (ISO). *See* VULNERABILITY. (2) In computer security, the characteristic of a resource which implies its value or importance, and its vulnerability to accidental or deliberate threats. *See* ACCIDENTAL THREAT, DELIBERATE THREAT, SENSITIVE SYSTEMS.

sensitivity and criticality. In computer security, a method developed to describe the value of an information system by taking into account the cost, capability, and jeopardy to mission accomplishments or human life associated with the system. (AFR).

sensitivity assessment. In computer security, a study of the data to determine level of protection required. (AFR).

sensitivity label. (1) In data security, a security level associated with an object. *See* OBJECT, SECURITY LEVEL. (2) In computer security, a piece of information that represents the security level of an object and that describes the sensitivity (e.g. classification) of the data in the object. Sensitivity labels are used by the TCB as the basis for mandatory access control decisions. (DOD). *See* MANDATORY ACCESS CONTROL, OBJECT, TCB. *Synonymous with* SECURITY LABEL.

Sentinel. In computer security, a virus that terminates and stays resident, infects COMMAND.COM, COM, EXE and OVL files, corrupts file linkage, affects run-time operation, corrupts program, OVL and data files. *See* VIRUS NAMES.

separate and mediate. In computer security, a principle for structuring secure systems in which entities of different security classifications are kept separate except when performing operating operations that require access to entities from more than one level. Such accesses must be performed by trusted reference monitors which ensure compliance with some externally imposed security policy. *See* REFERENCE MONITOR CONCEPT.

separation of duties or functions. In procedural security, the structuring of system-related jobs so that each has as little security exposure as is feasible for efficient operation. For execution of critical tasks, the intervention of more than one person should be required. In general the opportunity for any one person to subvert or damage the system must be minimized. *See* COMPUTER FRAUD CONTROL, DUAL CONTROL, SPLIT KNOWLEDGE.

separation of privilege. In computer security, principle of separation of privilege, one of the principles of secure systems. *See* PRINCIPLES OF SECURE SYSTEMS, SEPARATION OF DUTIES AND FUNCTIONS.

sequential card reader. In physical security, a card reader for access control, with associated keypad, which requires both an authorized access card and entry of a coded keypad sequence before entry or exit is granted. *See* CARD READER.

sequential switcher. In physical security, a video switcher facility for selecting camera views and dwell times to a pre-programmed sequence. *See* DWELL TIME, HOMING SEQUENTIAL SWITCHER, VIDEO SWITCHER.

serial communication. *See* SERIAL TRANSMISSION.

serial computer. In computing, a computer in which events occur one after the other with little or no provision for simultaneity or overlap. *Compare* PARALLEL COMPUTER.

serial interface. In data communications, an interface, e.g. between a DTE and a modem, which can only pass data in serial transmission form. *See* DTE, MODEM, RS-232C. *See* SERIAL TRANSMISSION.

serial transmission. In data communications, a method of information transfer in which each bit of a character is sent in sequence. *Compare* PARALLEL TRANSMISSION.

server. In computing, a unit at a node of a network that provides a specific service for network users, e.g. a printer server provides printing facilities, a file server stores user files. *See* COMMUNICATION SERVER, DISK SERVER, FILE SERVER.

service bureau. In computing, an organization that provides computing or data processing services for other individuals or organizations.

service data unit. In data communications, the information passed from one layer to its peer layer in the Open Systems Interconnection Reference Model. Control information is added to the service data unit, to form an interface data unit, when it is passed from the layer N to layer N-1. *Compare* PROTOCOL DATA UNIT, INTERFACE DATA UNIT. *See* OPEN SYSTEMS INTERCONNECTION.

service machine. *Synonymous with* INTERNAL SUBJECT.

service message. In data communications, a message, passing between two terminal points, containing or seeking information concerning other messages. *See* CRYPTOGRAPHIC SERVICE MESSAGE.

service provider. In data communications, a term used in the Open Systems Interconnection Reference Model. Layer N is a service provider to layer N+1. *Compare* SERVICE USER. *See* OPEN SYSTEMS INTERCONNECTION.

service type. *Synonymous with* FACILITY TYPE.

service user. In data communications, a term used in the Open Systems Interconnection Reference Model. Layer N+1 is a service user of the service provided by layer N. *Compare* SERVICE PROVIDER. *See* OPEN SYSTEMS INTERCONNECTION.

session. In computing, an activity for a period of time; the activity is access to a computer/network resource by a user; a period of time is bounded by session initiation (a form of log on) and session termination (a form of log off). (DCID).

session key. In key management, a cryptographic key used only for a limited period, e.g. a user session at a terminal, and then discarded. Session keys are the lowest level keys used in a key hierarchy and are not used as key-encrypting keys. *Compare* TRANSACTION KEY. *See* KEY-ENCRYPTING KEY.

session layer. In data communications, a layer in the ISO Open Systems Interconnection model. This layer allows the two communicating parties to establish sessions. It can provide a variety of services, regulating flows between communicating processes that can only transmit data in one direction at a time, providing token management for critical operations that cannot be undertaken simultaneously, inserting checkpoints in data streams so that operations may be restarted from intermediate points in the case of communication failure etc. *Compare* APPLICATION LAYER, DATA LINK LAYER, NETWORK LAYER, PHYSICAL LAYER, PRESENTATION LAYER, TOKEN

MANAGEMENT, TRANSPORT LAYER. *See* HOST, OPEN SYSTEMS INTERCONNECTION.

session security level. In computer security, the low water mark of the security levels of: the user, the terminal, a level specified by the user, and the system from which the session originates. (DCID). *See* LOW WATER MARK, SECURITY LEVEL.

set. (1) In mathematics, an operation on a bit, in binary arithmetic, to adjust its value to 1. *See* BIT. (2) In mathematics, a collection of elements with a common property.

settlement. In banking, a transfer of funds to complete one or more prior transactions which were subject to final settlement. (ANSI).

shadow. In key management, a segment of a key used in the threshold technique. *See* THRESHOLD.

Shake. In computer security, a virus that terminates and stays resident, infects COM files, affects run-time operation, corrupts program and OVL files. *See* VIRUS NAMES.

shannon. *See* INFORMATION CONTENT.

Shannon's five criteria. In cryptography, suggestions for the criteria of secure systems proposed by Shannon in the 1940's:

- the amount of secrecy offered;
- the size of the key;
- the simplicity of enciphering and deciphering operations;
- the propagation of errors;
- extension of the message.

See ERROR PROPAGATION, INFORMATION THEORY.

Shannon's Law. In communications, a law that provides a measure for the capacity of a communication line in terms of its bandwidth and signal to noise ratio. According to this law the maximum transmission in bits per second is given by:
$W \log_2 (1 + SN)$ where, W = bandwidth and SN = signal to noise ratio. *See* BANDWIDTH, SIGNAL TO NOISE RATIO.

shareware. In software, programs that are copyrighted and issued with a request that a modest donation be made to the supplier if they prove to be of value to the user. The supplier may also provide a better version or a manual upon receipt of a license fee. *See* BULLETIN BOARD.

sharp eyed cashier. In banking, pertaining to dishonest cashiers who use their knowledge, and/or positions to obtain information, in order to commit fraud. For example, observing and noting the entry of customer PINs. *See* PIN.

shell site. *Synonymous with* COLD SITE.

shielded cable. In communications, an inner conductor surrounded by an outer grounded metallic braid to protect signals from interference. *See* COAXIAL CABLE, INTERFERENCE.

shielding effectiveness. In electronics, the measure in decibels of the absorbing property of a conductive shield. In the U.S. computing devices must comply with FCC emission regulations and special electrically conductive plastics are used for this purpose. *See* CONDUCTIVE SHIELDING, DECIBEL, TEMPEST PROOFING.

shift. In cryptography, the difference in alphabetic position between a plaintext character, in a translation cipher, and the corresponding ciphertext character. *See* TRANSLATION CIPHER.

shift codes. In codes, a method of increasing the number of characters which can be associated with a given number of bits. If a 6 bit code is used then 64 characters may be allocated. However, if two of these characters are designated as 'shift' and 'unshift' then they may produce the effect of a shift to and from an alternative character set giving a total of 124 available characters. *See* ESCAPE CODE.

shift factor. In communications security, the average shift distance of segments in a given permutation when time element scramblers are employed for voice scrambling. *See* TIME ELEMENT SCRAMBLER, VOICE SCRAMBLING.

shift register. In hardware, a register designed for the shifting of data to the left or right. *See* REGISTER.

shouldering. *Synonymous with* SHOULDER SURFING.

shoulder surfing. In computer security, a method of obtaining knowledge of user passwords, log on procedures etc., by looking over the shoulder of a terminal user.

shrink-wrapped license. In computing, a contract supplied by a software house which is visible through the transparent wrapping around the box of diskettes and documentation. The contract will stipulate conditions under which the software may be used and is deemed to come into effect once the wrapping has been torn. The validity of this technique is very questionable in most countries. *See* SOFTWARE HOUSE. *Synonymous with* HAT BOX, TEAR-ME-OPEN.

SIC. In banking, Standard Industry Codes, developed by the Bank of England.

Sieve of Eratosthenes. In mathematics, a method of finding prime numbers with a lower value than a specified integer. The complete set of integers up to the specified value are written. Every second number after 2 is crossed out, then every third number after 3 is similarly crossed out (if it is uncrossed). The process is repeated for every fifth number after 5 etc. The numbers remaining at the end of the process are prime numbers. *See* PRIME NUMBER.

signal. (1) An intentional time-varying physical phenomenon conveying information. (2) The physical embodiment of a message. (3) A short message, as in a control signal.

1	2	3	4	5	6
7	8	9	10	11	12
13	14	15	16	17	18
19	20	21	22	23	24
25	26	27	28	29	30
31	32	33	34	35	36
37	38	39	40	41	42
43	44	45	46	47	48
49	50	51	52	53	54
55	56	57	58	59	60
61	62	63	64	65	66
67	68	69	70	71	72
73	74	75	76	77	78
79	80	81	82	83	84
85	86	87	88	89	90
91	92	93	94	95	96
97	98	99	100		

sieve of Eratosthenes
If the sieve is arranged in six columns (modulo 6), then only the first and fifth columns contain primes because the numbers in the third column are divisible by three and the numbers in the other columns are divisible by two.

signal element. In data communications, the basic unit by which data is communicated along a channel. Each unit is a state or condition of the channel representing one or more bits of digital information. A unit may be a DC pulse, or an AC signal of certain amplitude, phase or frequency which is recognized and translated by the receiving equipment.

signalling. In communications, the transfer of digits and call set up/clear down instructions between the telephone and central office, or exchange, or between one central office and another. *See* CENTRAL OFFICE.

signal quality detector. In data communications, a signal provided by synchronous modems indicating whether or not there is a high probability of an error in the received data. *See* SYNCHRONOUS MODEM, RS-232C.

signal to noise ratio. In communications, the ratio of the power of the required signal to that of the unwanted noise. *See* NOISE.

signature. *See* DIGITAL SIGNATURE.

signature analysis. In access control, a biometric technique based upon the analysis of a signature or the manner in which it is written. Machine recognition of signatures has been an active area of research since the 1970's. Template signatures can be stored with some 100 bytes, false accept/reject rates of 1 per cent have been reported.

Given the variability of written signatures some systems update the stored template to that corresponding to the last successful login. The use of stored templates of the written pattern of a signature, and the associated problems of developing acceptable levels of Type 1 and Type 2 errors, when the genuine signature may be subject to significant variations, renders such systems vulnerable to moderately competent forgers.

A more secure form of signature verification is based upon the dynamics of the production of the signature. These dynamic systems can measure the time to complete sections of the signature, variations in pen pressure during the production of the signature, pen accelerations etc. If such user characteristics of the signature production are captured, a forger requires considerably more information than a mere copy of the written signature.

Many different technologies for measurement of signature dynamics have been tested and reported. A U.K. National Physical Laboratory (NPL) system sampled the position of the pen employing a digitizer based upon pressure membranes. The Stanford Research Institute used an instrumented ballpoint with a strain gauge to measure drag forces in the X and Y directions and pressure in the Z direction. SRI also developed a platen to measure such data with any pen. IBM produced a device with accelerometers embedded in the pen. The Battelle Memorial Institute measured the velocity of the pen by means of a magnetic tip and a series of energized secondary coils. More recently the Midland Bank trialled a system developed by Rolls-Royce Business Ventures Ltd. which monitors the sound emitted by a pen as it is written.

The false reject of such devices can be measured by individual users inputting their signatures, and Type 1 errors of the order of 1 per cent were obtained. The measurement of Type 2 errors, however, presents a problem of some complexity. Clearly the difficulty lies in the development of a large number of statistical tests covering various competent forgers. The factors influencing the false accept rate would include: length of the signature, competence of forger, facility to study the production of the signature dynamics, coaching by legitimate user, facility for experimentation.

The most elementary form of Type 2 testing is to simply play each signature in the stored file against all other signatures and test for the number of false accepts. More sophisticated trials have been held with, at least amateur, forgers making their best attempts to fool the system. IBM for example reported, in 1983, trials involving 2133 forgeries and a false accept rate as low as .28 per cent.

The automatic recognition of signatures has much to commend it in terms of user acceptability, there are few people who would find such a method presented physical problems or was socially unacceptable. With reasonable security precautions, the attacker is presented with serious problems and a user can change their stored signature if there were reason to believe that the digitized form had been compromised. *See* BIOMETRICS, TYPE 1 ERROR, TYPE 2 ERROR.

signature construction. In cryptography, the cryptographic transformation of data to ensure data origin authentication. (ISO). *Compare* SIGNATURE DECONSTRUCTION. *See* DATA ORIGIN AUTHENTICATION, DIGITAL SIGNATURE.

signature deconstruction. In cryptography, the reversal of signature construction to produce data from which it is possible to determine whether a signature is valid or not. (ISO). *Compare* SIGNATURE CONSTRUCTION. *See* DIGITAL SIGNATURE.

signature service. In data security, a protection against repudiation and forgery. *See* DIGITAL SIGNATURE, FORGERY, REPUDIATION.

significant modification. In computer security, any modification to the facility or system that impacts the operation or affects the security measures of the system. Determination of impact is a subjective evaluation and depends on the environment where the system operates. (AFR).

sign in. *Synonymous with* LOG IN.

sign on. *Synonymous with* LOG ON.

simple mail transfer protocol. In data communications, an electronic mail protocol originally developed for ARPANET. *See* ARPANET, ELECTRONIC MAIL, X.400.

simple security property. In computer security, a Bell-La Padula security model rule allowing a subject read access to an object only if the security level of the subject dominates the security level of the object. (DOD). *See* BELL-LA PADULA MODEL, DOMINATE, OBJECT, READ ACCESS, SECURITY LEVEL, SUBJECT.

simplex. In communications, pertaining to communication in one direction only. *Compare* DUPLEX, HALF DUPLEX.

simplicity. In computer security, principle of simplicity, one of the principles of secure systems which states that the accuracy of security measures, incorporated in hardware and software, can be more readily checked if those measures are simple and small. *See* PRINCIPLES OF SECURE SYSTEMS.

simulation. In computer security, copying a computer process in order to become familiar with it with a view to altering it.

simultaneous transmission. In data communications, a technique for the transmission of control characters, or data, in one direction whilst messages are being received in the other. *See* DUPLEX.

single address message. In communications, a message to be delivered to only one destination.

single-level device. In computer security, a device that is used to process data of a single security level at any one time. Since the device need not be trusted to separate data of different security levels, sensitivity labels do not have to be stored with the data being processed. (DOD). *Compare* MULTILEVEL DEVICE. *See* SECURITY LEVEL, SENSITIVITY LABEL.

single point of failure. In computing, any part of a system which is vital to its operation and one in which failure would cause a failure in the total system because it cannot be bypassed. Systems should be designed with sufficient redundancy to avoid this situation.

single stroke bell. In physical security, an alarm device that rings only once each time operating energy is applied. *Compare* VIBRATING BELL.

single supervised system. In physical security, a system in which the source of power for the trouble signal is unsupervised. *See* TROUBLE SIGNAL.

single voiding card reader. In access control, a card reader used for access control in which one or more access control codes may be removed from the system. *See* CARD READER.

sink. *Synonymous with* DATA SINK.

sink tree. In data communications, the set of all paths to a destination in a communication network, when fixed routing tables are used. *See* ROUTING TABLE.

SIOP-ESI. Single Integrated Operational Plan - Extremely Sensitive Information; a DOD. *See* SPECIAL ACCESS PROGRAM. (DODD).

SITA high level network. In data communications, Société Internationale de Télécommunications Aéronautique, a network serving airlines with a combination of packet and message switching facilities. *See* PACKET SWITCHING, MESSAGE SWITCHING.

site polling. In data communications, a technique in which all the terminals at a given location are polled as a group, with the local controller acting as the supervisor for this purpose. *See* POLLING.

Skism. In computer security, a virus that terminates and stays resident, infects COM, EXE and OVL files, affects run-time operation, corrupts program and OVL files. *See* VIRUS NAMES.

slave. In computer networks, a remote system or terminal in which the functions are controlled by a central master system.

slice network. In data communications, a self-contained modular unit, capable of being located in as many places as necessary or convenient, which, in the event of being cut off from the rest of the system, will continue to operate independently. Such units will carry out processing functions normally handled by centralized operating centers.

sliding window protocol. In data communications, a modified form of a stop and wait protocol. The sending host is allowed to have multiple unacknowledged frames outstanding simultaneously. Successive frames are given sequence numbers in a given range with numbers being reused to prevent them growing without bound. The sending host maintains a record of unacknowledged frames and retransmits them after a specified time out interval, or receipt of negative acknowledgement frames from the receiver, a limit on the maximum permitted number of unacknowledged frames ensures flow control. *Compare* STOP AND WAIT PROTOCOL. *See* FRAME, NEGATIVE ACKNOWLEDGEMENT.

sliding window system. In communications security, a method of reducing the time delay associated with time element scramblers. The permutations are selected so that the maximum shift of segments is limited, thus it is not necessary to store the whole frame before permutation at the receiver and transmitter. *See* SHIFT FACTOR, TIME ELEMENT SCRAMBLER, VOICE SCRAMBLING.

slotted ring. *See* MESSAGE SLOT.

Slow. In computer security, a virus that encrypts itself, terminates and stays resident, infects COM, EXE and OVL files, affects run-time operation, corrupts program and OVL files and file linkage. *See* VIRUS NAMES.

smart card. In access control, a plastic card with similar dimensions to a magnetic stripe card that has electronic logic in the case of a stored data card, or a microprocessor for cards with processing capabilities.

The stored data card provides for the secure storage of data so that, unlike the magnetic stripe card, its contents can be neither copied nor modified in an unauthorized manner. The card with a processing capability has an embedded microprocessor in addition to data storage capabilities. The microprocessor is controlled by a program permanently stored in a ROM (Read Only Memory). Some cards have the capability of downloading code into an EPROM (Electrically Programmable Read Only Memory). The microprocessor provides an in-built intelligence which permits the card to enter into a fixed dialogue with a host computer. Such processing power can not only identify the user to the host computer, but it can also provide the card holder with a challenge/response mechanism to authenticate the host and thus obviate masquerade attacks.

Development of Smart Cards.
In 1974 a patent for a plastic card containing microelectronics was filed by a French inventor, Roland Moreno of Innovatron. Development was continued on the smart card and licenses were granted to other firms. In 1982 trials were organized in the French cities: Blois, Caen and Lyons to test the use of electronic payment cards in three typical environments.

In 1984 the Carte Bleue network, the French branch of the Visa card system, and the Credit Agricole network, with a total population of 10 million card holders, implemented a nationwide system for payment with hybrid cards. French Telecom also made use of the payphone card.

Smart cards have also been employed for access control. The Pentagon conducted a study for the introduction of a smart card ID system for Defence establishments and PX stores worldwide. The smart card may also be employed in conjunction with videotex and home banking systems. The US retailing chain J C Penny acquired the First Bank home videotex system, allowing trials to be undertaken with smart cards on the chain's computer network, in cooperation with other U.S. banks. More recently smart card readers have been installed in pay TV decoders.

Technology of Smart Cards.
There are in current use two basic types of smart cards:

- wired logic card;
- a card containing one or more microprocessors.

The wired logic card, e.g. the Flonic card developed by Flonic-Schlumberger, is similar in appearance to a magnetic stripe card and contains an electronic circuit encapsulated within the thickness of the card. The in-built circuitry provides a secure store and the facilities to perform simple computations. Thus access to the stored data is controlled, and the stored data may be updated by the appropriate card reader.

The conventional microprocessor card, e.g. CP8 originally developed by Cii Honeywell Bull, has a single embedded 8 bit microprocessor, RAM, ROM and EPROM or EEPROM (Electrically Erasable Read Only Memory) memory. The ROM contains the stored instructions, and all access to the stored data is controlled by the microprocessor. There is no external means of intercepting the data, flowing on the microprocessor bus, thus ensuring high security. Both EPROM and EEPROM memory provide nonvolatile data storage. EPROM technology allows data to be written but not thereafter erased, EEPROM does permit subsequent erasing thus allowing memory space to be reused by removing old data. Some smart cards have more than one microprocessor.

The range of smart cards may be further categorized as:

- memory cards;
- simple smart cards;
- smart cards;
- supersmart cards;
- contactless smart cards.

Memory cards may have storage capacities ranging from 50 kbytes to 1 megabit stored in RAM, EPROM or EEPROM, with or without a battery, but containing no on board processor. They are similar in size to credit cards but are always thicker and rigid, so that they are prone to breaking if bent.

Simple smart cards do not have an on board microprocessor but access to the internal memory (EPROM or EEPROM) is subject to physical protection, fuses, or logical protection controlled by in-built circuitry. These cards are of the same size and thickness of conventional credit cards.

Smart cards contain a microprocessor, RAM, ROM and EPROM, or EEPROM, memory, all accesses to the memory being controlled by the microprocessor. They are also of the same size and thickness as credit cards.

Supersmart cards have the same func-

tionality as a smart card but they also include a keyboard, LCD display and battery, thus resembling more a pocket calculator than a credit card. They are thicker than a credit card and rigid.

Contactless smart cards, unlike the cards described above, are not plugged into a card reader, but communicate by RF inductive interfaces. These cards are normally simply placed in a designated area on top of the reader, to this extent they are more user friendly and are less vulnerable to failure. Current contactless cards can comply with the thickness standards of smart cards and are sufficiently flexible to be carried in a wallet.

Standards

The International Standards Organization issued a standard for smart cards (ISO 7816) which comprises three parts:

- Part 1 - Physical characteristics;
- Part 2 - Dimensions and location of the contacts;
- Part 3 - Electronic signals and transmission protocols.

Part 1 defines the physical characteristics of the card, e.g. dimensions (0.68-0.84mm, 53.92-54.03mm, and 85.47-85.72mm). Part 2 of the standard defines 8 contacts, 2 of which are reserved for future use and the remaining 6 are designated:

- VCC - circuit supply voltage;
- RST - reset signal;
- CLK - clock signal;
- GND - zero voltage;
- VPP - programming voltage;
- I/O - data input/output.

VCC and GND are supply voltages, CLK provides a clock signal for cards operating in the synchronous modes, I/O provides the only channel for passing data to, or from, the card, RST resets the card in-built program and VPP is an optional control signal for use by the card.

The smart card is inserted into a reader, which supplies the necessary supply voltages, clock signals etc.; this reader then passes data between the smart card and a controlling unit over a RS232 interface. The transmission protocols are defined by ISO 7816/3; data may be transferred in synchronous or asynchronous mode.

The structure of a typical smart card is illustrated in Fig. 1. The memory comprises RAM, ROM and EPROM (or EEPROM). The volatile RAM storage holds data developed during the processing of a transaction, ROM holds the card program instructions that control the function of the card. The EPROM may contain additional card program subroutines and card data.

The data stored in the card memory is logically divided into three categories:

- free read and write;
- restricted access - the data transmitted from the card only if access is granted by the card controlling program, e.g. after

PIN checking;
- forbid access - secret data used only by the card programs, e.g. cryptographic keys used in encryption processes.
- manufacturer's fabrication zone- which cannot be written to.

Each card contains data unique to the card. At the manufacturing stage a unique serial number is stored in the free read and write area. The card may then by personalized by the card issuer. At this stage one or more secret card issuer codes are written in the forbid access area; the data is then locked by blowing internal fuses so that it cannot thereafter be overwritten.

The user PIN is stored in the forbid access area, and the card can be protected against PIN experimentation. Each time an incorrect PIN is entered, a counter is incremented; when the counter attains a prespecified value, the use of the card is blocked. Normally the

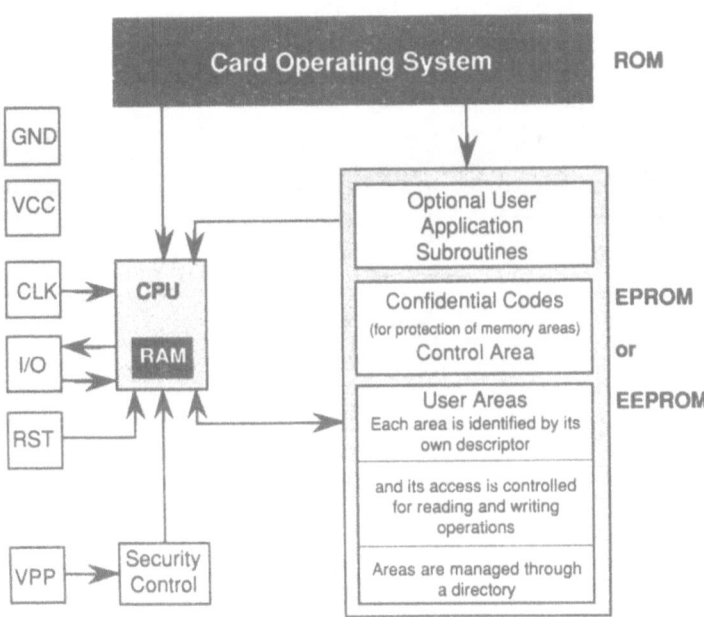

smart card
Fig. 1 Smart card memory.

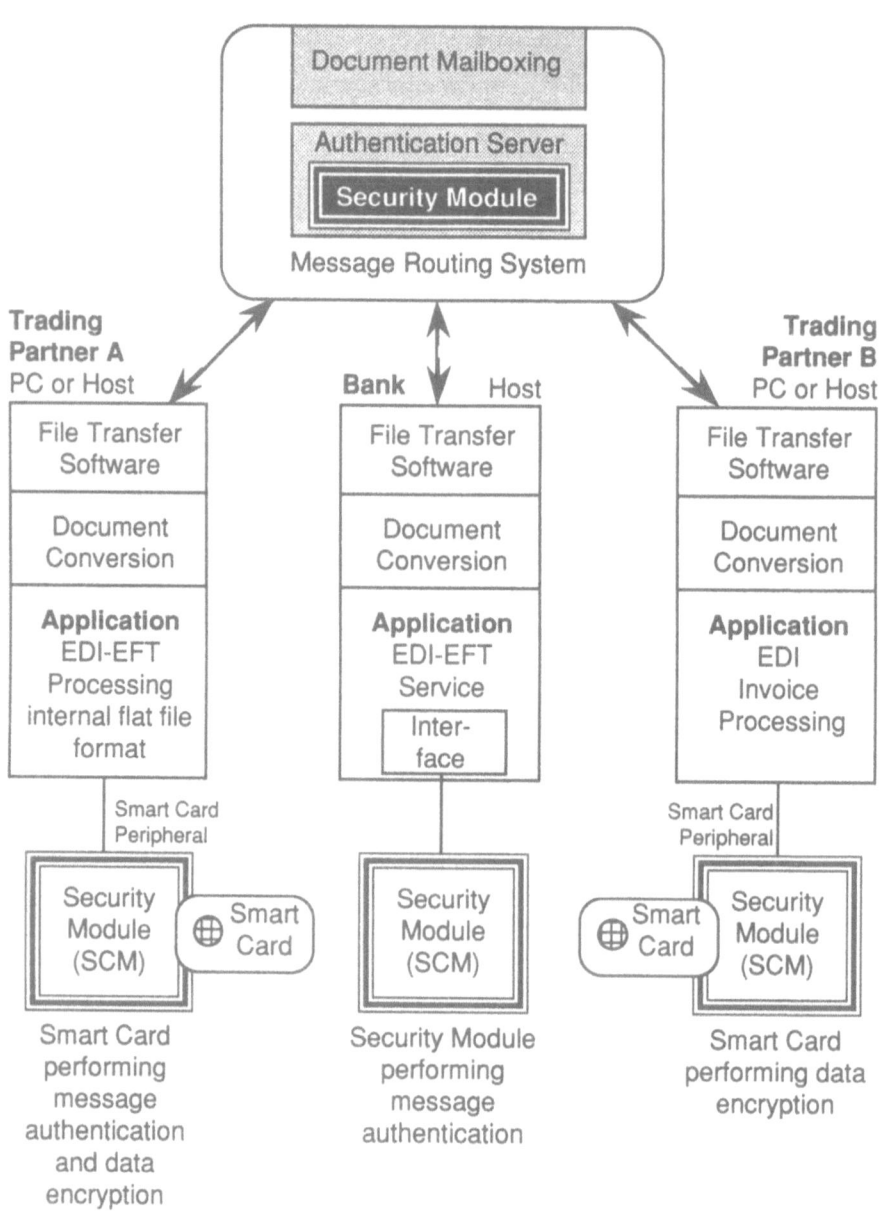

card issuer code, known only by the issuing bank, must be entered in conjunction with the PIN, to return the card to normal operation; experimentation of card issuer codes is inhibited in a similar manner to that of PINs.

The significant advantage of the smart card, from the security viewpoint, is that the card is capable of implementing its own security policy. The card will be presented with data, on its I/O line, from the card reader. In the set up stages, of a transaction, this data may serve to authenticate the card holder and the device communicating with the card. The card holders will identify themselves by entering their PINs on the keyboard connected to the reader. The communicating device, e.g. a remote host, may authenticate itself by a challenge response dialogue. These authentication processes will require the card processor to exploit secret data, stored in EPROM, that is accessible only to that processor. With current technology it is considered that any attempt to gain access to the secret stored data, by some form of direct attack on the card, is beyond the technical capability of a potential attacker.

The facility of smart cards to undertake encryption processing will render them valuable in areas including, and extending beyond, current consumer financial applications and access control. Use of smart cards for encryption processing has the following advantages:

- the processing is undertaken in a tamper proof environment;
- the associated encryption keys are securely stored and, in some cases, their value need not be available in any external device;
- the encryption facility has an in-built access control, i.e. employing the PIN mechanisms;
- the card is carried by the user thus, unlike cryptographic devices in personal computers,

is never left unattended and subject to potential misuse;
- the encryption facility and in-built cryptographic keys can be used by the card holder at any terminal containing an appropriate card reader.

The current common encryption algorithms available for smart cards are DES, Feal, RSA and Fiat-Shamir. In the case of symmetric ciphers, such as DES or Feal, the card may be employed, as an access control device, to ensure the secrecy of messages, to authenticate or to sign messages.

Application of Smart Cards
The application areas may be broadly classified as the overlapping areas:

- electronic purse;
- banking transactions;
- access control;
- personalized files;
- personalized encryption device;
- Electronic Data Interchange.

Electronic Purse
The electronic purse is simply a stored data card that is initially charged up with a specified number of value units. The consumer purchases the card and uses it every time that a transaction is to be enacted. The card reader checks the validity of the card, records the transaction and decreases the stored value by an amount corresponding to the value of the transaction. When the stored value is reduced the zero the consumer either simply discards the card, as for some payphone card systems, or takes it to a card issuer organization and pays for the card to be recharged.

Banking Transactions
Banking transaction applications include the abovementioned electronic purse, but are more generally aimed at some means of transferring money between users', and traders', bank accounts. The smart card offers two main advantages, as

compared with the magnetic stripe card, for such banking transactions, i.e. higher security and stored updated transaction data.

The secret data stored in smart cards is inaccessible to the unauthorized user. Moreover the smart card can enter into security protocols, such as challenge response which require a processing capability at the card end.

The second advantage, of the smart card, is that sensitive information can be both protected and updated, e.g. the client's currently available balance can be updated after each transaction. This feature can provide an assurance to the trader that not only is the client the legitimate card holder, but also that the client's credit limit has not been exceeded by previous transactions.

The enhanced security provided by the smart card can lead to renewed interest in home banking systems. Such systems have been bedeviled by the high cost of secure home terminals. With the encryption facilities, and secure storage of secret data, provided by smart cards the requisite level of security can now be achieved with relatively simple home terminals.

Access Control

The smart card can meet the demands of many access control applications. In particular they have the following advantages from an access control viewpoint:

- low cost of token and reader;
- protection against PIN experimentation;
- immunity to copying;
- active security protocols;
- protection against masquerading hosts;
- protection against untrusted hosts.

The cards can be protected against PIN experimentation by internal counters, which record the number of incorrect PIN entries, and block off the card after a prespecified number of such attempts. The card can thereafter only be reactivated by authorized security staff.

Unlike many access tokens each smart card has a fixed unique identifier, and the internal secret codes can neither be copied or modified, with the level of technology available to a potential attacker.

Sophisticated access control protocols, such as challenge response demand a degree of processing at the user end. Such processing involves use of secret data that should not be revealed outside the token; the smart card is ideally suited to this form of protocol.

Such protocols involve two stages of authentication. Users first prove their identity to the card, by keying in the PIN on the card reader terminal, and then a challenge response dialogue takes place between the card and the host.

With symmetric cipher systems, e.g. DES, the host computer issues a challenge in the form of a random number that is received, encrypted with a secret key, and returned to the host. The host retrieves the secret key, corresponding to the userID, and likewise encrypts the random number. If the two sets of ciphertext are identical, the user is authenticated. An eavesdropper would gain no benefit from the data exchanged in the login dialogue.

In a similar protocol, using public key cryptography, the card encrypts the random number with the RSA secret key; the host retrieves the public key corresponding to the userid, decrypts the returned ciphertext with the public key, stored with the userid, and checks the result against the original random number. The Fiat-Shamir dialogue similarly provides for a dialogue that differs for each login, but is less computationally demanding than RSA.

The challenge response technique can be used in both directions, thus allowing the user to authenticate the host. With public key protocols each user can be supplied a copy of the host's public key, a process involving fewer security hazards than the mass distribution of a host secret key, as would be required with DES challenge response dialogues.

The conventional password system of user authentication also suffers from the disadvantage when a user accesses an untrusted host, i.e. a computer system that cannot be trusted with the user's confidential data. Any technique, designed to overcome this problem, involves a dialogue to provide proof of identity, without revealing the secret information held by the user. Such a technique normally requires a user device, that can securely store secret information and undertake a degree of local processing. The Fiat-Shamir techniques described above do not require the user to reveal their secret information, the login dialogue merely enables a genuine host to satisfy itself that the user does, indeed, have access to the requisite secret information.

Personalized File

Smart cards can have local storage capacities ranging from tens of kilobytes up to the megabit level. They therefore can be used to hold extensive, sometimes sensitive, personal data such as medical history or student assessment records. Such storage may be provided as a value added service to (say) a medical insurance card used to transact payments.

Personalized Encryption Device

The smart card may be used as a personalized encryption device for PCs. The user inserts a personalized smart card into the particular PC and uses the processing power of the smart card to encrypt and decrypt sensitive files. The main disadvantage of this technique, compared with PC encryptor boards, lies in the comparatively low data rate on the communication line to the card reader.

The encryption device can also be used to authenticate, or check the authenticity of, messages. A smart card with a DES key and algorithm can be used to compute a MAC for a message with the user's key, or check the MAC for a received message. Thus the smart card could be employed by executives to give an electronic authority to a transaction, or check the authenticity of a received transaction. Similarly smart cards with public key facilities can provide a genuine digital signature for a message.

Electronic Data Interchange

An EDI system employing smart cards is illustrated in Fig. 2 The in-built security of EDI systems demands that transactions are protected against modification, loss, unauthorized disclosure, injection, replay and repudiation. Cryptography is thus an essential feature of such systems and key management will be of prime importance to the security of the system. However, if the cryptographic facilities are built into the terminal then an organization will be held responsible for all transactions emanating from that terminal; terminal access control will then be a major security concern. On the other hand, if the cryptographic facilities are contained within a manager's smart card, inserted in a card reader linked to the terminal, then an unattended terminal will be a less inviting target for attack.

Future Trends

There are two scenarios in the future of smart cards, market expansion in the size and number of application areas and technological developments in the card.

The smart card is likely to be dominated by the consumer market, which is dictated by price and consumer acceptability. To this extent one can reasonably forecast that the smart card will replace the magnetic stripe card in the consumers wallet. One particular advantage is that the multi-application nature of smart cards will mean that one such card can replace the mass of magnetic stripe cards now resident in wallets and purses.

Another important development in smart cards lies in the replacement of the card PIN, with a user's biometric template. With the user template stored on a smart card, then the biometric reader can ensure that the person presenting smart card is indeed the legitimate card holder, without having to retrieve the user's template from a central database. *See* ASYNCHRONOUS TRANSMISSION, CHALLENGE\RESPONSE, CONTACTLESS SMART CARD, DES, DIGITAL SIGNATURE, EDI, EEPROM, ELECTRONIC PURSE, EPROM, FEAL, FIAT-SHAMIR ALGORITHM, ISO 7816, LCD, MAC, MAGNETIC STRIPE CARD, MICROPROCESSOR, NONVOLATILE STORAGE, PIN, PUBLIC KEY CRYPTOGRAPHY, RAM, ROM, RSA, RS232-C, SUPERSMART CARD, SYMMETRIC CIPHER, SYNCHRONOUS TRANSMISSION, TEMPLATE, USER ID, VIDEOTEX, WIRED LOGIC CARD.

smart terminal. In computing, a terminal which provides additional features to those of a dumb terminal, in general such a terminal will have some memory and processing power and can provide formatted displays, graphic displays, upload and download facilities etc. *Compare* DUMB TERMINAL. *See* DOWNLOAD, UPLOAD.

SMF. In computer security, a data security package. *See* DATA SECURITY PACKAGE.

SMIB. *See* SECURE MANAGEMENT INFORMATION BASE.

smoke detector. In physical security, a device that senses the presence of particles of combustion. *See* COMBINATION SMOKE DETECTOR, IONIZATION SMOKE SENSOR, PHOTOELECTRIC BEAM SMOKE DETECTOR.

SMTP. *See* SIMPLE MAIL TRANSFER PROTOCOL.

SNA. *See* SYSTEM NETWORK ARCHITECTURE.

snapshot. In auditing, pertaining to the observation of different processing steps in a processing cycle. *See* TAGGING.

Snefru. In cryptography, a one-way hash function. *See* ONE-WAY FUNCTION.

s/n ratio. *See* SIGNAL TO NOISE RATIO.

societal vulnerability. In computer security, the possibility of loss, injury or the denial of equal rights to a significant segment of the population, as well as potential weakening of social stability, or risk to national sovereignty as a result of dependence on computer based technology. (AFIPS).

soft error. In computing, an error in reading data from a magnetic disk which can be corrected by rereading the sector or by moving the read write head back and forth. *Compare* HARD ERROR.

softlifting. In computer security, illegal copying of licensed software for personal use. *See* SOFTWARE PROTECTION.

software. The programs, procedures, routines and possibly documents associated with the operation of a data processing system. *Compare* FIRMWARE, HARDWARE.

software analysis. In computer security, software errors are not only a source of nonmalicious errors in a system they can also be exploited as security flaws. The analysis of existing software can be assisted by software tools; generally such tools can be categorized as static analysis and dynamic analysis tools. *See* DYNAMIC ANALYSIS, STATIC ANALYSIS, SOFTWARE TOOL.

software creep. In computing, the ad hoc, unauthorized copying of a program for another user but without a profit motive. *Compare* PIRACY.

software development life cycle. In computing, the phases of the software development life cycle are: initiation, definition, design, programming, test and operation.

software engineering. In computing, a broadly defined discipline that integrates the various aspects of programming, from writing code to ensuring that budgets are met, in order to produce efficient and cost effective software. *See* SOFTWARE.

software house. In software, an organization offering software support services to users. *See* SOFTWARE.

software interface functions. In computer security, TCB operations that can be invoked by software. (MTR). *See* TCB.

software interrupt. In computing, an interrupt caused by a high priority program requiring the services of the CPU. *Compare* HARDWARE INTERRUPT. *See* INTERRUPT, CPU.

software license. In computing, an agreement between a user and a vendor of software describing the user's rights to the software. *See* SHRINK-WRAPPED LICENSE, SOFTWARE.

software maintenance. In computing, the improvements and changes required to keep programs up to date and ensure effective operation. *See* SOFTWARE.

software package. In computing, a set of programs for a specific purpose, often written by a software house.

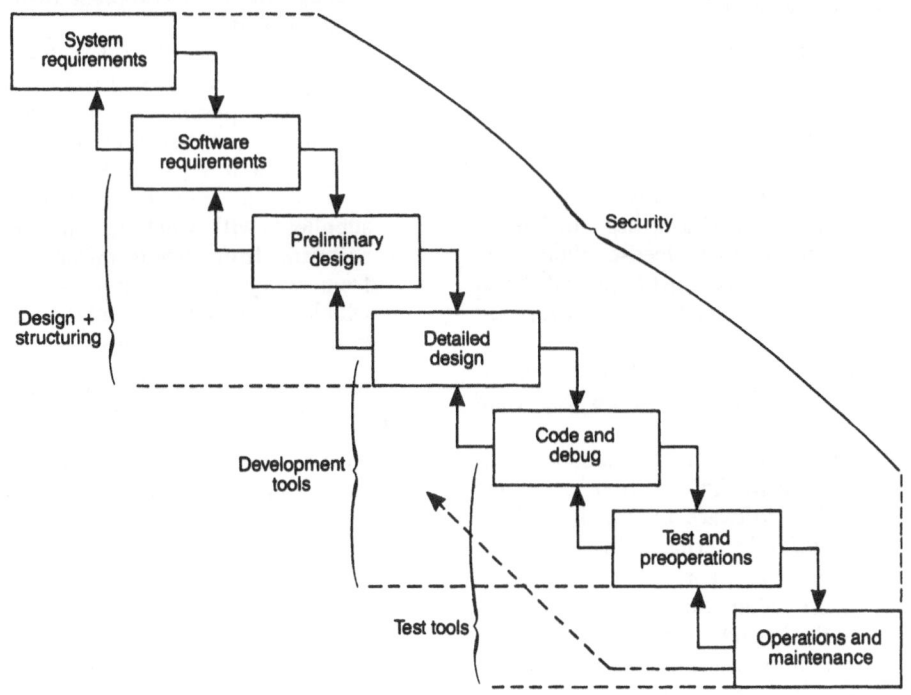

software development life cycle

software piracy. *See* PIRACY.

software protection. In computer security, the adoption of both legal and technical methods to prevent the unauthorized use or exploitation of software. Technical methods usually employ some means of preventing a copied program from being executed. Software may be protected by the intellectual property laws in some countries, but this is usually uncertain and limited. As a result it has become traditional for software suppliers to supplement and enhance that protection by appropriate contractual provisions contained in the software license.

The legal basis for contractual protection.
From a purely legal viewpoint view suppliers have three basic intentions which they aim to achieve by means of a contract with a purchaser, so far as protection is concerned.

- To define the extent to which the purchaser can use the software, on the basis that anything else would constitute an infringement of copyright. Thus the purchaser is granted a limited license under the copyright and any use outside the terms of that license should, in theory, be actionable provided that such use constitutes a restricted act, such as reproduction, translation or adaption within the meaning of the appropriate copyright legislation.
- To maintain the confidentiality of any secret information contained in the software by the imposition of suitable terms. Most countries have some sort of protection of confidential information but this will depend upon the extent to which the information is not in the public domain. The imposition and enforcement of suitable terms can enable confidentiality to be maintained in software, particularly software which has a limited distribution.
- To have a contractual remedy against the recipient of the software. The software supplier may well want to have a contractual remedy against a purchaser, in the event that it has no remedy as a result of the law of copyright or confidentiality, and also where any exclusive rights do not extend to the problem with which the supplier is concerned.

The interests to be protected
Suppliers want to sell the maximum number of their software packages. To achieve this a supplier will want:

- every user to buy their own software package;
- in the case of customer who has many computers, such as a large corporate user, to sell a software package for each computer owned by the customer;
- to limit the use of each software package to the personal use of the particular purchaser, especially where the purchaser is one of a group of a large number of companies. In addition, software suppliers will want to stop the software from being misused or from being used for purposes for which the suppliers could expect to make sales themselves.

This means that a supplier wants to prevent:

- unauthorized copying, whether for use within the customer's organization, or as a straightforward software piracy for profit;
- unauthorized use on a local area network or remote access entry systems;
- the use of the software for the development of competing products.

Traditional software license agreement.
As a practical matter the way in which contractual protection can be applied depends very much on the type of software. Traditionally computer software has always been supplied under license. The supplier would generally have a standard form of license agreement which the end user customer was required to sign before being allowed possession of the software. This type of contract is still widely used but it can only be used in circumstances where a customer and the supplier, or the supplier's agent, are both in a position to sign the agreement. This is still the case where an end user purchases a sophisticated software system, often tailored to the user's specific requirements, or is buying an integrated software/hardware system.

On the other hand such arrangements are no longer appropriate for mass market software for use with microcomputers, and in particular for the home computer market. Nowadays such software is generally sold to an end user by a computer store, or high street dealer, who may be at the end of a distribution chain well removed from the original software supplier. In this situation, particularly with software costing about the same as a compact disk, it is unrealistic or commercially unacceptable for the end user to be expected to sign an agreement.

To overcome this problem software suppliers have tried to develop new techniques to impose contractual conditions upon end users. In particular, throughout the world, distributors of software have followed the technique originally developed in the United States of 'shrink-wrapped license agreements' whereby the customer is deemed to have accepted restrictions on use simply by tearing open a sealed package containing the diskette.

In many countries, however, this technique is not likely to be legally recognized, since it may be considered to place an undue onus on an unsuspecting purchaser of software.

Shrink-wrapped license agreement
The object is to impose terms of use, similar to those contained in traditional license agreements, when the customer purchases software packages from high street dealers. The shrink-wrapped, or tear-me-open, license agreements were devised to try to meet the need for the customer to purchase software as simply as possible.

The manufacturer packs the software in such a way that the user has, in order to obtain access to the diskettes, to open a wrapper or envelope on which the terms of the so-called license agreement are printed. The envelope is sealed so as to direct the end user to the terms of the license agreement, together with a statement that opening the diskette package will indicate the purchaser's acceptance of the limitations. The position is reinforced by the inclusion of suitable wording on the pack making it clear to the end user that by buying the pack he or she is accepting the terms of the contract which it contains.

The legal theory behind this method is that the end user has bought outright the diskettes, manuals and other physical manifestations of the package but only obtains a limited license to use the programs. In practice it would prove difficult in many jurisdictions, such as the United Kingdom, for the manufacturer to enforce any limitations directly against an end user because of the problems of the privity of the contract, bearing in mind that it is the dealer who is the other party to the actual contract of sale.

The terms of the shrink-wrapped agreement
A shrink-wrapped license agreement usually contains the provisions listed below.

● *Conditions of purchase.* The license will first make a general statement along the lines that the product is sold subject to limitations on permitted use customary in the sale of microcomputer software for personal use. It will also be expressly brought to the user's notice that the terms of the agreement are set out on the product and that opening the diskette package indicates acceptance of the limitations. It is also common for there to be a statement that if the end user does not accept the limitations, the product should be returned to the dealer and the purchase price refunded.

- *Permitted uses.* The license agreement will usually include provisions whereby: the license granted is for personal use only; the software is only to be used on any item of compatible hardware owned or used by the purchaser; and sometimes the software is to be used only on one microcomputer at any one time.

- *Uses not permitted.* The license then sets out uses which are not permitted under the license. These include: use of the software on a multiple processor or multiple site arrangement; the use of the software in a computer service business or for remote access entry; the making of copies of the diskettes and associated documentation, except possibly for security purposes; the making of alterations to the software; the right to grant sublicenses; disassembly or decompilation; the making of translations of, or modifications to, the software for use with non-compatible hardware.

Quite apart from the validity of these terms as a matter of contract or copyright law, in some jurisdictions there might also be antitrust considerations, particularly in the United States. *See*

COPY PROTECTION, COPYRIGHT, DISKETTE, EXECUTE PROTECTION, LOCAL AREA NETWORK, SHRINK-WRAPPED LICENSE, SOFTWARE LICENSE.

software quality. *Synonymous with* COMPUTER SOFTWARE QUALITY.

software redundancy. In reliability, that part of the program that would not be necessary if the system were guaranteed to be fault-free.

software security. In computer security, pertaining to general purpose software, e.g. operating system, utility, software development tool, and applications programs and routines which protect data or information handled by a data processing system and its resources.

software security certification. In computer security, the evaluation of a given computer system and all related personnel and facilities from the perspective of a particular application. The basic objective of this process is to certify that the degree of security provided, by the computer environment in which the application is operated, is compatible with the level of security required by the application. *See* CERTIFICATION.

software tool. In computing, a program that is used to facilitate the development, or analysis, of other programs. Most operating systems provide: editors, to produce and modify source program files, translators, to convert from high or low level languages to machine language, linking loaders to assemble separately compiled modules into the form suitable for execution and debuggers for the study of programs containing errors.

SOIC. U.S. Senior Official of the Intelligence Community.

Solano. In computer security, a virus

that terminates and stays resident, infects COM files, affects run time operation, corrupts program and OVL files and file linkage. *See* VIRUS NAMES.

SOM. In data communications, a character in a poll response that precedes the address, or addresses, of any data stations other than the master station that are to receive the message. *See* POLLING.

something the user has. In access control, a technique by which access is granted on the basis of possession of some physical object or token. *Compare* SOMETHING THE USER IS, SOMETHING THE USER KNOWS. *See* TOKEN.

something the user is. In access control, a technique by which access is granted on the basis of a physical characteristic of the user, e.g. fingerprint, or some behavioral characteristic, e.g. performance of writing a signature. *Compare* SOMETHING THE USER HAS, SOMETHING THE USER KNOWS. *See* BIOMETRICS. PIN.

something the user knows. In access control, a technique by which access is granted on the basis of knowledge possessed by the user, e.g. password or PIN. *Compare* SOMETHING THE USER HAS, SOMETHING THE USER IS. *See* PASSWORD, PIN.

SON. Statement of Need.

sonic motion detector. In physical security, a device which detects the presence of an intruder by a disturbance in a pattern of audible signals generated in the protected area. *Compare* ULTRASONIC MOTION DETECTOR. *See* MOTION DETECTOR, PROTECTED AREA.

sonogram. In communications security, a three dimensional graphic representation of a sound signal. The two axes represent time and frequency whilst the amplitude is indicated by gray scale of the graph, i.e. black indicates high amplitude, and white low amplitude. *See* VOICE SCRAMBLING.

sonograph. In communications security, a device for producing a sonogram. *See* SONOGRAM.

Sorry. In computer security, a virus that terminates and stays resident, infects COMMAND.COM and COM files, affects run time operation, corrupts program and OVL files. *See* VIRUS NAMES.

source. In data communications, a point of message entry into the system. *Compare* SINK.

source authorization. In data security, the authorization given to a sender to transmit a high priority or sensitive message. This authorization is a countermeasure against network flooding. *See* FLOODING.

source code analyzer. In computer security, a software tool, used in static evaluation, which provides details on those specific characteristics of the source program, e.g. cross reference testing, variables which can exercise control decisions. *Compare* CODE REVIEW, PENETRATION STUDY. *See* SOFTWARE TOOL, SOURCE PROGRAM, STATIC EVALUATION.

source code. In computing, the original code of a user's program prior to being translated, e.g. compiled, assembled, interpreted. *Compare* OBJECT CODE. *See* SOURCE LANGUAGE.

source code escrow. *See* ESCROW AGENT.

source language. In computing, a high level computing language in which the user's program is written. *Compare* OBJECT LANGUAGE.

source program. In computing, a computer program written in a source language. *See* SOURCE CODE, SOURCE LANGUAGE.

source suppression. In communications security, the careful design of circuitry and layout so that no compromising signals are emitted. *Compare* ENCAPSULATION. *See* TEMPEST PROOFING.

SOW. Statement of Work.

space. (1) A blank column or character. (2) In communications, an impulse, or absence of an impulse, to signify a binary zero condition. *Compare* MARK.

space division multiplexing. In communications, the grouping of more than one physical transmission path. In landline communications, many wire pairs may be combined in one cable; in satellite communications, an antenna can focus a number of spot beams to different geographical locations. *Compare* TIME DIVISION MULTIPLEXING. *See* MULTIPLEXING.

space division switching. In communications, a method for switching circuits in which each connection through the switch takes a different physical path. *Compare* TIME DIVISION SWITCHING.

space protection. *Synonymous with* AREA PROTECTION.

spacial redundancy. *Synonymous with* PROTECTIVE REDUNDANCY.

span sensor. In physical security, a sensor than covers a straight and narrow area between two points, e.g. a photoelectric sensor. *See* PHOTOELECTRIC SENSOR.

Special. *See* HDM.

special access programs. In computer security, any programs imposing need-to-know or related security requirements or constraints which are beyond those normally provided for the protection of information classified in one of the three security classification designations; i.e., Confidential, Secret, or Top Secret. Such a program includes but is not limited to, special clearance, adjudicative, or investigative requirements, special designation of officials authorized to determine need-to-know, or special lists or briefings of personnel determined to have a need-to-know. SIOPESI is an example of a DOD Special Access Program. Other sources of additional access control or other pertinent security requirements, not generally applicable to the same security classification category within DOD include: (a) the Atomic Energy Act of 1954; (b) procedures based on International Treaty requirements; and (c) programs for the collection of foreign intelligence or under the jurisdiction of the National Foreign Intelligence Board or the U.S. Communications Security Board. (OPNAVINST). *See* NEED TO KNOW, SIOP-ESI.

specialized common carrier. In communications, a U.S. organization, not a telephone company, authorized by a 1971 FCC decision to provide a domestic point-to-point communication service on a common carrier basis. *See* COMMON CARRIER, FCC, POINT-TO-POINT.

special markings. In data security, markings that are not classification levels (but rather) are used on certain classified documents to indicate that the document has special access or handling requirements. (DOE). *Synonymous with* HANDLING CAVEATS, HANDLING RESTRICTIONS.

special purpose. Pertaining to systems and devices that have been specifically designed for use in a limited set of applications.

specification. A technical description of the desired behavior of a system, as derived from its requirements. A specification is used to develop and test the implementation of a system. *See* REQUIREMENT.

speech invertor. In communications security, a form of voice scrambling which interchanges the high and low frequencies of the voice signal. The voice waveform is amplitude modulated with a carrier signal, and the lower sideband is transmitted. If a sinusoidal signal of frequency f_m is amplitude modulated with a carrier frequency f_c the lower sideband frequency is $f_c - f_m$. Thus the high frequency components of the original signal appear as the low frequency components of the transmitted signal. The change introduced by this technique is probably insufficient to reduce the residual intelligibility to a satisfactory level. Moreover an interceptor can reverse the scrambling process to reveal the original message. *See* AMPLITUDE MODULATION, BAND SHIFT INVERTOR, CARRIER, RESIDUAL INTELLIGIBILITY, VOICE SCRAMBLING.

speech recognizer. In computing, a system that receives spoken word and identifies the message. The system output can then be used to initiate appropriate actions or responses. *Compare* SPEECH SYNTHESIZER.

speech scrambling. *Synonymous with* VOICE SCRAMBLING.

speech synthesizer. In man-machine interfaces, a system which produces the sound of spoken words according to stored text or commands. The current methods fall into two categories, stored digitized sound waveforms and formant synthesis. *See* FORMANT.

SPEED. In banking, an acronym in Bahasa Malaysia for the automated interbank clearing house system in Malaysia. *See* BANKING NETWORKS.

split knowledge. (1) In procedural security, a technique in which two or more parties hold data that must be combined in order to reveal a security parameter or to undertake a sensitive operation. *See* SEPARATION OF DUTIES OR FUNCTIONS, THRESHOLD. (2) In key management, a condition under which two or more parties separately have key components which, individually, convey no knowledge of the resultant cryptographic key. The resultant key exists only within secure equipment as the automatically generated exclusive-or'ed result of the full length key components which each individual entered separately and confidentially. (ANSI). *See* CRYPTOGRAPHIC KEY, EXCLUSIVE OR, ANSI X9.17 - 1985.

split site. In risk management, pertaining to the use of two sites to perform the data processing functions of a company so that the essential functions can continue to be performed if one of the sites ceases to be operational. The capability of the smaller of the two sites must be sufficient to perform all essential functions. The two sites should be sufficiently close to maintain essential liaison after the disaster event, but also sufficiently separated to ensure that they are not both affected by the same event. *Compare* HOT SITE.

spoofing. (1) In data security, assuming the characteristics of another computer system or user, for the purpose of deception. (2) In key management, the interception\modification of exchanged keys by an attacker. If two parties employ public key cryptography to exchange DES keys (say), then the normal exchange might be as described below.

- Alice requests Bob's public enciphering key.
- Bob responds to this request and sends encrypting key E_B to Alice.

- Alice then sends a DES data, or key encrypting, key K_A encrypted under E_B, i.e. $eE_B(K_A)$ to Bob.
- Bob receives $eE_B(K_A)$ and decrypts it with D_B, Bob's private deciphering key, to reveal K_A, which is then used for subsequent communication with Alice.

A spoofer intercepts and modifies communication between the parties. In this case the chain of events are:

- Alice requests Bob's public enciphering key.
- The spoofer intercepts this message, returns the spoofer's public encrypting key, E_s, to Alice and then forwards the request for Bob's public enciphering key.
- Alice forwards the DES key K_A, encrypted under E_s, to Bob and this message is, once again, intercepted by the spoofer.
- Meanwhile Bob has responded to the request for the public enciphering key E_B, which is yet again captured by the spoofer.
- The spoofer decrypts $eE_s(K_A)$ with D_s and encrypts the same, or a different, DES key with Bob's public key E_B.
- The encrypted message is then sent to Bob.
- Alice and Bob now undertake communications with a key, or keys, supplied by the spoofer who intercepts these message and reads or modifies them at will.

Even if the spoofer only operates for a limited period substantial damage may accrue to the two parties. A form of defence against the spoofer involves either a direct separate line of communication or agreed passwords exchanged over a secure channel. The parties can authenticate their messages and retain authentication data. If Bob authenticates the key E_A and retains the authentication block, then Alice can perform a similar authentication function on the received

key. A telephone call between the two parties, to check the authentication blocks, would reveal any modification of messages relating to keys.

If the two parties have previously exchanged passwords then a spoofer's operations can be detected. Alice encrypts her password, P_A, with the key currently used for communication with Bob, but only half of the encrypted block is forwarded to Bob. Bob likewise forwards half of the encrypted block of password P_B. When these two halves have been received by each party they forward the second halves of the encrypted blocks, decrypt the whole message and check the prearranged passwords.

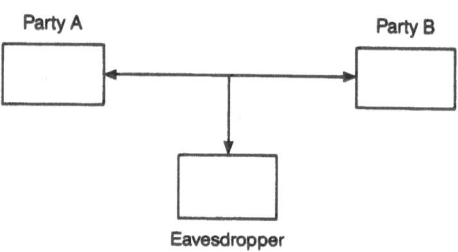

Eavesdropper

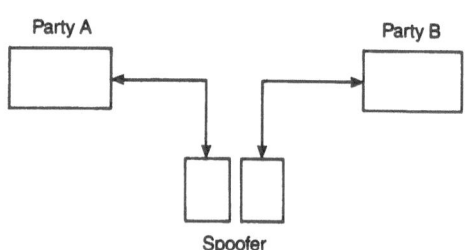

Spoofer

spoofing

The eavesdropper has to tap onto a communications link and monitor traffic, whereas the spoofer inserts himself into a link in such a way that the parties are given the impression of direct communications. The spoofer will try and share one key with party A and another key with party B, thus breaking the communications security. Spoofing bypasses the formidable task of deciphering traffic through cryptanalysis, an issue which the eavesdropper must confront with enciphered data.

The spoofer, who decrypts with one key and re-encrypts the messages with a second key for onward transmission, is now in a quandary. Parties A and B will not transmit the second half of the encrypted password blocks until they have received the first half from the other party. The spoofer cannot, however, sensibly decrypt and re-encrypt the half blocks received for onward transmission, any message sent by the spoofer for the first half block could not be subsequently joined with the second half block to decrypt as the known password. *See* DES, DIFFIE-HELLMAN TECHNIQUE, KEY-ENCRYPTING KEY, PUBLIC KEY CRYPTOGRAPHY. (3) In computer security, the deliberate inducement of a user or a resource to take an incorrect action. (FIPS). (4) In data communications, a technique to enable a multiplicity of computers to deal with a variety of terminals. Software emulators running on microprocessors in the channel interfaces make the network appear to the terminal as its own type of computer, and the terminals appear to the computer as its own type of terminal. *See* CHANNEL, EMULATOR, SOFTWARE.

spoofing program. In computer security, a section of malicious code which masquerades as the operating system, presenting a log on screen and tricking users into revealing their passwords. *See* MALICIOUS CODE.

spray paint. In database security, a technique employing cryptographic checksums to ensure that the security classification, or data, of a database record cannot be undetectably altered by an attacker. A MAC is computed for the message comprising the record and its classification, using a secret key. The technique is so named because a record is indelibly 'colored' with its classification. *See* MAC. *Synonymous with* INTEGRITY LOCKING.

spurious association initiation. In

communications security, an attack in which PDU's from a previous legitimate message are replayed or an association is established under a false identity. *Compare* DENIAL OF MESSAGE SERVICE, MESSAGE STREAM MODIFICATION. *See* PDU, REPLAY.

spurious key decipherment. In cryptography, a meaningful message, produced by the decipherment process on a given ciphertext message, which may or may not differ from another meaningful message produced by decipherment of the same ciphertext with a different key. If decipherment of ciphertext message C1, with key K1, produces meaningful plaintext message P1, then a spurious key decipherment message P2 is produced by decipherment of C1 with a different key K2; P2 may be the same as P1. *See* CRYPTOGRAPHIC KEY. *Synonymous with* FALSE SOLUTION.

SPX. *See* SIMPLEX.

Spyer. In computer security, a virus that terminates and stays resident, infects COM, EXE and OVL files, affects run-time operation, corrupts program and OVL files. *See* VIRUS NAMES.

SRN. In banking, System Reference Number, a number that identifies the message within a service. (ANSI). *Synonymous with* SSN.

SSN. In banking, System Sequence Number. *Synonymous with* SRN.

SSO. *See* SYSTEM SECURITY OFFICER.

stack. In computing, a structure in which items are added at the end of a sequential list and can only be retrieved from the same end. Thus a LIFO strategy is employed. *Compare* QUEUE. *See* LIFO.

stack pointer. In computing, a storage location holding the address of the most recently stored item in a stack. *See* STACK.

Staf. In computer security, a virus that terminates and stays resident, infects COMMAND.COM and COM files, affects run-time operation, corrupts program and OVL files and file linkage. *See* VIRUS NAMES.

stale message. *Synonymous with* RE-PLAY.

standalone terminal. In data communications, a terminal that can be directly connected via a modem and is not, therefore, a member of a cluster. *See* MODEM.

standards. In data security, common methods and protocols for data protection which enable the secure exchange of data between parties which may not belong to the same organization. The standards in data security cover cryptographic algorithms, the mode of use of such algorithms and the communication of secure messages. The bodies concerned with data security standards include Federal Telecommunications Standards Committee, NIST, NSA, ANSI, BSI, DIN, AFNOR and ISO. A specific subcommittee of the ISO, TC 97/SC20, was established to consider data security standards. DES was adopted by the U.S. government as a standard for symmetric data encipherment and was then accepted as the American national standard called the Data Encryption Algorithm. In addition to standards for cryptographic algorithms there are requirements for standards on the modes of use of such algorithms, e.g. ECB, CBC, CFB and OFB. These modes of use are subject to Federal Information Processing Standard (1980) and an American national standard (1983). The OSI architecture provides a standard for data communication and the role of encryption within that architecture is also be subject to a

standard. The Federal Telecommunication Standard 1026 provides a precise definition of the implementation of encipherment at the physical layer and ANSI has issued a standard defining implementation at the physical and data link layers. In the banking field ANSI X9.8 describes the management of PINs, X9.9 deals with the application DES to the authentication of financial messages and X9.17 is concerned with key management for wholesale banking. The Federal Telecommunications Standard 1027 defines the physical security requirements for equipment using DES. *See* AFNOR, ANSI, ANSI X9.8 - 1982, ANSI X9.9 - 1986, ANSI X9.17 - 1985, BSI, CBC, CFB, DATA LINK LAYER, DIN, ECB, FIPS, NIST, NSA, OFB, OSI SECURITY, PHYSICAL LAYER.

standby. In reliability, a condition in which a complete resumption of stable operation is possible within a short time. *See* COLD STANDBY, WARM STANDBY, HOT STANDBY.

standby equipment. In reliability, a duplicate system to be used if the primary unit becomes unusable as a result of malfunction. *See* STANDBY.

standby facility. In risk management, a facility that does nothing until the primary one is lost. Possible variations include a facility doing routine work ready to take over in an emergency.

star. In data communications, a network topology in which each node is connected only to one central controller. This network is commonly employed when a number of terminals are connected to a single host computer and the majority of traffic is concerned with host/terminal rather than terminal/terminal communications. However this topology suffers from disadvantages:

● a breakdown at the host disrupts

- all traffic;
- throughput is limited by the host capacity;
- the cost of cabling may be very high;
- there is no alternate path in case of failure in the line between a host and a terminal.

Compare RING. *See* LOCAL AREA NETWORK.

Star Dot. In computer security, a virus that terminates and stays resident, infects COM files, affects run-time operation, corrupts program and OVL files and file linkage. *See* VIRUS NAMES.

star property. In computer security, a Bell-La Padula security model rule allowing a subject write access to an object only if the security level of the subject is dominated by the security level of the object. (DOD). *See* BELL-LA PADULA MODEL, DOMINATE, OBJECT, SECURITY LEVEL, SUBJECT. *Synonymous with* CONFINEMENT PROPERTY, STAR SECURITY PROPERTY.

star security property. *Synonymous with* STAR PROPERTY.

start bit. In codes, a bit used in asynchronous transmission preceding a serial character and signalling the start of that character. *Compare* STOP BIT. *See* ASYNCHRONOUS TRANSMISSION.

start element. *See* START BIT.

start of header. In data communications, a control character used at the beginning of a sequence of characters that constitute the address or routing information for the message. *See* HEADER.

start of text. In data communications, a transmission control character that terminates a message heading and indicates that successive characters relate to the

text of the message. *Compare* END OF TEXT.

start-stop envelope. In data communications, a string of data elements comprising start elements, binary data and stop elements used in asynchronous communications. The envelope can arrive at any time, the receiver remains in an idling mode until the start element arrives and reverts to the idling mode after the stop element is received. *See* ASYNCHRONOUS TRANSMISSION, START BIT, STOP BIT.

state. In mathematics, an abstraction of the total history of a system, usually in terms of state variables.

statement. In computing, a meaningful expression used to specify an operation and is usually complete in the context of the language used.

static analysis. In computer security, a method of software analysis in which the source code is analyzed without executing it. The software tools of static analysis may be classified:

- code analysis;
- structure analysis;
- module interface analysis;
- event sequence analysis.

Code analysis is a syntactic check of source code that is effectively an extension of the compilation process. Such checking can reveal the existence of programming errors such as variables that are used but not initialized or variables that are initialized but not used. Such checking is performed by many modern compilers but it is a useful check for software developed under older and less powerful compilers.

Structure analysis may be used to develop graphs of the program which reveal flaws such as incorrect nesting of loops, unreferenced labels and unreachable statements. Module interface analysis checks for semantic defects across boundaries; this analysis can detect inconsistencies in the use of global data structures and parameters.

Event sequence analysis examines specified events to ensure that they are in the correct sequence, e.g. opening, writing and closing a file. *Compare* DYNAMIC ANALYSIS. *See* COMPILER, COMPLEXITY ANALYSIS, CONTROL FLOW ANALYSIS, DATA FLOW ANALYSIS, PATTERN DIRECTED ANALYSIS, GLOBAL, LABEL, SOFTWARE TOOL.

static data. In banking, data which will not be subject to frequent change, e.g. customer details, as opposed to that relating to transactions.

static dump. In computing, a dump performed at a particular point in time relative to a machine run, e.g. at the end of the run. *See* DUMP.

static evaluation. In computer security, a detailed examination and analysis of the system documentation and code in order to detect deliberate traps or other unauthorized modifications. The usual techniques of static evaluation include: code review, penetration studies and source code analyzers. *Compare* DYNAMIC TESTING. *See* CODE REVIEW, PENETRATION STUDY, SOURCE CODE ANALYZER.

station. In data communications, an input or output location of a communication system, it will contain the sources and sinks for the messages and those elements that control the message flow on the link.

statistical database. In database security, a database containing aggregate information concerning large subsets of entities, e.g. census data. Such data can be used by an attacker to reveal information concerning individuals unless one of the techniques of inference control are employed. *See* DATA PROTECTION, INFERENCE CONTROL.

statistically unique. In banking, pertaining to a situation in which there is an acceptably low statistical probability of an item (e.g. key or code) being duplicated by chance or intent. (SAA).

statistical time division multiplexing. In data communications, a version of time division multiplexing in which time slots are only allocated to active terminals. This technique increases the number of terminals that may be connected to a given capacity channel. A buffer memory assembles data and is usually sufficient to store channel characters if traffic temporarily exceeds the multiplexer data link rate. *See* MULTIPLEXER, TIME DIVISION MULTIPLEXING.

statmux. *See* STATISTICAL TIME DIVISION MULTIPLEXING.

status poll. In computing, a request, initiated by a computer, for information on the current status of a terminal. *See* POLLING.

STDM. *See* STATISTICAL TIME DIVISION MULTIPLEXING.

stealth virus. In computer security, a virus that seeks to hide its presence by taking over control of the computer. *See* VIRUS.

ST&E. *See* SECURITY TEST AND EVALUATION.

steganography. In data security, the concealment of the existence of messages, literally covered writing. In data security this can take the form of filling in intermessage gaps with padding characters, thus although the existence of the communication link is not concealed an attacker is denied information on when messages are being transmitted. *Compare* CRYPTOGRAPHY.

ST&E tools and equipment. In computer security, specialized techniques, procedures, criteria, standards, programs, or equipment accepted by qualified ST&E personnel for uniform or standard use in testing and evaluating the secure features of ADP systems or networks. (OPNAVINST). *See* ST&E.

STI. *See* SCIENTIFIC AND TECHNICAL INFORMATION.

Stone-90. In computer security, a virus that infects COMMAND.COM and COM files, affects run-time operation, corrupts program and OVL files. *See* VIRUS NAMES.

Stoned. In computer security, a virus that terminates and stays resident, infects floppy disk boot sector and hard disk partition table, affects run-time operation, corrupts boot sector and file linkage. *See* VIRUS NAMES.

stop-and-wait protocol. In data communications, a flow control algorithm in which the sending host awaits acknowledgement, from the receiving host, that error-free frames have been received before transmitting further frames. *Compare* SLIDING WINDOW PROTOCOL. *See* FRAME, HOST.

stop bit. In codes, a bit, used in asynchronous transmission, indicating the end of the character. *Compare* START BIT. *See* ASYNCHRONOUS TRANSMISSION. *Synonymous with* CABOOSE.

stop element. *See* STOP BIT.

storage object. In computer security, an object that supports both read and write accesses. (DOD). *See* OBJECT, READ ACCESS, WRITE ACCESS.

storage protection. *See* MEMORY PROTECTION.

store and forward. In data communications, a system that stores message packets at intermediate points prior to

further transmission. *See* COMPUTER NETWORK, PACKET, MESSAGE SWITCHING.

stream cipher. In cryptography, a method of encryption with the capability of providing perfect secrecy. The plaintext is encoded into numbers, usually binary, and a key stream of random numbers is combined with the plaintext to form the ciphertext. The receiving end is supplied with an identical key stream of random numbers and the mathematical inverse combination of ciphertext and key stream reveals the plaintext. If the key stream of binary numbers is added modulo 2 to the plaintext then the operation of encipherment and decipherment are identical.

This technique does not require that the plaintext be formed into blocks, with a blocksize determined by the cryptographic algorithm designer, the plaintext may be enciphered in segments of any desired length even down to bit-by-bit encipherment. It is therefore valuable in transmission systems where the messages may need to be encrypted character by character or even bit-by-bit.

The major practical disadvantage of this technique lies in the requirement of the secure transmission of key streams, of the same length as the messages, between sender and receiver. In practice a shorter secret key is used to generate pseudorandom bit streams at the transmitter and receiver. To avoid a possible confusion in terminology between the secret key, and the key stream generated, the term cryptographic bit stream is commonly used to describe the stream of random binary digits produced by the generator.

If an attacker can gain access to a portion of the plaintext, P, and corresponding ciphertext, C, then the cryptographic bit stream, KS, used to encrypt the plaintext can be easily determined. For example, if modulo 2 addition is used to produce the ciphertext from the plaintext and cryptographic bit stream:

$C = P +_2 KS$. Hence $KS = C +_2 P$.

Clearly the same cryptographic bit stream should not be used to encrypt different messages. If the cryptographic bit stream is generated by an algorithm based upon a secret key then it must be guaranteed that a knowledge of one segment of the cryptographic bit stream cannot be used to determine other segments; moreover the cryptographic bit stream must be generated from different initial conditions so that the cryptographic bit stream is not repeated in successive invocations of the algorithm.

The initial condition is normally determined by the initialization vector, IV, which can be transmitted in clear as a preamble to the message. In general the IV should not be repeated in successive messages since any such repetition will produce identical cryptographic bit streams. If plaintext messages are highly formatted then an attacker can assemble plaintext/ciphertext segments for each IV. Suppose that the IV comprises only 1 byte, then the attacker can develop 256 codebooks of plaintext/ciphertext pairs.

The IV is used to generate a block of ciphertext, part, or whole, of which is selected as the first segment of the cryptographic bit stream. Feedback from the cryptographic bit stream, plaintext, ciphertext or some combination thereof is then used to provide the initial condition for the generation of the second segment of the cryptographic bit stream.

The error extension properties of the cipher depend upon the quantity selected for feedback. If the cryptographic bit stream alone is selected for feed-back

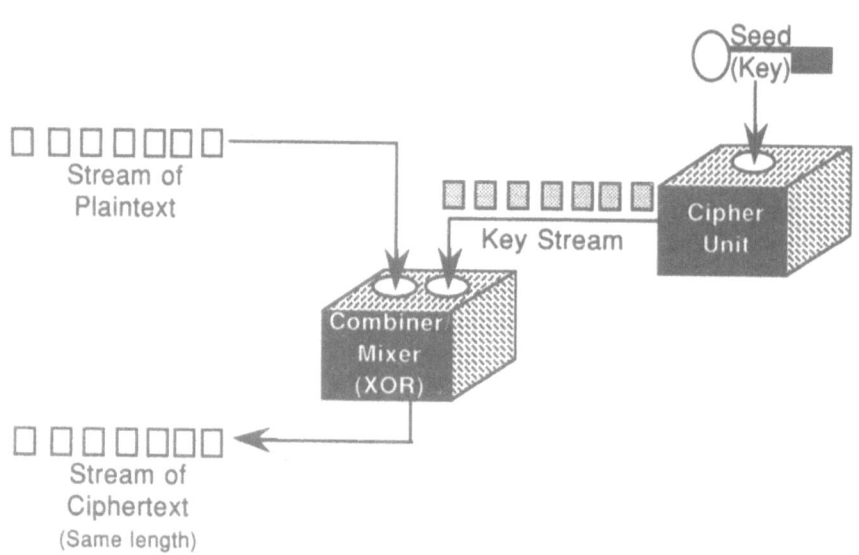

stream cipher

then there is no error extension. In this case the cipher provides no form of authentication; an attacker can modify the ciphertext and produce identical changes in the corresponding received ciphertext. Feedback from the plaintext or ciphertext will provide a degree of error extension which at least signals that the received ciphertext is not identical with that transmitted. *Compare* BLOCK CIPHER, BLOCK CIPHER CHAINING. *See* AUTHENTICATION, CRYPTOGRAPHIC BIT STREAM, CIPHER BLOCK CHAINING, CIPHER FEEDBACK, ERROR EXTENSION, INITIALIZATION VECTOR, KEY STREAM, MODULO ARITHMETIC, PERFECT SECRECY, VERNAM CIPHER.

stream cipher chaining. In cryptography, a stream cipher in which feedback is employed to generate the cryptographic bit stream. Stream ciphers which employ a cryptographic bit stream independent of the ciphertext exhibit neither error extension nor self synchronization. If the cryptographic bit stream is independent of the transmitted ciphertext then an attacker can directly influence the received plaintext, bit-by-bit. The use of feedback from the ciphertext to the generation of the cryptographic bit stream ensures that a one bit change in the ciphertext, either accidentally or deliberately induced, affects more than one bit in the received plaintext, thus providing an indication of the ciphertext change. Stream ciphers without plaintext or ciphertext feedback also provide no means of error recovery when an error in the ciphering process causes differences in the cryptographic bit streams at the transmitting and receiving ends. Chaining in stream ciphers can produce the necessary degree of self synchronization. *Compare* BLOCK CIPHER CHAINING, OUTPUT FEEDBACK. *See* CIPHER FEEDBACK, CRYPTOGRAPHIC BIT STREAM, ERROR EXTENSION, SELF-SYNCHRONIZING, STREAM CIPHER.

strength. In key management, a prop-erty of a key generation process. If the strength of a key generation process is at least equal to that of the resulting keys used then no advantage is gained from attacking the key generation process rather than the corresponding encryption algorithm. *See* CRYPTOGRAPHIC KEY, KEY GENERATION.

Striker. In computer security, a virus that infects COM files, corrupts boot sector, data files and file linkage, affects run-time operation. *See* VIRUS NAMES.

string. In computing, a sequence of characters that can correspond to textual message.

stripe reader. In computing, a device that reads the data encoded on the magnetic stripe of credit cards, etc. and inputs the information into a computer. *See* MAGNETIC STRIPE CARD.

stripping. In data communications, the process of extracting the essential information elements of a message by removing the header and tail parts of the message envelope. *See* HEADER, TAIL.

strong intersymbol dependence. In cryptography, a property of a block cipher in which every bit of the output block is a sufficiently complex function of every bit of the input block and key. A DES message comprising a single 64 bit block exhibits strong intersymbol dependence. *Compare* INTERSYMBOL DEPENDENCE. *See* DES.

structural redundancy. In reliability, a form of hardware redundancy applied at a gate level where multiple parallel paths are established between input and output. *Compare* MODULAR REDUNDANCY.

structure analysis. *See* STATIC ANALYSIS.

STU-III. In communications security, a secure telephone system using end-to-end secret key encryption. *See* END-TO-END ENCRYPTION, SECRET KEY ENCRYPTION.

stub. In computing, an artefact, usually software, that can be used to simulate the behavior of parts of a system. It is usually employed in testing software that relies on those parts of the system simulated by the stub. Stubs render it possible to test a system before all parts of it have been completed.

STX. *See* START OF TEXT.

subject. In computer security, an active entity, generally in the form of a person, process, or device that causes information to flow among objects or changes the system state. (DOD). *Compare* OBJECT.

subject security level. In computer security, a subject's security level is equal to the security level of the objects to which it has both read and write access. A subject's security level must always be dominated by the clearance of the user the subject is associated with. (DOD). *See* DOMINATE, SECURITY LEVEL, SUBJECT.

sub-key. In cryptography, a 48 bit key, produced from the 56 bit cryptographic key, used for one of the 16 rounds of DES encryption or decryption. *See* CRYPTOGRAPHIC KEY, DATA ENCRYPTION STANDARD. (2) In database security, a form of record-oriented encryption. The encrypted record is a single function of all its field values; each field being encrypted/decrypted with a separate key. Each field decryption key will decrypt only the corresponding field in the record.

Subliminal. In computer security, a virus that terminates and stays resident, infects COMMAND.COM and COM files, affects run-time operation, corrupts program and OVL files. *See* VIRUS

NAMES.

subroutine. In computing, a sequence of instructions to perform an action that is frequently required in a program, or set of programs, e.g. to sort a set of strings into alphabetical order.

subschema. In databases, the application programmer's, or end user's, view of the data. *See* SCHEMA.

subscriber's unit. *Synonymous with* AUTHORIZED ACCESS CONTROL SWITCH.

subset. A set of elements, each one of which is a member of another given set. *See* SET.

substantive testing. In computer security, the checking of a large volume of transactions, so that the auditor can verify that the transactions are correct. Normally undertaken if compliance testing has revealed weaknesses in the system. *Compare* COMPLIANCE TESTING.

substitute character. In codes, a control character put in place of a character that is recognized to be in error or cannot be represented on a given device.

substitution box. *Synonymous with* S BOX.

substitution cipher. In cryptography, a cipher in which each character or fixed group of characters is substituted by another character or group of characters. *Compare* TRANSPOSITION CIPHER. *See* CIPHER, CRYPTOGRAPHY, MONOALPHABETIC CIPHER, POLYALPHABETIC CIPHER.

summary processing. In computing, a redundant process using a summarized amount. This is compared for equality with a control total from the processing of the detailed items. *See* REDUNDANT PROCESSING.

summation check. In codes, a check

based upon the comparison of the sum of digits of a numeral with a previously computed value to indicate any accidental change in the value of a digit during transmission or transcriptions. *See* CHECKSUM, REDUNDANCY CHECKING.

Sunday. In computer security, a virus that terminates and stays resident, infects COM, EXE and OVL files, affects run-time operation, corrupts program and OVL files. *See* VIRUS NAMES.

supercomputer. In computing, an extremely powerful mainframe computer used for complex mathematical calculations demanding high speed and storage, e.g. weather forecasting.

superencipherment. (1) In cryptography, multiple encryption. *See* MULTIPLE DES ENCIPHERMENT. (2) In data security, a technique in which a plaintext message is first encoded, i.e. each word or phrase is changed to a preselected code, and the resulting encoded message is then enciphered. *See* CIPHER, CODE, CRYPTOGRAPHY.

superimposed circuit. *Synonymous with* SUPERPOSED CIRCUIT.

superincreasing series. In mathematics, a series of integers in which each term is greater than the sum of all preceding terms. Hence with a set of ordered integers $(a_1, a_2... a_n)$, for each term:

$$a_j > \sum_{i = 1, j-1} a_i$$

See KNAPSACK CIPHER.

superposed circuit. In communications, an additional channel obtained from one or more circuits, usually provided for other channels, in such a way that all the channels can be used simultaneously and without mutual interference. *Synonymous with* SUPERIMPOSED CIRCUIT.

supersmart card. In access control, an enhanced form of smart card with an inbuilt keypad and display. The supersmart card is more secure than a conventional smart card, which must rely upon the keypad and display on the smart card reader. If the smart card reader has been illicitly modified then the user has no assurance that the message displayed is a true reflection of the transaction, that the keys depressed will send signals corresponding to those keys, or that the card PIN will not be captured en route to the smart card. Thus a user may unwittingly:

- authorize a financial transaction when the amount of the transaction differs from that displayed;
- reject a transaction but that rejection is recorded as an authorization;
- reveal the card PIN.

Compare SMART CARD. *Synonymous with* INTELLIGENT TERMINAL.

superuser. In computer security, the system administrator in Unix systems who has extensive access privileges to system and user files and commands. *See* UNIX.

supervised line. In physical security, a wired circuit that is subject to supervision.

supervised system. In physical security, a system that initiates a trouble signal when transmission of an alarm signal could be inhibited by a break, or a ground, in the wiring. *See* ALARM SIGNAL, TROUBLE SIGNAL.

supervision. In physical security, the electrical protection of a wired circuit between specified points. A change in the circuit such as to a break, cross connection, increase or decrease in current or resistance initiates an alarm signal. *See* ALARM SIGNAL, SUPERVISED SYSTEM.

supervisor state. *Synonymous with* EXECUTIVE STATE.

supervisory sequence. In data communications, a sequence of control characters that performs a defined control function.

supervisory signal. (1) In communications, a signal indicating whether a circuit is in use. (2) In communications, a signal that is used to indicate the various operating states of circuit combinations.

superzapping. (1) In data security, pertaining to operations which misuse the computer universal access program in order to bypass normal security arrangements and allow an attacker to make illegal modifications to programs or data. (2) In computing, the process of modifying a program by making a direct change to the object or machine code. *See* PATCH. (3) In computer security, a utility program designed to be used in an emergency by system operators. The program bypasses normal security controls and can delete information. (4) In computer security, pertaining to the use of a ZAP utility program which can modify programs, bypassing controls, to change programs or data stored in the computer.

SURIV01. In computer security, a virus that terminates and stays resident, infects COM files, affects run-time operation, corrupts program and OVL files. *See* VIRUS NAMES.

SURIV02. In computer security, a virus that terminates and stays resident, infects EXE files, affects run-time operation, corrupts program and OVL files. *See* VIRUS NAMES.

susceptibility. In computer security, the state or quality of being more exploitable due to a higher level of sensitivity of operations. (AR).

suspense account. In computing, a control total for items awaiting further processing. *See* SUSPENSE FILE.

suspense file. In computing, a file containing unprocessed or partially processed items awaiting further action.

SVC. *See* SWITCHED VIRTUAL CALL.

Sverdlov. In computer security, a virus that terminates and stays resident, infects COMMAND.COM, COM, EXE and OVL files, affects run-time operation, corrupts program and OVL files. *See* VIRUS NAMES.

Swap Boot. In computer security, a virus that terminates and stays resident, infects floppy disk boot sector, corrupts boot sector. *See* VIRUS NAMES.

sweeping. *See* ELECTRONIC COUNTER-MEASURES SWEEPING.

SWIFT. In banking, the Society for Worldwide Interbank Financial Telecommunications, a private international telecommunication service for banks. (ANSI). *See* BANKING NETWORKS.

Swiss 143. In computer security, a virus that infects COMMAND.COM and COM files, affects run-time operation, corrupts program, OVL and data files. *See* VIRUS NAMES.

switched network backup. In communications, an optional facility enabling a user to specify an alternative path if the primary path is, for some reason, not available.

switched network. In communications, any network that uses switching to establish connections. *See* SWITCHING.

switched virtual call. In data communications, a connection between two terminals which is created only when it is required, following a call set up procedure. *See* PACKET SWITCHING, VIRTUAL CALL SERVICE.

switching. In communications, the provision of point-to-point connections between dynamically changing sources and sinks. *See* SOURCE, SINK, CIRCUIT SWITCHING, MESSAGE SWITCHING, PACKET SWITCHING.

switching center. In communications, a location that terminates multiple circuits and has the capability of transferring traffic between circuits or interconnecting circuits. *Synonymous with* SWITCHING OFFICE.

switching office. *Synonymous with* SWITCHING CENTER.

Sylvia/Holland. In computer security, a virus that infects COM files, corrupts program and OVL files. *See* VIRUS NAMES.

symmetric algorithm. In cryptography, a cryptographic algorithm employing the same value of key for both enciphering and deciphering or for both authentication and validation. (ISO). *Compare* ASYMMETRIC ALGORITHM. *See* AUTHENTICATION, VALIDATION. *Synonymous with* ONE-KEY CRYPTOSYSTEM, SYMMETRIC CIPHER, SYMMETRIC CRYPTOSYSTEM.

symmetric cipher. *Synonymous with* ONE-KEY CRYPTOSYSTEM, SYMMETRIC ALGORITHM, SYMMETRIC CRYPTOSYSTEM.

symmetric cryptosystem. In cryptography, a cipher system in which the enciphering and deciphering keys are equal, or one can easily be deduced from the other. *Compare* ASYMMETRIC CRYPTOSYSTEM, PUBLIC KEY CRYPTOGRAPHY. *Synonymous with* ONE-KEY CRYPTOSYSTEM, SYMMETRIC ALGORITHM, SYMMETRIC CIPHER, SYMMETRIC KEY SYSTEM.

symmetric key system. In cryptography, a cryptosystem that depends on the secrecy of a single key (or key pair) used for both encryption and for decryption. (ANSI). *Compare* ASYMMETRIC KEY SYSTEM. *Synonymous with* ONE-KEY CRYPTOSYSTEM, SYMMETRIC CRYPTOSYSTEM.

SYN. In data communications, a transmission control character used in a binary synchronous communication link to establish synchronization between the sending and receiving equipment. *See* BINARY SYNCHRONOUS COMMUNICATIONS.

sync. *See* SYNCHRONOUS.

sync bit. In data communications, a bit used for synchronization. *See* BIT, SYNCHRONIZATION.

synchronization pulses. In electronics, pulses sent to receiving equipment, by transmitting units, to keep the two units in step. *Synonymous with* SYNC PULSES.

synchronous. Pertaining to two or more processes that require common physical occurrences, e.g. timing pulses for their operation. *Compare* ASYNCHRONOUS.

synchronous data link control. In data communications, IBM's data link control protocol for SNA. It is a discipline for managing synchronous, code transparent, serial-by-bit information transfer over a link. SDLC conforms to subsets of the Advanced Data Link Control Procedures of ANSI and the High Level Data Link Control of the ISO. *See* ADCCP, ANSI, BIT, HDLC, PROTOCOL, SERIAL TRANSMISSION, SYNCHRONOUS TRANSMISSION, TRANSPARENT.

synchronous data network. In data communications, a network in which the timing of all network components is controlled by a single timing source.

synchronous idle character. In data communications, a transmission control character used by DTE's for synchronism or synchronous correction, particularly when no other character is being transmitted. *See* SYNCHRONOUS DATA NETWORK, DTE.

synchronous modem. In data communications, a modem with an internal clock, which produces a continuous stream of data at a fixed transmission rate. Synchronization is required at the bit, byte and message level. *See* BIT, BYTE, MODEM, SYNCHRONOUS TRANSMISSION.

synchronous stream cipher. In cryptography, a stream cipher in which the next state of the cryptographic bit stream depends only upon the previous state and not upon the input. *See* CRYPTOGRAPHIC BIT STREAM, OUTPUT FEEDBACK, STREAM CIPHER.

synchronous transmission. In data communications, a transmission method in which each bit is transmitted according to a given time sequence. It can provide a higher bit rate than asynchronous transmission but requires that the receiver and transmitter maintain exact synchronization over an extended period. *Compare* ASYNCHRONOUS TRANSMISSION. *See* BIT RATE.

sync pulses. *Synonymous with* SYNCHRONIZATION PULSES.

syntax. (1) The interrelationship of characters or groups of characters independent of their meaning, interpretation or use. (2) In computing, the grammatical rules governing the use of a language.

Syslock. In computer security, a virus that encrypts itself, infects COM and EXE files, corrupts program, OVL and data files. *See* VIRUS NAMES.

SYSOP. In computing, SYStems OPerator, the operator of a bulletin board who is responsible for the nature of the information provided. *See* BULLETIN BOARD.

system. (1) In computing, an interdependent collection of components that can be considered as a unified whole, for example, a networked collection of computer systems, a distributed system, a compiler or editor, a memory system. (2) In computing, an assembly of computer and/ or communications hardware, software and firmware configured for the purpose of classifying, sorting, calculating, computing, summarizing, transmitting and receiving, storing and retrieving data with the purpose of supporting users (TNI).

systematic ranges. In database security, a form of result based perturbation in which the statistics are represented as a range of values rather than an individual rounded value. *Compare* SYSTEMATIC ROUNDING.

systematic rounding. In database security, a form of result based perturbation in which the statistic is rounded to the closest integer multiple of a fixed rounding base. *Compare* CONTROLLED ROUNDING, RANDOM ROUNDING. *See* INFERENCE CONTROL, RESULT BASED PERTURBATION, PERTURBATION, SYSTEMATIC RANGES.

system authentication. In authentication, the process of verification of the validity of the system to which access was gained and to which classified information is to be transferred. *See* MASQUERADING.

system card reader. *Synonymous with* ON LINE CARD READER.

system code. *Synonymous with* CARD IDENTIFICATION CODE.

system high. In data security, the highest security level supported by a system at a particular time or in a particular environment (TNI). *Compare* SYSTEM LOW. *See* SECURITY LEVEL, SYSTEM HIGH SECURITY MODE.

system high security mode. (1) In computer security, a mode of operation where all personnel with access to the automated system have a security clearance, but not a need-to-know for all the material then contained in the system. A system operates in the system high security mode when the central computer facility and all of its connected peripheral devices and remote terminals are protected according to the requirement for the highest classification of material contained in the system. In this mode, the system design and operation must provide for some internal control of concurrently available classified material in the system on the basis of need-to-know. (AFR). *Compare* MULTILEVEL SECURITY MODE. *See* DISCRETIONARY ACCESS CONTROL, NEED TO KNOW, MANDATORY ACCESS CONTROL. (2) In computer security, the mode of operation in which system hardware/software is only trusted to provide need-to-know protection between users. In this mode, the entire system, to include all components electrically and/or physically connected, must operate with security measures commensurate with the highest classification and sensitivity of the information being processed and/or stored. All system users in this environment must possess clearances and authorizations for all information contained in the system. All system output must be clearly marked with the highest classification and all system caveats, until the information has been reviewed manually by an authorized individual to ensure appropriate classifications and caveats have been affixed. (DOD). *Compare* MULTILEVEL SECURITY MODE. *See* DISCRETIONARY ACCESS CONTROL, NEED TO KNOW, MANDATORY

ACCESS CONTROL. (3) In computer security, a mode of operation wherein all users having access to the AIS possess a security clearance and formal access approval, but not necessarily a need-to-know, for all data handled by the AIS. (DODD). *See* AIS, NEED TO KNOW.

system integrity. In computer security, the state that exists when there is complete assurance that under all conditions an ADP system is based on the logical correctness and reliability of the operating system, the logical completeness of the hardware and software that implement the protection mechanisms, and data integrity. (FIPS). *See* DATA INTEGRITY, SYSTEM INTEGRITY PROCEDURES.

system integrity procedures. In computer security, the procedures established for assuring that the hardware, software, and data in an ADP system maintain their state of original integrity and are not tampered with by program changes. (FIPS). *See* SYSTEM INTEGRITY.

system low. In computer security, the lowest security level supported by a system at a particular time or in a particular environment (TNI). *Compare* SYSTEM HIGH.

system manager. In computing, the ADP official who is responsible for the operation of an ADP system. (FIPS).

system network architecture. In data communications, IBM's network architecture for distributed data processing. It allows any distributed system to access any host processor in the network through multisystem networking facilities. It also provides the architecture for distribution between multiple processors, as well as between one or more processors and remote intelligent communication systems.

Compare OSI, PROCESSOR INTERCON-NECTION. *See* MULTISYSTEM NET-WORKING.

system penetration. In computer security, a violation or circumvention of operating system safeguards. *See* OPER-ATING SYSTEM, PENETRATION.

system saboteur. In computer security, a person who deliberately causes an error in the operating system so as to render it at least unreliable. *See* OPER-ATING SYSTEM.

systems analysis. In computing, the analysis of an activity or system to determine if and how the system may be improved using computer systems. *See* STRUCTURED SYSTEMS ANALYSIS.

system security audit. In computer security, the process of a security evaluation of systems either on a conceptual basis or on the basis of an examination of an actual implementation. The objectives of the audit are to identify security weaknesses and to propose corrective technical, organizational or procedural measures.

System Security Officer. In computer security, the person responsible for ensuring that security is provided for and implemented throughout the life cycle of an AIS from the beginning of the concept development phase through its design, development, operation, maintenance, and secure disposal. (DODD). *See* AIS.

system users. In computer security, users with direct connections to the system and also those individuals without direct connections who receive output or generate input that is not reliably reviewed for classification by a responsible individual. The clearance of system users is used in the calculation of the risk index. (DOD). *See* RISK INDEX.

T

table. In computing, a collection of data in a form suitable for ready reference, frequently stored in consecutive storage locations or written in the form of an array.

table restriction. In database security, a form of memoryless control in which complete tables of statistics are restricted to minimize the possibility of personal disclosure. In a lattice model this restriction implies that tables at the lower level, i.e. containing more dimensions, will be restricted. *See* LATTICE MODEL, INFERENCE CONTROL, MEMORYLESS CONTROL.

TAC. *See* TERMINAL ACCESS CONTROLLER.

tagged keys. In key management, a technique of including function identifiers within cryptographic keys. DES keys comprise 64 bits but only 56 of these bits can be independently selected, the other 8 bits are used for parity checking. Tagged keys employ the 8 spare bits to convey information on the function of a key employed in a key management system, e.g. data key for encipherment, key-encrypting key etc. The tagged keys are encrypted with key-encrypting keys, for normal use, and cannot therefore be observed or modified by an attacker. When the tagged key is revealed within a tamper-resistant module, the tag is checked to ensure that it corresponds to a valid key for the proposed operation. In the case of a valid key the tag bits are replaced by the appropriate parity bits prior to use of the key in the encipherment or decipherment operation. This technique thwarts attacks in which (say)

a MAC key, encrypted under a MAC master key, is revealed by misuse of data decryption facilities in secure modules. *Compare* CONTROL VECTOR. *See* CRYPTOGRAPHIC KEY, DATA ENCRYPTION STANDARD, PARITY BIT, RE-ENCIPHER FROM MASTER KEY.

tail. (1) In computing, a specified data item indicating the end of a list. *See* LIST. (2) In data communications, a series of codes to denote the end of a message.

tailgating. In access control, the practice of using one access card for successive use by two or more individuals. *See* ANTI-PASSBACK. *Synonymous with* PIGGYBACKING.

Taiwan. In computer security, a virus that infects COM files, corrupts program and OVL files. *See* VIRUS NAMES.

Taiwan3. In computer security, a virus that terminates and stays resident, infects COMMAND.COM, COM, EXE and OVL files, affects run-time operation, corrupts program, OVL and data files and file linkage. *See* VIRUS NAMES.

Taiwan4. In computer security, a virus that terminates and stays resident, infects COMMAND.COM, COM, EXE and OVL files, affects run-time operation, corrupts program, OVL and data files. *See* VIRUS NAMES.

take-grant access control. In access control, a form of capability system in which subjects and users have the privileges of passing on tickets.

In the take-grant model new users may be added to the system, new files created, or deleted, access rights passed from a file owner (say) to allow another user to read or modify the file, or an owner may allow another user to take all the owners privileges to a file, including bestowal privileges. These actions are formalized in the take-grant model by Create, Remove, Grant and Take rules.

- Create - the action of this rule is to create a new subject or object. The subject creating the node will select a set of rights for that subject/object which will be a subset of all possible rights.
- Remove - this rule reduces the set of privileges that one subject/object has in respect to another.
- Grant - rights may be bestowed with this rule.
- Take - this rule allows a subject to decide which subset of privileges it wishes to accept.

See CAPABILITY.

tamper-proof. In data security, pertaining to a device that is designed to protect its contents or functions against physical attack. Such devices contain a number of internal detectors, e.g tilt detectors, light detectors which will erase stored data, e.g. cryptographic keys, in the event that efforts are made to effect illegal access. The term tamper-resistant is now preferred because it more accurately describes the degree of protection provided. *See* TAMPER-RESISTANT MODULE.

tamper-resistant module. In data security, a device in which sensitive information, such as a master cryptographic key, is stored and cryptographic functions are performed. The device has one or more sensors to detect physical attacks, by an adversary trying to gain access to the stored information, in which case the stored sensitive data is immediately destroyed. *See* KEY.

tape. *See* FOIL.

tape dialer. In physical security, a device that automatically reports an alarm to one, or more, remote locations by dialing specified telephone numbers and playing a tape recorded message. *See* TELEPHONE DIALER.

tape streamer. In computing, a magnetic tape transport designed primarily for reading or writing continuous streams of data, as in backup operations. It is mechanically simpler and hence cheaper than start/stop units. *See* BACKING STORAGE.

target of evaluation. In information security, the system or product to be evaluated against security criteria. *See* INFORMATION TECHNOLOGY SECURITY EVALUATION CRITERIA.

tariff. In communications, the published set of rates, rules and regulations relevant to the equipment and services provided by a telecommunications common carrier. *See* COMMON CARRIER.

task. In programming, essentially an application program but it need not be a fully fledged program; it may be a subroutine or subprogram called by an application program for its own use.

TBDF. *See* TRANSBORDER DATA FLOW.

T carrier. In communications, a hierarchy of Bell Telephone digital communication systems designated T1, T2 and T4.

TC 11. A technical committee of IFIP concerned with security and protection of information processing systems. *See* IFIP.

TC 68/SC2. In data security, an ISO committee for secure banking standards.

See ISO.

TC 97/SC17/WG4. In data security, a working group of an ISO committee dealing with standards for physical properties and interface of smart cards. *See* ISO, SMART CARD.

TC 97/SC20. In data security, an ISO committee for data security standards. *See* ISO.

TCB. *See* TRUSTED COMPUTING BASE.

TCB Subset. In computer security, a trusted computing base subset M is a set of software, firmware and hardware (where any of the three could be absent) that mediates the access of a set S of subjects to a set O of objects on the basis of a stated access policy P and satisfies the properties:

- M mediates every access to objects in O by subjects in S;
- M is tamper resistant;
- M is small enough to be subject to analysis and tests, the completeness of which may be assured.

See BLUE BOOK, REFERENCE MONITOR CONCEPT, TRUSTED COMPUTING BASE.

TCP. *See* TRANSMISSION CONTROL PROTOCOL.

TCP/IP. In data communications, Transmission Control Protocol (TP)/Internet Protocol (IP). These protocols form part of a suite of communications protocols developed as part of the original ARPANET (Advanced Research Projects Agency Network) project in the U.S.A. This work commenced in the late 1960's under the auspices of the United States Department of Defense (DoD).

The Transmission Control Protocol (TCP) is similar in concept to the Transport Layer protocol in the OSI Reference Model. (TCP/IP is functionally equivalent to the Class 4 Transport protocol of the OSI Reference Model). TCP/IP provides a reliable connection-oriented service between host computer systems over a communications network, i.e. TCP/IP is an end-to-end (or host-to-host) protocol. TCP/IP is designed to operate over a communications network which may comprise one or more concatenated subnetworks. These subnetworks may not be reliable, e.g. transmission packets may be lost, corrupted or arbitrarily delayed.

The Internet Protocol (IP) is a set of procedures designed to enable messages to be routed between host computer systems across multiple sub-networks. It provides a connectionless (datagram) service and is similar in function to the internetwork protocol developed as an adjunct to the Network Layer protocol in the OSI Reference Model. *See* CONNECTIONLESS SERVICE, DATAGRAM, INTERNET, OPEN SYSTEMS INTERCONNECTION.

TCSEC. *See* TRUSTED COMPUTER SECURITY EVALUATION CRITERIA. *Synonymous with* ORANGE BOOK.

TDF. *See* TRANSBORDER DATA FLOW.

TDM. *See* TIME DIVISION MULTIPLEXING.

tear-me-open. *Synonymous with* SHRINK WRAPPED LICENSE.

technical and office protocol. In standards, specifies standards, and options within standards, appropriate to a local area network and terminals, computing resources, etc. for office and engineering environments. *Compare* MANUFACTURING AUTOMATION PROTOCOL. *See* LOCAL AREA NETWORK, OPEN SYSTEMS INTERCONNECTION.

technical data. Classified or unclassified information of any kind that can be used, or adapted for use, in the design, production, manufacture, repair, overhaul, processing, engineering, development, operation, maintenance, or reconstruction of goods or munitions; or any technology that advances the state of the art or establishes a new art in an area of significant military applicability in the United States. The data may be tangible, such as a model, prototype, blueprint, or an operating manual, or may be intangible, such as a technical service or oral or visual interactions. (DODD). (2) Recorded information related to experimental, developmental, or engineering works that can be used to define an engineering or manufacturing process or to design, procure, produce, support, maintain, operate, repair, or overhaul material. The data may be graphic or pictorial delineations in media such as drawings or photographs, text in specifications or related performance or design type documents, or computer printouts. Examples of technical data include research and engineering data, engineering drawings, and associated lists, specifications standards, process sheets, manuals, technical reports, catalog-item identifications, and related information and computer software documentation. (DODD).

technical policy. In computer security, the set of rules regulating access of subjects to objects enforced by TCB subset. (NCSC). *See* BLUE BOOK, TCB SUBSET.

technical security. Equipment, components, devices, and associated documentation or other media that pertain to cryptography, or to the securing of telecommunications and automated information systems. (NSDD-145)

technical vulnerability. In computer security, a hardware, firmware or software weakness or design deficiency that leaves an automated information system open to potential exploitation either externally or internally, thereby resulting in risk or compromise of information,

alteration of information, or denial of service. Technical vulnerability information, if made available to unauthorized persons, may allow an AIS to be exploited, resulting in potentially serious damage to national security. (DOD). *See* AIS. DENIAL OF SERVICE, VULNERABILITY.

technological attack. In computer security, an attack that can be perpetrated by circumventing or nullifying hardware and software access control mechanisms, rather than by subverting system personnel or other users. (FIPS). *See* ACCESS CONTROL MECHANISMS.

technology. The technical information and know-how that can be used to design, produce, manufacture, use, or reconstruct goods, including technical data and computer software. The term does not include the goods themselves. (DODD). *See* KNOW-HOW.

telebanking. In banking, a facility to perform client banking transactions over a communication network, e.g. videotex, interactive cable television. *See* HOME BANKING SECURITY, SELF BANKING, VIDEOTEX.

telecommunications. (1) A general term expressing data transmission between a computing system and remotely located devices via a unit that performs the necessary format conversion and controls the rate of transmission. (DODD). (2) Any transmission, emission, or reception of signs, signals, writing, images, sounds or other information by wire, radio, visual, or any electromagnetic systems. (FIPS). (3) The preparation, transmission, communication, or related processing of information by electrical, electromagnetic, electromechanical, or electro-optical means. (NSDD-145) (4) Essentially communications over a distance. The technology of the transmission may take one of three forms, i.e. electrical signals along a conductor, electromagnetic radiation or light signals passing along an optical fiber. The signal may, in some cases, have the same shape as the originating signal but in many cases the information to be transmitted modulates a carrier wave. *See* MODULATION, FIBER OPTICS.

telecommunications and automated information systems security. In computer and communications security, protection afforded to telecommunications and automated information systems in order to prevent exploitation through interception, unauthorized electronic access, or related technical intelligence threats, and to ensure authenticity. Such protection results from the application of security measures (including cryptosecurity, transmission security, emission security, and computer security) to systems that generate, store, process, transfer, or communicate information of use to an adversary, and also includes the physical protection of sensitive technical security material and sensitive technical security information. (NSDD-145) *See* AUTHENTICATION, TEMPEST PROOFING, VAN ECK PHENOMENON, WIRETAPPING.

teleconferencing. In applications, the use of computer networks and communication systems to enable participation in conferences, or joint projects involving close cooperation, by workers separated geographically. At one level the participants are supplied with computer terminals and they intercommunicate, not necessarily simultaneously, over data communication networks. The operation of the system is controlled by a manager, or management system, responsible for the distribution of information to relevant participants. More sophisticated systems provide video links, voting systems, recording of conference activities, etc.

teleinformatic services. In communica-

tions, a CCITT term encompassing all record type non voice, or non speech telecommunication services, e.g. telex, videotex, facsimile. *See* VIDEOTEX, FACSIMILE, COMMON CARRIER.

telemetering. In data communications, the remote metering of domestic utility consumption. *See* TELEMETRY.

telemetry. In data communications, the transmission of signals derived from measuring devices over long distances.

telemonitoring. In data communications, the remote monitoring of, usually domestic, measuring devices using a telecommunication link, e.g. reading electricity meters. *See* TELEMETERING.

telephone dialer. In physical security, a device that automatically telephones a central station and reports an alarm condition. *See* DIGITAL COMMUNICATOR, TAPE DIALER. *Synonymous with* DIALER.

telephone intrusion. In computer security, the intrusion into a computer system by dial-up access; a common form of attack by hackers. Such attacks have increased in recent years due to:

- facilities of dial-up networks;
- availability of penetration equipment;
- intruder expertise;
- bulletin boards.

Increases in telephone network facilities in recent years have allowed intruders to dial directly into computer systems from many parts of the world permitting, for example, intruders in the Middle East and Europe to dial-up computers in the U.S. The decreasing cost and increasing power of personal computers and modems allows even teenagers to acquire sophisticated intrusion equipment. Hackers sometimes display an extremely high level of technical expertise and pirate bulletin boards allow such hackers to disseminate their knowledge, acquired passwords, intrusion software etc.

Defense against dial-up attacks include special software, administrative practices and add-on hardware. The operating security facilities should be fully exploited and vendor supplied passwords, which often convey a high level of privilege, should be deleted. Administrative routines include disconnecting modems in periods when legitimate users do not require access, enforcement of good password practices, logging attack events, limiting the number of log on attempts and concealing information about the computer system until password controls have been satisfied. It is suggested that no entry be permitted on a call after one unsuccessful log on attempt, but the system should invite retry attempts so as to collect information on the intruder. However, caution must be exercised to avoid charges of entrapment.

Add-on security devices may be categorized as one and two-end systems. One-end systems are installed either at the host computer or, less commonly, on the legitimate user's terminal. Port protection devices are connected at the host computer; security modems for user terminals incorporate security features integrated into the modem.

Two-end devices provide enhanced security with the presence of security hardware at both ends of the legitimate telephone connection, such devices communicating with each other to perform security functions.

The development of new telephone services, such as ISDN, that provide the caller's telephone number to the called user may provide a significant advance against telephone intrusion. The called computer system may simply refuse to accept calls unaccompanied by the calling number, and check all calling numbers against an authorized list. *See* CALL BACK, ISDN, ONE-END DEVICE, PASSWORD, PPD, SECURITY MODEM, TWO-END DEVICE.

telephone scrambler. *See* VOICE SCRAMBLING.

telephone tap. In communications security, an electronic listening device. *See* ELECTRONIC LISTENING DEVICE, WIRETAPPING.

teleprocessing. (1) In data communications, pertaining to an information transmission system that combines telecommunications, ADP systems, and man-machine interface equipment for the purpose of interacting and functioning as an integrated whole. (FIPS). *See* TELECOMMUNICATIONS. (2) In data communications, data processing combined with telecommunications, e.g. the use of a telephone network to connect a remote terminal to a computer or to interconnect two computers. *See* TELEPROCESSING SECURITY.

teleprocessing security. In data security, the protection that results from all measures designed to prevent deliberate, inadvertent, or unauthorized disclosure, acquisition, manipulation, or modification of information in a teleprocessing system. (FIPS). *See* TELEPROCESSING.

teletext. In videotex, a method of transmitting information, stored on a computer, to domestic television sets suitably adapted. In broadcast services the data signals are transmitted in conjunction with normal TV programs.

teletext decoder. In videotex, a device to enable a domestic TV set to display teletext information. *See* TELETEXT.

TELNET. In data communications, a remote login protocol developed for ARPANET. *See* ARPANET, PROTOCOL.

Telpak. In communications, a pricing arrangement giving a bulk rate for multichannel paths on a two point or multipoint basis.

Tempest. (1) In computer security, a short name referring to investigations and studies of compromising emanations. It is sometimes used synonymously for the term 'compromising emanations' for example TEMPEST tests, TEMPEST inspections. (AFR). *See* COMPROMISING EMANATIONS, TEMPEST CONTROL ZONE, TEMPEST PROOFING. (2) In computer security, the study and control of spurious electronic signals emitted from ADP equipment. (DOD). *See* ADP, TEMPEST PROOFING.

Tempest control zone. In computer security, the contiguous space that surrounds equipment and distribution systems and is under sufficient physical and technical control to preclude interception of compromising emanations. Sufficient physical and technical control is the degree of control that enables the security forces responsible for protecting a controlled space to detect, investigate and remove any person or device of a suspicious nature which is detected therein. (DOE). *See* COMPROMISING EMANATIONS, TEMPEST.

Tempest proofing. In communications security, the prevention of undesirable radiation emission from a computer system which might otherwise enable an eavesdropper to record confidential information. Electromagnetic emission can escape by a variety of routes and to eliminate this risk, source suppression and encapsulation are used, together with shielding of all cables. Fiber optic cables do not radiate electromagnetic radiation. *See* CONDUCTIVE SHIELDING, ENCAPSULATION, FIBER OPTICS, SOURCE SUPPRESSION, VAN ECK PHENOMENON.

template. In access control, a digitized form of a biometric measurement of a users characteristic, e.g fingerprint. The user's template is stored and compared with the measured template when access or authorization is requested. *See* BIOMETRICS.

temporal separation. *See* ISOLATION ENFORCEMENT. *Synonymous with* PERIODS PROCESSING.

tera. A million million, i.e. 10^{12}.

term. (1) In banking, the period of time that a facility has to continue until maturity. (2) A word or expression that has a precise meaning, in some uses, or is peculiar to a science, art, profession or subject.

terminal. (1) In peripherals, an input/utput device for transmitting and receiving data on a communication line. (2) In communications, a point in the system where information can be transmitted or received.

terminal access controller. In data communications, a form of interface message processor that can be called directly by a terminal. *See* INTERFACE MESSAGE PROCESSOR.

terminal authentication device. In computer security, a two-end device designed to authenticate a specific user terminal. Matching pairs of devices are inserted in the communication channel. For example, one is installed between the terminal and modem and the other is attached to the host computer port. The host end device generates challenges to the unit connected to the terminal. *See* CHALLENGE/RESPONSE, TELEPHONE INTRUSION, TWO-END DEVICE.

terminal handler. In data communications, a part of a data network that services simple, character stream terminals.

terminal identification. In computer security, the means used to establish the unique identification of a terminal by an ADP system. (FIPS).

terminal key. (1) In key management, a key-encrypting key supplied to the terminal and used for the encryption of session keys. *Compare* SESSION KEY. *See* MIDNIGHT ATTACK. (2) In key management, a cryptographic key in the transaction key system used to derive keys used for transaction security. *See* TRANSACTION KEY SYSTEM.

terminal thief. *Synonymous with* HACKER.

Terror. In computer security, a virus that terminates and stays resident, infects COMMAND.COM, COM, EXE and OVL files, affects run-time operation, corrupts program and OVL files, formats or overwrites all or part of disk. *See* VIRUS NAMES.

test. In banking, a code in a message between sender and receiver used to validate the source of a message that may also validate certain elements of the message such as amount, date and sequence. The code is the result of a bilaterally agreed upon method of calculation. (ANSI). *See* AUTHENTICATOR, MESSAGE AUTHENTICATION, TEST KEY.

test amount. In banking, the total of the integral parts of all the amounts and quantities in a message.

test data. (1) In auditing, sample transactions processed from master records used to judge the effectiveness of the system and programmed controls. (2) In computing, data prepared solely to test the accuracy of the programming and logic of a system. Test data is used to prove each branch and combination of branches of a program and should, therefore, be as comprehensive as possible. Deliberate errors should be introduced into the test data, such as inserting alphabetic characters in numeric fields, to ensure that these errors are detected by the program. At the end of the test run the output will be checked against expected results of processing

the data to see if they are compatible. *See* DYNAMIC TESTING.

Tester. In computer security, a virus that terminates and stays resident, infects COMMAND.COM and COM files, affects run-time operation, corrupts program and OVL files. *See* VIRUS NAMES.

test key. In banking, sets of characters and method of computation designed to be known only to the correspondent parties. When the sets of characters are used according to the agreed upon method, the result will be the test. (ANSI). *See* AUTHENTICATOR, MESSAGE AUTHENTICATION, TEST.

text. In communications, the information content of a message.

text compression. In data communications, pertaining to the elimination of redundant data, e.g. leading zeros, trailing blanks, from a message. *See* DATA COMPRESSION, HUFFMAN CODE.

The Buddy System. In risk management, a risk analysis methodology. *See* RISK ANALYSIS METHODOLOGIES.

theoretically secure. In cryptanalysis, a system that is secure even when the cryptanalyst has unlimited time, facilities and funds.

third normal form. In databases, a property of a relation in a relational database. A relation is in third normal form if it is in second normal form and every nonprime attribute of the relation is nontransitively dependent upon each candidate key of the relation. In effect this requirement states that each field should only depend upon the primary key and not upon any other fields within the relation. An example of a relation not in third normal form is dept-number, project-number, project-name, project-completion-date with dept-number the key. Project-completion-date is functionally dependent upon projectnumber and, if there is only one project per department, project-number is functionally dependent upon the key deptnumber. Since a number of projects can have the same completion date there is a transitive dependence between project-completion-date and the key. A relation that is not in third normal form presents problems in the running of the database, e.g. it would not be possible to store a completion date for a project until the project is assigned to a department. *Compare* FIRST NORMAL FORM, SECOND NORMAL FORM. *See* CANDIDATE KEY, FUNCTIONAL DEPENDENCE, NONPRIME ATTRIBUTE, NORMAL FORMS, RELATIONAL DATABASE, TRANSITIVE DEPENDENCE.

third party transfer. In banking, a transfer in favor of a party other than the sender or receiver. (ANSI).

threaded tree. In computing, a tree in which additional pointers assist in the scan of the tree. *See* TREE, POINTER, SCAN.

threat. (1) In computer security, the means through which the ability or intent of a threat agent to adversely affect an automated system, facility, or operation can be manifest. Categorize and classify threats as follows:

Categories	Classes
Human	Intentional
	Unintentional
Environmental	Natural
	Fabricated

(AFR)

See THREAT AGENT, VULNERABILITY. (2) In risk management, a potential violation of security. (ISO). (3) In computer security, any circumstance or event with the potential to cause harm to the ADP system or activity in the form of destruction, disclosure, and modification of data, or denial of service. A threat is a potential for harm. The presence of a threat does not mean that it will necessarily cause actual harm. Threats exist because of the very existence of the system or activity and not because of any specific weakness. For example, the threat of fire exists at all facilities, regardless of the amount of fire protection available. (OPNAVINST). *See* DENIAL OF SERVICE. (4) In risk management, an aspect of the system environment that, if given an opportunity, could cause a harmful event to occur. *Compare* SAFEGUARD. *See* HARMFUL EVENT, MATRIX METHODOLOGY, VULNERABILITY.

threat agent. In risk management, methods and things used to exploit a vulnerability in an information system, operation, or facility, for example, fire, natural disaster, and so forth. (AFR). *See* THREAT.

threat analysis. In cryptography, the process of subjecting cryptographic operations, e.g. in a key management scheme, to a series of hypothetical attacks. *Compare* CRYPTANALYSIS. *See* KEY MANAGEMENT.

threat monitoring. In computer security, the analysis, assessment, and review of audit trails and other data collected for the purpose of searching out system events which may constitute violations or precipitate incidents involving data privacy matters. (FIPS). *See* AUDIT TRAIL.

threat team. In computer security, a team composed of key employees in an organization who search for threats and vulnerability in a system and who create possible scenarios for attacking the system. *See* THREAT MONITORING, TIGER TEAM.

three-layer architecture. In key management, a system in which a key-encrypting key is manually distributed and this key is used to encrypt a second layer key-encrypting key which is subject to automated distribution. Data keys are third level keys, encrypted under the second level key-encrypting key, for automated distribution. *Compare* TWO-LAYER ARCHITECTURE. *See* ANSI X9.17 - 1985, CRYPTOGRAPHIC KEY, DATA KEY, KEY-ENCRYPTING KEY.

threshold. In key management, pertaining to a technique to safeguard master keys against exposure and destruction. Many key management schemes use hierarchies with a single master key at the top level. If this key is exposed then the whole system is vulnerable to illegal action; on the other hand if the only copy of it is destroyed then the encrypted information is inaccessible to the legitimate users.

If copies of the master key are distributed to trustworthy keepers then the risks of key betrayal are inevitably increased. The threshold technique attempts to ameliorate this problem by distributing parts of the key around trustworthy custodians. The key (K) is broken into a number n (say) of pieces, termed shadows. This decomposition of the key is performed in such a manner that:

- if any m of the shadows are available then it is easy to compute the key K;
- the key K cannot be computed with m-1, or fewer shadows.

Thus if no more than m-1 of the custodians lose their key pieces, or conspire together to construct the key K, then the key cannot be exposed. On the other hand if one or more shadows are accidentally lost then the key can still be reconstructed provided that at least m shadows are available. The decomposition technique, which achieves the prop-

erties listed above, can be performed with specified mathematical methods. *See* CRYPTOGRAPHIC KEY, SECRET SHARING.

throughput. A measure of the amount of useful work performed by a system in a given period of time.

ticket. In access control, a term used in the Kerberos system. It performs a similar task to a certificate in an asymmetric cipher system. The ticket contains, name of client and server, network address of client, expiry lifetime, timestamp and a DES session key to be used between the client and server. The ticket is then encrypted with a secret key known by the ticket issuing server, and the server that the client wishes to access. The ticket is forwarded to the client. *See* CERTIFICATE, DATA ENCRYPTION STANDARD, KERBEROS, SYMMETRIC CIPHER.

tie line. *Synonymous with* TIE TRUNK.

tie trunk. In communications, a point-to-point communication channel linking PBX systems or switchboards. *See* POINT-TO-POINT. *Synonymous with* TIE LINE.

tiger team. In computer security, a group of people authorized to test the overall security of a system by 'illicit' entry or other means. *See* THREAT TEAM.

time and space requirements. In mathematics, an order of magnitude measure of the computational requirements involved in the solution of an algorithm. The time, or space, requirement is said to be polynomial time if it is of the order of n^t where t is a constant and n characterizes the size of the input. If t = 0 the requirement is constant, if t = 1 it is linear, if t = 2 it is quadratic etc. If the time, or space, requirement is of the order of $t^{f(n)}$, where f(n) is polynomial, then the requirement is exponential.

time bomb. In computer security, a form of Trojan Horse with a malicious action that is triggered to occur at specific times or dates. *Compare* LOGIC BOMB. *See* MALICIOUS CODE, TROJAN HORSE.

time-date stamp. In data security, a field in a message indicating the time and date of origin. *See* REPLAY.

time-dependent password. In access control, a password that is valid only at a certain time of the day or during a specified interval of time. (FIPS). *See* PASSWORD.

time-derived channel. In data communications, a channel derived by time division multiplexing. *See* TIME DIVISION MULTIPLEXING.

time division multiple access. In data communications, a technique in a time division multiplexing system in which a stream of time slots are allocated to users according to their demand. *Compare* FREQUENCY DIVISION MULTIPLE ACCESS. *See* TIME DIVISION MULTIPLEXING.

time division multiplexing. In communications, a method of allocating a high capacity channel to a number of sender recipient pairs. The information from each sender is allocated time intervals in the main channel and the sections of messages are interleaved, with those from other users, at the channel input. The message segments are separated and the complete messages are reconstructed at the receiving end. The decreasing cost of digital circuitry has rendered time division multiplexing cheaper than frequency division multiplexing which requires expensive analog filter circuits. However it can only be used for digital signals. Analog signals such as voice must be converted into digital form by PCM before they can employ this technique. *Compare* FREQUENCY DIVISION MULTIPLEXING. *See* ANALOG SIGNAL, DIGITAL SIGNAL, PACKET SWITCHING, PCM.

time division switching. In data communications, a switching method for time division multiplexed channels. Data enters a switching stage in one time slot and emerges in another. For switching of pulse code modulation channels, each time slot contains one coded sample, e.g. 8 bits. *Compare* SPACE DIVISION SWITCHING. *See* TIME DIVISION MULTIPLEXING, PULSE CODE MODULATION.

time element scrambler. In communications security, a form of voice scrambling based upon time division multiplexing techniques. The voice signal is divided into frames of a few hundred milliseconds and the frames subdivided into segments of 20 - 60 milliseconds. Scrambling is performed by permuting the order of segments in a frame. The permutations employed are changed in a sequence known only to the transmitter and receiver. *See* TIME DIVISION MULTIPLEXING, VOICE SCRAMBLING.

time limit cutout. In physical security, a system that limits the duration of an alarm signal by the provision of a fixed or variable time interval. *See* ALARM SIGNAL.

time out. (1) In computing, a time interval allotted for certain operations to occur. (2) In computing, a terminal feature that logs off a user if an entry is not made before the end of a specified time interval. *See* LOG OFF.

time redundancy. In reliability, a technique in which a part of a program is used to doublecheck critical computations. Either the same subprogram is repeated or a different algorithm is employed. *Compare* SPACIAL REDUNDANCY.

time sharing. In computing, a technique that enables a computer to handle simultaneous users and peripherals. Each computer operation is performed in sequence but the high speed of operation, together with the time slice technique, gives the appearance of a simultaneous multiuser service.

time slice. In computing, a non preemptible interval of processor time allocated to a specific task in a time shared system. All the tasks receive time slices in rotation until they are completed, thus no one task can monopolize the processor. *See* TIME SHARING.

time stamp. *See* TIME-DATE STAMP.

Tiny. In computer security, a virus that infects COMMAND.COM and COM files, affects run-time operation, corrupts program and OVL files. *See* VIRUS NAMES.

Tiny-133. In computer security, a virus that infects COMMAND.COM and COM files, affects run-time operation, corrupts program and OVL files. *See* VIRUS NAMES.

TLS. *See* TOP-LEVEL SPECIFICATION.

TMR. *See* TRIPLE MODULAR REDUNDANCY.

T network. In electronics, a network comprising three elements interconnected in the shape of a letter T.

TNF. *See* THIRD NORMAL FORM.

TNI. In communications security, the Trusted Network Interpretation of the Trusted Computer System Evaluation Criteria. *Compare* TCSEC.

TOCTTOU problems. In computer security, Time Of Check To Time Of Use, a class of security problems that can arise from illegal changes, after a check has been performed. For example, a request to an operating system is checked and found to be valid but a parameter of the request is then changed before it is performed. *See* ASYNCHRONOUS ATTACKS.

TOE. *See* TARGET OF EVALUATION.

token. (1) In access control, a physical device necessary for user authentication. (2) In access control, a physical object that must be held by a person requesting access, e.g. a badge, magnetic stripe card. *See* SOMETHING THE USER HAS. (3) In data communications, a pattern of bits that must be received by a station before it is allowed to broadcast a signal. *See* TOKEN BUS, TOKEN RING.

token authenticator. In access control, a pocket sized computer that can participate in a challenge/response authentication scheme. *See* CHALLENGE/RESPONSE.

token bus. In data communications, a protocol for local area network employing a linear or tree shaped cable. The stations are connected in a logical ring; each station has the address of the two stations on either side of it in this logical ring; they receive a token from one neighboring station and forward it to the next in the ring. Stations are only allowed to transmit when they hold a token. *Compare* IEEE 802.3, TOKEN RING. *See* LOCAL AREA NETWORK, TOKEN.

token management. In data communications, a technique employed to ensure that two systems do not attempt the same operation simultaneously. Only the system in possession of the single token is allowed to perform the critical operation. *See* TOKEN BUS, TOKEN RING.

token ring. In data communications, a

ring network architecture in which each node awaits the arrival of a control token, from the upstream node, before sending a message towards the next downstream node. Only one token is on the ring at any one time; when a node with a message to send receives a token it transmits its message followed by the token, which is passed from node to node until it arrives at one with a message for transmission. *Compare* CARRIER SENSE MULTIPLE ACCESS - COLLISION DETECTION, TOKEN BUS. *See* CONTROL TOKEN, IEEE 802.5, LOCAL AREA NETWORK.

TOP. *See* TECHNICAL AND OFFICE PROTOCOL.

top down method. A method of designing a system, or computer program, commencing with a simple overall structure, then successively refining the description of each subcomponent, in a similar manner, until a detailed structure is obtained.

top-level specification. A non-procedural description of system behavior at the most abstract level. Typically a functional specification that omits all implementation details. (DOD). *See* DESCRIPTIVE TOP-LEVEL SPECIFICATION, FORMAL TOP-LEVEL SPECIFICATION.

topology. In communications, the form of interconnection of nodes in a network. *See* BUS, NODE, RING, STAR.

Top Secret. *See* CLASSIFICATION.

top secret clearance. In access control, Department of Defense clearances which are designated top secret clearance based on a current background investigation (TS(BI)), or top secret clearance based on a current special background investigation (TS(SBI)). Top secret clearance based on a current background investigation requires an investigation that consists of a national agency check, person-

al contacts, record searches and written inquiries. It typically includes an investigation extending back five years, often with a spot check investigation extending back fifteen years. Top secret clearance based on a current special background investigation requires an investigation that in addition to the investigation for a TS(BI) includes additional checks on the subject's immediate family (if foreign born) and spouse and neighborhood investigations to verify each of the subject's former residences in the United States where the subject resided six months or more. It typically includes an investigation extending back fifteen years. *Compare* CONFIDENTIAL CLEARANCE, MULTIPLE CATEGORIES, ONE CATEGORY, SECRET CLEARANCE, UNCLASSIFIED INFORMATION, UNCLEARED. *See* CLEARANCE.

TP. *See* TRANSFORMATION PROCEDURE, TRANSACTION PROCESSING.

Traceback. In computer security, a virus that terminates and stays resident, infects COM and EXE files, corrupts program and OVL files. *See* VIRUS NAMES.

trace packet. In data communications, a packet that causes a report, on each stage of its progress through the network, to be transmitted to the network control station. *See* NETWORK CONTROL STATION, PACKET SWITCHING, PACKET SWITCHING NETWORK.

tracker. In database security, a technique used by attackers to subvert a system employing query set size control. A request for a small set of records is deliberately padded with extra records until the query set is large enough to meet the query set size control criteria. The effect of the padding records is then subtracted by the attacker from the released statistics. *See* INFERENCE CONTROL, QUERY SET, QUERY SET SIZE CONTROL, RECORD.

tractable. In complexity theory, pertaining to a problem that is solvable in polynomial time. *Compare* INTRACTABLE. *See* TIME AND SPACE REQUIREMENTS.

trade cycle. *Synonymous with* BANKING CYCLE.

traffic. In communications, the signals or messages handled by a communications system.

traffic analysis. (1) In communications security, the inference of information from observation of traffic flows (presence, absence, amount direction and frequency). (ISO). *See* TRAFFIC FLOW CONFIDENTIALITY, TRAFFIC PADDING. (2) The process of monitoring lines, not intercepting the information being transmitted but determining the rate of transmission. (AFR). (3) In communications security, a form of passive attack in which the intruder observes the source and destination address, frequency and length of messages. Countermeasures to traffic analysis are aimed at masking the patterns in messages that reveal origin/-destination address, message length etc. Link encryption automatically provides security against traffic analysis since the message headers, as well as message contents, are encrypted. In the case of end-to-end encryption the degree of protection against traffic analysis depends upon the level at which encryption is applied. It is virtually impossible to mask the traffic at host-to-host level, to do so would require duplication of messages to all hosts thus producing a traffic overload on the network. If encryption is applied at a high level, e.g. at individual user level, then all subsequent message header records must be added in cleartext. In this case traffic analysis will produce precise information at a user level. On the other hand if the messages are encrypted at a lower level then the traffic patterns within the host

will be masked. *See* END-TO-END ENCRYPTION, LINK ENCRYPTION, NETWORK ENCRYPTION, OSI SECURITY, PASSIVE ATTACK, TRAFFIC FLOW SECURITY, TRAFFIC PADDING. *Synonymous with* VIOLATION OF TRANSMISSION SECURITY.

traffic flow confidentiality. In communications security, a confidentiality service to protect against traffic analysis. (ISO). *See* TRAFFIC ANALYSIS.

traffic flow security. In communications security, the protection that results from those features in some cryptographic equipment that conceal the presence of valid messages on a communications circuit, usually by causing the circuit to appear busy at all times, or by encrypting the source and destination addresses of valid messages. (FIPS). *See* CRYPTOGRAPHIC EQUIPMENT, ENCRYPT, TRAFFIC ANALYSIS, TRAFFIC PADDING.

traffic padding. (1) In communications security, the generation of spurious instances of communication, spurious data units and/or spurious data within data units. (ISO). *See* TRAFFIC ANALYSIS. (2) In communications security, a technique used to disguise traffic flows; it includes padding messages out to standard lengths, generating spurious messages and spurious connections. *See* TRAFFIC ANALYSIS, TRAFFIC FLOW SECURITY. (3) In communications security, the generation of spurious instances of communication, spurious data units and/or spurious data within data units. (ISO).

trailer. (1) In computing, a label at the end of a magnetic tape giving summary statistics of data recorded. (2) In computing, a record at the end of a file containing summary information on the constituent data records. *See* FILE, MAGNETIC TAPE, RECORD.

tranquility. In computer security, a security model rule stating that the security level of an active object does not change. (MTR) *See* OBJECT, SECURITY LEVEL, SECURITY MODEL.

transaction. (1) In banking, a dialogue between a terminal and acquirer conducted under one set of cryptographic keys, the transaction key set. (SAA) *See* FUNDS TRANSFER TRANSACTION, TRANSACTION KEY SET. (2) In databases, a discrete unit of work. It may involve updating a number of fields in the database and it must be executed in its entirety to avoid inconsistencies in the data. *See* FIELD.

transaction code. In data processing, a field within a transaction record that designates the nature of the transaction. *See* FIELD, RECORD.

transaction driven system. In computing, a mode of operation in which the arrival of a transaction causes an interrupt of batch processing activities as resources are diverted to deal with the transaction. *See* TRANSACTION PROCESSING.

transaction key. (1) In banking, a cryptographic key used to encrypt and decrypt data in a message and to compute (or verify) the message authentication code associated with that message. A transaction key is statistically unique to two specific parties (e.g. the terminal and acquirer) and is valid only for the duration of a single transaction. (SAA). *See* ACQUIRER, KEY MANAGEMENT, MESSAGE AUTHENTICATION CODE, STATISTICALLY UNIQUE, TRANSACTION. (2) In key management, a key used to encipher the data of a single transaction. *Compare* SESSION KEY. *See* DECOUPLING KEY.

transaction key set. In banking, a set of one or more concurrently valid transaction keys derived from a single key register value and a single source of decoupling keys. In card based mode the source of the decoupling keys is the card presented for the current transaction. Different decoupling keys being generated in order to achieve mutual security between parties to the transaction. (SAA). *See* CARD BASED MODE, DECOUPLING KEY, KEY REGISTER, TRANSACTION KEY.

transaction key system. In key management, a scheme, described in Australian Standard 2805.6.2, developed for EFTPOS networks. It differs from the conventional master-session system and does not require session keys to be downloaded, encrypted under key-encrypting keys.

The environment for the scheme comprises EFTPOS terminals in retailers premises, acquirers and card issuers. An EFTPOS terminal passes transactions to the acquirer which cryptographically processes the message and forwards it to the appropriate cardissuer for PIN checking and transaction authorization.

The scheme is designed so that:

- PINs are not revealed even if the session keys between terminal and acquirer are compromised;
- transaction authorizations can only be issued by the card issuer, even if the session keys between terminal and acquirer are compromised.

There are effectively two sets of cryptographic keys/variables employed by the terminal. One set is based upon a current terminal key, known only by the terminal and acquirer. The second set are derived from 'Other Card Data' known only by the terminal and card issuer.

An initial terminal key is manually loaded into the terminal and the acquirer system. When a transaction is undertaken, the customer details are read from the card. These details include the Primary Account Number and Other Card Data. The terminal key is used, together with the fields of the PAN and constants, to produce a privacy key Kpr, a

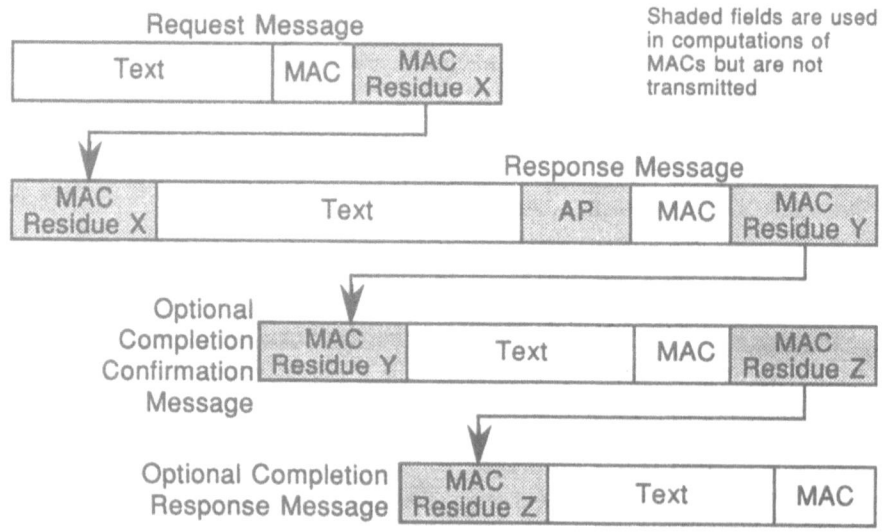

Shaded fields are used in computations of MACs but are not transmitted

transaction key system

MAC key KMAC and a PIN encrypting key KPE. In each case a one-way function is employed.

The transaction request message is produced including the Primary Account Number; a MAC is formed with KMAC and the message is transmitted, the MAC residue is stored. The acquirer develops a response message, which includes the request message MAC residue when the response MAC is computed, but this MAC residue is not transmitted with the response. This technique cryptographically links the request and response messages.

When the transaction is completed the terminal key is updated using the one-way function, current terminal key and request/response message MAC residues. Thus the terminal update is a function of the transaction, but employs data that is not actually transmitted.

The Other Card Data (OCD) is a specified field on the magnetic stripe card. It is read by the terminal, known by the card issuer, but not transmitted to the acquirer. The OCD is employed, together with other information such as the PAN, transaction amount, terminal identifier, message sequence number etc. in the development of a card key KC and authorization parameter AP.

The PIN is first encrypted with KC and then KPE. The acquirer decrypts the PIN block with KPE and forwards eKC(PINblock), encrypted under a session key for the acquirer-card issuer link, to the card issuer. The card issuer computes KC from the OCD etc., decrypts the PIN block, checks the PIN, computes an authorization parameter based upon Other Card Data, transaction amount etc. to the acquirer. This AP, like the MAC residue, is included in the acquirer-terminal response message, for MAC'ing, but is not transmitted.

The merchant can thus be assured that the authorization message was developed using an AP that could only have originated with the card issuer. *See* ACQUIR-

ER, EFTPOS, KEY MANAGEMENT, ONE-WAY FUNCTION, OTHER CARD DATA, PIN, PRIMARY ACCOUNT NUMBER.

transaction number. In banking, a security technique in home banking in which a customer is supplied with a batch of random numbers by post. Each successive customer initiated transaction must include the next transaction number in the batch, in addition to account number and PIN. This technique ensures that a wiretapper cannot obtain sufficient information from one transaction to initiate a subsequent fraudulent transaction. *See* HOME BANKING SECURITY.

Transaction/Payment Message. In banking, a message containing either an instruction to the recipient to make a payment or notification that a payment has been made. It includes bank transfers and customers' transactions.

transaction processing. In computing, a mode of computer usage in which the user enters data and commands from a remote terminal, often over a communication link. The results of the actions are displayed on the terminal. A similar mode of action to multi-access computing; it is often employed when the user is operating with a specific application package. *See* TRANSACTION DRIVEN SYSTEM.

transaction set. *See* ANSI - X.12.

transaction trail. *Synonymous with* AUDIT TRAIL.

transborder data flow. In data communications, the flow of data between countries, or states, and therefore passed from one jurisdiction to another. This represents an area of considerable complexity in the light of differing legislation on data protection, copyright, etc. in the various parts of the world. *See* COPYRIGHT, DATA PROTECTION, SOFTWARE PROTECTION, TRANSBORDER RESTRICTIONS.

transborder restrictions. In data communications, pertaining to restrictions placed upon the flow of encrypted data across a country's borders. Outside the United States this matter is usually the responsibility of a central government agency, often the PTT.

The regulations may deal with be either:

- prohibition on the transborder flow of encrypted data;
- transborder flow of encrypted data which is permitted if the cryptographic key is registered with the data protection agency;
- imposition of no restrictions.

The OECD has adopted a minimum set of protection standards, that a member country must satisfy, described in its publication, Guidelines Governing the Protection of Privacy of Transborder Data Flows of Personal Data. *See* DATA PROTECTION, TRANSBORDER DATA FLOW.

transceiver. In hardware, a bus driver that can pass data in both directions hence combining a transmitter and receiver action. *Compare* RECEIVER TRANSMITTER. *See* BUS DRIVER.

transfer. *See* FUNDS TRANSFER, FUNDS TRANSFER TRANSACTION.

transformational coding. In codes, the application of a strict set of rules in the transformation of data into a coded form.

transformation procedure. In formal models, a term used in the Clark-Wilson model, A transformation procedure is a routine that is permitted to update a constrained data item in accordance with the certified procedures. *See* CLARK-WILSON MODEL, CONSTRAINED DATA ITEM.

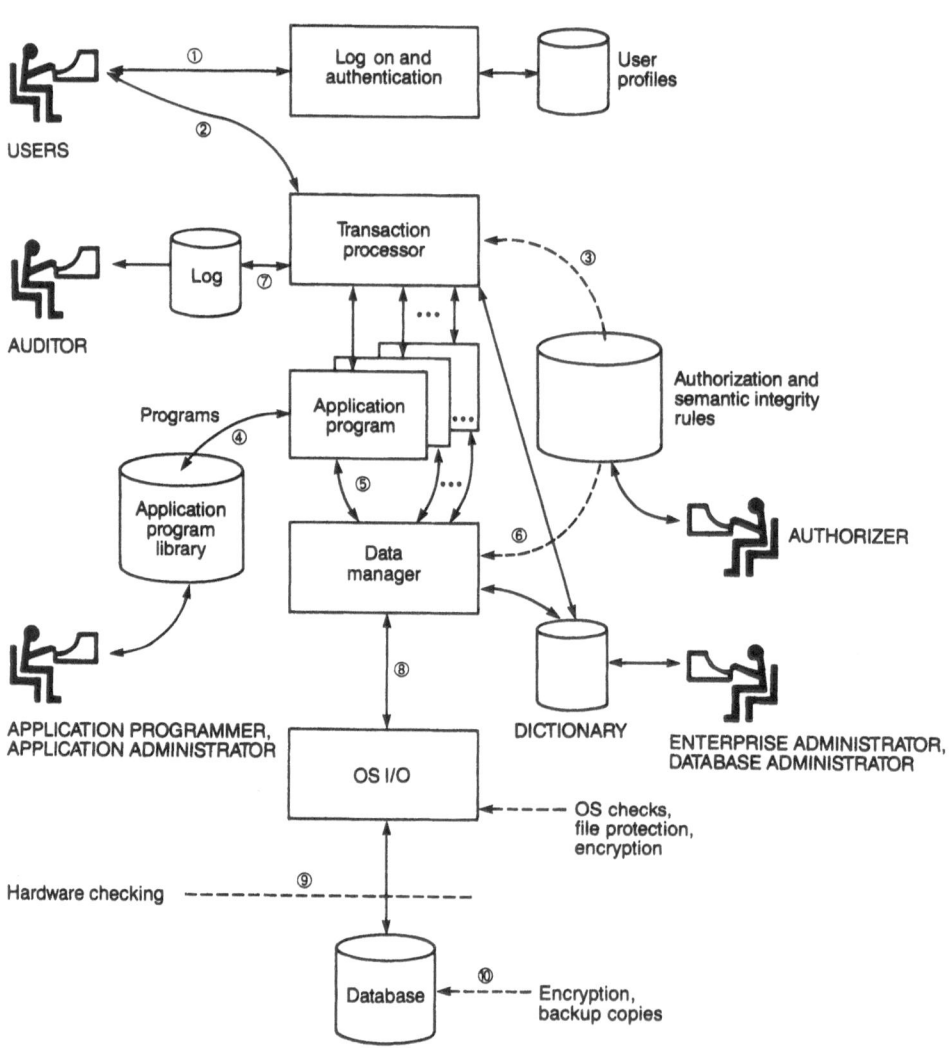

USERS

AUDITOR

Transaction processor

Log on and authentication

User profiles

Log

Programs

Application program

Application program library

Data manager

Authorization and semantic integrity rules

AUTHORIZER

APPLICATION PROGRAMMER,
APPLICATION ADMINISTRATOR

OS I/O

DICTIONARY

ENTERPRISE ADMINISTRATOR,
DATABASE ADMINISTRATOR

OS checks,
file protection,
encryption

Hardware checking

Database

Encryption,
backup copies

transaction processing
Some of the safeguards that can be built into a database system. (1) User logs on and is authenticated; (2) user attempts transaction, (3) and it is validated. The transaction may involve retrieval of programs from a library (4) and requests for data (5) go to the database management system (DBMS). Authorization is checked once more (6) and the DBMS maintains a log of access to the database (7). Once database access requests are validated, they are translated to I/O calls and passed to the operating system (8). Hardware can provide additional protection (9), and data may be encrypted (10). Reproduced with permission of IBM Corp.

transitive dependence. In relational databases, an indirect dependence between attributes. Suppose A, B and C are three attributes or distinct collections of attributes of a relation R. If C is functionally dependent on B and B is functionally dependent on A then C is functionally dependent on A, if A is not functionally dependent upon B or B is not functionally dependent on C then C is transitively dependent upon A. *See* FUNCTIONAL DEPENDENCE.

translation cipher. In cryptography, a very simple form of substitution cipher in which each enciphered character is a fixed distance, in the alphabet, from the corresponding plaintext character. For example with a shift of 5, F replaces A, G replaces B etc. *Synonymous with* ADDITIVE CIPHER. *See* CAESAR CIPHER.

translator. In communications, a device that converts information from one system of representation into another, e.g. converting dialed digits into call routing information.

transmission. (1) In banking, a data sequence, e.g. answerbacks and messages, transmitted between two parties, and operating from the time of the establishment of a connection, to its termination. (ANSI). (2) In communications, the action of sending information from one location to another leaving the source information unchanged.

transmission control protocol. In data communications, a transport protocol for a connection oriented network. *See* TCP/IP, TRANSPORT LAYER.

transmission window. In communications, the wavelength at which a fiber optic cable is most transparent.

transmitted data. In data communications, a data path for the data transmitted from a computer. *Compare* RE-

CEIVED DATA. *See* RS-232C.

transmitter. In access control, a method based upon a possession of the user. A low powered radio transmitter is carried by the user and emits a coded signal which grants access to a physical area and/or enables a terminal; the terminal is automatically disabled when the transmitter is removed from the vicinity. The transmitter requires daily battery recharging thus rendering it of limited value to a thief. *Compare* CODED KEY. *See* ACCESS CONTROL, PROXIMITY CARD READER.

transmitter signal element timing. In data communications, a signal used with synchronous modems for transmitted data. The modem may provide a clock signal transmitter signal element timing (DCE source) or the computer equipment may generate the timing signal on transmitter signal element timing (DTE source). *Compare* RECEIVER SIGNAL ELEMENT TIMING. *See* RS-232C, SYNCHRONOUS MODEM, TRANSMITTED DATA.

transparent. (1) Pertaining to a process, or procedure, invoked by a user without the latter being aware of its existence. *Compare* VIRTUAL. (2) In communications, pertaining to a network or facility that allows a signal to pass through it without a change.

transparent data communication code. In data communications, a mode using a code independent protocol. Correct functioning is independent of the code or character set. *See* TRANSPARENT.

transponder. In communications, a device that receives and retransmits signals. In satellite communications the received signals are amplified and retransmitted at a different frequency. *Compare* RESPONDER.

transport layer. In data communications, a layer in the ISO Open Systems Interconnection model. This layer accepts messages from the session layer, splits them into smaller segments, if necessary, and ensures that they arrive correctly at the receiving transport layer. The transport layer should perform this function in the most efficient manner, and shield the session layer from any changes in the hardware technology. *Compare* APPLICATION LAYER, DATA LINK LAYER, NETWORK LAYER, PHYSICAL LAYER, PRESENTATION LAYER, SESSION LAYER. *See* BIT STREAM, OPEN SYSTEMS INTERCONNECTION.

transposition cipher. In cryptography, a cipher in which the characters are reordered but not individually disguised. *Compare* SUBSTITUTION CIPHER. *See* CIPHER, CRYPTOGRAPHY.

trapdoor. (1) In computer security, a hidden software or hardware mechanism that permits system protection mechanisms to be circumvented. It is activated in some non-apparent manner (e.g. special 'random' key sequence at a terminal). (DOD). (2) In computer security, a breach created intentionally in an ADP system for the purpose of collecting, altering or destroying data. (FIPS). (3) In computer security, a condition existing in the system software or hardware which can be triggered to subvert the software or hardware security features. Basically, the condition is prompted internally (such as, by a counter, a date or time value, or any specific set of pre-established circumstances) or externally (such as, by a remote terminal or application program input message). (AR). *See* TIME BOMB, TROJAN HORSE.

trapdoor one-way function. In mathematics, a function that can be easily computed but the computation of the inverse function is infeasible unless certain specific information, employed in the design of the function, is available.

Thus two large prime numbers may be multiplied together to form a product but it may be computationally infeasible to derive the factors given only the value of the product. Knowledge of one factor in this case would constitute the trapdoor information. *See* PUBLIC KEY CRYPTOGRAPHY.

Treaty of Schengen. In legislation, an agreement signed by France, Germany, the Netherlands, Luxembourg and Belgium on the establishment of an automated system to exchange police intelligence. *See* DATA PROTECTION, DATA PROTECTION EC.

tree. *See* TREE STRUCTURE.

tree database. *Synonymous with* HIERARCHICAL DATABASE.

tree structure. In computing, a series of connected nodes without cycles. One node is termed the root and is the starting point of all paths, another one or more nodes, termed leaves, terminate the paths. A path from any node towards a leaf will never pass through any individual node more than once. It can be used to represent hierarchical structures, e.g. a family tree.

Trellis coding. In data communications, a protocol employing forward error correction used in some high speed modems. *See* FORWARD ERROR CORRECTION, MODEM.

tribit. In data communications, three consecutive bits. In phase modulated systems a tribit is represented by a phase change of 0, 45, 90, 135...... 315 degrees. *See* PHASE MODULATION.

tributary station. In data communications, any station, other than the control station on a multipoint circuit. It can communicate with the control station only when polled or selected by it. *See* MULTIPOINT CIRCUIT, POLLING.

trigram. In cryptanalysis, a triple of successive letters. *See* BIGRAM.

triple modular redundancy. In reliability, a form of modular redundancy using three active units in parallel. The outputs of all three units are compared and the system output is obtained by taking a majority vote of the three unit outputs. *Compare* DUAL REDUNDANCY, HYBRID REDUNDANCY, NMR. *See* MODULAR REDUNDANCY.

TRM. *See* TAMPER-RESISTANT MODULE.

Trojan Horse. (1) In computer security, a computer program with an apparently or actually useful function that contains additional (hidden) functions that surreptitiously exploit the legitimate authorizations of the invoking process to the detriment of security. For example, making a 'blind copy' of a sensitive file for the creator of the Trojan Horse. (DOD). (2) In computer security, a computer program that is apparently or actually useful and that contains a trapdoor. (FIPS). *See* TRAPDOOR. (3) In computer security, a program inserted by an attacker in a computer system. It performs functions not described in the program specifications, taking advantage of rights belonging to the calling environment to copy, misuse or destroy data. For example, a Trojan Horse in a text editor might copy confidential information in a file being edited to a file accessible to the attacker. *See* LEAKAGE, TROJAN HORSE DIRECT RELEASE, TROJAN HORSE LEAKAGE.

Trojan Horse direct release. In database security, a form of threat in which a Trojan Horse causes classified data to be released to a user with a lower security classification. The unauthorized data is released because it is effectively labelled with a lower security classification by the Trojan Horse. This can be achieved by changing the security label, placing the data in a record or field with a lower classification or failing to update a security classification as the classification of the data increases. *Compare* DIRECT ACCESS, INDIRECT ACCESS, TROJAN HORSE LEAKAGE. *See* FIELD, RECORD, TROJAN HORSE.

Trojan Horse leakage. In database security, a form of threat in which a Trojan Horse causes the system to apparently respond to an authorized query but actually responds to a different query, i.e. one requiring a higher security classification. The unauthorized data is encoded into authorized data returned to the user. *Compare* DIRECT ACCESS, INDIRECT ACCESS, TROJAN HORSE DIRECT RELEASE. *See* TROJAN HORSE.

trouble condition. In physical security, a situation in an alarm system in which supervision is lost due to a short circuit, power failure etc.

troubleshoot. (1) To seek, locate and repair equipment malfunctions. (2) In programming, to debug. *See* DEBUG.

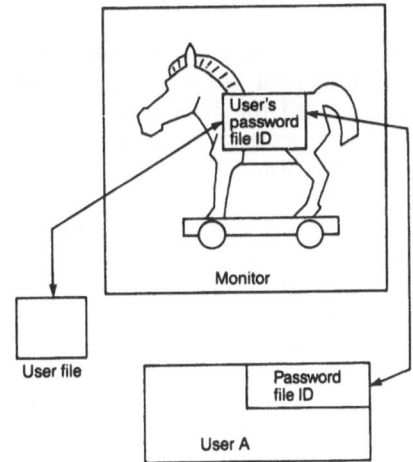

Trojan Horse
In this example of a Trojan Horse, a software performance monitor evaluates a software program, as well as gathering sensitive data associated with the program. Reproduced with permission of IBM Corp.

trouble signal. In physical security, a signal that arises as a result of a problem, e.g. circuit break or ground, in a device or wiring associated with a fire alarm system. *Compare* TROUBLE CONDITION.

trunk. In communications, a circuit, or channel, interconnecting two exchanges or switching units, capable of being switched at both ends and provided with the necessary signalling and terminating equipment.

trust. The belief that a system meets its specifications. *See* SPECIFICATION.

trusted. In data security, pertaining to software and hardware systems that have been designed, and verified, to avoid compromising, corrupting or denying sensitive information. *See* COMPROMISE, CORRUPT DATA, DELAY/DENIAL OF SERVICE, TRUSTED COMPUTING BASE.

trusted channel. In communications security, a mechanism by which two NTCB partitions can communicate directly. This mechanism can be activated by either of the NTCB partitions, cannot be imitated by untrusted software, and maintains the integrity of information that is sent over it. A trusted channel may be needed for the correct operation of other security mechanisms. *See* NTCB PARTITION.

trusted communications path. In communications security, a mechanism by which a network subject can communicate directly with the trusted computing base. This mechanism can only be activated by the network subject or the TCB and cannot be imitated by the untrusted software. *See* TRUSTED COMPUTING BASE.

trusted computer security evaluation criteria. *Synonymous with* ORANGE BOOK.

trusted computer system. In computer security, a system that employs sufficient hardware and software integrity measures to allow its use for processing simultaneously a range of sensitive or classified information. (DOD). *See* ORANGE BOOK, TRUSTED, TRUSTED COMPUTING BASE.

trusted computing base. In computer security, the totality of protection mechanisms within a computer system - including hardware, firmware, and software - the combination of which is responsible for enforcing a security policy. It creates a basic protection environment and provides additional user services required for a trusted computer system. The ability of a trusted computing base to correctly enforce a security policy depends solely on the mechanisms within the TCB and on the correct input by system administrative personnel of parameters (e.g. a user's clearance) related to the security policy. (DOD). *Compare* NETWORK TRUSTED COMPUTING BASE. *See* SECURITY POLICY, TRUSTED, TRUSTED COMPUTER SYSTEM.

trusted functionality. In computer security, that which is perceived to be correct with respect to some criteria, e.g. as established by a security policy. The functionality shall neither fall short nor exceed that of the criteria. *See* SECURITY POLICY, TRUSTED.

trusted identification forwarding. In communications security, an identification method used in networks where the sending host can verify that an authorized user on its system is attempting a connection to another host. The sending host transmits the required user authentication information to the receiving host. The receiving host can then verify that the user is validated for access to its system. This operation may be transparent to the user. (DOD).

trusted path. In computer security, a mechanism by which a person at a terminal can communicate directly with the TCB. This mechanism can only be activated by the person or the TCB and cannot be imitated by untrusted software. (DOD). *See* TRUSTED SOFTWARE, TCB.

trusted process. In computer security, a process that can affect system security. It is sometimes but not always endowed with privileges to override kernel-enforced rules. The protection capabilities or characteristics of a trusted process must be reliably demonstrated to comply with stated requirements, through formal verification when possible. Trusted processes are sometimes used to execute NKSR software. (MTR). *Compare* UNTRUSTED PROCESS. *See* NKSR, SECURITY KERNEL.

trusted products. Products certified by Director, NCSC for inclusion on the Evaluated Products List. (DODD). *See* EVALUATED PRODUCTS LIST, NCSC.

trusted software. In computer security, the software portion of a TCB. (DOD). *See* TRUSTED, TRUSTED COMPUTER SYSTEM, TRUSTED COMPUTING BASE, TRUSTED PROCESS.

trusted subject. (1) In computer security, a subject that is part of the TCB. It has the ability to violate the security policy, but is trusted not to actually do so. For example in the Bell-La Padula model a trusted subject is not constrained by the star(*) property and thus has the ability to write sensitive information into an object whose level is not dominated by the (maximum) level of the subject, but it is trusted to only write information into objects with a label appropriate for the actual level of the information (TNI). *See* BELL-LA PADULA MODEL, OBJECT, STAR PROPERTY, SUBJECT. (2) In computer security, a subject that is permitted to have simulta-

neous view- and alter-access to objects of more than one sensitivity level. (NCSC). *See* BELL-LA PADULA MODEL, ORANGE BOOK.

trusted system. A system employing sufficient integrity measures to allow its use for processing intelligence information involving sensitive intelligence sources and methods. (DCID). *See* TRUSTED, TRUSTED COMPUTER SYSTEM, TRUSTED COMPUTING BASE, TRUSTED PROCESS.

trustworthiness. Assurance that a system deserves to be trusted. *See* TRUST.

TSW. *See* TELESOFTWARE.

TTAP. In computer security, Trust Technology Assessment Program, a U.S. program directed towards the security assessment of products with minimal assurance requirements. It was developed with the goals of assisting the international recognition of product evaluations, minimizing time and cost of product assessment and maximizing product availability. *Compare* TCSEC. *See* FC-FIPS, MFSR.

tuned circuit card. *See* PROXIMITY CARD READER.

Tunes. In computer security, a virus that terminates and stays resident, infects COM and EXE and OVL files, affects run-time operation, and corrupts program and OVL files. *See* VIRUS NAMES.

tuning. To optimize the performance of a system by fine adjustment.

tunneling attack. In computer security, an attempt to exploit a weakness in a system at a low level of abstraction.

tuple. In mathematics, a related set of values. *See* N-TUPLE.

turnkey system. In computing, a complete system designed for a specific user. With large, complex systems the user needs only to switch on the system, the prime contractor accepting full responsibility for system design, installation, supply of hardware, software and documentation. With software packages the user need not be aware of the operating system; upon loading the disk all operating instructions will be displayed to the user. *See* OPERATING SYSTEM.

twisted pair. In communications, a cable produced by twisting together two individually insulated thin conductors. This arrangement reduces the capacitance between the wires.

two-dimensional scrambler. In communications security, a form of voice scrambler which permutes the signal in both the time and frequency domain. The speech signal is split into frames and each frame has a number of segments. The signals within each segment are transformed to the frequency domain and the frequency components permuted. The segments themselves are also permuted with the frame. *Compare* DISCRETE FOURIER TRANSFORM SCRAMBLER. *See* VOICE SCRAMBLING.

two-end device. In computer security, a device installed at both the host computer, and legitimate user, end of the telephone connection to provide protection against telephone intrusion. Current devices provide authentication of the user terminal or location and data transmitted, and concealment of the transmitted data. User authentication is normally provided by some form of token possessed by the user; such tokens enable the user to enter a dynamic password. Terminal authentication demands a unit in the terminal which can automatically enter a challenge/response dialogue with the host computer. Data authentication is performed by the production of a MAC over the message

contents and data concealment is produced with link encryption. *Compare* ONE-END DEVICE. *See* CHALLENGE/RESPONSE, DYNAMIC PASSWORD, LINK ENCRYPTION, MESSAGE AUTHENTICATION, MESSAGE AUTHENTICATION CODE.

two-key cryptosystem. *Synonymous with* ASYMMETRIC CRYPTOSYSTEM. *See* PUBLIC KEY CRYPTOGRAPHY.

two-layer architecture. In key management, a system in which a key-encrypting key is manually distributed and this key is used to encrypt data keys that are subject to automated distribution. *Compare* THREE-LAYER ARCHITECTURE. *See* ANSI X9.17 - 1985, CRYPTOGRAPHIC KEY, DATA KEY, KEY-ENCRYPTING KEY.

two-wire circuit. In communications, a circuit comprising two conductors insulated from each other, thus providing a go and return channel for signals of same frequency. *Compare* FOUR-WIRE CIRCUIT.

TX. *See* TRANSMITTER.

Tymnet. In data communications, a U.S. public packet switching carrier. *See* PACKET SWITCHING.

type. In programming, pertaining to the range of values and valid operations associated with a variable.

Type I. In cryptography. *See* NSA COMSEC MODULE.

type accreditation. In computer security, official authorization by the DAA to employ a system in a specified environment. This authorization includes a statement of residual risk, delineates operating environment, and specific use. It is performed when multiple copies of a system are to be fielded. (AFR). *See* DAA.

Type 1 cryptographic product. In cryptography, a product endorsed by the NSA to secure classified information. *Compare* TYPE 2 CRYPTOGRAPHIC PRODUCT. *See* NSA.

Type 2 cryptographic product. In cryptography, a product endorsed by the NSA to secure only unclassified information. *Compare* TYPE 1 CRYPTOGRAPHIC PRODUCT. *See* NSA.

Type 1 error. In access control, an error in a biometric system that causes a request, from an authorized user for access, to be rejected. *Compare* TYPE 2 ERROR. *See* BIOMETRICS.

Type 2 error. In access control, an error in a biometric system that causes a request, from an unauthorized user for access, to be accepted since the biometric measurement is incorrectly matched with that of an authorized user.

Compare TYPE 1 ERROR. *See* BIOMETRICS.

Type 1 magnetic media. In electronics, magnetic media with coercivity factors not exceeding 325 oersteds. (DOD). *See* COERCIVE FORCE, OERSTED.

Type 2 magnetic media. In electronics, magnetic media with coercivity factors exceeding 325 oersteds, possibly as high as 750 oersteds. (DOD). *See* COERCIVE FORCE, OERSTED.

Typo Boot. In computer security, a computer virus that affects run-time operation and corrupts boot sector. *See* VIRUS NAMES.

Typo/Fumble. In computer security, a computer virus that terminates and stays resident, infects COM files, affects run time operation, corrupts program and OVL files. *See* VIRUS NAMES.

U

UA. User Agent. *Compare* MTA, MTS. *See* USER AGENT.

UCC1. In access control, a data security package. *See* DATA SECURITY PACKAGE.

UDAC. *See* USER-DIRECTED ACCESS CONTROL.

UDI. *See* UNCONSTRAINED DATA ITEM.

UL. *See* UNDERWRITERS LABORATORY.

ultimate beneficiary. *Synonymous with* BENEFICIARY.

ultrasonic motion detector. In physical security, a form of intrusion detection device in which ultrasonic waves are transmitted. The presence of an intruder is detected as the moving body affects the frequency of signals reflected back to the sensor. *Compare* SONIC MOTION DETECTOR. *See* MOTION DETECTOR.

ultraviolet fire detector. In physical security, a fire detector that is activated by an increase in ultraviolet radiation emitted by a flame. Such fire detectors are responsive to a limited range of frequencies and therefore less susceptible to false alarms e.g. electrical discharge. *Compare* PHOTOELECTRIC BEAM SMOKE DETECTOR.

unapproved software. In computer security, all software that has not been formally identified, evaluated, and examined by competent personnel to ensure that the software performs to exact specifications. (AR). *Compare* TRUSTED SOFTWARE.

unary operation. In mathematics, an operation on only one operand, e.g. negation that reverses the sign of a term. *See* OPERAND.

unauthorized disclosure. In data security, the process of making information available to unauthorized individuals, entities or processes.

unbalanced transmission. In data communications, a technique employing one wire for each signal and a common return path for all signals. *Compare* BALANCED TRANSMISSION.

unbreakable cipher. *See* PERFECT SECRECY.

Unclassified. In data security, the lowest level of classification of data and hence one that normally requires no protection against unauthorized disclosure. *See* CLASSIFICATION.

unclassified information. In data security, a U.S. Department of Defense clearance for personnel who are authorized to access sensitive unclassified, e.g. For Official Use Only, information, either by an explicit official authorization or by an implicit authorization derived from official assignments of responsibilities. *Compare* CONFIDENTIAL CLEARANCE, MULTIPLE CATEGORIES, ONE CATEGORY, SECRET CLEARANCE, TOP SECRET CLEARANCE, UNCLEARED. *See* CLEARANCE.

uncleared. In data security, a U.S. Department of Defense clearance for personnel with no clearance of authorization. Access is permitted to any information for which there is no specified controls, e.g. openly published information. *Compare* CONFIDENTIAL CLEARANCE, MULTIPLE CATEGORIES, ONE CATEGORY, SECRET CLEARANCE, TOP SECRET CLEARANCE, UNCLASSIFIED INFORMATION. *See* CLEARANCE.

unconditionally secure. In cryptanalysis, pertaining to a cipher that cannot be broken, even with an unlimited amount of ciphertext available to the cryptanalyst. Formally this requires that the key equivocation never approaches zero even for extremely long messages. *See* INFORMATION THEORY, KEY EQUIVOCATION, PERFECT SECRECY.

unconfirmed service. In data communications, a service in which the sender issues a request and an indication of the request is passed to the intended recipient, but no confirmation is returned to the sender. *Compare* CONFIRMED SERVICE.

unconstrained data item. In formal models, a term used in the Clark-Wilson model to refer to an entered data item, prior to the necessary checking for conformation with the rules of a constrained data item. *Compare* CONSTRAINED DATA ITEM. *See* CLARK-WILSON MODEL.

undecidable. In mathematics, pertaining to a problem for which no algorithm can be written for its solution. *Compare* INTRACTABLE.

Underwriter's Laboratory. In physical security, a U.S. nonprofit making testing laboratory that tests and certifies categories of equipment for safety and reliability.

unicity distance. In cryptology, the minimum length of ciphertext message for which the key equivocation approaches zero. The unicity distance of a ciphertext message is the amount of ciphertext that is theoretically required to uniquely determine the key. *See* CRYPTOGRAPHIC KEY, KEY EQUIVOCATION.

unipolar. In data communications, pertaining to a signal that has excursions from zero to either a positive or negative value but not both, e.g. it consists of a stream of positive pulses only. *Compare* BIPOLAR.

unique identification. *Synonymous with* FINGERPRINT.

unit buffer terminal. In communications, a terminal that does not have a communication buffer.

universal quantifier. In mathematics, a symbol employed in predicate calculus, and relational calculus, that is read as 'for all'.

universal set. In mathematics, the total set of elements that have a specified property, e.g. 0, 1, 2...9, is the universal set of non-negative, single digit integers. *See* SET.

universal signature. In authentication, a digital signature that can be validated by the receiver and does not require an arbiter. *Compare* ARBITRATED SIGNATURE. *See* DIGITAL SIGNATURE.

Unix. A trademark, in computing, a general purpose multiuser operating system suitable for use in a wide range of mini- and microcomputers. It originated in the Bell Laboratories in 1969, for the PDP-7 minicomputer, and it became extremely popular amongst computer scientists. Unix encompasses a range of programming tools that provide a rich, productive environment for the development of software by a team of programmers. Unix is highly portable and its use is rapidly expanding in the personal computer fields. It is a multi-user system, providing facilities for sharing system resources (disk space, CPU time, etc.) and protection mechanisms for user files. For each file users can specify individual read, write and execution privileges to themselves, members of group and all other users. The system is also multitasking, allowing the user to relegate programs requiring no user interaction to background processing whilst interacting with the foreground program.

unprotect. In computer security, a program that overcomes software protection features and copies specific 'protected' software. *See* SOFTWARE PROTECTION.

untrusted. In computer security, pertaining to a system that is not verified with respect to its security properties. *Compare* TRUSTED.

untrusted process. In computer security, a process whose incorrect or malicious execution cannot affect system security. Verification is usually not applied to untrusted processes. (MTR). *Compare* TRUSTED PROCESS.

update inconsistency. In databases, a phenomenon that can arise in a multiuser database. The sequence of events is:

- Alice retrieves a record;
- Bob retrieves the same record;
- Alice updates a field of the record and writes it back to the database whilst Bob still has the retrieved record;
- Bob updates a different field of the same record and writes it back to the database overwriting Alice's update.

Lockout is employed to avoid this situation. *See* FIELD, LOCKOUT, RECORD.

upload. In computing, to send a file from a smaller computer or local one to a larger or remote computer. *Compare* DOWNLOAD. *See* FILE TRANSFER.

uptime. In computing, the time that a computer is available for normal operation. *Synonymous with* AVAILABLE TIME.

upward compatibility. In computing, the capability of one computer to execute programs written for another but not vice versa.

usability. In computing, the effort required to learn, operate, prepare input and interpret output of a program.

usage. In data security, pertaining to the integrity of data, specifically the set of protective countermeasures to assure and maintain validity of data and to provide for its continued existence and recoverability. *See* COUNTERMEASURE, DATA INTEGRITY.

usage sensitive pricing. In communications, charges for service based upon usage.

USASCII. In codes, USA Standard Code for Information Interchange. *Synonymous with* ASCII.

USASI. United States of America Standards Institute.

user. (1) In communications security, any person who interacts directly with a network system. This includes both those persons who are authorized to interact with the system and those people who interact without authorization (e.g. active or passive wiretappers) (TNI). *Compare* SUBJECT. *See* WIRETAP. (2) In operations, an organizational or programmatic entity that receives service from an information technology facility. A user may be either internal or external to the agency organization responsible for the facility, but normally does not report to the manager or director of the facility or to the same immediate supervisor. (OMBC) *Compare* CUSTOMER. *See* INFORMATION TECHNOLOGY FACILITY. (3) In operations, any person or organization who has access to an automated system via communication through a remote device or who is allowed to submit input to the system through other media. 'Users' are not those persons or organizations defined as customers. (AFR). *Compare* CUSTOMER. (4) In computer security, people who can access an AIS either by direct connections (i.e. via terminals) or indirect connections (i.e. prepare input data or software or receive output that is not reviewed for content and classification by a responsible individual). (DODD). *See* AIS. (5) In computer security, any individual who is able to operate any equipment that can access the ADP system or input commands to the ADP system or receive output from the ADP system without intervention of an authorized reviewing official. Note that a user may not necessarily be an authorized user of the ADP system. (DOE). *See* ADP. (6) In computer security, any person who interacts directly with a computer system. (DOD). (7) In computer security, the person, function or organization that receives and uses the output of a computer application. User functions are outside the physical boundary of the computer facility, but the user may directly interface with the system via a terminal. *See* END USER.

user acceptability. In computer security, principle of user acceptability, one of the principles of secure systems which states - security measures should not unduly interfere with the work of users whilst, of course, fulfilling all necessary security constraints. *See* PRINCIPLES OF SECURE SYSTEMS.

user agent. In data communications, a process in the CCITT X.400 standard for message handling. The user agent has a role analogous to the user of a postal system who inserts a letter into an envelope, addresses it and then posts it. *Compare* MESSAGE TRANSFER AGENT. *See* X.400.

user alternative plan. In risk management, the set of plans for use by the user of an application when the processing of that application has been disrupted. *See* CONTINGENCY PLANS.

user authentication. *See* ACCESS CONTROL, AUTHENTICATION.

user-directed access control. In access control, access control in which users (or subjects generally) may alter the access rights. Such alterations may, for example, be restricted to certain individuals by the access controls, thus they may be limited to the owner of an object. *Compare* ADMINISTRATIVELY DIRECTED ACCESS CONTROL. *See* DISCRETIONARY ACCESS CONTROL.

user friendly. Pertaining to any system designed to be used without extensive operator training and that seeks to assist the user to gain maximum benefit from the system.

user id. (1) In computer security, a unique symbol or character string that is used by an ADP system to uniquely identify a user. The security provided by a password system should not rely on secrecy of the user id. (DOD). *Compare* NETWORK USER IDENTITY. *See* ADP, PASSWORD, PIN. (2) In operations, a user identification code enabling a computer to recognize, and allocate charges to, a user.

user profile. (1) A description of the essential parameters of a user with respect to a given system. (2) In computer networks, a definition of the user type of interaction with a network, supplied by the user as a set of parameters, or options, at registration.

user programs. In computing, a group of programs written by the user as compared with manufacturer supplied software. *See* APPLICATION PROGRAM.

users group. A group of users who agree to share programs, exchange information, etc, on a class of computer systems. *Compare* CLOSED USER GROUP.

USSR. In computer security, a virus that encrypts itself, infects EXE files, affects run time operation, corrupts program and OVL files. *See* VIRUS NAMES.

UU. Unauthorized user.

V

V. *See* V-Series recommendations of CCITT.

V.1. In standards, a CCITT recommendation for equivalence between binary notation symbols and the significant conditions of two condition code.

V.2. In standards, a CCITT recommendation for power levels for data transmission over telephone lines.

V.3. In standards, a CCITT recommendation for international Alphabet Number 5 for transmission of data and messages. *See* International Alphabet Number 5.

V.4. In standards, a CCITT recommendation for general structure of signals of International Alphabet Number 5 for data and message transmission over public telephone networks. *See* International Alphabet Number 5.

V.5. In standards, a CCITT recommendation for standardization of data signalling rates for synchronous data transmission in the general switched telephone network.

V.6. In standards, a CCITT recommendation for the standardization of data signalling rates for synchronous data transmission employed on leased telephone-type circuits.

V.10. In standards, a CCITT recommendation for electrical characteristics for unbalanced double-current inter-change circuits for general use with integrated circuit equipment in the field of data communications.

V.11. In standards, a CCITT recommendation for electrical characteristics for balanced double-current interchange circuits for general use with integrated circuit equipment in the field of data communications.

V.13. In standards, a CCITT recommendation for answer-back unit simulators.

V.15. In standards, a CCITT recommendation for use of acoustic coupling for data transmission.

V.16. In standards, a CCITT recommendation for medical analog data transmission modems. *See* MODEM.

V.19. In standards, a CCITT recommendation for modems for parallel data transmission using telephone signalling frequencies. *See* MODEM.

V.20. In standards, a CCITT recommendation for parallel data transmission modems standardized for universal use in the general switched telephone network. *See* MODEM.

V.21. In standards, a CCITT recommendation for 300-baud modem standardized for use in the general switched telephone network. *See* MODEM.

V.22. In standards, a CCITT recommendation for a specification for 1200 bit per second modems. *Compare* Bell 212A. *See* bits per second, CCITT, MODEM.

V.22 bis. In standards, a CCITT recommendation for a specification based on

541

a 600 baud line signalling rate using quadrature amplitude modulation. In this standard each phase angle of the QAM star represents four consecutive bits. The combination of 600 signal changes per second with 4 bit patterns per signal then produces a rate of 2400 bits per second. *Compare* V.BB, V.22. *See* BAUD, BITS PER SECOND, QUADRATURE AMPLITUDE MODULATION.

V.23. In standards, a CCITT recommendation for 600/1200 baud modem standardized for use in the general switched telephone network. *See* MODEM.

V.24. In standards, a CCITT recommendation comparable with RS-232C. *See* RS-232C, V.28.

V.25. In standards, a CCITT recommendation comparable with RS-366. *See* RS-366.

V.26. In standards, a CCITT recommendation for 2400 bit/s modem standardized for use on four-wire leased circuits. *See* MODEM.

V.26 bis. In standards, a CCITT recommendation for 2400/1200 bit/s modem standardized for use in the general switched telephone network. *See* MODEM.

V.27. In standards, a CCITT recommendation for 4800 bit/s modem standardized for use on leased circuits. *See* MODEM.

V.27 bis. In standards, a CCITT recommendation for 4800 bit/s modem with automatic equalizer standardized for use on leased circuits. *See* MODEM.

V.27 ter. In standards, a CCITT recommendation for 4800/2400 bit/s modem standardized for use in the general switched telephone network. *See* MODEM.

V.28. In standards, a CCITT recommendation which defines electrical signal characteristics comparable with those of RS-232C. *See* RS-232C, V.24.

V.29. In standards, a CCITT recommendation for 9600 bit/s modem for use on leased circuits. *See* MODEM.

V.30. In standards, a CCITT recommendation for parallel data transmission systems for universal use on the general switched telephone network. *See* MODEM.

V.31. In standards, a CCITT recommendation for electrical characteristics for single-current interchange circuits controlled by contact closure. *See* MODEM.

V.32. In standards, a CCITT recommendation for a specification based on 2400 baud signal rate using quadrature amplitude modulation. Each phase angle of the QAM star represents five consecutive bits. The combination of 2400 signal changes per second with a 5 bit pattern per signal change produces 12000 bits per second; however, the effective data bit throughput will only be 9600 bits per second since one out of five of the transferred bits is used for error correction. *Compare* V.22 BIS. *See* BAUD, BITS PER SECOND, QUADRATURE AMPLITUDE MODULATION.

V.35. In standards, a CCITT recommendation for data transmission at 48 kilobit/s using 60 to 108 kHz group band circuits.

V.36. In standards, a CCITT recommendation for modems for synchronous data transmission using 60 to 108 kHz group band circuits. *See* MODEM.

V.37. In standards, a CCITT recommendation for synchronous data transmission at a data signalling rate higher than 72 Kbit/s using 60 to 108 kHz group band circuits.

V.40. In standards, a CCITT recommendation for error indication with electromechanical equipment.

V.41. In standards, a CCITT recommendation for code independent error control system.

V.50. In standards, a CCITT recommendation for standard limits for transmission quality of data transmission.

V.51. In standards, a CCITT recommendation for organization of the maintenance of international telephone-type circuits used for data transmission.

V.52. In standards, a CCITT recommendation for characteristics of distortion and error rate measuring apparatus for data transmission.

V.53. In standards, a CCITT recommendation for limits for the maintenance of telephone-type circuits used for data transmission.

V.54. In standards, a CCITT recommendation for loop test device for modems. *See* MODEM.

V.55. In standards, a CCITT recommendation for specification for an impulsive noise measuring instrument for telephone-type circuits.

V.56. In standards, a CCITT recommendation for comparative tests of modems for use over telephone-type circuits. *See* MODEM.

V-299. In computer security, a virus that infects COM files, affects run time operation. *See* VIRUS NAMES.

V-555. In computer security, a virus that terminates and stays resident, infects COMMAND.COM, COM, EXE and OVL files, affects run time operation, corrupts program and OVL files and file linkage. *See* VIRUS NAMES.

V800. In computer security, a stealth virus that encrypts itself, terminates and stays resident, infects COM files, affects run time operation, corrupts program and OVL files and file linkage. *See* VIRUS NAMES.

V-801. In computer security, a virus that terminates and stays resident, infects COMMAND.COM, COM, EXE and OVL files, affects run time operation, corrupts program and OVL files and file linkage. *See* VIRUS NAMES.

V-961. In computer security, a virus that terminates and stays resident, infects COMMAND.COM and COM files, affects run time operation, corrupts program and OVL files. *See* VIRUS NAMES.

V2000. In computer security, a virus that terminates and stays resident, infects COMMAND.COM, COM, EXE and OVL files, affects run time operation, corrupts program and OVL files and file linkage. *See* VIRUS NAMES.

V2100. In computer security, a virus that terminates and stays resident, infects COM and EXE files, affects run time operation, corrupts program, OVL and data files and file linkage. *See* VIRUS NAMES.

vaccine. In computer security, a software product designed to detect a virus. Some products also claim to remove the virus. *See* ANTI-VIRAL MEASURES.

Vacsina. In computer security, a virus that terminates and stays resident, infects COM, EXE and OVL files, affects run time operation, corrupts program and OVL files. *See* VIRUS NAMES.

VAD. Value Added Distributor.

validation. (1) In cryptography, the process of checking the data integrity of a message, or selected parts of a message. *See* DATA INTEGRITY. (2) That portion of the development of specialized ST&E, procedures, tools, and equipment needed to establish acceptance for joint usage by one or more DOD components or their contractors. Such action will include, as necessary, final development, evaluation, testing, leading to acceptance by senior ST&E staff specialists of the three Military Departments or a Defense Agency, and approval for joint usage by the Deputy Under Secretary of Defense for Policy Review. (OPNAVINST). (3) In computer security, the performance of tests and evaluations in order to determine compliance with security specifications and requirements. (FIPS). (4) In programming, a check on input data for correctness against set criteria, e.g. format, ranges, etc. May be performed manually or automatically. *See* VALIDITY CHECKING.

validity checking. (1) In programming, a procedure to check that a code group is actually a character of the particular code in use. (2) In programming, a data s-creening procedure wherein data input records are checked for range, valid representation etc. *See* REASONABLENESS CHECK.

valid password. In access control, a personal password that will authenticate the identity of an individual when presented to a password system or an access password that will allow the requested access when presented to a password system. (FIPS). *See* PERSONAL PASSWORD, PASSWORD.

value added network service. In communications, a communication service using the communications networks of a common carrier for transmission and providing added data services with separate additional equipment. Added services may include store and forward message switching, terminal and host interfacing; the users include some who do not belong to the organization providing the service.

value added service provider. In communications, a service, such as a database enquiry facility, offered over a value added network but marketed and supported by a separate organization from the VANS company. *Compare* CLOSED USER GROUP. *See* VANS.

value date. In banking, the date the transfer entry to an account is considered effective; either the day the instruction is received or some future date as stipulated by the sender. (ANSI) *Compare* PAY DATE.

value of service pricing. In communications, a pricing system in which the charges are related to the value of the service, to the user, rather than the costs of the supplier.

vandalware. *Synonymous with* MALWARE.

van Eck phenomenon. In computer security, pertaining to radiation from a VDU. Van Eck reported that signals sent to a VDU have a high voltage level and the electromagnetic radiation of such signals is relatively strong; moreover the frequencies are in the UHF range. Under optimum conditions this radiation can be received as far as 0.66 to 1.25 miles away, and translated to readable display. The radiation can be detected and displayed with a UHF television set modified with low cost standard electronic components. The van Eck phenomenon is therefore of some concern in computer security fields and its effect was demonstrated on a television program. *See* COMPROMISING EMANATIONS, TEMPEST PROOFING.

VANS. *See* VALUE ADDED NETWORK SERVICE.

VANS security. In data security, a Value Added Network Service poses specific security problems for the operators. In general, these security problems arise because:

- the operator cannot ensure that the users implement the security measures and procedures;
- it is difficult to control access to terminals which may be located in shops, homes etc.;
- it is difficult to assign liability when a user transaction fails, e.g. a message is lost due to communication link failure.

The potential dangers, to a VANS operator, due to system misuse or component malfunction are:

- loss of service revenue;
- claims from users or third parties;
- loss of public confidence.

Loss of revenue can from arise from equipment malfunction which denies user access, fraudulent bypassing of billing procedures etc. Claims from users or third parties may occur if unauthorized access is made to private data, if a transaction or message is modified, e.g. in an EFTPOS transaction, or if messages, or data, are lost due to component or communication system failure. Loss of public confidence is of particular concern because the publicity, given to a reported misuse by a hacker, may be out of all proportion to the actual or potential damage associated with the attack but can nevertheless cause a loss in actual or potential business from users.

The controls that can be employed to minimize the above mentioned dangers need to be considered in relation to the cost of the control vis-a-vis the risk of revenue loss. The cost of controls is measured not only in terms of enhanced equipment, software, communication costs, etc. but also relate to reductions in user friendliness. The available controls are:

- access control;
- system development;

- backup and resilience;
- cryptography and message authentication;
- independent reviews.

Access control may be considered under two headings: logical access and physical access. There are a wide variety of classes of users, with varying levels of access privileges, in VANS systems: systems programmers, maintenance engineers, users, potential clients at demonstrations, etc. A regular discipline on passwords, deletion of privileges when staff resign, nonavailability of cleartext PINs in transmission, deletion of passwords used in demonstrations etc. are all necessary to enforce logical access control.

Physical access control is particularly important since havoc can be caused by malicious damage wrought by vandals, terrorists, disgruntled employees etc. who need have no prior knowledge of the system nor computing expertise. Card keys, closed circuit television, site location of unattended units, alarm systems for unattended equipment, withdrawal of access privileges from ex-employees etc. are all components of a sensible access control strategy.

It is essential that the system development phase should be conducted, and monitored, to avoid both accidental and deliberate bugs being carried over to the live system. This involves:

- The use of appropriate structured design and development methodologies.
- The implementation of quality control procedures including independent reviews of all software modules.
- An independent review of system design by a security specialist.

A simple and direct form of attack on a system is to cause the loss of a facility, or interference on a communication path. If spurious data is introduced into a communication channel, carrying encrypted data, then the operator may conclude that there is a fault in the cryptographic equipment and take it off line, in order to maintain service. The options to be considered in the provision of backup systems are:

- the use of a backup site;
- the distribution of processing facilities over a number of nodes to obviate the risk of a total system failure by an event at one site;
- the use of fault tolerant hardware;
- diverse routing of communication channels.

Cryptography may be employed to disguise or authenticate sensitive or financial data. Such schemes require that the cryptographic keys used for transmitted messages be changed frequently; the associated key management schemes must be designed for the VANS environment in which the terminals will often be in unsupervised and insecure locations. Cryptography may not be a valid solution in certain VANS applications, e.g. home banking, where the user terminals must be cheap and user friendly. *See* ACCESS CONTROL, AUTHENTICATION, CARD KEY, CCTV, CRYPTOGRAPHY, DISGRUNTLED EMPLOYEE, EFTPOS, HACKER, HOME BANKING, KEY MANAGEMENT, VANS.

VAR. Value Added Retailer.

variable. In programming, a quantity that is named in the program and can assume any value, within a valid range for its type, and may be operated upon by any valid operator for that type. The name given to a variable is a string of characters which is used to denote the particular memory location in which the current value of the variable is held. The translator of a source program assigns the memory location to the named variable.

variable length record. In data structures, a record that can have a length independent of the length of other records

with which it is associated. Such a record could contain repeating groups. *Compare* FIXED LENGTH RECORD.

varying density holographic card. *Synonymous with* OPTICAL DENSITY CARD.

VASP. *See* VALUE ADDED SERVICE PROVIDER.

V.bb. In standards, a CCITT recommendation for a specification for 4800 bits per second data transmission over voice grade, telephone line compatible modems. *See* VOICE GRADE CHANNEL, MODEM, V-SERIES RECOMMENDATIONS OF CCITT.

Vcomm. In computer security, a virus that infects EXE files, affects run-time operation, corrupts program and OVL files and file linkage. *See* VIRUS NAMES.

VDU. *See* VISUAL DISPLAY UNIT.

vector. (1) A variable that has magnitude and direction. (2) In data structures, a quantity represented by an ordered set of numbers, e.g. a one-dimensional array.

veincheck. In access control, a biometric technique that scans the subcutaneous veins in a subject's hand, or wrist. The device comprises an infra red scanner and an electronic camera; the subject places their hand in the scanner and the image of the veins recorded by the camera is digitized and compared with a corresponding stored digitized image. Equal error rates of 0.1% have been claimed. *See* BIOMETRICS, EQUAL ERROR RATE.

verification. (1) In computer security, the documentation of penetration or attempts to penetrate an actual on-line system in support or in contradiction of assumptions developed during system review and analysis. (AR). *See* VERIFICATION. (2) In computer security, the process of comparing two levels of system specification for proper correspondence (e.g. security policy model with top-level specification, TLS with source code, or source code with object code). This process may or may not be automated. (DOD). *See* OBJECT CODE, SOURCE CODE, TLS.

verify. (1) To determine whether an operation on data has been performed accurately. (2) In computing, a facility which verifies that the data written to disk has been correctly recorded. The user commands 'Verify on' which then verifies all disk write operations until the user cancels with a 'Verify off' command.

Vernam cipher. In cryptography, an early stream cipher developed for the printing telegraph in 1917. The plaintext characters are encoded into binary and punched on a paper tape; a set of random numbers, also expressed in binary form are similarly punched onto a second tape. The two tapes are read in synchronism, the numbers added modulo 2 and hence a corresponding ciphertext tape is produced. The receiving end is supplied with a tape containing the same cryptographic bit stream and the plaintext is revealed by modulo 2 addition of the ciphertext and cryptographic bit stream. *Compare* VIGENÉRE CIPHER. *See* CRYPTOGRAPHIC BIT STREAM, MODULO ARITHMETIC, STREAM CIPHER.

version number. In computing, an indication of the enhancements contained in a particular offering of an operating system.

vertical redundancy check. *See* LONGITUDINAL REDUNDANCY CHECK.

vibrating bell. In physical security, an alarm device that rings continuously as long as operating energy is applied. *Compare* SINGLE STROKE BELL.

vibrating horn. In physical security, an electrically operated horn which produces an acoustic alarm signal by the action of a vibrating armature against a metal diaphragm.

vibration detector. In physical security, a sensor, employing a tuning fork or delicately balanced mercury or ring contacts, which activates an alarm when vibrated or moved. The tuning fork devices are sensitive to specific vibrations, e.g. those associated with breaking glass.

Victor. In computer security, a virus that terminates and stays resident, infects COMMAND.COM, COM, EXE and OVL files, corrupts program, OVL and data files and file linkage. *See* VIRUS NAMES.

video motion detector. In physical security, a device, used in conjunction with a CCTV system, which can detect a change in a received image. The image is encoded digitally and stored, changes in any part of the successively stored images indicate a movement within the area of view.

video switcher. In physical security, a CCTV switching device for re-routing signals from video cameras to monitors. The switcher enables users to sequence or bridge camera inputs. *See* BRIDGING SEQUENTIAL SWITCHER, CCTV, HOMING SEQUENTIAL SWITCHER, SEQUENTIAL SWITCHER.

videotex. A term which is used generically to cover teletext, a broadcast videotex service as well as viewdata, a wired videotex service. Videotext was first introduced in the late 1970's and a number of public services were implemented. Videotex technology was designed to forge a link between members of the general public and a centralized computer. In its most advanced form it can bring massive reference library, computer power and extensive communication facilities into the home. The term videotex covers two separate technological developments: viewdata and teletext. In the former case a communication link, providing simple two-way communication, is established between the user and host computer through a telephone network. With teletext the information flow is simplex, broadcast over TV wavebands in conjunction with normal television programs. *See* TELETEXT, VIEWDATA.

videotext. The display of textual material on a CRT screen or television set. *Compare* VIDEOTEX.

Vienna/648. In computer security, a virus that infects COM files, corrupts program and OVL files. *See* VIRUS NAMES.

view. (1) In databases, a multivalued function from a set of relations to a relation, or set thereof. In effect a view saves a user from having to manipulate stored data. For example if a database stores the weights of individual items in a ships cargo, and the number of each type of item then the user may issue a request for the total weight of the cargo as if it were a stored item, rather than having to retrieve the individual items of data and perform the computation. The views approach gives an impression, to users, that such derived data is stored in the database in a manner most suited to the user's requirements. *See* MULTILEVEL DATABASE SECURITY. (2) In databases, the subset of a database that is made available to a particular user. *See* ACCESS CONTROL. (3) In databases, that portion of the database that satisfies conditions specified in a query. (NCSC).

viewdata. In videotex, an interactive information service using a telephone link between the user and a host computer. The user employs a special terminal or an adaptor linked to a domestic TV set. *Synonymous with* INTERACTIVE VIDEOTEX.

violation of transmission security. *Synonymous with* TRAFFIC ANALYSIS.

Violator. In computer security, a virus that infects COMMAND.COM and COM files, affects run-time operation, corrupts program, OVL and data files. *See* VIRUS NAMES.

virtual. In architecture and data communications, a description of a facility that is offered to a user, or system, as if it were a physical reality. *Compare* TRANSPARENT.

virtual call service. In data communications, a packet switching service in which a logical link is set up prior to transfer. Packets are transferred over the logical link, some of them contain no data but are used for supervisory purposes. During the data transfer phase, packet sequence and flow control operations are performed. *See* FLOW CONTROL, PACKET SWITCHING, PACKET SWITCHING NETWORK, VIRTUAL CIRCUIT.

virtual circuit. In data communications, a circuit which comprises a path established from source to destination in the network. For the duration of the call all packets, which are not individually addressed, are transmitted through this virtual circuit and arrive in the same order as delivered. *Compare* DATAGRAM, PACKET SWITCHING, PACKET SWITCHING NETWORK.

virtual machine. In computing, a simulation of a computer and its associated devices by another computer system.

virtual memory. (1) In computing, a technique which allows the processor to employ its full address space even though it exceeds the physical main memory available. The virtual memory space exists on disk, when the processor addresses a portion of its address space, outside the main memory, special hardware locates the required page on disk and transfers it to a section of the main memory. *See* ADDRESS SPACE, PAGE. (2) In computer security, virtual memory systems provide a mechanism to enforce access control. The physical memory is shared amongst users but pages of virtual memory can be assigned to individual users or processes. A page entry table can specify the access type (Read, Write or none) that is allowed from each access node. *See* ACCESS CONTROL.

virtual password. In access control, a password computed from a passphrase that meets the requirements of password storage (e.g., 64 bits for DES). (FIPS). *See* PASSPHRASE, PASSWORD.

virtual terminal. In peripherals, an ideal terminal that is defined as a standard for the purpose of uniform handling of a variety of actual terminals. A terminal processor thereafter converts the signals of the real terminal to conform to the standards of the virtual terminal. *See* TERMINAL.

virtual terminal protocol. In data communications, a protocol that allows programs to access terminals over a network independent of the type of terminal in use. *See* NETWORK VIRTUAL TERMINAL, PROTOCOL.

virus. (1) In computer security, a form of malicious code that can infect other programs by modifying themselves to include a possibly evolved copy of itself. (2) In computer security, a form of malicious code which is 'self-propagating Trojan Horse, composed of a mission component, a trigger component and a self-propagating component. (NCSC). (3) In computer security, a form of malicious code which:

- is a set of instructions, programmatic or otherwise, that propagate themselves through computer systems and/or networks, and
- deliberately set up to do things unwanted by the legitimate owners of those systems.

Introduction

A statement on early virus research work was published by Cohen in 1984 and in this paper Cohen gave a pseudo language description of a typical virus.

The action of the virus program is first to seek another executable file and check if the virus signature string, in this case '1234567', is present at the beginning of the file. If this signature is present, then

**program virus := **

{1234567;

**subroutine infect-executable := **
  {loop: file = random-executable;
  if first-line-of-file = 1234567
    then go to loop;
  prepend virus to file;
  }

**subroutine do-damage := **
  {whatever damage is desired}

**subroutine trigger-pulled := **
  {return true on desired conditions}
**main-program := **
  {infect-executable;
  if trigger-pulled then do damage;
  }

next:}

Cohen Virus

the file has been infected and the next-executable file in the directory is examined. If, and when, an uninfected file is discovered, virus code is written to the beginning of that file.

The next stage of the viral action depends upon the presence of a time or logic bomb in the virus code. The trigger mechanism is checked, e.g. the time\date is checked for Friday 13th; if the appropriate trigger condition is satisfied then the malicious action is performed, e.g. formatting disks, as specified in the viral code. The executable file, infected with the virus, may cause further viral infection whenever it, in turn, is executed.

A virus does not necessarily have an associated time/logic bomb and malicious action. Experience of virus attacks indicates however, that harmful side effects may develop as viruses spread into new environments, even if there is no in-built malicious code.

The code given above describes only one possible class of viruses. It is not necessary for the virus code to be attached to the beginning of the executable file, moreover more than one executable file could be infected every time the virus code is executed.

In discussing the spread, detection, protection etc. of viruses it is important to distinguish between the action of a specific virus and that of some future theoretical virus. It is always possible to deal with a known virus because it has specific properties and actions, e.g. in the example above the presence of the virus can be detected by the existence of the '1234567' signature at the beginning of the file.

In the most general case, however, the person stipulating the defence mechanism, provided against a virus, must base that mechanism upon some attribute of the virus. This can then lead a virus designer to produce a program, which infects other programs, but does not possess that attribute. At this stage it is not possible to point to an attribute that must always be present in an arbitrary virus and must always be absent from arbitrary legitimate code. There is therefore no known test which can unambiguously identify a virus, and Cohen has suggested that it is theoretically impossible to develop such a test.

The spread of a virus will accelerate through a computer system as each infected program further infects others when it is executed. Even if only limited sharing of information is allowed in a system, the virus will spread by the transitive nature of information flow. Thus if A can share information with B then all the information available to A, and all the information available to B, may be affected by a virus initially planted in A's files, even if only one file is shared by A and B. Similarly if B shares information with C then the virus can eventually affect all C's files.

Types of Viruses.
Viruses developed to date may have one or more of the attributes: overwriting, non-overwriting, source code, memory resident, boot sector, and personal computer. The most prevalent viruses are undoubtedly the boot sector viruses which attack personal computers.

Overwriting Viruses.
The overwriting virus is, to date, comparatively rare; its action is illustrated in Fig. 1. A carrier program is introduced into the computer system, wittingly or unwittingly. The virus part of the carrier comprises three sections:

- S, virus signature.
- I, infection routine.
- M, malicious action code.

When the carrier program is executed the virus begins its action. The signature S may simply comprise a jump instruction to the code section I; the first action of the infection routine is to find an executable file and load it into memory. The executable file should be such that upon execution, control will be transferred to the first byte. The infection routine will then check for the presence of the signature S; if this is present then the infection routine will seek another executable file and load it from secondary storage into main memory. If the signature S is absent then the infection routine will overwrite the first section of executable code with its three sections S, I and M, and then write the file back to secondary storage.

The next stage of viral action depends upon the malicious code section, M. If this section is included in the virus then a malicious action, e.g. modifying files, may be undertaken unconditionally or dependent upon a trigger mechanism, e.g. time bomb or logic bomb. Thereafter control is passed to the remainder of the carrier program.

When the infected program is run the virus will seek to infect a further executable file, when control passes to the remainder of the user program, however, this program will crash or behave abnormally. The virus may disguise its presence by causing an error message, e.g. parity error, to be displayed, thus leading the user to believe that some system malfunction had occurred.

Overwriting viruses have two important characteristics:

- the length of infected programs is not changed by the presence of the virus;
- the infected program will behave abnormally upon execution, either crashing or causing error messages.

Non-overwriting Viruses.
A non-overwriting virus normally increases the length of the infected software but it can allow the program to execute normally after the virus has performed its action. The operation of a non-overwriting virus is illustrated in Fig. 2.

The virus code comprises three sections, S, I and M, as for the overwriting virus discussed above. In addition there is a MOV instruction which causes data to be copied from one section of memory to another.

The virus initially seeks an executable file which does not contain the virus signature S, indicating that it has not yet been infected. The virus then selects an initial portion of that file, Part 1 in the diagram, which is exactly the same length as the virus sections S, I and M. This Part 1 section is then copied to the end of the program, and a MOV routine is appended to the end of that. Then the virus code, S, I and M is written at the beginning of the file, overwriting Part 1. The virus then passes control to its malicious code M, and thereafter to the carrier program itself.

When the infected user program is invoked it is copied into main memory; the virus code, S, I and M is executed, causing a further infection and any malicious actions associated with M. Control is then passed to the MOV routine at the end of the program. The MOV routine copies the Part 1 section, near the end of the program, to the beginning, overwriting the virus section S, I and M. Control is now passed to the beginning of the user program which executes normally.

Non-overwriting viruses have two important characteristics:

- the length of infected programs is usually increased by the presence of the virus;
- the infected program will behave normally after the virus has performed its action. If the virus performs no noticeable malicious action then its presence will be masked.

Source Code Viruses.
A source code virus is written into the source code of a carrier program and it attacks the source code of other programs. Any undergraduate could write a source code virus in BASIC. The action of such a program is described below.

- Upon execution of the virus the directory is examined for .BAS files;
- The name of a .BAS file is read by the virus and checked against the contents of a file containing the names of files infected to date;
- The selected, uninfected file is chain merged with the virus program;
- The uninfected file is overwritten with the program produced above by chain merging;
- The name of the file just infected is written into the file containing the list of infected files.

Source code viruses have two significant advantages, at least from the viewpoint of the virus developer:

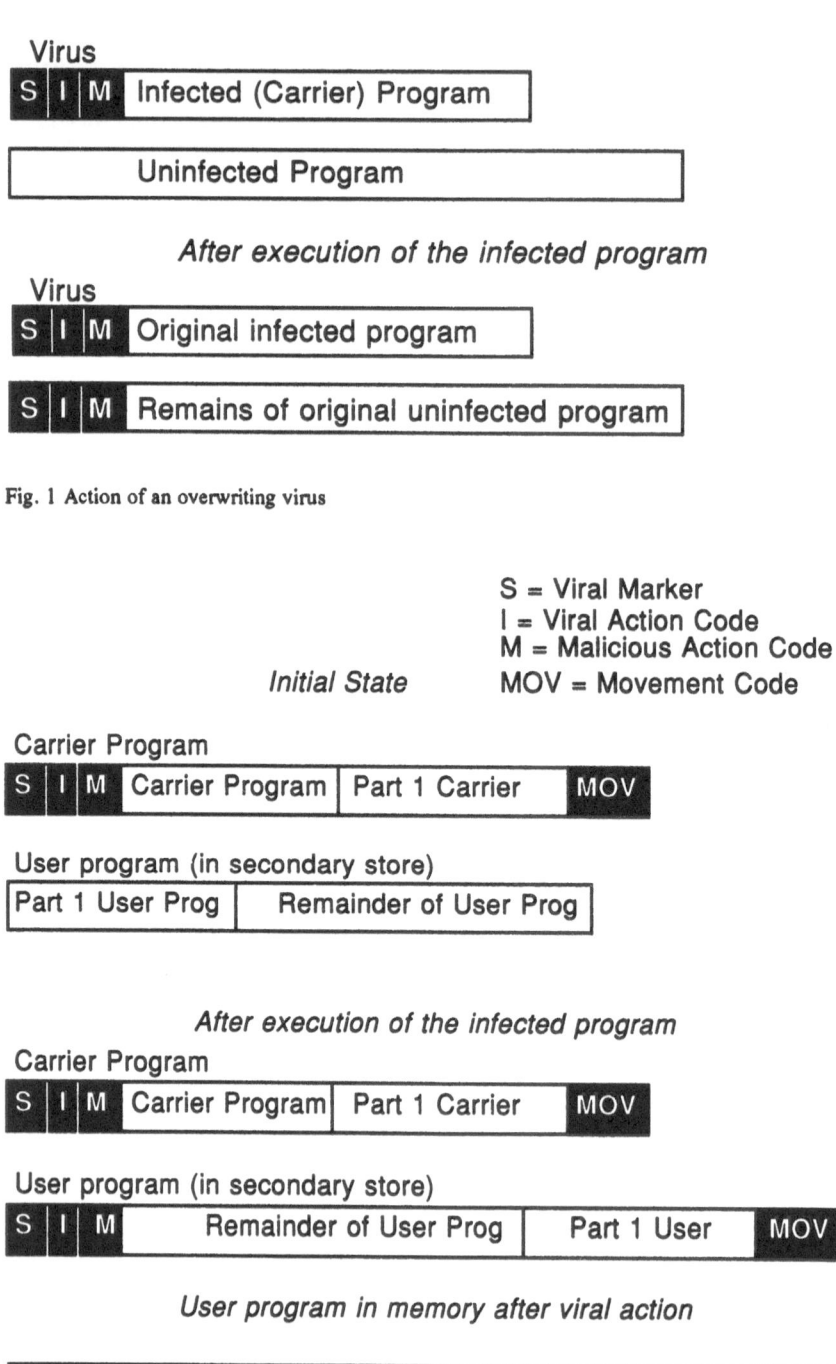

Fig. 1 Action of an overwriting virus

Fig. 2 Action of a non-overwriting virus
virus

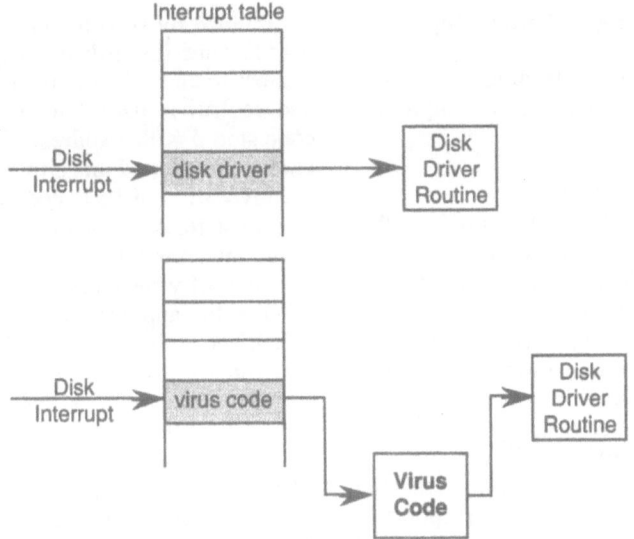

Fig. 3 Virus diverts control from disk driver to virus code.

Before loading Memory Resident Virus

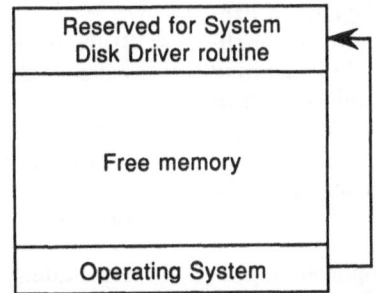

After loading Memory Resident Virus

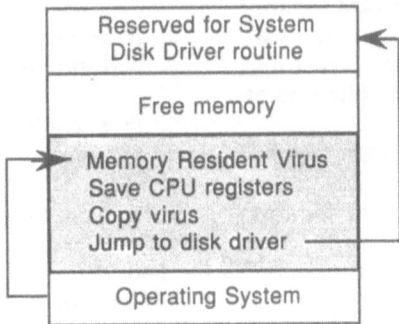

Fig. 4 Memory resident virus
virus

- they are portable between operating systems;
- the conventional technique of disinfecting programs by recompilation will fail.

Memory Resident Viruses.

Virus designers have the problem that their code must be invoked by the unsuspecting user before the first user program is infected. Once this hurdle has been overcome then the infection will spread as users invoke their own infected programs.

Memory resident viruses can overcome this problem, of first invocation, by exploiting the in-built flexibility of personal computer architectures. One essential feature of computers is the interrupt facility, which can produce the invocation of code which does not lie within the sequence of instructions of an application program.

When an application program is executed there is an interaction of the application code and that of the operating system. Whenever the application program needs to interact with some aspect of the computer, e.g. read a keyboard input, output data to a printer, input data from a magnetic disk etc., it invokes a section of code, termed a driver, in the operating system. The application program must know where to find the driver, and when the action requested by the driver is completed, the operating system must know where to find the next application program instruction to be executed. This handover and handback of control is performed by the interrupt architecture of the computer.

When the application program requires data from the disk it simply raises a disk interrupt. Control is passed to the disk driver and the state of the application program is saved during the execution of the driver code. When the disk driver has read the data from the disk, the application program state is restored and execution continues.

In personal computers the linkage between a disk interrupt and the disk driver is provided by an entry in a table held in RAM. Thus the disk interrupt causes an address to be read from the interrupt table and control is passed to the disk driver code stored at that address. Virus designers have exploited this situation to ensure the invocation of their code (see Fig. 3). The virus replaces the disk driver address in the interrupt table, with the address of a section of virus code.

When the application program requests a disk action it raises the disk interrupt. The entry in the interrupt table has been changed from the disk driver address to that of a section of virus code. Thus the virus code is invoked by the disk request, when the virus has performed its actions control is passed on to the disk driver so that the user is unaware of the infection.

The action of such memory resident virus may be illustrated by the pseudo code:

If the virus is not already resident in memory then

   replace at least one interrupt, terminate and stay resident

execute original program

New interrupt

   If uninfected file found then infect that file

   If trigger condition applies then perform malicious action

   Pass control to original interrupt program

A common form of memory resident viruses in the personal computer sector is the boot sector virus. The boot sector is the first sector to be read when a floppy, or hard, disk is booted; a section of virus code stored on the disk can therefore take control before any further action is taken by the user. The virus then attacks the personal computer system (see Fig. 4.).

One of the most virulent, early boot sector viruses was the Brain, or Pakistani virus. Basit Alvit, a nineteen year old Pakistani dealer in personal computers produced the virus, and incorporated a copyright notice giving the name, Brain Computer Services, address and telephone number in the virus code. Alvit claimed that he had only given one copy of the virus to a friend. It somehow migrated to the United States and versions of it appeared at the University of Delaware, University of Pittsburgh, George Washington University, University of Pennsylvania and Georgetown University. The virus normally contains no damage mechanism, although in some circumstances there is a side effect which can destroy data sectors on a disk. There are many versions of the Brain virus throughout the world and damage has been reported from some mutations of this virus.

The Brain virus resides partly in the boot sector of a floppy disk and partly in three clusters marked bad sectors.

Personal Computer Viruses.
The first reports of virus attacks occurred in the personal computer sector. It is clear that personal computers are a much greater risk than mainframes from virus attacks for the reasons listed below

- there is widespread sharing of floppy disks and software amongst personal computer users; some of the software being derived from unknown sources;
- there are massive numbers of users of a very restricted range of personal computer operating systems, e.g. MS.DOS;
- a virus developer has unlimited opportunity to gain access to all details of the operating system, and unlimited opportunity to experiment with the virus;
- many personal computer users have virtually no knowledge of computing and are unlikely to detect the early symptoms of a virus attack;

- personal computers are widely used on college campuses, a good breeding ground for computing pranksters.

The Brain virus proved to be but one of a myriad of personal computer viruses. Between 1988 and late 1990 there were innumerable media reports of new forms including inter alia: Macintosh, LeHigh, Amiga, Israeli, Bouncing Ball, Marijuana.

Most of these viruses were of the boot sector variety. In mid 1900 reports of a new breed of stealth viruses were reported, of which the 4096, also known as 4k, IDF (Israeli Defence Forces) and Frodo was the most common. The stealth virus seeks to hide its presence by taking over control of the machine. In the case of the 4096 virus, the virus goes memory resident and thereafter traps disk interrupts. When executable files are infected their length is increased by 4096 bytes. The virus actually disinfects files on the fly to hide the infection; if an infected .COM file is copied to a file with a different extension then the file is disinfected as it is copied, hiding the evidence of the infection. The virus has a time bomb set to any date between 22nd September and the 31st December, the former date is the birthday of Frodo, a character in Tolkien's novel the Lord of the Rings. The virus intended to display a message '-Frodo lives' when the time bomb is triggered, but the virus has a program bug which simply causes the computer to hang up.

The stealth viruses promise to become larger and more sophisticated. They point to the danger of allowing the virus to assume control of the computer before a search for the virus is commenced. *Compare* BLOB, CHECK KITING, COOKIE MONSTER, FLYING DUTCHMAN, FRENCH ROUNDOFF, LOGIC BOMB, STEALTH VIRUS, TIME BOMB, TROJAN HORSE, WORM. *See* MALICIOUS LOGIC, VIRUS NAMES.

Virus-90. In computer security, a virus that terminates and stays resident, infects

COM files, corrupts program and OVL files. *See* VIRUS NAMES.

Virus-101. In computer security, a virus that encrypts itself, terminates and stays resident, infects COMMAND.COM, COM, EXE and OVL files, infects floppy disk boot sector, corrupts program and OVL files. *See* VIRUS NAMES.

virus names . In computer security, there appear to be seven ways in which a viruses may be given a name:

- text strings located in virus;
- original source code;
- size of virus code;
- similarity;
- virus action;
- trigger date;
- best guess.

Some viruses have text strings embedded in the virus code, e.g. the Stoned virus contains the phrase 'your computer is now stoned'. In other cases the virus is named within the virus source code itself, e.g. Dark Avenger. Commonly viruses are named by their length, e.g. the 4096 virus increases the length of the infected file by 4096 bytes. Many viruses are mutations of earlier versions and given correspondingly similar names. For example, mutations of the Stoned virus are termed Stoned II, Stone A etc. Some viruses are named according to their action; the DIR-II virus affects the directory entry of the infected file, No-INT does not exploit DOS interrupts to infect the computer. The trigger date for virus malicious action is commonly used to name the virus, hence the Friday 13th virus. Finally the person discovering the virus may decide upon a best guess, thus Michelangelo was so named because the trigger date corresponded to Michelangelo's birthday. *See* VIRUS.

visual display unit. In peripherals, a device for the display of computer output in soft copy form. The display technologies include CRT, LCD, LED and plasma panel.

vocoder. In communications, a device used to reduce the bandwidth requirements of voice signals.

voice analysis. In access control, a biometric technique based upon recognition of a user's voice. Biometric systems that identify users by their voice patterns have two significant advantages. Firstly they are acceptable to the majority of users and secondly they can capture the user signal over telephone networks. Linear predictive coding techniques are commonly employed to process the voice data to provide a digital template. Enrolment typically involves the repetition of a PIN or password three times. When requesting access the user repeats the password and access time is of the order of 20 seconds. The system may update the voice template with successful access thus improving the stored template with usage. Type 1 and Type 2 error rates as low as .1% and 0.001% have been claimed by vendors. *See* BIOMETRICS, TYPE 1 ERROR, TYPE 2 ERROR.

voice answer-back. In peripherals, an audio response unit that can link a computer system to a telephone network to provide voice responses to enquiries. *See* SPEECH SYNTHESIZER.

voice band. In communications, the band of frequencies permitting intelligible transmission of human voice, usually in the range 300 - 3000 Hz. *See* VOICE SCRAMBLING.

voice bank. In communications, a recording system which can store spoken material for ready access.

voice grade channel. In communications, a channel suitable for the transmission of speech, facsimile, analog or digital data with a frequency range in the voice band, generally about 300 - 3000 Hz. *See* HZ, VOICE BAND.

voice mail. In communications, a system in which spoken information is digitized and stored either in a network memory or in the appropriate apparatus at the destination for the message. The spoken message is later retrieved by the called party. *See* VOICE STORE AND FORWARD. *See* COMPARE ELECTRONIC MAIL

voice print. In access control, a digitally recorded signal which identifies the voice characteristics of an individual and is used for identification purposes. *See* VOICE ANALYSIS.

voice scrambling. In communications security, the enciphering of voice communications. Voice scrambling techniques may be classified as analog or digital. Traditionally voice scrambling was applied to conventional analog signals on telephone lines but developments in ISDN now provide for digital transmission of voice signals and this development has significant implications for voice scramblers.

Analog voice scrambling involves a transformation on the analog signal, to be transmitted, and this transformation may be considered to operate in the frequency or time domain, or indeed both.

Frequency Domain Scramblers.
Frequency domain scramblers involve transformations of the constituent frequencies of the voice signal. The frequency distribution of the input signal, which lies in the audio frequency range i.e. 300 - 3000 Hz in the case of telephone communications, is modified for transmission. At the receiving end the frequency distribution of the received signal is reconverted to its original form.

These techniques can provide protection against the casual or intentional eavesdropper but are vulnerable to the determined, well equipped interceptor. The difficulties faced by the designer, of such scrambling devices, include the high degree of redundancy in normal speech, the ability of the trained interceptor to extract meaningful information from highly garbled voice transmissions and the requirement that the scrambling process should not significantly impair transmission quality after unscrambling.

The speech invertor was an early scrambling device and it effectively produces a mirror image of the voice frequency spectrum (see Fig. 1). Consider two frequencies at the lower (300 Hz) and higher (3000 Hz) ends of the range. If the amplitudes of these signals are V_L and V_H then the signals are represented by $V_L.\sin(2\pi300t)$ and $V_H.\sin(2\pi3000)$ respectively. The scrambler multiplies the voice signal by a carrier signal $V_c.\sin(2\pi f_c t)$ and the two aforementioned signals are transformed into:

$$V_L.\sin(2\pi300t).V_c.\sin(2\pi f_c t)$$
$$V_H.\sin(2\pi3000t).V_c.\sin(2\pi f_c t)$$

Each of these signals comprise a lower and upper sideband frequency Thus:

$$V_L.\sin(2\pi300t).V_c.\sin(2\pi f_c t) =$$
$$0.5V_L V_c((\cos(2.\pi(f_c - 300)t) -$$
$$\cos(2.\pi(f_c + 300)t))$$

The higher sideband frequencies (e.g. $(f_c + 300)$ lie above the audio frequency range and are filtered out. If the carrier frequency is 3300 Hz, and the carrier amplitude V_c is equal to 2, then the two original speech signals are transformed into scrambled signals,

$$V_H((\cos(2.\pi. 300)t)) \text{ and}$$
$$V_L((\cos(2.\pi.3000)t)),$$

i.e. the high and low frequency signal amplitudes are swapped in the scrambled output.

Speech invertors garble the voice signal but provide no real secrecy, because an interceptor merely has to perform the same signal processing, as that undertaken by the legitimate receiver, to obtain the original signal.

The concept of a secret key, shared between the sender and receiver, can be introduced in the frequency inversion process by the use of band shift invertors. In this case a higher frequency carrier signal is employed so that the inverted signal contains frequencies in the range 3000 to $(f_c - 300)$ Hz, whilst there are no signals between 300 and $(f_c - 3000)$ Hz. The upper range of inverted signals is then shifted to the lower end of the spectrum.

For example, if f_c is 4500 Hz then the inverted signal lies within the range 1500 - 4200 Hz. The band 3000 - 4200 is then frequency shifted to fill the band 300 - 1500 Hz (See Fig. 2).

In cyclical band shift invertors the carrier frequency (f_c) is changed, every 10 - 20 milliseconds, in accordance with the output of a pseudorandom number generator. The sender and receiver need only agree upon a pseudorandom number generator, its seed and synchronization of carrier frequency changes.

Bandsplitters (See Fig. 3), also known as bandscramblers, provide far greater segmentation and re-arrangement of the voice signal spectrum. In this case the spectrum is split into a number of equal width bands and these bands can be both re-ordered and, optionally, inverted. For example, in a 5 band unit the original ordering 12345 can be changed, by frequency shifting, to 42153, moreover bands 2 and 3 can be inverted. There are 120 possible permutations of the 5 bands and for each permutation there are 32 arrangements with individual bands inverted or not. Thus the scrambler can employ 3840 ($= 120 \times 32$) possible arrangements of the voice signal for the 5 band case.

However, many of the rearrangements of the input signal will be so close to the original that the residual intelligibility will be unacceptably high. For example, the bands corresponding to the first formant contain a high proportion of the voice signal energy, if the interceptor can locate these two bands then there is a good chance of making sense of the scrambled message.

The performance of the bandsplitter can be improved by selecting only those combinations of inversion and re-ordering which most effectively disguise the voice communication. This set of permutations/inversions can then be stored in a ROM and the sequence of ROM outputs selected by a pseudorandom number generator, at intervals of a few hundred milliseconds. The potential number of permutations can be enhanced by increasing the number of bands in the spectrum, but an excessive splitting of the voice frequency spectrum can cause an unacceptably high impairment of the unscrambled signal.

In general the frequency scrambling techniques are susceptible to determined attack and it is difficult to ensure that the residual intelligibility will be sufficiently low; the human brain is extremely adept at extracting meaningful messages from garbled voice signals. These techniques are therefore mainly employed when the scrambler is merely required to provide a degree of privacy.

Time Domain Scramblers

Time element scramblers use time division multiplexing techniques to re-order the signal in terms of the time domain. In this case the voice signal is divided into time frames and each frame is further subdivided into segments.

A complete frame is stored, by the scrambler, and the individual segments are then permuted. The scrambled frame is transmitted to the receiver which assembles the whole frame, performs an inverse permutation and outputs the reassembled frame as the unscrambled speech (See Fig. 4).

The process of storing and re-ordering segments is performed by subjecting each portion of the signal, corresponding to one segment, to an analog to digital conversion, storing the resultant set of bits

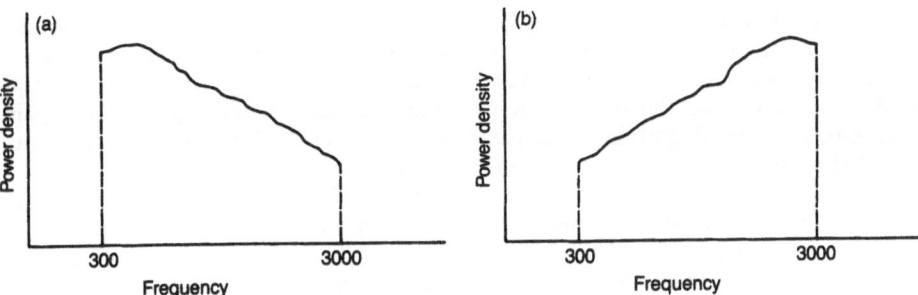

voice scrambling
Fig. 1. Frequency inversion.

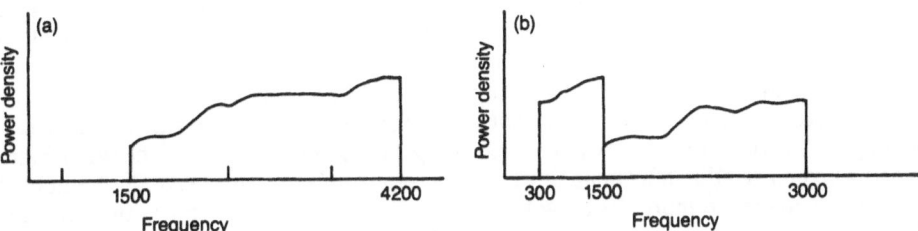

voice scrambling
Fig. 2. Band-shift inverter.

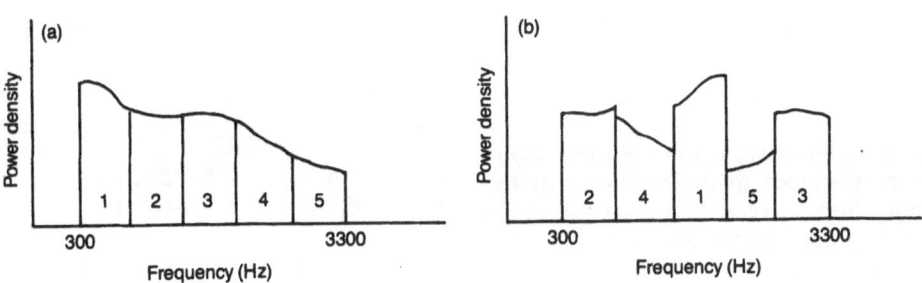

voice scrambling
Fig. 3. Bandsplitter: (a) original ordering of subbands; (b) scrambled spectrum.

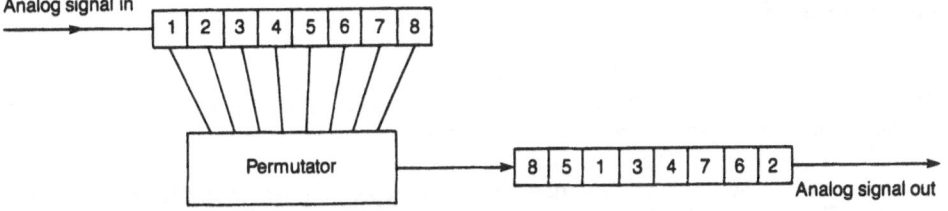

voice scrambling
Fig. 4. Time division multiplexing.

and repeating the process until a complete frame has been stored. The binary numbers representing each segment are then permuted in store and the resultant segment numbers are output in sequence, subjected to digital-to-analog conversion and transmitted to the receiver.

The performance of the scrambler depends upon the length of a frame, the number of segments in the frame and the permutations of the segments. From a security viewpoint the frame should be as long as possible; if this frame length is less than that of recognizable speech components the residual intelligibility will be insufficiently low. On the other hand the scrambling process introduces an additional delay of 2 frame lengths; this delay can cause annoyance to users conducting a conversation, similar to that experienced on satellite telephone links, if the frame lengths are more than few hundred milliseconds.

The cause of the delay may be illustrated by the typical permutation given below:

Scrambler input	1 2 3 4 5 6 7 8
Scrambler output	8 5 1 3 4 7 6 8
Unscrambler input	8 5 1 3 4 7 6 2
Unscrambler output	1 2 3 4 5 6 7 8

If, as in this case, the last segment (8) is to be permuted to the beginning of the frame then the scrambler must collect the whole frame before the first scrambled segment (i.e. 8) is transmitted. The unscrambler must similarly reckon on the possibility that the last segment of the received frame will correspond to the first segment of the unscrambled frame and likewise store the whole frame before outputting the first segment. The delay can be reduced by using the sliding window system which sets a limit on the displacement of any one segment.

The number of segments must be high enough to provide a large number of permutations, otherwise an interceptor could easily unscramble the message by exhaustively testing the complete set of possible permutations. However, increasing the number of segments, for a given frame length, reduces the segment length and this can produce significant impairment of the quality of the unscrambled message.

Not all permutations will cause a sufficient scrambling to disguise the message from a trained interceptor. The shift factor, which is a measure of the average displacement of the permuted segments, provides one indication of the degree of scrambling. For example, in the permutation 12345678 to 21345678 just 2 segments are displaced by one unit giving a shift factor of 1/4. This permutation would, clearly, provide a high degree of residual intelligibility.

Displacing pairs of segments, interposing one or more segments between pairs of segments etc., also leave the scrambled frame in a state vulnerable to the interceptor. A significant number of permutations thus prove to be inadequate for security purposes.

The number of useful permutations is further reduced by the necessity to eliminate certain pairs of permutations. Consider, for example, consider the pair of permutations:

TP1	TP2
1 2 3 4 5 6 7 8	1 2 3 4 5 6 7 8
5 3 7 1 6 2 8 4	4 3 7 1 6 2 8 5

The receiver must contain the inverse of these permutations in order to restore the scrambled message back to its original form. The inverses are:

RP1	RP2
1 2 3 4 5 6 7 8	1 2 3 4 5 6 7 8
4 6 2 8 1 5 3 7	4 6 2 1 8 5 3 7

An interceptor might well also store the inverse permutations and use a sonograph to test the effect of these inverses on the intercepted signal. If the interceptor tries RP2 on TP1 then the result is 12354678. This is sufficiently close to the original signal (only segments 5 and 4 are reversed) for interception purposes.

It is clear that permutations TP1 and TP2 should not both be used by the scrambler. The permutations should therefore be tested against one another to remove unsatisfactory combinations; this process is known as mutual security.

The scrambler might either produce permutations, by some form of pseudorandom number generator, and use an algorithm to reject unsatisfactory permutations, or alternatively store all satisfactory permutations in a ROM and select them in a pseudorandom fashion.

If the former method is employed then the generation, testing, rejection, regeneration, re-testing etc. must be performed in a few hundred milliseconds in order to ensure that a permutation is available for the next frame. Moreover this technique cannot use the mutual security method to reject unsatisfactory pairs of permutations.

The ROM technique sets a limit on the total number of permutations that can be economically stored but it does overcome the problem of selecting satisfactory permutations in real time and can, moreover, use mutual security methods.

The receiver must not only perform the inverse permutation of each frame but it must also ensure that the division of the received signal corresponds to the same frames as that of the transmitter. Synchronization signals must therefore be transmitted and such signals may take the form of initial or continuous synchronization.

In the former case the synchronization signal is sent only at the beginning of the message. Continuous synchronization signals, on the other hand, are transmitted continuously throughout the message. The major advantages of continuous synchronization are:

- the receiver may decipher the message even in the case of late entry, i.e. the beginning of the message is not available;
- the receiver can automatically switch between scrambled and clear

messages by detecting the presence, or otherwise, of the synchronization signals. These signals are often located in a narrow frequency band and can therefore render the system vulnerable to a denial of service attack.

Two-Dimensional Scramblers

Scramblers may combine time and frequency scrambling techniques. A segment of the voice message to be scrambled is divided in to time/frequency elements. These elements are then permuted within the time/frequency space (See Fig. 5).

Elements X11 through to X51 are five frequency bands all contained within the same time element X1. Time element X2 has five frequency bands X12 through to X52 associated with it etc. After the time/frequency elements have been repositioned the resulting signal is transmitted in place of the original speech.

The figure shows the new time/frequency map. The legitimate receiver must restore the time/frequency elements to their original positions in order to unscramble the voice message. Such schemes result in scrambled speech with low residual intelligibility and are difficult to cryptanalyze. However the quality of the unscrambled speech is impaired because the segmentation process in both the time and frequency domains introduces discontinuities which distort the speech signal.

Discrete Fourier Transform Scrambler

A mathematical transformation, known as the discrete Fourier transform (DFT), may be exploited for speech scramblers. The voice message is digitized and the resulting speech samples are then grouped into equal length frames.

The number of speech samples in each frame is normally made equal to a power of two, in order to simplify the transformation operation; typically it is chosen to be equal to 256. Each speech frame is transformed into the frequency domain using the DFT, resulting in 256 transform components.

These transform components represent the frequency content of the speech frame, and those transform components which correspond to frequencies communication path bandwidth, are then permuted. The remaining transform components are set to zero. Thus ensuring that the significant frequency components are retained when the scrambled signal is transmitted.

The number of transform components permuted is usually in the order of 88. Following permutation, the transform components are transformed back to the time domain, using the inverse Fourier transform, and the resulting time samples converted from digital to analog form for transmission.

The receiver synchronizes the incoming scrambled speech frames and performs the inverse of the scrambling operation. The Fourier transform signals undergo an inverse permutation, and the inverse Fourier transform is applied once again to recover the speech time samples.

The discrete Fourier transform scrambler has a low residual intelligibility, producing a scrambled signal which bears little resemblance to speech. However some information still remains in the form of the energy variation of the voice signal. Some intelligibility may be extracted from this information. The recovered voice quality is very good but may suffer impairment over a poor communications link.

The number of potential permutations is very high with 88 transform components, giving the DFT scrambler an advantage over the time element and bandsplitter type scramblers, that permute no more than 32 elements. Hence the DFT technique is less susceptible to a cryptanalytic attack which tests for each scrambling permutation.

Characteristics of Analog Scramblers
An effective voice scrambling system will produce scrambled speech with low resid-

ual intelligibility. However, speech signals are highly redundant and the human brain is adept at extracting intelligibility from garbled voice signals. Moreover the speech recovered from unscrambled signals should not suffer significant impairment; it should be acceptable to the person at the receiving end in terms of sound quality and should also allow the speaker to be recognized.

The analog scramblers characteristically have high residual intelligibility with the possible exception of discrete Fourier transform and two-dimensional scrambling techniques. The recovered speech quality is good provided the degradation due to the communications link is not severe. Equalization is often necessary to compensate for the link.

The analog scramblers described above have as their scrambling algorithm permutation of either frequency or time domain elements. In the case where a fixed permutation is used many of these systems have been successfully attacked using the redundancy of speech. Automated attacks, which require only the scrambled speech, can be conducted on the bandsplitter, discrete Fourier transform scrambler and time element scrambler.

If the contents of a ROM used to store scrambling permutations is discovered by a cryptanalyst, the restricted list may allow an exhaustive trial of each permutation. The ROM also provides a basis for comparison when the interceptor is able to derive an estimate of the permutation using cryptanalysis.

Digital Scramblers
In digital encryption, for an analog channel, the analog signal is first digitized (analog to digital conversion). The digital bits are then compressed using a speech coder to generate a data signal at a suitable bit rate. The speech coding compresses the speech, in order to ensure that it lies within the transmission channel bandwidth. The bit stream is then encrypted and the resulting encrypted stream is transmitted over the voice channel. When

the standard analog telephone channel is used the encrypted bit stream is converted to an analog signal by a modem. The reverse process is conducted at the receiving end.

The speech coder causes some degradation in the quality of the unscrambled speech. Typically the digital encryption algorithm is a stream cipher such as a block cipher in output feedback or cipher feedback mode.

Cipher feedback is self-synchronizing, but it suffers from error propagation. If a noisy communication channel is employed then the error propagation effectively increases the noise at the receiver, and this can produce an unintelligible unscrambled output. Output feedback does not exhibit error propagation and is suitable for highly redundant speech signals where errors in individual bytes can be easily tolerated.

X51	X52	X53	X54	X55	X56	X57	X58
X41	X42	X43	X44	X45	X46	X47	X48
X31	X32	X33	X34	X35	X36	X37	X38
X21	X22	X23	X24	X25	X26	X27	X28
X11	X12	X13	X14	X15	X16	X17	X18

voice scrambling
Fig. 5 Matrix for two dimensional scrambling.

X43	X37	X25	X11	X17	X38	X22	46
X26	X18	X36	X58	X48	X12	X33	X52
X53	X24	X14	X42	X28	X57	X31	X16
X41	X13	X56	X32	X51	X47	X15	X34
X35	X44	X21	X23	X54	X45	X27	X55

voice scrambling
Fig. 6 A Two dimensional scrambling permutation.

However, the output feedback form of stream cipher is not self-synchronizing, and noisy communications channels, causing loss of synchronization, will again render the output unintelligible. Continuous synchronization is therefore required with the synchronization signals sent at regular or pseudorandom intervals. Flywheeling may be employed to enable the receiver to deduce both the expected time of synchronization updates and the synchronization information.

Digitally scrambled signals will have the characteristics of white noise and the

transmitter may well continue to send white noise signals, during lulls in traffic, to deny traffic flow information to the interceptor. On the other hand the interceptor may be able to gain useful plaintext information from any consistent background noise, e.g. an air conditioner, at the transmitting end. This noise will be enciphered during pauses in speech and the interceptor can eventually gain a significant amount of plaintext and corresponding ciphertext information.

The interceptor is also aided by the high redundancy of speech signals which provide opportunities for the frequency analysis of the scrambled messages.

The design voice scramblers for conventional telephone circuits is constrained by the requirement that the scrambled signal takes the form of a analog signal within the 300-3000 Hz bandwidth. For a digital scrambler on a broadband digital network, such as broadband ISDN, it may not be necessary to compress the speech prior to encryption. On such a communication network it is possible to design a voice scrambler which has low residual intelligibility in the scrambled speech, provides excellent quality of recovered speech and is secure from cryptanalysis. *See* BAND SHIFT INVERTOR, BANDSPLITTER, CARRIER, CIPHER FEEDBACK, CONTINUOUS SYNCHRONIZATION, CRYPTOGRAPHIC BIT STREAM, CYCLICAL BAND SHIFT INVERTOR, DENIAL OF SERVICE, ERROR PROPAGATION, FLY WHEELING, FORMANT, Hz, INITIAL SYNCHRONIZATION, MUTUAL SECURITY, OUTPUT FEEDBACK, PSEUDORANDOM NUMBER, RESIDUAL INTELLIGIBILITY, ROM, SEED, SELF SYNCHRONIZING, SHIFT FACTOR, SLIDING WINDOW-SYSTEM, SONOGRAPH, SPEECH INVERTOR, TIME DIVISION MULTIPLEXING, TIME ELEMENT SCRAMBLER, TRAFFIC ANALYSIS. *Synonymous with* SPEECH SCRAMBLING.

voice store and forward. In communications, a system that transmits and stores voice messages for playback on demand. *See* STORE AND FORWARD, VOICE MAIL.

volatile storage. In computing, storage media in which the stored data is lost when the power supply is removed. *Compare* NONVOLATILE STORAGE.

volume. In computing, a storage medium holding data that can be mounted or demounted as a complete unit, e.g. a disk pack.

volumetric sensor. In physical security, pertaining to an intrusion sensor that detects an intruder in a specified three-

dimensional space. *See* INTRUSION DETECTOR.

von Neumann. In computing, pertaining to the architecture of a conventional computer. It is characterized by: a single computing element incorporating processor, communications and memory, linear organization of fixed size memory cells, one level address space of cells, low level machine language, sequential, centralized control of computation and primitive input output capability. *Compare* PARALLEL PROCESSING.

Voronezh. In computer security, a virus that encrypts itself, terminates and stays resident, infects COMMAND.COM, COM, EXE and OVL files, affects run-time operation, corrupts program, OVL and data files. *See* VIRUS NAMES.

vostro account. *Synonymous with* LORO ACCOUNT.

V-Series recommendations of CCITT. In standards, a series of recommendations relating to data communications over analog channels. *Compare* X-SERIES RECOMMENDATIONS OF CCITT. *See* PROTOCOL STANDARDS.

VTP. *See* VIRTUAL TERMINAL PROTOCOL.

vulnerability. (1) In risk management, a weakness in automated system security procedures, administrative controls, internal controls, and so forth, that could be exploited by a threat to gain unauthorized access to information or disrupt critical processing. (AFR). (2) In risk management, a weakness in the physical layout, organization, procedures, personnel, management, administration, hardware, or software that may be exploited to cause harm to the ADP system or activity. The presence of a vulnerability does not in itself cause harm; a vulnerability is merely a condition or set of conditions that may allow the ADP system or activity to be harmed by an attack. (OPNAVINST). *See* ADP, TECHNICAL VULNERABILITY. (3) In risk management, any security weakness or flaw existing in a system. The susceptibility of a system to a specific threat attack or harmful event, or the opportunity available to a threat agent to mount that attack. *Compare* SAFEGUARD, THREAT. *See* COUNTERMEASURE, HARMFUL EVENT, MATRIX METHODOLOGY, VULNERABILITY ASSESSMENT. (4) In information security, a property or security weakness of a target of evaluation which may be exploited to overcome a countermeasure. *See* CONSTRUCTION VULNERABILITY, EXPLOITABLE VULNERABILITY, INFORMATION TECHNOLOGY SECURITY EVALUATION CRITERIA, OPERATIONAL VULNERABILITY, POTENTIAL VULNERABILITY, TARGET OF EVALUATION.

vulnerability assessment. (1) In risk management, a review of the susceptibility to loss or unauthorized use of resources, errors in reports and information, illegal or unethical acts, and/or adverse or unfavorable public opinion. (OMBC). (2)

In risk management, a measurement of vulnerability which would include: (a) The susceptibility of a particular system to a specific attack. (b) The opportunity available to a threat agent (methods or things which may be used to exploit a vulnerability (such as fire)) to mount that attack. A vulnerability is always demonstrable but may exist independently of a known threat. In general, a description of a vulnerability takes account of those factors under friendly control. (AR). *See* THREAT, THREAT AGENT, VULNERABILITY. (3) In risk management, a review of the susceptibility to loss or unauthorized use of resources, errors in reports and information, illegal or unethical acts, and adverse or unfavorable public opinion. Vulnerability assessments do not identify weaknesses or result in improvements. They are the mechanism with which an organization can determine quickly the potential for losses in its different programs or functions. The schedule of internal control reviews should be based on the results of the vulnerability assessments. (DODD). *See* INTERNAL CONTROL REVIEW.

W

W-13. In computer security, a virus that infects COM files, affects run-time operation, corrupts program and OVL files. *See* VIRUS NAMES.

WACK. In data communications, Wait before transmitting positive ACKnowledgement. A signal sent by a receiving station to indicate that it is temporarily not ready to receive.

WADS. *See* WIDE AREA DATA SERVICE.

WAN. *See* WIDE AREA NETWORK.

warm site. In risk management, a system similar to a cold site except that it has telecommunications facilities. *Compare* COLD SITE, HOT SITE.

warm standby. In reliability, a backup system that can be switched into operation within a few seconds of an active system malfunction. *Compare* COLD STANDBY, HOT STANDBY.

watermark tape. In access control, a material used for magnetic stripes that is designed to increase the difficulty of manufacturing counterfeit cards. A permanent magnetic watermark is induced into the material by exposing it to an appropriate varying magnetic field whilst the magnetic particles are held in a resinous lacquer, the material is then dried thus fixing the orientation of the magnetic particles. One track of the card is used to check the watermark and the track is subjected to a constant magnetic field before reading. Thus any attempt to counterfeit the watermark pattern by magnetizing a conventional magnetic stripe is thwarted by the erasing effect of the constant magnetic field. *Compare* SANDWICH TAPE. *See* MAGNETIC STRIPE CARD.

wavelength division multiplexing. In communications, a technique that is identical to frequency division multiplexing. The term is applied to the use of different wavelengths for the light signals along an optical fiber. *See* FIBER OPTICS, FREQUENCY DIVISION MULTIPLEXING.

WDM. *See* WAVELENGTH DIVISION MULTIPLEXING.

weak bits. In computer security, a technique in which bits with intermediate polarization values between those of a binary 1 and a binary 0 are prerecorded onto a master floppy disk, along with the software to be protected. When a weak bit is read, the disk controller on a microcomputer will sometimes interpret it as a 1 and sometimes as a 0. A special test program will check for this statistical variation by reading the sector concerned several times and hence determining if a master disk is being used. If a weak bit is read and then copied across to another disk, along with the protected program, it will be written as a true binary digit and the test program will not detect any variation, in consecutive reads, and therefore conclude that a copy is being used; it will then prevent the program from being executed. *See* EXECUTE PROTECTION, FINGERPRINT. *Synonymous with* FUZZY SECTOR TECHNIQUE.

weak key. In cryptography, a DES key that produces the same transformation in the encipherment and decipherment process, i.e. double encipherment reproduces the original plaintext. The weak keys for DES are

0101010101010101,
FEFEFEFEFEFEFEFE,
1F1F1F1F0E0E0E0E and
E0E0E0E0F1F1F1F1.

Note that when the parity bits are removed from these keys their regular structure becomes apparent, e.g.

0101010101010101 becomes 000000000000000.

Some key management schemes provide users with restricted encipherment or decipherment facilities and weak or semiweak keys could be exploited by an attacker. Compare semiweak key. *See* DES, DUAL KEY, KEY MANAGEMENT.

Whale. In computer security, a stealth virus that encrypts itself, terminates and stays resident, infects COM-MAND.COM, COM, EXE and OVL files, affects run time operation, corrupts program, OVL and data files and file linkage. *See* VIRUS NAMES.

what if. In applications, an interactive decision making technique in which one or more independent variables in a model are given specific values and the output is computed. The results often lead to a change in the model itself.

White Book. *See* INFORMATION TECHNOLOGY SECURITY EVALUATION CRITERIA.

white card fraud. (1) In banking, a form of credit card fraud using a counterfeit credit card. A blank white plastic card, with a magnetic stripe, is manufactured and the stripe is encoded with the details contained in a genuine client's credit card; such information being obtained illegally from the appropriate financial institution. The cards are then used to obtain money from ATMs. The perpetrator may also emboss the account number or other information on the card. *See* ATM. (2) In banking, a form of fraud in which a stolen credit card is heated, e.g. by boiling in water; the old embossed digits are pressed out and new numbers re-embossed.

white noise. In communications, an unwanted random signal with equal power over all frequencies. *See* NOISE.

white noise emitter. In computer security, a device to provide a degree of protection against compromising emanations. The device fits onto the back of a VDU and emits random radio signals. The device can, however, cause interference with other electronic equipment in the vicinity and an eavesdropper may be able to filter out the noise with correlation techniques. *Compare* RANDOM LINE SWITCHING. *See* COMPROMISING EMANATIONS, VAN ECK PHENOMENON.

wide area data service. In data communications, an AT&T service that makes unlimited dial up use of telegraph grade circuits, within a particular geographic area, available to subscribers for a fixed monthly fee.

wide area network. In data communications, a comprehensive multimode network connecting large numbers of terminals and computers spread over a wide area. *Compare* LOCAL AREA NETWORK, MUNICIPAL AREA NETWORK.

wideband channel. In data communications, channels that operate to 50 Kbits per second, speed can be increased up to 168 Kbits per second with special modems. *See* BIT, MODEM.

Wiegand effect. In access control, a magnetic effect used in some access control systems. A special ferromagnetic wire, formed into a permanently tensioned helical twist, experiences sudden reversals of magnetic field when exposed to an external magnetic field; such reversals can be converted into electrical pulses. *See* MAGNETICALLY ENCODED CARD.

window. (1) In computing, pertaining to a software technique that facilitates the movement of data between packages. The concept is intended to provide extremely user friendly systems for executives who can view the contents of different packages in 'windows' on the VDU screen and cut and paste information from one into another. (2) In data communications. *See* SLIDING WINDOW PROTOCOL.

windows. *See* WINDOW.

wipe through card reader. In banking and access control, a card reader in which the card is wiped through an open slot in the read head device. *See* CARD READER.

wire center. In data communications, a device that allows a local area network, with a ring architecture, to maintain limited communication when there is a cable break. If a cable break is detected, a bypass relay operates in the wire center and effectively shorts out the section of cable and station affected by the break, allowing communications to continue with the remaining stations in the ring. *See* LOCAL AREA NETWORK, RING.

wired logic card. In access control, a form of smart card containing an electronic circuit encapsulated within the card. *See* SMART CARD.

wire service. In data communications, any telecommunication service over which messages or transmissions can be sent to subscribers (e.g. Telex, TWX, SWIFT, BankWire, Fedwire). (ANSI) *See* BANKING NETWORKS, BANKWIRE, FEDWIRE, SWIFT.

wiretap. (1) In communications security, the attaching of an unauthorized device, such as a line tap, tape recorder, or computer terminal, to a communications circuit for the purpose of obtaining access to data. (ANSI). (2) In communications security, a technique to intercept a communications line to get information. Wiretapping may be performed in active or passive modes:

- Active - the attaching of an unauthorized device, such as a computer terminal, to a communications circuit for the purpose of obtaining access to data through the generation of false messages or control signals, or by altering the communications of legitimate users.
- Passive - the monitoring and/or recording of data which is being transmitted over a communication link.

See ACTIVE WIRETAPPING, PASSIVE WIRETAPPING. (2) In communications security, a means of unauthorized interception of messages. The purpose of passive wiretapping is to disclose message contents without detection, whilst active wiretapping involves the deliberate modification of messages, sometimes for the purpose of injecting false messages, injecting replays of previous messages, (e.g. to repeat a credit transaction) or deleting messages. Authentication protects against message modification and injection of false messages by making it infeasible for an opponent to modify or create messages that meet the authentication criteria. *Compare* BETWEEN-THE-LINES ENTRY, PIGGYBACK ENTRY. *See* ACTIVE WIRETAPPING, BROWSING, PASSIVE WIRETAPPING.

wiretapping. *See* WIRETAP.

Wisconsin. In computer security, a virus that encrypts itself, infects COMMAND.COM and COM files, affects run-time operation, corrupts program, OVL and data files. *See* VIRUS NAMES.

WNINTEL. In data security, Warning Notice-Intelligence Sources or Methods Involved.

Wolfman. In computer security, a virus that terminates and stays resident, infects COMMAND.COM, COM and EXE files, affects run-time operation, corrupts program and OVL files. *See* VIRUS NAMES.

word. In data structures, a group of bits, bytes or characters, considered as an entity, and capable of storage in one memory location.

word-frame counter. In data communications, a unit to count the number of words in a frame as they are received. It may also count the number of frames. *See* FRAME, WORD.

word length. In data structures, the number of bits, bytes or characters in a word. *See* WORD.

work factor. In computer security, an estimate of the effort or time that can be expected to be expended to overcome a protective measure by a would be penetrator with specified expertise and resources. (FIPS). *See* RESOURCE.

workstation. An intelligent terminal with facilities designed for specific tasks, e.g. word processing, computer aided design.

worm. (1) In computer security, a form of malicious code that can replicate itself without requiring a host program to carry the infection. Networks are vulnerable to worm attacks, a worm enters a node of a network, causes local problems at the node and sends copies of itself to neighboring nodes. *Compare* VIRUS. *See* MALICIOUS CODE, MORRIS WORM. (2) In software protection, a program written by a software publisher that will invoke a penalty if unauthorized use of a program is detected. At best the worm will halt the protected program, at worst it will cause a small amount of corruption each time it is run, eventually leading to a disk crash. Worms are dangerous because they can be activated accidentally. *Compare* VIRUS. *See* DISK CRASH.

WORM. In peripherals, Write Once Read Many times, an optical compact disk, that allows new data to be written on a blank surface. The absence of erasability facilities can be tolerated in personal computers given the high storage capacity of the disk. These devices are ideal for storing a complete audit trail for both legal and financial information.

worst case condition. In cryptanalysis, the worst case condition, from the cryptographer's viewpoint, is when the cryptanalyst has a complete knowledge of the cipher system, has accumulated a considerable volume of ciphertext and knows the plaintext equivalent of a certain amount of the ciphertext.

write. In computer security a fundamental operation that results only in the flow of information from a subject to an object. (DOD). *Compare* READ. *See* OBJECT, SUBJECT.

write access. In computer security, permission to write an object. (DOD). *Compare* READ ACCESS. *See* OBJECT, WRITE.

X

X. A prefix for standards used by CCITT and ANSI. In this dictionary the CCITT standards are listed below under X., e.g. X.25. ANSI standards are listed under ANSI e.g. ANSI X9.9. *See* ANSI, X-SERIES RECOMMENDATIONS OF CCITT.

X.1. In standards, a CCITT recommendation for international user classes of service in public data networks.

X.2. In standards, a CCITT recommendation for international user facilities in public data networks.

X.3. In standards, a CCITT recommendation for packet assembly/disassembly facility (PAD) in a public data network. *See* PAD.

X.4. In standards, a CCITT recommendation for general structure of signals of International Alphabet Number 5 code for data transmission over public data networks. *See* INTERNATIONAL ALPHABET NUMBER 5.

X.20. In standards, a CCITT recommendation for interface between data terminal equipment (DTE) and data circuit terminating equipment (DCE) for start/stop transmission services on public data networks. *See* DCE, DTE, PUBLIC DATA NETWORK.

X.20 bis. In standards, a CCITT recommendation for V.21-compatible interface between data terminal equipment (DTE) and data circuit terminating equipment (DCE) for start-stop transmission services on public data networks.

See DCE, DTE, V.21.

X.21. In standards, a CCITT recommendation for an interface specification to a public data network using synchronous transmission on a digital telephone network and the communication equipment will provide bit and byte timing signals. The specification includes protocols for making and answering calls and for transmission and reception of data using full duplex synchronous transmission. *See* BYTE, FULL DUPLEX, SYNCHRONOUS TRANSMISSION, X.26, X.27.

X.22. In standards, a CCITT recommendation for Multiplex DTE/DCE interface for user classes 3-6. *See* DCE, DTE.

X.24. In standards, a CCITT recommendation for definitions of interchange circuits between data terminal equipment and data circuit-terminating equipment on public data networks. *See* DCE, DTE.

X.25. In standards, a CCITT recommendation for the interface between data terminal equipment (DTE) and data circuit terminating equipment (DCE) for terminals operating in the packet mode on public data networks. *See* DATA COMMUNICATIONS, DCE, DTE.

X.26. In standards, a CCITT recommendation in respect of the electrical specification for X.21, corresponding to RS-422A. *Compare* X.27. *See* CCITT, RS-422A, X.21.

X.27. In standards, a CCITT recommendation in respect of the electrical specifications for X.21, corresponding to RS-423A. *Compare* X.26. *See* CCITT, RS-423A, X.21.

X.28. In standards, a CCITT recommendation for DTE/DCE interface for a start-stop mode data terminal equipment a c c e s s i n g   t h e   p a c k e t assembly/disassembly facility (PAD) on a public data network situated in the same country. *See* DCE, DTE, PAD.

X.29. In standards, a CCITT recommendation for procedures for the exchange of control information and user data between a packet mode DTE and a packet assembly/disassembly facility (PAD). *See* DTE, PAD.

X.30. In standards, a CCITT recommendation for standardization of basic mode-page-printing machine in accordance with International Alphabet No 5. *See* INTERNATIONAL ALPHABET NUMBER 5.

X.31. In standards, a CCITT recommendation for characteristics, from the transmission point of view, at the interchange point between data terminal equipment and data circuit terminating equipment when a 200-baud start-stop data terminal in accordance with International Alphabet No 5 is used. *See* BAUD, DCE, DTE, INTERNATIONAL ALPHABET NUMBER 5.

X.32. In standards, a CCITT recommendation for answer-back units for 200 bauds start-stop machines in accordance with International Alphabet No 5. *See* BAUD, INTERNATIONAL ALPHABET NUMBER 5.

X.33. In standards, a CCITT recommendation for standardization of an international text for the measurement of the margin of start-stop machines in

accordance with International Alphabet No 5. *See* INTERNATIONAL ALPHABET NUMBER 5.

X.40. In standards, a CCITT recommendation for standardization of frequency-shift modulated transmission systems for the provision of telegraph and data channels by frequency division of a primary group.

X.50. In standards, a CCITT recommendation for fundamental parameters of a multiplexing scheme for the international interface between synchronous data networks. *See* MULTIPLEXING, SYNCHRONOUS DATA NETWORK.

X.50 bis. In standards, a CCITT recommendation for fundamental parameters of a 48 Kbit/s user data signalling rate transmission scheme for the international interface between synchronous data networks. *See* BIT, SYNCHRONOUS DATA NETWORK.

X.51. In standards, a CCITT recommendation for fundamental parameters of a multiplexing scheme for the international interface between synchronous data networks using 10-bit envelope structures. *See* BIT, SYNCHRONOUS DATA NETWORK.

X.52. In standards, a CCITT recommendation for a method of encoding anisochronous signals into a synchronous user bearer. *See* ANISOCHRONOUS TRANSMISSION.

X.53. In standards, a CCITT recommendation for numbering of channels on international multiplex links at 64 Kbit/s. *See* BIT, MULTIPLEXING.

X.54. In standards, a CCITT recommendation for allocation of channels on international multiplex links at 64 Kbit/s. *See* BIT, MULTIPLEXING.

X.60. In standards, a CCITT recommendation for common channel signalling for circuit switched data applications.

X.61. In standards, a CCITT recommendation for signalling system No 7 - data user part.

X.70. In standards, a CCITT recommendation for terminal and transit control signalling system for start-stop services on international circuits between anisochronous data networks. *See* ANISOCHRONOUS TRANSMISSION.

X.71. In standards, a CCITT recommendation for decentralized terminal and transit control signalling system on international circuits between synchronous data networks. *See* SYNCHRONOUS DATA NETWORK.

X.75. In standards, a CCITT recommendation for terminal and transit call control procedures and data transfer system on international circuits between packet-switched data networks.

X.80. In standards, a CCITT recommendation for interworking of interchange signalling system switched data services.

X.87. In standards, a CCITT recommendation for principles and procedures for realization of international user facilities and network utilities in public data networks. *See* PUBLIC DATA NETWORK.

X.92. In standards, a CCITT recommendation for hypothetical reference connections for public synchronous data networks. *See* SYNCHRONOUS DATA NETWORK.

X.93. In standards, a CCITT recommendation for hypothetical reference connection for packet switched data transmission services.

X.95. In standards, a CCITT recommendation for network parameters in public data networks. *See* PUBLIC DATA NETWORK.

X.96. In standards, a CCITT recommendation for call progress signals in public data networks.

X.110. In standards, a CCITT recommendation for routing principles for international public data services through switched public data networks of the same type. *See* ROUTING.

X.121. In standards, a CCITT recommendation for international numbering plan for public data networks.

X.130. In standards, a CCITT recommendation for provisional objectives for call set-up and clear-down times in public synchronous data networks (circuit switching). *See* CIRCUIT SWITCHING, SYNCHRONOUS DATA NETWORK.

X.132. In standards, a CCITT recommendation for provisional objectives for grade of service in international data communications over circuit switched public data networks.

X.150. In standards, a CCITT recommendation for DTE and DCE test loops for public data networks in the case of X.21 and X.21 bis interface. *See* DCE, DTE, X.21, X.21 BIS.

X.180. In standards, a CCITT recommendation for administration arrangements for international closed user groups (CUG). *See* CLOSED USER GROUP.

X.200. In standards, a CCITT recommendation for OSI Reference Model for CCITT applications. *See* OSI.

X.210. In standards, a CCITT recommendation for OSI Layer Service definition convention. *See* OSI.

X.400. In data communications, a standard for message handling systems which includes specifications for the network architecture, protocol structure, implementation detail, message transfer elements and content protocols. X.400 is a fully developed application layer of the open systems interconnection model and it introduces the concept of sub-layers termed user agents (UA) and message transfer agents (MTA).

The user agent is analogous to the user of a postal system who addresses and posts a letter. The message transfer agents are effectively the sorting offices which provide for the distribution and final delivery of the message. The MTAs as a group are termed the message transfer system (MTS).

The three major protocols within X.400 are the relay protocol P1, the message header and body protocol P2, and the submission protocol P3. The user interface is not defined, thus allowing considerable flexibility in the manner in which the message is written, displayed, stored and retrieved.

A typical message has an envelope and a message content which comprises the message header and body. The P2 protocol refers to the message header, including elements such as: originator, recipient, subject, copy recipients, reply-to indication, reply-by indication, priority, sensitivity, expiry date, blind copy, specification of delivery time, delivery notification address, cross references to other messages, obsolete message references and reply-to message reference. P2 also defines the various body parts of the message including, telex, voice, fax, teletex, videotex.

The P3 protocol covers the envelope standard for the transmissions between the user agent and the message transfer agent. Thus the user sends the message body and address to the user agent who adds the P2 header, to the P2 body, and places it in a P3 envelope.

The P1 protocol refers to the envelope standard when the message is being routed from one message transfer agent to another. The MTA accepts the message in the P3 envelope from the UA, and encloses the P2 header and body in a P1 envelope for transfer to the next MTA. At the receiving end the MTA accepts the P1 envelope, and transfers the P2 header and body into a P3 envelope for submission to the receiving UA. The latter accepts the P3 envelope and passes the P2 body to the receiver.

It is anticipated that the main application area of X.400 will be in office systems using connections between personal computers and networks.

The specific advantages of X.400 to OEMs and their customers are listed below.

- Reduced development costs resulting from the use of clearly defined specifications.
- Purchase of off-the-shelf software reducing development times.
- OEM development staff need less specialist knowledge of proprietary communications systems.
- Users will not be locked into individual manufacturers.
- Elimination of wasteful conversion between different services.
- Modular expansion.
- Reduction in telephone usage.
- Reduction in paper usage.

See APPLICATION LAYER, BLIND COPY, ELECTRONIC MAIL, OPEN SYSTEMS INTERCONNECTION, MTA, MTS, OEM, PROTOCOL, P1, P2, P3, UA.

X.435. In standards, a CCITT standard EDI Messaging System and Services, which governs the transmission of EDI documents over X.400 electronic mail systems. *Compare* ANSI X12. *See* EDI SECURITY, ELECTRONIC MAIL, ELECTRONIC DATA INTERCHANGE, X.400.

Xmas tree. In computer security, a worm attack that took place on an IBM electronic mail network in which a

Xmas tree was drawn on user's screens. *See* WORM.

X-modem. In software, an asynchronous file transfer protocol that works with almost any microcomputer and host. The protocol is in the public domain and is widely used on bulletin board systems. Data to be transmitted is assembled into 128 byte blocks, the last block being padded with blanks if necessary. LRC is used for block checking and each frame has a sequence number so the receiver will acknowledge and then ignore duplicate frames. *See* BULLETIN BOARD, FRAME, LRC.

XON-XOFF protocol. In data communications, a standard protocol employed when information is transferred from one computer to another, or to a peripheral. The protocol usually requires a full duplex data link. When the receiving computer, or peripheral, can no longer receive data, e.g. when a computer is required to service another higher priority task, it sends an XOFF ASCII control character which instructs the transmitting computer to await an XON character. *See* ASCII, FULL DUPLEX, PRIORITY, PROTOCOL.

XOR. *See* EXCLUSIVE OR.

X-Series recommendations of CCITT. In standards, a series of recommendations for data transmission over public-data networks. *Compare* V-SERIES RECOMMENDATIONS OF CCITT. *See* PROTOCOL STANDARDS.

Y

Yankee Doodle. In computer security, a virus that terminates and stays resident, infects COM and EXE files, affects run time operation, corrupts program and OVL files. *See* VIRUS NAMES.

Yankee-2. In computer security, a virus that infects COM and EXE files, affects run time operation, corrupts program and OVL files. *See* VIRUS NAMES.

Yellow Book. In computer security, the Department of Defense Technical Rationale Behind CSC-STD-003-85. It provides guidance for applying TCSEC to specific environments. *Compare* BLUE BOOK, ORANGE BOOK, RED BOOK. *See* TCSEC, RAINBOW SERIES.

Younger Committee. In legislation, a U.K. committee that considered the problems of data protection and privacy and reported in 1972 *See* DATA PROTECTION, DATA PROTECTION - U.K., PRIVACY.

Z

Zero Bug. In computer security, a virus that terminates and stays resident, infects COM files, affects run time operation, corrupts program and OVL files. *See* VIRUS NAMES.

zero effort rate. In access control, pertaining to a biometric device that has been desensitized to the point where it will accept any input signal as that corresponding to an input from an authorized user. *Compare* EQUAL ERROR RATE. *See* BIOMETRICS.

ZeroHunt. In computer security, a stealth virus that encrypts itself, terminates and stays resident, infects COM files, affects run time operation, corrupts program, OVL and data files. *See* VIRUS NAMES.

zeroization. In computer security, a method of degaussing, erasing or overwriting electronically stored data. *See* DEGAUSS, OVERWRITING.

zero knowledge proof. In cryptography, a method by which Alice convinces Bob that she knows some fact without revealing the fact to Bob; indeed it would be computationally infeasible for Bob to determine the fact with the information provided by Alice. *See* CHALLENGE/RESPONSE, FIAT-SHAMIR ALGORITHM. *Synonymous with* MINIMUM KNOWLEDGE PROOF.

zero order correlation immune. In cryptography, a sequence formed by a nonlinear combination of sequences produced by a set of linear feedback shift registers is said to be zero order correlation immune if it is statistically dependent upon one of the input sequences. *See* LINEAR FEEDBACK SHIFT REGISTER.

zoning. In physical security, a technique in which a protected building is divided into areas; any alarm initiating device in such an area can be programmed to signal an identifying code and/or indicate on an annunciator the area of the fire.

ZSI. Zentralstelle für Sicherheit in der Informationstechnik, the German Information Security Agency.

Subject Index

577